MARTIN LUTHER KING, JR.
AND THE CIVIL RIGHTS MOVEMENT

Edited by David J. Garrow

A CARLSON PUBLISHING SERIES

The Walking City

THE MONTGOMERY BUS BOYCOTT, 1955-1956

Edited with a Preface by David J. Garrow

INTRODUCTION BY
J. MILLS THORNTON III

CARLSON
Publishing Inc

BROOKLYN, NEW YORK, 1989

Library of Congress Cataloging-in Publication Data

The Walking city : the Montgomery bus boycott, 1955-1956 / edited with
a preface by David J. Garrow ; introduction by J. Mills Thornton,
III. —
    p.   cm. —(Martin Luther King, Jr. and the Civil Rights
Movement : 7)
    Includes bibliographies and index.
    1. Montgomery (Ala.)—Race relations. 2. Segregation in
transportation—Alabama—Montgomery—History—20th century. 3. Afro-
–Americans—Civil Rights—Alabama—Montgomery—History—20th
century. I. Garrow, David J., 1953-   . II. Series.
F334.M79N48   1989   89-9869
323.1'196073076845—dc20
ISBN 0-926019-03-1

Typographic design: Julian Waters

Typeface: Bitstream ITC Galliard

The index to this book was created using NL Cindex, a scholarly indexing program from the
Newberry Library.

For a complete listing of the volumes in this series, please see the back of this book.

Printed on acid-free, 250-year-life paper.

Manufactured in the United States of America.

Contents

Series Editor's Preface

The Montgomery Bus Boycott of 1955-1956 is one of the most important events in twentieth century Afro-American history, and the works collected in this volume—especially Ralph D. Abernathy's never-before-published 1958 thesis and memoir of the protest—represent an extremely valuable and indeed essential resource for the study and understanding of the Montgomery boycott's importance.

Mills Thornton's significant introduction to this volume accurately and provocatively emphasizes the importance of local strengths, local concerns, and local influences to the emergence, evolution, and resolution of the Montgomery protest. The primacy of such local aspects in the development and growth of black activism all across the South during the 1950s and 1960s is increasingly being better and better appreciated by scholars of the civil rights movement. In the Montgomery context that appreciation was significantly advanced by the 1980 publication in the *Alabama Review* of Professor Thornton's own landmark analysis of the boycott; it was even more decisively underscored in 1987 by the publication of *The Montgomery Bus Boycott and the Women Who Started It: The Memoir of Jo Ann Gibson Robinson*, a primary source of signal importance.

Ralph Abernathy's 1958 thesis ranks with Mrs. Robinson's memoir in importance and significance, and its publication here marks the first time it has been made available to a readership of more than two or three movement scholars. Abernathy's portrait is important not simply because of Abernathy's own major role in the boycott and his closeness, then and later, to Martin Luther King, Jr., but also because of how close in time it was written to the boycott's occurrence, hardly eighteen months after the boycott's successful conclusion. As more and more years have passed since both the mid-1950s and the mid-1960s, scholars who have actively pursued oral history recollections of the movement have more and more come to realize the tremendous extent to which contemporaneous or relatively close-in-time recollections are far richer, far more detailed, and far more accurate and dependable than recollections offered ten, twenty, or more years later. In this regard in particular, Abernathy's thesis and memoir represents a true gem whose historical significance will endure for decades to come.

Although far less well known than Abernathy, Reverend Edgar N. French was another of the Montgomery ministerial activists who played a crucial role in the founding of the Montgomery Improvement Association and the institutionalization of the boycott, and his little-cited 1962 memoir of the protest merits historical appreciation to almost the degree that Abernathy's and Robinson's landmark accounts do. Likewise, as Professor Thornton correctly points out in his introduction, the little-known essay by Preston Valien, along with the contemporaneous journalistic accounts by participant-observers L. D. Reddick, Thomas R. Thrasher, and Norman W. Walton, also represent primary sources of considerable value.

Lastly, my own brief 1985 essay emphasizing the primary importance of Mrs. Robinson and the Women's Political Council to the boycott's instigation, the 1979 article by Dominic Capeci, and the 1968 and 1981 theses by Thomas Gilliam and Steven Millner, all represent notable secondary analyses and contributions, although not on the scale offered by Professor Thornton's 1980 paper. All in all, the unpublished theses and sometimes little-noted articles that make up this volume represent an extremely significant contribution to civil rights historiography. I am deeply pleased with the scope and richness of this volume, and trust that it, like the other seventeen volumes that make up Carlson Publishing's series on *Martin Luther King, Jr., and the Civil Rights Movement*, will help encourage additional scholarly study and appreciation of both the Montgomery boycott and the wider movement in which Montgomery was such a crucial, early chapter.

David J. Garrow

Chronology

1953

November
> Racial liberal Dave Birmingham elected to the Montgomery City Commission, with 53% of the vote.

Late 1953
> Black civic activists, led by Women's Political Council Members (primarily Jo Ann Robinson) meet with City Commissioners to present complaints about the buses.

1954

March
> The City Commission agrees to change policy of buses only stopping at alternate blocks in black areas, but insists that they cannot change seating policy.

May 17
> Supreme Court decision on *Brown v. Board of Education of Topeka*.

May 21
> Jo Ann Robinson writes to Mayor W. A. Gayle on behalf of the Women's Political Council stating that a boycott of the buses is being considered.

September
> Martin Luther King, Jr. assumes his duties as pastor of the Dexter Avenue Baptist Church.

1955

February 23

Candidates forum sponsored by E.D. Nixon's Progressive Democratic Association at which all candidates for City Council face questions from blacks about bus policies and inadequate recreation areas.

March 2

Claudette Colvin arrested for refusing to give up her bus seat for a white passenger. Black leadership decides hers would not be a good test case.

March 21

Election for City Commissioners held. Clyde Sellers, who had run a race-baiting campaign, defeats Dave Birmingham and Frank Parks defeats George Cleere.

June

Black representatives meet again with city and bus company officials, who insist that nothing can be done about bus seating practices.

October 21

Mary Louise Smith arrested for not vacating her bus seat when ordered to do so by bus driver.

December 1

Rosa Parks arrested for not obeying a bus driver's order to give up her seat to a white passenger. Jo Ann Robinson, E. D. Nixon, and other blacks see this as perfect opportunity for protest and begin planning boycott of buses.

December 2

Black leadership (primarily ministers) caucus meets, with Reverend L. Roy Bennett presiding. They are presented with *fait accompli* of mass distribution of flyers announcing boycott scheduled for Monday the 5th.

December 5

One-day black boycott of buses is over 90% successful.

An afternoon meeting of leaders names the protest organization the Montgomery Improvement Association, and nominates Martin Luther King, Jr. president.

An evening mass meeting decides to continue the boycott until bus policies are changed. Martin Luther King, Jr., newly elected president, gives moving speech.

December 8

Negotiations between MIA leaders, City Commissioners, and bus company officials. Initial demands presented by MIA ask only for more equitable seating plan, not for abolition of segregated seating.

December 17 and 19

Negotiations on these two days include a committee of 16 appointed by Mayor Gayle. It becomes clear that no compromise is possible. This committee never meets again.

1956

January 6

City Commissioner Clyde Sellers publicly announces that he has joined the White Citizens Council.

January 9

Negotiations between MIA officials and City Commissioners. Neither will modify their position.

January 21

False settlement announced by City and denied by leaders of the Montgomery Improvement Association.

January 24

Mayor W. A. Gayle and City Commissioner Frank Parks announce that they have joined the White Citizens Council.

January 26

King arrested and jailed for speeding.

January 27

King's "kitchen experience" provides him with the strength and courage to continue the protest in spite of increasing hostility.

January 30

King's home is bombed. His calming speech defuses hostile crowd.

February 1

Browder v. Gayle suit filed in federal court by MIA challenging the constitutionality of bus segregation.

E.D. Nixon's home bombed.

February 20

Negotiations between MIA and City Commission arranged by the Men of Montgomery. A "compromise proposal" is presented by the City and subsequently rejected by vote of the Association membership. No further serious efforts by the City are made to negotiate.

February 21

Leaders of the boycott are indicted under Alabama's anti-boycott law.

March 19

King is first indicted boycott leader to be tried. He is convicted and fined $500 and $500 court costs or 386 days in jail. His conviction is appealed and other cases are held over pending a decision.

May 11

MIA's federal court suit (*Browder v. Gayle*) begins in Montgomery.

June 5

The federal district court rules that bus segregation is unconstitutional. City officials appeal to the Supreme Court.

June 11

U. J. Fields, secretary of the Montgomery Improvement Association, resigns from the organization and accuses members of misuse of funds.

November 13

Belatedly, the City files for and wins a temporary injunction to halt the car pool. From now until the end of the boycott there is no organized transportation provided.

The Supreme Court affirms the lower court ruling holding the City's bus segregation unconstitutional.

November 14

Mass meeting of MIA decides to discontinue boycott as soon as Supreme Court decision is implemented.

December 21

With official notification to the City of the Supreme Court decision, the buses are desegregated and blacks begin riding for the first time in over a year. The first bus is boarded by Martin Luther King, Jr., Ralph D. Abernathy, and Glenn Smiley. The driver's greeting—"We are glad to have you this morning."

1957

January 10

Violence erupts with six bombings—the homes of Reverend Ralph D. Abernathy and Reverend Robert Graetz and four churches—the Bell Street Baptist, the Hutchinson Street Baptist, the Negro First

Baptist, and the Mount Olive Baptist. Bus service is suspended for the "protection of life, limb, and property of the people of Montgomery."

Late January

An unexploded bomb containing twelve sticks of dynamite, with the fuse still smoldering, is found of the porch of King's home.

May 30

The men arrested for bombings are found not guilty by an all white jury.

First Among Equals: The Montgomery Bus Boycott

J. MILLS THORNTON, III

The Montgomery Bus Boycott of 1955-56 shares a number of characteristics with the civil rights crusades which swept across other Southern cities—Tallahassee, Tuskegee, Greensboro, Albany, Birmingham, St. Augustine, Selma, among the best known of them—in the decade after the Bus Boycott ended. They share a quite generally aroused and resolute black citizenry; an often confused and nearly always deeply hostile white political leadership; a frightened and hesitant, but frequently somewhat more moderate, white business community. They share violence, increasing racial polarization, national and international press attention, and the newly crucial role of federal authority, commonly in the persons of federal district judges. Above all, they share the example—inspiring or terrifying—of Martin Luther King, Jr., who seems, both in the narratives of some historians and in the memories of some participants, almost to embody the civil rights movement in himself. Perhaps these similarities account for the tendency to think of the Bus Boycott as simply the first in a line of events produced by black direct action in the South which would eventually revolutionize American race relations, a line which would culminate in the enactment of the Civil Rights Act of 1964, the Voting Rights Act of 1965 and the Fair Housing Act of 1968.

The Bus Boycott as a movement, however, also contains elements which will on first examination appear to distinguish it sharply from its successors. These elements seem to me to be at least as instructive as the similarities. In fact, as we shall see, they do remind us that each of the civil rights crusades in each of the towns and cities is unique, and warn us of the dangers of too readily grouping them together. In the first place, King's importance in any of these episodes may be very easily overstated. In Tallahassee, Tuskegee and Greensboro, it is only his example with which we are dealing, in any case. In Albany, Birmingham, St. Augustine and Selma, he and his organization came into the city in response to the invitation of local black leaders to assist them in effecting goals of local importance, whatever may have been the national implications of their decision to do so. In Montgomery, however, King's role was even more completely than elsewhere a function of local circumstance. He played no significant part in creating the Boycott. That honor belongs to E. D. Nixon, Jo Ann Robinson, Rufus Lewis, Fred Gray and other Montgomery blacks who, unlike King, could be considered community leaders in 1955. Indeed, King's nomination as the president of the Montgomery Improvement Association by Rufus Lewis on the afternoon of the Bus Boycott's first day, grew not out of any particular sense on Lewis's part of King's potential for leadership, but simply from the fact that King was Lewis's pastor, and Lewis very much wanted to replace the group's acting president, L. Roy Bennett, with someone else. King did thereafter give the Boycott wise and inspirational direction, and thus gained growing fame for himself. But it was the Bus Boycott which made the 26-year-old minister into a leader—almost despite himself—more than the leader who drew attention from beyond the city's boundaries to the movement.

In the second place, the national and international press attention which would follow King in later years, and would play so decisive a role particularly in Birmingham and Selma, was far less apparent in Montgomery. The Camel News Caravan with John Cameron Swayze and the CBS Evening News with Douglas Edwards were fifteen-minute programs in which the announcer essentially read a summary of the reports carried by the newspaper wire services. Film of the events described was rare in 1955, and reports from the scene of an incident even rarer. National television coverage of the Bus Boycott was, therefore, an inconsequential factor in its course. But even newspapers played no very important role. The white press—unlike the black press—was slow to discover the momentousness of the story. Except for a single report on a large rally of the White Citizens Council at the Alabama State Coliseum on February 10, the Bus Boycott did not reach the front page of the New York *Times*, for instance, until the state's indictment of the city's black leadership on February 21 for violation of the Alabama Anti-Boycott Act—more than two and a half months after the Boycott's commencement on the preceding December 5. And by the following summer, the Boycott had again dropped from view, reappearing only when the U.S. Supreme Court ruled favorably in November on the boycotters' suit to compel the integration of the buses. For most of the year that the Boycott lasted, therefore, Montgomery's blacks carried on their protest with surprisingly little notice from the outside world.

The most telling difference between the Bus Boycott and its successors in other Southern cities, however, is that its goal only rather slowly became racial integration. Initially, the boycotters simply sought the adoption by the Montgomery bus company of the plan of seating segregation in use in Mobile. Montgomery's black leaders, in particular the Negro Women's Political Council, had been asking for this reform since 1952. The election of the candidate supported by blacks in a special municipal election in 1953, his success in obtaining the hiring of black officers by the city police force in 1954 and the rectification in the same year of black complaints that buses would not stop at every corner in black neighborhoods, had given black leaders strong hope that the city government could be induced to respond to blacks' requests. But the election of a hard-line segregationist as police commissioner in 1955, and the failure of the city to try to clarify the bus seating regulations after the arrest of a black teenager for violation of the bus segregation ordinance that spring, moved black leaders to search for a means outside the electoral process to force white politicians to pay attention to the needs of black citizens. When the circumstances of the teenager's arrest were duplicated in December in the arrest of Mrs. Rosa Parks, this search produced acceptance of the idea of a boycott of the buses.

The Bus Boycott thus grew out of the events of municipal politics in Montgomery, and the efforts of blacks, largely disfranchised, nevertheless to use politics to ameliorate the practice of segregation in their community. The U.S. Supreme Court's decision in 1954 that the racial segregation of public schools was unconstitutional formed a part of the background to the Bus Boycott, of course, but the Boycott's initial goal was not to extend integration to the buses; its goal at first was to make the city commission take blacks' desires seriously. As a result, a majority of the executive board of the Montgomery Improvement Association, the organization established to run the Boycott, proved extremely reluctant to abandon the path of negotiations with the city commission, or to move beyond the modest reform proposal first advanced in 1952. The association's attorney, Fred Gray, began urging the filing of an integration suit in federal court early in the Boycott, but as late as January 23, almost two months after the Boycott had begun, the executive board once again voted to delay filing the suit, and ordered one last approach to the city commission. Only after the bombing of the home of the association's president, Martin Luther King, on January 30, was the board finally pushed into authorizing the suit. It was filed on February 1.

All three of these elements that appear on first inspection to distinguish the Bus Boycott so decisively from other Southern civil rights crusades— the fact that King came quite late to the leadership of the protest, rather than having had a part in organizing it; the fact that national press coverage played only a relatively minor role in creating or sustaining the movement; and the fact that integration became a goal of the boycotters only some two months into the protest, and only as a rather reluctant response to white intransigence and violence—derive the clarity with which we may see them in this circumstance from the fact that Montgomery was the first of the direct action campaigns. In 1955, King was a young minister rather than a civil rights leader. The national press was as yet ill-prepared, institutionally and intellectually, to understand and to report direct action efforts. And for local black leaders in the South, the dream of universal integration was a far distant and still a seemingly unrealistic goal; their aims were for the present shaped by the quiet efforts at black community advancement within the framework of segregation to which they had devoted themselves for so many years.

And yet, there is a deeper level at which these elements that appear to establish the Boycott's uniqueness, actually can teach us truths about the other civil rights crusades as well. Each of them owed its creation to local leadership, was shaped by local concerns, and was successful, to the extent that it was so, because of the devotion and zeal of the local black citizenry. The national civil rights organizations—in particular King's Southern Christian Leadership Conference, but also the Student Nonviolent Coordinating Committee, the Congress of Racial Equality and, to a lesser degree, the National Association for the Advancement of Colored People— acted to knit the local crusades together into a national movement, and to supply them with national goals. But these national goals were always added onto the local crusades, rather than generating the demonstrations in the first place. The Birmingham demonstrations of 1963, for instance, were undertaken not to pass the Civil Rights Act of 1964 but to force downtown department store owners to integrate their store facilities and to hire black clerks. The Dallas County Voters League launched the Selma demonstrations of 1965, similarly, in order to obtain alteration of the procedures of the Dallas County Board of Voting Registrars, even if the League's partners in the SCLC were really seeking national voting rights legislation instead. By seeing these local crusades primarily as episodes in a national movement with national aims, we distort them.

Even the role of the national press may be exaggerated. It is true that its coverage was essential both in giving Southern blacks generally a feeling of being part of a common struggle, and in communicating to Americans outside the South a sense of Southern blacks' plight. It was this latter development which led to the spread of the federal commitment to the civil rights cause beyond the courts into the federal government's political arms, first to the executive branch and finally to the Congress. And in this process, coverage of events in Birmingham and Selma was unquestionably crucial. Nevertheless, important civil rights crusades took place in a number of towns —Tuskegee, Nashville and Danville, for instance—with very little national coverage. And in Albany, the national coverage worked, if anything, to diminish public sympathy for blacks' cause.

The point, then, is that the extent of local black support for the crusade largely determined its ability to persevere and to prevail, and that local support was rooted in local concerns far more than in any desire to subserve the national civil rights organizations' broader strategies. Both the press and the civil rights organizations saw the local movements chiefly as contributing to the shaping of federal policy, and that was the source of their interest in them. But the participants in the demonstrations by and large derived their enthusiasm and dedication from the prospect of effecting specific changes in their own municipalities. Thus the Bus Boycott, for all its exceptional characteristics, in fact foreshadows in important ways the direct action campaigns that were to come.

These observations lead us to the Bus Boycott's final lesson. The Boycott was undertaken in the context of general black disfranchisement. It represented an effort to find some way to influence the city government outside the electoral process. But with the re-enfranchisement of blacks after 1965, the context changed. Often we hear it said that the civil rights movement ended at about the time of King's assassination in 1968. This notion originates in the misleading conception of the civil rights movement as an escalating series of municipal demonstrations aimed at extracting federal legislation or presidential initiatives. But once we comprehend the sense in which the civil rights movement may be understood as discrete municipal campaigns arising in various towns and cities at particular times because of local circumstances and needs—the sense in which the participants, as opposed to the national civil rights organizations and the national press, understood it—then we may see the "end" of the civil rights movement through new eyes. The truth is that the civil rights movement, conceived in these terms, has never ended. After the national legislative goals had been achieved, the attention of the national press shifted elsewhere, and the national civil rights organizations withered or died. The re-enfranchisement of blacks, too, made demonstrations and other types of direct action less often necessary. But the local struggles in the cities and towns across the South that had given birth to the various municipal crusades continued, and continue at this moment, though now usually fought out less dramatically within electoral politics. The Bus Boycott and its successors represent, at least in very significant part, the efforts of citizens legally disfranchised for half a century to give expression to their political will. Today those efforts persist just as vigorously throughout the region, but because their form is now more ordinarily American, observers have erroneously concluded that the spirit of the civil rights movement is no longer to be found. Once we appreciate the decidedly local character and goals of the various civil rights campaigns, we can see that this belief is contradicted in virtually every single Southern municipal election.

The Bus Boycott, in sum, has much to teach us. The works included in this volume cast substantial new light upon an episode whose examination can greatly clarify the recent history both of the South and of the United States as a whole. All of these accounts have had only limited circulation heretofore, and three are published here for the first time. Six of them—the contributions by Ralph Abernathy, Edgar French, Thomas Thrasher, Lawrence Reddick, Norman Walton, and Preston Valien—are probably best characterized as primary sources. Of these, the most significant certainly is Abernathy's, though it has never before been printed. Abernathy was, of course, King's closest associate and friend throughout the Boycott, and King's successor as president both of the Montgomery Improvement Association and, later, of the Southern Christian Leadership Conference. This work was a master's thesis which Abernathy submitted to the sociology department of Atlanta University only a year and a half after the Boycott's end. Because Abernathy was a candidate for a degree in sociology, he felt himself compelled in writing the thesis to adopt the peculiar conventions of that discipline. Therefore, even though the thesis is in effect a memoir,

Abernathy structures it as if it were based on interviews with "informants." By far the majority of it, however, is derived from an "interview" with himself, and simply recounts his own recollections of the events. The remainder is based upon his conversations with his MIA associates.

Edgar French, too, was one of the MIA's founders. His article, however, is a memoir in form as well as in fact. Initially published in 1962, it contains our only direct evidence of the origins of the three demands that became the Boycott's foundation, and that were subsequently adopted as the demands of the Tallahassee boycott as well.

The articles by Thomas Thrasher, Lawrence Reddick and Norman Walton were published in the midst of the Boycott. Thrasher, a white Episcopal priest, headed the Montgomery chapter of the Alabama Council on Human Relations, the state's affiliate of the Southern Regional Council and its most important interracial organization. His reflections, which appeared in March, 1956, stress the critical importance of rumors and misunderstandings in shaping the Boycott's course. Reddick and Walton were both professors of history at Alabama State College, a Montgomery public institution of higher education for blacks. Reddick's account of the Boycott's beginning also appeared in the spring of 1956. Reddick became a friend and advisor of Martin Luther King's, later helped King compile his own account of the Boycott, *Stride Toward Freedom* (1958), and wrote the first biography of King, *Crusader Without Violence* (1959). After a group of undergraduates from Alabama State staged a sit-in at the snack bar in the basement of the Montgomery County Courthouse in February, 1960, an enraged Governor John Patterson and his state board of education ordered Reddick fired from his teaching position, apparently in the belief that he had had a hand in fomenting the trouble; for this action Alabama State was placed under censure by the American Association of University Professors. Walton began the publication of his history of the Boycott, "The Walking City," in the *Negro History Bulletin* in October, 1956; it appeared in five installments in that journal, concluding in January, 1958. Based chiefly upon reports in the Montgomery newspapers, it was the first full narrative of the movement.

The final contribution which should probably be classed as a primary source is the article by Preston Valien, a sociologist at Fisk University in Nashville, Tennessee. Though the article first appeared in 1961, it was written in the summer of 1957, and the extensive interviews upon which it is based were conducted at the very height of the Boycott by Valien and his colleagues and graduate students at Fisk. His principal associate in this project was Inez Adams. The records of the interviews themselves are now housed in the Amistad Research Center at Tulane University in New Orleans, and they make fascinating reading. Students of the Boycott have not as yet sufficiently exploited them.

The remaining five contributions represent the research of scholars in more recent years. Two are here receiving their initial publication. The work by Thomas J. Gilliam was a master's thesis in history presented to Auburn University in 1968. It was the first thorough exploration of the movement by a historian not actually a participant in it. The study by Steven M. Millner was a doctoral dissertation in sociology submitted to the University of California at Berkeley in 1981, and just revised for inclusion in the present volume. It emphasizes, as do the articles by Professor David Garrow and by the present writer, the especially important role played in the Boycott by Montgomery's black women. This point has recently received emphatic support with the publication by the University of Tennessee Press of the memoirs of Jo Ann G. Robinson, *The Montgomery Bus Boycott and the Women Who Started It* (1987).

The final three articles have appeared elsewhere, but are not readily available to all students of the period. The article by Dominic J. Capeci, Jr., was initially published in *The Historian* in 1979. That by David J. Garrow is from *Southern Changes*, the journal of the Southern Regional Council, and appeared in 1985. And the contribution by this writer was first published in the *Alabama Review* in 1980, and in 1987 was reprinted in Sarah Woolfolk Wiggins, editor, *From Civil War to Civil Rights: Alabama, 1860-1960* (University of Alabama Press).

J. Mills Thornton III
University of Michigan, Ann Arbor

The Walking City

The Walking City: A History of The Montgomery Bus Boycott

NORMAN W. WALTON

Part I

Introduction

Montgomery, Alabama is an agrarian city nestled in the middle of the cotton kingdom. It is the capital city of Alabama proud of its heritage and its Civil War contributions. Most of the people are proud too, proud of their southern way of life. Here, the historical Huntingdon College and the Alabama State College play an important role in the development of an enriched community life. Just a few miles east of Montgomery is the famed Tuskegee Institute which stands as a monument of the work of Booker T. Washington.

There is a strange silence about the city, no major factories or industries. The usual sound of whistles, clanging of bells and the hustle and bustle which often are a part of a city with a population of 100,000 are missing here. But this is it, the heart of Dixie, the cradle of the Confederacy, THE WALKING CITY.

Today Montgomery is one of the sore spots of race relations in the world. One can almost feel the undercurrent of tension in the air as he travels upon its streets. The city has indicted twenty-four Negro ministers of the Gospel and sixty-six other persons. To arrest a Negro minister in the south where

3

the hardships and tribulations have made many Negroes become deeply religious is a crime, but to arrest twenty-four is almost an unforgivable act against God. These twenty-four "Holy Men," as they were called by their constituents, have added new fuel to the doctrine which is destined to become a rallying cry in the South's struggle over segregation. It is the doctrine of "passive resistance."

Henry D. Thoreau originated the idea in his church in Massachusetts about 110 years ago. When Thoreau refused to pay his poll tax, he was thrown in jail. His famous essay on "Civil Disobedience" presents the theme that if the government is wrong the least a man can do is refuse to cooperate with it. He wrote, "It is not a man's duty, as a matter of course to devote himself to the eradication of anything even the most enormous wrong. He may still properly have other concerns to engage him; but it is his duty at least to wash his hands of it."

In the past 100 years or more the idea has traveled around the world. It worked to topple the British in India as it went and today it has come to America. Mahatma Gandhi, the great leader of India, without an army or political alliance, used the theory of Thoreau, which he called "passive resistance" and gained political independence for India. The doctrine based on spiritual and moral principles declares that love is the force that holds people together. As a leader of the Congress Party in India, he fought for the dignity and equality of man. He led a successful boycott against the English salt regulations.

Today "passive resistance" has become the cry of Montgomery's 50,000 Negroes in their struggle for the dignity of man. Negroes throughout the nation, and oppressed people all over the world are watching Montgomery, watching and waiting with great anticipation for what they hope will become a universal weapon to champion the cause of downtrodden and degraded people in their struggle for the dignity of man on earth.

What mysterious phenomenon of the "winds of nature" swept this doctrine to the heart of the South, or why Montgomery has become the testing ground for this weapon in America cannot be answered. Nevertheless these are some of the facts about the movement as they have unfolded here in the deep South.

The Beginning

On December 1, 1955, a tall light-skin Negro seamstress, employed by a downtown department store, was making a routine trip to work on a city bus. The bus, being filled with passengers, carried fourteen whites and twenty-four Negroes seated in the accustomed areas on the thirty-six seat vehicle.[1] It was reported that the bus operator sought to equalize the seating by asking some of the Negroes to move to the rear. Mrs. Rosa Parks argued she was not in the white section since the bus was filled from the back to the front. It is interesting to note that the Montgomery City code states:

Section 10, Chapter 6 of the Code of the City of Montgomery 1952

Every person operating a bus line in the city shall provide equal but separate accommodations for white people and Negroes on his buses by requiring the employees in charge thereof to assign passenger seats on the vehicles under their charge in such a manner as to separate the white people from the Negroes, where there are both white and Negro passengers on the same car; provided, however, that Negro nurses having charge of white children, sick or infirm white persons, may be assigned seats among white people.

Nothing in this section shall be constructed prohibiting the operators of such bus lines from separating the races by means of separate vehicles if they see fit.

Section 11, Chapter 6 of the Code of the City of Montgomery 1952

Any employee in charge of a bus operated in the city shall have the power of a police officer of the city while in actual charge of any bus, for the purpose of carrying out the provisions of the preceding section.

Under these circumstances Rosa Parks was arrested by J. F. Blake, the bus driver in charge when she refused to move from her seat which Blake said was in the white section of the bus. As stated above in the City Code of Montgomery 1952, the bus driver has special police power to make arrests on the bus he operates. Policemen who arrived later confirmed Blake's

5

charges that the woman was seated in the white section of the bus, and refused to move to the rear.

The arrest of Rosa Parks, who was secretary to the local chapter of the NAACP, was resented by the Negro population in general. The resentment seemed not to have been because of this one incident, but this was the "straw that broke the camel's back."

On Friday when the Negroes of Montgomery heard of Mrs. Parks' arrest, thousands of circulars were distributed urging Negroes not to ride the city buses on the following Monday in protest to the arrest. On Monday night about 5,000 Negroes met at the Holt Street Baptist Church and adopted a resolution which asked the citizens of Montgomery not to ride the bus until a satisfactory seating condition had been worked out. The resolution stated that no method of intimidation would be used to prevent anyone from riding the buses. A car pool was organized to aid in getting the people to and from work. It was reported that all Negro cab operators in the city told their drivers to charge only 10 cents a head for certain hours during the day in an effort to make the boycott effective.[2]

In the meantime, more than a dozen motorcycle police were assigned to trail the buses. Hundreds of Negroes lined the streets to cheer when the emptied buses passed followed by two motorcycle police. It was reported that the "old unlearned Negroes" were confused. It seemed that they could not figure out if the police would arrest them or protect them if they attempted to ride the buses. Rumors were spread that they would be arrested instead of protected. The few Negroes who boarded the buses were more confused. They found it difficult to get off without being embarrassed by other Negroes who waited at the bus stops throughout the city. Some were seen ducking in the aisles as the buses passed various stops in order not to be seen.

Anti-Bus Sentiment Crystallized

Although many Negroes expressed openly their sentiment against the bus company, others were less vocal and others still would rather suffer while evils were sufferable than go through the hardships of righting them. Thus in the beginning much of the sentiment against the bus company was promoted by a minority of the Negroes who devoted time and service to molding public opinion. They presented a long line of abuses which were easily obtained from those who rode the buses. In the streets, over the telephone, in the cabs and in the schools and churches they related their varied unpleasant experiences with the bus company.

On December 8 a group of Negro leaders met for four hours with representatives of the bus company and the city to discuss the issue. Rev. M. L. King who was later branded as the "boycott boss" was selected as spokesman for the Negro delegation. Rev. King is the 27 year old pastor of the historical Dexter Avenue Baptist Church of Montgomery. He holds degrees from Morehouse College, Crozer Theological Seminary and Boston University where he earned his doctorate.[3]

The Rev. M.L. King, speaking for the Negroes, proposed that patrons be seated on a first come first served basis with no section reserved for either race. Negroes would continue to seat from the rear to the front and the whites from the front. He suggested that there would be no reassignment of seats once the bus was loaded. He laid down two other conditions sought by Negroes: more courteous service by the bus drivers to Negroes and the hiring of Negro bus drivers on predominantly Negro routes.

The boycott conference failed to find a solution to the problem. Many Negroes felt that one more day of rain might send the Negroes back on the buses. Some Negroes were unhappy about walking in the rain while others rode in big cars. One irritated college student who walked into a campus building quite wet stomped her feet at the door and yelled, "boycott or no boycott if it rains tomorrow, I am going to ride a bus." After the second day the novelty of the movement had worn off. This was serious business. Thus it appears that the decision to slash bus runs in the Negro sections did more to crystallize the movement than any act thus far. The Negro could not ride if he desired to. There were no buses to ride.

The act of taking the buses off the lines in Negro areas united the feet but the minds were left to the press. Perhaps the most influential organ in Montgomery for molding public opinion was the daily newspaper, the *Montgomery Advertiser*. On the editorial page of this paper is a section commonly known as "Tell It To Old Grandma." Here the opinions and expressions of the people of the area could be found. These expressions did much to classify the people of the area as pro-boycott or anti-boycott.

As Montgomery approached the Yuletide season, there was indeed a oneness among Negroes that had never existed before. The so-called "big Negroes" were carrying maids to work in their new cars and they talked together and laughed together. The Negro who remarked to the college professor, after hearing the word boycott, boycott, boycott, "I don't see what the boycott has to do with the buses, anyway," had something in common with the professor. Maybe not a spirit of Christmas but an "esprit de corps" which brought them together. This spirit of unity was expressed in the attitude of a maid when she declared, "I'll walk until my feet fall off before I ride the bus again."

One Negro, obviously from the country, said "this is where I was bred and born." Another was sure that walking had cured her illness and most of the maids walking claimed to feel the schoolgirl figure returning. A Negro bandleader wrote the boycott song:

> Ain't gonna ride them buses no
>   more
> Ain't gonna ride no more
> Why in the hell don't the white
>   folk know
> That I ain't gonna ride no more.

The Negro had come to realize that there was something religious and noble about this movement. To them it promoted the brotherhood of men. The nonviolence doctrine which had come to dominate the thinking of its leaders gave the movement a Christian attachment. It was their religious duty now not only to go to church, visit the sick, and to pray, but they must also attend the mass meetings. To the Negro of Montgomery, Christianity and boycott went hand in hand. Later, Adam Clayton Powell, Negro Congressman of New York, declared "the movement in Montgomery is religious not political; politicians come and go, but faith and God march forward."

Whites Aid Boycotters

It is not unusual to find members of the white race giving aid to such movements, and there are evidences to show that many white people were in sympathy with the movement in Montgomery, but the climate of opinion at the time was not favorable to express their feelings. One might be branded as a "Nigger lover" for even the smallest overt act of sympathy with the movement. Disregarding these conditions, however, many whites gave "lip service" to the cause and many gave money and their time and service to aid the protest. The lip service ranged from the emotional expression of individuals like those of an ex-bus driver who declared that "as long as the bus boycott is on, it will be a dreary rainy day, when I have sprained my ankle and less than 45 cents cab fare, before I board one of those yellow rolling cell blocks again," to the very scholarly letters like the one of Mrs. J. Morgan.[4] Perhaps one of the most energetic white workers in the movement was Rev. Robert S. Graetz, pastor of the all Negro Lutheran Church in Montgomery. His activities with the boycott caused him to receive many threatening calls. As reported in the *Montgomery Advertiser* some of the calls ran afoul to the state's profanity law. One irritated fellow called to say, "Pastor if I were you I wouldn't call myself a pastor. You are a no good S.O.B." Another hoped that he would have a son-in-law as black as the blackest Negro that ever originated from the wilds of Africa.[5]

Appeal to the People

On December 25, the *Montgomery Advertiser* carried the Negroes declaration of grievances against the bus company. The document brought forth many of the bitter experiences of the Negroes who had at various times been pushed around on the buses. The document accused the operators of discourtesy, and unfairness in seating of passengers. The doctrine stated that in many instances the operators have passed up passengers standing at the stop to board the bus. They have also collected fares at the front door and after commanding Negro passengers to enter by the rear door, have pulled off and left them standing there. It told of a Negro mother, with two small children in her arms, who put them on the front seat while she opened her purse for the fare. The driver ordered her to take them off, and without giving her a chance to place the children elsewhere, lunged the vehicle forward, causing the small children to be thrown into the aisle of the bus. In this document the movement was officially crowned as "non-violent"; a movement of "passive resistance" depending on moral and spiritual forces. It further expressed the willingness of the Negroes to arbitrate and felt that this could be done with men of goodwill, but it was difficult to arbitrate with those whose public pronouncements were anti-Negro. This document was a great victory for the Negroes of Montgomery and for the cause in general.

The New Year came in with little hope to ease the crippled transportation system of Montgomery. By this time the ministers of the city had been branded as the leaders of the protest. Perhaps the assumption stems from the overt activities of the ministers in the movement. It was being suggested in the community that the Montgomery Improvement Association should be checked to see if they were violating any laws of the state. On December 13, the *Montgomery Advertiser* carried an editorial entitled, "Action and Reaction, a Two Edge Sword," in which the editor declared that Negroes should reckon with the facts of life. First the white man's economic artillery is far superior, and commanded by more experienced gunners; second, the white man holds all offices of government machinery. There would be white rule as far as the eye can see.[6] The Negroes were beginning to feel the sting of this whip. On January 9, a Montgomery attorney called attention to the press to the state law against boycott. He stated that Title 14, Section 54 of the Alabama Code, provided that when two or more persons unlawfully enter into an understanding for the purpose of preventing the operation of lawful business, they shall be guilty of a misdemeanor.

Perhaps the best summary expression of the situation in Montgomery by January 1956 was given by Rev. Thomas R. Thrasher, Director of an Episcopal Church in the City, when he declared, "the only universal thing about our community is fear . . ."

Get Tough Policy

On January 22, the City Commissioners shocked the Negro population of Montgomery by stating that it had met with a group of prominent Negro ministers and had reached a solution to the problem. When it was learned that these problems of transportation had been solved the Negro leaders were confused; they knew nothing about the meeting. Later it was revealed that three Negro ministers had been called to the Commissioners' office to discuss "another issue about some type of insurance" and that they had been "hoodwinked into it." Negro ministers mobilized their forces to spread the news that the boycott was not over. By the next morning, the news had been circulated and almost everyone was aware of the Commissioners' act. Even the newsboys who delivered the morning's paper rapped on the doors to warn the readers, "don't believe that stuff about the boycott on the front page."

Such an attack on the City Commissioners which virtually called them liars could not be stomached. This was the last straw. Perhaps the concept of "southern honor" is a figment of the imagination, but to most white southerners it is a very real and cherished thing to protect at all cost.

The Commissioners instituted their "get tough policy" by declaring that it was time to be frank and that the vast majority of the whites in Montgomery "do not care whether a Negro ever rides a bus again if it means that the fabric of our community is to be destroyed, and that the Commission would stop pussyfooting around with the boycott." They further declared that "the Negroes have made their beds, let them sleep in them."[7]

Jitney Service Denied

Faced with this intransigent attitude on the part of the Commissioners and convinced that the difficulties in the transportation among Negroes were becoming more serious, it became evident, by then, that the system could not continue on a "share a ride" policy. Complaints were more numerous than before because it was becoming more difficult to catch a ride. Perhaps it was this situation coupled with a pressing need for a more organized system that provoked the proposal of the Montgomery Transit Lines. On January 2, 1956, a Negro group asked for permission to set up special transportation service owned and operated by Negroes; however, the Commissioner denied the request on the grounds that there was plenty transportation available in the city. On April 2, the Negroes asked again to be granted a bus franchise, but were denied.

King Arrested for Speeding

By now it seemed, to the Negroes, that this action of the City Commission was a part of an organized conspiracy to harass and intimidate them with the police department leading the attack. In this atmosphere, Rev. M. L. King was arrested for speeding. Negroes gathered at the scene of the arrest and were upset over the customary procedure of frisking a person, being arrested, for weapons. As the officer searched Rev. King, one of the bystanders remarked "That's a shame a'fore God they is searching the preacher."

Another Negro borrowed one of the Governor's expressions to answer a statement made by one of the arresting officers at the trial, that the car left before he could get the license number, the Negro declared "Hogwash, I ain't never seen a car yet that can outrun a motorcycle in a crowded city, it's just hogwash."

King's Home Bombed

On January 30, Rev. King's home was bombed. This convinced the Negro that this was indeed serious business. Immediately a crowd gathered outside the house which was the parsonage of the Dexter Avenue Baptist Church. They refused to leave when police attempted to disperse the crowd. King came out later to address the crowd, and told them to go home. "I am all right and my wife is all right." Someone from the crowd called, "let us see her" and Mrs. King came out and stood with her husband. King continued to innoculate the Negroes with the serum of passive resistance. "We believe in law and order, don't go get your weapons. He who lives by the sword will perish by the sword." He assured the crowd that if he was stopped the movement would not stop because God was with the movement. As he finished, the crowd cheered him, shouting "Amen" and "God bless you." "We are with you all the way, Reverend."

The Police Commissioner attempted to address the group and immediately a roar of disapproval was heard throughout the crowd. Police officers sought to get the attention of the Negroes by yelling, "Be quiet, the Commissioner is talking," but the Negroes seemed not to have heard them. Shortly Rev. King turned to the crowd, raised his hand and said "hear the Commissioner" and immediately there was quietness throughout the group. Like Gandhi of India, King had become the Mahatma, a great soul, and for the Negroes of Montgomery he was "Bapo," the father. Later when E.D. Nixon's home was bombed, the Negroes were more convinced that "we ain't gonna ride dem buses no more."

Negroes Filed Anti-Segregation Suit

It appears that this get tough policy of the Commissioners and the recent bombings caused the Negroes to seek an additional method of adjusting their grievances. Thus, on February 1, 1956, five Montgomery Negro women filed suit in the U.S. District Court asking the courts to declare Alabama and Montgomery's transportation laws unconstitutional.

This bill of complaint charged that Negroes have been deprived of their rights, privileges and immunities under the 14th Amendment in seeking "to compel the plaintiffs and other Negro citizens to use the bus facilities" under threats and harassment. It specifically accused the defendants of a conspiracy to interfere with the civil and constitutional rights of the Negro citizen. However, less than two days after the suit, Jeanette Reese, one of the five women who filed the complaint, told the Mayor that she didn't know what she was signing and that she didn't want anything to do with the "mess." Thus on March 8, Attorney Fred Gray withdrew the name of Jeanette Reese from the anti-segregation suit.[8]

Boycott Attorney Under Pressure

In the meantime, Attorney Fred Gray was having trouble with the local draft board. It seems that Gray had been exempted from military service since 1948 because he was classified by the draft board as a practicing minister. If Gray was not a practicing minister, he was subject to disciplinary action. Attorney Gray was also indicted by the Grand Jury for unlawful practice because of the suit filed in U.S. District Court seeking to overthrow Montgomery and Alabama's transportation laws. The case did not materialize because the unlawful practice charge against Fred Gray was tossed out of court.

Grand Jury Reports

By now the situation in Montgomery had reached the breaking point. And though there were many appeals for peace, they seemed to have fallen on deaf ears. The fat was in the fire. Already the Montgomery County Grand Jury had been selected to determine whether Negroes who were boycotting the buses were violating the law. This jury, including 1 Negro and 17 whites, found that the boycott was illegal and the violators should be punished.[9]

13

PART II

Mass Arrest of Boycotters

On February 22 deputies began the arrest of all persons connected with the boycott who were violating the state law . . . the arrests which were to shock the world. A total of ninety-three persons were arrested under the law. Twenty-four were ministers. For almost two days the courthouse was crowded with Negroes going in and out. They were given a number and fingerprinted and photographed. The whole procedure seemed to have everyone confused because surely there had been nothing like it in Montgomery's whole history. Negroes who were expected by all past action in history to be afraid and attempt to deny the charge, virtually placed themselves under arrest. There seemed to have been some supernatural force that gave them strength. Many Negroes after hearing that their names were on the list went straight to the courthouse. Others went to inquire if they were on the list. One Negro leader, after being told he was not listed, became angry and insisted on knowing why he was not. It was indeed a day of honor to be arrested. Thurgood Marshall, General Counsel for the NAACP, declared "up until the indictment was handed down by the Montgomery County Grand Jury, there was a local problem growing out of the spontaneous resentment of the people. Now it has become our case and we intend to fight it."[10]

In the meantime the City Commissioners had proposed a final compromise which would end the boycott. The arrest and compromise came when Rev. King was out of the city, but at a mass meeting led by Rev. Ralph Abernathy, the compromise, which was the same as the one which had been refused by Negroes, was voted down.

Boycotters in the Court

The trial of 93 Negroes charged with illegally boycotting the Montgomery City Lines began on March 19, 1956. About 500 Negroes waited in the halls and outside the small courthouse which was to be the scene of the trial. The Rev. M. L. King, Case No. 7399, pastor of the Dexter Avenue Baptist Church and recognized spokesman of the boycott, was the first to be tried.[11]

On the first day of the trial, the State Prosecuting Attorneys produced testimony and bookkeeping records to show that several thousand dollars had been spent by the Montgomery Improvement Association to finance automobile rides for Negroes who had boycotted the Montgomery City Lines, Inc. Mrs. Erna Dungee, wife of a Negro doctor and financial secretary of the Association, affirmed financial records presented by Assistant Circuit Solicitor R. E. Stewart. Mrs. Dungee testified Association checks were paid to eight service station operators for gasoline purchases for operation of the transportation service. Particular attention was given to the check of $5,000 made out to cash and endorsed by King. Mrs. Dungee testified the money was simply a transfer of funds from Alabama National Bank in Montgomery to Citizens Trust Company in Atlanta, Georgia.[12] King had explained this move in a mass meeting; he said it was to prevent the tying up of funds by local officials.

The Defense Attorneys, Arthur Shores, Peter Hall, Ozell Billingsley, Fred Gray, Charles Langford and Robert Carter, objected to the admission of the bookkeeping records on grounds that the records, deposit slips, and checks were photostatic copied and not the best evidence, and that the records of the Improvement Association were "immaterial and irrelevant."[13] Judge Carter overruled the objection and admitted the evidence. He explained that there was enough evidence at that time to connect the material with a charge of conspiracy against the defendant.

After the state had completed its case, the Negro Defense Attorneys immediately sought to throw out all of the prosecution's evidence as insufficient to prove that King violated Alabama anti-boycott law. "Even if the state had proved such action," Gray continued, "no evidence was produced to show the Negroes did not have a just cause or legal excuse."[14] Again Gray restated that the law itself, under which King was brought to trial, was unconstitutional in that it violated the Federal Constitution.

Replying to the Negro Attorneys, Circuit Solicitor William F. Thetford said both the Alabama and U.S. Supreme Court have held that the boycott law was not in violation of freedom of speech or assembly.

Judge Carter overruled this request of the Negro Lawyers and stated that he thought the state had established a "prime facie" case of conspiracy but did not say if King was connected with it.[15] The state had attempted to show that Negroes were threatened and intimidated to keep them from riding the buses, by presenting Negroes who were later to be called "black Judases" to testify that they had been threatened and intimidated.

On March 21, Rev. Martin L. King testified in his defense that he had not encouraged Negroes to boycott the buses and that his attitude was "Let your conscience be your guide." He described the Montgomery Improvement Association as an organization created to improve the general status of Montgomery, improve race relations, and uplift the "general tenor of the community."[16] He agreed that the officers of the Association were M. L. King, President; L. R. Bennett, Vice President; U. J. Fields, Recording Secretary; and E. D. Nixon, Treasurer. King also supported the statement that about $3,500 a week was being spent to support the bus boycott.

King was questioned by City Solicitor William Thetford on the facts about the formation of the boycott and said he couldn't remember what group drew up the petition or the recommendations that were presented at the first mass meeting, nor could he remember whether the agenda for the meeting at the Holt Street Baptist Church was drawn up that afternoon or that night. "In any event," he said, "the plan reflected the wishes of the 4,000 Negroes present at the December 5 mass meeting."[17] When asked if there were any white persons who were members of the Montgomery Improvement Association, King said that he didn't know because "We don't keep our records on the basis of race." However, he admitted that Graetz was a member.

Rufus Lewis, First Chairman of the Transportation Committee that operated the car pool, explained how the committee arranged a system of free transportation for Negroes financed by contributions made at church services and mass meetings. He said approximately 43 pick up and dispatch stations were set up to accommodate persons who could not get transportation otherwise.

One of the difficulties of the state was its own witness, the Rev. U. J. Fields, pastor of the Bell Street Church and Secretary of the Montgomery Improvement Association. He refused to swear the oath to tell the truth because it was against his religion, but he promised the Judge he would tell the truth. Most of his answers were in the tune of "My memory does not serve me well enough to answer" or "the words do not make sense to me now."

The Defense Attorneys used 28 witnesses to show Negroes were mistreated while riding the buses. Mrs. Thelma Glass of the Women's

Political Council testified her group had tried for six years to get the City Commission to arrange more favorable seating conditions on the buses and were refused. Mrs. Sadie Brooks, member of the Civic Federation Club, testified she heard a Negro passenger threatened because he did not have the correct change. "The driver whipped out a pistol and drove the man off the bus."

Georgia Gilmore said when she boarded a bus, a driver yelled out at her, "come out nigger and go in the back door." When she stepped off the bus to comply, the driver drove away. She continued, "when they count the money, they do not know Negro money from white money."

The Rev. Robert S. Graetz, 27 year old white pastor of the Trinity Lutheran Church in Montgomery testified for the defense. He declared that King was not in favor of threatening or intimidating anyone who chose to ride the buses.

Richard S. Jordan testified that his wife had been forced to move to make way for white ladies at the capitol just going two blocks. He also objected to being called "nigger" and "boy." Della Perkins said she had been called "ugly black ape" by a driver. Many of the Negroes wore crosses on their lapels reading "Father, forgive them."

Scores of newspaper reporters representing publications in the United States, India, France, and England covered the trial. The reporter from the farthest distance was M. V. Kamath, special correspondent of the press in India, LTD, which is the AP of India. The *New York Post* sent down two artists to cover the trial. They were Harvey Dinnastein and Burt S. Luenman. Farrel Dobbs, who was a candidate for President of the United States in 1948 and 1952 on the Socialist Workers Party ticket, was covering the trials for a labor weekly. He stated, "I believe their (the Negroes) demands are democratic and certainly they are entitled to full equality as citizens. I am interested in the trial because of the demand for democratic rights which our group adheres to strongly." Negro Congressman Charles C. Diggs (D-Mich) was present. He brought more than $5,000 contributed by residents of Detroit to aid the boycotters.[18]

Rev. King was convicted on March 22, on a charge of violating the state's Anti-Boycott Law and was fined $500 and court costs by Judge Eugene Carter, the equivalent of 386 days at hard labor in the County of Montgomery. Carter ordered a continuance in 89 other cases of Negroes charged with the same violation until a final appeal action was complete in the King case. Hundreds of Negroes and whites, including newspapermen, television cameramen, and photographers waited outside the courthouse to greet King. As King and his beautiful wife left the courthouse, they encountered a lively demonstration on the sidewalk and in the streets. The crowd waving and clapping their hands and chanting "Long live the King," "God bless you," and "we ain't gonna ride the buses no more." King's remarks were, "we will continue to protest in the same spirit of nonviolence and passive resistance using the weapon of love."

Judge Carter left town for a "welcomed rest" after the court ordeal. Negroes knew that even though he sought refuge in isolation, he could not erase the stain of injustice from his conscience. Nor would the nation allow him to forget, because the people were already branding him as a "butcher of democracy."

In New York, Rabbi William Rosenblum stated that the conviction of the leader of the nonviolent protest "emphasizes some of the amazing contradictions upon which the American people and the world as a whole should ponder. The Judge who imposed the sentence upon this fine Christian minister is himself a Christian Bible Class teacher, a mason, and a member of the American Legion."[19]

In New Jersey, a young Evangelist, Russell Roberts, started sleeping, fasting, and praying in his Shiloh Baptist Church pulpit in sympathy with the Montgomery, Alabama bus boycott. He thrived off one quart of vegetable juice a day and declared, "I will live and sleep and pray and fast in my pulpit for as long as God gives me strength." Roberts lost 15 pounds as he continued for 11 days to pray for the rights of all people.[20]

The pro-boycott sentiment extended throughout the nation and gained momentum when a group of prominent clergymen led by Adam C. Powell called upon every Negro man, woman, and child to join in a National Deliverance Day of Prayer. Powell told a Harlem church rally he might resign from Congress and devote himself to a nationwide prayer movement against segregation, if his March 28 Deliverance Day extended itself successfully. He would ask President Eisenhower to join in the prayer day on the steps of the White House and would confer with Cardinal Spellman.[21] In the Negroes' great anxiety to aid the movement in Montgomery, it was rumored that sympathizers throughout the nation would stop work for an hour and pray. However, Dr. Joseph H. Jackson, President of the National Baptist Convention, told Powell the work stoppage idea was completely erroneous. He declared that we are interested in prayer only, and

Powell concurred by declaring, "we are not emphasizing anything that will cause tension or ill will."

Most Negroes in the nation seemed to have been in favor of the National Deliverance Day Movement, but some of the leaders felt that a more effective program for the boycotters would include some financial support. In the light of this idea, it was suggested that instead of demonstrating to show sympathy that March 28 would be a day every American Negro would give one hour's pay to support the protest.

In the South, the pro-segregationists rallied their forces to combat the proposed "Day of Deliverance." George W. Cheek of Selma, Alabama felt the Negroes were not sincere in posing such a deep "love" for those who "hate" them so intensely. He warned the southern whites to beware of outside influence like Adam C. Powell of New York who suggested a day of prayer for the deliverance of Montgomery Negroes from the wickedness of their white friends. About the prayer day, he declared, "Let them pray, they should pray! But praying till the crack of doom will not bring integration."[22]

Decision, Confusion and Protest

On April 23, 1956, the Supreme Court banned racial segregation by refusing to review a decision by the U.S. Circuit Court in Richmond stating that segregation on intrastate buses in Columbia, South Carolina violated the Federal Constitution. The decision by the Supreme Court caused a great deal of confusion throughout the nation. Some believed it abolished all segregation on intrastate media, others believed it abolished all segregation on intrastate travel only in South Carolina, and still others believed the court made no decision on the question but merely returned the appeal to the lower court where it had apparently not been completed. Immediately the many pro-segregation leaders branded the U.S. Supreme Court decision outlawing segregation on public buses as an "unwarranted invasion of state and municipal rights" and a new step in "Federal dictatorship." On April 23, the Superintendent of the Montgomery Lines posted orders to his drivers not to enforce segregation on the buses. On the other hand the City Commission issued a warning that it expected the bus company and other persons to abide by Alabama Laws, and that they would enforce the City Laws to maintain segregation. An angry city bus driver threatened an Associated Press photographer who attempted to take a picture of the bus. He declared, "If you take my picture, G— D— you, I'll kill you." Another driver declared, "I feel like driving this bus straight into the river."[23] A National City Lines, Inc. representative, parent of the Montgomery City Lines, stated that the company would not enforce segregation and the company would help its drivers, if they were arrested.

In the meantime, the Negroes, in a mass meeting, declared, "We will never go back to Jim Crow buses." They adopted a resolution, read by Rev. King, which declared:

> Whereas the public officials of . . . Montgomery and . . . Alabama have indicated . . . that they intend to . . . use all means available, including the arrest of bus drivers and passengers who refuse to abide by and obey the segregation law . . . it is . . . agreed that the conditions heretofore existing remain the same because of the position taken by our public officials.
>
> Be it therefore resolved that we, the Negro citizens of Montgomery, Alabama . . . will continue to carry on our Mass Protest . . ."

On May 9, Circuit Judge Walter B. Jones issued an injunction against further compliance with the bus company's integration order. To this Benjamin W. Franklin, Vice President of National City Lines, stated: "We will obey the injunction of the court." This statement by the National City Lines representative created a favorable climate for peace between the city officials and the National City Lines.

On May 11, 1956, a three judge Federal Court panel aired the anti-segregation suit filed by attorney Fred Gray. City attorneys worked diligently with the theme, "If Segregation Barriers are Lifted, Violence will be the Order of the Day." To these assertions, Judge Rives of the panel asked, "Can you command one man to surrender his constitutional rights, if they are his constitutional rights, to prevent another man from committing a crime?" This statement brought a new confidence to the Negroes in their struggle and kindled their hopes that justice was residual in the courts.

The three judge panel studied and deliberated on the case for a few weeks and then on June 4, 1956, declared the city bus segregation laws of Alabama unconstitutional. Thus the city continued operating under conflicting orders of two courts—the Federal Court injunction requiring desegregation and a Circuit Court injunction ordering maintenance of separate seating of races. City attorneys promised to appeal the case.

In the meantime, the Negroes of Montgomery continued to walk and passively resist the injustices which would destroy the dignity of man. Somehow they seem to be sure that here in THE WALKING CITY the battle for the preservation of democracy in America and the world was being fought.

By now the Montgomery boycott had continued so long until it was hardly news. The routine of share a ride or walk, mass meetings every Monday and Thursday nights had become a part of the Negroes' way of life. Moreover, the Negro people had become adjusted to being in the spotlight. Within the space of one year, no less than a dozen nationally known Negroes had spoken to Montgomery audiences. They included such prominent men as Dr. Archibald Carey, Congressman Adam C. Powell, Thurgood Marshall, Dr. Samuel Procter, Kelly Miller Smith, J. Pious Barber, Benjamin Mays, Congressman Clarence Diggs, Clarence Mitchell, Vernon Johns and many others. There can be no doubt that these great leaders of the Negro race did much to arouse and to stimulate the desire for first class citizenship among the Negroes of Montgomery.

NAACP Banned in Alabama

In 1909, as a result of a series of race riots which had shocked the nation, and under the leadership of Mary White Ovington, William English Walling, Dr. W. E. B. DuBois, Dr. Henry Moskowitz and Oswald Garrison Villard, the NAACP was founded. In the first year of its existence, the NAACP launched a program to widen the industrial opportunities for Negroes, to seek greater police protection for Negroes in the South, and to carry on a crusade against lynching and lawlessness.

Down through the years, it championed the cause of the Negro in his struggle for equal opportunities. In 1915, in the case of Guinn vs. United States, the Supreme Court, after hearing the arguments of Moorfield Storey, declared the Grandfather Clauses in the Maryland and Oklahoma Constitutions to be repugnant to the Fifteenth Amendment. In 1917, in the case of Buchanan vs. Warley, the court declared unconstitutional the Louisville Ordinance requiring Negroes to live in certain sections of the city. In 1923, in the case of Moore vs. Dempsey, the court ordered a new trial in the Arkansas Courts for a Negro who had been convicted of a murder.[24]

The Association undertook to secure in the courts the rights which Negroes could not otherwise obtain. Encouraged by its success in the cases involving the Grandfather Clauses, residential segregation, and the Arkansas peons, it sought to break down the practice of the Southern States of excluding Negroes from democratic primaries. It succeeded in the case of Nixon vs. Herndon in having the Supreme Court of the United States declare null and void a Texas Statute which excluded Negroes from the democratic primaries in the State. In 1944, the Association won a victory for Negro suffrage in the case of Smith vs. Allwright, when the Supreme Court decided that the exclusion of Negroes from the Democratic Primary was a clear violation of the Fifteenth Amendment. Thus, many Negroes came to regard the Court as the most reliable safeguard of the rights of all citizens, and the NAACP as an agent of protest for their rights.

Though there had been many unfavorable expressions about the operations of the NAACP, there had never been such an effort on the part of a Southern state to curb its activities, as was made during the first six months of 1956. Perhaps, it was because the NAACP was threatening the Southern way of life and seemed to be biting at the core of southern pride—white supremacy.

As part of this southern move against the NAACP, and at the request of Attorney General John Patterson, Circuit Judge Walter B. Jones issued a temporary injunction against the NAACP and declared it would remain in effect until further notice. Patterson said the NAACP has "never qualified under the law of this state to do business in Alabama as a foreign corporation." The injunction, among other things, charged the NAACP with helping to organize and support the boycott of the Montgomery Bus Lines by Negroes, also with employing or paying two Negro women to enroll in the University of Alabama. Patterson also charged that the activities of the NAACP "are causing irreparable injury to the property and civil rights of the residents and citizens of the State of Alabama," and that "they tend to bring about violations of the law and breaches of the peace."[25]

On June 2, 1956, the Alabama Chapter of the Association for the Advancement of Colored People stated that it would comply with the court order, temporarily banning NAACP activities in the State. Most of the state officials of the NAACP claimed that they would abide by all provisions of the injunction which was handed down by Judge Walter B. Jones. In reply to Attorney General John Patterson's charge that the NAACP never qualified under the law of Alabama as a foreign corporation, Roy Wilkins said copies of the NAACP's certificate of incorporation and constitution were mailed "some time ago" to Patterson, who had requested them. Wilkins said further, "We received a letter thanking us for these items and asking for some names and addresses to complete my files." There was no mention of compliance with or violation of Alabama Law.[26]

Reactions to the anti-NAACP injunction were immediate and varied. Ruby Hurley, regional secretary of the NAACP, said that "insomuch as we are law abiding citizens, we will abide by the injunction handed down by Judge Jones." Roy Wilkins, Executive Secretary of the NAACP, said the Association "did not organize the Montgomery Bus Protest, but we joined the rest of the country in hailing the people who did." He continued, "Nor did the NAACP employ Autherine Lucy or Polly Myers Hudson to enroll at the University of Alabama." Wilkins also declared about Patterson's petition and charges that, "These allegations appear to be efforts to deny the right of protest against intolerable and degrading treatment of citizens and to deny also the right of organized protest and legal action in the courts to serve admission of a qualified and accepted applicant to a tax supported school."[27]

Dr. G. A. Rodger, Jr., of Anniston, State NAACP President, commented that the Attorney General "cannot quench the quest for full citizenship by 900,000 Alabama Negroes through injunctions." Nor will it make Negroes ride segregated buses in Montgomery.

In Birmingham, Alabama on June 5, 1956, more than 500 "cheering, handclapping Negroes" met and organized the Alabama Christian Movement for Human Rights. This movement was dedicated to wiping out racial segregation. Rev. F. L. Shuttlesworth said, "The only thing we are interested in is uniting our people in seeing that the laws of our land are upheld according to the constitution of the United States." He continued, "Our citizens are restless under the dismal yoke of segregation."[28] The formation of the new group seemed to have been in answer to the temporary injunction granted by Circuit Judge Walter B. Jones of Montgomery, in which the NAACP was outlawed in Alabama.

The real answer to the anti-NAACP injunction came on June 12, 1956 when it was announced by the Board of Directors of the NAACP, that the organization would not be intimidated by the Alabama injunction and promised to fight the ban in the courts and in the arena of public opinion. Dr. Channing Tobias directed the NAACP attorneys to take the necessary legal steps to obtain a hearing on merits of the Alabama injunction at the earliest possible time with a view of dissolving the court's restraining order.

The NAACP Board declared the injunction was a direct violation of the American tradition and Constitutional Principle of Freedom of Association.[29]

The Fields Episode

On June 11, 1956 Rev. U. J. Fields, secretary to the Montgomery Improvement Association, was reported to have resigned his office. He accused the members of the Association of misappropriating funds, and "misusing money sent from all over the nation." He stated that the workers were "irresponsible" and declared that he could no longer be identified with a movement in which "the many are exploited by the few." He felt that the Association no longer represented what he stood for and that it had taken on a "bigness, which many of the persons involved were not used to." Moreover, he thought the leaders of the movement had become "too egotistical and interested in perpetuating themselves." Fields said industries, labor unions and churches all over the nation, plus "all kinds of social and political organizations," have been sending contributions to Montgomery Improvement Association to support the boycott and much of it is being kept by the persons who handle it and are "using it for their own purposes."[30]

This accusation against the MIA by Rev. Fields made many Negroes fear that this was the beginning of the end for the passive resistance movement in Montgomery. Until now, the Negroes had stood as a stone wall against a common foe. That had been the secret of their strength. It had been impenetrable without one little leak. Time after time, the whites had attempted to seek out a weak link and destroy the Movement, but without success. This accusation, then, was more than the pro-segregationists could bargain for. Rev. U. J. Fields, Pastor of the Bell Street Baptist church and one of the founders of the MIA, had turned traitor. It is understandable then why the pro-segregationists show little enthusiasm for the issue; they must be shrewd and diplomatic lest they lose their treasure. One small bit of overt anxiety might send the prize scrambling back into the fold.

The next two weeks were weeks of diplomatic maneuvering and undercover agreements. The Rev. M. L. King, President of the MIA was out of the city at the time. He and the Rev. Abernathy, pastor of the First Baptist Church, had gone to California to vacation, preach, and attend business obligations. The psychological unrest forced upon him after hearing the decision, and his pressing desire to be in Montgomery at this crucial time, caused him to cancel his appointments and return immediately to the city.

In the meantime, the perturbed emotions of the Negroes to the announcement were being overtly expressed—on the streets, in the churches, in the schools, in the cabs and almost every place they assembled; they talked about the "damnable Fields, the modern Judas." A Negro maid remarked, "I jest wish I could git my hands on 'im." Another exclaimed, "He must be a fool." Still another exclaimed, "The white folks have been stealing from us all this time and ain't nobody said nothing." The members of the Bell Baptist Church, which he pastored, expressed their sentiment in a very convincing way—they kicked him out. Even the school children knew him as a traitor to the cause, and as a villain with a "smiling cheek." This personal interest in the Movement, increased by the accusation of Fields, explains why the Negroes began to gather at the Beulah Baptist Church June 18 at 3 p.m. for a 7 p.m. Mass Meeting. By five o'clock the church was filled, and in the ninety degree temperature, which was considerably hotter in the church, they sat there, singing, praying and waiting . . . About 7 o'clock, the Rev. M. L. King entered the Church with Rev. Fields. The King received a standing ovation. They, the Rev. King and Rev. Fields, sat on the stage together. A Negro said, "Look at that devil sitting right next to Rev. King." King addressed the people with an eloquence that swayed the audience therein; he told the crowd, "I guess I know more about the MIA than anyone else, and I know of no misappropriation of funds–not one cent." He expressed his regret that Fields' statement had been publicized because it opened new avenues of investigation; but what had been done could not be undone. He asked the crowd, in the light of the true spirit of the passive resistance movement, to be forgiving toward Rev. Fields. He reminded the crowd of the words of Christ:

"Let he who is without sin cast the first stone."

Again, he innoculated the audience with a serum of "love" and explained that the nonviolence movement meant not only no physical violence, but no spiritual violence. One can kill a man in his heart. He appealed to the crowd to be forgiving as God had been. Thus, when he introduced the Rev. Fields, instead of the expected boos and sneers, there was a strange, hushed silence in the church.

Fields stood before the audience and began to pray. "Lord, help us to live in such a way from day to day, that even when we kneel to pray, our prayers will be for others . . ." An occasional "Amen" was heard throughout the audience. He asked the audience to forgive him for making the mistake and assured them that the statement was not true and that he had no available evidence that money meant for the MIA had been misplaced, or misused. The magic spell seemed to have engulfed the audience, and instead of booing him, they cheered him. The prodigal son had returned. Hundreds of persons who were gathered about the church talked of many things. Some agreed that they had witnessed a great event and a great man. An old man remarked, "He shore got guts." Another man said he was a fool to go before the audience because only a fool would have such a thing. Still others expressed the sentiment that all the "perfumes of Arabia" could not cleanse him of this deed.

Those who had hoped for a break in the Movement may find a lesson in history. History is rich with instances in which substantially unlike interests and diverse personalities find themselves working for a common object. One such instance was the breach between Frederick Douglass and William L. Garrison, in their struggle for the emancipation of slaves.

Garrison had found Douglass and had secured him to lecture for the Abolitionists and there had developed a strong friendship between them. When Douglass raised money to purchase his freedom, many of the Abolitionists criticized the transaction as a tacit recognition of the right "To Traffic in Human Beings." Garrison had justified the Negotiation. However, while on a speaking tour of the West, the hardships of the trip—exposure to rains, finally overcame Garrison and he became ill in Cleveland and was unable to proceed on schedule. He insisted that Douglass continued the tour. Douglass failed to write and inquire about Garrison's health. The Breach had come.

Later, Douglass started a new paper, the *North Star*, against the will of Garrison, who accused him of using money given to fight slavery for his personal recognition and who disagreed with him on some constitutional problems. The breach was irrevocable.

Thus, two great men fought diligently for a common cause—Garrison with his *Liberator* and Douglass with the *North Star*—would hardly speak when they chanced to meet.

Economic Effect of Boycott on Negro Population

Since the early days of the American Republic, money has been the hub of our economy. Perhaps the most important effect of the boycott on the community life of Montgomery is the pecuniary readjustments it is making among the people. Wealth that had for decades been flowing in one stream, is changing its course. Today instead of flowing from Negro to white, it flows from Negro to Negro. There is no doubt that this economic factor played a major role in the dissention and protest in Montgomery.

During the early phase of the boycott, taxicab service formed the cornerstone of the movement. Their increase in number is an index to the pecuniary upsurge in the business. Evidence will support the fact that there are many new and additional cabs on the streets of Montgomery. It is probably the "cabbiest" city of its size in the United States. There are no less than eighteen Negro cab companies in Montgomery.

Negro Cab Companies Spring 1965, Approximate Number of Cabs

New Deal	26
People Cab Co.	17
Original Queen	15
Dependable	8
Blue and Gray	7
Watts Cab Co.	7
Porter Cab Co.	6
Town Service Cab Co.	5
Blue Diamond	5
State Cab Co.	5
Lane Cab Co.	4
Henderson Cab Co.	3
United Cab Co.	3
Quick Service	3
Scott Cab Co.	2
Community Cab Co.	2
Fair Price	1
Sims Cab Co.	1

Outside Aid to Transportation

The transportation system in Montgomery, which was severely torn up during the early phase of the protest, was reconstructed, to a large degree, with the aid of more than fifteen new station wagons. These brand new 1956 cars, which were the property of the Negro churches, lifted the Negroes' spirits as well as their feet. The name of a church was painted on the front and sides of each station wagon along with a cross. The mere sight of these "rolling churches," as they are called, because many of the passengers sing hymns on their way to work, gave Negroes the spiritual uplift they needed. One old lady walking along the streets saw a loaded station wagon pass her by. With a smile on her face she exclaimed, "Dat's my church going thar," and began walking faster than ever. These station wagons were more than just rides for the Negro to and from work, they represented a moving symbol of the spirit of the protest that was in the hearts of all Negroes. This spirit burned anew with the sight of a station wagon, keeping alive the flame of protest from mass meeting to mass meeting.

Of no less importance was the upsurge in Negro business. It was common knowledge that many Negroes found it difficult to get downtown and found it easier to shop at the neighborhood stores, particularly if they were owned by Negroes. Negro theaters located in the downtown area felt the sting of the protest. Even Wild Bill Hickock wasn't worth walking two miles to see. Thus the neighborhood business, be it gas station or grocery store, got a new front or was able to buy fresher vegetables and meat because of the quick turnover. Moreover the thousands of dollars per week which had left the Negroes' hands and perhaps went to the bus company was now being spent among Negroes. The clubs, the stores, the cleaners and almost every Negro business shared directly or indirectly in the new income. Even the newspaper boys got a share of the profit. Sometimes there were as many as ten newspaper boys working the various mass meetings selling the *Afro-American*, the *Courier*, the *Defender*, *Jet* and other Negro publications. One professional Negro asked a newsboy what the *Afro-American* stood for in the front page of the paper. The newspaper boy replied, "I don't know what dat is, but here is Rev. King's picture on the front page. Wanna buy one?"

Achievements of Boycott

It is obviously too early to evaluate the accomplishments of the Negroes and Democracy in this passive resistance movement. Moreover, the fluid situation at the time makes it impossible to see the protest in its proper perspective; however, it may be reasonably safe to make these statements:

1. During the boycott, the Negroes of Montgomery became of age. As James E. Pierce, Professor of Political Science at the Alabama State College, stated, "The Negro matured in a space of four days. On December 1st, he was a boy, but on Monday, December 5 he had become a man. This complicated matters for the white man; he knew how to deal with the boy but could not handle the man." Perhaps this lack of understanding stems from the fact that there had been little contact between the races in the South for almost a hundred years. The maximum contact most whites have with Negroes is through the house servants or unscrupulous politicians. Thus, they must judge all Negroes by the actions of these persons. Moreover, the house servant is a confused Negro who must possess a dichotomous personality and be a master at "common psychology." He lives in the luxurious white home during the day and in many instances sleeps in shacks at night. He eats the best of food at work, watches TV in color, walks on expensive rugs and lounges on soft chairs. He uses the extension covered telephone and good perfume. He hates whites who are not as wealthy as his employers and with his small salary tries to live as his employer, trading at exclusive downtown stores, etc. On the other hand Negro teachers never really know the white teacher and Negro doctors know very little about white doctors in the South. Thus, during the boycott, for the first time in history, the white man sat down to talk with the Negro as a man, which brought them to the shocking realization that the Negro had grown up "while they slept."

2. A second interesting observation is the fact that the Negro leaders finally caught up with the masses. The lower elements, the proletariat, were ready and waiting for the leadership of the educated and intelligent groups.

3. A third vital accomplishment of the protest was the solidifying of the ministry, which had been divided along many lines. They are united as one and willing to follow their chosen leader with an enthusiasm which is astounding. Moreover it has bridged the gap of religious denominations in Montgomery. The Baptists, Methodists, Catholics, Lutherans, Seventh Day

Adventists, and Presbyterians and many others sang and prayed together, perhaps for the first time in America's history.

4. Dr. M. L. King has given new interpretation to the fight. He has insisted on a spiritual and moral movement, with love as the guiding light, and people of humble birth and limited training can understand. Love and suffering can be the tools in the struggle for the dignity of oppressed people throughout the world. Rev. Ralph Abernathy, pastor of the First Baptist Church of Montgomery, expressed the true spirit of the movement when he urged the Negroes to "Keep alive the spiritual side of the movement. If we concentrate on the political side, we are lost . . . but the long arm of God extends to everybody. We have as much access to Him as they."

5. It has closed the gap between the Negro groups based on education, income and position. In Montgomery, there is unity, the lowest person doing her humble task, rides to work in a Cadillac, a jalopy or a truck. The college professor talks with the maid and the drunkard with the minister, but with a common interest that brings them together.

Even more significant than these achievements was the projection of the Negroes' struggle, for the dignity of man, into the international sphere. Oppressed people throughout the world saw the boycott as a fight for the hope of the human race. It is of utmost importance to the people of the world, that American Democracy withstand the slings and arrows of segregation and the vicissitudes of world affairs and emerge strong. The Montgomery boycott has aided in shocking America into a realization of this urgency and helped to discipline her to become worthy of world leadership.

PART III

If the summer of 1956 seemed hotter than ever before to the Negroes of Montgomery, Alabama, it was indeed a part of the order of things in this southern city. The intrigue, unrest and foul play which was present almost everywhere added new fuel to the tension. For the Negroes, the anxiety and the desire to know more about their status in the struggle for the dignity of man increased the strain.

Insurance Trouble

The car pool, which had operated for months with only slight handicaps, was now under somewhat formal attack. Insurance agents, blaming the high risk involved in insuring taxi service station wagons, refused to insure them. Thus the churches found it difficult to secure insurance for their church station wagons. This action on the part of the local insurance agents provoked Reverend Robert Graetz, one of the white ministers working with the boycott, to charge there was a conspiracy to boycott, by denying liability insurance. However, the *Montgomery Advertiser* felt that Graetz had developed a persecution complex because of his "loneliness as the only white minister in the boycott."[31] It further declared that "the boycott automobiles including these shiny new station wagons masquerading as church cars had been guilty of notoriously bad driving resulting in a number of accidents" and that the "police in recent months have bent over backwards to avoid arrests for any but the most outrageous examples of carelessness or violation of the law."[32] After reading these words one Negro sat down in the street, tore his paper into bits and burned it. Another Negro reading the same paper nearby, after witnessing the act, ran over and threw his paper on the fire and exclaimed, "take this one too, darn it."

In the meantime, on July 1, the Rev. C. K. Steele, president of the Negro Intercivic Council in Tallahassee, Florida, said that 14,000 Negroes would boycott downtown merchants unless "police intimidation" was halted.[33] He felt that the city police had decided to "run us out of town" and that they seem not to recognize that "we are in town to pay bills and give business and patronage to stores that are friendly to us." A few days later the City Commission of Tallahassee ordered the police to crack down on drivers of automobiles in the car pool. They were to start arresting Negro car pool drivers for any violations of state law governing public carriers. Tallahassee's city attorney, James Messer, said most of the car pool drivers were not carrying the proper license tags, and only a few of the drivers were licensed as chauffeurs.[34] Negroes of Montgomery felt an evil wind blowing their way.

The Battles of the Brains

On June 27, 1956, the attorneys for the NAACP filed legal protests in the circuit court to kill the order restraining the operation of the NAACP in Alabama. It charged that the attorney general had no cause for action and the injunction deprived the organization of constitutional rights, including the due process of law, freedom of speech and assembly, and equal protection of the law. The Negro attorneys further said that the Alabama branch was separate and independent from the National Organization.[35] On the other hand, the Attorney General, John Patterson, continued his attack on the NAACP.

On July 5, he filed a petition seeking to force the NAACP to supply detailed information on its operation in Alabama.[36] He sought to compel the NAACP to furnish a list of all contributors to the Association in Alabama during the past 12 months, including names and addresses of persons authorized to solicit membership and contributions. The petition also sought to secure correspondence, telegrams and other records pertaining to the NAACP and the Negro Women (Authurine Lucy and Polly Myers Hudson) who sought admission to the University of Alabama. The attorney general decided the NAACP's records were the best evidence to determine whether the organization was illegally doing business in Alabama.[37] Patterson had gained a temporary injunction on the grounds that the NAACP never registered as a foreign corporation and is not legally qualified to engage in business in Alabama.

When the argument was heard in the court, the Negro attorney, Arthur Shores, contended that the production of NAACP records would amount to forcing the organization to give evidence against itself which was prohibited by the constitution. Attorney Shores contended Patterson could not know what records he needed until the hearing. Shores described the effort as a "fishing expedition."[38]

Nevertheless, on July 11, Judge Jones ordered the NAACP to produce certain documents by 10 a.m., Monday, July 16, for inspection of state authorities. Included in the information the NAACP was ordered to produce was the following: Copies of the charters of Alabama chapters, a list of all paid members in Alabama, names of all people authorized to solicit funds, a list of all real and personal property owned in the state, and a list of Alabama officers of the NAACP.[39]

Later, Judge Jones gave the Negro attorneys extended time to produce the records of the NAACP, because of the annual meeting of the Alabama Bar Association. The new date was 10 a.m., July 25.

Acting before the deadline set by Judge Jones on July 20, the NAACP filed a petition denying that it was doing business in Alabama in violation of any state law. It further charged that the state was seeking to prohibit citizens of Alabama from pursuing their rights which they say constitutes a denial of freedom of speech and freedom of assembly.[40]

The NAACP failed to deliver the records as requested by Judge Jones and was immediately fined $100,000 for contempt of court. It seemed at this point the Association records would remain a secret.

In the meantime, Negro attorneys asked the Alabama Supreme Court to stay the action of the lower court, but the Alabama Supreme Court declined the request. Negro attorneys argued Judge Jones made 10 errors in his orders starting with the issuance of the injunction and going through with the levying of the fine. On the other hand, state attorneys were busy trying to map strategy to collect the $100,000 fine levied on the NAACP. There was to be no sympathy for the Association even though they had offered to surrender some of the records to Judge Jones, but said that its 14,566 Alabama members had to be protected.[41]

At this time the situation in Montgomery seemed to have reached the breaking point. Gallows were erected on Court Square in downtown Montgomery, to hang the NAACP, and pro-integrationists in effigy. For a while two figures hung high over this square, one the NAACP, and the other was labeled, "I talked integregration." Of no less importance in understanding the incident was the sign painted on the frame structure which read "Built by union labor." It was reported that passers-by expressed more curiosity than approval of the incident. One small girl apparently enjoying the demonstration, asked, "Mommy, is that all?" When asked by a bystander if this was a prank or joke, one of the demonstrators replied, "Hell, no. We did this to show how serious we feel about the segregation issue."[42]

On the other hand, struggle between the White Citizen's Council of North Alabama led by Ace Carter and the W.C.C. of South Alabama led by Sam Englehardt continued, and the gap grew wider between the two sections. Around July 7, 1956 Carter invaded Montgomery to induce members to join the North Alabama Council and promised to put an end to the boycott. When informed of Carter's activities in Montgomery, Englehardt said, "We can't stand to have a rabble rouser like him (Carter) in Montgomery, Alabama."[43]

This action pleased many Negroes, for as one old Negro man said, "as long as they fight themselves they can't fight us." So the boycotters continued to walk and protest peacefully for the dignity of Man.

Car Pool Destroyed

Following the pattern that had been used in the Florida protest, on October 30, 1956, the City Commission unanimously set in motion machinery to obtain a Circuit Court injunction against continued operation of the car pool. Mayor W. A. Gayle introduced the resolution instructing the City's Legal Department "to file such proceedings as it may deem proper to stop the operation of car pool or transportation systems growing out of the bus boycott."

Negro attorneys attempted to steal the ball from the city lawyers by filing a request for an order restraining the city from interfering with Negro car pool operations, but U.S. District Judge Frank M. Johnson refused to grant the request.

In the meanwhile the city's Legal Department had filed an injunction to halt the car pool. The city's petition was directed against the MIA and several churches and individuals. It asked the court to determine and grant compensation for damages growing out of the car pool operation. The city contended it lost $15,000 as a result of car pool operations. The city receives 2 per cent of the bus company revenues, which meant the bus company had lost about $750,000 by November 1956.[44] Moreover the petition alleged the car pool was illegal, that it operated without a license fee, and without a franchise and with poor drivers. Further, the car pool created many police problems; it was a "public nuisance" and a "private enterprise" operating without approval of the city.

Attorney Peter Hall of Birmingham raised the question that if the car pool was illegal, as the city contended, why hadn't the drivers and dispatchers been arrested and tried in city court. Hall told the court, "They would have had the Negroes in jail long ago if it were illegal." The whole discussion boiled down to this: Was the car pool a "private enterprise" operating without a license as the city contended? Or was it a voluntary "share the ride" plan provided as a service by Negro churches without profit or finance?

The answer came to the Negroes of Montgomery and the nation when on November 13, 1956, the city won a temporary injunction in State Court to halt the motor pool until further notice.[45]

To add to the confusion in November the Supreme Court wiped out Alabama's state and local laws requiring segregation on buses. It affirmed a decision on a special three-judge U.S. District Court in Montgomery which had ruled that enforced segregation of whites and Negroes on Montgomery buses violated the Federal Constitution's guarantees of due process and equal protection of the law. It also cited a subsequent decision outlawing segregation in public parks and playgrounds and public golf links. The Supreme Court acted without listening to any argument; it simply said, "The motion to affirm is granted and the judgment is affirmed."

Reactions to the decision were immediate and varied. Mrs. Susie McDonald, a 78-year-old Montgomery woman, said, "We were badly treated on the buses but now they've given us justice." Reverend Martin Luther King called it "a glorious daybreak to end a long night of forced segregation." On the other hand, President Jack Owens of the Alabama Public Service Commission said that "to keep down violence and bloodshed, segregation must be maintained." Senator Lister Hill of Alabama said, "Every lawful means to set aside the ruling should be used."[46] Mrs. Rosa Parks, the 43-year-old seamstress whose arrest started the boycott, commented the decision was a "triumph for justice." Negro attorneys immediately requested the U.S. District Judge Frank M. Johnson for an order to permit them to continue their car lift until the boycott ended. It was believed by many that the boycott would be called off at the next mass meeting. The Negroes felt there was no basic need to continue the car pool in face of the Supreme Court ruling.

Negro attorneys attempted to speed up the effective date of the mandate ending state and local laws requiring segregation on buses. The high court's mandate would not become effective until formal notice reached the lower court. This would normally take about 30 days. A prompt filing of the court's ruling would have the effect of permitting an earlier and final determination of four anti-segregation cases which were pending in Alabama. One justice of the Supreme Court had the authority to grant or deny the petition. On November 20, 1956, Supreme Court Justice Hugo Black of Alabama, after consulting with eight other Supreme Court Justices, denied the request of the Negro attorneys. The ruling held the bus segregation decision would be handled just as any routine decision.[47]

35

The refusal brought "no real disappointment" to the Negroes of Montgomery. Reverend King decided "we were optimistic enough to hope for the best but realistic enough to know it was possible the court would deny the request." He continued, "The protest will continue. We don't intend to return to segregated buses."[48]

On November 15, the boycott ended officially when Negroes at two mass meetings approved the recommendations made by the executive board of the SIA to call the boycott off and return to the buses on a non-segregated basis.[49] The two mass meetings were held to allow a greater number of Negroes to vote on this matter. About 8,000 people crowded the two churches and voted unanimously to end the boycott. However, it was suggested that the Negroes wait for the mandate to come from the Supreme Court to the lower court. This was necessary, King said, to prevent the reactionary element from plunging "us into needless harassment and meaningless litigation." King continued, "we must take this not as victory over the white man but a victory for justice and democracy. Don't go back on the buses and push people around . . . We are just going to sit where there's a seat."[50]

Reverend S. S. Seay broke into tears during the invocation. Many old souls couldn't stand the strain; they began to shout and cry out all over the church. With eyes closed and tears streaming down his cheeks, Reverend Seay said, "wherever the Klans may march, no matter what the White Citizen's Councils may want to do, we are not afraid because God is on our side."[51]

Outside the church thousands stood in the chilly weather. Mothers had many small children wrapped in blankets so that they too could witness the history-making event. The transportation system was no longer operating—the car pool was broken up, but the Negroes pledged to share a ride for a few more days until the mandate reached Montgomery.

Though the Negroes at the mass meeting sang and prayed and voted to end the boycott, it was not the usual atmosphere of a mass meeting. There seemed to be a mysterious strangeness in the air, for this was to be the last of the usual mass meetings. Almost a year of protest had created a new entity in this city—the Mass Meetings. Here, the doctors, maids, preachers, drunkards, professors, and the coalman prayed together and sang together. Here too, the Baptists, Methodists, Seventh Day Adventists, Presbyterians, Catholics and all other religious denominations had sung together and prayed together as one in a common cause. This apparent mixed emotion of joy and sadness might have stemmed from the fear that this was the end, the end of a movement that had given a new birth to the Negroes of Montgomery.

The Acid Test

Although the Negroes of Montgomery continued to walk and protest the injustices, there seemed to have been a growing need for the religious influence in the movement. Intimidations appeared on every hand. There was no concrete evidence to show that the beating of two or three Negroes by public officials, and the death of at least one were due to the general tension arising out of the situation in Montgomery, but many Negroes were sure that this was the case.

To add to the horror and the problems of the Negroes, was the devilish act of throwing acid on new cars owned by Negroes. This acid would peel the paint off the car and leave an unsightly appearance. Though there were some ten or more cases of such incidents, and although the police promised to investigate the situation, the Negroes were of the opinion that this too could be added to the long line of abuses which they must endure in their struggle for the dignity of man.

Thus by the 15th of December 1956 the jubilant Christmas spirit had not reached the Negroes of Montgomery; they continued to walk and pray. The Non-Violence Institute which had just concluded and which had emphasized the religious and moral power of man, had tremendous influence on the Negroes and seemed to have directed their everyday life.

PART IV

The Supreme Court had spoken—segregation on the buses was unconstitutional in Montgomery and in the state of Alabama. Many southerners were unable to accept the decision as the law of the land—they cried loudly and continuously that the Supreme Court invaded the natural rights of a State. In Montgomery reconsideration was asked by the city of Montgomery and the Alabama Public Service Commission, on the grounds that the Supreme Court's decision did not answer various "vital" law questions and that it had taken from Alabama the State's police power. On the matter, the President of the Alabama Public Service Commission hinted that the Commission would issue an order designed to "preserve peace and harmony" on the buses in Alabama. Reverend M. L. King noted that there was nothing totally new in the decision. King said, "We have had close (racial) contact in elevators, stores, and banks for many years through custom."

The plea of the City of Montgomery and the Alabama Public Service Commission was in vain. On December 17, the Supreme Court refused to reconsider its decision banning racial segregation on local buses. It stated it was mailing the official notice to a special federal court in Montgomery, Alabama.[52]

Eve of Desegregated Buses

It is interesting to mention at this time the attitude of some of the bus riding people of the city toward the Supreme Court's decision.

On December 18, a reporter attempted to sample the attitude of the people toward the decision. He rode the bus throughout the day and talked with the drivers and passengers about the decision. Many of them laughed as they affirmed the statement, "The Negroes got what they wanted." Others wanted to know what the White Citizen's Council was doing about it, and questioned the use of "all that money they were getting from everyone." When an old Negro got on the bus and joked with the driver, the driver commented to the reporter, "Now there's another good Negro. Most of the old ones are."[53] Others felt that this was only the Negroes start toward integration; soon he would start pushing to get into schools. Then, it would be too late to stop them.

On December 18, 1956, the City Commissioners issued a segregation statement in which they expressed the attitude of the Commissioners on the issue. The statement was widely publicized. It declared:

> This decision in the Bus case has had a tremendous impact on the customs of our people here in Montgomery. It is not an easy thing to live under a law recognized as constitutional for these many years and then have it suddenly overturned on the basis of psychology . . . The City Commission, and we know our people are with us in this determination, will not yield one inch, but will do all in its power to oppose the integration of the Negro race with the white race in Montgomery, and will forever stand like a rock against

social equality, intermarriage, and mixing of the races under God's creation and plan.[54]

The *Montgomery Advertiser*, on December 20, 1956, interpreted this statement to mean, "The jig is up; it is up to the white citizens whether they ride buses in the new order." It was felt that the proposal to evade the decision, such as establishing a fleet of station wagons for white pick-up service—organized as a club and permissible under the city ordinance, would not be adequate. Further, it concurred in a statement made earlier by Reverend M. L. King, that the trains which pull in and out of Montgomery, the planes which fly over the city and the elevators are desegregated.[55]

In the meantime, Montgomery Negroes were preparing to go back on the buses as soon as the Supreme Court's order outlawing segregation on the buses reached Montgomery. The MIA requested police protection in the "danger zones" which were referred to as the ends of bus runs and dark streets. Moreover, the MIA suggested that special police be secured to protect the buses during the hours after dark, and warned that violence in the city "will lead to a long and desolate night of bitterness which will bring shame to generations unborn."[56]

In addition to these safety measures the Negroes of Montgomery had been attending a "school" which instructed members how to return to integrated buses. Some of the suggestions by the school official were: Do not deliberately sit by a white person unless there is no other seat. If cursed, do not curse back. If pushed, do not push back. In case of an incident, talk as little as possible. If you feel you cannot take it, walk for another week or two.

On December 20, 1956, the bus integration order reached Montgomery.[57] Separate writs of injunctions were served by U. S. Marshals, first on the Alabama Public Service Commission, then the Montgomery Police Chief, G. J. Ruppenthal and others. The Public Service Commission notified all other bus companies operating in Alabama that the injunction applied to Montgomery alone. And that all other companies must continue to enforce segregation. This appeared to have been a necessary move for the segregationists, because the Alabama Christian Movement For Human Rights in Birmingham, led by Reverend F. L. Shuttlesworth, had already written the Birmingham City Commission requesting an immediate end of "segregated buses in Birmingham."[58]

Desegregated Buses By Law

It is interesting to note that even though many leaders of Montgomery and the South declared "violence would break out if the buses were integrated," the first few days passed without violence. Two minor incidents were recorded as the integrated buses rolled the streets of the "Walking City." A Negro woman told of having been slapped by a white man after she alighted from a bus. Another incident was reported when a well-dressed Negro boarded a bus and took a front seat, and called out to other Negroes to do likewise. He was called a troublemaker by white passengers as he got off.[59] The *Montgomery Advertiser* reported, "The calm but cautious acceptance of this significant change in Montgomery's way of life came without any major disturbance." Police Chief G. J. Ruppenthal said, "It was just another Friday before Christmas for us." A sales girl, who took a seat beside a Negro woman, although there were other seats available, commented, "I figure if they stay in their place and leave me alone, I'll stay in mine and leave them alone."[60]

Reverend M. L. King, Jr., President of the MIA, declared that we have just started to work for the dignity of man. He outlined three possible new goals to strive for as recreation opportunities, voting, and education. He appealed to the Negroes to go back to the buses now that they were desegregated. Perhaps this stemmed from the fact that many Negroes were not riding the buses because of the increased fare, which became necessary during the boycott. King said, "I'd rather pay $200 to ride an integrated bus than to pay one cent to ride a segregated bus."

R. J. Cartwright, manager of Mobile Bus Lines, Inc., announced that the Mobile Transit System had ceased trying to enforce the city's bus segregation ordinances.[61]

Violence Wholesale

By December 28, 1956, a new pattern of intimidation was taking shape for the citizens of Montgomery. The first few days of peaceful compliance with the new law had given way to a reign of terror. City buses were being fired on throughout the city by snipers in poorly lighted sections of the city. It was reported that a teen-age colored girl was beaten by four or five white men as she alighted a bus near her home. Tension, which had been somewhat relaxed for the Christmas holidays, was being regenerated throughout the city. The fat was thrown into the fire on December 28, 1956, when a pregnant Negro woman was shot in both legs while riding a bus. Doctors were afraid to remove the bullet for fear of losing the baby. However, the bullet was removed and she was released from the hospital January 27, 1957.[62] Many Negroes and whites refused to ride the buses. The Montgomery City Commission ordered the suspension of night runs by city line buses for a week. No runs could begin after five o'clock in the evening. The snipers had won.

In an effort to halt armed attacks on racially integrated city buses, additional policemen were added to the force. Police Commissioner Clyde Sellers said, "We feel that with the additional new officers, we will be able to maintain order."

Moreover, Governor James E. Folsom said that the highway patrol was "ready to swing into action" if needed to maintain "good order" in racially tense areas.

On January 21, 1957, the curfew was extended another week—the Commission declared an "emergency exists" and said the curfew is necessary to protect the health, life and property of the citizens of Montgomery.[63]

The psychological warfare continued among the people of Montgomery. Propaganda leaflets flooded the Negro and white communities. An effort to divide the Negroes was made by a group who began on January 3, distributing handbills in Negro neighborhoods urging Montgomery Negroes to rebel against M. L. King, referred to as Luther. "We get shot at while he rides. He is getting us in more trouble everyday. Wake up. Run him out of town." Below are three of such circulars as they appeared on the streets of Montgomery. Although this material reads as though it was written by disgruntled Negroes, most of the colored people called it a "white scheme to divide the Negroes."[See page 42.]

The Negroes of Montgomery appeared to have become hardened to this type of intimidation. They were not easily frightened. The once feared K.K.K. could hardly incite the Negroes or make them uncomfortable. During the peak of the propaganda warfare in the city, it was reported that a little Negro boy was seen on a cold night, standing before a burning cross warming his chilled hands. A college teacher reported this incident. One day the K.K.K. paraded the streets of Montgomery. They were all over the city, in the streets, in the stores, on the square, on the buses, etc. A college professor gave two college students a ride, and to make conversation he

"White Scheme to Divide The Negroes"

DRAFT DODGER
NAACP TROUBLEMAKER

This is the disgrace to our people. Such a person in the white race is an outcast, as you well know. Many complaints are now being heard, we are losing jobs, relief is limited.

The White man celebrates July 4th as Independence Day. Some Negroes have been discharged for minor offenses and Whites hired. By July 4th we are told there will be no jobs left for Negroes.

Many believe it's a Communist inspired plot being led by King, Abernathy, Graetz, Nixon and Gray. They ride high, eat good, stay warm and pilfer the funds. We walk and suffer in many ways.

Let's run these five out of the state before we all have to leave.

Are You Tired of Walking?
SURE YOU ARE . . . BUT WE WALK WHILE OUR LEADERS RIDE . . . IN BIG CARS TOO!

W H Y ?

Because They're Playing Us For Suckers While They Get Rich On Our Money!

NO WONDER THEY WANT TO KEEP THE BOYCOTT GOING . . . NO WONDER THEY DON'T TELL US THERE ISN'T A CHANCE IN THE WORLD OF BREAKING SEGREGATION IN MONTGOMERY

WAKE UP — GET SMART

We'll Be Walking To Work Till Judgement Day If They Have Their Way . . . We'll Be Losing What Friendship We Have Left And Making Our Situation Worse Instead Of Better If They Have Their Way . . . We'll Be The Joke Of The Whole Country . . . Walking While Our Leaders Ride In Big Cars . . . Walking While Our Leaders Get Rich On Our Money!

DON'T SWALLOW THEIR MESS ANYMORE!

Don't Be A Fool — It's Our Money & Our Feet!

LOOK OUT!
Liver Lip Luther
Getting Us In More Trouble Every Day
FUNNY BULLETS
ON
FUNNY TERMS
FROM
FUNNY PLACES
We Get Shot At While He Hides
Wake Up! Mess Is His Business Run Him Out Of Town!

We been doing O K. in Montgomery before outside preachers were born!

Ask rev. King's pappa & mamma if they like his doings -- ask him if they going to help in Atlanta.

Better quit him before it is too late!

asked, "Did you see the K.K.K. downtown?" The girl looked shocked and answered, "No, are they down there?" "Yes," said the professor, "they are all over the place, they are dressed in white robes with red insignias." "Oh," exclaimed one of the girls, "I thought they were with the United Appeal." Here in Montgomery this type of intimidation, at least, had lost its sting.

The Movement Spreads

In Birmingham, Asa Carter was outlining his plan for the "Minute Men" who were pledged to maintain segregated buses. The machinery was simple. If a white woman was insulted on the bus she was simply to call a number and "Minute Men" would board the bus—not for violence but "for good race relations and to relieve the tension" which meant, as the Negroes interpreted it, trouble for them.[64]

The Negroes in Birmingham, seemingly jealous of the achievement made in Montgomery, continued their attack on the segregated buses. Already twenty-two Negroes, who had pledged to test the city's bus segregation laws, had been arrested and charged with violating the city's bus segregation ordinance. Attorney Arthur D. Shores, who had been with the Montgomery boycott, was to defend the Negroes. He, too, was being intimidated. On January 3, Shores returned to his home to find a seven-foot metal man of the land of Oz leaning against his home. He called the police.[65]

The movement for dignity of the Negro continued to spread throughout the South. Reverends Martin L. King, C. K. Steele, and F. L. Shuttlesworth, Negro leaders, called a meeting on January 10, in Atlanta to "coordinate and spin the campaign for integrated transportation in the South." The conferences were called because "we have no moral choice, before God, but to delve deeper into the struggle—and to do so with greater reliance on nonviolence and with greater unity, coordination, sharing and Christian understanding."[66]

A few days later, the Negro ministers of Atlanta began a "love, law and liberation" movement to end racial seating barriers on the buses. Here, about 100 Negro ministers pledged to test the Atlanta bus segregation law by riding the bus on a nonsegregated basis. Many of them did and six Negro ministers were arrested.[67]

In Tallahassee, the City Commission knocked out the racial segregation section of the city bus franchise and substituted a passenger assignment ordinance. Under the new plan the bus driver would issue tickets to riders assigning them to seats. The passengers would be required to occupy these seats under penalty of $500 fine or 60 days in jail. They could, of course, have their fare refunded.

The Bombs Explode

Although the movement was spreading, the Negroes in Montgomery, the core of the struggle, were reaping the whirlwind of the decision. On January 10, 1957, the city was shocked by six bombings which left four Negro churches and two pastor's homes seriously damaged. The homes of Reverend Robert Graetz and Reverend Ralph Abernathy, the Bell Street Baptist Church of which Reverend U. J. Fields was pastor, Hutchinson Street Baptist Church, the Negro First Baptist Church, and the Mount Olive Baptist Church were victims of this devilish act.[68] During the early morning hours, Negroes and a few whites mingled together to view the damages; tension increased as they came together. Some spoke militant words at whites who came to view the scene of broken glass, fallen bricks and splintered wood. At Abernathy's home Negroes pushed by police and entered the house to give aid to Reverend Abernathy's wife and small baby who were in the house at the time of the bombing. While the crowd was assembled at the Abernathy home the First Baptist Church was bombed. By now tension was almost at the breaking point. Nobody was doing much talking—indeed there was not much to be said. One old man remarked, "When they bomb the house of the Lord we are dealing with crazy people." Another replied, "I am ready for whatever comes now." One got the impression from the attitude of the crowd that assembled Negroes were not afraid but appeared to be disgusted.

The Governor, James E. Folsom, made a pre-dawn inspection of the bombings. He commented that he didn't think they wanted to kill anyone, but stated, "Any person or group of persons that would bomb the house of the Lord endangers the life of every man, woman and child in Montgomery."[69] Governor Folson said that a $2,000 reward would be offered for information leading to the arrest of persons guilty of the violent action.

The Montgomery City Commission suspended all bus service for an indefinite period of time for the "protection of life, limb and property of the people of Montgomery."[70]

BOMBED CHURCHES AND PARSONAGES
$64,180.00 TOTAL ESTIMATED DAMAGE

This city of about 110,000 people was without public transportation. However, there was some discussion by two city attorneys and U.S. District Judge Frank M. Johnson, Jr., about a suggested new all-white bus system for Montgomery. Earlier in the year, the City Commission had refused to license a Negro bus jitney service on the grounds that Montgomery City Lines was offering adequate service.[71]

The Rebel Club, a white group, requested a franchise to operate a non-profit bus line for transportation of members only. No mention of race was made in the memorandum filed with the City. The group proposed to charge each member $1 for a membership fee and fifteen cents for each ride.[72] On February 27, 1957, the question of whether the city of Montgomery could license an all-white bus line was still not settled because a three-judge Federal Court refused to rule on the matter. However, two of the judges expressed the opinion that it would be unlawful to operate the bus line on a segregated basis.[73]

There is evidence to show that many sober thinking whites could not sanction violence to maintain segregation. The Men of Montgomery, a powerful white group, called on the citizens to stop violence. "Violence by white or colored cannot be tolerated . . . We urge that no stone be left unturned to bring these cowards to justice and that they be punished to the fullest extent of the law."[74]

The *Alabama Journal* warned the people that "dynamite is not the answer." It stated no one knew whether the dynamite is being used by "those opposed to race mixing or by those who shed more crocodile tears, seek more money, more sympathy from Northerners, but ask the people to 'stick to legal procedure.'"[75] Others thought it was a disgrace to democracy to let a cowardly element in any community prevent buses from operating. Negro ministers pledged to hold service as usual in some of the bombed Negro churches. Reverend Ralph Abernathy said, "We will pray that the President of the U.S. will say just a word to us. It would help us so much." However, Reverend Ralph D. Abernathy said that night service at his First Baptist Church had been halted "because we feel it might endanger the lives of our congregation." Reverend U. J. Fields, who held service in the borrowed basement of another church, said, "Some of those in responsible positions had contributed to violence by advocating opposition to integration." Reverend Robert Graetz preached a sermon entitled, "How Often Shall We Forgive."[76]

In the meanwhile, the police department continued its investigation of the bombings. An unexploded dynamite bomb was found beneath an old iron bridge. They referred to it as the "ditching type of dynamite." Negroes attempted to provide some type of security for themselves. It was reported that the Negro volunteer guards were keeping watch over four Negro churches. They were, of course, unarmed to comply with the law.

Bombing Continued

On January 28, 1957, two Negroes, Vurlie Wilkins and Sammuel Wallace were arrested on disorderly conduct charges at the scene of the bombing of the People's Service Station and Cab Stand and a residential home located at the corner of High and Jackson Streets. Both men were later found guilty of "trying to incite a riot." Arresting officers reported that Wallace cursed the police and used obscene language at the scene of the bombing. The explosion did extensive damage to the home of Allen Robertson, a 60-year-old Negro hospital worker. This was the tenth dynamite blast linked with the integration situation within the past year.

Another unexploded bomb was found on the porch of Reverend M. L. King's home; however, the house was unoccupied. The bomb, consisting of 12 sticks of dynamite, had the fuse still smoldering when Assistant State Toxicologist, Dr. Van V. Pruitt, disarmed it.

King Reveals Vision

The twelve sticks of dynamite which were found on Reverend King's porch did not shatter his belief in the cause of nonviolence. The following Sunday, with a greater determination to win justice for his people, King revealed for the first time that he had "a vision" telling him to lead the movement against segregation without fear. He told his congregation that he had never really suffered until he accepted the leadership of the movement. The suffering was so great at one time until he was at the point of almost surrendering. King said, "I went to bed many nights scared to death by threats against myself and my family. I could not sleep and I didn't know where to turn." "Early on a sleepless morning in January, 1956," King continued, "rationality left me. There in my kitchen, almost out of nowhere, I heard a voice say, 'Preach

47

the gospel, stand up for the truth, stand up for righteousness.' Since that morning I can stand up without fear. Tell Montgomery they can keep shooting and I am going to stand up to them. If I die tomorrow morning, I would die happy because I've seen the mountain top. . . ."

Reaction to King's vision was varied. A Negro man remarked, "I knew it was something behind him because no man could stand up to these white folks like he's doing unless God was with him." In the church, many Negroes who wanted to shout held their emotions. Upon seeing a white reporter remove his glasses and wipe his eyes (perhaps to be sure of his notes) tears began to flow throughout the church. On the other hand a white man writing in the local paper remarked, "King might have heard the devil in his kitchen."

The struggle in The Walking City engulfed almost everyone. Bob Underwood, news director and announcer for a local television station, was shot as he left his studio. He reported it was the result of Negro resentment of his reporting of news. He said he had received threats "from Negroes who are not satisfied with the way I treat the Negro news."

Underwood said he had received many threats about his children. He reported the anonymous voice said, "I see your two kids riding their silver tricycles everyday. They look like nice kids. If you don't want anything to happen to them . . ." At this point the newsman hung up the phone.

The investigation of the bombings continued under a veil of secrecy, but there were hints that a break would come soon. A total of $4,000 reward was being offered for information leading to the arrest and conviction of the bombers. On January 31, 1957, the arrest of seven or eight white men in connection with the bombings shocked the entire city of Montgomery. Detective J. D. Shows was given credit for his keen memory in helping solve the bombings. He had recognized Henry Alexander, who was arrested in the round-up of the suspects at the scene of the bombing of the People's Taxi Stand.

Those charged were Henry Alexander and Raymond D. York, accused of dynamiting the occupied home of Reverend Ralph D. Abernathy. Alexander was also charged with the bus shooting and the explosion at the service station. Sonny Kyle Livingston, Jr. was charged with dynamiting one of the churches. Three were charged with conspiracy—a misdemeanor—they were Eugene Hall, Charlie Bodiford and Donald Dunlap. All these men were released on bonds ranging from $250 to $13,000. The charges of the men were passed over in City Court without testimony to the Montgomery

County Grand Jury. One Negro was listed on the panel of fifty prospective jurors but his name was not drawn.

Although seven men had been arrested in connection with the bombings, many Negroes felt there was little hope for a conviction. The case of Emmett Till was still fresh in their memories. Moreover, the defense was already mobilizing its strength. A group organized and known as the Alabama Segregation Defense set out raising money in a door-to-door campaign. They proposed to fill many molasses buckets with money. However, on February 11, 1957, the City Commission refused to extend a soliciting permit to the Alabama Segregation Defense Fund which was trying to raise $60,000 for legal assistance for the accused men. A permit had been granted February 5, 1957.

The attorneys for the defendants were mobilizing their strength. They declared, "We have discussed these charges with our clients and they all state emphatically that they are innocent. They are convinced that these charges were directly inspired by the NAACP (which has been outlawed in Alabama) of which Reverends Martin Luther King, Jr. and Ralph Abernathy are admitted nationwide leaders.

By spring of 1957, as the Negro looked back over more than a year of nonviolent struggle for the dignity of man, Montgomery Negroes could correctly visualize themselves as an integral part of the struggle for freedom throughout the world. This strong moral position was assumed as the Negroes became more articulate in the area of peace and freedom for the world. The Negroes of Montgomery spoke of freedom and democracy in Africa and Asia. They seem to bear personal witness to the struggle in Africa, through the eyes of their leader, Rev. M. L. King, who had made the trip to Africa in March, 1957, to witness the birth of the Negro State of Ghana. These rich experiences that the Negroes of Montgomery had undergone gave evidence of the growing maturity of the southern Negro, and the willingness of the Negro to accept the responsibility they must share in the achievement of the great dream of the entire world.

PART V

Bombers in the Court

Justice in the court for the Negro in the South is a recent idea. It occurred to only a few Negroes during their struggle in Montgomery. Most of them believed it was an attractive goal but very difficult to reach. Nonetheless the wheel of justice had been turning in Montgomery, Alabama during the Spring of 1957, grinding out the arrest of seven white men charged with the bombing of Negro homes and churches a few months earlier. By June, however, three of the men arrested were already released. They were Eugene Hall, employee of the mechanical department of the *Alabama Journal*, Charlies Bodiford Forman of a local furniture company, and Donald Dunlap, heating and plumbing worker.

Consequently, few Negroes were optimistic enough to think the remaining four men would be punished. Rev. Martin Luther King, leader of the boycott, declared at a mass meeting, "No matter which way the court decision goes . . . keep the faith in the future . . . Don't despair in our struggle because Providence is on our side."[77]

After months of delay because of legal procedures and the illness of the defense attorney John Blue Hill, partner in law, Circuit Clerk John Matthews announced the trial date had been set for May 27, 1957.[78]

On the 20th of May the two men were arraigned in circuit court. Both men were charged with dynamiting the home of Rev. Ralph Abernathy.

Britt also faced another indictment for the bombing of a Negro taxicab station on January 27, 1957. The two felony cases were to be tried under a State law which prohibits setting off dynamite "in, under, or dangerously near" an occupied dwelling.[79] Defense attorney asked that the two men be tried separately. Both of the men pleaded innocent.[80]

It was thought that the other two defendants, James O. York, an IBM operator, and Henry Alexander, a plumber, would be tried the week of June 3, 1957; however, the trial was later set for August 7, 1957, and then reset for November. This continuance was a mutual agreement among the prosecutor, defense, and court officials because of the heat and crowded conditions of the courthouse. These two men faced possible death sentences for bombing the inhabited home of Rev. Ralph Abernathy, a Negro minister.

On the 20th of May the trial of Britt and Livingston began. It was the opinion of many that the conduct of this trial and the decision would have great impact on the passing of the pending civil rights bill which had been amended by pro-southerners to include the famous "jury trial clause." Its national and international significance did not appear to disturb the defendants. From the first day of the trial these men appeared calm and felt sure of a favorable verdict. Every action by the defendants seems to have been made with confidence. Occasionally Livingston held his small daughter on his lap; he was a family man. The defense witnesses also were not disturbed about the trial. Many of them played checkers while they waited to testify.[81]

Contrary to expectation the defense attorney did not ask for a separate trial for the two defendants. The defense attorney immediately attacked the bomb confessions. The attorney declared the "state's so-called confessions which they will introduce as evidence are not worth the paper they are written on." He continued, "These confessions were obtained under shocking circumstances . . . the police used coercion, brutality, gestapo tactics and brainwashing methods to obtain them." He accused agitators of causing the trouble and declared, "These agitators are the tools of the NAACP bent on destroying our civilization . . . they don't just want integration of buses and schools, they want mongrelization and intermarriage."[82]

Moreover, the defense charged that the Montgomery Negroes bombed their own churches to win sympathy and financial support for their campaign against racial segregation.[83]

Perhaps the most confusing bit of logic presented by the defense attorneys was their appeal for acquittal warning that the verdict would determine "our very civilization and our way of life . . . and an acquittal would also serve notice to Negroes that the whites of the South would no longer tolerate attacks on their segregation laws." Hill declared the verdict must go down in history as saying to the Negroes that YOU SHALL NOT PASS.[84] Then after establishing an alibi for the defendants the defense rested its case.

On the other hand, evidence was presented at the trial that Livingston met with Britt and others at Britt's home the night of January 9 to discuss plans for the bombing. They agreed to rendezvous at a downtown cafe where dynamite was passed out by Britt and James D. York. Then they drove to the Hutchinson Street Baptist Church. Livingston got out and tossed a bomb on the church steps and drove off.[85] It was also reported that Livingston told Detective Shows that "They've let me down. They were supposed to have me out in ten minutes after I got in jail. I am ready to tell you all about it." Shows testified Livingston showed them to an abandoned well where he said they would find 17 sticks of dynamite and some bombing material but Shows failed to find anything. These are some of the questions asked Livingston and his replies.

Q. What kind of car did you ride to the Hutchinson Street Baptist Church in?

A. A yellow Oldsmobile convertible.

Q. What did the bomb look like?

A. I imagine it was from six to ten sticks of dynamite wrapped around a rod approximately eighteen inches (long) which had two fuses and two caps.

Q. Did you light both of these fuses?

A. Yes.

Q. Did you get out of the car to light them?

A. No.

Q. Did you get out of the car to throw them?

A. Yes.

Q. How was the dynamite held to the rack?

A. It was taped together . . . it looked like masking tape.[86]

Prosecuting attorney William F. Thetford warned the jury, "If you turn these men loose under the evidence the State has presented, you say to the Ku Klux Klan, if you bomb a Negro church or home it's all right . . . The next thing you know it will be your house because it's a sword that cuts both ways."[87]

Once again a new wave of tension swept over the city as its citizens waited for the verdicts. The waiting gave way to emotional over expressions when on May 30, 1957, after one hour and thirty-five minutes the all white jury announced the verdicts of not guilty for both Britt and Livingston.

Repercussions

Reaction to the verdicts were varied and confusing; however, the Negroes were almost unanimous in their disapproval of the verdicts. Although some expressed disappointment in the jury for not finding the two men guilty, most of them seemed to have expected the decision. One Negro remarked, "I would have really been shocked if they had found them guilty."

Bob Murphy writing in the *Montgomery Advertiser* declared, "The women cried and the men cheered. Almost all the people in the courtroom yelled, clapped, shouted, and shook hands in agreement."[88] Livingston and Britt declared, "We knew we were innocent, so we weren't afraid of the jury's verdict . . . God was on our side."[89]

Numerous men made wager on the outcome of the jury. One man bet the jury would not take longer than two hours to reach a verdict. Some bettors waged as high as 100 to 5 on acquittal.

Of more significance were the responses of the southern newspapers to the verdicts. Many of these papers denounced the jury for blundering and accused the jurors of lending aid to the cause of the Negro on the national scene, in their struggle to get the civil rights bill through Congress. The *Chattanooga Times* declared,

> . . . The Montgomery case will certainly raise arguments by proponents of the civil rights bills which are sponsored by President Eisenhower as to just what a "trial by jury" means in the South when the Negro question is involved . . . This trial by jury takes its place alongside the trial of the Emmett Till murder case in Mississippi. Trial by jury is the foundation of our system of justice . . . Its integrity must be safeguarded.[90]

Virginius Dabney, editor of the *Richmond Dispatch*, stated ". . . If the two men tried in Montgomery were guilty the jurors would do far more to uphold our 'way of life' by convicting them (Britt and Livingston) than by setting them free."[91]

On the other hand the *Charleston News and Courier* would not say that the Montgomery jury did or did not make an error but declared, "One error on the part of a judge or jury is not sufficient reason for destroying a bulwark of our freedom (trial by jury)."[92] It appears here that even men who approved the justice of a not guilty verdict could possibly see and fear the danger of the action to the southern way of life. Where democratic principles conflict with the southern traditions—Southerners stand firm.

The Tuskegee Crisis

While the Negroes of Montgomery continued their struggle for the dignity of man a new flame of protest was ignited less than fifty miles from Montgomery. The boycott fever had hit Tuskegee, Alabama, the land of Booker T. Washington, who during his lifetime had hammered out a system of compromise for the Negroes and whites of the South. Tuskegee was considered the cradle of the "Washington Theory" and generation after generation had held on tenaciously to the doctrine. As late as 1957 the cultural and educational center of Alabama could boast of no more than 400 registered voters. Though Negroes outnumbered whites in Macon County and had made somewhat great economic advancements, the law, the institutions, the courts, in fact, the city was administered by whites. It took an act of the State legislature to uproot the Tuskegee community and move the people to action.

During the month of June 1957 Senator Sam Engelhardt of Macon County introduced a bill in the legislature which would reduce the city limits of Tuskegee to eliminate virtually all predominantly Negro residential areas from the Municipal boundaries. This move was perhaps stimulated by the growing interest of the Southern Negro leader in Negro suffrage. On June 13, 1957, a campaign to prepare three million southern Negroes for voting in the 1958 election was announced by Rev. M. L. King. Voting clinics were set up across the South "to help Negroes overcome the continued and artificial obstacles to their registering and voting."

The "Engelhardt Bill" became law with no attempt by Governor Folsom to veto it on July 13, 1957.[93] It went through both the House and Senate without a dissenting vote. Senator Engelhardt later, on July 16, introduced a bill aimed at abolishing Macon County. The County would be divided among Montgomery, Elmore Bullock, Lee and Tallapoosa Counties.[94] Many southerners were not in favor of such drastic action against Tuskegee. The *Montgomery Advertiser* explained the logic of the bill in an editorial which declared, "Senator Sam Engelhardt's pie-slice proposal for abolishing Macon county is the wrong approach, but it could lead to an eminently worthwhile process—the systematic reduction of a number of counties in Alabama . . . Extending this logic to all other counties where more than half the population is Negro. The following thirteen should also be abolished: Barbour 54% Negro, Bullock 74%, Choctaw 53%, Dallas 65%, Greene

83%, Hale 70%, Lowndes 82%, Marengo 70%, Monroe 51%, Perry 68%, Russell 52%, Sumter 76%, and Wilcox 79%."[95]

The Little Boycott

It was in protest of these bills and with the Montgomery boycott as a guide, that the Negroes of Tuskegee began boycotting the white merchants of that city. On June 25, a mass meeting was called, as had been the pattern in Montgomery, to urge Negroes to boycott Tuskegee's white merchants. C. G. Gomillion, President of the Tuskegee Civil Association declared, "We will buy goods and services from only those who will recognize us as first class citizens . . ." About the Board of Registrars he declared, "We have to hunt and find a Board of Registrars in their hiding places." Gomillion listed the objectives of the boycott: 1. To halt enactment of the City Limits bill. 2. To try to get a Board of Registrars which would function more effectively. 3. To stimulate a greater interest among local Negroes in "their plight."[96]

Dr. Stanley H. Smith, a Tuskegee Institute Sociology professor, urged the Negroes to "Continue the fight." He continued, "The education of the white citizen is so lacking that they don't know how to fulfill their duties and responsibilities as citizens."[97]

The die was cast for a successful protest, but could Tuskegee follow Montgomery in their protest? Many were sure it could but others were afraid of the heterogeneous group of Negroes in the community. This fear seemed justifiable when it was reported that the Negro boycott was losing momentum. It appeared to have been the rural Negro element which prevented almost certain success of the boycott and subsequent economic death of many businesses there. It was further reported that "goon squads" were intimidating Negroes, frightening them away from the stores. Police Chief O. H. Hodnett declared, "There would be more rural Negroes there (in Tuskegee) if they were not afraid . . . I had one Negro woman to ask me if she could go in a white store and pay a bill."[98]

By September the Tuskegee boycott was in full swing. Despite the Attorney General John Patterson's eleven-day probe and his personal raid of the Tuskegee Civic Association, his seizure of records, memberships, lists and other literature, the flame of protest flares high in Tuskegee. THE SPIRIT OF THE WALKING CITY BURNS ANEW.

NOTES

1. *Montgomery Advertiser*, December 6, 1955.
2. *Montgomery Advertiser*, December 6, 1955.
3. Dexter Avenue Baptist Church (unpublished).
4. *Montgomery Advertiser*, December 12, 1955.
5. *Alabama Journal*, January 4, 1956.
6. *Montgomery Advertiser*, December 13, 1955.
7. *Montgomery Advertiser*, January 24, 1956.
8. *Montgomery Advertiser*, March 8, 1956.
9. *Alabama Journal*, February 22, 1956.
10. *Chicago Daily Defender*, February 23, 1956.
11. *Montgomery Advertiser*, March 20, 1956.
12. *Alabama Journal*, March 20, 1956.
13. *Alabama Journal*, March 2, 1956.
14. *Ibid.*
15. *Alabama Journal*, March 2, 1956.
16. *Montgomery Advertiser*, March 2, 1956.
17. *Alabama Journal*, March 22, 1956.
18. *New York Times*, March 23, 1956.
19. *New York Times*, May 25, 1956.
20. *Chicago Daily Defender*, March 4, 1956.
21. *New York Tribune*, March 5, 1956.
22. *Montgomery Advertiser*, March 1, 1956.
23. *Alabama Journal*, April 25, 1956.
24. John H. Franklin, *From Slavery to Freedom*.
25. *Alabama Journal*, June 2, 1956.
26. *Alabama Journal*, June 2, 1956.
27. *Ibid.*
28. *Montgomery Advertiser*, June 6, 1956.
29. *Montgomery Advertiser*, June 12, 1956.
30. *Montgomery Advertiser*, June 1, 1956.
31. *Montgomery Advertiser*, September 18, 1956.
32. *Ibid.*
33. *Montgomery Advertiser*, July 18, 1956.
34. *Ibid.*
35. *Montgomery Advertiser*, June 27, 1956.
36. *Alabama Journal*, July 5, 1956.
37. *Alabama Journal*, July 9, 1956.
38. *Montgomery Advertiser*, July 9, 1956.
39. *Montgomery Advertiser*, July 11, 1956.
40. *Montgomery Advertiser*, July 20, 1956.

41. *Alabama Journal*, August 1, 1956.
42. *Montgomery Advertiser*, August 5, 1956.
43. *Montgomery Advertiser*, July 8, 1956.
44. *Ibid.*, November 1956.
45. *Alabama Journal*, November 13, 1956.
46. *Birmingham Post Herald*, November 14, 1956.
47. *Montgomery Advertiser*, November 20, 1956.
48. *Ibid.*
49. *Alabama Journal*, November 15, 1956.
50. *Montgomery Advertiser*, November 15, 1956.
51. *Alabama Journal*, November 16, 1956.
52. *Alabama Journal*, December 17, 1956.
53. *Montgomery Advertiser*, December 18, 1956.
54. *Ibid.*, December 18, 1956.
55. *Ibid.*, December 20, 1956.
56. *Montgomery Advertiser*, December 23, 1956.
57. *Alabama Journal*, December 20, 1956.
58. *Montgomery Advertiser*, December 22, 1956.
59. *Montgomery Advertiser*, December 22, 1956.
60. *Ibid.*
61. *Mobile Register*, December 23, 1956.
62. *Montgomery Advertiser*, January 27, 1957.
63. *Ibid.*, January 21, 1957.
64. *Birmingham Post Herald*, January 1, 1957.
65. *Ibid.*, January 4, 1957.
66. *Atlanta Constitution*, January 10, 1957.
67. *Atlanta Constitution*, January 10, 1957.
68. *Alabama Journal*, January 10, 1957.
69. *Alabama Journal*, January 10, 1957.
70. *Montgomery Advertiser*, January 11, 1957.
71. *Alabama Journal*, January 11, 1957.
72. *Alabama Journal*, January 11 and 26, 1957.
73. *Ibid.*, February 27, 1957.
74. *Montgomery Advertiser*, January 11, 1957.
75. *Ibid.*
76. *Montgomery Advertiser*, January 28, 1957.
77. *Montgomery Advertiser*, May 28, 1957.
78. *Ibid.*, May 7, 1957.
79. *Alabama Journal*, May 7, 1957.
80. *Ibid.*
81. *Montgomery Advertiser*, May 30, 1957.
82. *Alabama Journal*, May 27, 1957.
83. Montgomery, Alabama, May 30, 1957.
84. *Alabama Journal*, May 30, 1957.
85. *Montgomery Advertiser*, May 30, 1957.

86. *Ibid.*
87. *Alabama Journal*, May 30, 1957.
88. *Alabama Journal*, May 30, 1957.
89. *Montgomery Advertiser*, May 30, 1957.
90. *Ibid.*
91. *Chattanooga Times*, June 2, 1957.
92. *Richmond Times Dispatch*, June 2, 1957.
93. *Charleston News and Courier*, June 4, 1957.
94. *Alabama Journal*, July 16, 1957.
95. *Montgomery Advertiser*, July 18, 1957.
96. *Montgomery Advertiser*, July 8, 1957.
97. *Ibid.*, July 9, 1957.
98. *Montgomery Advertiser*, July 7, 1957.

Alabama's Bus Boycott

REV. THOMAS R. THRASHER

MONTGOMERY, ALABAMA

The facts of our local situation are essentially simple. Yet various members of our community, both white and Negro, believe things that make it enormously complex.

Last December 1 in the early evening, one of the buses of the Montgomery City Lines passed through Court Square, in the heart of town, and headed for the stop in front of the Empire Theatre. On board the thirty-six passenger bus twenty-four Negroes were seated, in the traditional manner from the rear forward, and there were twelve whites seated in the front. Some people of each race were standing in the aisle. The bus driver has since testified that there were no empty seats. Yet today, many weeks later, there are many who believe that four Negroes were asked to get up in order to allow one white person to sit down.

At the Empire Theatre stop a number of white passengers were waiting to board the bus. The driver of the bus, as was the practice when in his judgment it was necessary to "equalize facilities," requested four Negroes, including Mrs. Rosa Parks, to give up their seats. No charge of discourtesy has been made against this bus driver. Three of the Negroes rose and moved toward the rear. Mrs. Parks, a seamstress at a local department store and a highly respected member of the Negro community, refused. She said later that she acted on a sudden impulse, probably arising from the fact that she was tired. There are substantial numbers of people here in Montgomery who believe that she was a willing participant in a trumped-up plot.

The driver, seeing that Mrs. Parks was adamant, called a policeman, who led her off the bus and escorted her to the police station. There she was booked on a charge of violating the city's segregation law and the trial was set for the following Monday, December 5. She was released on bond.

At this point the facts become somewhat less precise. On Saturday, December 3, a number of mimeographed and typed circulars were distributed in the Negro sections of the community calling on citizens to stage a one-day protest by not riding the city buses the day of the trial. I have never been able to determine just who initiated this planned boycott, and there are innumerable conflicting rumors about it. But on Sunday, the day before the trial, there was a news story in the local paper that carried the information far more widely than the original circulars had. A number of Negro ministers, it is known, referred to it in their sermons that day.

On Monday three-quarters or more of the usual Negro riders stayed off the buses. The extent of the protest was noticeable, for the fifty thousand Negroes who live in Montgomery constitute about forty percent of the population and made up nearly seventy-five percent of the bus passengers. This was an act of passive resistance on a monumental scale, which could not be passed off as simply a product of outside interference, agitation, or intimidation. There was no widespread absenteeism from work that day; the protesters went to their jobs by Negro taxis, wagons, or by foot over long distances.

That same day, Mrs. Parks appeared at the city court with her lawyer. The city prosecutor asked that the charge against her be based not on the city segregation ordinance but on a state law giving bus drivers authority to assign or reassign passengers in accordance with segregation practice. Mrs. Parks was found guilty and fined ten dollars and costs, a total of fourteen dollars. (The law permits a maximum fine of five hundred dollars.) She appealed her case.

Meeting at the Building

That night, according to a newspaper account, approximately five thousand Negroes overflowed the protest meeting at the Holt Street Baptist Church. Forty-seven Negro ministers are said to have been present. There was a good deal of hymn singing and speechmaking, none of it inflammatory, according to the newspaper report, but all of it defiant. From the story it appears that there was a general welling-up of grievances in which the specific case of

Rosa Parks was all but forgotten. But those members of our community who believe that the whole thing was staged by outside influences generally do not believe that the local press has given an accurate reporting of the facts.

The meeting accomplished three things. First, a resolution was adopted to continue the bus boycott indefinitely and calling on "every citizen of Montgomery regardless of race, color, or creed to refrain from riding buses owned and operated in the city of Montgomery, by Montgomery City Lines, Incorporated, until some arrangement has been worked out between said citizens and the Montgomery City Lines." Second, those present were urged to make their cars available in assisting others to get to work. An organization was formed on the spot—the Montgomery Improvement Association—and a board of directors was named. Its chairman was Dr. Martin Luther King, the twenty-seven-year-old minister of the Dexter Avenue Baptist Church. Dr. King, though Southern born, holds a Ph.D degree from Boston University. The board of directors included several other Negro ministers.

Finally, the meeting addressed three proposals to the Montgomery City Lines as the basis for ending the boycott:

1. More courteous treatment of Negro passengers.
2. Seating on a first come, first served basis, with Negroes continuing to sit from the rear of the bus and whites from front to rear.
3. Negro bus drivers to be employed on predominantly Negro runs.

By the next day the boycott was close to ninety-five percent effective, a figure that has been maintained with remarkable consistency ever since. A car pool began to take shape. On telephone poles and in other public places, unsigned and unidentified schedules were posted. For a time the police didn't know what they were. Actually, they listed the forty pickup points at which some two hundred and fifty cars were operating from 6 to 8:30 a.m. and 3 to 6 p.m. To avoid violating city regulations concerning taxis, this rather sizable carlift charged no fares but collected funds for gas at the churches and at rallies, which have been held with regularity. Other funds undoubtedly came in from outside the South, a fact that some members of our community choose to dwell upon. Some also believe that the Negroes secretly pay ten-cent fares to the drivers and won't admit it when the police question them.

By Wednesday, December 7, neither side had made any contact with the other. The Alabama Council on Human Relations, a biracial organization of which I am a member and which was holding its semi-annual meeting that day, decided to offer its "good offices" to bring about a meeting between the Negro leaders and bus company and city officials. The mayor accepted our suggestion and a meeting was set for the next day at the City Hall. There the Negro group presented its three demands. The attorney for the bus company replied that the company would always investigate formal complaints of discourtesy but asserted that the discourtesy was often provoked. He rejected the other proposals as contrary to city law and inappropriate. The mayor called on the bus company officials and the Negro leaders to work their problems out. Everyone else withdrew and these two groups continued the discussion for a time—but without success.

Though their meeting adjourned without even an agreement to meet again, I feel that at least two good effects stemmed from it. It was the first proof, small but significant, that the parties to the dispute could sit down together. Further, it helped to ease the pent-up frustrations which in the first days of the boycott had provoked several cases of stoning and even firing upon the buses. After this first meeting there was only one further incident of that nature.

Again at our request, the mayor arranged a meeting for Saturday, December 10, so that the Negro leaders could meet the representative of the National City Lines of Chicago, owner of the local bus company. This representative had come to Montgomery to look into the trouble, we learned, but had not approached the boycott leaders. To this meeting the mayor invited a larger number, including a prominent leader of the local White Citizens' Council. After again listening to a recital of the grievances and to a statement disclaiming authority under city and state laws by the National City Lines representative, the mayor appointed a committee to try to reach a solution.

The committee failed in its purpose. The Negro group felt that some of the members, including the White Citizens' Council leader, were not appointed in good faith; the white group felt that the Negroes were not ready to negotiate in good faith. Not being a member of the committee, I can only report what I have read in the press regarding its deliberations. The voting was reported to have been eight white against eight Negro on matters where they disagreed. Unanimous concurrence was achieved on the proposal that more courtesy on the busses was in order. On this note the committee broke up after only two meetings.

Montgomery returned to a state of affairs in which there was no communication between the two groups—only mounting tension and the grim, ever-present fact of the boycott.

The Christmas season passed and there were reports that some businesses were off by thirty per cent or more. But this was rumor, not confirmed fact, and there were other stories that some businesses were booming. The bus company had raised its fare by fifty percent. Negro leaders hailed this as evidence of the boycott's success, while white leaders pointed out that local rates had been below those elsewhere. The bus company had long since suspended routes going into predominantly Negro neighborhoods. A number of bus drivers were furloughed. On January 6, the police commissioner dramatically entered a meeting of the White Citizens' Council and announced that he was paying his $3.50 membership fee. "I wouldn't trade my Southern birthright for one hundred Negro votes," he declared.

A 'Get Tough' Policy

There were false hopes on January 21, when the city commission announced that after a conference with unidentified "prominent Negro ministers" a plan had been reached for ending the boycott. Next day the hopes were dissipated. The leaders of the boycott announced that they had not been present at the City Hall meeting and didn't know who had. Subsequently, there were recriminations between the three Negro ministers who had been present and the city commissioners. The ministers said that they had gone there on other business and had not entered any agreement. The commissioners, in turn, accused them of double-dealing. It was at any rate clear that the three ministers had not been prominent in the boycott movement. And the boycott continued.

On January 24 the mayor issued a statement: "We have pussyfooted around on this boycott long enough and it is time to be frank and honest . . . The Negro leaders have proved they are not interested in ending the boycott but rather in prolonging it so that they may stir up racial strife. The Negro leaders have proved that they will say one thing to a white man and another thing to a Negro about the boycott . . . [They] have forced the boycott into a campaign between whether the social fabric of our community will continue to exist or will be destroyed by a group of Negro radicals who have split asunder the fine relationships which have existed between the Negro and white people for generations . . . What they are after is the destruction of our social fabric . . . The white people are firm in their convictions that they do not care whether the Negroes ever ride a city bus again if it means that the social fabric of our community is destroyed so that Negroes will start riding the busses again." He called on white citizens to refrain from carrying their domestic servants to and from work in their cars and thus contributing to the boycott.

That same day it was announced that the mayor and the remaining city commissioner had joined the White Citizens' Council. On the following day there were reports that a "get tough" police was being initiated. Scores of Negroes driving volunteer cars were given tickets for minor traffic violations. On Thursday, January 26, Dr. M. L. King, the boycott leader, was arrested for going thirty-five miles an hour in a twenty-five mile zone. His case is on appeal. The following day King's house was bombed, causing minor damage. Neighbors said the explosive had been thrown from a passing car. Some members of the white community believe firmly that the incident was staged by the Negroes themselves. Both the mayor and the police commissioner went promptly to the scene, and stated firmly that the culprit would be caught and prosecuted. Dr. King exhorted the Negroes who had gathered not to resort to violence.

"We believe in law and order," he said. "Don't get panicky. Don't get your weapons. He who lives by the sword will perish by the sword. Remember that is what God said. I want it to be known the length and breadth of this land that if I am stopped this movement will not stop."

Two days later, a dynamite cap exploded in the front yard of a Negro who had not been prominent in the boycott but who was active in the local N.A.A.C.P. For a time the whole community realized the grim possibilities of the situation, and reason held back emotion. The arrests and issuing of tickets by the police slacked off as suddenly as they had started. The White Citizens' Council added five hundred dollars to the reward offered by the city commissioners for information leading to the arrest and conviction of the bomb throwers.

On February 1, the whole dispute moved into the courts. That day five Montgomery Negroes filed suit in the U.S. District Court asking that state and local segregation laws pertaining to transportation be declared unconstitutional. This, of course, is a far broader challenge than had been posed by the boycott itself.

Subsequently, the grand jury indicted the Negro lawyer who had brought the cases to court because one of the five plaintiffs, a young Negro woman, testified that she had not known what he was asking her to do. If convicted, the lawyer can be disbarred for false representation.

This same grand jury on February 21 indicted about one hundred Negroes for participating in the boycott. The indictment cited a state anti-conspiracy act passed in 1921 to deal with coal-mining strikes in Birmingham. While the anti-conspiratorial features of the act have never been tested in the courts, its anti-picketing provisions have been declared unconstitutional. Among those indicted was Mrs. Parks, who had refused to pay the fourteen-dollar fine and was sentenced to serve a jail sentence instead for the indictment that led to the boycott.

As these legal battles went forward, it was announced that secret efforts at a compromise in the dispute by a businessmen's organization, the Men of Montgomery, had been unavailing. There are some who believe that they might have succeeded if these court indictments had not been threatening.

A Sudden Deafness

As the painful weeks have passed, the facts of the situation have become more rather than less obscure. There is, for example, the recurrent rumor of goon squads operating among the Negroes to force them to obey the boycott. Thus far only one arrest has been made on this count—a Negro youth picked up for preventing a Negro woman from boarding a bus. She testified in court that he was helping her across the street and the charge was dropped. If there has been widespread intimidation among Negroes, the police have been unable to get evidence of it.

There have been rumors in the Negro community that white employers were going to discharge them on a certain day, and rumors in the white community that all the Negroes were going to quit on a certain day.

Businesses have been damaged severely by rumors circulated among white people that they had contributed to the N.A.A.C.P. or rumors among Negroes that they had contributed to the White Citizens' Council. In a few cases businesses have been caught in a crossfire of rumor. Some say that competitors have been starting these rumors.

If there is anything universal in our community it is fear. The businessman's fear lest his business be destroyed by some false move or baseless rumor. The Negro's fear for his safety and his job. The clergy's fear that their congregations may be divided by the tense feelings generated by our situation. The politician's fear that he may do something disapproved of by the majority of voters. And finally the whole community's fear that we may be torn asunder by a single rash act precipitating interracial violence.

Time after time during these past weeks I have felt as if I were living in a nightmare, one of those where you speak and nobody hears, where you wave your arms and nobody pays any attention. This nightmare extends to the whole community. White and black stand on opposite sides of an invisible line, and there seems no possible way of communicating across the barrier, a barrier which is there and isn't there, which in a sense both of us have made and of which we both are victims. The Negroes are people who have helped us, taught us, nurtured us, made us laugh, made us weep, and have given us depth of understanding. But the patterns of our past communication are breaking, and new patterns are not yet formed. We know them, and yet in our knowing we are aware that we know them not. The nightmare persists even when we hear words and see gestures. They speak. We do not understand.

As I look at this tragic situation involving me and my fellow Southerners of both races, I can only ask God's mercy and pity on us all. No one of us is wise enough to predict what our relationships will be or how they will be worked out. There is only one thing of which I am fully certain. It is that there must be a mutual facing of our common problem. We must get at the facts of our situation and not simply believe any rumor that happens to fit our prejudices. Having gotten the facts, we must then sit down together and negotiate practical solutions.

The missing element in our community's attempts to cope with the situation has been the lack of recognized agencies for interracial communication, cooperation, and understanding. In the past a dreary fate awaited any person or group who made even tentative steps in this direction. One of the encouraging recent developments has been the growth of our Alabama Council on Human Relations, an affiliate of the Southern Regional Council, which provides a meeting point for men and women of good will from both races.

I am not Pollyanna enough to think that the Alabama Council can meet and effectively deal with such crises as the recent ones in our state. We are too few and too weak. However, we are fully convinced that the fundamental method we propose—that white and Negro must sit down together—is the only way to avoid recurring crises of even greater severity. This may sound like a simple point but sometimes in complex situations the simple points are overlooked.

As a Southerner born and bred, I am deeply moved by the plight of all Southerners of both races. All of us know that no easy, pat solutions will solve our problems. Our experience in Montgomery, a city known in the past for its good race relations, shows us that change, any change, will be painful for some of us, and that sudden change may operate in reverse and bring about what is not wanted. The Negro is surely regretful to see his bus boycott contribute to the growth of the White Citizens' Council.

The white Southerner cannot be indifferent to the feelings and aspirations of the Negro, for though he is politically impotent here, we are beginning to see that he is exceedingly important humanly and economically to the maintenance of "our social fabric."

Our situation in Montgomery gives strong evidence of the need for patience in negotiation. Sometimes in labor-management disputes the only thing the two groups have in common is a belief that negotiations should continue. We have not even had this much in Montgomery. There is much to be learned of the art of negotiation, but mainly we need a will to find a solution.

The most disturbing factor in the whole situation is the growth of the White Citizens' Council, an organization pledged to nonviolence but dedicated to thwarting the Supreme Court decision on integration. Its main argument seems to be that if vigilance is relaxed in any measure there will be wholesale intermarriage across racial lines. The situation is complex enough without muddying the waters with such arguments as these. The question before us is not intermarriage but simple human rights for a vast section of the human family.

The Bus Boycott in Montgomery

L. D. REDDICK

Suddenly, Montgomery, Alabama, has become one of the world's most interesting cities. It is a handsome little town, restful for an ex-urbanite. In its center is a spacious circle with gently flowing water-spray, covered by soft lights in the evening. From it one looks down the main avenue to the white marble Capitol. Here markers tell the visitor where Jefferson Davis stood when he swore allegiance to the Southern Confederacy.

But it is not the White House of the Confederacy, preserved in Montgomery by aged daughters of the Lost Cause, that attracted the newspaper men, sociologists, and just plain visitors who have been floating in and out these past few weeks. It is the bus boycott. The metropolitan dailies have on the scene what have been jokingly called "war correspondents covering the Southern front." And there are journalists from Japan, England, France.

With all the odds against it, the Negro community of Montgomery has initiated and sustained what is easily the most creative approach yet made to the crisis in race relations. And even those of us who have watched developments unfold day by day are reluctant to say that we understand fully what we see or that we can predict the outcome of it all.

Before last December, a visitor to Montgomery would have noticed Negroes standing up in the city buses, while there were empty seats right before them. Somebody could then explain that according to local practice, these unoccupied seats were reserved for "whites only." No matter how packed a bus might be with Negro passengers, they were prohibited from sitting in the first 4 seats (which hold about 10 persons). Theoretically, the last 3 back seats (holding about 10 persons) were similarly reserved for Negroes. In fact this was not so. Moreover, if white passengers were already occupying all of their reserved seats and additional white passengers boarded the bus, Negro passengers, sitting in the unreserved section immediately behind the whites, might be asked to get up and "move back" by the bus driver. At times this was done courteously; all too often it was an undisguised insult.

Race relations in Montgomery have traditionally been "good" in the sense that Negroes have seldom challenged their state of subordination. The structure of the society was more or less set. Opposition seemed futile. Personal difficulties might be adjusted through some prominent Negro, who would speak with an influential white person. This was the established pattern of paternalism; and it did not disturb the status quo.

But for some reason on Thursday afternoon, December 1, 1955, Mrs. Rosa Parks refused to "move back" when she was ordered to do so by the bus driver. She was *not* sitting in the section reserved for whites (as the *New York Times* mistakenly reported) but in the first seat of the unreserved section. At the time every seat in the bus was taken. So the command for her to "move back" meant that she would have to stand while a white male passenger, who had just taken the bus, would sit. And so she was arrested and for a brief moment jailed.

Mrs. Parks was ideally fitted for her role. She is attractive and quiet, a churchgoer who looks like the symbol of Mother's Day. Her trial was set for the following Monday, December 5. Out of nowhere, it seems, written and mimeographed appeals appeared in the Negro community, saying: ". . . This has to be stopped . . . if Negroes did not ride the buses they could not operate . . . every Negro stay off the buses Monday in protest of this arrest and trial."

Only a fraction of Negro bus riders saw these unsigned appeals but one of the notices did fall into the hands of the local paper, which put it on the front page. Negroes laugh when they tell about this. They say that the newspaper was mostly interested in letting the white folks know what the Negroes were up to. But through this story many Negroes got the news of the Monday plan for the first time. At the Sunday church services, Negro ministers hammered home their endorsement of the projected one-day "protest"—as they consistently called the boycott.

Physically, Montgomery is ideally fitted for a bus boycott. It is just 27.9 square miles in area. Its population, 130,000, is about 40 percent Negro. Most residents *could* walk to most places in the city.

The judge who tried Mrs. Parks, had he looked into his crystal ball, would have probably dismissed the case. Instead, he found her guilty, fining her $14. She appealed.

All day long on December 5 Negroes stayed off the buses. They did so with such enthusiasm that there was a general feeling that "we ought to continue this."

The Negro ministers had hastily scheduled a mass meeting for Monday evening. Normally, the church holds about 1,500 persons. Hours before meeting time, 7:00 p.m., people began filling up the place. By 7 o'clock every seat had been taken and some 3 or 4 thousand standees overflowed into the street. Outdoor loudspeakers were set up.

Nobody expected such a response. The Negro ministers, rising to the occasion, improvised a declaration of principles. Amid the singing of hymns and some first class oratory—led by Rev. M. L. King, Jr.—the audience unanimously adopted the following declaration as read by Rev. Ralph Abernathy: Negroes were not to resume riding the buses until (1) courteous treatment by bus operators was guaranteed; (2) passengers were seated on a first come, first serve basis—Negroes seating from the back of the bus toward the front while whites seat from the front toward the back; (3) Negro bus operators were employed on predominantly Negro routes.

Then without the usual money-raising salesmanship, the crowd—inside and outside of the church—filed in and placed dimes, quarters and dollars on the collection table. This was altogether spontaneous.

Since the Negro ministers were cagey about revealing who was directing the movement, that seemed to whet the appetite of the reporters. As a matter of fact, at this very point everything was *ad hoc* and tentative. The emergence of King and Abernathy was almost by chance. No leader was calling the shots. As Abernathy said later, it was never "a one-man show." The indignation and demands for action by the "common people" swept everyone along like a flood.

II

There had been a long history of abuse by the bus operators. Almost everybody could tell of some unfortunate personal experience that he himself had had or seen. Montgomery Negroes were fed up with the bus service in particular and, like Negroes throughout the South, with race relations in general. The outrage of the Emmett Till murder was alive in everybody's mind. The silence and inaction of the Federal Government, in the face of the daily abuse, beatings and killings of Negro citizens, was maddening. Negroes have no faith at all in Southern law-making and law-enforcing agencies, for these instruments of "justice" are in the hands of "the brothers of the hoodlums who attack us."

Negroes themselves wanted to get into action. Here and elsewhere they were willing to fight it out—if the fighting was "fair." But Negroes knew on whose side the police and the lily-white militia would be when they came in to "put down disorder." And after that—there would be the local judges and juries. To remain human, the Negroes simply could not stand by and do nothing. Under the circumstances, the channel into which the Negroes of Montgomery have poured their energies and resentments is the best answer thus far to the question of what to do. Here is organized struggle and group solidarity. It is legal, nonviolent and effective.

And so the one-day boycott passed into an indefinite protest that, as of this writing, has run for fourteen weeks.

Both the press and the police expected violence. Early newspaper stories started off in this fashion: "Negro goon squads reportedly have been organized here to intimidate Negroes who ride . . . in violation of a Negro boycott . . ." This was untrue.

The police were equally sure of the image in their minds. Accordingly, they arrested a college student, saying that he had pulled a Negro woman from a bus as she was attempting to get on it. In court it came out that the two were good friends and that they were merrily crossing the street, arm in arm, near a bus. She had told the cops this before the arrest was made but the police believed that there were goons—there had to be—so they saw what they were looking for: "believing is seeing."

The first reaction of the bus company officials was one of arrogance. They pretended that the Negroes were demanding that the company violate the law. This was absurd. The law required segregation, but did not specify the manner of seating so long as it was segregated. The bus company summarily rejected the proposal of the Negroes.

The city commission sided with the bus company, condemning the boycott and declaring that "first come, first serve" would be illegal. And so almost everybody—the bus company, the city commissioners and the white public—expected Negroes to be back on the buses in a few days.

This was only the first of a series of misjudgments on the part of the city fathers. All along they demonstrated that their conception of the Negro was the stereotype of the tired field hand or the witless house servant who could be cajoled or forced to do what the white folks wanted him to do. Even now, after 14 weeks of "education," the commissioners seem not to comprehend the intelligence, resourcefulness, and resolve of the people with whom they are dealing.

III

The ex-bus riders soon found themselves face to face with a practical problem: since the buses were taboo, how were the Negroes to get about the city? At first, they called upon the taxis for cheap-rate jitney service. The police stopped this by warning the taxis that by law they must charge a minimum fare of 45 cents. Next, private cars began giving "friends" a lift, along the bus routes. The charge was 15 cents for "gasoline expense." The cops stopped this, too, by insisting that drivers had to have a taxi permit and license.

In reply, the Negroes organized a voluntary motor pool. Almost overnight Montgomery saw a network of private cars spread over the city, picking up and depositing passengers, from dawn until early evening. It was a marvel of quick organization. Even the local press had to concede that the pick-up system moved with "military precision." Some transportation problems that the bus company had grappled with for twenty years were, apparently, solved overnight.

The police searched the books for laws that would dry up the motor pool. One old rule forbade more than three persons to sit on the front seat of an automobile. Lights, brakes, even the position of license tags, were checked by the police frequently. Minor regulations that are seldom invoked in this normally easy-going town were resurrected and severely enforced. Negro taxi drivers really caught it!

The Negro community of Montgomery has neither its own radio station (as does Atlanta, Ga.) nor a widely-read local newspaper. Communication is by word of mouth and through churches mainly. This is probably why frequent mass meetings have proved a necessity. The pattern was established during the first week of the boycott: mass meetings each Monday and Thursday evening. It has been adhered to ever since.

These twice-a-week get-togethers are the soul of the boycott; the Montgomery Improvement Association is the brains. The meetings are rotated from church to church. The speakers, in turn, represent the various denominations. Thus the ground is cut from under any institutional or sectarian jealousy. Rev. King and Rev. Abernathy make it plain by their words and by their sharing of the speakers' platform that they are not self-appointed "leaders" but only "spokesmen" of the movement. Incidentally, the people have "fallen in love" with King, a boyish-looking Ph.D. They look upon Abernathy, also young and an M.A., as a tower of strength. These two men symbolize the poise, the thoughtfulness and the ability of the independent ministers. They are the real and obvious leaders of this mass upsurge. The more vulnerable intellectuals stay discreetly in the background. Rufus Lewis, an ex-football coach and presently a civic-minded businessman, is the cool-headed chairman of the motor pool committee.

People come hours ahead of time to get a seat at these mass meetings. A few read papers and books while waiting, but mostly the audiences sing. Hymns such as "Onward Christian Soldiers," "Abide With Me," and "Higher Ground" are moving but the really stirring songs are the lined, camp-meeting tunes, of low pitch and long meter. These seem to recapture the long history of the Negro's suffering and struggle.

IV

By 7 p.m., the time the meeting starts, virtually every inch of space is taken, including standing room. Often as many listeners are outside as inside. Many others do not come at all because they know they cannot get near the church. It is curious that meetings were never scheduled in different parts of the city or at different hours on the same night or rotated to different parts of the city on different nights in order to accommodate the crowds. This suggestion was made but the planning committee never got around to it or concluded that "the people prefer to be together," as several persons had said.

The mass meeting pattern is relatively simple: songs, prayers, latest news and plans, a "pep talk," collection. Often the pastor in whose church the meeting was held would preside or, after preliminary remarks, would turn the meeting over to some official of the Montgomery Improvement Association.

The meetings are serious but thoroughly relaxed. There are quips and jokes—a great deal of genial humor. All classes are present in the audiences but the bulk of the attendants are working class people. It is here that morale is built and sustained. Unity is expressed in words and in the little kindnesses that the people show to each other. The automobile-owning folk, who never rode the buses, and the maids and day-laborers, who depended upon the buses, have come to know each other. The interdenominational, interclass integration of the Negro community has called forth much comment. Moreover, the mass meetings have given many persons someplace to go; something to think about; something to absorb their energies. There is high purpose these days in the Negro community.

Few whites attend these meetings although they are open to all. Aside from a Lutheran minister who has a Negro congregation, no local white preacher had publicly identified himself with the Negro cause. Many, of course, give assurances privately. A few are in "hot water" for real or suspected sympathies with the boycotters.

But the main force that keeps the people and their leaders together is the idea of the movement itself. These people know that they are fighting a big battle and that it is a vital part of a larger war. Messages and money contributions from many parts of the nation as well as from remote parts of the world have confirmed this belief.

At first, the demands of the boycotters were limited—courtesy, fair play, fair employment. These were all within the segregation laws of the city and state. At one point, the Negroes would have called off the boycott for just the "first come, first serve" agreement. That day, of course, has long since passed.

Apparently to impress the Negro community with what it could lose, the bus company abruptly stopped all service to Negro neighborhoods. This was supposed to bring Negroes on their knees, crying for the buses. But nobody was impressed. Instead, doubtful would-be bus riders were pushed into the motor pool. The water, they found, was just "fine." On second thought, the bus company decided to reestablish the discontinued lines. So the buses were put back on the routes in the Negro area. They continued to roll empty.

For about a month negotiations were on and off. Neither side would yield. The boycott held its own. This meant that 75 percent of the bus riding public was "out," and it cut some $3,000 from each day's revenue. Moreover, fewer whites—probably out of sympathy with the boycott—seem to be riding.

To counteract this economic squeeze, the mayor called on the white public to support the buses. The so-called White Citizens Council solicited contributions for the poor suffering bus company. No figures were ever given out but the general impression is that very few persons were willing to subsidize the National City Lines, an economic giant that is spread out over the cities and towns of the Middle West and South and has its main office in Chicago. A forced subsidy was made possible by raising the bus fare from 10 to 15 cents. At which point, additional whites stayed off the buses.

V

To break the impasse, the city commission pulled a fast one. On Sunday, January 22, the Negro community was astounded to read in the morning paper that a settlement had been reached. The article said: "The above agreement is concurred in by all three members of the City Commission, as well as by representatives of the bus company and the group representing the Negroes of Montgomery." The terms of the "agreement" were: (1) courtesy to all; (2) white reserve section at the front of the bus, Negro reserve section at rear of bus; (3) special, all-Negro buses during the rush hours. "First come, first serve" would obtain for the unreserved, middle section. The city commission stated that it had nothing to do with the question of employment. The declaration of courtesy carried no machinery for assuring its practice. In short, this latest "agreement" was merely a restatement of the *status quo ante bellum*. Nevertheless, it sounded like a settlement and many persons who read the story felt that the boycott was over. Some whites were jubilant. Some Negroes were ill. Why had the "leaders" given in?, they asked.

A careful reading of the article raises the question whether it was just poor reporting or something much worse. For example, the names of the "prominent ministers" were not given. Other omissions were equally strange. If this was a release from the city commission, would any newspaper naively print such an important front-page story without first checking with the known Negro representatives, who had been negotiating with the bus company and city commission for weeks? Obviously, this announcement was a calculated maneuver to get the ex-bus riders back on the buses Sunday morning. Perhaps once the spell of not riding was broken, the boycott would dissolve.

The Negroes foiled this maneuver by a combination of luck and quick action. The story had been sent out Saturday evening by the Associated Press. As it came over the wires into the office of the *Minneapolis Tribune*, the reporter Carl T. Rowan, who had been down to Montgomery to cover the boycott, did what any good reporter would do: he called Rev. M. L. King, Jr. to verify the story.

King was amazed. He knew absolutely nothing about any settlement. Rowan then contacted one of the Montgomery commissioners who confirmed the story but refused to give the names of the Negro ministers involved. Under prodding, the commissioner did reveal the denomination of the ministers. Rowan then called King again. This clue was enough. King and his colleagues by a process of checking soon identified the "three prominent Negro ministers." It turned out that they were neither prominent nor members of the negotiating committee.

It was now late Saturday night. Like minute men, the ministers of the Montgomery Improvement Association went themselves or sent messages to all of the night clubs and taverns in the Negro community, informing the Saturday night revellers of the attempted hoax. Rev. King himself humorously stated that he got a chance to see the insides of many a night spot! Result: word got around so well that the next day the buses rolled empty as usual. At the Sunday morning services, the ministers excoriated the "fake settlement" and repeated that the "protest" was still on. The commissioners lost face. The Negroes were brought closer together.

By the next day, the "three prominent Negro ministers" had publicly repudiated the commission's press announcement. One of the three stated before an open meeting that he had been "tricked" into the conference on the basis of a telephone invitation, asking that he join in a discussion of group insurance for the city. This man said that neither he nor the other two Negroes present agreed to any settlement, declaring that they were unauthorized to speak for the ex-bus riders.

Few persons thought that these three Negro ministers would dare challenge the veracity of the city fathers; but they did. This, everybody was sure, would make front page news. But the local press reduced the sensational disclosure to a bare statement of denial that was buried near the

77

end of a long story. When the local dailies did not print his statement, one of the three ministers purchased space for a three-inch ad saying: "The rumor that is out that I agreed with the commissioners on the proposal that they issued is an untrue statement." These words have never been contradicted.

Things now took a turn for the worse. The mayor and the other commissioners embarked upon a "get tough" policy. With a show of anger the mayor denounced the boycott, declared that the white people did not care if another Negro ever rode the buses again, and called upon white employers to stop taking their Negro employees to and from work. He said that white businessmen informed him that they were discharging Negro workers who were participating in the boycott. All three commissioners let it be known that they had joined the White Citizens Council. Even the timid member of the trio mustered up enough bravado to go on television and join the "get tough with Negroes" act. All this, of course, was the traditional, Confederate, flag-waving appeal to white supremacy.

It was to be a field day. The police would "cut the legs off" the boycott by a campaign of arrests for real and imaginary traffic infractions. Negro drivers, who appeared to be in the motor pool, would be questioned about their employment, the balance due on the purchase of their automobiles, and the firms with which they had their insurance.

VI

For a moment the protest movement seemed to be wavering. Again, Negroes saw that the very instruments of law and order were being used against them. Surely, a man had a right to give someone a ride in his own automobile. Persons who had not received a traffic ticket in years were booked. Some ex-bus riders, while waiting to be picked up, were told that there was a law against hitchhiking; others were accused of "loud talking," walking on lawns and "congregating in white neighborhoods." The daily press printed next to nothing about the wholesale arrests and harassment.

Under such heavy blows the voluntary pick-up system began to weaken. Some drivers were already tired; others disliked "tangling with the law"; still others feared that they could not stand much more provocation without striking back.

The high point of the "get tough" operation was the arrest of Rev. King himself. But if this move was intended to frighten King, it fell flat. He calmly submitted to arrest and jailing. At first, he was not to be let out on bond. The news spread through the Negro community like wildfire. Negroes began rushing down to the jail in such numbers that King was released without having even to sign his own bond.

Meanwhile, a group of Negro business and professional men asked the city for permission to operate a jitney service. This was turned down on the grounds that sufficient transportation was already available. The mayor said, let them ride the buses now rolling empty through the streets. A strange stand for one who didn't care if another Negro ever rode a bus again!

But the city did care. It stood to lose part of the $20,000 in taxes it received from the bus company each year. Downtown merchants cared, too, for some of their businesses were off by as much as a third since the boycott had begun. Most of all, the bus company cared—each day it cared more and more. It let it be known that it would agree to any seating arrangement that the city commissioners would approve.

The worst was yet to come. The inflammatory appeals seemed to give the signal to the violent elements. A stick of dynamite was thrown on the porch of Rev. King's home. The job was amateurish; the damage slight; the intent vicious. Within minutes hundreds of Negroes flocked to King's home; also the police. It was at this moment that nonviolent resistance almost faded. Many Negroes wanted to launch a counter-offensive. Rev. King, standing on the front porch of his "bombed" home, pleaded with the angry Negroes: "We are not harmed. Do not get your weapons. Let us not answer hate with hate, violence with violence. But we will continue to stay off the buses." Probably this saved the city from a race riot.

There had been other incidents. Some Negro and white high school students had clashed; one or more cars of white youths had made commando raids on the nearby Negro college, dashing through the campus with lights out, throwing out bags of water, eggs, rocks, and a tiny flaming cross. One evening the commandos were ambushed and bombarded with bricks. Another commando car was captured by special police. Another clumsy bomb-thrower hit the fence of E. D. Nixon, the president of the local NAACP chapter.

This flurry of violence had no noticeable effect on the boycott. The leaders were careful but nobody seemed to be at all afraid. On the other hand, it helped convince the patient hopefuls that an all-out fight was the only kind that made any sense.

For two months the Negroes had clung to the hope of a settlement on the basis of their limited demands. But the failure of negotiations and the crude brutality of the "get tough" policy convinced the most conservative ex-bus riders that an attack had to be made upon bus segregation itself. Accordingly, on February 1 a suit was filed in the local federal courts, asking for the end of bus jim crow on the grounds that it is contrary to the 14th Amendment of the Constitution of the United States. Furthermore, the court was asked to stop the city commissioners from violating the civil rights of Negro motorists and pedestrians.

This was a sobering jolt for the city commissioners. The "get tough" police evaporated overnight. The city fathers, who had been making speeches at the drop of the hat, lapsed into their usual quietude.

VII

Meanwhile, a fresh effort was made to reopen negotiations. This time a white businessmen's club intervened. Many of them had stores that had been hurt. It is estimated that the boycott has cost Montgomery $1,000,000. The businessmen's club met several times, separately, with the city commission and a committee from the Montgomery Improvement Association. Chicago Negroes had thrown a picket line around the offices of the parent bus company, so it was more willing than ever to come to terms. The city commissioners, however, remained adamant. They seem to feel that they cannot afford to yield. So the best that the businessmen could offer was little more than the old "fake" settlement that had been palmed off on the "three prominent Negro ministers."

Some of the drivers in the motor pool were becoming exhausted. Twelve or thirteen weeks of free, voluntary service, four or five hours per day, is fatiguing. Most of these drivers have jobs and other obligations. Several of the leaders felt that maybe the boycott might as well be called off since in the end the courts would settle the issue. Understandably, people were becoming battle-weary. For over three months, life has been like a military operation for the Negro Improvement Association.

So the leaders, though reluctantly, submitted the proposals of the businessmen to the rank and file at one of the mass meetings. The answer was an almost total rejection. Out of approximately four thousand persons present, *only two* voted in favor of calling off the boycott. The morale of the masses, once again, revived the morale of the leaders.

To date the latest move to break the boycott has been the indictment of the leaders of the Improvement Association. This was based on an old anti-labor law of doubtful constitutionality. And again nobody was frightened.

Nobody tried to hide. Many inquired of the sheriff's office: "Is my name on that Grand Jury list?" If it was, the caller let it be known that he would come down immediately. Confident, orderly, loyal to each other, the Negroes again manifested their collective will and *esprit de corps*.

As for the future, nobody can be sure. The white people of Montgomery have been amazed by the group discipline of the Negro community and by the intelligence and organization with which the boycott has been maintained. "I didn't think they had it in them," is a frequent comment.

Many whites who would like to see the boycott ended and who feel that the demands of the Negroes are reasonable, are afraid to admit this. They fear that to "give in" on this means that "all" is lost. There are sincere apprehensions that desegregation at any one point will lead to general racial integration—and that means intermarriage! An absurd goblin hovers over every white household. The politicians and White Councils exploit these fears. The chief weakness of the movement for desegregation is that so little is done to remove the unfounded alarms of the thousands who in desperation are flocking to the hate organizations.

The fact is that desegregation has been magnified so greatly in the minds of so many Americans, both Negro and white, that they do not realize how ordinary and natural a nonsegregated society is. Nonsegregation already prevails in many areas of Southern life—the supermarkets, for example—with scarcely passing notice. Negroes seem to feel that desegregation will work overnight miracles. Southern whites feel that it will precipitate disaster. They are both wrong. It is neither so glorious nor so dangerous as pictured, even in terms of the values of the opposing groups. A nonsegregated society is merely a crude, basic precondition for creating a social order in which the higher sensibilities can flourish.

We are all indebted to the Negroes of Montgomery. They say that they are confident of ultimate victory. In a sense, they have already won. They have given us a magnificent case study of the circumstances under which the philosophy of Thoreau and Gandhi can triumph. Moreover, the boycott movement has brought something new into the lives of the Negroes of Montgomery. They would be loath to give it up. Whenever the boycott ends, it will be missed.

March 15, 1956

81

The Montgomery
Bus Protest as
a Social Movement

PRESTON VALIEN

Many of the generalizations on social movements now current in the sociological literature stem from the insights of Robert E. Park and his students. In one of his many brilliant papers on collective behavior, Park wrote:

> . . . the crowd dissolves with the occasion that brings it into existence. How the transition is made from this passing, ephemeral and spontaneous organization to a more formal, permanent, and self-conscious one, such as we have in the strike, in revolution, and in social movements generally, neither Le Bon nor any later writer, with the possible exception of Theodor Geiger, has really attempted to explain . . .
>
> A social movement . . . seems, when looked at casually, to be a mere series of episodes–public meetings, discussions, accompanied by intermittent clashes and minor encounters with the existing order . . .
>
> No doubt every social movement tends to pass through a series of typical phases. Every political action, including war, revolution, and reform, assumes at the outset the character of a collective gesture. What takes place is expressive merely. Someone is agitated and his very agitation makes him, without any ulterior motive on his part, an agitator. If his sentiments thus expressed find an echo in other minds, this expression assumes the character of 'public sentiment.' Public sentiment thus aroused expresses itself, perhaps, in a spontaneous and unpremeditated public demonstration. At this point the necessity for some organization and direction makes itself felt. Agitation turns out to be a serious business. What was a gesture assumes the form of a political movement. It becomes important that the movement be directed with foresight in order that it may achieve its end. In attempting to direct such a

83

social movement the leaders develop some sort of technique for maintaining discipline within the ranks and strategy in dealing with the enemy outside.[1]

Thus, there is much in a story of the Montgomery bus protest that throws light on political strategy, public opinion, and on all the conscious devices and unconscious mechanisms by which morale is maintained in conflict groups.

In a dynamic society such as is characteristic of the United States, social relationships are in a state of constant flux and change, and it is one of the tasks of social science to delineate, describe, and explain objectively this process. Social change presupposes the modification of social situations in such a manner that a new structure of social relationships emerges, and such change frequently grows out of what. Park calls the organization and direction of public sentiments as it passes through a series of phases or stages and assumes the form of social movement. Conceived of in this manner, the research efforts of the sociologist should be directed toward the description and analysis of the set of factors which are constantly modifying the character of social situations.

The obvious fact is that in the South today the social situation which we know as the racial order is changing. For present purposes, we may speak of two channels through which these changes are being made evident. The first we may designate as "institutional," that is changes which take place within the context of pre-established understandings, customs, traditions, rules, or laws. The second channel for such social changes we may designate as "extra-institutional" or "non-institutional." By this we mean changes which take place as a result of collective behavior *outside* the context of regulated group activity. This would include collective action such as boycotts, social protests, and mass movements. The so-called "institutional" changes have been widely studied and are fairly well understood; the "extra-institutional" changes have been generally less studied and are less well understood. Yet, it is highly important that we understand these changes if we are to place social behavior in a meaningful context, especially with reference to racial desegregation in both the North and the South.

Recent sociological literature contains many excellent surveys of specific desegregation situations, but these tend generally to be more idiographic than nomothetic in presentation, more concerned with programs and policies than with social processes and social interaction. The Department of Social Sciences of Fisk University has been attempting to study desegregation situations within a nomothetic frame of reference, utilizing two conceptual approaches. One approach has been an attempt to study the desegregation process as a social movement while the second has been an attempt to study the differential perceptions of Negroes and whites. The first is reflected in a study of the Montgomery, Alabama bus protest as a social movement, and the other is represented by studies of the different perception by whites and Negroes of the same social situation with respect to desegregation in Montgomery, Alabama; St. Louis, Missouri; and Clinton, Oak Ridge, and Nashville, Tennessee, as well as a broad-gauged national study of conflicting social norms where the racial factor is introduced. Space will permit here only a broad sketch of the materials from the Montgomery bus protest.[2]

It appeared rather early after it began in December, 1955, that the Montgomery bus protest might provide a natural laboratory for the study of what might be regarded as the natural history of a social movement. A social movement is defined here as a concerted action or agitation with some degree of continuity, by a group which is united by somewhat definite aims, follows a designed program, and is directed at a change of patterns and institutions of the existing society. Often sociologists have come to the study of social movements after these movements have run their course, but Montgomery provided an opportunity to study one in the process of formation and subsequent operation.

Several generalizations regarding social movements seemed to warrant testing or at least documenting with empirical evidence in connection with the Montgomery bus protest, and some of these will be presented here with supporting material from our field interviews.

1. *While a social movement begins with a concrete precipitating incident, it is usually the result of an accumulation of known or shared incidents on the part of the participants.* Two typical interviews regarding the background of bus incidents in Montgomery earlier than the precipitating incident of December 1, 1955, will serve to illustrate the accumulation of known or shared incidents. One respondent gave the background of the precipitating incident in the following words:

> For a number of years people here have suffered indignities. There are very few people who ride the buses who haven't at some time suffered the indignity of having to give their seat to some white person whether there were other seats or not. So, you see, this is something mutual. It concerns all of the people.

Through the years colored people have been moving back without saying anything and those who outwardly disapproved would get off the bus and wait for another one. This was the case until last year when one of our school girls over at Booker Washington refused to move. The bus driver asked for her seat and the two seats across the aisle. The other three young ladies immediately stood, but little Claudette Colvin stated that she was tired of standing for white folks every morning, so she kept her seat. The motorman circled the block then called the police. A young policeman, about 26, forcefully arrested her. Bless her heart, she fought like a little tigress. The policeman had scars all over his face and hands.

We (a group of representatives from the various organizations) went down to settle the affair. The motorman admitted that he was wrong; however, they did have a trial and she was found guilty of assault and battery and was sentenced to one year probation to her parents. We talked to the bus company officials about their bus policy, and they were very nice and humble and willing to cooperate; but until this day they haven't done a thing that they said they would. We have talked and filed petitions and all we've received are empty promises.

Now when Mrs. Parks was arrested, to others as well as myself, it was a shock. As you may already know, Mrs. Parks is local secretary of the NAACP, wonderful church worker, graduate of State (Alabama State Teachers College), respectable and above all she *is a lady*. When I asked her what happened, she said that she did not move. There were no other seats; however, she stated that if there had been, she had made up her mind never to move again. She was very quiet about the whole matter.

Another respondent, while acknowledging favorable treatment which she had received, indicated the impact of known or shared incidents in the following statement:

From my own experiences over a period of years I have witnessed several incidents wherein the bus drivers were quite nasty to Negro patrons, and I've also witnessed very nice bus drivers. In fact the drivers in this vicinity are very nice to me. Several times they've pulled away from the stop, but will wait across the street if they should see me coming, and I always thanked them with a smile because they didn't have to stop. On the other hand, there are two cases I remember very distinctly. In the first case, I was going out Maxwell Road, and there were four young colored ladies sitting on the first two horizontal seats and two white airmen got on the bus. The bus driver yelled, 'Let me have those seats.' There were no other seats in the back, so the girls had to stand. The airmen were very much embarrassed. They didn't care to take the seats, and said so everyone could hear them: 'I never heard of such . . . women stand while men sit.' In the next case, the two seats across the aisle from the colored lady were vacant, but the driver demanded that she move, because a white man could not sit opposite a colored lady. In this case, however, there was a seat or at least part of a seat in back. I say part of a seat because the woman sitting there weighed around 250 pounds, which means she left only about half of the second seat vacant, and the woman whom the driver asked to move back weighed nearly 200. Anyway, she refused to move. The driver called her a few nasty names and asked her to come up to the front of the bus. She told him, 'If you want me, you'll have to come back here, and if you do, the undertaker sure will dress you.' The other people on the bus told her to move back; there was no use in getting in trouble over something like that. So she finally moved back.

Now about five years ago there was a teacher who had a teenage daughter arrested because she refused to move. I don't know exactly how the case came out, but I do know they left town.

So you see, things have been piling up over a period of years, and those people are not going to give up easily. The people on all levels are helping. Even the drunks will not ride the buses. They say they'll walk and use bus fare money for more wiskey. I cannot help but remember how pleased I was when I learned about the 'boycott.' I was downtown when someone handed me one of the leaflets, and I said, 'Thank God! At last it has come.'

2. *While a social movement begins with a concrete incident, it develops an ideology which progressively becomes more idealistic with the passage of time.* The initial proposals of the Negro bus protesters in Montgomery were (a) more courteous treatment of Negro bus passengers, (b) seating on a first-come, first-served basis, with Negroes continuing to sit from the rear of the bus and white from front to rear, and (c) hiring of Negro bus drivers on predominantly Negro lines. As late as April, 1956, the Reverend Martin Luther King was writing, "We seek the right, *under segregation*, to seat ourselves from the rear forward on a first-come, first-served basis."[3] But in January, 1957, he was writing in cooperation with sixty Negro leaders, "All over the world men are in revolt against social and political domination. The age old cry for freedom and human dignity takes on a significance never experienced before. For in a very real and impelling sense no man, no nation and no part of the universe is an island unto itself. Asia's successive revolts against European imperialism, Africa's present ferment for independence, Hungary's death struggle against Communism, and the determined drive of Negro Americans to become first-class citizens are inextricably bound together. They are all vital factors in determining whether Twentieth Century mankind will crown its vast material gains with the achievement of liberty and justice for all, or whether it will commit suicide through lack of moral fiber."

"We advocate nonviolence in words, thought and deed; we believe this spirit and this spirit alone can overcome the decades of mutual fear and suspicion that have infested and poisoned our Southern culture." Translated into popular terms, the official slogan of the movement, "Justice without violence," became "If you don't let them make you mad, you can win."

3. *In order for a social movement to develop and persist, it must make effective use of certain social mechanisms.* In perhaps what is the most definitive general treatment of social movements in the literature, Herbert Blumer stated that a social movement grows and becomes organized through five mechanisms: (a) agitation, (b) development of *esprit de corps*, (c) development of morale, (d) the formation of an ideology, and (e) the development of operation tactics. Some of these mechanisms have already been touched upon as they relate to the Montgomery bus protest, but others deserve further consideration. *Esprit de corps*, for example, may be regarded as the development of group solidarity and allegiance through promoting enthusiasm and collective feelings on behalf of the movement. *Esprit de corps* is promoted in three ways: (1) the development of ingroup-outgroup relations, (2) the formation of informal fellowship associations, and (3) the participation in formal ceremonial behavior. The weekly mass meetings with songs, poems, cartoons, hymns, and membership cards illustrate the ceremonial behavior which developed in connection with the Montgomery movement. The following is a typical interview statement illustrating the nature and strength of ingroup-outgroup relations:

I wurk fur two families, and dey stay next doe to each other. Let me tell you about one fust.
    The fust one, her husband is a busdriver. Fur a week after the boycott started nothing happened. Den one evening I was bout to leave the other lady's house and the othern came to the fence and told me to come by her house when I finish, she had something fur me. Said she had some bacon grease. She told me don't let her husband see it cause he told her don't gimmie nothing else. I told 'er if her husband seyd don't gimmie nothing else, den don't gimmie nothing else. Den she sayd, 'Irene, what happen at the meeting last night?' I told 'er we sung and prayed. She looked at me and tole me I was telling a damn lie. I seyd back to 'er, 'Now listen, I know we did sung and prayed, and if you don't believe me you go to de meeting fur yoself,' and I seyd to myself, 'She must take me fur a fool, think I'll come back here and puke everything my folks seys to her, and then just for some little old stinking bakin grease at dat.'

Esprit de corps is promoted also by informal associations on the basis of fellowship, and these were fostered by the mass meetings and by the car pool to which many professional Negroes contributed both their vehicles as well as their services as drivers. College professors, maids, ministers, and drunkards all shared the intimacy of the mass meetings and the conveniences and inconveniences of the car-pool facilities. The following account of a mass meeting illustrates some of the social mechanisms which were utilized in the development of *esprit de corps*:

Report on Mass Meetings

Hymn . . . . *Onward Christian Soldiers*
Prayer
Hymn . . . . *Plant My Feet on Higher Ground*

First Speaker:

It is time for the white man to realize that he is not dealing with a child. Even the 'Uncle Toms' are tired of being 'Uncle Toms,' and this reminds me of something which was supposed to have happened in Mississippi a couple of years ago.

The whites in Mississippi wanted to show to the world that they were not as bad as they were said to be. So they went all over Mississippi searching for 'Uncle Toms.' Finally they dug up the best one they had in the state and told him that he would be put on television, that the whole nation would see him and that he must tell them what wonderful relations exist between white and colored folks in Mississippi. Finally the day came, and he was on television. He looked at the white folks all around and said, 'Did you say I'll be heard in Boston, New York, Chicago, Philadelphia, and all over the world?'

Yes, now tell people how wonderful it is here.

You really mean I'm on all over the country, and that's the God sent truth?

Yes.

HELP!!!

So you see, 'Uncle Tom' is fed up too.

Second Speaker:

Some of our good white citizens told me today that the relationships between white and colored used to be good, that the whites have never let us down and that the outsiders came in and upset this relationship. But I want you to know that if M. L. King had never been born this movement would have taken place. I *just happened* to be here. You know there comes a time when time itself is ready for change. That time has come in Montgomery, and I had nothing to do with it.

Our opponents, I hate to think of our governmental officials as opponents, but they are, have tried all sorts of things to break us, but we still held steadfast. Their first strategy was to negotiate a compromise and that failed. And now they are trying to intimidate us by a get-tough policy and that's going to fail too because a man's language is courage when his back is against the wall.

We don't advocate violence. WE WILL STAY WITHIN THE LAW. WHEN WE ARE RIGHT, WE DON'T MIND GOING TO JAIL. (The applause rang out like a great clap of thunder.) If all I have to pay is going to jail a few times and getting about 20 threatening calls a day, I think that is a very small price to pay for what we are fighting for (applause very loud and long).

We are a chain. We are linked together, and I cannot be what I ought unless you are what you ought to be.

This good white citizen I was talking to said that I should devote more time to preaching the gospel and leave other things alone. I told him that it's not enough to stand in the pulpit on Sunday and preach about honesty, to tell people to be honest and don't think about their economic conditions which may be conducive to their being dishonest. It's not enough to tell them to be truthful and forget about the social environment which may necessitate their telling untruths. All of these are a minister's job. You see, God didn't make us with just soul alone so we could float about in space without care or worry. He made a body to put around a soul. When the body was made in flesh, there became a material connection between man and his environment, and this connection means a material well being of the body as well as the spiritual well being of the soul is to be sought. And it is my job as minister to aid in both of these (roaring applause).

Third Speaker:

The 'Get-Tough Policy' will not stop us (loud nos and amens). I want you to know that there is only one sure fire way to deal with Mr. Sellers–BY THE VOTE. He was put in by the lack of your vote. So pay your poll tax now and get ready to vote.

Fourth Speaker:

The next Mass Meeting will be held at the Day Street Baptist Church, and if I can't see you there, I'll meet you in the city jail (loud laughs and applause).

You know they have on the car tags 'Heart of Dixie.' *Well, let's walk until Dixie has a Heart* (roaring applause).

Fifth Speaker: Minister from Mobile

We have for you $500.43. That $0.43 is to let you know that some more is coming. Just fight on and with God on our side we cannot lose. And no matter what the other side does, one thing it cannot do–THEY CANNOT PICK YOU UP AND PUT YOU BACK ON THE BUSES (thundering applause).

Pep Talk:

When I was a boy my mother used to take a string and tie it around her waist to hold her dress up so it wouldn't get wet in the morning dew when she trudged her way into the cotton fields. But more than that I remember what she used to sing. I haven't heard it in over 30 years, but I think it's time to sing it again in our hearts. She used to sing, 'O Freedom, O Freedom Over Me. Before I'd be a slave, I'd be buried in my grave and go home to my Lord and be free.' That is how I feel, and we can be free.

You know, if a man doesn't want to sit beside me because I'm dirty, that's my fault. If he doesn't want to sit beside me because I'm loud, that is my fault too, but if he doesn't want to sit beside me because *I am black*, that's not my fault because God made me black, and my white brother is discriminating against God and His will. But even though they are, we must love them. We must love Mr. Sellers and Mr. Gayle for God said that we must love our enemies as ourselves. Let's not hate them for with love in our hearts and God on our side, there are no forces in hell or on earth that can mow us down.

I had a book which was so interesting that I gave it to the city officials to read. It's a book on great powers, the stories of men who ruled and conquered by force only to lose later. Men like Alexander the Great, Napoleon and Hitler were discussed, men who lived by the sword. Their empires are no longer, but have perished. But there was a man who was passive, who taught that love and faith could move mountains and more mountains. And unto this day that empire which was built by a man who said while dying on the Cross, 'Forgive them, O Lord, for they know not what they do'—that is the empire of Jesus Christ! He was asking forgiveness for the men who crucified Him, drove nails through his Hands and put thorns on His head. So we forgive Sellers and Gayle, but we do not give up.

There were two armies once, and they both gave out of ammunition. The soldiers said to the General in one army, 'What are we going to do?' The

91

General replied, 'Retreat.' In the other army the soldiers asked the same question and the General replied, 'Forward March!' They won the battle. So we are going to 'Forward March' to a victory whether Mr. Sellers is bluffing or not. And if any of you are scared, keep your fears to yourself. Get your flat shoes and *walk*. Heaven knows how much it will help.

Announcements; Hymn; Benediction.

Ministers and adherents of different Negro religious denominations sang and prayed together in one another's houses of worship at the weekly mass meetings which were rotated among different churches. The following statement which appeared in *The Christian Index*, official organ of the Christian (formerly Colored) Methodist Episcopal Church, on April 4, 1957, indicates the recognition of the growth of denominational cooperation. The statement cites an open letter from a group of Negro Methodist ministers in Birmingham who wanted to assure the Negro Methodist laity that Methodist ministers were actively cooperating in the Montgomery bus protest despite the fact that the elected leaders of the bus protest were chiefly Baptist.

An Open Letter to All Methodists

Negro ministers, especially in the South, have assumed the lead in a great spiritual movement for rights and freedom of all people. Some have already risked their lives at the hands of racial extremists. Their churches and homes have been bombed. Their wives and children have been injured and have barely escaped death. But they grow more courageous and more effective.

One of the "by products" of this movement has been the close fellowship and cooperation between the Negro ministers of different denominations. Despite the fact that practically all of the elected leaders are of one denomination, there has been the closest support and cooperation from ministers of other denominations. This team work among the ministers has been so genuine and effective that only a few have questioned the fact that the president of each movement in the different cities happens to be a Baptist minister.

The following "open letter to Methodists" from the Methodist ministers in Birmingham illustrates the team work among these ministers; it also indicates that the Methodist ministers and other Negro ministers fully share the leadership for freedom:

We are sure you are aware of the great struggle for the freedom of the communicants in your branch of Methodism here in Montgomery, Alabama. Efforts have been made by some, inside and outside of Montgomery, to discredit the service and interest of the representatives of various branches of Methodism during this great struggle.

You can be well assured that the leading ministers in all branches of Methodism have acquitted themselves in this struggle with a degree of integrity, loyalty, and devotion which is unsurpassed for the leading ministers of any other denomination.

Perhaps you have not heard this before due primarily to the modesty of the Methodist ministers. The first meeting held that initiated the bus protest in Montgomery was presided over by a minister of the African Methodist Episcopal Zion Church. Nine of the ministers arrested were Methodist pastors and one Presiding Elder.

The time has come for Methodists to further prove to the world that their hearts are big. We are in a great struggle here to repair and rebuild four Baptist churches that were bombed on January 10. A special committee has been appointed to direct this campaign and to supervise the disbursements of this fund to those churches in accordance to their needs.

A Methodist minister is the chairman of this committee and a Methodist is the secretary-director of this campaign. We call upon you Methodists all over America to send offerings or donations to Committee for Aid of Bombed Churches, Montgomery Improvement Association, 530 S. Union St., Montgomery 8, Alabama.

> Rev. J.W. Bonner, Committee Chairman
> Rev. Harold A.L. Clement, Secretary-Director
> Rev. J.W. Hayes and S.S. Seay

Endorsed by the Methodist Ministerial Alliance; other officers of Alliance not named above: Revs. R.W. Hilson, President; A.S. Bannister, 2nd Vice President; J.B. Kelly, Assistant and Corresponding Secretary; A.W. Murphy, Parliamentarian, and W.J. Powell, Reporter.

While *esprit de corps* gave life, enthusiasm, and vigor to the movement, the development of morale was necessary to give it persistency and determination in the face of adversity. Morale is based upon a set of convictions which includes a strong belief in the purpose of the movement, coupled with a faith in the ultimate attainment of its goal. Revealing a high degree of morale, a Negro domestic servant responded as follows when asked what had her white employer said about the bus protest.

> She never seyed anythang about the buses but once, and dat waz right after we stopped riding 'em. One day she says to me, 'Dealy, why don't you ride the bus? Dat Rev. King is jest making a fool outta you people.'

I seyed back to her, 'Don't you sey nothing about Rev. Kang. You kin sey anythang else you won't to, but don't you sey nothin about Rev. Kang. Dat's us man and I declare he's a fine un. He went to school and made somethin out of hisself, and now he's trying to help us. Yall white folks done kept us bline long enough. We got our eyes open and now us sho' ain't gonna let you close 'em back. I don't mean to be sassy, but when you talk bout Rev. Kang I gits mad.'

'I ain't gonna get back on the bus till Rev. Kang sey so, and he seys we ain't going back til they treat us right.'

Another domestic servant reported an exchange with her white employer which may reflect the fact that, in 1950, 63 percent of employed Negro females of Montgomery were in domestic service while 61 percent of the employed white females were in clerical service.

You see, I work out in Cloverdale (elite section of town) for Mrs. Powell and she hates it, but it sure ain't nothing she can do about it. She said to me when I went to work that Wednesday: 'Susie you ride the bus, don't you?' I said, 'I sure don't.' She said, 'Why, Susie, they haven't done anything to you.' I said, 'Listen Mrs. Powell, you don't ride the bus, you don't know how those ole nasty drivers treat us and further when you do something to my people you do it to me too. If you kick one, if you can get around to me you'll kick me too. My mother taught me, Mrs. Powell, to treat thy neighbor as thy self, but I don't have anything in my heart but hatred for those bus drivers.' 'Susie, don't feel that way. I've always been nice to you.' 'That's true, Mrs. Powell, if I get sick for a couple of days, you come by to see me, pay me and bring my food, but if I stayed sick 2 or 3 weeks, would you do it?' "Course I would, Susie, but I just can't see white and colored riding together on the buses. It just wouldn't come to a good end.'

'I'm going to tell you this, Susie, because I know you can keep your mouth shut. In the White Citizen Council meeting, they discussed starving the maids for a month. They asked us to lay off our maids for a month, and they'll be glad to ride the buses again. If they do it I still want you to come one day a week.'

'Well, Mrs. Powell, I just won't come at all and I sure won't starve. You see, my husband is a working man, my son and daughter have good jobs, and my daddy keeps plenty food on his farm. So, I'm not worried at all, 'cause I was eating before I started working for you.'

'Susie, that ole Rev. King and Ole Graetz should be run out of town. They keep this mess going. You know, I heard that Rev. King is going to take all your money and go buy a Cadillac with it. He's going from door to door asking for $2. Susie, don't give him $2.'

'Who ever told you that, Mrs. Powell, told you a lie, but if he did, it ain't no more for me to pay $2 than it is for you to pay $3.50 for the White Citizen thing.'

'And you know, Susie, Old Rev. King wants people to go to church together and I just can't see it.'

'Mrs. Powell, I didn't ask you to come to my church and I ain't particular about going to yours, but a church is a house of worship and the doors should be open to everybody. You don't want to go to church with us when down in the 5th Ward until a couple of years ago, you couldn't go in or leave after dark 'cause all those white men and women were down there after these colored people.' She stood there looking at me like a sick chicken, then hurried off, talking about she had to go to work. She didn't say anything more after that. I came right home and called Rev. Abernathy, my pastor, and told him about them talking about firing maids. You know our pastors tell us what to do. They lead us in a Christian way. We just act nice and quiet.

It seems apparent that the development of morale in a social movement is essentially a matter of linking a sectarian attitude toward obstacles to the movement with a religious faith in the moral rightness of the movement. The linkage of this sectarian attitude with religious faith is clearly illustrated in an incident involving three Negro ministers of Montgomery who were called down to the city hall by the city commissioners during the bus protest on the pretext of discussing insurance. Although these ministers had not been active in the bus protest movement, when they arrived at City Hall, the commissioners presented them with a proposal to end the boycott without granting the requests of the Negroes. The ministers claimed later that they had not agreed to the proposals, but after they left, the commissioners announced to the newspapers that a settlement had been reached. When one of the newspapers checked with the protest leaders, it was found that they knew nothing about the settlement and word was quickly spread in the Negro community that the protest was still in force. The interesting point here is the secular reaction of church members of the three ministers which is typified by this response.

I'm a member of Rev. Brown's church and I felt bad when I heard it, to think some of your folks dat you been sitting under in church will sell you out. Dat's bad. I believe in giving every man his right, but if it's true dat he sold us out, he got to leave dat church. If you wrong you jest wrong if it's my daddy, and he's dead, he's just wrong. He looked guilty in church Sunday morning. I didn't say anything cause I didn't know the whole thing. Dey said on the radio dat he wuz paid and you have to tell the truth on the radio cause people can sue you for lying on 'm, so it must be true.

But Rev. Brown ain't no fool. He's too old a man to let dem folks do him like dat. He got two churches and he didn't have to sell us out to get some money. He knowed he didn't know nothing about insurance, so when old Sellers called him, all he had to do wuz say I ain't on de committee and call

Rev. King. He knowed he ain't set through no meeting fur 2 hours and didn't say nothin. Silence is consent anyway. I heard dat dey beat Rev. Smith up and dat dar weren't but two members at his church Sunday. Dey told him, dat they didn't need 'em and I heard dat dey beat him up. Dem young boys said dey wuz going to beat Rev. Brown up too. If day said it, dey'll do it. He better stay close. I wouldn't won't dem to kill 'em but it'd be okey if day just pull his britches down and tap him a few times.

4. *Another generalization which we sought to document is that a social movement passes through several stages usually with changes of leadership in each of the contending sides as each stage develops.* The stages suggested usually include: initial protest, collective organization, negotiation (including litigation), and institutionalization.

The empirical evidence supports this generalization with some qualifications as to the leadership aspects. The initial protest was organized by a women's political club, but the ministers were called upon when a continuing organization was desired. Lawyers entered at the stage of negotiation. One of the leaders of the Women's Political Council gave this account of the development of leadership in the bus protest:

Respondent: I was called and asked if I would help in initiating a one day 'boycott' and of course I was willing. I was sent a large stock of leaflets which I distributed among my workers, and they in turn put them on porches without ringing door bells in order to keep the finger off of any persons.

Interviewer: Excuse me, but when you say workers, to whom do you have reference?

Respondent: Well, in the Women's Political Council we sort of work in areas which are broken down into sub-areas and within these there are persons who know the people a little better than I, and who can reach some which I cannot, and these are called workers.

Interviewer: When did the ministers get into the movement?

Respondent: The ministers did not take over until the following Monday after Mrs. Parks' arrest. There was a meeting and Rev. M. L. King was unanimously chosen chairman of the Montgomery Improvement Association. I think he is doing a wonderful job for a man of his age (27) and his small degree of experience. The same may be attributed to Lawyer Gray who is working with us too. Their minds are much older than they are biologically. They are doing wonderful jobs. The movement has been a great success up to this point and I'm sure it will be even greater for the working people, the ones whom the bus corporation is dependent upon are the ones who keep this movement going. The leaders could do nothing by themselves. They are only the voice of thousands of colored workers. Where the lawyers are concerned, though, the voice is very important for this movement could not have happened with great success at any other time in Montgomery.

Interviewer: Why?

Respondent: It couldn't have happened because we did not have any Negro lawyers. The situation here has been pathetic—to be considered for an appointment with city officials you had to have a lawyer. With a lawyer they cannot brush you aside because he knows the law as well or better than the city officials. Lawyer Gray keeps us within those boundaries of the law so there will be no backfiring.

There is objective evidence to demonstrate the stage of institutionalization. On November 27, 1956, the Montgomery Improvement Association which was the sponsoring organization of the bus protest issued the following announcement: "During the week of December 3, 1956, the MIA will observe its first anniversary by conducting an Institute on Non-Violence and Social Change. Some of the outstanding thinkers and personalities of the nation have been invited to Montgomery to participate in this Institute. This is not to be construed as a victory celebration; rather it will be a week in which we will seek to rededicate the community and the nation to the principle of nonviolence in the struggle for freedom and justice." During April, 1957, a further announcement was made that "The Montgomery Improvement Association, which spearheaded the Montgomery bus boycott for more than 381 days and achieved its goal of desegregation on public transportation carriers through the decision of the U.S. Supreme Court, has become a permanent organization and is in need of an executive secretary." Applicants were solicited and a decent salary was promised. The following objectives were outlined for the permanent organization:

1. Civic education and participation on a non-partisan basis
2. Community relationship (interracial and intraracial)
3. Education for individual competence
4. Improvement of economic status
5. Health
6. Recreation
7. Law enforcement
8. Public relations
9. Spiritual enrichment

10. Cultural development

Institutions grow up, as Everett Hughes has pointed out, because social movements never quite accomplish all they undertake to do. There is always "unfinished business"—something still to be done which is eventually turned over to a committee or to a secretariat and eventually to a corps of permanent functionaries. This, at any rate, is one way in which institutionalization takes place in a secular society.

In conclusion, it should be said that while the Montgomery bus protest assumed international importance, social scientists are not journalists looking for the headline event. They seek an accurate and adequate understanding of man's conduct among men by constantly attempting to relate the events which they study to a class of similar events. Viewing the Montgomery bus protest as a social movement may contribute to this end.

This paper was written in August, 1957, at the request of the senior editor.

NOTES

1. Robert E. Park, *Society* (Glencoe, Ill.: The Free Press, 1955), pp. 31-32.
2. In the Montgomery Negro community interviewing was done by three graduate students—Willie Mae Lee, Donald Ferron, Harold Jones—and the author of this paper. Interviewing in the white community was carried out by Anna Holden and Inez Adams. Other faculty members who have participated in the formulation of the study and other aspects of the project include J. Masuoka, R. L. Yokley, and Bonita Valien.
3. Martin Luther King, "Our Struggle," *Liberation* (April, 1956), pp. 3-6.

The Natural History
of a
Social Movement

The Montgomery

Improvement

Association

RALPH D. ABERNATHY

This paper was originally written as an M.A. thesis in the Department of Sociology at Atlanta University, August, 1958. It has been edited for publication, but otherwise is presented here as it was written.

Ralph D. Abernathy is Pastor of the West Hunter Baptist Church in Atlanta, Georgia. One of the central figures in the boycott, as well as Martin Luther King, Jr.'s closest friend, he was Dr. King's chosen successor as president of the Southern Christian Leadership Conference.

Contents

ONE

Introduction

This study represents an attempt to describe and analyze the character and processes of a social movement—The Montgomery Improvement Association. The study of social movements is one of the specialized fields of sociological science, falling within the broad area of "collective behavior." The field of collective behavior stems from observation about group influence over the behavior of individuals who act together toward some reasoned or unreasoned goal.[1]

Collective behavior refers to the characteristic of groups rather than separate individuals. But the field is not identical with the study of groups. Moreover, it can be sharply contrasted with institutional behavior in which the acts of individuals are guided by the culture and norms of the larger society. Collective behavior develops its own norms which are not envisaged in the larger society; people acting collectively in this fashion may even modify or oppose the broad norms.[2] In this connection, Herbert Blumer states:

> . . . the student of collective behavior seeks to understand the way in which a new social order arises, for the appearance of such a new social order is equivalent to the emergence of new forms of collective behavior . . . collective behavior is concerned in studying ways by which the social order comes into existence, in the sense of emergence and solidification of new forms of collective behavior.[3]

Every social movement can be received as a collective effort to establish a new order of life. They rest upon a condition of unrest and obtain their power from dissatisfactions of individuals over life conditions and hopes, wishes and aspirations for a better way of life.[4] In addition, every social movement, whether of the reform or revolutionary variety, has at least one well defined objective or goal which it seeks to obtain. Then, too, a social movement is marked by continuity to promote a change or wrest a change in the society or group of which it is a part. Finally a social movement follows a life-cycle.[5] The life-cycle consists of a series of successive stages from the inception to the success or final form of the movement. As such, it is well to view movements from a temporal and developmental perspective, from which one can delineate stages in the career of the movement.

For the study of social change in minority-majority group relationships, and more particularly race relations in the South, Louis Wirth felt that sociologists can come closest to the actual minority problems that plague the modern world by analyzing the major goals toward which the ideas, the sentiments and actions of minority groups are directed.

Wirth remarked:

Viewed in this way minorities may conveniently be typed into: (1) pluralistic; (2) assimilationist; (3) secessionist; and (4) militant.

A pluralistic minority is one which seeks toleration for its differences on the part of the dominant group.

The assimilationist minority puts no such obstacles in the path of its members but looks upon the crossing of stocks as well as the blending of cultures as wholesome end products. Since assimilation is a two-way process, however, in which there is give and take, the emergence of an assimilationist minority rests upon a willingness of the dominant group to absorb and of the minority group to be absorbed.

The secessionist minority represents a third distinct type. It repudiates assimilation on the one hand, and is not content with more toleration or cultural autonomy . . .

The militant minority has set domination over others as its goal. Far from suffering from feelings of inferiority, it is convinced of its own superiority and inspired by the lust for conquest. While the initial claims of minority movements are generally modest, like all secessions of power, they feed upon their own success and often culminate in delusions of grandeur.

The initial goal of an emerging minority group, as it becomes aware of its ethnic identity, is to seek toleration for its cultural differences. By virtue of this striving it constitutes a pluralistic minority. If sufficient toleration and autonomy is attained the pluralistic minority advances to the assimilationist stage, characterized by the desire for acceptance by and incorporation into the dominant group. Frustration of this desire for full participation is likely to produce (1) secessionist tendencies which may take the form either of the complete separation from the dominant group and the establishment of sovereign nationhood, or (2) the drive to become incorporated into another state with which there exists close cultural or historical identification. Progress in either of these directions may in turn lead to the goal of domination over others and the resort to militant methods of achieving that objective. If this goal is actually reached the group sheds the distinctive characteristics of a minority.[6]

The Problem

The specific movement under study is that of a "minority group" movement—The Montgomery Improvement Association. According to Wirth's ideal topology, this movement is more like that of an "assimilationist movement," although the movement contains some of the ingredients of a "pluralistic minority."[7]

The study is guided by a series of hypotheses which can be stated in the form of questions for investigation:

1. What was the nature of life conditions out of which social unrest and personal dissatisfaction emerged in Montgomery?
2. What are the perceptible stages in the life cycle of the movement?
3. What are the discernible mechanisms and means through which the movement grew into an organization?
4. What appears to be the predictable future of the movement?

Methodology

The role of participant observation was employed as the chief technique for gathering information and pertinent data. In employing this technique of investigation it has been observed that:

. . . [in] participant observation, more than in any other technique, analysis of the data should proceed simultaneously with their collection. This requirement may be explained as follows: since participant observation is usually resorted to as an exploratory technique, the observer's understanding of the situation is likely to change as he goes along. This, in turn, may call for changes in what he observes, at least to the extent of making the content of observation more specific; and often the changes called for may be quite radical. These changes in the content of observation are not undesirable. Quite the contrary; they represent the optimum use of participant observation. But, if the data are not analyzed as the observation proceeds, the observer is not in a position to make these changes as rapidly as he should.[8]

In designing a study-project of a social movement in which playing the role of a participant observer is relied upon there are several elements of the situation that must be taken into account.

A social situation is characterized by:

1. The participants
2. The consequences of the interaction between participants
3. The means used in the interaction and in the goal-directed activity
4. The initiating event or stimulus
5. The incentives or other factors which maintain the situation or keep the activity going
6. The constraints imposed on the participants
7. The context of the situation
8. Regularities and recurrences
9. Length of time for which it lasts
10. Significant omissions
11. Deviations from what is usual in such situations
12. Inconsistencies[9]

This list in its entirety does not apply to every act of the observer. Moreover, events in a social movement unfold much too rapidly to permit consideration of the multi-dimensions of every occurrence.

Other methods used in this study involved:

1. the statistical compilation of relevant materials, especially those pertinent for development of clues and leads for observation;
2. the examination of documentary materials such as reports of municipal, county, state and federal governmental agencies;
3. the construction of social base maps for pinpointing physical and social distances;
4. the chronicling of events and activities—actions and reactions—as revealed in newspaper accounts.

Conceptual Scheme

The "Natural History" approach to the study of human behavior, was the frame of reference selected for the study of the social movement—the Montgomery Improvement Association.

Hopper explains that:

> The Natural History method is nothing more or less than an account of an evolutionary process—a process by which not the individual but the type evolves.[10]

Dawson and Gettys[11] have developed a conceptual scheme for studying the social processes of a social movement. They suggest that a social movement passes through four stages in its development:

(1) The preliminary stage of mass (individual) excitement and unrest.
(2) The popular stage of crowd (collective) excitement and unrest.
(3) The formal stage of the formation of issues. The formation of public and formal organization.
(4) The institutional stage of legalization and societal organization.[12]

It should be stressed, however, that in considering the "natural history" through which the Montgomery Improvement Association has passed, the interest and attention are focused, not on the stages, but rather on the social and psychological mechanisms and means through which the movement gained strength and was able to grow into a social organization. Herbert Blumer[13] postulates that it is convenient to group these mechanisms under five heads:

> (1) the nature of the agitation as expressed through the leadership; (2) the development of *esprit de corps*; (3) the development of morale; (4) the formation of an ideology; and finally, (5) the development of operational tactics and strategies.

Conceptually, it is necessary to emphasize that neither the four stages of a social movement, nor the mechanisms through which it grows, are clear-cut and mutually exclusive. The concept "stage" is simply a means of describing dominant tendencies; it makes no pretense of dealing with absolutely delineated periods.

The assumption is that in a social movement, ". . . the behavior of individuals [is] under the influence of an impulse that is common and collective, an impulse, in other words, that is the result of social interaction."[14] Under such conditions the behavior of individuals is characterized by unrest[15] and crowd-mindedness[16] which becomes contagious,[17] and individuals enter into *rapport*, thus socializing the restlessness of the individuals.

The Setting
Montgomery, Alabama, and the Social Conditions Behind the Movement

Montgomery, commonly referred to as "the cradle of the Confederacy" and the capital city of Alabama, covers a land area of 26.1 square miles; it ranks as one hundredth in population. In 1950 the population of Montgomery was 106,525 persons of which 26.7% was Negro. Between 1940 and 1950, the population increased by 36.4%; however, the increase in the white population was considerably greater than that of the Negro segment of the population.

The 1950 census reports 32,315 dwelling units in the city, 39.7% of which are dilapidated and without running water, private toilets and bath facilities. Only 40.1% of the dwelling units are owner-occupied, meaning of course, that almost two-thirds of the homes are rented.

In 1954, the Bureau of Vital Statistics reported 3,146 live births over 1,096 deaths. When this natural increase of population is combined with the tremendous rate of immigration which exceeds out-migration, it becomes obvious that the city of Montgomery is growing very rapidly.[18]

Race relations in this traditional Southern Ante-Bellum city, which was once the official headquarters of the Confederacy, have been under the impact of rapid social change. World War II served only to speed up the processes, heighten the tension, and sharpen the issues of Negro-white relations. As a result there was an increase in racial tensions, fears, and aggressions which opened up the basic question of racial segregation and discrimination, Negro minority rights, and democratic freedom as they were practiced in the city. The issues became more and more acute and developed into a serious impasse through the deepening of fears, and the insistence by Negroes on the improvement of their status, and the welfare of the nation as a whole.

Negroes in the city became increasingly sensitive and resentful toward acts of discrimination and segregation. They felt that all forms of discriminatory practices, evasions of the law, and intimidations of Negro citizens should be abolished.

The Supreme Court decision of 1954 declaring segregation in the public schools unconstitutional deepened the dissatisfaction of both white and Negro individuals over the state of affairs in their city. Generally, Negroes began to seek a way to implement the decision, and most whites, particularly the political leaders, started to look around for ways and means to circumvent, nullify or resist the court decrees.

The social conditions underlying the Montgomery situation in 1956 are explained dramatically in a personal document given by one of the key figures of the movement. He states:

As you know Montgomery is a small town; however, it is the third largest city in the state of Alabama. We have a population of 130,000 with a three to two ratio of whites and Negroes. We have approximately 50,000 Negroes in the city of Montgomery. Across the years, it has been known as a non-industrial city. Montgomery is just a shopping center for what we call the Black-Belt areas.

We have two colleges here, one white and the other Negro; a state capitol, two air bases, a regional office and a Veterans hospital. These institutions provide the main sources of income. About seventy-five to eighty per cent of the Negroes in the city are employed in service occupations.

We have a neat class system in Montgomery, perhaps due to the college population, and other professional groups. The several classes before our movement were very sharply divided. The masses were described as a group of complacent and satisfied hard-working domestics. The leadership was also terribly divided.

However, Negroes in 1955 faced what they felt to be a common problem—the deplorable conditions on city buses. The Women's Political Council, a group of middle-class Negro women in the city, began some agitation in an effort to clarify the seating policy on our buses. Montgomery, unlike Birmingham and some of the other cities, did not have the big glaring signs that divided Negroes and whites into various sections of the bus. The bus drivers had the authority to determine where imaginary lines of racial division should be. Yet, paradoxically, on all buses the first ten seats were reserved for whites, and then, of course, the drivers determined if the Negroes could occupy the other seats, or if Negroes would be required to get up and give their seats to white passengers. Now this created a serious problem because Negro seating was never secure, not even near the rear. It was the custom that if white passengers got on the bus, the driver would demand Negro seats, and if they didn't get up they would be taken from the bus and thrown into jail. No white passenger was allowed to stand while Negroes were seated. This created resentment that was common to virtually every Negro because just about every one of them, especially the masses, rode the buses to work and, of course, back home again.

During the month of March, 1955, a fourteen-year old Negro school girl, Miss Claudette Colvin, was dragged from a bus, handcuffed, arrested, and thrown into jail. Miss Colvin occupied a seat in what was commonly used as the Negro section. When the bus driver demanded that she give up her seat to a white man, she refused. This incident aroused more discontent and unrest in the community.

We held several conferences following her arrest with the city officials, and the officials of the bus company. We asked that they do two things: change the seating policy to a first come, first served basis; that is, with Negroes beginning from the rear and whites from the front with no reserved seats for either group. Wherever the two races met, this would constitute the dividing line. The officials said this could not be done legally. Then we asked that they clarify the seating policy and publish it in the paper so that each person would know where his section was, so that once a Negro got on the bus and was properly seated in the Negro section he would not have to worry about getting up, giving his seat to a white passenger. After several conferences, bus officials refused to clarify this policy.

Then later in the year we had another arrest—a young Negro woman who refused to vacate her seat for a white passenger. This happened during the month of July.

Finally, on December 1, Mrs. Rosa Parks, who had lived in Montgomery all of her life, was arrested. She had served as secretary of the local branch of the NAACP, and as secretary to the Civic Improvement League. Mrs. Parks was an industrious civic worker and church-goer in the community. She was requested to give her seat to a white man despite the fact that she was sitting in what was normally thought of as the Negro section of the bus. She refused and was taken from the bus and put into jail. This occurred on Thursday evening, December 1, 1955.

On Friday, December 2, before I got out of bed, I received a telephone call about five o'clock in the morning from Mr. E.D. Nixon. Mr. Nixon had been an aggressive and fearless fighter for the rights of Negro people in Montgomery for many years. He is a pullman porter; he does not have a formal education; but he is a very courageous man. Mr. Nixon informed me of Mrs. Parks' arrest; I was surprised to hear it. He told me that he thought that we should do something because we had taken enough. 'Now is the time to stay off of the buses,' he said 'and show the white people that we will not tolerate the way we have been treated any longer.' I agreed with him.

In an article appearing in a national magazine about the situation in Montgomery out of which the social movement emerged, Montgomery is described as "a testing ground arising from the Supreme Court order on bus desegregation." The author states:

The Negroes here decided suddenly last December to stand up against Southern Jim Crow—against paying fares at the front door but having to enter the bus by the rear door to avoid contact with white passengers, of walking along the outside of the bus—after paying their fares—and being deliberately abandoned by grinning white drivers, of suffering in silent humiliation epithets from the drivers like 'black ape,' 'black cow,' and 'dirty nigger.'

So, on December 5, 1955, Montgomery's Negroes, who made up 40 per cent of the town's population but about 70 per cent of the paying bus traffic, simply decided to stop riding the buses. Four days before that decision, a 42-year-old seamstress, Mrs. Rosa Parks, had been arrested under city and state segregation laws, for refusing a bus driver's order to give up her seat and move back in the bus. For all the community's Negroes, Mrs. Parks' arrest was the determining blow.

Resentments in the making for more than one hundred years crystallized into collective action. Most of the white community pooh-poohed the Negro boycott, and predicted that 'them shiftless, no-account niggers' would not last the week out before they would start climbing back into the buses—at the back end.[19]

The depth of the sensitivities and dissatisfactions of Negroes over the bus situation is told by Reverend Martin Luther King, Jr., the spiritual and philosophical leader of the movement, in his testimony at the trial of ninety

111

men and women in a local court. When asked to relate unpleasant experiences of Negroes on the Montgomery City Lines Bus and to state what bus drivers would say to Negroes, he remarked:

They said they didn't like standing up over empty 'white seats.' They didn't like having to get up and give their seats to whites. They didn't like having to go to the front door of the bus to deposit their dimes, then going out again to the rear door to re-enter. They didn't like how the buses often took off while they were going to the back door, taking their dimes away with them. They didn't like the fact that in predominantly Negro areas buses just didn't stop at each corner as scheduled. They didn't like the way some drivers started the bus before a Negro passenger could get both feet on the ground. Most of all, they didn't like the way many bus drivers talked to them. 'Go on round the back door, N——r.' 'Give up that seat, boy.' 'Get back, you ugly black apes.' 'You people ought to watch the door 'fore it closes.' 'I'm gonna show you niggers that we got laws in Alabama.' 'N——r, next time you stand up over those white people I'm gonna throw you over to the law.' 'I hate N——rs.' 'N——r? Git back.' 'Pack 'em in the back, N——rs,' 'I don't care if you git killed long as this bus don't git hurt.' 'Say, shine.' 'Hey, boy.' 'Y'all N——rs oughta open your mouth up.' 'Y'all black cows and apes, git back.'[20]

Finally, a local white minister, Reverend Thomas Thrasher in a copyrighted story gives his interpretation of the state of affairs in December, 1955, that led to the specific social movement—The Montgomery Improvement Association. He writes:

Last December 1 in the early evening, one of the buses of the Montgomery City Lines passed through Court Square, in the heart of town and headed for the stop in front of the Empire Theatre. On board the thirty-six passenger bus, twenty-four Negroes were seated, in the traditional manner from the rear forward, and there were twelve whites seated in the front. Some people of each race were standing in the aisle. The bus driver has since testified that there were no empty seats. Yet today, many weeks later, there are many who believe that the bus was substantially empty, while others believe that four Negroes were asked to get up in order to allow one white person to sit down.

At the Empire Theatre stop a number of white passengers were waiting to board the bus. The driver of the bus, as was the practice when in his judgment it was necessary to 'equalize facilities,' requested four Negroes, including Mrs. Rosa Parks, to give up their seats. No charge of discourtesy has been made against this bus driver. Three of the Negroes rose and moved toward the rear. Mrs. Parks, a seamstress at a local department store and a highly respected member of the Negro community, refused. She said later that she acted on a sudden impulse, probably arising from the fact that she was tired. There are substantial numbers of people here in Montgomery who believe that she was a willing participant in a trumped-up plot.

The driver, seeing that Mrs. Parks was adamant, called a policeman, who led her off the bus and escorted her to the police station. There she was booked on a charge of violating the city's segregation law and the trial was set for the following Monday, December 5. She was released on bond.[21]

TWO

Social Unrest
and
Popular Excitement

It has been suggested that when a society breaks up into mass individual excitement and unrest, certain social and psychological processes are necessarily preliminary to the introduction of a social movement. In Chapter One some of the conditions underlying the breakdown of the social structure and controls in the city of Montgomery were given. During this stage Negroes began to manifest, more and more, their dissatisfactions with the conditions and events as they affected their lives. There was a general restlessness which expressed itself in the behavior of individual Negro men and women. In addition to the "cultural drift" of social change in race relations, individual restlessness began to spread by the process of socialization. This behavior manifested itself in the following manner: (1) increased tension and irritability among Negroes, (2) increased talk of dissatisfaction and yearnings for better life conditions (reform), (3) increased threats of revolts, and (4) increased circular reaction—milling, interpersonal interstimulation—wavering of attention from one individual to another, line of action to another, or one object to another.

Under such conditions of diffuse discontent, Negroes became suggestible and susceptible to the milling processes and circular interaction.[1] In the milling process—crowd-like conduct—there are signs of wandering of individuals of all class levels, deviant behavior among all those caught up in the excitement, balked dispositions and mental preoccupations among individuals, and wish repression among those suffering from discontentment.

The Milling Process

Under the conditions described above, people began to "mill" and engage in "circular reaction." Milling is a distinct characteristic of restless individuals. Out of this milling process a collective impulse is formed which dominates all members of the crowd. "The Crowd," says Le Bon, "is a slave to its impulses . . . they will always be so imperious that the interest of the individual . . . will not dominate them." Milling always occurs in the early stages of a social movement. This is precisely the basic psychological mechanism from which restless individuals fit together the random character of their separate and uncertain acts into a collectivity for action.

In the early stage of the Montgomery Improvement Association movement there was tremendous random-like behavior in that people just did not know what to do. The restlessness was individualized and diffuse; it had no sense of direction. People would gather in large numbers at any point of excitement or upon any spectacular or unusual happening. One such event took place the evening Reverend King was arrested. An informant gives the following version of this event which illustrates the crowd-like behavior and milling process of Negroes during the initial stage of the movement:

> When Reverend King was arrested, I got a call at headquarters that King was being arrested on the corner of Grove and Jackson. I drove over to Grove and Jackson Street and I really broke the law because I wanted to get there before they took him down. They had called the squad car and it had already taken him to jail. Then I proceeded to go to the jail house. When I got to the city jail, I asked to see him. The Sergeant on duty told me that I could see him the following morning at nine o'clock; it was five o'clock in the afternoon. I said well if I couldn't see him I would like to 'go his bond.' He replied that I would have to go to the courthouse and bring him back a certified statement saying I was a qualified bonder. I said that the courthouse was closed, and he said it would open again tomorrow at nine o'clock. This was bad news for me. I asked how much was his bond, and he said one hundred dollars. I didn't have a hundred dollars in my pocket. I went to my church office, not far away, and called my wife. I told her to look around and see if she could find a little money about the house because we had to get King out of jail. I also called Mrs. King and informed her.
>
> When I got back to the jail some twenty-five or thirty other individuals had gathered at the jail, and they said they weren't leaving.

They declared that if they kept Reverend King there overnight then they were going to stay on the jailhouse steps all night and have prayer. They were just walking around in the place. Some of them began to sing, not disorderly, but just singing.

Then we got up a purse from the various persons there to make up King's bond; this man having ten dollars and another fifteen dollars and finally I got enough, ($100). They gave it to me and I went in and said to the Desk Sergeant who was looking out the window all the time, 'I have the money now. Will you let me go his bond?' After seeing and hearing the people on the outside, they decided that the best thing to do was to get rid of him. So they let him out without a bond, and I don't think he even signed his release.

This was the real crucial period: people would leave home going to the grocery store and wind up in jail. Nobody would know their whereabouts and sometimes they wouldn't let them call. They jailed them for such simple things as making a left-turn in a turn-right-only zone. They would take Negroes to jail and carry their cars and impound them.

Social Contagion

As a consequence of collective excitement resulting from the milling process and circular interaction, the discontent among individuals spreads; it becomes contagious—"everybody catches the feeling." Accordingly, activity increases; there is a heightened state of expectancy; moreover the collective excitement is given a focus which captures the attention of restless individuals. Rumor and scandal become widespread, and a literature emerges which identifies the new leadership, and the guilty groups and individuals who are responsible for the state of affairs.

Under such conditions the minority group takes on an "oppression psychosis" out of which it begins to fabricate social myths and an "in-group-out-group" consciousness. Thus, discontented minority individuals begin to look about for remedies to relieve their distressful situations.

The development of an in-group feeling, along with an "oppression psychosis" is expressed in the interview materials given by a distinguished Baptist minister and perhaps the most effective leader of the movement in respect to strategies and operational tactics. He states:

As I said already the first ten seats were reserved for whites and the Negro passengers couldn't sit in those seats although they were

117

unoccupied; if they were empty, that is, if not a single white person was seated in one of the seats, and although the aisles were jammed, Negroes had to stand up over those empty seats even during the rush hours. Negroes would pay their fare from the front of the bus then get off and board the bus from the back door. Profane language was used by the bus driver even toward Negro women, such as 'black apes,' 'black cows;' they would look in the rear view mirror saying '. . . all right give me that seat.' All of us had suffered on these buses. It was humiliating.

The Brethren (ministers) turned out in large numbers. There were about seventy-five persons at our first meeting—some sixty were ministers, and about eight women were in the group. At this meeting we thought it would be in good taste to let Reverend H. H. Hubbard, an elderly minister and president of the Baptist Ministers Conference, open the meeting; however, he was not to preside. Reverend Hubbard opened the meeting with an old, long hymn; the reading of a scripture, and a prayer. Then he turned the meeting over to Reverend L. R. Bennett, Pastor of the Mount Zion A.M.E. Zion church. Reverend Bennett came forward and stated that he was glad to see the large number of persons that had turned out. He was so autocratic and dictatorial in his manners that several people became insulted and left the room; he was obviously a poor person to preside over this type of meeting. It was then apparent that we had made a mistake.

We decided to prepare a second handbill that would announce a call meeting. We agreed that this meeting would be at the Holt Street Baptist Church on Monday evening, December 5. We also divided the city into various districts and assigned individuals to pass out handbills in the various Negro sections in order that the people might be persuaded not to ride the buses on Monday, but to come to the mass meeting on Holt Street on Monday night. We also got it over to the ministers that they were to go to their respective congregations on Sunday morning urging Negroes not to ride the buses. For further instructions they were to come to the mass meeting. At the close of this meeting Reverend M. L. King and I were delegated the responsibility of getting out the handbills. While drawing up these handbills, we discussed this whole problem of Reverend Bennett as the presiding officer even though we wanted a Methodist to preside. It was clear that he was not the man. Reverend King's criticism of Bennett was that he had set the stage for a movement that was to involve too many preachers in key roles and not enough of the lay people in the community.

So we distributed handbills on Saturday and they circulated. One Negro woman got a handbill and turned it over to her white mistress for whom she worked. The mistress turned it over to the city authorities, and they gave it to the *Montgomery Advertiser*. The whites laughed and made fun of us; they printed the handbill on the front page of the Sunday morning paper, thus, we got free front page coverage. One elderly Negro woman said she didn't get a handbill but upon seeing the handbill printed verbatim in the paper, she got the message; she knew that she was not supposed to ride the buses.

Late Sunday evening, the Police Commissioner appeared on local television and radio stations. His purpose, as he so stated, was to assure Negro people that he would give them police protection if they rode the buses on Monday morning. It had been reported to him, he claimed, that there were Negro goon squads organized to keep Negroes from riding the buses, and he was speaking to assure them that it was all right to ride. A Negro woman later testified at the mass meeting that she neither got the Sunday morning paper, nor did she get to church. Therefore, she didn't know about the bus situation. She didn't even know that a protest had been called. But when she heard the Commissioner assuring her that it was all right to ride the buses (he had said that he would never sell his southern heritage while running for office for a single 'nigger' vote,) she knew that it wasn't all right.

From this you can see that we got excellent newspaper, radio, and even television coverage.

The Commissioner also said that there would be two squad cars—one in front and one behind every bus that rolled on Monday morning. This worked in our favor; Negroes who had not really been swept into the spirit of the movement, upon seeing policemen riding behind the buses, felt they were there to force them to ride, and rebelled against it by joining those who were walking.

Later, in one of our mass meetings we had another testimony from one of the female 'walking citizens.' She said she went up to the bus stop to wait for a bus, but a policeman was standing there; she had never found any ease standing near a white cop because 'they always beat up our heads and locked us up.' She actually thought the policeman was there to 'beat her up,' so she moved on. She did not wait for a bus. Morning morning we discovered the buses were ninety per cent empty.

On the morning of Mrs. Parks' trial, of course, we went down to the City Court. I could not get in; there were too many people. Policemen were there and they looked very bitter. They demanded that people get off the street and not block the sidewalks. They were overly disgruntled. The trial was soon over, and Mrs. Parks was fined ten dollars and the cost. The case was appealed, however. Immediately following, a group of us met in Attorney Gray's office to discuss the trial. We talked so long the attorney told us that he needed his office, so we moved over in the adjacent room—the office of the Home Mission Board of the A.M.E. Zion Church—and talked and talked.

In an interview with the wife of one of the religious leaders of the movement concerning her own sensitiveness, restlessness and in-group feelings about her early experiences in the bus boycott, she remarked:

Experiences undergone in previous years helped prepare us for the racial incidents that were bound to come . . . It is not a feeling to rejoice about . . . I had no idea that I would be involved, nor my husband . . . I was frightened but I am realistic . . . We are dealing with a sick man who in his feverish hysteria is capable of committing any kind of deed . . . But it's something we don't worry about.

Another aspect of this early incipient collective effort was the Negroes' compensation of laughing at both himself and white people. This circular emotional interstimulation within the Negro group reinforced their collective excitement that was beginning to move toward formal organization. An article appearing in a national weekly, *Time*, (February 6, 1956), under the caption, "Negroes Laughing?" illustrated the contagious nature of the protest movement and the reactions of the white majority to the "happy-go-lucky" myth of Negroes:

For more than fifty days the Negroes of Montgomery, Alabama have boycotted the city buses, protesting segregated transportation (*Time*, January 16). Last week Montgomery's Mayor W.A. Gayle reacted in a way that showed how much the boycott—95% effective—was hurting. He first announced that he and his fellow members of the City Commission had joined the extremist White Citizens' Council. Then he announced a policy of no surrender on the boycott: 'We have pussyfooted around on this boycott long enough and it has come time to be frank and honest. There seems to be a belief on the part of the Negroes that they have the white people hemmed up in a corner and they are not going to give an inch until they can force the white people of the community to submit to their demands—in fact, swallow them all.' (The Negroes demand seating in buses on a first-come, first-seated basis, with white seating from the front backward, Negroes from the back forward).

Mayor Gayle was specially vexed about the white families who give car rides to their Negro help, or pay their taxi fare. He said that the cooks and maids who boycott the buses 'are fighting to destroy our social fabric just as much as the Negro radicals who are leading them. The Negroes are laughing at white people behind their backs . . . they think it's very funny and amusing that whites who are opposed to the Negro boycott will act as chauffeur to Negroes who are boycotting the buses. When a white person gives a Negro a single penny for transportation or helps a Negro with his transportation, even if it's a block ride, he is helping the Negro radicals who lead the boycott. The Negroes have made their own bed, and the whites should let them sleep in it.'

It is at this point that milling has accomplished the initial purpose of the protest movement; the precesses of milling and social contagion establish sufficient rapport so that restless individuals are united into a collective mass. Thus, the foundation has been laid for further developments.

A news report taken from *The New York Times Magazine* (March 3, 1957, p. 11), describes the contagious character of the movement:

Enter a Negro church any Sunday. The minister reads the prayer, slowly, and a single finger, then a foot, tap out the rhythm. Swiftly, the congregation picks up the crescendo: 'Hear our prayer, O Lord!' But it's no longer the old-style religion, no longer the way of escape from terrible realities. There is a sound now more than a cry; there is the ring of a deep conviction.

The words and music are old—yet strangely new—as massed voices sing:
Thou has made us willing,
Thou has made us free,
By Thy grace divine,
We are on the Lord's side.
And this is the remarkable strength of the Negro in Montgomery: his conviction, so vivid in his face, that he must at last win because he is on God's side.

Popular Excitement

As the movement develops, it is worked by an intensification of milling. However, behavior is not quite so random and people begin to develop more definite notions of the causes of their difficulties, and of what can and should be done to resolve them. In minority group movements, virtually every individual so identified gets caught up in the excitement; excitement becomes contagious; it is now the popular thing to do and the accepted way to act. Old patterns begin to give way and the excited individuals begin to prepare for new patterns of behavior.

In this connection, an informant and leader in the community wrote:

At this time, it was apparent to us that we would have to take this all the way to the Supreme Court, and we would have to walk alone for a length of time. A special prayer meeting was called. We prayed that we might have the courage to endure until the grievances were granted. In the second prayer, we prayed for 'strength to keep our protest non-violent, even if our opponents inflicted violence against us—that we might receive it, but that we may never become violent physically or in spirit.' The third prayer was centered around praying to God 'to give us the ability to love our opposers'; and the fourth prayer, we prayed that God would 'give us the strength to endure and drink the bitter cup of persecution.' These were the texts of the prayers with the minister coming forward to lead a prepared prayer. We would then ask the congregation to pray to that specific end. That did a great deal of good for the people. We started off by asking for strength to endure; and to prepare ourselves for long suffering. At the close of this prayer meeting, I think, from then on we left determined.

Reverend would always make it clear that ours was a non-violent protest. With the help from the other ministers, the protest gained national and international significance. Then, we had no other alternative but to adhere to a doctrine of non-violence, with ministers following closely in the teachings of Christ and learning again about Gandhi and the philosophy of non-violence. This became the definite ideology and pattern of our movement.

We made an appeal to churches for additional funds, and funds began to come in from all across the nation. We decided that we would supplement the car pool system by purchasing some station wagons.

Another illuminating array of data, illustrating the reinforcements given the people through the preliminary stages of collective excitement can be seen in the personal document that follows:

We, M. L. King, and I, went to the meeting together. It was drizzling rain; I had been working up until the last minute on the resolutions. I was given instructions: one, to call off the protest, or two, if indicated, to continue the protest until the grievances were granted. We had had a successful 'one-day protest,' but we feared that if we extended it beyond the first day, we might fail; it might be better after all to call the protest off, and then we could hold this 'one-day boycott' as a threat for future negotiations. However, we were to determine whether to continue the protest by the size of the crowds. If we found a large number of persons at the church this would indicate that Negroes would be interested in continuing the protest. But, if there were only a few, we felt that Negroes were not sufficiently interested, and that they might return to the buses the next day even in spite of our wishes.

When we got about twenty blocks from the church we saw cars parked solid; we wondered if there was a funeral or a death in the community. But as we got closer to the church we saw a great mass of people. The *Montgomery Advertiser* estimated the crowd at approximately seven thousand persons all trying to get in a church that will accommodate less than a thousand. It took us about fifteen minutes to work our way through the crowd by pleading: 'Please let us through—we are Reverend King and Reverend Abernathy. Please permit us to get through.'

Once we broke through the crowd there was another ten minutes of picture-taking coupled with flashing lights, cheering and hand-clapping. Those inside applauded for at least ten minutes.

It was apparent to us that the people were with us. It was then that all of the ministers who had previously refused to take part in the program came up to Reverend King and me to offer their services. This expression of togetherness on the part of the masses was obviously an inspiration to the leadership and helped to rid it of the cowardly, submissive, over timidity.

We began the meeting by singing *Onward Christian Soldiers, Marching as to War.* Then Reverend Alford, who later resigned from our movement because he felt that the bus boycott should be halted, and that Negroes should, for the sake of peace accept segregated seating again, offered a prayer which was soul-stirring. Next Reverend U. J. Fields, who likewise eventually broke with our movement but for other reasons (he believed we had misappropriated funds)—read a scripture from the thirteenth chapter of First Corinthians. After which Reverend King made one of his now famous statements:

> 'There comes a time when people get tired of being trampled over by the iron feet of oppression. There comes a time when people get tired of being pushed out of the glittering sunlight of life's July and left standing in the piercing chills of an Alpine November.'

He has said this many times since, but we heard it on that evening for the first time; it was beautiful.

Mrs. Rosa Parks was presented to the mass meeting because we wanted her to become symbolic of our protest movement. Following her we presented Mr. Daniels, who happily for our meeting had been arrested on that day. The policemen alleged that he tried to prevent a Negro woman from riding the bus, while he claimed he was only assisting her across the street. The appearance of these persons created enthusiasm, thereby giving added momentum to the movement.

We then heard the resolutions calling for the continuation of the boycott. The resolution stated: Negro people and people of good conscience are to refrain from riding the buses until their grievances were granted; (1) more courtesy on the part of the bus drivers; (2) first-come, first-served seating policy; and (3) the employment of Negro bus drivers on predominantly Negro bus routes. These three resolutions were unanimously and enthusiastically adopted by the 7,000 individuals both in and outside the church. We closed the meeting by taking an offering with people marching down the aisles giving their nickels, dimes, quarters, and dollars for freedom. The *Montgomery Advertiser* described the movement the next morning under the heading—'Hymn Singing Negroes of Montgomery, Alabama.'

Thus, the foregoing data points out that the social unrest had reached the level of popular excitement. Following this first meeting, the leaders were no longer afraid; they were no longer fearful of their pictures in the papers because they knew they were not standing alone. They now felt that they had the whole community behind them; the people had rallied to make them their leaders. This was a spontaneous expression of dissatisfaction; the people had given its leaders the courage to stand up in the face of what appeared then to be insurmountable opposition to their restlessness. It was within these conditions that the restless dissatisfactions and frustrations of separate individuals became socialized and/or collectionized in a state of popular excitement.

THREE

Formal Organization of the Montgomery Improvement Association

"Transition from the popular to the formal stage marks a crucial point in the development of a revolutionary movement."[1] Excitement and *esprit de corps* are not sufficient for a movement to gain sufficient momentum. To persist, they must be complemented by other social psychological mechanisms—morale, ideology, as well as techniques of operation if the movement is to avoid disintegration. Just because people become excited over their individual restlessness and reinforce each other through milling (crowd mindedness) and social contagion, these alone are not adequate to serve as the foundation for enduring social change. Issues must be formulated and procedures must also be formalized. A social movement in order to persist must develop roots deeper than mere sensationalism, fashionable rituals and popular fads. It must come to appeal to the essential desires of a heterogeneous people.

In the development of a formal organization the minority group is confronted with the following problems:

1. The fixation of motives (attitudes) and the formulation of specific aims, values, and objectives;
2. The resolution of differences between "radicals," "conservatives," and "moderates";
3. The continuation of communication between the "in-group" and "out-group";
4. The consideration of invasion (violence from the "out-group"), internal rebellion, and lack of political experience;

5. The desertion of lukewarm supporters, and the elimination of overly conservative members;

6. The position of the movement in respect to 'left' (communism) and 'right' (fascism)—both of which create uncontrollable radicalism in mass behavior;

7. The development of a set of norms stated in the dogma, and formally expressed in ritual, together with a marked increase in the use of shibboleths;

8. The danger of conservatives, "lukewarm" minority group members playing roles as "quislings" and "Fifth-columnists;"

9. The selection of programs, leaders, doctrines and traditions; and

10. The danger of conflict within the ranks of the leadership.

Due to the character of events and fluidity of the situation, the problems and issues listed above cannot be discussed as separate categories; each interpenetrates all the others during this most crucial point in the development of the movement. Perhaps it is more convenient, then, to describe this stage of the movement under three headings: (1) discussion and deliberation, (2) formulation, and (3) formalization.

Discussion and Deliberation and Formulation

In the formal stage of a social movement issues emerge about which there are sharp differences of opinion. Publics must be formed to discuss these issues out of which a "public opinion" is derived.[2]

Discussion is an effort to interpret issues; it is marked by debate, dispute, and the conflict of interests. However, it gives the participants an opportunity to sharpen their self-consciousness and critical sensitivities through careful consideration of pertinent facts, arguments and counter-arguments.

In regard to the selection of issues and the subsequent processes and mechanisms of clarification, give-and-take discussion and opinion formation, one of the leaders describes the problem in the following manner:

We drew up this particular document that stated our grievances: (1) the lack of courtesy on the part of the bus drivers, (2) a seating policy of first-come, first-served with Negroes beginning in the rear and whites in the front of the bus, and (3) the employment of Negro bus drivers on predominantly Negro bus routes.

The next problem that confronted us was to get this before the committee before three p.m. This meeting was composed of only community leaders, that is, presidents of selected key organizations. The big problem was how we would get the grievances across to them. We decided that Reverend Bennett, who was incidentally my personal friend, might reconsider his previous ruling that no one would be allowed to discuss issues except himself, and at least hear me. When I would get the floor I would tell the group that Mr. Nixon could not be with us at our Friday night meeting, and since he had been a leader in the community for quite some time we ought to have a word from him.

The strategy was that Mr. Nixon would arise and say that he had nothing to say and would ask Reverend French to read the grievances and proposals for organization. We knew that once we got the floor it would be adopted, because the newly formed committee, though excited as it was had had sufficient time to work out an agenda for the meeting. It was equally obvious that Reverend Bennett, the temporary chairman who wanted to do all the talking had nothing on his mind to offer.

We arrived at the meeting immediately after Reverend Bennett had given the devotion. He then reiterated: 'We are not going to have any talking. I am not going to let anybody talk; we came here to work and to outline our program.' I tried to get the floor, but he said, 'Well, Ab, although you're my good friend, I'm not going to even let you talk—so sit down.'

At this time the president of the National Association for the Advancement of Colored People sounded an alarm. He exclaimed, 'Don't go any further; we have some stool pigeons (subversives) in the house. They just walked in and they are here to get our strategy to take it back to the white man; don't go any further.' Against this warning it was suggested that we take a poll of the committee to see who was present, and what organization each person represented. Finally, however, a motion prevailed that we elect an executive committee that would go into secret session in the pastor's study and work out a program for the mass meeting. We gave it the authority to do so without reporting to the larger group for satisfaction. Eighteen persons were chosen.

This meeting was adjourned and the eighteen selected committee retired to the pastor's study. Going up the steps, I had an opportunity to say to Reverend Bennett in a rather disgusted tone of voice, 'Well old buddy you've mistreated me and we've been friends all along. Why is it that you won't let me have the floor now? I have something I think is just exactly what you need if you'll just listen.' After much needling, he agreed reluctantly and promised that as soon as we got the meeting underway he might recognize me. Then I dropped back and started talking to Reverend King. I told him that we had worked out a proposal for permanent organization of the movement which included the election of the officers and a statement of aims and objectives. He was very happy to hear this. 'But who will be the president?' King asked. I said, 'Well, I feel that we owe it to Mr. Nixon for he has been a fearless fighter in the city. Even though he is not a lettered man, he is not afraid to stand up and fight.' 'Perhaps,' King replied, 'Mr. Lewis might make the better man.' Well, there we were trying to decide whether to elect Lewis or Nixon. By this time Bennett opened the meeting and was calling for me to say what I had to say. I presented Nixon who in turn asked Reverend French to read the proposal. The Committee adopted it verbatim; all agreed that the proposed organization with its purposes was exactly what we needed.

The next item that came before the committee was the name and structure of the permanent organization. Several names were submitted, among them such names as 'The Community Coordinating Council', the 'Civic Council,' etcetera. These names were so closely akin to that of the White Citizens Council, a pro-segregation organization, that the group did not approve them. After considerable debate, during which time other suggestions were made, the committee reached an impasse and a motion was made to table. I stated an unreadiness. I don't know whether this was correct according to *Roberts Rules of Order* or not, but I asked that they indulge me, because I felt that I had an appropriate name that had just come to me. I said that if I could just get this name before the group I was confident that they would adopt it. I gave the name—The Montgomery Improvement Association.

I felt that we had too many organizations such as the 'Willing Workers,' the 'Loyal Ten,' and the 'Faithful Five,' that really did not reflect the name of the city. We wanted an organization that would be just as important as the Montgomery Kiwanis Club, the Montgomery Chamber of Commerce, or the Montgomery Lions Club. Furthermore, we wanted a name that would stick, a name that would help us to be a part of the city of Montgomery. We also wanted an organization that would not confine its program to the bus situation, but rather one that would be concerned with the total social, economic, spiritual and political improvement of all the people.

The name, Montgomery Improvement Association was adopted. Thus on this day, December 5, 1955, the social movement took on organizational form. The next question before the committee was the election of a president.

King and I were still puzzled as to what we might do to guide the group to elect one of two men—Lewis and Nixon. Each one of them had a substantial following in the city. However, their interests were divided and they had never gotten together on any important issues. This was the basis of our dilemma and concern for we wanted an organization that would promote unity and not one that would highlight and bring to the fore old scars of conflicting group interests. The house was open to receive nominations. Mr. Rufus Lewis, the man who Reverend King thought should be the president, arose and said, 'Mr. Chairman, I wish to move that my pastor, Reverend Martin Luther King, Jr., be chosen as president of this organization.' It came as a surprise to me and I believe likewise King was caught off guard because neither he nor I expected him to be chosen. I had not even paid him the courtesy of suggesting that it might be possible.

The next problem was to set up a program for the seven o'clock meeting. King, the newly elected president, took the chair and presided. Reverend A.W. Wilson, pastor of the Holt Street Baptist Church where the mass meeting was to be held, reported some very frustrating information. He stated that he had had calls from reporters and that they wanted to attend the meeting. They had put pressure on him, he said, and he didn't know what to tell them other than the doors of Holt Street Church were always open to everybody. We certainly did not want to be labelled as conducting closed meetings in the church.

Furthermore, the really threatening thing about it was that television reporters would be there to take pictures of this entire meeting. We didn't like this for it posed a great problem of getting participants for our program. Reverend King said that he had another meeting and could not preside over the entire meeting, but he would at least give his blessings to the occasion. Reverend Bennett said that he would run late, and wouldn't be able to preside. We asked other persons if they would offer prayer. Some of them said they were hoarse, but would read the scripture. At this point, Mr. Nixon took the floor saying, 'I want to get faith. I am just ashamed of you. You said that God has called you to lead the people and now you are afraid and gone to pieces because the man tells you that the newspaper men will be here and your pictures might come out in the newspaper. Somebody has got to get hurt in this thing and if you preachers are not the leaders, then we have to pray that God will send us some more leaders.' He really made an arousing speech that made the ministers angry, and Reverend Alford said, 'I will pray the prayer.' Reverend Fields added, 'I will read the scripture.' I agreed to read the resolution. We finally got the participants for our program and we closed this three o'clock meeting with almost time enough to go home and have dinner before getting into the seven o'clock meeting.

The process of formulation must be seen as not only the result of discussion and deliberation, but also a continuation of resolving differences of opinion through argumentation and critical analysis of lines of action. As policies begin to take shape, programs must be formulated to implement them, along with an increasing differentiation of functions and role behavior on the part of the leadership. This process is vividly portrayed in a personal document dictated by one of the leaders of the movement. He relates that:

On the morning of December 6, a Tuesday, we moved into the second day of the protest and everyone was greatly encouraged over the successful mass meeting. On Monday night we had a caucus after the mass meeting. I had taken it upon myself, along with Reverend King, to mail copies of the resolutions to the Mayor of the city, and the bus officials. This document stated that we were ready to negotiate and to hold conferences with both the city and bus officials or any other designated group.

We had been cautioned by several persons that city officials were going to put somebody in jail. We knew we had some people who did not want to go to jail, so we mailed the resolutions unsigned, in plain envelopes about 12:30 that night. We just wanted them to get a copy of what we had agreed upon so they would at least know what our disposition was toward the situation. After this, we would remain silent, waiting for them to call us in for a conference. We waited all day Tuesday and the buses were even more empty than they were Monday. We waited through Wednesday and we did not hear from them. Finally on Thursday, the Alabama Council on Human Relations, through its Montgomery Branch, contacted the city officials and suggested that it would contact our Association officials with their approval to see if our organization would agree to a meeting; the city officials agreed. However, neither the city official nor our organization would take the initiative to call such a meeting, so the Alabama Council called one. The three persons responsible for this meeting were the Reverend R. Keyes, Doctor H. Council Trenholm, President of Alabama State College, Mr. Thomas Thrasher, pastor of the Episcopal Church here in the city of Montgomery. We met with the city officials for our first negotiating session on Thursday, the 8th of December, 1955.

At this meeting we were addressed by the mayor who was also presiding; he was casual and friendly. He received us in his chamber. The manager of the local bus company and two city commissioners were also in attendance. There were five of us from the Montgomery

Improvement Association. The Mayor gave us a 'nice talk.' He told us that he had received a copy of the resolution, but he did not know where he had gotten it from. He reminded us that we were asking for more courtesy and suggested that a good way to receive courtesy is to give courtesy. He charged that the Negro people had not been courteous and if the riders would be courteous, then the drivers would be courteous; that we ought to understand that if we would just teach our people to be courteous, he was sure that the bus drivers would be courteous. And as far as first come, first served, they could not adopt this because the statutes of the state of Alabama make mandatory segregation on the buses. Concerning the employment of Negro bus drivers, he nor any other city officials did not have anything to do with employment policies of a private company. Such matters were left solely to the discretion of the bus company. The bus company official, however, didn't say a word. He didn't talk very much during the entire session; he may have said about two words. He had an attorney there who proceeded to back up the position of the Mayor. In regard to first-come, first-served, to change the policy, he said, would violate the laws of the city of Montgomery and the laws of the state of Alabama.

We pointed out to them that the city of Mobile, Alabama had a policy and practiced first-come, first-serve, for many years, and that the buses were owned and operated by the same bus company—The Chicago City Line of Chicago, Illinois. Both cities are in the state of Alabama and if this can happen in Mobile, why not in Montgomery?

After the Mayor and attorney gave us their positions through lecturing to us, they urged us to go on back and to forget it. Return to the buses, they said, and they would also forget it, if we did.

However, we could not return to the buses without some kind of satisfaction. We made this clear to the Mayor and others present. So the Mayor said he would appoint a citizens committee that would deal with the problem. During the following days—Saturday, Sunday, Monday, Tuesday, Wednesday, Thursday and Friday—the bus protest grew larger and larger.

We came to our second session, meeting this time with the mayor's committee on Saturday of the following week. The Mayor opened this meeting by presenting the persons in attendance. There were eight persons representing our group, and the mayor had invited eight whites and two Negroes. The Negroes, who were supposed to have wealth and property in the city, had been hand-picked by the Mayor as leaders in the community. The first thing we did in this meeting was to question the selection of the two Negroes whom the mayor had appointed to this committee. We let the Mayor know that we had appointed our own representatives and that he could not choose our representatives.

This committee was chaired by the Reverend Parker, Pastor of the First Baptist Church for whites. On the committee was Reverend Russell, Pastor of one of the Presbyterian churches of the city. (Reverend Russell is a brother of U.S. Senior Senator Richard B. Russell of the state of Georgia). Also, the Reverend E. Frazier, a Methodist white minister was on the committee, and we surely anticipated that with these Christian ministers on the committee we would easily locate common ground for fruitful negotiation. But it was soon apparent to us that these ministers were segregationists and accordingly wanted us to go back to the buses under the same objectionable conditions; they too, had been hand-picked by the Mayor just like the two Negroes. There was a business man on the committee from a furniture store, a community civic leader, and an official of the Parent-Teacher Association.

We did not get very far with this committee. Reverend Frazier made a very persuasive speech in favor of segregation. He was very dynamic and forceful. I am sure if he had been talking for integration the committee would have adopted his recommendation. He is quite a speaker, a man of tall stature, robust, with a deep voice, and quite persuasive. Despite his forcefulness, however, he did not move us. We finally adjourned the meeting around five o'clock after having spent all day Saturday at the Chamber of Commerce in downtown Montgomery.

We met again on Monday and we used the strategy of beginning the meeting by moving that this Citizen Committee recommend more courtesy on the part of the bus drivers and the seating policy, first-come, first-served. Reverend Frazier gave an unreadiness and arose to offer a prepared substitute motion of some three or four typewritten pages that turned out to be another speech. We now had eight Negroes and eight white members on the committee. When a vote was taken the eight whites voted to adopt Reverend Frazier's motion and the eight Negroes voted against it; so there we stood—another impasse.

Finally, the pastor of the First Baptist Church said that he did not see any need for a further meeting; if he saw such a need, he would call it. Later, we learned he called the white division of the committee and they reported to the Mayor that we could not reach any agreement. Following this we made no further negotiation, as we expanded and extended our protest movement.

Formalization

The social movement during the third stage of developments proceeds to the level that may be called formalization. When formalization is attained, the wishes—attitudes and values—have crystallized, and policies have been worked out so as to contain the minority-conscious group. The movement thus becomes a formal part of the behavior of individuals in preparation for the subsequent and final stage of institutionalization. The formalization of the protest movement might best be seen in the analysis of the organization of a "car pool" to transport Negroes to and from work.

The spokesman continues:

So we decided to purchase those station wagons in the names of the various churches in the community in order that we would have a good "pick up system." In the weeks that followed, we purchased about eighteen or twenty station wagons. We felt that those churches had given to the Association large sums of money and we could purchase them out to the sums they had contributed.

This, of course, increased the efficiency of our car pool. These station wagons worked on a full time basis, and we were able to employ various persons to drive these wagons. Many of these persons had not been employed at all and it really created a new job for them. In other cases, a large number of ministers drove the wagons; some of the pastors of various churches drove their own wagons. We would grant compensations to many which served to increase incomes.

However, it was not very long before we discovered that we could not get insurance for the wagons. This posed a great problem because the various companies were cancelling contracts once they discovered these wagons were being used in the car pool of the Montgomery Improvement Association. The collision insurance did not pose such a problem, but the real problem came with liability insurance. After trying several companies, finally, through the Alexander Insurance Company, we made contact with Lloyds of London, the oldest insurance company in the world. We were able to get liability insurance from them. This brought satisfaction to all of us, because the problem of insurance almost wrecked our car pool.

At this stage we thought of working out some kind of compromise. We were able to prepare a document with the 'Men of Montgomery.' We were successful in getting it approved by our group, but the 'Men of Montgomery' were not able to get a unanimous approval from their group. That ended these negotiations. We had come through the winter in spite of great hardships. The summer was not as severe as we had anticipated. A large number of school teachers who had been out during the regular year were free to drive in our car pool. Many of the persons had worked out of the community and others had worked here in the city and they were now offering their services to drive. We had a large number of teachers coming in from summer school at State College and they placed their cars at the disposal of the car pool. We were able to give some gasoline because funds were coming in from all over the country. We spent more than $5,000 a week just to operate our car pool. This covered gasoline, oil, salaries which we paid to some individuals who drove, and repair on automobiles. The individuals would make applications to the transportation committee if they needed tires, and the transportation committee decided on the basis of the number of hours they had been driving, whether to give them a tire, tire and a half, or two tires or whatever the case might be. We spent a lot of money on transportation.

The car pool operated in full force during the normal working hours of four a.m. until eight p.m. Fewer cars were made available for the later working shifts up to eleven p.m. Then the car pool would close and persons who got off later would have to make private arrangements with ministers or friends for transportation.

A great deal of pressure was exerted to get the people to ride the buses. The mayor of the city called upon all of the white people to stop cooperating with the protest and called upon the white women to refrain from transporting their maids. 'Don't give them any assistance whatever,' he urged. A Negro woman gave an explanation in one of our mass meetings. (Often we would let them talk and tell some of their experiences and speak on the topic, 'Why I am with the protest and why I favor integration.') She testified when asked 'How did she come to work?' that she replied that her pastor brought her. The employer told her if she didn't start riding the bus she was going to fire her. The domestic said 'I will save you the trouble of firing me because I quit. You don't have anything to do with how I get to work.' She quit and walked out of the house. A neighbor across the street saw her leaving and called her by her first name and asked her where she was going. She told her she had just been fired. The neighbor said, 'Come on in, you have just been hired. I have been wanting to hire you for a long time.'

The pressure wasn't too bad because of the vast unity among the Negro people of Montgomery. If an individual was fired because of participation in the movement, the person who was hired the next day was also a sympathetic participant. There was no escape for white employers.

There were other incidents of boycotting in the city. For example, a local milk company and the Coca Cola Company. In one instance where the son of a supermarket owner beat up a Negro one Saturday night, the Negroes completely stopped patronizing his store. False rumors would get out and the Negroes would start boycotting.

FOUR

Social Psychological Mechanisms of the Social Movement

Throughout the entire life-cycle of the social movement as it passes through the idealized stages of its "natural history," the means and mechanisms by which it attains its objectives might be grouped under the following: (1) leadership, (2) *esprit de corps*, (3) morale, (4) ideology, and (5) operating tactics.[1]

Leadership

The mechanisms employed by the leadership in any social movement must be suited to the dominant psychological moods of the participants. Men who emerge as leaders must be able and skilled in the use of such devices as agitation, suggestion, imitation and propaganda. Blumer has shown that there are two types of leaders who correspond to two types of situations in which they function. He states:

> Agitation [leadership] operates in two kinds of situations. One is a situation marked by abuse, unfair discrimination and injustice, but a situation wherein people take this mode of life for granted and do not raise questions about it . . . The other situation is one wherein people are already aroused, restless and discontented, but where they are too timid to act or else do not know what to do.
>   . . . Agitators [leaders] seem to fall into two types corresponding roughly to these two situations. One type . . . is an excitable, restless, and aggressive individual . . . The second type . . . is more calm, quiet, and dignified. He stirs the people not by what he does, but by what he says.

139

. . . The function of agitation [leadership] . . . is in part to dislodge and stir up people and so liberate them for movement in a new direction.[2]

The leadership of the Montgomery Improvement Association was, in the main, of the calm, quiet, and dignified type. However, there were some who were more excitable, restless, and aggressive. Reverend Martin Luther King, Jr, is recognized, not only as the spiritual and philosophical leader of the movement, but also as symbolic of the desires and aspirations of its participants. Ethel L. Payne, writing in the *Chicago Defender* (May 19, 1956, page 18, "The Story of Reverend Martin L. King") describes the leadership of the movement and gives some personal characteristics of Reverend King:

. . . At his birth, there were no trumpets sounded; but who can tell at what moment divine power singles out a newborn child for a role in destiny?

At 27, he is very young for the test of whether he has achieved greatness. Certainly, history will not deny that he was there when the hour demanded leadership.

Once, a man named Mordecai was moved to say of his adopted daughter, Queen Esther, when she used her persuasive charm to save the Jews from annihilation, 'Who knows but thou art come into the Kingdom for such a time as this?'

THE DAY—DECEMBER 3

It must have been the night of December 3 when young M. L. had leadership thrust upon him. Mrs. Rosa Parks had been arrested two evenings before.

At the insistence of E.D. Nixon, one of the city's leading civic leaders, who had gone down and got Mrs. Parks released on bond, a meeting was called of the Minister's Alliance to discuss action. Nixon felt that if it could happen to a woman like Mrs. Parks whose character was above reproach and who was highly respected in the community, this was an indication of a general pattern of increased intimidation against Negroes no matter who they were.

Nixon had called 284 people whom he felt had some influence in community affairs.

LEADERSHIP NEEDED

The ministers gathered at the Holt Street Baptist Church were all in accord that something needed to be done. Their determination needed to be crystallized and somebody needed to take the leadership.

It was at the moment that M.L. King, Jr, walked in and all eyes turned in his direction. By common accord, they agreed that he should be the one.

He was young, he had intelligence, he presented a calm and fearless appearance. He was a newcomer, only a little over a year in his first pastorate, the Dexter Avenue Baptist Church.

'You're the one,' they said. The chosen one answered quietly, 'If you think I can do the job, I don't mind trying.'

Martin Luther King, Jr, was born in Atlanta, Georgia, January 15, 1929, the second of three children of Martin, Sr., and Alberta Williams King. Martin, Sr., 'inherited' the pastorate of historic Ebeneser Baptist Church from his father-in-law, the late Reverend Adam Daniel Williams, a militant figure in Atlanta life for more than 35 years.

NATURAL BORN LEADER

What makes Martin Luther King, Jr. a natural born leader, as Thurgood Marshall describes him, are some rare combinations of qualities. He is genuinely modest and self-effacing without the overtones of the deliberate aesthetic.

He is honest, sincere and dedicated and he has the ability to translate into dramatic but simple terms the struggles of the people.

Besides this, he combines eloquent oratory with a phenomenal brilliance in sermonizing, building his themes like a master builder uses bricks.

The result is to inspire passionate fellowship from a people who were thirsty for leadership. To them, Martin Luther has become a knight in shining armor. Outside the courtroom after his conviction on a conspiracy charge a woman cried, 'Long live the King' and the cry was taken up by 500 throats.

NAIVE HONESTY

It is his almost naive honesty and modesty which has made the ministers and the other leaders of the protest movement unite together with no friction or signs of jealousy. The people are proud of his Southern background and his northern training brought back to be put to use where it is most needed.

Reverend King's words, photograph and personal characteristics have appeared in virtually every newspaper and most magazines around the world. *Time* Magazine (February 18, 1957, pages 17-20) assesses the impact of Reverend King, the man and leader of the movement:

. . . He is a scholarly, 28-year old Negro Baptist minister, the Reverend Martin Luther King, Jr, who in little more than a year has risen from nowhere to become one of the nation's remarkable leaders of men.

Most of all, Baptist King's impact has been felt by the influential white clergy, which could—if it would—help lead the South through a peaceful and orderly transitional period toward the integration that is inevitable. Explains Baptist Minister Will Campbell, one time chaplain at the University of Mississippi, now a Southern official of the National Council of Churches: 'I know of very few white Southern ministers who aren't troubled and don't have admiration for King. They've become tortured souls.' Says Baptist Minister William Finlator of Raleigh, North Carolina: 'King has been working on the guilt conscience of the South. If he can bring us to contrition, that is our hope . . .' Sturdy (5 feet, 7 inches, 164 lbs.), soft-voiced Martin Luther King describes himself as 'an ambivert—half introvert and half extrovert.' He can draw within himself for long, single minded concentration on his people's problems, and then exert the force of personality and conviction that makes him a public leader. No radical, he avoids the excess of radicalism, e.g., he recognized economic reprisal as a weapon that could get out of hand, kept the Montgomery boycott focused on the immediate goal of bus integration, restrained his followers from declaring sanctions against any white merchant or tradesman who offended them. King is an expert organizer, to the extent that during the bus boycott the hastily assembled Negro car pool under his direction achieved even judicial recognition as a full-fledged transit system. Personally humble, articulate, and of high educational attainment, Martin Luther King, Jr., is, in fact, what many a Negro—and, were it not for his color, many a white—would like to be.

Even King's name is meaningful: he was baptized Michael Luther King, son of the Reverend Michael Luther King, Sr., then and now pastor of Atlanta's big (4,000 members) Ebenezer Baptist Church. He was six when King, Sr, decided to take on, for himself and his son, the full name of the Protestant reformer. Says young King: 'Both father and

142

I have fought all our lives for reform, and perhaps we've earned our right to the name . . .' King's Crozer career was extraordinary. He graduated first in his class, was named the seminary's outstanding student, was president of the student body (the first Negro so honored), and earned a chance to go on to Boston University for his Ph.D. His doctoral thesis: *A Comparison of the Conceptions of God in the Thinking of Paul Tillich and Henry Nelson Wieman.*[3]

As indicated above, the leadership was not wholly confined to ministers. One of the most dynamic leaders of the movement was E.D. Nixon, a pullman porter and a native of Montgomery. The *Chicago Defender* (May 26, 1956, page 18), published an interesting personality profile of Nixon, in respect to his background, fighting career for the rights of Negroes and role in the bus boycott movement:

. . . A Pullman porter for more than 30 years, Nixon is a natural-born organizer and a fierce resenter of tyranny in any form.

Born in Montgomery, 56 years ago, he runs to Chicago and the four days he is at home are devoted to intense civic and church work.

FOUNDED POLITICAL UNIT

He was a founder of the Progressive Democrats and is its president. Mrs. Parks is an active member of the organization. In the 20 years of its existence, Nixon has arranged to place 2,200 Negro names on the voters' registration list in Montgomery. Speaking in his rapid-fire clipped voice, he says with pungent meaning: 'There's nothing wrong with Montgomery that 10,000 Negro votes can't cure.'

A tall, raw-boned man of blunt directness, Nixon has both tenacity and stamina; so that, long ago before the bus crisis, he was meeting threats and turning them back in language sometimes as picturesque as a Missouri mule skinner.

After a talk with Mrs. Eleanor Roosevelt in World War II, USO clubs which had excluded Negro servicemen, changed their policy to take them in. Nixon was responsible for the Louisville and Nashville Railroad's spending $22,000 to change its methods of selling tickets to Negroes. Formerly Negroes were required to go to the back of the station to a dingy little office and wait until somebody got good and ready to serve them.

143

TAUGHT TO FIGHT

Nixon is president of the Montgomery division of the Brotherhood of Sleeping Car Porters. He says the brotherhood taught him to fight; but anybody who knows him can tell you that he has always been aggressive about basic rights.

He also headed, for many years, the state conference of the NAACP, and he and Mrs. Parks are the two most active members in the local branch . . .

But despite the vigorous and aggressive leadership provided the movement by Nixon, the key leaders came from the Negro ministers of Montgomery, including the Methodist Ministerial Alliance and the Baptist Ministers Conference. The symbolic personalities in addition to Reverend King were Reverend R. D. Abernathy, Reverend L. Roy Bennett, Reverend U. J. Fields, Reverend R. J. Glasco, Reverend Robert Graetz, Reverend H. H. Hubbard, Reverend H. H. Johnson, Reverend W. J. Powell, Reverend S. S. Seay and Reverend A. W. Wilson.

In addition, there was a great deal of leadership given the movement outside the city of Montgomery. In addition to organizations and agencies sympathetic with the aims and objectives of the bus boycott effort, several outstanding nationally known personalities gave the movement their personal attention. One notable example is the work of A. Clayton Powell. Of Congressman Powell's activities, the *Atlanta Journal* (April 3, 1957) stated:

Representative Adam Clayton Powell disclosed Wednesday he is soliciting all House Members for contributions to help rebuild Montgomery, Alabama Negro churches bombed in recent racial strife.

Powell, New York Democrat and one of three Negro members of the House, is telling members their contributions will be treated with secrecy. Those who might be embarrassed at home by gifts may send cash in a 'plain white envelope' either to him or the offices of the fund drive in Montgomery, Powell says.

The drive is for $100,000 to repair four Negro churches and two Negro parsonages damaged in controversy over a boycott by Negroes of the city's segregated bus system.

Esprit de Corps and Morale

Leaders of a social movement have the problem of intensifying rapport as a means of transforming a mass of individuals into a psychological unit. To control the mass, leaders must establish, build and maintain an *esprit de corps* within the group. It is the only way of organizing and integrating loyalty to a movement—by making people think that they belong together and are identified with and engaged in a common undertaking. Thus, *"esprit de corps is a very necessary means of developing unity and solidarity in a movement."*[4] Blumer[5] states that *esprit de corps* in a social movement is developed chiefly in three ways: the development of an in-group-out-group relation, the formation of informal fellowship association and participation in formal ceremonial behavior.

In regard to morale, it can be thought of as giving persistency and determination to a movement. While *esprit de corps* gives life, enthusiasm, and vigor to a movement, morale gives it purpose, a belief and faith in the ultimate attainment of its goals, a willingness to undergo hardship in the struggle, and a deep conviction that the movement is a sacred mission.

> Together these convictions serve to give an enduring and unchangeable character to the goals of the movement and a tenacity of its efforts. Obstructions, checks, and reversals are occasions for renewed efforts instead of for disheartenment and despair . . ."[6]

In addition to personal document and "participant observation," a vast number of such accounts have appeared in news releases. One such report appeared in the *Afro-American Weekly* (May 5, 1956) under the caption "4,000 Vow to Walk 'til Bitter End":

> 'We will never go back on Jim-Crow buses.' Making the above declaration with vociferous applause and unanimous approval, citizens of Montgomery Thursday night vowed to continue the bus boycott until justice and democracy prevails.
>
> More than 4,000 perspiring men, women and children over-taxed the Day Street Baptist Church for a mass meeting at which the decision was made.
>
> By a standing vote, with no dissenters, the members of the Montgomery Improvement Association approved the 200 word resolution urging continuance of the boycott.

The resolution was read by the Reverend Martin Luther King, president of MIA, who hurried to the meeting after an executive session of the MIA officers at which the resolutions were drawn.

The seven-part resolution cited the April 23 decision of the U.S. Supreme Court declaring unconstitutional intrastate bus transportation in South Carolina.

It pointed to orders of the National City Lines, parent organization of the Montgomery City Lines, to cease enforcement of the local laws, requiring segregation on city buses.

It also called attention to the change of bus policy in other southern cities, notably Richmond, Virginia, Little Rock, Arkansas and Dallas, Texas.

Then the resolution pointed out that Montgomery city officials have indicated, both orally and in writing, that they 'intend to and will use all means available to continue segregation of local buses.'

It said that city officials have said they would do this even if it is necessary 'to arrest bus drivers and passengers who refuse to abide by and obey the segregation laws of Montgomery.'

This, the resolution pointed out, means that 'conditions heretofore existing remain the same because of the position taken by our public officials.'

And because of the position, the resolution concluded: 'We, the colored citizens of Montgomery, do now and will continue to carry on our mass protest until such time as the matters (stated above) are clarified; and we hereby authorize and direct the officers and board of directors of the Montgomery Improvement Association to do any and all acts that it deems necessary to perfect our desires.'

The Rev. Mr. King hardly completed reading the resolutions before the Rev. B. D. Lambert jumped up from his sitting position on the floor near the front of the church and made a motion to adopt it.

'God is on our side and we will never go back on Jim-Crow buses,' the Rev. Mr. Lambert declared. He lamented the fact that city officials did not and apparently would not do what the highest court of the land had asked that they do, but suggested that they may be forced to do so come May 11.

May 11 is the trial date for the court suit testing the constitutionality of Montgomery City and Alabama state laws on public transportation.

The youthful passive resistance leader emphasized that whatever victories may come will not be a victory for the 50,000 Montgomery citizens nor the 16,000,000 American colored citizens alone, but a 'victory for justice and for democracy the world over.'

'Let us not abuse our new rights and continue to walk with heads high,' he concluded.

Others who spoke at the rally were the Reverends A. Sanders, R. J. Glasco, B. J. Sims, Ralph D. Abernathy, W. J. Powell, R. W. Hilson, M. C. Cleveland, and Dr. M. D. Jones, who presided . . .

Those who tried it two hours earlier were rewarded with standing room on the main floor, while the 'late comers' were forced into the basement where a public address system was erected, or had to stand outside and listen through the open window . . . Cars were parked for blocks around the church, though many walked to the meeting. Another mass meeting is scheduled for Monday night at the Holt Street Baptist Church . . .

Emory O. Jackson, a Negro newspaper reporter and an influential personality in the state, and more particularly in Birmingham, Alabama describes (the *Atlanta Daily World,* December 11, 1955) a protest mass meeting, the implicit purposes of which were to develop an *esprit de corps*, and to enhance the morale of Negroes in the movement:

A crowd estimated at 5,000 Monday night, which overflowed the Holt Street Baptist Church pastored by the Rev. A.W. Wilson and poured into the surrounding streets, heard oratory from a trio of distinguished ministers promise leadership that would keep them from being 'trampled by the iron feet of oppression.'

The crowd came there to 'get further instructions' for withholding patronage from the bus line in a mass protest growing out of the December 1 arrest of Mrs. Rosa Parks, seamstress, church worker and civic leader. The protest was also expanded to include Fred Daniels, a 19-year-old student of Alabama State College, who was reportedly arrested December 5 on charges of allegedly trying to prevent a woman from catching the bus.

Dr. Martin Luther King, the Ph.D. degree pastor of fashionable Dexter Avenue Baptist Church, presided and delivered the keynote address. The audience sang 'Onward Christian Soldiers' and 'Leaning on the Everlasting Arms' to open the meeting.

The Rev. W. F. Alford, pastor of Beulah Baptist Church, offered the prayer and the Rev. U. J. Fields, pastor of Bell Street Baptist Church, read the 34th Psalm and the scripture lesson.

The Rev. King in stating the purpose of the meeting described it as 'serious business' growing out of a determination as 'American citizens to exercise our citizenship to the fullness of its meaning.'

He said the time had come to take the idea of freedom from 'this paper to thick action.' 'We have come,' he declared, 'to get this bus situation corrected.' He asserted that the alleged mistreatment-on-buses problem had 'existed over endless years' and created 'a paralysis which is crippling the spirit.'

'There comes a time when people get tired of being trampled by the iron feet of oppression,' he asserted.

DR. KING SPEAKS

The eloquent Dr. King then riddled what he called the erroneous version of the incident. 'There is no reserved section on the bus.' (Stories published in the general press said that Mrs. Parks would not surrender her seat and move back into the colored section of the bus when the bus driver instructed her to do so.) He said legal scholars had informed him that the Montgomery bus seating law had never been clarified.

He then mentioned the circumstances under which 'this fine, Christian woman of integrity and character was arrested and carried to jail.'

Dr. King urged the group 'to work together and stick together.' He said there was coming 'a daybreak of justice, freedom and equality.' He added, 'Justice is love in calculation.' He asserted they were ready to use the 'tools' of persuasion although there comes a time when legislation and coercion have to be used.

'Work and fight until justice runs down like water,' he urged, 'but perform peacefully, within the law and as law-abiding citizens,' he counselled. 'In all of our actions we must stick together,' he warned.

'Unity,' Dr. King admonished his hearers, was the key to success. He declared the group's leadership was determined 'to gain justice on the buses of the city of Montgomery.'

Bitterly he assailed those who would compare their techniques with the KKK [Ku Klux Klan] and WCC [White Citizens Council]. He said there had not been and there would not be any (1) cross burning, (2) lynchings, (3) defying the constitution of the nation, (4) violence and (5) attack on the United States Supreme Court.

The force and intensity of the effort of the leadership for morale extended beyond the city limits of Montgomery. Speaking in Cleveland, Ohio before a crowd of over two thousand persons at a prayer-protest rally, the Reverend Bennett, one of the early leaders in the bus protest movement, admonished

148

his cohorts to "stick together" . . . "we decided to go to jail together." He declared:

> Perhaps you've heard that Negroes will not stick together. Well, if you hear it again remember Montgomery, Alabama.
>
> December 23 was the last of the meetings we had with city officials. They refused any compromise on our first two points. On the third they said union rules would take a little time for any integration of Negro drivers into the union.

NEGROES HAVE WALKED AND WALKED

> Since then Negroes in Montgomery have walked and walked. In a sense it is a spiritual movement and a passive movement . . . While we are walking, the bus line has lost $3,500 a day. Imagine, $3,500 a day for 91 days. We're going to fight until we can sit down where we darn please . . .

The *Chicago Defender* (April 4, 1956) reports one of the many activities of Reverend Ralph D. Abernathy, chief leader in respect to operational tactics and strategies. However, his efforts were primarily that of morale building:

> Rev. Ralph D. Abernathy, indicted leader of the heroic movement of the 50,000 Montgomery Negroes against the buses will give a first hand report of the bus boycott. Roy Wilkins, national executive secretary of the NAACP, will give an up-to-the-minute picture of the struggle of the embattled Negroes of the South for dignity, justice and freedom.

ALL FAITHS HELP

> The 'Hour of Prayer' will be conducted by the ministry of Chicago with representatives of all denominations and religious groups participating. The 'Hour of Prayer' is co-chaired by Rev. A. Lincoln James and Rev. Archibald J. Carey, Jr.
>
> 'Negroes in the South are giving us and the rest of the world an inspiring performance,' said the labor leaders. But they added, 'We know from bitter past experience it will take more than raw courage by Negro leaders and the fighting spirit of their followers to stand up long against the superior political and economic power of White Citizens' Councils'.

149

Another aspect of Reverend Abernathy's leadership and strategic role in morale building is revealed in the *Afro American* (March 3, 1956, page 8).

Numerous national organizations and prominent individuals throughout the United States have strongly protested to city officials here against bus segregation and have vigorously encouraged the Montgomery Improvement Association in its effort to wipe out discrimination on municipal buses.

Most of the letters of encouragement were addressed to the Rev. Ralph D. Abernathy, while those condemning the actions of the police and city officials were sent to these officials and published as open-to-the-public protests.

The Emergency Civil Liberties Committee, New York City, of which Clark Forman, director, is spokesman, offered not only encouragement to the bus segregation protestants, but aid to them in their defense 'in any way which seems feasible.'

'As you are not only defending the rights of colored persons but of all Americans, this committee extends its sympathy for the indictment of you and others under an ordinance which we consider to be clearly unconstitutional. The attempt of the authorities in Montgomery to break up a boycott by invoking an ordinance which is clearly unconstitutional should be resisted by all who believe in the Bill of Rights,' the telegram continued.

'The ECLA will do everything in its power to see that these cases get a fair hearing, and, if necessary, be carried to the Supreme Court . . .'

Ceremonial behavior, in group feelings of oppression and intensification of morale as the result of Negro pastors preaching passive resistance is revealed in a news report (*New York Times*, February 21, 1956):

Montgomery's Negro ministers, twenty-four of them under indictment in the current bus boycott—preached the doctrine of passive resistance today.

And in their churches special collections were taken up, as they have been for the last eleven weeks, to help support the car-pool that transports Negroes to and from work.

In the sermons today there was a new and stronger emphasis, however, perhaps the result of the solidarity the city's Negroes have shown in the face of last week's ninety arrests.

The boycott, which began as a protest against what was considered unfair segregation, now was being equated with an attack on all segregation . . .

The Rev. Martin Luther King., Jr., president of the organization that has led the bus protest, returned after two weeks out of the city to his pulpit in the Dexter Avenue Baptist Church, a red-brick building almost at the foot of the State Capitol.

'A GREAT STRUGGLE'

'Integration is the great issue of our age, the great issue of our nation and the great issue of our community . . .'

'We are in the midst of a great struggle, the consequences of which will be world-shaking,' he said. 'But our victory will not be a victory for Montgomery's Negroes alone. It will be a victory for justice, a victory for fair play and a victory for democracy.'

'Were we to stop right now, we would have won a victory because the Negro has achieved from this a new dignity. But we are not going to stop. We are going on in the same spirit of love and protest, and the same dignity we have shown in the past.'

'There is something deep down in our Christian faith that says that man, however low, can be lifted . . . No man will so exploit me, no man so trample me, that I will not believe there is hope in human nature.'

'Even though there are men standing on the sinking sands of injustice, even though there are men standing on the sinking sands of exploitation, I will not believe that deep down within the teachings they've been brought up under—and stand up for what is right. I'm not worried about the death of oppression; I'm not worried about the death of segregation. I know segregation cannot survive for God will get into the hearts of men. Ultimately the most prejudiced mind in Montgomery, the most prejudiced mind in America, will become a loving mind. And twenty-four years from now men will look back and laugh, even at segregation.'

'We have to be very careful that no one exploits this movement. We all know,' he said, 'that the Till case was exploited too much. We need money, but we're not going to do anything and everything to get it. No one is going to get fat on this, and no one is going to get any handouts.'

Rev. Ralph D. Abernathy, chairman of the negotiating committee that failed in the last attempts to settle the boycott, told his congregation of supporting telegrams and financial contributions that had come from all over the country. 'The telegrams told us to hold out, keep the faith and keep moving,' he said. In the morning's mail, he added, there had come $1,200 in contributions to help support the protest, some of it from northern white people.

250 AT CHURCH SERVICES

'Our white friends are with us, you don't have to make this fight alone,' he told the 250 worshippers at the Negro First Baptist Church. 'Our method is one of passive resistance, of non-violence, not economic reprisals,' he declared. 'We have nothing against the bus company. It can run buses as long as it want to—but it will run them without Negroes until it gives us justice. Let us keep love in our hearts, but fight until the walls of segregation crumble. And when they crumble, I don't intend to be in heaven, but right here in Montgomery.'

The Negro Interdenominational Ministerial Alliance, headed by the Rev. L. Roy Bennett, pastor of the Mount Zion African Methodist Episcopal Church, has played a leading role in organizing the bus protest. The actual direction of it, however, has been through the Montgomery Improvement Association headed by Reverend King.

Ideology

The ideology of a social movement consists in a body of doctrines, beliefs, and myths which provide direction and ability to withstand the opposition.

Ideology consists of (1) objectives and purposes of a movement, (2) criticism and condemnation of the existing life conditions which the movement is attacking, (3) defense doctrines to justify the movement, (4) the myth of the movement, and (5) a body of beliefs dealing with policies.

Turner and Killian[7] state:

The success of the entire movement hinges on what happens at this point in its evolution. If objectives (values) that were formulated in doctrine written in the constitution, and expressed in ritual and ceremony are really attitudinally accepted and become the bases for behavior, the goals of the movement have been assimilated and victory has been relatively complete.

The basic ideology of the Montgomery Improvement Association was one of passive resistance and non-violence. The essential elements of this ideology is revealed in an article in the *New York Herald Tribune* (March 2, 1956) in which it is reported that Reverend King "bids all Negroes to emulate Gandhi." He said:

We can't slow up. We have our self-respect. We are on the highway of freedom, to the goal of equality, and we can't slow up because we have a date with destiny.

Discussing the methods of non-violence and passive resistance which have brought national notice to the city where he is pastor of the Dexter Avenue Baptist Church, Dr. King declared that 'The 50,000 Negroes there have borrowed from a little brown-skinned man in India, Gandhi, the message that brought the British Empire to its knees.'

SAYS PLAN CAN WORK

He explained that 'we have proved in Montgomery that it can work in America. What we are doing is refusing to cooperate with injustice. We are refusing to spend our money.'

Dr. King spoke in the partially completed Concord Baptist Church at 823 March Avenue in the Bedford-Stuyvesant area of Brooklyn. He addressed an overflow crowd of 2,500 persons meeting under the auspices of the National Association of Business and Professional Women, a Negro organization.

'The next step on the way to complete freedom in this country' he said, 'is for all Negroes to emulate the Montgomery experiment. Let us take a stand for the elimination of all segregation. It is evil. It is slavery covered up with niceties,' he declared.

"We stand together" is another element of the ideology. In this, there is the blending of *Old Time Religion* with the determination to achieve racial equality. Three stanzas of a song set to the tune of *Give Me That Old Time Religion* were sung repeatedly at mass meetings:

We are moving on to Victory
We are moving on to Victory
We are moving on to Victory
With hope and Dignity
We will all stand together . . .

> Until we are all free
> Black and white both are brothers . . .
> To live in harmony.

The influence of Gandhi and his ideas on non-violence upon the ideology is reported by Edward P. Morgan in the *New Republic* (February 24, 1956, page 7). Under the title "The Ghost of Gandhi Walks Montgomery Streets," he writes:

I would respectfully suggest to the civic leaders of Montgomery, Alabama, that if they can find the time they would be doing themselves and the nation a service to bone up a little on what they may have forgotten about recent history.

Do you remember the symbol of the wizened little man with loin cloth and spinning wheel? Do you remember how the world used to hang on the suspenseful news of Mohandas K. Gandhi's latest passive resistance bout with the British; how Americans, with their instinctive affinity for the underdog, cheered quietly as the Mahatma won round after round with the Viceroy, whether it was on a boycott of foreign goods, defiance of the salt tax or the longer deeper protest against the core of the matter, the denial of freedom?

And the British in their exasperation fell back on measures which did little more than eloquently confess the desperately embarrassing bankruptcy of their position. They threw Gandhi in jail. Not once but many times. Then he fasted and his weakness from it only gave his followers strength.

Who would have thought to look at him that in the frail bones of this wisp of a human being lay the marrow of independence of a nation? Ah, but there's the clue. For the passion of righteousness, by stubborn, enduring but gentle defiance, can transform a puny man into a giant. Who would have thought, looking back just 90 days that a $14 fine against a Negro seamstress named Mrs. Rosa Parks for refusing to move to the Jim Crow section of a municipal bus in Montgomery, Alabama, would galvanize a show of passive resistance that may become a symbol in another struggle for independence?

For this in essence is what the racial issue is all about. It is not a sinister conspiracy of black hordes to impress a pagan supremacy on genteel citizens of lighter skin. It is not a swaggering ultimatum, bloodshot with passion as so many seem to fear, that a Negro shall marry your sister. It is the insistence, springing from the innards of some of the gentlest souls God ever fashioned to choose their own seat on a

154

municipal bus, to travel afoot or on horseback, in a Cadillac convertible or to stay at home. Pierced by this simple shaft of truth, the city fathers of Montgomery, Alabama, can do nothing more than fall back in consternation, as the British did in India, and clap the leaders of the Negro community into jail. And yet really they have done more, far more. What they have done, rather pathetically in fact, is to reveal the transparency of the sincere but mistaken claims of white supremacy. For who has had the superior record of civilized behavior in this tortured episode? From which side came the extremism and the ugly little bursts of violence, and from which side the restraint? The record is not on the side of the white citizens.

It just happens that the U.S. Government is about to exploit an exhibit on the way America lives. Although far from perfect, it is a capsule picture of the upward growth of American life. It will be shown in India. It may arouse interest there. But another exhibit has preceded it: the press accounts of the Montgomery story. It needs no prophet to foretell which exhibit will make the deeper impression on the disciples of Gandhi.

The ideology of the movement of Montgomery provided it with a philosophy and a psychology. It gave the movement a set of values, convictions, criticisms, arguments and defenses in respect to direction, justification, weapons of attack, and inspiration. Moreover, the ideology places the movement on a plane of respectability and prestige—an appeal to the intelligentsia as well as the masses. In other words the movement through its ideology could now be termed popular and successful.

Writing in *Phylon* (First Quarter, 1957, pages 25-34), Reverend Martin L. King, Jr, gave the direction, inspiration, arguments, convictions, and philosophy, the ideology as it were, of the movement when he wrote:

Those of us who live in the Twentieth Century are privileged to live in one of the most momentous periods of human history. It is an exciting age filled with hope. It is an age in which a new social order is being born. We stand today between two worlds—the dying old and the emerging new . . . We are all familiar with the old order that is passing away. We have lived with it for many years. We have seen it in its international aspect, in the form of colonialism and imperialism. There are approximately two billion four hundred million (2,400,000,000) people in this world, and the vast majority of these people are colored—about one billion six hundred million (1,600,000,000) of the people of the world are colored.

. . . But there comes a time when people get tired. There comes a time when people get tired of being trampled over by the iron feet of oppression. There comes a time when people get tired of being plunged across the abyss of exploitation where they experience the bleakness of nagging despair.

We have also seen the older order in our own nation, in the form of segregation and discrimination. We know something of the long history of this old order in America. It had its beginning in the year 1619 when the first Negro slaves landed on the shores of this nation. They were brought here from the soils of Africa. And unlike the Pilgrim Fathers who landed at Plymouth a year later, they were brought here against their wills. Throughout slavery the Negro was treated in a very inhuman fashion. He was a thing to be used, not a person to be respected . . .

Living under these conditions, many Negroes came to the point of losing faith in themselves. They came to feel that perhaps they were less than human. The great tragedy of physical slavery was that it lead to mental slavery. So long as the Negro maintained this subservient attitude and accepted this 'place' assigned to him a sort of racial peace existed. But it was an uneasy peace in which the Negro was forced patiently to accept insult, injustice and exploitation. It was a negative peace. True peace is not merely the absence of some negative force—tension, confusion, or war; it is the presence of some positive force—justice, goodwill and brotherhood. And so the peace which existed between the races was a negative peace devoid of any positive and lasting quality.

. . . Along with the emergence of a 'New Negro,' with a new sense of dignity and destiny, came that memorable decision of May 17, 1954. In this decision the Supreme Court of this nation unanimously affirmed that the old Plessy Doctrine must go. This decision came as a legal and sociological death blow to an evil that had occupied the throne of American life for several decades. It affirmed in no uncertain terms that separate facilities are inherently unequal and that to segregate a child because of his race is to deny him equal protection of the law. With the coming of this great decision we could gradually see the old order of segregation and discrimination passing away, and the new order of freedom and justice coming into being. Let nobody fool you, all of the loud noises that you hear today from the legislative halls of the South in terms of 'interposition' and 'nullification,' and of outlawing the NAACP are merely the death groans from a dying system. The old order is passing away, and the new order is coming into being. We are witnessing in our day the birth of a new age, with a new structure of freedom and justice . . . Now as we face the fact of this new, emerging world, we must face the responsibilities that come along with it. A new age brings with it new challenges. Let us consider some of the challenges of this new age.

First, we are challenged to rise above the narrow confines of our individualistic concerns to the broader concerns of all humanity. The New World is a world of geographical togetherness. This means that no individual or nation can live alone. We must all learn to live together, or we will be forced to die together . . .

A second challenge that the new age brings to each of us is that of achieving excellency in our various fields of endeavor. In the new age many doors will be opening to us that were not opened in the past, and the great challenge which we confront is to be prepared to enter these doors as they open . . .

A third challenge that stands before us is that of entering the new age with understanding goodwill. This simply means that the Christian virtues of love, mercy and forgiveness should stand at the center of our lives. There is the danger that those of us who have lived so long under the yoke of oppression, those of us who have been exploited and trampled over, those of us who have had to stand amid the tragic midnight of injustice and indignities will enter the new age with hate and bitterness. But if we retaliate with hate and bitterness, the new age will be nothing but a duplication of the old age. We must blot out the hate and injustice of the old age with the love and justice of the new. This is why I believe so firmly in non-violence. Violence never solves problems. It only creates new and more complicated ones. If we succumb to the temptation of using violence in our struggle for justice, unborn generations will be the recipients of a long and desolate night of bitterness, and our chief legacy to the future will be an endless reign of meaningless chaos . . .

This is why I am so impressed with our motto for the week, 'Freedom and Justice Through Love.' Not through violence; not through hate; no, not even through boycotts; but through love. It is true that as we struggle for freedom in America we will have to boycott at times. But

157

we must remember as we boycott that a boycott is not an end within itself; it is merely a means to awaken a sense of shame within the oppressor and challenge his false sense of superiority. But the end is reconciliation; the end is redemption; the end is the creation of the beloved community. It is this type of spirit and this type of love that can transform oppressors into friends. It is this type of understanding goodwill that will transform the deep gloom of the old age into the exuberant gladness of the new age. It is this love which will bring about miracles in the hearts of men . . .

Now the fact that this new age is emerging reveals something basic about the universe. It tells us something about the core and heartbeat of the cosmos. It reminds us that the universe is on the side of justice. It says to those who struggle for justice, 'You do not struggle alone, but God struggles with you.' This belief that God is on the side of truth and justice comes down to us from the long tradition of our Christian faith . . .

So we must continue the struggle against segregation in order to speed up the coming of the inevitable. We must continue to gain the ballot. This is one of the basic keys to the solution of our problem. Until we gain political power through possession of the ballot we will be convenient tools of unscrupulous politicians. We must face the appalling fact that we have been betrayed by both the Democratic and Republican parties. The Democrats have betrayed us by capitulating to the themes and caprices of the southern Dixiecrats. The Republicans have betrayed us by capitulating to the blatant hypocrisy of right-wing reactionary northerners. This coalition of Southern Democrats and Northern right-wing Republicans defeats every proposed bill on civil rights. Until we gain the ballot and place proper public officials in office this condition will continue to exist. In communities where we confront difficulties in gaining the ballot, we must use all legal and moral means to remove these difficulties.

We must continue to struggle through legalism and legislation. There are those who contend that integration can come only through education, for no other reason than that morals cannot be legislated. I choose, however, to be dialectical at this point. It is neither education nor legislation; it is both legislation and education . . . Another thing that we must do in pressing on for integration is to invest our finances in the cause of freedom. Freedom has always been an expensive thing.

History is a fit testimony to the fact that freedom is rarely gained without sacrifice and self-denial. So we must donate large sums of money to the cause of freedom . . .

Another thing that we must do in speeding up the coming of the new age is to develop intelligent, courageous and dedicated leadership. This is one of the pressing needs of the hour. In this period of transition and growing social change, there is a dire need for leaders who are calm and yet positive, leaders who avoid the extremes of 'hot-headedness' and 'Uncle Tomism.'

Finally, if we are to speed up the coming of the new age we must have the moral courage to stand up and protest against injustice wherever we find it. Wherever we find segregation we must have the fortitude to passively resist it. I realize that this will mean suffering and sacrifice. It might even mean going to jail. If such is the case we must be willing to fill up the jail houses of the South. It might even mean physical death. But if physical death is the price that some must pay to free their children from a permanent life of psychological death, then nothing could be more honorable. Once more it might well turn out that the blood of the martyr will be the seed of the tabernacle of freedom . . .

There is nothing in all the world greater than freedom. It is worth paying for; it is worth losing a job; it is worth going to jail for. I would rather be a free pauper than a rich slave. I would rather die in abject poverty with my convictions than live in inordinate riches with the lack of self respect. Once more every Negro must be able to cry out with his forefathers: 'Before I'll be a slave, I'll be buried in my grave and go home to my Father and be saved . . .'

Freedom must ring from every mountainside. Yes, let it ring from the snow-capped Rockies of Colorado, from the prodigious hilltops of New Hampshire, from the mighty Allghenies of Pennsylvania, from the curvaceous slopes of California. But not only that. Let freedom ring from every mountainside—from every mole hill in Mississippi, from Stone Mountain of Georgia, from lookout Mountain of Tennessee, yes and from every hill and mountain of Alabama. From every mountainside let freedom ring.

Operating Tactics

Finally, tactics is the fifth mechanism essential to the development of a social movement. They develop along three lines: gaining adherents, holding adherents and reaching objectives. Tactics are always dependent upon the nature of the situation in which the movement is operating, and always with reference to the cultural, religious, socio-economic, and political background of the movement. They are almost by definition flexible and variable, taking their form from the exigencies of circumstances and the ingenuity of the people.

Tactically the movement must develop a public opinion favorable to its aims. At the same time it must influence public opinion and make converts. In this sense a social movement operates much like that of a religious crusade.

In addition to gaining tactical vantage points of attack and attaining respectability, a social movement must establish its strength among people inside its own rank; these are people usually of a lower class who have been long suffering from economic deprivations.

But in the end most social movements, especially like that of the Montgomery Improvement Association must bring about social change by (1) a reaffirmation of the ideal values of a society, and (2) by avoiding compromise with traditional values incompatible with its aims and objectives, and introducing a new set of essentially religious values.

A dramatic illustration of 'on the spot' and improvised operational tactics appears in a personal document taken from a series of interviews with an informant, and also a leader in the movement. He stated:

. . . We had just received a call that they have just bombed Reverend King's home, which was some three blocks away. My first act was to send a committee over to his home to see if his wife and baby were safe. When they returned and we informed Reverend King, he went home. But before leaving, Reverend King appealed to the people to remain calm and not to worry about him. We stayed behind in the mass meeting. I think this was the most dramatic part in our meeting.

When King arrived home and discovered that his wife and baby had not been injured, he returned outside to face the large crowd that had gathered. The mayor of the city, who was there within ten minutes after the bombing, made a speech as did the police commissioner. Then Reverend King spoke. This was our first demonstration of non-violence and passive resistance. Reverend King appealed to the people, some five or six hundred who were standing around the house, to put down their weapons and to go home. 'He that fightest by the sword shall perish by the sword.' This became the most dramatic incident in the Montgomery Improvement Association.

A few days after that the home of Mr. Nixon was also bombed. We then decided that we would not be bombed into subjection. After this they [city officials] began to search the statutes trying to find some way to stop us. They finally found an old anti-boycott statute passed during the 1920s designed for mine strikes in Birmingham, Alabama. Nevertheless, this led to the mass arrests. They arrested twenty-four ministers in all, a total of ninety individuals. The arrests came on the twenty-second of February, George Washington's birthday. This day, we felt, had been selected because the banks were closed and we couldn't get any money to bail Negro citizens out of jail. Soon after our arrest, I believe our movement developed into its full maturity and fully recognized the meaning of a philosophy of non-violence. For as soon as we were out of jail, it was apparent to everybody, that we could not win this struggle by fighting back. We had to be willing to suffer and we would have to be emancipated from our fears. Representatives of the FOR (Fellowship of Reconciliation) came into Montgomery and began to leave books and to discuss Gandhi's philosophy of non-violence. In the beginning of our protest we had asked our people not to fight back and not to fire on the buses because it was so impractical. We didn't have any weapons, we didn't have any ammunition. They stopped selling us even shells for shotguns to go hunting with.

I never will forget those threatening telephone calls and letters of intimidation, threatening with such violent statements as 'we would not live until morning;' that 'they were on their way to get us;' that 'they were going to kill us and members of our families.'

Finally, one morning M. L. King and I got together to discuss the matter. We felt we ought to be ready just in case these threats were real. I asked King if he had any means of protection for him and his family. He said the only weapon he had was a butcher knife. He asked, 'What do you have?' I said, 'The only thing I have is a razor.' We decided that we should go downtown together and buy some weapons for our protection. In the meantime, King's members brought him guns and ammunition. When this happened, I had to go downtown alone and try to buy a pistol. I found out that none of the white merchants were selling weapons to Negroes, not even shells.

So it was dramatized to me and others spearheading the movement that counter violence, that is, fighting back with weapons of physical destruction, was incompatible with Christian doctrine. Moreover, even if we wanted to employ forces of violence, we did not have the means or the materials for militant minority tactics. Finally, Negro minorities in the United States, due to economic deprivations, and limited social participation are not sufficiently organized, or have not had adequate experience in tactical military campaigns to accept threats of the dominant white society to engage them in physical combat.

FIVE

Toward
Institutionalization:
A Summary

The final stage in the development of a social movement is the period in which institutionalization takes place. In order to avoid the stigma of "rebels," the newly gained power of the movement must be legalized or organized, and become an integral part of the political structure. When this is attained, that is, when the attitudes and values of the leadership have become a part of the legal and political foundations of the social order, a new society has been formed, and accordingly, the movement has been consummated. Blumer[1] states:

> In the institutional stage, the movement has crystallized into a fixed organization with a definite personnel and structure to carry into execution the purposes of the movement. Here the leader is likely to be an administrator.

It is convenient to give a chronological summary to the major events during the life-cycle, "natural history," as it were, of the social movement in Montgomery, up to this point. It will be remembered that Montgomery, Alabama traditionally has been a bi-racially structured community. As the "Cradle of the Confederacy," the community is controlled by social norms—rules, regulations, folkways, mores, and institutions—that accorded all Negroes inferior status roles and all whites superior status—social privileges, authority and power.

The regulation for city bus seating in Montgomery required separate reserved sections of the bus for white and Negro riders. Whites could sit at the front and Negroes at the rear of the buses in designated seats. Negroes were forced to stand on buses when seats were vacant in the white sections.

This created resentment, discontent and indignation on the part of virtually all Negroes who were forced to ride the buses.

On December 1, 1955, Mrs. Rosa Parks, a Negro seamstress, was arrested on a Montgomery bus when she took an empty seat in what was believed to be the Negro section of the bus and later refused to relinquish it to a white passenger.

Following the initial protest, Negro leaders, through the newly organized Montgomery Improvement Association, asked the company for three concessions, at the same time emphasizing that the movement was not an attempt to break down segregation on the buses. Negroes petitioned for (1) more courteous treatment from bus operators (the group claimed that Negroes had suffered innumerable indignities from bus operators and white patrons over a period of many years), (2) seating on a "first-come, first-served" basis with Negroes seating from the rear and whites seating from the front (seating now is at the discretion of the bus driver by "reserved seat" sections), and (3) employment of Negro drivers on predominantly Negro lines as driver vacancies occur.

The bus company officials answered (1) no recent reports of discourtesies had been received, (2) failure to provide reserved sections for the races would not fulfill legal "separate but equal" requirements of the state (Negroes claim that other Alabama cities operate the transit system on a first-come, first-served basis), and (3) the company would not hire Negro drivers within the next ten years or more.

On December 17, the city commissioners appointed a committee to advise them on the bus situation. The committee was composed of eight Negroes and eight whites. These Negro committee members were chosen by the protest group. The selection of two additional Negro representatives by the Mayor was bitterly opposed by the Negro leadership.

Negotiations failed when white members of the commission refused to consider abandoning the reserved seat sections and allowing service on a "first-come, first-served" basis. Instead, the compromise offered the Negroes was a plan by which the first ten seats on each bus would be reserved for whites only and the ten seats nearest the rear of the buses for Negroes. If the reserved seat sections were filled, then the few remaining seats between the reserved sections could be occupied on a first-come, first-served basis.

On January 24, 1956, Mayor W.A. Gayle issued a statement:

We have pussyfooted around on this boycott long enough and it is time to be frank and honest . . . The Negro leaders have proved they are not interested in ending the boycott but rather in prolonging it so that they may stir up racial strife. The Negro leaders have proved that they will say one thing to a white man and another to a Negro about the boycott . . . [They] have forced the boycott into a campaign between whether the social fabric of our community will continue to exist or will be destroyed by a group of Negro radicals who have split the fine relationships which have existed between Negro and white people for generations . . . The white people are firm in their convictions that they do not care whether the Negroes ever ride a city bus again if it means that the social fabric of our community is destroyed so that Negroes will start riding the bus again.

He called on white citizens to refrain from carrying their domestic employees to and from work in their cars.

The same day it was announced that the mayor and a city commissioner had become members of the White Citizens' Council. The other two commissioners had joined the organization previously.

On January 26, Reverend M. L. King, the boycott leader, was arrested for going thirty-five miles an hour in a twenty-five mile an hour speed zone.

On January 27, Reverend King's home was bombed, causing minor damage.

On January 29, a dynamite cap was exploded in the front yard of E.D. Nixon, a Negro leader in the protest.

On February 22, more than ninety Negroes were indicted on charges of violating Alabama's boycott laws.

On March 22, Reverend King was convicted on a charge of violating the boycott law. He was fined five hundred dollars plus five hundred dollars for court costs. The conviction was appealed.

On April 23, the U.S. Supreme Court remanded a Circuit Court ruling concerning bus segregation in South Carolina. The Montgomery City Lines, Incorporated, announced it would end segregation on buses in the city, but police commissioner Clyde Sellers said he would order the arrest of any passenger or bus driver involved in race mixing.

On June 5, a three-judge federal court declared Alabama and Montgomery laws requiring separate seating of the races unconstitutional. The Montgomery Board of Commissioners and Alabama's attorney general appealed the decision to the United States Supreme Court.

On November 13, the United States Supreme Court unanimously ruled Alabama and Montgomery bus segregation laws unconstitutional. The court affirmed the ruling of the three-judge Federal District Court, which was made some time ago, that segregation on public transportation in Montgomery and Alabama was unconstitutional. When this affirmation was promulgated, Negroes who had boycotted city buses for eleven months, voted to ride public transportation carriers again, this time on a non-segregated basis. The thirteenth month of the boycott was well under way before actual integration on buses took place, however, because the Court gave the contesting groups—the city and state—time to file petitions requesting "reconsideration of the ruling."

Such petitions were filed by both city and state officials, but the Court refused to act upon the petitions. When the mandate was received by the Federal District court on Thursday, December 21, and filed, segregation laws affecting public transportation were officially dead and Negroes boarded city carriers on Friday, December 22, for the first time in thirteen months.

For a few days integration worked smoothly and without incident. Both races appeared indifferent and seemingly accepted the inevitable. Bus drivers, who had been "furloughed without pay" for months, were noticeably happy.

These developments placed the movement at the point of institutionalization. It must now establish formal offices, organized groups, defined situations and a new body of sanctions. Behavior of Negroes must be channelized into a body of common expectations—rules and norms. The leadership must build for the people what R.E. Park[2] has called a "network of accommodative arrangements." Moreover, a set of values must be attached to these "accommodative expectations," and people must be given social prescriptions as to how to adhere to them. This means that the people must change their conceptions of themselves in relation to each other and to the "out-group;" their dispositions and subjective moods must fit the new society.

One of the leaders of the movement assesses the situation in the following manner:

> Montgomery, Alabama has now really made history. Not only have we solved the problem for Montgomery, but also for the whole South. Eternally and everlastingly, it is now unconstitutional to segregate people because of race. This came like a great reward for all of our walking. We cannot go out and celebrate and say that we have won a victory because it is not our purpose to humiliate and embarrass white people.

In non-violence, one never seeks to humiliate, embarrass or destroy his opponent.

We have become an organization concerned with the total freedom of the people here in Montgomery. I might say, also, that the movement has spread all over the South. Our sister cities in Alabama have also tried to adopt movements like the Montgomery movement; they have tried to pattern after our organization. As a result, we have organized the Southern Christian Leadership Conference, which is the Montgomery Improvement Association serving primarily as a co-ordinating association. The next item on our program is to attack recreational facilities in Montgomery. We hope to have that cleared along with segregation in the public parks and swimming pools and all other recreational facilities. We have a program for public education, too.

. . . We feel the problem of registration and voting will be a continuous process; we will have to work on it over and over again.

Yes, we are now a full-fledged organization with a central office building, definite officers, and we are building a program for continuing our efforts.

Finally, this study has been an attempt to apply the natural approach as a scheme for describing and analyzing the processes and mechanisms of a social movement. It is apparent from the foregoing data analyses that the social movement of the Montgomery Improvement Association has passed through perceptible stages of development. It is now on the threshold of becoming a social institution which is the completion of the life-cycle of a movement. The persistence of the Association as a social institution will be influenced by the following:

(1) The services of the leadership—who must now become executive administrators;
(2) The organizational form—division of labor, social values, culture, and "scheme of life;" and
(3) The redefinition of attitudes and values of the masses served by the institution.

Notes

CHAPTER ONE

1. R.T. La Piere, *Collective Behavior* (New York, 1938); Ralph H. Turner and Lewis M. Killian, *Collective Behavior*, (Englewood Cliffs, New Jersey, 1957), pp. 4-12.
2. Herbert Blumer, "Collective Behavior," *Principals of Sociology*, Alfred McClung Lee (ed.) (New York, 1953), PP. 167-222.
3. Blumer, *op cit.*, pp. 168-69.
4. *Ibid.,* p. 199.
5. Turner and Killian, *op cit.*, p. 309.
6. Louis Wirth, "The Problem of Minority Groups," in *The Science of Man in World Crisis,* Ralph Linten (ed.), (New York, 1945), pp. 354-58, 360-364.
7. See Ernest W. Burgess and Hower Locke, *The Family* (New York, 1953).
8. Marie Johoda, Morten Deutsch and Stuart W. Cook, *Research Methods in Social Relations* (New York, 1955), p. 135.
9. *Ibid,.* pp. 136-138.
10. Rex P. Hopper, "The Revolutionary Process: A Frame of Reference for the Study of Revolutionary Movements," *Social Forces,* XXVIII (March, 1950), pp. 270-79.
11. C.A. Dawson and W.E. Gettys, *Introduction to Sociology* (rev. ed.) (New York, 1935), Chap. 19.
12. Hopper, *op cit.,* pp. 271-276.
13. Blumer, *op cit.*, pp. 203-214.
14. Robert E. Park and Ernest W. Burgess, *Introduction to the Science of Sociology* (New York, 1921), p. 865.
15. *Ibid.*, p. 866.
16. *Ibid.*, p. 871.
17. *Ibid.*, p. 874.
18. For a statistical summary of Montgomery in respect to population, housing characteristics, vital statistics, retail trade, building and construction, selective services, manufactures, banking, city government, city employment, municipal revenue, city school system, hospitals and climate, see U.S. Department of Commerce, Bureau of the Census, *County and City Data Book* (Washington, D.C., 1956), pp. 364-371.
19. George Barrett, "Montgomery Testing Ground," *New York Times Magazine,* (December 12, 1956), p. 8.
20. *Pittsburgh Courier,* (March 31, 1956), p. 2.

21. *The Reporter,* (March 8, 1956).

CHAPTER TWO

1. See Blumer, *op cit.*, for a definition of "milling" and "circular reaction."

CHAPTER THREE

1. For a discussion of the features of a public and an elementary collective grouping, and the process of the formation of a collective opinion (Public Opinion), see Blumer, *op cit.*, pp. 189-97; also see Walter Lippman *Public Opinion* (New York, 1922).
2. Walter Lippman, *loc cit.*

CHAPTER FOUR

1. Blumer, *op cit.,* p. 203.
2. *Ibid.*, pp. 204-205.
3. Harvard Theologian Tillich stresses the transcendence of God, i.e., that God is outside all things, while Neo-Naturalist Philosopher Wieman stresses the imminence of God, i.e., that God is within all things.
4. Turner and Killian, *op cit.*, p. 314.
5. *Ibid.*, pp. 206-208.
6. *Ibid.*, p. 209.
7. Turner and Killian, *op cit.*, p. 318.

CHAPTER FIVE

1. Blumer, *op cit.*, p. 203.
2. Park and Burgess, *op cit.*, Chapter 10.

Bibliography

BOOKS

Brinton, Crane. *The Anatomy of Evolution.* Englewood Cliffs, New Jersey; Prentice-Hall, Inc., 1952

Cantril, Hadley. *The Psychology of Social Movements.* New York: John Wiley and Sons, 1941.

Edwards, Lyford P. *The Natural History of Revolution.* Chicago; University of Chicago Press, 1947

Heberle, Rudolf. *Social Movements: An Introduction to Political Sociology.* New York: Appleton-Century-Crofts, Inc., 1951

Hook, Sidney. *The Hero in History: A Study in Limitation and Possibility.* New York: The John Day Company, 1943.

Hunter, Floyd. *Community Power Structure: A Study of Decision Makers.* Chapel Hill: University of North Carolina Press, 1953.

LaPiere, R.T. *Collective Behavior.* New York: McGraw-Hill Book Company, 1938.

LeBen, Gustave. *The Crowd: A Study of the Popular Mind.* London: T.F. Unwin, 1897.

Lippmann, Walter. *The Phantom Public: A Sequel to "Public Opinion."* New York: The Macmillan Company, 1930.

_____. *Public Opinion.* New York: Penguin Books, 1946.

Mannheim, Karl. *Ideology and Utopia,* translated by Louis Wirth and E.A. Shils. New York: Harcourt, Brace and Company, 1936.

Morton, Robert K. *Mass Persuasion: The Social Psychology of a War Bond Drive.* New York: Harper and Brothers, 1946.

Park, Robert E. and E.W. Burgess. *Introduction to the Science of Sociology.* Chicago: University of Chicago Press, 1924.

Ross, E.A. *Social Psychology.* New York: The MacMillan Company, 1908.

Serel, Georges, *Reflections on Violence,* translated by T.E. Hulme and J. Roth. Glencoe Illinois: The Free Press, 1950.

Turner, Ralph H. and Lewis M. Killian. *Collective Behavior.*

171

Englewood Cliffs, New Jersey; Prentice-Hall, Inc., 1957

Weekler, J.E. and T.E. Hall. *The Police and Minority Groups.* Chicago: The International City Managers Association, 1944.

Wolf, Hazel Catherine. *On Freedom's Altar: The Martyr Complex in the Abolition Movement.* Madison: University of Wisconsin Press, 1952.

ARTICLES

Abel, Theodore. "The Pattern of A Successful Political Movement." *American Sociological Review,* II (1937), 347-52.

Becker, Howard. "Unrest, Culture Contact, and Release During the Middle Ages and the Renaissance," *Southwestern Social Science Quarterly,* XII (1931), 143-55.

Blumer, Herbert. "Collective Behavior," *Principles of Sociology,* Edited by Alfred McClung Lee. New York: Barnes and Noble, Inc. 1951.

Carr, Lowell Juilliard. "Disaster and the Sequence-Pattern Concept of Social Change," *American Journal of Sociology,* XXXVIII (1932), 207-18.

Dekany, E. "Une Forme 'Elementaire' de la Vie Sociale: Le Public," Revue Internationale de Sociologie, XLIV (1936), 263-77.

Gerth, Hans. "The Nazi Party: Its Leadership and Composition," *American Journal of Sociology,* XLV (1940), 517-41.

Lemon, Sarah McCulloh. "The Ideology of the 'Dixiecrat' Movement," *Social Forces,* XXX (1951), 162-71.

Park, Robert E. "Collective Behavior," *Encyclopedia of the Social Sciences,* III (1930), 631-33.

Parsons, Talcott. "The Role of Ideas in Social Action," *American Sociological Review,* III (1938), 652-64.

Polansky, Norman, R. Lippit, and F. Redl. "An Investigation of Behavioral Contagion in Groups," *Human Relations*, III (1950), 319-48.

The Beginnings of a New Age

EDGAR N. FRENCH

The ground-swell of social unrest erupted like a great volcano in the city of Montgomery, State of Alabama, December 5, 1955. The city, the state, the nation, and the world were struck dumb by the unusual, unexpected, and undreamed of phenomenon which followed the arrest, trial and conviction of what might have been "just another Negro citizen." Newspapers, radio, and television spread the news: "Negroes Boycott Buses in Montgomery, Alabama." While this message was relayed around the world, the white City Fathers asked, "Where are our Negroes? These are strange people, far different from the Negroes we have known." Little did they realize that a combination of conditions and circumstances which had existed for many years had, slowly but surely, cast a new Negro to replace the old Negro in the South.

The State of Alabama is proud of its geographical location. The license plate on every motor vehicle in the state bears the inscription "Heart of Dixie." Likewise the city of Montgomery takes pride in its history, boasting of the fact that it is the cradle of the Confederacy. Even though the guns of the Civil War were silenced almost a hundred years ago and the breach in the union was declared mended, the freedom for which the war was waged and won had not been fully realized by the southern blacks or whites in 1955, nor fully realized even to this date.

What precipitated the Montgomery crisis? This is a question many people have asked, but only the over-zealous, over-confident or foolish dare to offer a conclusive answer. After years of reflection on the movement, or "boycott," as it was called, this writer can offer only his personal view, as a participant, of the circumstances and conditions which precipitated the breakthrough, a breakthrough that crystallized the attitudes of the Negro people into a mass protest against local customs.

The conditions existing in other cities and states which were causing the oppressed people to seek relief through the courts were also to be found in Montgomery, Alabama. Here, too, the white citizens were of the opinion that the Negro had no rights which the white man was bound to respect. Here, too, the gospel of the Fatherhood of God and the Brotherhood of Man was proclaimed from pulpits, as the voices of Negroes and whites, separately assembled in their respective churches on opposite sides of Dexter Avenue, blended in the air to the pleasure of passers-by as each group sang, "Jesus, Lover of My Soul, Let Me to Thy Bosom Fly."

The laws of the white worshippers made mandatory some line of demarcation wherever whites and Negroes assembled. The *Plessy vs. Ferguson* decision, which gave legal sanction to the dual system of education under the doctrine of separate but equal, also gave sanction to the denial of educational opportunity for Negro children. Denial of educational opportunity led to denial of job opportunity, and economic inequality to social inequality.

It would be a mistake to assert that the Negro citizens of this southern metropolis had not tried to free themselves from the shackles which had bound them through the years prior to the Supreme Court decision of 1954. The desire for freedom and first-class citizenship had become the obsession of every man and woman of color who had felt the piercing pangs of oppression. But every effort put forth to break segregation and discrimination was met by double and sometimes triple counter-attack by the white citizens.

By 1953, there was a peculiar kind of social unrest. The common people were voluntarily discussing their desire to exercise fully and freely their rights as citizens and to be treated and respected as human beings. It was not at all uncommon to hear a colored citizen say, "We have been in *this* all of our lives! WE are tired of *this*! We want somebody to lead us out of *this*! We are willing to do whatever is necessary. We want somebody to tell us what to do and show us how to do it . . ." In order to understand fully what the people meant by "this," one would have had to live in Montgomery prior to December, 1955. But some understanding can be gained by taking a look at the circumstances which gave rise to an historic movement.

There are two means of public conveyance in Montgomery: taxi and bus. It is unlawful as well as improper for a white cab operator to pick up a Negro passenger, unless the passenger is a Negro woman and the cab driver has immoral designs. It is next to impossible to describe to the average

American citizen the internal turmoil that seizes an individual when he is refused a needed service because of his color or race.

A line of demarcation separated the racial groups on the Montgomery buses which carried thousands of people to their destinations daily. The dividing line sometimes took the form of a sign designating the area for Negroes and the area for whites. More often than not, on predominantly Negro streets, separation of races was declared in terms of a number of seats reserved for "whites only." This, Negroes had learned, was the ideal; in reality, the line of demarcation was an imaginary line which existed only in the mind of the bus operator. Wherever his whims dictated, the dividing line was located. The determining factor of his whims was the number of white passengers boarding the bus at each stop. The flexibility of the line became apparent at stop number two, number three, and so on.

It was also not uncommon for bus drivers to pass by Negroes waiting at bus stops, because they knew whites were waiting several blocks ahead. Often, since Negroes could not easily pass whites who were standing in the front of crowded busses, they were forced to pay their fares and proceed to the rear for boarding. Many a Negro passenger was left standing without his fare, as the operator, failing to open the rear door, drove away.

Since the Civil War, Negroes have sought legal redress from the magistrates to the State Supreme Court, although they could easily foretell what the verdict would be. Case after case was squashed, thrown out, or, when tried and appealed, the verdict of lower courts was sustained. The Supreme Court decision of 1954 restored hope to a people who had come to feel themselves helpless victims of outrageous and inhuman treatment.

This new-found hope expressed itself in the events surrounding the arrest and conviction of Mrs. Rosa Parks, a Negro seamstress. On December 1, 1955, after working and shopping, Mrs. Parks boarded a bus, paid the fare and took a seat in what was designated at that point as the area for Negroes. Soon the line of demarcation shifted to the rear of Mrs. Parks and she was ordered by the driver to move accordingly. A white man was standing by, awaiting her seat. She refused to move. Officers were summoned and Mrs. Parks was placed in jail.

Mrs. Rosa Parks was a typical American housewife who shared in the support of her household by working as a seamstress in a downtown department store. As a member of the Methodist Church, she was held in high esteem by her fellow parishioners. Although mild-mannered and soft-spoken, the warmth and radiance of her personality bespoke her presence in

175

almost any setting. The reason given by Mrs. Parks for her refusal to move when ordered to do so was, "My feet were hurting. I'd been working and shopping all day and I was tired."

The news of the arrest of Mrs. Parks was immediately seized upon as a means of giving united expression to the new-found hope which had stemmed from the Supreme Court decision. The Negro Interdenominational Ministerial Alliance was called into immediate session, and to this meeting came other prominent civic and social leaders. In every heart and mind was the thought that now we must register our protest against the inhuman, unchristian, unlawful, and unethical indignities which we have suffered through the years.

A strange sense of community and group consciousness seized each person present. This same attitude would soon be realized in many places. Not only was Mrs. Rosa Parks arrested but every Negro in Montgomery felt arrested. The penalties which were soon to be pronounced on her, also awaited all other people of color, who dared to defy the "beasts of Ephesus." Group consciousness did not exclude from its consideration the whites, who later were to be referred to sympathetically and with various degrees of affection as "our white brethren." The group was mindful of the difficulty of holding another in a pit without actually restricting the holder's freedom. The action decided upon to gain our freedom had to be of such a nature as would point up the thoughtlessness of our oppressors.

The meeting opened on the note of the denial of our civil rights. It closed with the decision that we should register our protest against the arrest and trial of the latest victim of "cock-crowing White Supremacy" in Montgomery. No Negro was to ride a bus to work or to town, not even to the hospital, on Monday, December 5, 1955.

There were approximately three dozen people present at this meeting on Saturday, December 3rd, a number that was to multiply itself more than a thousandfold, two days later, on the evening of the fifth. This small group set itself the mammoth task of getting their protest decision over to the 50,000 Negroes who lived in the various sections of the large city. They divided the city into sections and assigned individuals to cover each section. The assignees were responsible for notifying everyone in their area. It was important that not one family should be missed. This seemed like a staggering, if not an impossible, assignment, but the self-appointed mailmen began their deliveries the same night. A prepared statement was to be placed under as many doors and in as many mail boxes as possible by late Saturday night. All Negro ministers were asked to announce the protest plan to their congregations on Sunday. All sermons were to be concerned with some aspect of social justice with emphasis upon what was happening in Montgomery—a wonderful challenge during Advent.

The Saturday night check-up revealed that much had been accomplished, though many women had twisted shoe heels, several had developed bunions, and all had tired legs. Overweight ministers assured themselves that walking was good for the waistline. Although there was not time for pastoral visits, ministers had been closer to the realities of living in slum areas than ever before. They had really been among poorly-clad and undernourished children, alcoholics, and many other forms of human deprivation they hardly realized existed. The stark evils of social and economic injustices experienced in these few hours made it easy for many of the ministers to discard their well-prepared manuscripts at the Sunday Worship hour, and to speak concerning the evils of their day. Many of the school teachers involved laid aside their economic and sociology text books the following Monday and taught absolute reality instead of superficial idealism.

A few brokenhearted, unpaid postmen reported at the end of that Saturday, that their area was too broad to cover. Some families had been missed. Some would call it fate, others might say luck, but for this hard-working group, God was on their side! One of the notices intended only for Negroes fell into the hands of a reporter for the local newspaper, *The Montgomery Advertiser*. With comments appropriate to inform every reader of the intention of the Negroes, the paper carried the words of the circular exactly as it was printed:

Another Negro has been arrested and thrown in jail because she refused to give up her seat on a bus . . . Trial will be held Monday, December 5 . . . No Negro will ride any city bus on Monday to work, to town or any place . . . Don't ride the bus Monday! Report to Holt Street Baptist Church, Monday night for further instruction.

The group gave a sigh of relief Sunday morning as they read this notice on the front page of a paper which reached almost every family in the city. Now *everyone* had the message. But would they respond?

The morning of December 5th found ministers out of bed at an hour unusual for most men of the cloth; they had to know if the message had really been understood. Buses were checked from 5 a.m. until the hour for the trial. No Negroes were riding! Really a few Negroes who were hard-pressed to get to their jobs might have ridden, but again providence came to the aid of those who were struggling for justice.

The white City Fathers felt confident that the group leading the protest was a "goon squad" designed to prevent, by force, Negroes from riding the buses. Arrangements were made for two police motorcycles to lead, and two squad cars to follow each bus into the Negro sections, presumably to haul in anyone deemed an interferer. The less-informed Negroes regarded this unusual spectacle as a plan to keep Negroes *off* the buses. Therefore, the plan of the City Fathers worked in reverse. The few colored people who went to the bus stops as usual, upon seeing the unusual spectacle of a police escort, were frightened away.

This first phase of the beginning of a new age for an oppressed people in the "Heart of Dixie" bore an outward sign of victory, although a long, hard struggle lay ahead. There was almost complete consensus that this was the time the Negroes should take a firm stand for their freedom. "We have proven to ourselves that we can stick together. We have shown the white people that we can stick together. Let us stand firmly until they know we mean business." Such statements were on the lips of the colored citizens milling about the streets. Many of these people took a holiday, their only reason being, "We want to celebrate!"

The "Kangaroo Court" ended. To no one's surprise, Mrs. Rosa Parks was found guilty and fined. The masses left the court scurrying for the Holt Street Baptist Church, where they had been directed to assemble for "further instruction." It was approximately five hours before the curtain was to rise on an epoch-making meeting.

Out of deep concern for what was to follow, three men sat down in the office of Home Missions, Brotherhood, Pension and Relief of the A.M.E. Zion Church to talk. These men were the Reverend Ralph D. Abernathy, who later became vice president of the Montgomery Improvement Association, Ed Nixon, who became treasurer, and myself, the elected corresponding secretary. After a sort of post-mortem of the trial which had just ended, I spoke of the danger of going to the mass meeting without specific directions or suggestions to present to the people who had responded one hundred percent to the first request. Everyone knew why he did not ride the bus on Monday, December 5, but should all ride again on December 6? If so, under what conditions? If not, why not?

Seemingly unaware of the fleeting moments, Abernathy and Nixon reviewed the bitter and painful experience Negroes had experienced in public transportation for many years. They ranged from harsh, inhuman insults; "monkey's cousins," "niggers," "cows," "black fools," "get in the back," to those who had been shot and killed because they registered their disapproval of such insolence. While these men talked, I scribbled notes on paper. The discussion ended and I turned to the typewriter. The silence was broken only by the clatter of the keys hammering out proposals which were to become the guiding principles for people struggling to form a new destiny:

We, the Negro citizens of Montgomery, shall continue to register our protest against man's inhumanity to man, and no one of us shall ride any city bus until the bus company agrees to:

1. Allow all patrons, White and Negro, to be seated on buses on a "first come–first served" basis. Negroes will be seated from the rear toward the front. White people will be seated from the front toward the rear. There are to be no signs or lines of demarcation and no one is to be asked to give up a seat.

2. Give assurance that Negroes will be accorded all the courtesy afforded any other patrons of the city lines and that no abusive and insulting language will be used by the bus operators. Negroes are to be guaranteed a dime's worth of service for a dime.

3. Since a large percentage of the bus patronage is Negro, Negroes who qualify should be employed to operate buses running into predominantly Negro sections.

Long before 7:00 p.m., on that Monday, December 5th, the people filled the church and streets for blocks around. Thousands of freedom-craving people awaited instructions. Dr. Martin Luther King, who had been elected president of the Montgomery Improvement Association, was the first to speak at the mass meeting. His personal zeal for freedom and his interpretation of the longing desires of those assembled, met with their hearty approval. Then the voice of Ralph D. Abernathy was heard as he clearly and forcefully read the resolution upon which the group was to act. The three proposals to the bus company had been turned over to a brilliant young attorney, Fred D. Gray, who was to form a resolution void of language which would needlessly lay the Negroes liable for suit. The resolution was approved without dissent, and with no questions raised. An insatiable thirst for freedom had seized everyone. A new dignity and a new destiny had been conceived.

Many southern whites regard themselves as masters, and Negroes as servants who are to obey their every command. Such was the case with the authorities of Montgomery. They *commanded* the Negroes to return to the buses, after which, they promised, they would give consideration to their grievances. "Negroes cannot force us to do anything," they said. "We have the economic and political power. We can crush you at will. We have laws you must obey. If we do not have a law on the books for the crime you are committing, we will make a law. Return to the buses and then we will talk with your leaders. Return or we will crush you!"

When this ultimatum was not obeyed, every conceivable attempt was made to deprive the Negro of even the third class citizenship which was reluctantly accorded him. The city police force was expanded to ensure that the job be well done. Colored drivers stopping to pick up their wives in the downtown area were given tickets for blocking traffic. Responsible drivers, followed by patrols, were given tickets for speeding, reckless driving, or whatever charge could be dreamed up at the moment. Negroes on the streets were attacked by groups of white men and beaten mercilessly. Negroes at home and in offices were harassed day and night by paid white telephone operators. Homes and churches were bombed. But an enlarged police force could "catch" nothing but innocent Negro drivers!

The beginning of this "get-tough policy," as the city officials called it, proved to be trying for the Negro citizens. We had preached, "Love your enemies," "Do good to those who hate you," "Render not evil for evil, but overcome evil with good." The time had come for the real test of these preachments. Were our people prepared to practice what they had been taught? Had we reached the point where our faith in the ultimate triumph of justice over injustice would enable us to stand firmly for what we knew to be right? We were mindful of the claims of those who had held that they were the controllers of the wealth and power of the state. But we could not forget the ancient writer who said, "The earth is the Lord's, the fullness thereof, the world and they that dwell therein." We would stand with the ancient writer.

The mass arrest of nearly one hundred people in one day followed. The firmness and passion of the struggling group came to the front. For the first time, police officers were confronted by Negroes who acted like men. Some informed the officers to expect them to report to jail at a certain hour. One retired colored widow instructed an arresting officer to return to his post, saying, "My chauffeur will drive me to jail." Many, who knew their names were on the list, reported to the jail voluntarily. Others went calmly, and sat chatting leisurely in the cells long after bonds had been arranged, doors had been opened, and they were free to go. Some, like myself, do not even know who signed their bonds.

This was strange and unusual behavior for Negroes. Less than a year prior to this event, they thought themselves defenseless against the unlawful cruelties of their oppressors. The swinging of a "headache stick," the flashing of a gun by a cop, or the threat of imprisonment had silenced thousands of voices that might have cried out for justice. All of the threats which had been used to suppress the Negro had lost their potency. Iron bars and the prison cell could be a pleasant sight if such meant freedom and first-class citizenship for all unborn generations of American children. The thirst for freedom had pushed all fears into the background. The desire for full-fledged citizenship had rendered null and void any acceptance of second-class citizenship. The aspiration, resolve, and determination expressed by Patrick Henry in the statement, "I know not what course others may take, but as for me, give me liberty or give me death," obsessed these people who had been denied. There was no room for doubt that they would ever again accept anything less than first-class citizenship. It was a hard decision to make after years of compromise and complacency during which the better educated Negroes in Montgomery, as well as in many other places in the South, knew they were not allowed participation in government. For them, the claim that democracy is "government of the people, by the people, and for the people," was in fact a false claim, for if it were not false, then they were not people. But it was sheer folly to think of registering and voting, even though they paid their taxes and respected all laws.

Their decision to act confronted the group with a larger problem: *How* to win the rights guaranteed by the Constitution of the United States? We all knew we would have to fight hard and long. We knew the enemy was strong, but we had to be stronger. To a great extent we were outnumbered; but this could be balanced by strategy. The oppressors were experts in inflicting physical harm, but we would not raise a hand to harm a hair on anyone's head. We all believed that love is stronger than hate. If we were to help those who were persecuting us, we had to win them by firmness and love. We would respect them, respect ourselves, and consequently demand respect from them.

The belief that outside interference was prompting the Negroes to behave in this unusual manner led to the early outlawing of the N.A.A.C.P. in the

State of Alabama, followed by accusations that Communists had infiltrated the Negro ranks. But the outlawing of the organization did not undermine its principles, for these were stamped indelibly upon the minds of thousands of Negro citizens. The City Fathers' claim of Communist infiltration was absurd. The only "Red" Negroes in Montgomery were those who did not agree with the philosophy of the White Citizens Council. Calculated from this point of view, there were 50,000 Negroes to be classified as communists. All disagreed with the White Citizens Council and made their positions crystal clear.

"Together we stand, divided we fall," became the byword of the protest. It was a guiding principle which led finally to success.

Going to and from work without riding buses presented a great challenge. To lessen the hardship, all who owned cars were asked to pick up their neighbors on their way to work. Voluntary car pools formed quickly. Those who had reasonable distances to go were encouraged to walk. Many walked five to seven miles daily. Business and professional men and woman, as well as housewives, who owned cars, cruised the streets and picked up people who were walking in the rain and cold, and drove them without pay to their jobs. Some who were picked up insisted upon giving a dime or a quarter to replenish the gas tanks and keep the wheels of freedom turning.

Wages paid Negro laborers were not adequate to cover the cost of cab fare to ride to work, and Negro cab operators were warned that their licenses would be revoked if they accepted reduced rates. The officers, therefore, reasoned that the voluntary car pool and pickup cars were accepting fees for their services. This led to a number of arrests for charging passengers without a license. It was useless for the driver and the passengers to say there was no money involved. The officer would tell the judge, "I saw the driver reach his hand toward the passenger, and the passenger reached his hand toward the driver. They had to be giving and receiving something." Upon this testimony by a white officer, the judge would levy a fine. It was not long before the Negroes learned the folly of telling the "whole truth and nothing but the truth" before the "bar of justice"—not even the judge believed the truth, or at least he did not act as though he did. Finally, one Negro opened the gateway to escape from this gross injustice, and all others followed. "Did you reach your hand toward the passenger as he was about to get out of your car?" the judge asked the driver. "I did," replied the driver. "What was the passenger giving you?" asked the judge. "A match," came the reply. The outwitted judge rapped his gavel, "Case dismissed!"

A similar pattern of response was adopted by Negroes who were questioned by their employers concerning their participation in the protest. The Negroes learned early that one type of truthful response meant they no longer had a job, but another, equally as truthful, brought them no harm.

"Say, John," the white customer said to the bootblack as "John" polished his shoes, "Are you having anything to do with this damn boycott?" "No, Cap'n," came the reply as the bootblack continued shining the shoes, not even looking up, "I ain't havin' nothin' to do with boycott, nothin' at all. I jest ain't ridin' no bus."

As the days grew into weeks and the weeks into months, the signs of strain were on every face. The novelty of the protest was over. There were no indications that consideration would be given any of the proposals that had been made. Instead, there were loud, strong statements denouncing our actions and promising that more hardships would be heaped upon us if we continued our rebellious actions.

By this time the tires were well worn on the cars. Many of the family cars had broken down and there were not enough funds to repair them. And, as in the beginning of the movement, all local communication media remained closed to us. We could not even buy space in the local newspaper for a statement to the general public. Not only was "freedom of the press" denied us, but "freedom of speech" as well. When the association contacted the radio and television stations asking to pay for the privilege of making a statement to the nation, the request was denied. To the Negro leaders it seemed that the white man had created a monster of which the white man, himself, was deathly afraid. They believed, as did the great President who said, "There is nothing to fear but fear itself."

The faith of the Negro in the unforeseen and the eternal had brought him through many seemingly impossible situations. This was, therefore, no exception. The word of the struggle did reach the outside world. Not many Negroes in the city asked for an explanation of how this publicity came about, nor did they try to explain the response of people everywhere whose generous contributions swelled the treasury from a few dollars to thousands. Their prayers and hopes were based on the belief that "God would make a way." When the way was opened they thanked God and walked in it.

The funds which came in abundance made possible the enlarging of the car pools, the purchasing of station wagons, the renting of a parking area downtown as a pickup station, the hiring of dispatchers, and the repairing of some of the cars which had been used in the early days of the struggle. This is not to say that these funds brought an end to sacrifice and suffering. Such would be far from the truth. There were many who never rode a car; until the end, they walked. But the contributions which came from so many people in many different places gave all renewed courage. The pain of the criticisms and insults hurled at them by the local whites was completely overcome by the expression of thousands who said by their actions, "We are with you to the end."

The new sense of dignity and worth of the individual conceived by the minority group in this Southern city expressed itself in many ways. The Negroes ceased to think of themselves as mere servants of their employers. They began to see themselves as important contributors to the economic, social, political, and spiritual progress of a great nation. The tremendous loss of revenue by the bus company in Montgomery focused the attention of the Negro upon the large part he played in the economic life of the city. The cooks, maids, and butlers gained new insights into their worth.

The Citizens' Council, in retaliation, recommended the firing of Negro help who refused to ride the buses. When thoughtless whites began to carry out this recommendation, important discoveries were made. The mistresses who turned their help away discovered, to their surprise, when the hour came for them to go to their business or social affairs that there was no one to care for little Betty and Paul; there were a thousand chores to be done about the house but there was no butler nor maid. Some maids, who were fired because they refused to pay for insults and for the privilege of standing over empty seats, found employment, either next door or further down the block in which they had worked for years. It was no surprise to them when they were called by the head of a neighboring family and given employment in the same hour they were fired, with this remark: "I have been watching you for a long time and have wanted so much to have you work for me."

The young and the old alike were spurred on by the desire for freedom. Those who became weak found strength in the determination of others, which expressed itself in the churches where thousands assembled for weekly mass meetings. For hours, the multitude sang the great hymns of the church. A favorite was, "Leaning on the Everlasting Arms." These meetings, to which thousands walked after walking to and from their jobs, served as a source of relief and rejuvenation. Many, whose backs were tired, whose feet were sore and whose legs were aching, went away from the meetings counting themselves fortunate for the opportunity of suffering for the cause of freedom.

One morning a very old lady was seen approaching a bus stop. It was obvious that she was walking with severe difficulty. Her destination was her doctor's office. The hour of her appointment was near. There was not a car belonging to the car pool in sight. A long wait for one to return proved to be in vain. As she started on her way, a bus approached. The dispatchers at the post prevailed upon her to take the bus. "Everyone would understand. We will be happy to explain the circumstances at the mass meeting," they assured her. "We think you are too tired to go on walking." The frail body, heavily taxed by years of hardship, moved slowly away, and to those who were encouraging her to ride the bus, she said, "I'll walk! I'll walk so someday all of God's children can ride in peace. Yes, my body is tired, but my soul is rested!" And she went on her way.

One bus driver told of an experience he had with a group of school children. It was a rainy day, and the weather was cold. Seeing the poorly-clad children walking in the rain and knowing they were not responsible for the boycott was more than he wanted to have on his conscience. Since there were no passengers on the bus, he stopped and invited them aboard, out of the rain. The response the children gave was indicative both of their involvement in the crises and of the inadequacy of their training in the neglected segregated schools. "Us ain't ridin' no bus today," cried one child. "Us boycotting," said another. And turning, they walked proudly on in the rain.

What was it that provoked this uprising and set 50,000 Negroes solidly against the status quo? There is much to be said for "the straw which broke the camel's back." The deprivations and inhuman injustices heaped upon the Afro-Americans in the South for generations had left their mark. The racial group had been so welded together by wholesale injustices that what happened to one happened to all. There had been years and years when Negroes were lynched in Montgomery, one or more at a time. Little had been said about the lynchings and nothing had been done at all. Some Negroes bemoaned the situation, but for the most part nurtured their anxieties and fears in their bosoms. The year 1955 stood in marked contrast to this long-ago period. Somehow people had finally found courage in the midst of adversities. No longer would they be silent. No longer would they fail to act.

Those who hold that the Negro was a coward and afraid to speak out for himself may be able to find some justification for their claim. It is not difficult for the intelligent person to understand that there is not much left when manhood is taken from a man, no matter what his race. Anyone who has been reduced to the status of a slave, bound by the legal and social customs of his society, and brow-beaten and indoctrinated by false ideas of White Supremacy from his infancy does well to stand at all on his feet. But this is not the whole story. For years the Negroes in Montgomery, as elsewhere, had been crying, but their voices had been unheard, except by God, and their tears had not been seen. Many brave souls had dared to stand up against the "beasts of Ephesus," only to be hanged, shot, or driven from the city. But now there were too many to kill, or drive away.

Most of the Negroes recognized their legitimate claim to the rights and privileges accorded the citizens of Alabama, and the city of Montgomery, including access to all public facilities. They knew, from as far back as they could trace their families, that they had split rails, cleared forests, planted and harvested crops, dug ditches, paved roads and built the city. The pay received for their labor hardly provided them with the bare necessities of life. But they had planned well and spent wisely the little they had earned. Many had been on foreign soil defending a nation and a people which had given only lip service to their rights in the democracy they were fighting to preserve. Those who returned brought back with them the desire to be respected for the services they had rendered and the sacrifices they had made. The newspapers, radio, and television brought into the homes of Negroes reports of current happenings from all over the world. The struggles of oppressed peoples for freedom everywhere evoked sympathetic response from companions in tribulation.

One must never underestimate the impact of the historic Supreme Court decision of May 17, 1954 on the Negroes throughout the South. However, history refutes any claim that this date marked the beginning of their struggle. The stony road leading to the decision bears the marks of disappointments, hardships, and setbacks. Legal battles were fought in courts where injustice seemed to triumph. Negro families had had their homes bombed, mortgages foreclosed, and had suffered other types of economic and social pressure, because they dared to demand equal educational opportunity for their children.

In spite of the agony and the heartache, parents in Southern States brought suits, and the legal staff of the N.A.A.C.P. continued to plead the cause of justice, citizenship, and constitutional rights for all Americans regardless of race or creed. The reward for these efforts and sacrifices came when the High Court decreed that separate, as it relates to school and similar institutions, is inherently unequal. The mandate that separation based on race is unconstitutional was the greatest pronouncement the Negro had heard since the Emancipation Proclamation and the Fourteenth Amendment. If the statement made by a doctor is representative of the thinking of others of his group, many southern whites looked with favor upon the decision. Said the doctor, "The Emancipation Proclamation freed the Negro physically; the Supreme Court decision of 1954 freed the white man's conscience. Many of us have never felt that what we have been doing has been right, but we had no good excuse to change."

If this man, and possibly others like him, viewed the Supreme Court decision as an excuse for agreeing to change, more can be said for those who suffered. For the Negro felt that the Court had finally opened a way to the land of freedom and opportunity for which he had longed and fought for some time. He knew that he had reluctantly obeyed state laws and city ordinances which deprived him of his constitutional rights. This, he had been told, is the duty and responsibility of all good citizens. Surely those who had preached obedience to the law should, themselves, be good examples of their preachments. Now that it was made very clear what the law was, would the changes be forthcoming?

It was not long before the intention of southern lawmakers was made unmistakably clear. The only law the white citizens of Alabama would obey was that made on their own Capitol Hill by their own state legislature. And the Negroes had come to realize that the Court would not and could not fight their battles for them. They did understand that they could use the legal arm to help secure the rights the courts said belonged to them.

The court decision outlawing segregation based on race in public education was pregnant with implications for the dawning of a new age and new horizons for people of color in the South. The reactions of the southern whites was a clear demonstration of the fact that they intended no changes, whatsoever, in the *status quo*. They were set on maintaining what they called "our Southern way of life." The Negroes, on the other hand, were definitely looking for change. They were determined to change some of the social patterns of the South. In order that this might be done they would have to develop the courage, the skill, and the understanding to bring about such changes in the patterns which are consistent only in their inconsistencies. For example, movie houses which admit whites only, may be attended by a Negro maid if she is escorting "Mr. Charlie's little Johnny." Negroes with bandannas on their heads and faking a peculiar accent have been admitted to "white-only" places under the disguise of Indians, Arabians, or some other nationality. Anyone, except an American Negro, is permitted to enter.

These social practices on the part of whites are generally thought of as being carry-overs from the days of slavery. Three hundred years would seem long enough for the race which claims superiority to all others to have discovered its grave error. But some have closed their eyes to reality, and have denied the obvious truth: given an equal opportunity, Negroes are capable of standing, head and shoulder, with representatives of any racial group. The Montgomery strugglers accepted the challenge of forcing their oppressors to recognize and respect this truth. A gradual process, yes, but a continuous process as well.

The bus boycott ended officially on December 20, 1956; it was on that date that the Supreme Court's mandate reached Montgomery. On December 21st, 1956, more than a year after Mrs. Rosa Parks' arrest, integrated buses operated for the first time in the history of the city. Even before the bus boycott case had reached the Supreme Court, Negroes were already thinking of other areas to be attacked. The fact that court cases concerning the rights of Negroes had been lost in the past was no deterrent to the determination of the people at this time. They would continue to use the strong arm of federal law to break the yoke of unconstitutional state laws. The dream of a way of life of which the Negroes had had only a taste was adequate to sustain them in their strivings.

The boycott was a decided victory for the people of Montgomery and for the whole of humanity. It was never regarded by the Negroes as a struggle of blacks against whites. Rather it was thought of as a struggle of justice against injustice. Those who possessed faith in humanity and faith in God believed that justice would triumph. Sustained by such a faith and fortified by a visible sign of assurance, the people of color would continue to press their claim for first-class citizenship. Discrimination in city and state-owned parks, playgrounds, swimming pools and golf courses would be attacked with renewed and intensified vigor. All first class citizens participate in state and Federal government. This meant that Negroes would have to demand the right to register and vote. They walked to gain the privilege of riding; by standing in line they would gain their opportunity of registering and voting. And finally, the most glaring of all types of segregation, segregation in Christian worship, could never escape severe criticism and firm attempts to correct the error. The fact that the eleven o'clock hour on Sunday morning is the most segregated hour of the week is of great concern to all who believe in the brotherhood of man.

When the boycott had ended, the next point of attack and the exact procedure to be followed were not specifically known. All only knew that the end of the boycott was the beginning of what was to be. The movement for freedom had gained such momentum that nothing could stop it. Even if the leaders of the movement had to fill an untimely grave, the volcano of social unrest would continue its eruptions, and the lava of love and nonviolent action would continue to force its way into the American conscience.

Edgar N. French, A.B. and B.D. (Livingstone College), M.A. (Columbia University), as an ordained minister of the A.M.E. Zion Church in Montgomery, Ala., helped to organize and served as secretary of the Montgomery Improvement Association, which directed the Montgomery bus boycott. A native of North Carolina, he has held pastorates in his home state and South Carolina and is now serving as college minister and director of guidance and personnel at Livingstone College, Salisbury, N.C. [1962 biography]

The Montgomery Bus Boycott of 1955-1956

THOMAS J. GILLIAM

This paper was originally written as an M. A. thesis in the Department of History at Auburn University in 1968. It has been edited for publication, but is otherwise presented as it was written.

Thomas J. Gilliam is a Research Associate at the Library of the University of West Florida. He received his Ph.D. from Auburn University, with a dissertation entitled, *The Second Folsom Administration: The Destruction of Alabama Liberalism, 1954-1958.*

Contents

Preface 1989

I was very young when I wrote this Thesis, 25, and the year was 1967—with the Vietnam War, the civil rights movement , and the Youth Culture all in full roar. I was a married graduate student with one child and another on the way and about as liberal as you could be and still stay in Alabama. I was a field organizer of an irregular, voluntary sort for the Freedom Democratic Movement and a year later wound up working the back roads for the Humphrey campaign.

My Thesis concerned *two* topics, really: the civil rights movement, which I supported and found fascinating, and raw political organization. What I truly wanted to know was how people got things done out there in the great world. The two "sides" in the Montgomery racial encounter had waged big league politics and I wanted to know how they did it, why one side won and the other lost.

How times have changed since then. The civil rights movement has triumphed and ought to be declared finished and accomplished. So, that means I was associated with a distinct winner. In 1988, like all good Southern conservatives, I supported the Bush campaign—another winner.

Dr. King and many of his friends and foes have gone now, but what a fight they made and how important it was. I was allowed to touch greatness by coming along behind King, tracing his steps through Montgomery, talking to people he talked with. I had an appointment to see him when he should return to Atlanta from Memphis in that awful April of 1968, but instead, with the rest of the world, I watched in horror as he was brought back to be laid to rest. It was impossible to believe that his career had lasted only 12 years.

Tom Gilliam
Cottage Hill, Florida
January, 1989

The Boycott Begins

Montgomery, Alabama, in 1955 appeared outwardly to be different in no significant way from scores of other medium-sized southern cities. Montgomery's population of 120,000, of which about 50,000 were Negroes, derived a living largely from three sources. First, there was the agricultural establishment of the surrounding black-belt region, which traded and sold in the city. A second important economic factor was the payroll of two near-by Air Force bases, Gunter and Maxwell Fields. A third source of support was the presence of the offices of state government. The contributions of these three sectors combined to make Montgomery a prosperous community and a leader in the affairs of central Alabama.

The city took a typical pride in its economic accomplishments, and it also believed itself fortunate in other areas of civic life. At least the white portion of Montgomery's population boasted fondly of the city's heritage as the first capital of the Confederate States. But despite this history, civic boosters also believed that their city offered a particularly successful example of good interracial relations. They pointed out that the incidence of friction between whites and Negroes over the years had been low, and that current relations could be characterized as "gentle, easy, and benign."[1]

This vista of apparent racial harmony gave little or no indication that Montgomery would shortly become the locale for what has been called "the myth event of the new cause" of civil rights.[2] Beyond the tranquility on the surface of things, there was among Negroes a potentially disrupting pattern of grievances and dissatisfactions. These irritants were resented by Negroes for many years, but it was only in the final month of 1955 that a unique combination of events and circumstances operated for the release of Negro feelings about them. The result was an agonizing and fiercely-contested boycott which divided Montgomery's two races for the 382 days of its duration. And compared to former days, when relations between them were "benign," they are divided still.

These several sources of dissatisfactions for Negroes were found in almost every area of daily life. In the economic sphere, for instance, they occupied a demonstrably inferior status to the one enjoyed by whites. The median

197

income for Negroes stood at $970.00, while the figure for whites was $1,730.00.[3] In politics Negroes thought they possessed only a limited franchise. In the whole of Montgomery County only about 1,800 of them were registered to vote.[4]

Disparities such as these, and others like them, seemed to Negroes to be only symptoms of the real problem. The cause of their depressed status could be found in the half-century old system of rigid and extensive racial segregation. If their situation were to be improved this system would have to be removed, or at least made less effective.

This system of segregation was felt in almost every area of social life, including public transportation. Since Montgomery's black people possessed fewer economic resources they were forced to rely heavily on the city's single bus line for everyday transportation. Reflecting this dependence, it was estimated that Negro patronage accounted for about 70% of the revenue of Montgomery City Lines, Inc., the private company which operated buses under a city franchise.[5] It was here that Negroes encountered the indignities of segregation most frequently. For about 17,000 regular Negro patrons, it meant an intimate contact with the system at least twice on every working day.

Segregated seating on buses was enforced by two governments. The city had passed an ordinance on the subject in 1900, while the state had imposed a similar law after devising the new Constitution of 1901. The Montgomery City Code ordered all bus lines in the city to:

> . . . provide equal but separate accommodations for white people and negroes . . . by requiring the employee in charge thereof (on each bus) to assign passengers seats . . . in such a manner as to separate the white people from the Negroes, where there are both whites and negroes on the same car . . .[6]

There was one exception to this charge; Negro nurses caring for white children, or for "sick or infirm white persons" were allowed to sit with their wards in the white sections. The Code also permitted a bus company to enforce segregation by using separate vehicles for each race, if desired.

A companion section to the above gave the bus driver "the power of a police officer of the city" while on duty. Thus, his assignment of seats carried the sanction of law. The ordinance made it illegal for anyone to refuse to obey the driver's assignment to the section reserved for that person's race, "if there is such a seat vacant."[7] This last phrase proved to be a point of sore contention in future months.

The previous Alabama statute on this matter, as codified in 1940, also ordered "equal but separate accommodations." It was a more stringent measure than the Montgomery ordinance, providing for distinct partitions between sections reserved for the two races. These partitions were to be "constructed of metal, wood, strong cloth, or other material."[8]

An amended act was passed in 1947 which did not call for such partitions, but which did order the maintenance of separate sections on buses. The driver was given the power to eject anyone who refused to sit in the proper area for his race. Such refusal to comply was classified as a misdemeanor, subject to a maximum fine of $500.00.[9]

Montgomery City Lines, Inc., as previously mentioned, operated buses under an exclusive franchise granted by the city. This firm had been in Montgomery since 1935, and had gradually worked out a practical system of separation through experience and with the cooperation of the City Commission.[10] There were about fourteen different routes drawn through the city. On several of these segregation was only a minor problem, since in some areas buses were frequented mostly by members of one or the other races. In some sections where Negroes and whites were expected to be present each in substantial numbers, the company often ran a bus marked "special," which signified that it was for Negroes only, again eliminating concern over segregation. However, Montgomery's residential and business sections were so juxtaposed, that some buses had to provide for carrying great numbers of both races.[11]

The most important route serving both races was one which crossed the popular Negro section of Washington Park and South Jackson Street. This route also passed by Alabama State College, a Negro institution, then touched a white residential and commercial section, before entering downtown Montgomery. It was on this run that most attention had to be given to segregation. It was also here that trouble over seating most often developed.[12]

On all other runs, but especially on this one, it was standard policy that at least the first ten seats on the bus be reserved exclusively, and at all times, for whites. There were thirty-six seats to a bus, so this left almost three-fourths of the bus at the potential disposal of Negroes. But, the preserving of the front ten seats for whites was a strict rule. This was accomplished by using the concept of a "line of demarcation," or "dead line," behind which Negroes were obliged to sit. This demarcation line, however, was a shifting one, due to the exigencies of the route. As the bus traveled through areas where the usual proportion of white and black passengers fluctuated, the driver could move the line forward or backward at his discretion. This was done to allow as many people as possible to find a seat. In any event, the last five seats resting against the rear panel of the bus were usually reserved for Negroes.[13]

The demarcation line was indicated by signs. Each row of seats was flanked by a metal pole, extending from floor to roof, which was used for support by standing passengers. Each pole also had a small metal placard attached to it, which could be manipulated by the driver. The placard showed a pointing arrow when exposed. An arrow pointing forward meant that all seats before that point were reserved for whites; one pointing rearward determined the area of Negro seating.[14] These signs, called "race boards" or "race signs," were generally detested by Negroes as the most tangible symbol of bus segregation.[15]

If enough whites boarded a bus to require more than the front ten seats, and if there were vacant seats in the rear of the bus, a driver could "equalize" the situation by requiring some Negroes to move to seats in the rear. It often happened in this situation that some Negroes, accustomed to the system, would voluntarily move to the rear when several whites came on. Sometimes, too, whites came on when all seats were taken; most of the time when this happened the whites simply had to stand in the aisle.[16]

There was little complaint about the cases such as the above. What annoyed Negroes most often was some drivers' practice of shifting the demarcation line rearward if several whites boarded an already-filled bus. When this occurred, Negroes sitting in front of the new location of this theoretical line were ordered to yield their seats to the white newcomers. To comply, the Negroes had to stand while the whites sat.[17] This was especially galling to black people, who felt that this happened an inordinate number of times. Some of them contended that the City Code stipulated that they could only be forced to move if there was a vacant seat for each of them to occupy in place of the one surrendered. They resented, too, the preemptory manner in which they were often told to give up their seats. If the driver was too busy to adjust the metal placard, he might instead call out, "Give me those seats back there!" This seemed to many Negroes simply a gratuitous humiliation added to the inequities of the system.[18]

The bus company was sensitive to the fact that many Negroes were dissatisfied with the theory of segregation, or with the practical aspects of its enforcement. The company realized that to have its best-paying customers forced to stand, while ten forward seats might be empty, was plainly inimical to good public relations. The firm knew it could operate at a profit, albeit a slender one, if its entire white patronage were removed. But the Negro population was an indispensable source of fares. The company definitely wanted to keep their good will.

On the other hand, though, the company had an obligation as the holder of a municipal franchise. It had to carry whites, as well. The local firm was a wholly-owned subsidiary of National City Lines, Inc., which was based in Chicago. The parent company held franchises in more than a dozen Southern cities and had developed a policy of letting each branch line operate in a manner consistent with local custom and preference. The officers of the Montgomery line knew that their existence as a firm depended on the good will of the white establishment. It was obvious that white public opinion demanded some form of segregation.[19]

The bus company, then, was pulled in different directions by two powerful considerations. It thought about at one time the possibility of dropping the ten-reserved-seat rule, as a sister firm in Mobile had done. However, when the subject was considered in detail it was realized that insurmountable difficulties required retention of the rule. For one thing, the routing of buses required at least one vehicle to serve racially contiguous sections. Other cities might escape this difficulty by judicious re-routing, but Montgomery's Negro and white sections were so juxtaposed that it could not be done here. Since both races would be present on buses in large numbers some room must be reserved for whites, as segregation laws required. For that reason the front ten seats were always kept for whites only.[20]

The company tried to lessen Negro objections by making it a policy to give both races a proportionate share of seating on any given bus. It asked drivers to be diplomatic about reassignment of seats. It was pointed out that whites, too, were prevented from occupying seats in the other race's section. The company claimed it had received more complaints over the years from whites who had to give up seats, than from Negroes. Existing seat regulations were believed by the company to be the best practical compromise measures.[21]

Negroes were dissatisfied with two other aspects of bus transportation which contributed to their general frustration. First, they resented the custom of hiring only white bus drivers. There had never been a Negro bus driver in Montgomery. Also, many of them felt that Negroes were frequently subjected to deliberate discourtesies by white drivers. These included the use of abusive language, surly non-cooperation with reasonable requests, and general disregard for the ordinary amenities. It was claimed that every Negro in Montgomery had a friend or relation who had suffered some distasteful experience on a bus.[22]

The bus company was aware of these complaints as well. It could not consider hiring Negro drivers, for reasons which will be dealt with later. But, it did ask drivers to guard against rude behavior to customers.[23]

There had been no concerted effort by Negroes to remedy this situation. Complaints had been lodged in the past by people involved in particular incidents, but no real attempt had been made to apply for redress by the Negro community as a whole, or by even a significant part of it. This was partly attributable to the concentration by Negro leadership on other problems. Then, too, there was a certain amount of division within the ranks of this leadership.

The extent of this division of leadership is difficult to gauge. Martin Luther King, Jr., later stated that there was a serious split among them when he had first come to Montgomery in 1954. He declined to describe the nature of the division, or to explain its origins. He believed, though, that the split was manifested by the large number of separate Negro groups operating in the community, all of which maintained exclusive programs for progress in civil rights. Other leaders, however, including some active on the scene for many more years than King, did not believe there was any deep or irrevocable division over personalities or methods. They saw the situation as simply a negative one in which there was considerable apathy toward any pooling of energies in a single, unified campaign. They point out that there had been no incident or cause for all groups to rally to, in the past. Cogent proof of this argument is the rapidity with which those groups united in December, 1955, once a sufficiently important incident offered itself.[24]

The failure of Negroes to combine in a single cause previously was not due to any want of ability or experience among the leaders of 1955. Whereas, in years past black people justly complained that their own leaders were usually subservient to, or even in the employ of, white interests, the leadership of the nineteen fifties was characterized as sober, straight-forward, and honest.[25]

Among the foremost of these was Edgar Daniel Nixon, known to the community as "E. D." Tall and gregarious, Nixon was a personable man who worked as a porter for the Pullman Company. He was president of that group. He had worked with Asa Philip Randolph in the nineteen forties and had been associated with the projected march on Washington at that time. He was also influential in the local and state-wide leadership of the National Association for the Advancement of Colored People, having been Alabama president a few years before. In 1955 he was chairman for the local branch's redress committee.

Nixon was deeply interested, too, in politics. In 1954 he made an unsuccessful bid for election to the Montgomery County Democratic Party Committee. Despite his failure in that attempt he was chairman of the Democratic Progressive Association, the Negro branch of the party in Montgomery. Also in 1954 he had tried to attend the party's Jefferson-Jackson Day Dinner, but had been refused. In the ensuing controversy Governor G. Mennen Williams of Michigan cancelled a speaking engagement at the affair in protest of Nixon's exclusion.[26] As a result of these many and varied interests, Nixon enjoyed the support and esteem of the masses of local Negroes.

Another powerful member of the black leadership group was Rufus A. Lewis, a successful businessman who held interests in a mortuary, a supper club, and other local properties. He was also known as the former football coach at Alabama State College, who was remembered for having led that team to its first victory over arch-rival Tuskegee Institute in 1934. Like Nixon, Lewis was influential in the NAACP, and gave much energy to problems of Negro voter registration. By helping to conduct voter clinics and by advocating the NAACP's legalistic approach to the attack on segregation, he received much support from professional and commercial classes in Montgomery.[27]

Several other persons, most of them young people, had also come into prominence locally. Mrs. Jo Ann Robinson, for example, worked with Lewis on voter education projects. She was a teacher at Alabama State, and was president of a powerful women's organization. She was able and intelligent, and deeply concerned with civil rights.[28] Ralph Abernathy, young pastor of the Negro First Baptist Church, largest in the community, had gained a favorable reputation through church work and by his work with the NAACP.[29] Another young leader was Fred David Gray, a tall and boyish-looking native of Montgomery. Gray had attended Alabama State College and Western Reserve University, and in June, 1954 received a law degree from Franklin Thomas Backus School of Law. He was one of two Negroes at the local bar, and was also a part time minister of the Holt Street Church of Christ. He was counsel for the local NAACP, and had great zeal for civil rights work.[30]

Added to the list of rising young leaders was the pastor of the Dexter Avenue Baptist Church. Dr. Martin Luther King, Jr., had come to Montgomery from Atlanta in September, 1954. As the holder of a doctorate from Boston University and a pastor of the most "fashionable" Negro church, whose congregation was largely composed of faculty members from Alabama State, King was soon a prominent man. He rapidly augmented his reputation by taking part in several campaigns for Negro progress, through his church, the NAACP, and other organizations. His keen intelligence and ability to speak well in public impressed the Negro community considerably.[31]

All of these leaders played conspicuous roles in the formation and guidance of the boycott. Their combination of talent and experience had a great deal to do with its ultimate success. But there were other less tangible factors which contributed to that success. An undertaking such as these people shouldered in 1955 might well have been impossible to achieve in an earlier decade. It was necessary for two developing currents to influence national life, before such a crusade would have succeeded.

The first of these necessary developments was the maturing of the Negro's own consciousness and understanding of his ability to gain acceptance of his demands through mass action. Also, if there could not be on the local level, there had to be nationally a favorable climate of attitude and opinion surrounding the topic of civil rights. Without the sustenance of a host of sympathetic whites, the Montgomery bus boycott could not have succeeded.

Any search for the causes behind this comparatively new favorable temper must take into account the importance of a number of supporting decisions by the Federal Courts. Whether in advance of the predominant national mood, or simply reflecting it, these courts considerably eased the task of acquiring civil equality for Negroes. The action of the Supreme Court of the United States was especially important in this respect. In at least a dozen cases between 1938 and 1955 that body whittled away the legality of the separate-but-equal doctrine, as embodied in earlier decisions. In *Morgan vs. Virginia* (328 U.S. 372), for example, the court struck down segregated seating on interstate buses in 1946. The importance of *Brown vs Board of Education* (347 U.S. 483) in 1954, as another example, does not need retelling. Only a month before the boycott in Montgomery began, in

November of 1955, the high court invalidated segregation in public parks and playgrounds, and in similar facilities.[32]

The rapidity with which units of the segregation system were falling was impressive. Shortly after the boycott began a United States Court of Appeals ordered the University of Alabama to admit Negroes to its classes.[33]

The effect of these rulings on the determination of Negroes to attack all forms of segregation is patent. One observer has said that, "What this released in the hearts and minds of Negroes began to express itself in Montgomery in December of 1955."[34] One of those prominent in the boycott assessed the impact of a "friendly" court by explaining that before the 1954 decision his people had been sure of "getting justice" only in the after-life; now the courts had shown them it was to be had on earth.[35]

The method of attacking bus segregation in Montgomery which was finally adopted had two sides to it. Negroes waged a boycott of buses and simultaneously pursued redress through the court. The tactic of going through the courts had been employed in civil rights cases with effectiveness before, but the idea of a boycott was less traditional.

Although the Negro leadership in Montgomery was apparently unaware of it, their predecessors had tried the boycott method in 1900, to no avail. This boycott was undertaken in response to the city's first segregation ordinance for public carriers, and evidently was spontaneous in nature. It was urged on Negro citizens by ministers, as it would be again half a century later but the 1900 boycott lacked a central organization to guide it, and ultimately faded out.[36]

More recently Negroes had used the bus boycott elsewhere, with limited success. Most notable were those in Harlem in 1941 and in Baton Rouge in 1953. In the latter case the city gave Negroes the use of vacant front seats, only to have the Louisiana Attorney General strike down the ordinance involved. Baton Rouge Negroes boycotted in retaliation, achieving almost 90% cooperation from their race for a while, although their efforts were unsuccessful.[37] In that same year Negroes in Memphis threatened to invoke a boycott in protest of alleged mistreatment by drivers, but this did not materialize.[38]

The decision to wage a boycott in Montgomery, then, was not the result of an original idea. Nor did the protest spring full-grown into being in December of 1955, when it ultimately began.

Some Negro leaders occasionally advocated some form of protest against bus segregation prior to that time. E. D. Nixon, in particular had been watching for the proper persons or incident, around which a protest could be built, for a year before.[39]

There were several incidents in 1955 that caused discussion of protest. In early March of that year a Negro teenager, Claudette Colvin, was ordered to give up her seat on a bus to a white person. When she refused, police were summoned and she was dragged off the bus "kicking and clawing." She was charged with violating the segregation ordinance, disorderly conduct, and assault and battery.[40] Many in the black community sympathized with this girl's outburst, and thought she had been treated too harshly. Nixon discussed the matter with J. E. Pierce, a well-known figure at Alabama State. The possibility of a boycott as a suitable mode of protest was alluded to, but no definite decision was made. Nixon arranged an interview with Miss Colvin and talked with her family. He decided, however, that she was not the sort of person who could best withstand the pressures sure to be exerted on any central figure in a protest, and left the matter alone.[41]

Rev. King, Mrs. Robinson, and Pierce, however, decided that nothing would be lost if an ad hoc committee were formed to discuss grievances with local officials. They were hopeful that some concessions might stem from the Colvin case. They were joined in this by Mrs. Rosa Parks, secretary to the local chapter of the NAACP. This group met with J. H. Bagley, manager of the bus company, and David Birmingham, the police commissioner. Although the talks were cordial nothing substantial came out of the them.[42]

In the next few months there were two similar arrests for violating the segregation ordinance. But, in neither case was sufficient interest aroused to spark a protest.

The occasion finally offered itself on Thursday, December 1, 1955. On that afternoon a bus was traveling through the downtown section with twelve whites and twenty-six Negroes seated. Several persons of each race were standing. At a stop by the Empire Theater several more whites boarded. The driver ordered four Negroes sitting in the row of seats immediately behind those occupied by whites to move to the rear. In effect he was ordering these four to stand, since no vacant seats were available. Three of the Negroes complied, but the fourth, Mrs. Rosa Parks, declined.[43]

Despite allegations made later by some whites that Mrs. Parks' refusal was planned in advance to deliberately provoke the protest it is evident that she made her decision on the spot. She later stated that she was tired after a hard day's work, and that to move would have been too inconvenient. But, admittedly, there was more prompting her refusal than sore feet. As she said,

"There had to be a stopping place, and this seemed to have been the place for me to stop being pushed around, and to find out what human rights I had, if any . . ."[44]

Mrs. Parks was taken to jail on a warrant signed by the bus driver. She was charged with violating the city's segregation ordinance.[45]

Shortly after her arrest someone at the jail telephoned E. D. Nixon. He was not available at the time, but soon returned the call to verify the message. He learned that Mrs. Parks was, indeed, being held, but he could not ascertain the charge against her. Nixon then called Clifford Durr, brother-in-law of Supreme Court Justice Hugo Black, and prominent local lawyer, who had been a member of the Federal Communications Commission. Nixon asked Durr to look into the matter and find out the charge against Mrs. Parks. Durr did so, and went with Nixon to the jail. Nixon posted bond of $100.00 for Mrs. Parks, then drove her home.[46]

Nixon was excited over the incident, for he had already realized that her arrest would make an excellent rallying-point for a protest. Mrs. Parks was very well-known among Negroes and was regarded as a sober and modest woman of impeccable reputation. Also, she was engaged in civil rights work, and had been in the NAACP for 15 years. Nixon discussed the subject with her and urged her to let him use her name in calling for a protest. This was surely, he said, the opportunity both had been seeking "to crack the situation that exists on the buses.""[47] Mrs. Parks agreed to this readily, and gave permission.[48]

Nixon returned home and mulled over the problem. He decided that only a boycott would entail enough dramatic demonstration to show the white community that the Negroes "meant business." All that remained was to enlist the support of the right people, whose endorsement would appeal strongly to the masses. He spent the rest of the night drawing up a list of these names.[49]

Nixon began telephoning these people early the next morning, which was Friday, December 2. His first call went to Ralph Abernathy, who immediately agreed to help. Rev. H. H. Hubbard was the second to consent. The third call produced the first hesitation; Rev. King wanted time to think the proposal over and asked to be called back later.[50] Others hesitated at first, as well. Nixon asked J. E. Pierce to contact all faculty members at Alabama State and to use his influence in securing their help. Pierce declined, because he felt that the Negro masses would not support even the one-day boycott that Nixon was proposing. But, later in the day, when Nixon's idea was gaining widespread acceptance, Pierce and King both agreed to participate.[51]

Nixon's call was first news of the arrest for many, who had not seen the item about it in the morning paper. The first reaction for most of these, on hearing the news, was indignation. Most responded quickly to his suggestion. For others who did know of the arrest, Nixon's appeal was simply a catalyst for their own inclinations.[52]

As the morning progressed others helped Nixon spread word of the arrest and projected boycott. Attention soon turned to the practical considerations of organizing for the project. Nixon, Abernathy, and King decided that there should be a meeting later in the day, where lay and clerical leaders could confer to work out details. King and Abernathy approached Hubbard, who was also president of the Baptist Ministerial Alliance, and got his consent to notify all of their follow Baptist preachers at an Alliance meeting set for that afternoon. Abernathy also went to a gathering of Methodist ministers and invited them as a group to come to an organization meeting.[53]

Nixon, meanwhile, called Jo Ann Robinson and Mrs. A. W. West, another woman active in various clubs. He asked them to enlist the help of their colleagues in women's clubs. They agreed, and calling in a third club-woman, agreed to get word to most of their members. More important, they took the initiative for broadcasting news of the boycott to the city at large. They mimeographed a number of unsigned pamphlets, which were distributed door-to door in the Negro residential areas.[54] The message printed on the circular was simple and direct:

> Another Negro has been arrested and thrown into jail because she refused to get up out of her seat on the bus and give it to a white person . . . This must be stopped. Negroes are citizens and have rights . . . This woman's case will come up Monday. We are, therefore asking every Negro to stay off the buses on Monday in protest of the arrest and trial. Don't ride the buses to work, to town, to school or anywhere on Monday.[55]

Later that evening, the meeting arranged by Nixon, King and Abernathy was convened at King's church. Almost fifty men were present, representing the ministerial groups, professional men, and businessmen. Nixon was not in attendance, since he had been scheduled to make his regular run as a porter for the railroad. Before he left that afternoon, he had asked that no permanent organization or officers be established until his return. Informally then, when time came for the meeting to begin, it was agreed that L. Roy

Bennett should preside over the discussion. Rev. Bennett was the president of the Interdenominational Ministerial Alliance, which included all Negro pastors, and was a respected figure. However, he proved to be inept at handling the assignment, and his arbitrary presiding provoked at least one man into leaving the meeting in disgust.[56] This experience would be recalled later by others, when it became necessary to choose a permanent leader for the Montgomery Improvement Association.

After Bennett was persuaded to step aside, discussion got underway. After some debate those present reached agreement on four important articles. First, it was decided that the boycott should be encouraged, and that for the time-being it should be designed to last only one day. Next, there should be a mass meeting of all Negroes on Monday night, following the boycott, to sample the sentiment of the masses about continuing the protest. Third, it was decided to print more pamphlets to ensure that everyone heard the proposals. Finally, in order to facilitate the necessary movement of Negroes to work and elsewhere on Monday, it was agreed that all Negro taxi companies would be asked provide cheap transportation for that day.[57]

To implement these decisions, A. W. Wilson offered the Holt Street Baptist Church, of which he was pastor, as the site for the mass meeting. Rev. W. J. Powell undertook to approach the cab companies. By Saturday night he had arranged for over two hundred individual vehicles to offer rides on Monday for ten cents per person. Rev. King headed a group which drew up the new circular, which was only different from the one already distributed by carrying word of the mass meeting. King arranged for the secretary of his church to mimeograph 7,000 of these by the next morning.[58]

After these things had been done, there was little to be done on Saturday, except to see that the leaflets were broadcast.

On Sunday morning one further effort was made to encourage support of the boycott. As had been agreed on via telephone and at the meeting Friday night, the majority of Negro ministers went before their congregations to urge cooperation. One white minister also joined the call. This was Rev. Robert Graetz, who was pastor of the all-Negro Trinity Lutheran Church, and who was active in civil rights work. His appeal to his parishioners was probably typical of others in the Negro community on that day. He told his listeners that he would be busy on Monday giving rides to boycotters. He hoped members of his church would follow his example. He warned, too, of the need for unity: "Let's try to make this boycott as effective as possible, because it won't be any boycott if half of us ride the buses and half don't ride. If we're going do it, let's make a good job of it."[59]

Despite the hopes of some Negroes that the coming boycott could be kept secret from whites, many had already learned of what was planned. An afternoon newspaper, the *Alabama Journal*, published a brief article about distribution of circulars on Saturday.[60] The *Montgomery Advertiser* featured the story on the front page of its Sunday morning edition. The *Advertiser* told of the scheduled mass meeting, but could learn little else of importance. It surmised that the protest was being instigated by leaders who had been "long prominent" in campaigns for voter registration. It also indicated its disapproval of the boycott method by describing it as "modelled along the lines of the White Citizens Council program."[61]

White officials were alerted on Saturday. J. H. Bagley, manager of the bus company, received a call from a housewife whose maid had given her a copy of the circular. Bagley went to the woman's house to get the pamphlet. After notifying Jack Crenshaw, the firm's attorney, Bagley called Clyde Sellers and told him of the contents. Sellers was the newly-elected member of the City Commission who had charge of the police department. He had replaced Dave Birmingham, who had talked to the Negro delegation concerned with the Colvin case.[62]

Sellers' first reaction to the news was unfavorable. He feared that Monday's event might lead to violence. He therefore called his chief of police, G. J. Ruppenthal, and ordered him to alert the force for possible trouble. Sellers also conferred with the other two commissioners, Mayor W. A. Gayle, and Franklin Parks, public works commissioner. They decided that the situation did not warrant any immediate official action on the city's part, at least for the time being. They decided to await further developments.[63]

By Sunday afternoon almost all of Montgomery's inhabitants had been informed as a result of the wide coverage given to the story by the press, radio, and television. Sellers appeared on television that afternoon with a disturbing announcement. He stated that officials had learned that several Negroes had been threatened with physical violence unless they cooperated with the boycott. He said these threats came from "goon squads" of other Negroes, who were determined to force acceptance of their will on their fellows. To counter this threat he had ordered motorcycle police to follow each bus that entered a Negro section on Monday. Patrolmen would also watch all bus stops closely, to allow anyone to ride, who wanted to.[64] This was the first charge that Negroes were willing to resort to violence to accomplish their ends. It would be repeated persistently for the next year.

Despite Sellers' charge, Negro leaders felt that his appearance had been of positive benefit to their project. His warning, along with the heavy attention devoted to the boycott by news media, had allayed one of their apprehensions. They were certain now that everyone in the black community who could possibly be reached had heard of the boycott. They believed that the whites had unwittingly aided their cause in this respect. As one leader commented, "All this, I would say, gave us about $10,000 worth of publicity."[65]

Both sides now awaited the decision of the mass of Negroes, who alone could say what would happen.

Monday, December 5, dawned clear, but with a "crisp and biting wind." At 5:30 A.M. the first bus pulled into Court Square in downtown Montgomery, to begin the day's run. At the first stop the driver noticed a crude sign attached to the wall of an empty shed, which normally was filled with Negroes waiting for buses. The sign read "Remember it is for our cause that you do not ride the bus today." No one boarded the first bus.[66]

Instead, Negroes clustered on street corners, waiting for rides from passing automobiles. Others jammed into the already overcrowded Negro cabs. Many others walked to work. Traffic was also especially heavy that morning, due to the numbers of whites going to pick up their Negro employees, mostly domestic workers. Montgomery motorcycle police went on duty at 6:30 A.M., and two of them followed each bus headed for a Negro section.

By mid-morning less than a dozen Negroes had been seen riding buses in the downtown area.[67] The response of the masses surpassed the expectations of their leaders. Some had been pessimistic about chances for success, but even those who had been optimistic were surprised at the magnitude of cooperation. Rev. King and others had decided that if 60% of the Negroes refrained from riding that day, then they could claim a victory. [68] The actual total was about 90%, according to bus company receipts. It was observed that most of those Negroes who did ride the buses were elderly.[69]

The majority of Negroes responded as they did for an uncomplicated reason. As one of them replied when asked later why she joined the boycott, "I stopped riding because I wanted better treatment. I knew if I would cooperate with my color I would finally get it."[70]

The Negro press echoed the jubilation and surprise felt by the leaders. They also shared the belief that victory was in sight if the protest could be

211

sustained. As one journalist wrote: "The thing that strikes this writer more than anything else is how the colored people cooperated . . . One thing I can say is the people of this capital city have made up their minds to stay together, and in a big way the other race is worried about it."[71]

TWO

Organization of the Montgomery Improvement Association

By mid-morning of December 5 it was evident that the boycott of buses was extremely successful, at least as a one-day proposition. Montgomery was at the time a place of mixed feelings about the day's event, of course, as news of what the Negroes were doing swept across town by radio, television, and from person to person.

There was much confusion in certain places as might be expected. J. H. Bagley was keeping close watch or the situation from his position at the bus company, and was very worried. He might have reflected that, only a few days before his major concern had been about the possibility of a strike by drivers if pending negotiations with their union were not concluded satisfactorily. That cloud still hung over his head, but now his firm was menaced from another direction, and in a way that might be fatal.[1] His office was swamped with calls from whites, who complained that they were without domestic help because buses were not stopping to take on Negroes. Bagley could only assure them of the contrary and charge that Negroes were spreading that rumor for their own ends.[2]

Another disturbing rumor was current in Negro quarters, to the effect that motorcycle police following each bus were really supposed to prevent Negroes from riding, not to encourage them. Apparently, many black people believed this, and it is credited with helping to make the protest effective.[3] While Bagley was busy trying to counter this rumor he received some ironic news. An assistant, whose function was to make periodic spot checks on the efficiency and courtesy of the lines's 74 drivers, made his regular report. It was the best such report in years, and every driver passed the test handily.[4]

At 9 A.M. that morning the focus of attention shifted to the City Recorder's Court, where Rosa Parks went on trial before Judge John Scott.

The courtroom and the halls and steps of the building were crowded with several hundred Negroes, who had come to witness her trial. Fred Gray stood as counsel for her, assisted by Charles Langford, another local Negro lawyer who was to play a significant role in the boycott.

As the trial opened Eugene Loe, City Prosecutor, asked for an amendment to the complaint against Mrs. Parks. He wanted her violation to be charged against the pertinent state law, rather than as a branch of the city ordinance.[5] This could possibly result in a fine of $500.00. Fred Gray objected to this, asserting that the state law didn't apply in this case and denying the usefulness of an amended charge. Judge Scott sustained Loe's motion. The City took testimony from only three of the eleven witnesses it summoned since the evidence against Mrs. Parks was patent. She was found guilty under the state segregation law, and fined $10.00, and assessed $4.00 in costs.[6]

After the verdict Gray announced his intention to appeal the case to the Montgomery Circuit Court. E. D. Nixon came forward to sign the appeal bond. Gray revealed nothing else of his plan for the case but the idea quickly took hold among the press and court officials that this would be the first stop in a series of appeals, leading to the United States Supreme Court. It was widely believed that Gray was planning to mount an attack against the entire concept of bus segregation.[7]

This was, in fact, what Gray had in mind. He was determined to exhaust every avenue of approach in the case, until the statutes and ordinances were voided. He believed that the Parks case was the vehicle to use, but later events were to force a change in his strategy.[8]

After the trial was concluded Nixon returned to the NAACP office. Ralph Abernathy and E. N. French, pastor of the A.M.E. Hilliard church, accompanied him. They fell into a discussion of the day's events and the boycott in general. They agreed that the boycott could probably be continued with success, as the high degree of cooperation among Negroes had shown that day. They also agreed that it should be carried on, at least until white officials conceded a list of demands satisfactory to the black community. They thought that any such list of demands must include settlement on three basic points: the problem of segregated seating; courteous treatment for Negro passengers; the hiring of Negro drivers. Further, they thought it advisable that a new organization should be constructed to sponsor and guide the protest until these aims were achieved.[9]

Other leaders in the black community were holding similar discussions. Rufus Lewis, for example, was talking with a group of his friends at the same time. They, too, wanted the boycott to continue, and thought it best that a new organization lead it.[10] This consensus on the need for a fresh sponsoring committee was based on an apprehension about white reaction to the boycott. As has been shown, almost all of Montgomery's Negro leaders were members of the NAACP; this group was, of course, the most active one in the area of civil rights. Nevertheless, it was judged that to operate the protest under NAACP auspices might be a serious mistake. To use that organization in such a capacity was to invite the immediate attention and disapprobation of the white community. Alabama whites detested the NAACP, and at the first raising of its standard in the boycott, were sure to savagely denounce its participation.

Another consideration prompted this decision for a new organization. There was an effort abroad in Alabama to attack the NAACP in the state courts. Negro leaders reasoned that if the organization were enjoined from conducting civil rights operations while it was leading the boycott, the result might be fatal to the protest. Those fears were justified, as it turned out. June 1, 1956, in the heat of the boycott, Judge Walter B. Jones of Montgomery Circuit Court issued just such an injunction and temporarily, at least, prohibited the NAACP from working in Alabama.[11]

There were other practical reasons for setting up a new guiding agency. It was hoped that such a device would have tactical benefits such as for a while confusing white officials about the identity of protest leaders, allowing the movement to "get on its feet." Certainly, too, a local group would be looked on a bit more favorably than would outsiders. Also, local leaders thought they could do a better job if unencumbered by outside control. Finally, they knew they could still solicit aid from the NAACP and other groups, no matter who controlled the boycott. The NAACP would not be so jealous or vindictive as to withhold aid, even if it were excluded from the protest.[12]

Having decided the question, all that was needed was an occasion for the leaders to get together and organize the new agency. Rev. L. Roy Bennett provided this. In his capacity as head of the Interdenominational Ministerial Alliance and as presiding officer at the meeting on Friday night, he asked the leaders to gather on Monday afternoon. This meeting was to set up plans for the large mass meeting scheduled for that night.[13]

About sixteen men responded to the call, and met in the pastor's study of the Mount Zion A. M. E. Church at 3:00 that afternoon. Their first move was to organize themselves into a committee to guide the protest.[14] Ralph Abernathy suggested a name for the group and thereafter they were styled "The Montgomery Improvement Association."

The members turned to election of officers, beginning with the post of president. The experience with Bennett's inept handling of the meeting of three days before pointed up the need for a president who could conduct the meetings with efficiency and tranquility, and who could competently work within the organization. The right man would be one who was friendly with the various groupings represented in the MIA, and acceptable to Nixon, Lewis, and other prominent leaders. The president should also be someone who could act as a liaison officer with the Negro masses explaining the MIA's requests and positions. The president, therefore, should be a man with a gift for public speaking, who had the confidence of the Negro public.[15]

Nixon, French and Abernathy had given thought to the right man for the job in their discussion earlier in the day. Nixon had decided not to seek the position, as he informed the other two, because of the consequent interference with his other activities. Furthermore, having observed Rev. King at various NAACP functions, he knew that the younger man was a magnificent public speaker. He thought that King would make a superior leader, and asked his friends to support him in his choice.[16]

Rufus Lewis, too, had decided that King was the best man for the office. He was a member of King's church, and greatly admired his pastor, both for his religious work and for his activities with the NAACP, and other groups. Also, Lewis feared that other individuals might try to gain control of the nascent organization to serve their own purposes and ambitions. He believed that Rev. King was completely disinterested in that respect. Therefore, before the meeting he asked his friends to vote for King.[17]

When nominations were opened for the post of president, Lewis immediately brought forward King's name. This was seconded, and very quickly approved by a unanimous vote. King stated later that the voting was accomplished so suddenly that he had little time to weigh the merits of the offer. He believes that, if he had reflected sufficiently, he would have declined the honor due to his other responsibilities. However, the spontaneity of the voting prompted him to accept, and he did so.[18]

The other officers were elected next. Rev. Bennett was made vice president; E. N. French became corresponding secretary; Nixon was given the treasurer's past; in a choice that was to be regretted later, a young, goateed minister, U. J. Fields, was made recording secretary; Erna Dungee, a secretary at the Mount Zion Church, was made financial secretary. It was next moved that nine other people, not present at the meeting, would be invited to join the MIA (as they later did). These twenty-five people, including the nine mentioned above, were to be designated together as the "executive board" of the MIA.[19]

After the work of organization was completed, the group turned its attention to the boycott. The first issue discussed was indefinite extension of the boycott, and there was some debate about this. It was pointed out that as a result of the one-day boycott they now had a tangible success that could be used as a bargaining lever in talks with whites. An attempt to carry on the protest might fail, thereby dissipating the value of what had already been attained.

However, the majority of the MIA argued in favor of prolongation. Many of them had felt from the start that more than a one-day affair would be necessary to get redress of their complaints. Moreover, their reading of the temper of the Negro people, as evinced by that day's action, convinced them that a continued effort could be sustained. And, if successful, that would allow the MIA to exert much more pressure on white officials. Therefore, when the question was polled, it was readily decided that they would ask the Negro public to continue the protest. This would be done at the mass meeting that night.[20]

To implement this decision, a resolutions committee was formed, charged with preparing a consonant document for presentation that night. This committee consisted of four ministers, King, Abernathy, R. J. Glasco, and A. W. Wilson, and the two lawyers, Gray and Langford.[21]

In discussing the idea of a formal resolution earlier, someone had suggested to the executive board that secrecy was necessary. It was asked that the MIA's recommendations be mimeographed, and handed out to the assembled crowd in silence, with no discussion of the subject allowed. This would keep the whites in the dark as to the MIA's plans. Another virtue of the idea was that it would protect the leaders from criticism by whites.[22] E. D. Nixon spoke out vehemently against any such surreptitious approach, arguing that subterfuges were ultimately of no real use. Further, this was no time to appear before the community as cowards. That attitude would jeopardize their effectiveness, and was intrinsically wrong anyway. He demanded that their resolutions and policies be offered in straight forward fashion. This stinging rebuke was convincing, and the motion was carried.[23]

As the resolutions committee worked on the document, it reached agreement on several matters. The three proposals discussed by Nixon, French, and Abernathy were approved as the basis for MIA demands. These proposals, pertaining to seating, courtesy, and hiring of Negroes, seemed reasonable and just and were thought to be items which whites would consent to.

The members of the MIA were certain that eventually they could have bus segregation declared unconstitutional by the Supreme Court. However, it was obvious that the necessary court battles and legal preparations would take time to conduct. In the meantime, it was just as obvious that it would be futile to demand integrated seating from local whites. But, to complicate things, it was also certain that the spirit of dissatisfaction rampant among Montgomery Negroes would prevent any return to the old, hated seating pattern. Therefore, if Negroes were to go back to the buses, the MIA would have to get whites to agree on some third, and intermediate, form of seating. As much as they despised segregation, this intermediate form would probably have to embody some aspects of the old way.[24]

The seating plan that they approved was one already used in several other Southern cities. It was called the "first-come-first served" arrangement. Under it, Negroes took seats in the rear of the bus and filled toward the front. Whites, conversely, sat in the front and filled toward the rear. Where the spaces occupied by the two races met was the location of the demarcation line. If all seats were taken when whites boarded the new comers would simply have to stand. No person could be compelled to yield his seat to another.[25]

This proposal, along with the call for courtesy toward Negroes and the hiring of drivers, went into the finished resolution. This paper asked whites and Negroes both to "refrain from riding buses until some arrangement has been worked out," with the bus company. Rufus Lewis had pointed out to the group that there was an urgent need for substitute transportation for the bulk of Negroes. Agreeing with him, the committee called for cooperation on this. All Negroes who owned automobiles were asked to give rides to others at no cost. White Negro employers were requested to see that their workers got transportation to their jobs, if they lived an excessive distance from the business.

Another section in the document also dealt with negotiation. The MIA pledged its willingness to send a delegation to meet with the bus company and city officials under reasonable conditions.

In an epilogue the committee attached to the document an avowal of non-violence, which read:

> Be it further resolved that we have not, are not, and have no intention of using any unlawful means or any intimidation to persuade persons not to ride the Montgomery City Lines buses. However, we call upon your conscience, both moral and spiritual, to give your whole-hearted support to this undertaking.[26]

In this way the MIA repudiated charges of "goon-squadism," which had been lodged by Police Commissioner Sellers, and others.

It was decided by the committee that Ralph Abernathy, who was most responsible for the resolution's final form, should present it for approval to the mass meeting.[27]

When the MIA set its approval of this document, it immediately came into legal jeopardy. In October of 1921 Alabama's governor, Thomas E. Kilby, had asked the state legislature for a law designed to prevent the recurrence of labor strife, such as had occurred in Birmingham two years before during strikes against coal and steel interests. Kilby believed that existing laws were not strong enough and wanted a sterner measure. The legislature responded by passing such a law which was not limited in application only to labor unions.[28] The law forbade "two or more persons" to enter into a "combination, conspiracy, agreement, arrangement, or undertaking," which was aimed at "hindering, delaying, or preventing" the operation of any lawful business, without a just cause. This act also prohibited the printing of any material to be used to support a boycott. Anyone violating the provisions of the law was subject to a maximum fine of $1,000.00 and six months in jail.[29]

A following section of this law had also prohibited union picketing. But, this part was struck down by the United States Supreme Court in 1940 in the case of *Thornhill vs. Alabama* (310 U.S. 514). Although there were some doubts as to whether the other anti-boycott sections would stand up in Federal Courts, the MIA was wary of prosecution under the act "right from the start." Accordingly, the leaders practiced caution when advocating continuance of the boycott. For example, in the resolution the word "boycott" was not mentioned. Among themselves and in public MIA leaders purposely used the designation "protest," and avoided the other whenever possible.[30] Interestingly, portions of the Negro press followed this practice, as well, at least for several weeks. They struggled along with several awkward euphemisms, including: "stay-off-the-bus campaign; "stop-riding-the-buses protest; "riders' strike; a "refuse-to-ride." Usually, though, they too simply referred to "the protest."[31]

Before adjourning, the organizational meeting of the MIA transacted further business. A transportation committee was suggested, to coordinate the unorganized efforts of individual Negroes along this line. Jo Ann Robinson nominated Rufus Lewis for the chairmanship of this group, since he had earlier shown an interest in the problem. His nomination was approved, and R. J. Glasco and W. J. Powell joined him as assistants. A finance committee was also chosen to help Nixon in his task as treasurer. Finally, the agenda for that night's mass meeting was worked out.[32]

By 7:00 that evening the Holt Street Baptist Church, site of the meeting, was completely filled. Besides the hundreds of people packed inside the building, a larger crew, estimated at from 3,000 to 7,000 Negroes, milled around in the street and sidewalk outside. Delegations were seen from other Alabama towns, including Mobile, Birmingham, and Tuscaloosa. Word of the meeting had evidently spread far and wide. Also among the crowd inside the church were four Negro policemen, sent as observers by Clyde Sellers. About half a dozen white reporters and cameramen were present. The turnout was so great that MIA leaders encountered a small traffic-jam outside, and were unable to get the meeting underway until 7:30.[33]

As the crowd finished singing "Onward Christian Soldiers," the first speaker, A. W. Alford, stepped forward to lead them in prayer.[34] It might be stated that, at this point, the MIA took control of the boycott. It simply assumed leadership in the face of an organizational vacuum. There was no conscious debate over the rectitude of calling or managing the mass meeting. The mass of Negroes were waiting to be led, and the MIA obliged them. A Negro journalist unconsciously recorded this coup when he described the opening of the meeting "The presiding officer merely assumed his position and the program went off."[35]

The prayer was followed by a scripture reading, then by an address from Rev. King, in his capacity as president of the MIA. He reviewed for the audience the events and grievances which led to the reaction over Mrs. Parks' arrest. He reminded them of the seemingly anomalous seating regulations on buses, and promised them that the MIA would employ "the tools of justice" to get these changed.[36]

Speaking in more general terms King sought to impress the crowd with the importance of non-violence in the campaign. His convictions on that point, gained after a long study of the principles and methods of Thoreau and Gandhi, were illustrated by examples from the life of Christ. He closed his speech by quoting Booker T. Washington's famous admonition, "Let no man pull you so low as to make you hate him," asking the crowd to love their white brothers, no matter what transpired in the coming days.[37]

After this speech Mrs. Parks and Fred Daniel were presented to the audience, amidst cheers and applause. Daniel was a young college student who had been arrested that day for allegedly restraining a Negro woman from riding a bus. He denied both the charge and the assertion that goon squads were being employed; he urged the use of non-violence.[38]

The climax of the meeting came when Ralph Abernathy rose to read aloud the MIA's resolution. When he finished he asked everyone in favor of its adoption to stand. It seemed to the leaders that the entire crowd stood in a body, and passage was declared to be unanimous. This was the mandate the MIA had hoped for and expected. This became the justification for their future actions, and was the proclaimed source of their authority.[39]

The final business at hand was to solicit contributions from the assembly to meet expenses. A collection was taken church-style, as Nixon and others circulated among the crowd. About $500.00 was given, the first cash donation to the MIA. As Nixon left the church with the money he asked white police in attendance to escort him for protection. In one of the last gestures of cooperation between the MIA and the police department, Nixon was driven home in a patrol car.[40]

The meeting closed with the singing of a patriotic song and a benediction by Rev. Bennett. As the crowd left the church there was much for observers to reflect upon. No one could doubt that the meeting was a meaningful event. Negroes had given unanimous enthusiastic response to the MIA's plans and had backed up their approval with a substantial gift of money. It was a certainty that the boycott would go on, and no end was in sight. Equally important, Negroes had shown a determination to approach the project with vigor and solidarity. The intensity of their sentiment impressed one white editor, who warned his readers, "The meeting was much like an old-fashioned revival with loud applause added. It proved beyond doubt there was a discipline among Negroes that many whites had doubted. It was almost a military discipline combined with emotion."[41] This was a perceptive assessment. The two attributes of religious fervor and rigorous discipline were important characteristics of the entire year-long boycott.

After the developments on December 5, four major problems confronted the MIA. First, it had set itself up to become an efficient instrument of control. Also, it had to establish a substitute transportation system to replace the bus line. Next, some way had to be found to discharge the enormous expense sure to be incurred by such a transportation system. Finally, it must find a successful formula for satisfying Negro demands, while yet allowing whites to make concessions in negotiations. As will be seen, the MIA solved the first three problems with great facility. The fourth, however, never yielded to solution, and caused much bitterness and frustration for both sides.

A Negro observer has stated that pro-boycott feeling in Montgomery was "promoted by a minority" of the black population, who "donated time and service to molding public opinion . . ."[42] Although the MIA's responsibility for the intensity of feeling is not that demonstrable, the organization can take credit for the "time and service" it gave to the protest. In the year that the boycott lasted, the executive board met on numerous occasions, often several times a week, to decide on practical matters. This board, which comprised the total membership of the MIA, was ultimately expanded to include forty-six people. Of these, twenty-four were ministers. There was only one white member, Rev. Robert Graetz, a West-Virginia-born liberal who was pastor of the all-Negro Trinity Lutheran Church. The rest of the members were representatives of the business and professional classes of the community. The executive board was the final decision-making body, and held all responsibility for actions. Implementation of its decisions was left to the president, or to the various committees involved. Questions referred to it were decided by majority vote. It has been stated that the success of the board was due to good relations obtaining within it, and to the willingness of its members to meet on an hour's notice, at any time of the day or night.[43]

Since such a large body might prove unwieldy for smaller matters, the MIA set up several committees responsible for specific areas of endeavor. There was a "strategy committee" of thirteen to sixteen members, which convened informally to decide on minor points of policy. This group included the most influential people in the MIA, and its officers, who belonged ex-officio. Its decisions, of course, were subject to approval by the larger board.[44]

There were three other major committees. A "negotiating committee" was set up, composed of about a dozen people, mostly ministers. This group was delegated to represent the MIA viewpoint discussions with white officials. Rev. King, as president, was chairman of the committee, and it was to this duty that he devoted much of his attention. King was considered to be the MIA's "spokesman," and was authorized to deliver their opinions at conferences. Rev. Abernathy was most active in this field, as were the two legal advisors, Gray and Langford.[45]

The other two committees, on finance and transportation, operated with a high degree of independence from the rest of the MIA, subject to recourse to the executive board.[46]

Rev. King's role as president was a major one. Although he did not enter into the operation of the finance and transportation committees to a great extent, he worked to maintain a general coordination between them. Each of those groups called on him for services from time to time, such as speaking for them, appealing for funds, and the like. His proficiency at these tasks made him invaluable.[47]

King proved also to be an able representative of the MIA with the Negro public. His manifest intelligence, his firm commitment to nonviolence and the cause of civil rights, and his ability to present the MIA's program in a warm and convincing manner soon won him the complete allegiance of the Negro masses in Montgomery. This confidence and support, in turn, allowed the MIA to assert truthfully at the bargaining sessions that it was speaking for most of the 50,000 black people in town. The Negro public looked on King and the MIA as the delegates, whom they had authorized to stand for them in confrontation with white groups. They did not feel, as whites sometimes implied, that they were being manipulated or maneuvered by the MIA. As one participant in the boycott put it, "We the Negroes, request the Rev. King, and not he over us (sic) . . . We employed him to be our mouth-piece."[48] This feeling of mutual support and dependence cemented the MIA and the masses together, for the benefit of both groups.

The MIA maintained these close relations through the holding of regular, frequent mass meetings. These were held each Monday and Thursday night at various Negro churches. In format and content these meetings strongly resembled church services, and helped to preserve the religious flavor of the protest. They invariably opened with prayers and hymns, followed by speeches similar to sermons, collections of offerings, and benedictions.[49]

The MIA used these meetings as a forum to report to the Negro public on its activities and to explain its proposals. Important questions were put to a vote of the audience, which gave leaders a continuing mandate. Programs and speeches were offered to bolster the masses' will to keep the boycott going. For example, one program featured a list of speakers who discussed the topic "Why I am with the Protest."[50] Such methods undoubtedly gave the protestors a better understanding of their own motives, and prepared them psychologically for the year-long ordeal.

In January of 1956 the MIA was forced to increase the number of mass meetings, due to the scarcity of seats available in any one church, and because of the magnitude of the turn-out every week. Thereafter until late 1956, the MIA held five simultaneous meetings every Thursday, besides the regular single Monday night session.[51]

Another area in which the MIA gained a large measure of success was in transportation. As early as December 5 it had been realized that transportation was crucial to continuation of the boycott, since the mass of Negroes had to have an alternative mode of travel to the bus line. This became especially urgent for the leaders after it was seen that negotiations with whites were to be protracted, as will be discussed later.

The majority of the 17,000 boycotting Negroes had arranged for their own transportation at the beginning. The bus company in a way encouraged this. On December 9, the company asked the City Commission for permission to close down its run in the most populous Negro districts, and to re-route six other runs to avoid Negro neighborhoods. The company claimed that it could not afford to keep these routes active, if no one was going to use them. The City Commission gave its consent to the petition.[52] As a result of this close-down, many Negroes could not now ride the buses if they wanted to.

Most of the Negroes were sharing rides to work or elsewhere, with neighbors or friends who owned cars. Private car pools were set up. There was a notable spirit of cooperation running though the black community, which helped to lessen transportation problems considerably. Also, whites, themselves, were of inestimable help in maintaining the boycott. Hundreds, perhaps thousands, of white men and women picked up their Negro domestic help every morning, and returned them in the evening. This incidental cooperation was fully appreciated by the MIA.[53]

For the first few days of the campaign many Negroes were also using taxis. The MIA had arranged for the cab companies to continue charging reduced rates. On week days the average taxi charged only ten cents per ride between the hours of 4:00 AM to 9:00 AM, and 3:00 to 11:00 PM.[54] However, Montgomery had a city ordinance which set a minimum fare of forty-five cents per ride for all taxis. On December 14 the city comptroller mailed out mimeographed warnings to all companies and operators, ordering them to abide by this provision.[55] This move caught the MIA by surprise, and especially its transportation committee, which hoped to continue the use of cheap cab rides as an adjunct to its own transportation system. The loss of this aid spurred the committee on in its efforts to develop that supplemental system.[56]

The committee began working feverishly about December 7, organizing a vast car pool to be controlled by the MIA. Rev. King was asked to appeal for volunteer drivers at a mass meeting, and he did so. The response was better than expected, as about 20 people donated either their services or their cars for the project. Some of these could only participate at limited times; others offered to drive throughout the day. Lewis and R. J. Glasco, his main assistant, drew up a schedule for each driver to follow, based on the time he would be available. Since several people were not able to drive, but had given use of their cars, the committee procured full-time drivers. There were usually from fifteen to twenty-five of those drivers, each of whom was hired at the rate of $4.00 per work day, which lasted from 6:00 A.M. until 6:00 or 7:00 P.M. This group included ministers, a few unemployed, and several retired persons.[57]

After securing an adequate number of drivers and vehicles the committee went to work on a map of Montgomery. Their purpose was to locate routes and points between which cars would shuttle. It was necessary to find a central point in downtown Montgomery, which could serve as a transfer area, where cars bringing in loads of passengers from Negro residential areas in the morning could transfer these riders to cars bound outward for white residential or commercial sections. In the evening, of course, the direction of this flow would be reversed, with cars bearing passengers from white neighborhoods transferring them to others headed for Negro sections. The committee was fortunate in finding an ideal spot for this central point. A Negro-owned parking lot at the intersection of Monroe and McDonough Streets was rented for $30.00 per month by the MIA. This lot, besides being well-situated, was also large enough to permit several cars to enter, take on or discharge passengers, and turn around at one time. This was important because the committee wanted to avoid blocking sidewalks or traffic while cars performed these functions. They feared that, otherwise, they would be subject to the worry and expense of frequent arrest by police, which might also lead to an injunction against the car pool as a public nuisance.[58]

The committee next located forty-three "dispatch stations" in Negro areas. At these stations Negroes could gather in the morning to await rides to the areas where they worked, or to the central lot, where they could transfer to other cars. Thirty-seven of these stations were in front of Negro churches, which kept their doors unlocked and their heat on for comfort on cold mornings. Riders were returned to these same stations in the evening.[59]

Forty-two "pickup points" were spotted conveniently across the white portions of Montgomery. These were located in nine divisions, each of which was served by a certain proportional number of vehicles dispatched from the central lot. Most of these pickup points were at strategic street intersections, but others were at stores, businesses, white churches, and schools familiar to the Negro population. In one instance the parking lot of a fashionable white country club was used. Also designated were the main gates of the two Air Force bases. Car loads of Negroes were dropped off at these points every morning. From here they could easily catch another ride, or walk to their jobs. Conversely, in the afternoon they would gather again at these points, to be ferried downtown or to their own neighborhoods.[60]

If a person were unable for some reason to get to one of the dispatch stations or pickup points, he could call the MIA headquarters and explain his destination. A dispatcher at headquarters would try to either route a car already in progress by that person, or send a special car to take him to the central lot.[61]

Regrettably, the MIA kept no records on the number of people served by this system. The pool picked up a considerable amount of the slack left over from share-a-ride systems, use of taxis, and the like. A reliable estimate puts the figure carried by the car pool each day as in excess of 1,000. Thus, the total figure for persons carried for the duration of boycott approached 200,000.[62]

The MIA provided fuel and oil for every car in the pool which needed it. Some people donated the gas they used, but others could not afford it. Therefore, anyone who requested was given a ticket at headquarters, which specified a quantity of fuel sufficient for that driver's route for the day. The committee arranged for credit at nine centrally-located service stations, which had lists of current MIA drivers, and which honored MIA tickets. All of these stations were Negro-owned, and none of the proprietors belonged to

226

the MIA. Each station was also large enough to prevent blocking of traffic by MIA cars.[63]

A Negro minister, J. H. Cherry, served as chief dispatcher at the central lot. Other dispatchers were assigned to various stations around town. One dispatching operation was carried on by the pharmacist of a Negro drug store. He provided benches in the store for those waiting for rides, to prevent blocking sidewalks. His dispatching calls, too, were sometimes phrased in code, because he suspected that his telephone was tapped by police.[64]

Clerical work was considerable. Bills for gasoline, garage bills, payment of full-time drivers, routing schedules, all created a load of paper work which was handled at the central transportation office. This was also MIA headquarters. A full-time staff which eventually included ten secretaries was used to handle this work. For the first few weeks of the boycott offices were situated in a supper club owned by Rufus Lewis. However, to prevent Lewis' license from being revoked for using a place of entertainment as a business office, the MIA soon sought space elsewhere. After temporary residence in a ministerial group's building, permanent offices were finally set up in the labor hall of a local Negro brick-layers' union. The MIA remained here for the duration.[65]

The transportation committee made sure every Negro knew of the car pool. Mimeographed schedules of the pool were posted in public places. Also, the work of the pool was constantly emphasized at mass meetings. During these sessions the public was given an opportunity to criticize the operation and to suggest changes.[66]

This system, of course, was expensive to run. To make matters more difficult the MIA could not charge for rides because the organization would then be liable for prosecution as an unlicensed jitney service. It was suggested, then, that every Negro riding in the pool contribute a small sum, say ten cents, for each time he rode. Such money was given during collections periods at mass meetings. Many people complied with the request and it helped to defray some of the costs.[67]

The pool continued in operation almost for the duration of the boycott. The idea worked well but there was some dissatisfaction with the necessary crowding of several people into each car. An appeal was made for more volunteers. This boosted the number of vehicles engaged to about 300. However, there were never really enough cars. Many people were still walking to work, or were otherwise inconvenienced. The transportation committee decided to supplement this system, and cut costs, by setting up its own jitney service.

Lewis and four others filed a petition with the City Commission, asking to be recognized as the Montgomery Transit Company. They asked to be allowed to use new station wagons on the routes in Negro sections abandoned by the bus company. They thought there was a good chance that the city would grant this, but they were to be disappointed. After a hearing in commission chambers on January 31, 1956, the City Commission unanimously denied their request. The Commission argued that there was adequate transport for Negroes available though the bus company, if they chose to use it.[68] Lewis and the others approached the Commission again in April with the same petition, but were again refused.[69]

After this second rebuff the committee decided to use the principle of the idea, if not the exact form. Lewis and Glasco were authorized to arrange the purchase of new station wagons for the MIA. They decided to patronize local Chevrolet and Ford dealers, since it was reasoned that a local purchase might contribute in some small way to better relations with the white community. After being offered attractive discounts, Lewis and Glasco bought about a dozen new cars. When philanthropic individuals and groups in other states heard of the committee's plan, four more were donated. Each of these cars was registered in the name of a different Negro church, although MIA funds were used in payment. These cars were manned by the full-time drivers and offered free rides beginning in late April, 1956.[70]

The car pool operated successfully until November 13, 1966. On that date a Montgomery Circuit judge, acting in a suit brought by the City Commission, temporarily enjoined the MIA from using the pool, which was characterized by the city as an unlicensed "private enterprise."[71] On that same day the United States Supreme Court, as will be seen, struck down segregation on the buses. For about a month after that, or until the Supreme Court's order reached local officials on December 21, Montgomery's Negroes were without a car pool. They made do for that period with private pools and by a resort to walking.[72]

As was expected the cost of maintaining the pool was high. Fund-raising, therefore, became a major activity of the MIA. Exact figures are not available as to how much the organization was spending on the pool or on other matters because the sum fluctuated from week to week, and because of the lack of surviving records. However, creditable estimates put the total cost of operations at about $5,000.00 per month, of which the pool consumed the major share.[73] The MIA set about securing money to cover these costs and actually succeeded in raising far more than was needed.

The finance committee under Nixon had the primary responsibility for getting this money. At first the only income was that collected at mass meetings. Several hundred dollars per week could be counted on from this source but more was needed. Fortunately as news of the boycott spread individuals and groups began to send in contributions. Most of these were from out-of-town or out-of-state Negroes. Some of these gifts were quite small, ranging as low as one dollar. On the other hand a Birmingham Negro church group gave a total of about $600.00 during the first month of the boycott.[74] A single church in Montgomery pledged and delivered $100.00 per week for the duration. A mysterious and anonymous female donor, who styled herself "The Club From Nowhere" also sent in $100.00 per week. These gifts were appreciated, and, taken together, made up a considerable sum. But the MIA felt it was necessary get more.[75]

The finance committee requested the MIA as a whole to set up a "speaker's bureau" to get additional funds. This was to take advantage of the expressed desire of civil rights groups and other organizations outside of Montgomery to get first-hand reports of what was happening, and to aid in the protest. King, Abernathy, Mrs. Parks, Nixon, Bennett, Pierce, and others regularly spoke before such groups. These occasions proved to be ideal for soliciting contributions. At one event before an NAACP audience in Cleveland, Rev. Bennett collected over $3,200.00 for the cause.[76] A Negro medical society in Atlanta gave another speaker $1,000.00.[77] The speaker's bureau was a great help to the committee in shoring up finances.

Although the NAACP as a national unit did not contribute monetarily, various local branches did send help. These local branches frequently sponsored fund-raising affairs for the speaker's bureau. Besides raising money, these events also helped to interest civil rights workers across the country in the MIA's campaign.[78]

Through these efforts the MIA collected by mid-February about $25,000.00 from all sources.[79] This figure cannot be broken down to ascertain the proportions given by different sources, because all gifts immediately went into the general fund, and records as to their origins were not kept. Nor can a single bank statement reveal the extent of the MIA's resources, since funds were deposited in several different banks. This practice was advised by Nixon, who feared that an injunction might be issued against the MIA in the future, which would freeze its accounts in Alabama institutions. Thus, the method was to deposit funds in the local Alabama National Bank for immediate safety, then to transfer money by check to other banks outside the state. The most favored outside bank was the Citizen's Trust Company in Atlanta, which was wholly Negro-owned. In fact, twelve other Negro banks were recipients of deposits, in an area stretching from Nashville to Philadelphia.[80]

Mid-February was the turning-point in the MIA's financial fortunes. On February 21 a Montgomery County Grand Jury brought in indictments against the leaders of the boycott, for violation of the state's anti-boycott law.[81] This resulted in a great deal of national publicity for the protest. Sympathy for the MIA ran high, and many groups were aroused to contribute, which had not done so before. Non-Southern whites became more interested at this time. When Rev. King was tried and convicted on that charge a month later the volume of contributions rose.[82]

In early March, for example, Nixon went to Detroit to address a convention of local presidents of the United Automobile Workers Union. He made a strong appeal for money, and was surprised at the response by the union leaders. The assembly pledged a total of $35,000.00 to the MIA, and gave Nixon a check for $7,000.00 of it. The remainder was sent in 90 days. About that same time Nixon telephoned a labor leader in Los Angeles and explained their financial needs. This man replied that he had no authority as union president to commit his group for any sum of $100.00 or over, without getting authorization from the membership. He did promise, though, to send along a check for $99.99 every week for ten weeks.[83]

Labor and civil rights groups were not the sole contributors during this period of increased interest. Northern professional and religious organizations chipped in, as well. These groups though could not match the sums provided by the better-financed interests mentioned above.

The indictment and trial of Rev. King, as well as the jeopardy of the other leaders, resulted in a financial wind-fall for the MIA. Before this occurred the organization was receiving about $10,000.00 per month in gifts; in the month following the indictment it is estimated that about $60,000.00 was given. By the time that King went on trial, the MIA enjoyed a surplus in its several accounts of over $50,000.00. For the year during which the boycott lasted, total donations amounted to about $225,000.00. The MIA probably retained a substantial surplus at the end of the boycott. The organization continued to function as a community agent after that time, as it still does today. Contributions to it, though, dropped off sharply after the dramatic event of the boycott while expenses for voter education projects and other schemes continued. In the first eighteen months of its existence the organization spent well over the $225,000.00 received in the first twelve months. Although no records were kept to indicate which group or classification of contributors gave the most, it is believed that organized labor probably deserved the honor.[84]

Although the MIA was forced to concentrate almost the whole of its energies on problems associated with the boycott, it might be mentioned that a few ancillary activities were undertaken. For example another committee was established to collect parcels of food for needy families at Christmas time. After that, the committee, which was headed by Rufus Lewis, also gathered shoes and clothing for the poor of the Negro community. Lewis also was chairman of yet another committee on registration and voting which sponsored a drive to increase participation in that area.[85]

Another committee was formed to study an intriguing proposal by Nixon. He urged that the MIA use its capital surplus, along with a large loan from the Federal Government, to establish a Negro bank. The bank building was to be a large, three-story structure containing office space for Negro professional men. The whole establishment, he argued, would be of as much benefit as a successful boycott, since capital development of the Negro section was as urgently needed as civil rights. However, the committee to look into the idea never decided on the matter, and nothing came of it.[86]

THREE

Failure of
Negotiations

When it was realized by both races in Montgomery that the boycott was going to continue until solutions were found to demands posed by the MIA the majority of each race began to express a set of opinions concerning the protest. Most Negroes justified the boycott as something proper, for which there had long been a need. Most of them gave whole-hearted support to the effort. Many whites, though, saw it as an uncalled for demonstration of civic irresponsibility on the part of Negroes and wanted to see it quickly ended.

It must be pointed out, however, that a small minority within each race dissented from its group's prevailing opinion. Some Negroes, for example, believed the boycott would ultimately be detrimental to the peaceful and harmonious relationships enjoyed with whites. They thought such tranquil relations were more important for the progress of their people than the rearrangement of bus seating patterns would be, which was the only advantage they could see coming from the boycott. It is probable that most Negroes who thought this way were elderly people, who had grown accustomed to their status on the buses. A persistent five to ten percent of the old customers continued to ride buses for the duration. Others who had little sympathy with the protest may have stayed off buses because of the social pressure exerted on them by the example of their neighbors, their church leaders, and prominent community leaders.[1]

A few whites sympathized with the aims of the protest but their number was extremely small. One of these, Juliette Morgan of Montgomery, told her views in a remarkable letter to the *Montgomery Advertiser* a week after the boycott began. She compared the boycott to Gandhi's "Salt March" in the conflict preceding Indian independence, and extolled the dignity of the Negro movement in Montgomery. She reminded whites that boycotts had been a conspicuous weapon in fomenting the American Revolution, and she warned them that history was being written before their very eyes.[2]

From time to time other sympathetic whites addressed the local newspapers with favorable sentiments towards the protest, although these were outweighed numerically by letters in opposition. A few whites supported their beliefs with action, on occasion driving into the central dispatch station of the car pool operated by the MIA, and offering rides to Negroes. Others offered encouragement to the MIA, and at least one anonymous white donor gave a large cash gift. However, it was believed that the largest part of the sympathizers resided at the local Air Force bases and were people raised outside the South.[3]

The dominant view of the boycott among whites was reflected, and doubtless influenced by, the two large local newspapers. The more important of these two was the *Montgomery Advertiser* published by Grover Cleveland Hall, Jr., who held to what could be characterized as a "moderate" position on racial matters. Hall's reputation for a rational approach to these problems won him appointment to the National Committee of the American Civil Liberties Union a month after the boycott began.[4] The *Advertiser*, under his direction, disapproved of the extreme policies and pronouncements of such groups as the White Citizens Councils, and particularly the call for economic reprisals against Negroes who agitated against the system of segregation. But, this disapprobation was also directed against the use of what was considered to be essentially the same threat, when employed by Negro boycotters. The *Advertiser* made its position clear on this point early along in December, when it advised the Negroes to consider the consequences of their actions. The primary concern, in the paper's view, was an increase in racial tension. Montgomery had fared well in this respect in the past; "Therefore it is rash to excite fears that become hostility. Strong measures beget strong measures." Reading the temper of the masses of whites, the *Advertiser* warned that, "Segregation sentiment dominates Montgomery, and will for a long time to come."

But, at the same time, the paper noted that the MIA claimed not to be asking for an end to segregation but only for some arrangement whereby Negroes could use vacant seats in the white section of the bus. It counselled, "If the grievance is confined to that, then attention should be given to it promptly. Any other grievance should be fairly heard."

Besides urging that the Negro side be heard, the paper also understood the necessity for tempering white reaction with moderation. In a prophetic observation, it wrote:

234

Montgomery has witnessed the dramatic event of the boycott with admirable and typical coolness. It is well. For protests of this kind are going to be a commonplace of our state and community for a long time to come, ours being a time of evolution in oldtime custom and usage.[5]

The *Advertiser* also raised the first public doubts as to the legality of the boycott method. Having approached William F. Thetford, Circuit Solicitor for Montgomery County, who confessed uncertainty on that issue, the paper printed the text of the anti-boycott law. It warned, however, that although the Alabama Supreme Court would probably uphold prosecutions under that statute, the United States high court probably would not. In another observation, this one inversely prophetic, it implied the futility of trying to enforce the law: "As a practical matter, we doubt that either the bus company or the solicitor will attempt to jail five thousand Negroes."[6]

These first reflections, coming before the emergence of the MIA as the guiding hand of the protest, were followed by others couched in stronger language. After the failure of the first negotiating session the paper sought to impress upon Negroes "two facts of life" which they overlooked in holding the bus company "hostage." These were that, first, "The white man's economic artillery is far superior, better emplaced and commanded by more experienced gunners. Second, the white man holds all the offices of government machinery. There will be white rule as far as the eye can see."[7]

The *Advertiser*, a morning newspaper, was financially connected with its afternoon counterpart, the *Alabama Journal*. The latter publication kept separate staffs and reporters, but usually took an identical editorial position to its larger sister. Reflecting the same disapproving stand, the *Journal* on occasion reprinted and approved portions of the *Advertiser's* comments on the boycott.[8]

Equally concerned about the situation was the Montgomery City Commission. W. A. Gayle, Franklin Parks, and Clyde Sellers concurred on the importance of getting the boycott over with as soon as possible. They saw at least four disastrous contingencies associated with a protracted protest. First, good interracial relations, which it was partially their responsibility to maintain, were bound to be disrupted by a lengthy boycott. Also, the bus company, which was an absolute necessity to the community in terms of transportation convenience and traffic abatement might be forced to abandon its local franchise for economic reasons. Third, they feared an immanent eruption of violence, provoked by the extremists of either race. And, from all of these causes, the good image which Montgomery enjoyed nationally might suffer irreparable damage.[9]

The majority of whites shared the Commission's apprehensions, and with good reasons. Business, especially in the downtown section, began to feel the effects of decreased Negro patronage almost at once. Even more alarming was the incidence of violence that accompanied the boycott from the beginning. This irritated Montgomery's whites, because it was inherently wrong, and because it always carried the possibility of spreading into something more serious.

Clyde Sellers' charge of roaming goon squads seemed for many to have been demonstrated on the day the boycott began. On that afternoon a nineteen-year old Negro, Fred Daniel, was arrested for allegedly pulling an elderly Negro woman away from a bus she was attempting to board. Fred Gray immediately rushed to Daniel's defense, and had the case dismissed after the woman in question testified that the youth was merely escorting her across the street.[10]

This explanation of the incident failed to still Sellers' suspicions. He ordered the police department to be especially watchful for attempts to intimidate non-boycotting Negroes. He and the other Commissioners believed that the MIA was sincere in its call for nonviolence, and that the Negro leaders were sufficiently honorable to decline such methods. However, the Commission doubted the MIA's ability to control other, more dangerous elements among the Negro population who were not as scrupulous.[11]

Also disquieting were isolated, but frequent, assaults on city buses in Negro areas. On the first night of the boycott someone fired on, and hit, a bus traveling through a Negro neighborhood. Rocks were thrown at another. At the end of the first week at least five buses had been hit by gunfire, and several more by rocks, bricks and other missiles.[12] Police investigations of these acts established no links with the MIA, which was considered blameless. Nevertheless, this situation made it more urgent to find a solution to the boycott, especially if the MIA proved unable to control the behavior of Negroes inclined to overt hostility.[13]

The need, then, for bi-racial discussions of grievances became quite apparent soon after the protest began. Despite this, neither side made the initial contact with the other. On December 7, Rev. King called a news conference, where he stated the willingness of the MIA, as pledged in the resolution approved at the first mass meeting, to meet with officials "any time we get an invitation." King also sought to reassure whites on the reasonableness of Negro demands by stating:

> We are not asking an end to segregation. That's a matter for the legislature and the courts. We feel that we have a plan within the law . . . We don't like the idea of Negroes having to stand when there are vacant seats. We are demanding justice on that point.[14]

The City Commission was equally willing to meet with the other side. However, they felt that, as representatives of the city, they were not required to approach the MIA. They preferred that the Negro organization come to them, perhaps at a regular Commission meeting.[15]

Jack Crenshaw, attorney for the bus company, also announced the line's readiness to negotiate on December 6, if that was what the boycotters wanted. However, as he had explained to a delegation at the time of the Colvin incident, there was really little use for such a meeting. The bus company only obeyed laws formulated by others; it could do nothing to change those laws. He preferred that Negroes work out a settlement with the city or state authorities, which the bus company would accept.[16] Crenshaw also hit out at the MIA, saying that before talks began, "I think they ought to get their house cleaned," a reference to alleged forceful tactics by boycott enforcers.[17]

By December 7, it appeared that prospects for an early meeting were not good. Fortunately, though, an outside force intervened to arrange for discussion. On that day the Alabama Council on Human Relations held its semi-annual conference. The Council, of which Rev. King was a member, was a bi-racial organization, the only one in Montgomery. It was composed mainly of ministers and was affiliated with the Southern Regional Council of Atlanta. In keeping with the spirit of that well-known liberal organization, the Montgomery group advocated equal opportunity for Negroes, gained through the scholarly study of racial problems. The Council was distressed at the failure of the two sides to communicate and voted that morning to act as an intermediary in establishing contacts.[18]

A three-man committee was authorized to bring this about. These were Rev. Robert E. Hughes, the Council's white executive director, Rev. Thomas R. Thrasher, local white minister, and Dr. H. Council Trenholm, Negro president of Alabama State College. They contacted Mayor Gayle and explained their purpose. Gayle accepted their "good offices," and suggested a meeting between the City Commission and the MIA at City Hall, at 11:00

A.M. the next morning.[19] Rev. Hughes relayed this invitation to King, who accepted for the MIA.[20]

At the appointed time on December 8 the negotiators gathered in Commission chambers. Present were the twelve-man negotiating committee of the MIA, the three representatives of the Alabama Council On Human Relations, the City Commission, and Bagley and Crenshaw for the bus company. Several reporters rounded out the assembly. W. A. Gayle presided, and opened the session by allowing Rev. Thrasher to speak for the intermediary group. Thrasher appealed to both sides to present their cases in a "factual and unemotional" manner, and declared that his group would remain neutral during the discussions.[21]

Gayle next asked for a representative of the Negro viewpoint. Rev. King came forward as president and spokesman of the MIA. This was his first introduction to the City Commission, and to other whites. These noted with surprise King's position within the MIA, having already seen that several older leaders were absent whom they had dealt with in the past and who had been expected to head the present delegation.[22]

King's statement began with citations of past mistreatment of Negroes on city buses. Having outlined the causes for the present protest, he promised that the MIA would work to keep it peaceful and decorous in character. He also disclaimed any desire to injure the bus company financially. He reiterated the MIA's concession to the segregation laws, and said that they were asking only for what was legal and just.[23]

Moving on to specific items, King outlined the three demands. First, the bus company should guarantee courteous treatment of Negro passengers in the future. Second, Negro drivers should be hired, and given routes in predominantly Negro sections. Finally, he asked that the bus line employ seating practices akin to those in effect in Nashville, Atlanta, Mobile, and other Southern cities.

This was the "first come-first served" rule. Using a large diagram prepared by Fred Gray, King illustrated the seating arrangement they preferred. This entailed Negroes sitting in the rear of the bus and filling seats forward. Whites would take the front seats and fill toward the rear. No seats would be reserved; where the two races met would determine their separate sections on that bus. In reply to a question by Crenshaw, King pointed out that if there were no whites aboard, and thirty-six Negroes were present, they would use all the seats. If whites came on in this situation, they would have to stand. If there were no vacant seats in the rear of the bus, Negroes could not be required to yield their seats to whites. In fact, once a bus was loaded there was to be no reassignment of seats, at all.[24]

A general discussion followed King's presentation. Both sides were eager to make objections or observations, but with such a large group present it was difficult to make any headway. Therefore, Gayle suggested that a few from each side withdraw, leaving the others to thrash out problems more effectively. He was among those who left the meeting, but before leaving spoke to both sides on the urgency of reaching a solution, advising "I want you to get in there and settle this thing."[25] Sellers, Parks, Bagley, and Crenshaw remained to represent the white interests. King, Gray, and a few other Negroes stayed behind for the MIA.[26]

The smaller group proceeded to tackle the three proposals separately. On the matter of courtesy, Sellers averred that it was a problem for the bus company alone, although he was of the opinion personally, that "you receive the type of treatment that you give."[27]

Crenshaw agreed that discourtesy by drivers was often a reaction to rudeness or misbehavior of riders. Nevertheless, it was company policy to investigate all such complaints, and to encourage drivers always to be courteous. But, there had been no recent cases of rudeness to Negroes reported to the management. Further, this aspect had not been mentioned by the defense in the trial of Mrs. Parks, and he wondered what was its pertinence to the boycott or to the issue at hand. Despite this, he stated that he was prepared to pledge that the company would try to improve in this respect in the future.[28]

On the next topic, that of Negro employment, the company was able to make no such concession. King had not specified that any certain number of his race be hired. He had demanded, though, that hiring policy be altered immediately in that direction. Sellers interjected that this, too, was outside the legitimate province of the city government, which had no legal right to tell any firm who it might, or might not, hire. Crenshaw stepped in and explained that this demand was impossible of fulfillment. The bus company had recently signed a new contract with the drivers' union. This contract, and the union's regulations, were quite specific in this area. If new drivers were needed, they must first come from the ranks of previous drivers who had been "furloughed," that is laid off. Also no qualified Negro had ever applied for a position with the company. Even if one did, Crenshaw doubted that he would be able to get through the training school operated by the Union. Furthermore, if a Negro did complete training, he could not be given a

239

route in a Negro district. Such routes were considered by drivers to be the choicest in Montgomery, because of the larger revenue contained in them. Union rules on seniority required that they be given to drivers with the largest past service. In short, to accede to the MIA's wishes would be to hazard economic suicide, by risking a drivers' strike.[29]

Crenshaw also elaborated another side of the problem. He cited the prevalence of a Southern custom, whereby only white drivers were used. He knew of no city in the region which employed Negroes. But he did extend a slight hope to the Negroes: perhaps his company could take on drivers of their race in the future, when such customs had become less stringent, perhaps in ten years. Fred Gray snapped back, "We don't mean ten years, we mean this year."[30]

Having reached an impasse on this point, the negotiators turned to the MIA's seating proposition. This was an area in which the city was involved, and Sellers spoke up in objection to the plan. The position he outlined was adopted by the City Commission as a whole, and was to be consistently retained for the duration of the controversy. Sellers stated that the first come-first served plan was patently illegal. In his view it violated explicit injunctions in the city and state laws that the two races be kept distinctly separate. He believed, contrary to the MIA's contention, that these laws demanded specific sections for the occupancy of either race. The new proposal was objectionable because it might result in all-Negro or all-white buses. Some room for each race must be preserved on every bus that was not a "special."[31]

Commissioner Parks next wondered aloud if the MIA proposal was really contrary to the law, and whether it might not be workable in some fashion.[32]

Jack Crenshaw, whom King now regarded as the Negroes' "most stubborn opponent",[33] sided with Sellers. Though still of the opinion that the City Commission had final responsibility on this subject, he believed that the first come-first served idea was inappropriate. It did not amount to complete integration, but was nevertheless in conflict with definite provisions, as Sellers had stated. He was also concerned with the dangers attendant upon a circumstance where whites boarded a bus to find all seats taken by Negroes, and being forced to stand. Therefore, he opposed the MIA's recommendation.[34]

Fred Gray, as legal counsel, answered these charges. Replying at length, he sought to disparage any legal doubts of Crenshaw and Sellers by arguing that the Act of July 1, 1947, was so constructed as to leave the practical enforcement of segregation to the individual municipalities and bus companies. Furthermore, the Act, when viewed in its full context, really pertained only to vehicles operated by the Alabama Public Service Commission. References in the Act to "ticket window", "waiting rooms," and the like, made Gray feel that it was intended to regulate only railroads, interstate or inter-city bus lines, and other such utilities under PSC regulation. If this were correct, then Montgomery could devise its own seating law.[35]

Crenshaw was not certain about the validity of this argument, and felt that the Act probably should be construed as applying to local buses. He and Gray, who knew and respected each other from professional association, argued this point. They decided that it might be useful to have this question submitted to the courts or to the state's Attorney General for a declaratory judgment.[36] W. A. Gayle and the other Commissioners discussed this possibility later, but for unexplained reasons decided not seek such a ruling.[37]

In a final bid for agreement, Crenshaw offered, on behalf of the bus line, to designate every other bus on Negro routes "special", which would carry only Negroes. The MIA delegates rejected this, as no real answer to the seating problem.[38]

Finally, after four hours of discussion the meeting came to a close. Agreement had been reached only on the matter of courtesy, which was probably the least important of the Negro proposals. Each side seemed adamant with respect to the other two problems, and each side came away with suspicions about the good faith of the other. Rev. King states that, as a result of this meeting, he conceived grave doubts about the willingness of whites to concede just demands.[39]

The City Commission came away convinced that the MIA was asking them to violate the law, which was clear and specific. Further, they guessed that the MIA was aiming at the ultimate destruction of bus segregation, if not through negotiation, then by an attack in the courts. The Commissioners thought it likely, from past decisions, that the United States Supreme Court would be responsive to the MIA viewpoint. Therefore, Gayle, Parks, and Sellers felt that it was not expedient for them to yield on the matter of seating. Even if they did give in here, the Negroes would likely go on to the Federal courts anyway. The Commission determined to remain firm, and await the Negroes' next move.[40]

241

Jack Crenshaw also thought the MIA could get what it wanted from the Supreme Court. He too was distressed at the lack of prospects for a quick settlement of the dispute. He believed he had done his best to satisfy both the demands of the MIA, and the requirements of the law. He was now convinced that there was little likelihood of a negotiated end to the boycott, because the MIA was not bargaining in good faith. Their insistence on having Negro drivers after he had shown the difficulties involved proved that they were not really willing to compromise.[41]

The first meeting had ended with no specific arrangements for convening another. During the next few days each side applied mild pressure. On December 10, for instance, King issued a statement to the press in which he repeated his group's contention that the city and the bus company could accept the MIA's demands if they really wanted to. He said there were no obstacles to resuming talks, and urged both sides to meet soon.[42]

Having already warned taxi companies about violating city ordinances, authorities now moved against the car pool. Police Chief Ruppenthal ordered his men to be especially watchful for over-crowded cars, under an ordinance which forbade more than three people in the front seat. Judge John Scott of Recorders Court warned publicly that offenders were subject to a fine of up to $100.00. Private cars, he said would probably receive a smaller fine, but taxis would suffer "somewhat higher" assessments.[43] The transportation committee of the MIA had about completed the switch from dependence on taxis to use of the car pool, by this time. Scott's warning gave them some pause, since they were forced to assign as many people as possible to each car in the pool.[44]

The MIA acted next to stimulate further talks. They had learned a few days after the first meeting that the local bus company was owned by National City Lines, Inc., of Chicago. The MIA wired the president of that firm and asked him to come to Montgomery or to send a personal representative, to enter into negotiations. He replied that a vice president would arrive in a few days.[45] This representative, K. E. Totten, flew into Montgomery on December 15. On the 16th he met with the City Commission to review the situation, but did not contact the MIA.[46]

In the meantime several people had approached the Commission, representing labor organizations, the Parent Teacher Association and other civic groups, who were anxious to bring about a settlement of the boycott. They asked the Commission to be allowed to take part in direct negotiations with the MIA, and hoped that they might succeed where the Commission had failed. Gayle, Sellers, and Parks discussed the idea. They decided that if these volunteers were organized into a special "Mayor's Committee," they might, indeed, get results. There was little to lose by the idea at any rate. Gayle therefore contacted a number of these people and appointed them to the special body.[47]

The Alabama Council on Human Relations also re-entered the picture. They asked the Commissioners to arrange another meeting as soon as possible.[48] Gayle contacted the MIA and told them of his new committee. He requested them to send a delegation to City Hall on the morning of December 17, to resume the talks.[49]

The executive board of the MIA met to consider its next move, and agreed to attend the meeting. There was some criticism in the Negro community of the first come-first served plan which, it was complained, "embraces all of the objectionable and despicable features of racial segregation." To those holding this view, about the only virtues of the plan were that it did not allow for the reassigning of Negroes to other seats, and that it prohibited the despised racial sign boards.[50] Despite this criticism, the executive board voted to retain the plan in their proposals. They did modify their stand on one point. They understood the seriousness of union objections to the immediate hiring of Negro drivers. Therefore, they decided that they would not ask for immediate acceptance, but only stipulate that applications by Negroes be considered, and that they be employed as vacancies occurred in the future.[51]

On the morning of the 17th the several representatives again gathered in Commission chambers. The Mayor's Committee was present, and consisted of the female head of the local Parent-Teacher Association, a member of the bus drivers' union, and several prominent white ministers. Among these were Dr. Henry E. Russell, a leading Presbyterian minister and brother of Senator Richard Russell of Georgia, and Dr. Stanley Frazier, a Methodist pastor whom Negroes regarded as "a well-known segregation advocate."[52] Dr. Henry A. Parker, pastor of the First Baptist church was appointed chairman of the group by Gayle. Mrs. Logan A. Hipp, Jr., a prominent social figure in Montgomery, was made secretary.

Present for the MIA were King, Abernathy, Jo Ann Robinson, H. H. Hubbard, Gray, Charles Langford and Rufus Lewis. But, unknown to the MIA, Gayle had summoned two other Negroes to the meeting, to join with the MIA in representing their race. One was P. M. Blair, the popular "Negro Mayor of Montgomery." The other was Dee Caffey, a successful dealer in real estate and insurance. Before the protest began, these two were considered by the white officials to be the real leaders of the Negro population. The City Commission had dealt with them as such for several years, and so it was felt that they deserved a place in negotiations.[53] Nevertheless, their inclusion irritated the MIA. King voiced this opposition and objected to their presence, as only the MIA spoke for Negroes in the boycott. Gayle allowed the two men to remain, despite King's objections.[54]

Also present were the three Commissioners, four representatives of the bus company, including Crenshaw and Totten, and Rev. Thrasher of the Alabama Council on Human Relations.

Mayor Gayle opened the meeting by summarizing the present status of the crisis, and by urging the contending parties to work together harmoniously. He said, "I want to see it settled as soon as possible," and hoped that the Mayor's Committee would fulfill its purpose by finding some recommendations to present to the Commission for approval.[55]

King spoke next, again outlining the MIA position. When he had finished, Gayle called on K. E. Totten to state the opinions of the National City Lines. Totten told the assembly that his company felt that it was up to the citizens of Montgomery to determine how their own segregation laws were to be handled with respect to buses. They were the only ones who could legitimately do so, and his firm was pledged to abide by whatever decision the people made. In further remarks he noted that the problem of discourtesy by drivers was not confined to Montgomery, but was one encountered by his firm in all of its franchises in the South and elsewhere. Furthermore, the driver was not always the one at fault; often, customers provoked his behavior by their own rudeness.[56]

This last observation angered King, who immediately "raised his voice." He charged that Totten was not looking at all sides of the matter, but only at the point of view presented by the City Commission. He said that frequent abuse of Negroes by drivers was a well-established fact that had been notorious for a long time. He also chided Totten for conferring previously only with the Commission, but not with the MIA.[57]

Not replying to King's outburst, Totten went on to explain that on the problem of seating, his company had to conform to local laws and customs wherever it operated. This rule applied also to the hiring of drivers. Ralph Abernathy answered the last point by revealing the modified stand on employment.[58]

After more general remarks Gayle and others again withdrew from the session. Left behind was the full Mayor's Committee, which after some

244

argument was evenly divided as to race, with eight whites and a like number of Negroes. As this group got down to specifics, James Bailey, a white member, offered the first resolution for consideration. The whites supported his thesis that, since Christmas was approaching, the seasonal good spirits and the need for extra transportation for shoppers warranted suspending the boycott until some time after the holidays. It was suggested that this suspension would also have a beneficial effect on white public opinion, as a sign of the MIA's good-will. Bailey moved, therefore, that the postponement be recommended, effective immediately, and to last until January 15th of the new year. A show of hands on this resolution, however, revealed that the Negroes were determined that no disruption of the boycott, which might be fatal to the momentum they had built up, be permitted. The vote was tied at eight to eight.[59]

Another resolution was then proposed, which got unanimous support. This was a declaration asking that courteous treatment be extended to all passengers on buses. Its passage excited no controversy.

Beyond this, nothing else was accomplished. The MIA's seating demands were discussed, but no effort was made to extract a vote on the matter. Therefore, the meeting was adjourned by Dr. Parker, with an agreement to meet again on the following Monday, December 19th. The Montgomery Chamber of Commerce had volunteered the use of its headquarters, which were more commodious than Commission chambers, and this site was approved for the next meeting.[60]

This next meeting was convened at the appointed hour and almost immediately the two sides were in conflict. Sitting among the white delegates was Luther Ingalls, a local lawyer who had a conspicuous hand in recently organizing the Middle Alabama chapter of the White Citizens Council. Ingalls had not been present at the meeting on the previous Saturday. Nor, as was natural, was he a popular figure among Negroes. Rev. King quickly challenged Ingalls' credentials and protested his presence. The latter explained that he had been appointed to the Committee by Gayle several days before. Unfortunately, he could not attend Saturday's meeting due to prior commitments. This failed to satisfy King, who replied, "The Mayor has been very unfair to add to the committee without consulting us."

King did not stop there. He also complained of the group's composition, stating that Gayle "has not appointed a representative committee of whites." He was disappointed that some of the members were obviously "anti-Negro," who had come to the meetings with certain "preconceived ideas." He felt, he said, that there was no use for any more discussions since their efforts were doomed to failure. He moved that the meeting be adjourned.

This outburst angered the white half of the Committee, who opened their own flood-gates of criticism. Mrs. Logan Hipp, "her voice shaking," hurled back her resentment at King's charge, stating that she "most certainly did not" attend the sessions with a closed mind. James Bailey was also indignant. He had been ready, he said, to approve "liberalization" of the city's segregation laws, "with certain conditions." He agreed with King's indictment on one point, saying "We have some whose minds are made up." In his view, "Rev. King is one of them."

King backtracked in the face of these vigorous retorts. He explained that he hadn't meant that all of the whites present were prejudiced; his statements had pertained to only a few. Dr. Parker spoke up, averring that, "If that's true, then you should not be here. Your stand has been made clear."[61]

After this uproar subsided and tempers were cooled, Parker argued against the motion for adjournment by reminding both sides of their serious purpose, and by pleading with each to continue discussions, and to learn to work with the other. It was agreed that they should go on.[62] A resolution on courtesy was already achieved; only two more points of contention remained, although these admittedly were more controversial than the other. The seating proposal was taken up first.

Rev. Frazier of the whites came forward with a suggestion that had the backing of his colleagues. He proposed that each bus be divided into distinct sections reserved for each race. These respective areas would be designated on each bus by a "conspicuously placed" race sign. On a particular run the number of seats allocated to either race would be determined proportionally, according to the "average patronage of each race" on that route in the past. If one race temporarily surpassed in numbers the availability of seats reserved for it, it could make use of the empty adjacent seats in the other section. These seats, though, would have to be surrendered if the other race needed them.[63]

The Negroes found this proposal "repugnant." Charles Langford voiced their disapproval, stating that the plan was little different than existing regulations. In his opinion it was no material improvement in their status. The other MIA delegates indicated their concurrence in this, so no vote was taken on Frazier's plan.[64]

King motioned that the Committee accept the MIA's seating plan. Walter Knabe, a white lawyer who represented the city on legal matters and who was sitting in on the Commission's behalf, opposed King's motion. He repeated the assertion that first come-first served was illegal. Fred Gray answered him with the familiar argument that state law left such matters to the cities, and that Montgomery's City Code was not prohibitively specific on seating. He emphasized again that the MIA was not asking for integration, but only that "all passengers be given that equality in seating which the law requires."[65] Gray's appeal failed to move the whites so, again, no vote was polled.

Since the meeting had lasted upwards of three hours, Rev. Parker decided to adjourn the session, even though there had been no discussion of hiring of Negro drivers. He proposed that another meeting would be called, but at an unspecified date.[66]

King states that he called Parker later in the day to apologize for the "misunderstanding."[67] Nevertheless, Parker called no more meetings. He reasoned that to do so would be futile since the last two sessions, totalling some five hours of debate (much of it on extraneous issues), "didn't get anywhere." For the next month Parker maintained that his Committee "stands ready to meet." But, it is probable that the firm adherence of the MIA to its demands, and the heated clashes in previous sessions, convinced white members that noting could be gained.[68]

In January of 1956 the white half of the Mayor's Committee submitted a report to Gayle which outlined their collective position. The issuing of this report signaled the tacit dissolution of the group, which never conferred together again. Though they had conceded on the matter of courtesy, they could not do so on the other points. As to seating they declared that they had "no authority to invoke any rule . . . that seeks to nullify or circumvent the spirit or the letter of the law." They endorsed Frazier's proportional plan as the best compromise accommodation. As to hiring Negroes, the whites decided that they had no right to ask the bus company to disregard prevailing Southern custom. To do so would "not be in the public interest."[69]

After the failure of this Committee as a vehicle of conciliation, there was a hiatus of several weeks' duration in communication between white and Negro leaders. K. E. Totten, apparently convinced that he could do nothing else to end the boycott, left Montgomery after the final session, although he promised to return if needed.[70] The Negro press announced that the MIA came away from these sessions "disgusted" with white proposals, and that the organization was preparing to re-think its strategy.[71] The City Commission, fortified by the support for its stand of the disaffected white Committee members, made no further efforts to resume negotiations. Each side, however, announced that it was ready to talk to the other at any time. Each admitted that it had no definite instance in mind.[72] As the rupture in communication continued, a minister characterized the existing state of affairs as one of "mounting tension and the grim, ever-present fact of the boycott."[73]

The MIA was the first to break this silence. On January 9 King requested a "top-level" meeting with the City Commission for the following day. He wanted the opportunity to present a slightly different version of the MIA's seating proposal. The Commission agreed, and a delegation met with them on the 10th for two hours. According to this modified plan seating would still be by the first come-first served method, with Negroes filling the bus toward the front and the whites filling toward the rear. But, whenever seats became vacant to the rear of them, Negroes would "voluntarily" move back to them. Similarly, whites would "voluntarily" shift to forward seats, when they became vacant. It was hoped this would remove some of the previously objectionable drawbacks, such as the possibility of some whites having to stand. Also, Negroes and whites would not occupy seats next to each other. The MIA pointed out that this plan was in effect extensively in the South, and in Mobile, Dothan, and Huntsville in Alabama.[74]

Mayor Gayle and the other Commissioners were not convinced that this addition to the plan altered its inadvisability. They refused to approve it, citing, as usual, the city and state laws. The MIA said in return, as they had before, that they were not asking that these old laws be broken, or that new laws replace them. They asked, instead, that the Commission simply re-interpret the laws. But, again no agreement was reached.[75]

No other attempt was made to promote a negotiated settlement for another month. When the new effort was made, it was undertaken in response to new impetus, provided by dramatic developments. As will be discussed later, the City Commission inaugurated its "get tough" policy on January 3rd. On January 30th King's home was bombed; E. D. Nixon's was hit two days later. On February 1st the MIA shifted the focus of its attack to the Federal Courts. Also, the atmosphere of antagonism between the races was growing at an alarming rate.

An influential group of whites stepped into the breach at this juncture, hoping that some way could still be found to resolve differences at the conference table. The "Men of Montgomery" was a newly-formed civic club composed of about one hundred successful business and professional leaders of the city. Headed by William R. Lynn, manager of a local television station, this group appealed publicly on February 8 for any suggestions on a way solve the boycott problem. Individuals or associations were urged to come up with proposals. Lynn's promotion of the appeal resulted in its wide coverage by the news media. He broadcast his telephone number, asking any interested party to call him at any time.

The Men of Montgomery also issued a joint declaration with the Montgomery Ministerial Alliance. They deplored the recent deterioration in inter-racial relations, and contrasted the Montgomery of a few weeks back, a proud and good place to live, with the town's present dilemma. They felt that the city was becoming virtually "a house divided against itself." They warned that the community was being hurt severely, both economically and morally. If steps were not taken the damage might be increased, and made permanent. Therefore, they asked every citizen to abide by three proposals. First, every one should "censor" his own words, to forestall unfounded rumors which were plaguing attempts to restore harmony. Second, neither side should threaten the other with reprisals or intimidations. Finally, both sides should pick "true representatives" to meet together.[76] This appeal, by such a powerful group, commanded attention. The MIA responded to the invitation, and met secretly with the Men of Montgomery on at least two occasions, although nothing in the way of new proposals was forthcoming.[77]

This group finally succeeded in bringing the two sides together for another confrontation. The Men of Montgomery urged this meeting on the Commission, which was bound to agree, and also worked out with them the "compromise proposal" which was offered to the MIA on Feb 20th. Under this plan courtesy to Negroes was guaranteed through periodic spot checks by riders of both races. Suggestion boxes would be installed on all buses. As to seating, the first ten spaces on each bus would be reserved for whites, the last ten for Negroes. Each race would fill toward the middle, and drivers could assign seats in the middle section as needed. Also, special buses would be assigned for the exclusive use of either race at peak hours. Finally, it was declared

Colored citizens are assured by the City Commissioners that there will be no retaliation whatsoever resulting from the bus boycott.[78]

The leaders of the MIA listened to these proposals, but did not commit themselves to acceptance. A mass meeting of Negroes was scheduled for that night, and the Commission's terms were offered to the crowd for a vote. Ralph Abernathy detailed the plan to them, and pointed out that it allowed Negroes few real concessions. Also, due to declining revenues, the bus company had recently instituted a raise in fares, which would remain in force even if this plan were accepted. Thus, Negroes would be paying more to ride in circumstances much like those they had chosen to protest.[79]

There was one other factor which worked on the crowd's consciousness that night, and which also operated against acceptance of the Commission's plan. One week before this date a Montgomery County Grand Jury had begun examining the boycott, to determine if its leaders were in violation of the anti-boycott law. The jury had been hearing evidence all week and it was widely expected that indictments of some sort would be returned shortly, as in fact, occurred the very next day. Therefore, the mood of the crowd was not favorable to this "compromise." When a vote was taken only two men in a number estimated at four thousand were in favor of acceptance. Afterwards Abernathy summed up the feeling of the Negro public, saying, "We have walked for eleven weeks in the cold and rain. Now the weather is warming up. Therefore we will walk on until some better proposals are forthcoming from our city fathers."[80]

After rejection of this plan, and the return of indictments against boycott leaders, local officials made no further serious efforts to negotiate an end to the protest. At this juncture many people hoped that state government might intervene. Even though the City Commission was directly responsible in the matter, the governor might offer fresh ideas or lend his moral authority and prestige to persuade both sides to reach a settlement. Those who had such a hope were destined to be disappointed.

Alabama's governor at the time was James E. Folsom, then serving his second term in office. Folsom was an enigmatic and highly controversial figure who hitherto had remained aloof from any involvement in the boycott. He traditionally drew much of his political support from his native section of northern Alabama, from labor, and from Negroes. Indeed, with this latter group he was probably the most popular white politician in recent years. Negroes liked his avoidance of "race baiting" and his resistance to Southern movements to "nullify" the Supreme Court's school decision of 1954. If he had chosen to speak out on the protest Negroes would have at least heard his proposals with respect.[81]

In fact, the Governor was sympathetic to the complaints which had sparked the protest in December. Privately he believed that there was little justification for requiring Negroes to ride in the rear of buses. Also, he had always thought that the segregation issue was largely a tool used by Black Belt politicians to draw the attention of northern Alabamians away from inequalities in legislative apportionment. He often lamented that while there were countless segregation statutes to enforce white rule in the Black Belt he was, by his reckoning, only the third governor in the state's history to come from the northern hill country. He considered it one of his primary aims in politics to institute a legislative reapportionment to redress the sectional imbalance.[82]

Despite his sympathy for Negro complaints against bus segregation Folsom refused to speak out publicly on the boycott for several months. There were several reasons for this, all of those associated with the precarious political situation in Alabama. First, Folsom well understood that the prevailing opinion among whites strongly favored segregation. He believed that nothing he could do would change this. Also, like most whites, he suspected that to yield to Negroes in the matter of buses where integration would be rather innocuous might lead to stronger assaults on other aspects of segregation where it was more important that the races remain separate.

Other reasons for his silence hinged on two projects which Folsom was urging in the early months of 1956. He had scheduled a special session of the state legislature for January, which was to consider his plan for reapportionment. Another special session was called for February, to take up proposals for dealing with school finances. Folsom was under heavy fire from opponents at the time because of his stand on the race issue, absenteeism from office, high personal expenses, and for various political reasons. He knew that if he committed himself at this time to any moderate stand on the boycott, he might offend many arch-segregationists in the state, and thereby ruin his chances of getting any program through the legislature. It was in February also that riots broke out at the University of Alabama's Tuscaloosa campus over the admission of Autherine Lucy. Folsom relied on campus police to quell the disorders instead of using state troopers, as many urged him to do. When the riots worsened Folsom was roundly criticized for "fiddling while the state burns."[83]

This strategy of maintaining a judicious silence did not have the desired benefits. Both sessions of the legislature were unproductive and Folsom considered them failures. Also, people did not see Folsom's position as one of neutrality, but as an indication that he approved the boycott. When the City Commission proclaimed its "get tough" policy in January, to be discussed later, Folsom had no comment to make about their statements. The *Advertiser* reported the public's dissatisfaction at Folsom's silence by writing, "Throughout the city, white residents were discussing the Commission's stand and many commented that 'our governor ought to take a stand like that instead of siding with Negroes.'"[84]

Folsom's reaction to this criticism was to propose the creation of a biracial commission to make recommendations on the race situation in general. Though endorsed by much of Alabama's press this idea never gained favor with the legislature and was soon abandoned.[85]

On the topic of the boycott Folsom did not speak out until the middle of March, when the problem had been irretrievably transferred to the courts. At that time he simply urged both sides to "bring about a settlement of the boycott so that life can return to normal in our capital city."[86] He also stated that he had been in "private" contact with Negro leaders and with Mayor Gayle three times each, but would not reveal any details.[87]

This mild pronouncement and some attempts at promoting negotiations were the sum of Folsom's efforts to solve the boycott. The assistant Attorney General of Alabama, MacDonald Gallion, did arrange a meeting of lawyers for both sides in late April. Langford, Gray, Crenshaw, and others talked over the issue involved but by this time no fresh alternative proposal were feasible and the meeting ended in failure.[88] After the break up of negotiations in January it is unlikely that any meaningful negotiations were possible. After this point the courts became the new arena of contest. It was here that the MIA finally saw realization of its demands.

FOUR

Rupture of Communications

In the aftermath of unsuccessful negotiations between officials and representatives of the MIA, Negroes and whites in Montgomery became further separated. Each side was convinced the other was clinging to untenable positions.

Most Negroes believed whites were stubbornly refusing to face certain realities. To them the MIA's demands represented social improvements their race needed and deserved in a new age. The City Commission was seen as the chief architect of stalemate. Negroes charged that the Commission refused to meet their demands, not out of a sincere concern for legal objections but because whites feared the consequences of yielding to Negroes. White people were afraid that if Negroes realized the extent of the latent economic power they possessed, a kind of Pandora's Box of civil rights would be opened, leading to new campaigns for equality in other areas.[1]

As this suspicion of motives intensified many Negroes began to lose patience. Soon after New Year's Rev. U. J. Fields, recording secretary of the MIA, warned whites of this feeling in a blunt letter to the *Advertiser*. He wrote that the MIA was not going to soften its demands because these were already compromises with what Negroes really wanted. He added that, "We should have demanded complete integration which does away with Jim Crow . . . Such unwarranted delay in granting our request will result in a demand for the annihilation of segregation . . ."[2]

The same newspaper printed an interview with Rev. King a few days later, in which he seconded Fields' views about the impossibility of compromise. King said that he, too, was an advocate of full integration because "segregation is evil, and I cannot, as a minister, condone evil." He admitted, though, that the current campaign was not designed to destroy the whole system, but only to secure "a small improvement" in the Negro's condition. Nevertheless whites should learn to see the boycott as part of a larger, inexorable world-wide movement for civil rights.[3]

Most white people, of course, were distressed at the impasse in negotiations, which they attributed to Negro intransigence. They did not consider the protest limited to attaining "a small improvement" for the Negro; ultimately, they feared it would lead to a breakdown of segregation.

This divergence in viewpoints was bound to contribute to a growing atmosphere of anger and frustration among both races. This is patently dangerous for the health of any community. In the early months of 1956, unfortunately the situation did not improve. Rather, through a series of events and circumstances, ill-feeling was increased.

For whites there was a tangible symbol of the boycott's destructiveness in the declining number of green and yellow city buses to be seen on Montgomery's streets. The bus company was in serious financial straits. Revenue had fallen to about twenty-two cents per mile driven by each bus, while costs stood at a constant forty-four cents per mile. Loyal white patrons continued to ride, and others sometimes dropped cash gifts into a bus' toll box. This was not enough to off-set the loss of Negro business, so the City Commission assisted the firm in several ways. First, in January, the company was allowed to increase fares by fifty percent. Several times the Commission also permitted cut-backs in the length or number of routes served, until eventually these were pared to a minimum. By March, for instance, the company operated only two buses on Sunday, one to each of the air force bases.[4]

Despite this assistance the company continued to lose money at an alarming rate, reported to be about $600.00 per working day.[5] Montgomerians feared they might finally be deprived to bus service unless the boycott was ended. In an effort to shore up finances the line began to practice strict economy by laying off about 35 drivers and putting about 70 buses in storage. The suffering that this brought about to the drivers and their families angered many whites. White labor union officials were particularly vehement in denouncing the boycott for this reason.[6]

Worsening relations were reflected by a spate of rumors which circulated through the town, and these probably served to increase tensions even more. An observer commenting on this problem pointed out that "the facts of our local situation are essentially simple. Yet various members of our community, both white and Negro, believe things that make it enormously complex."[7]

White people continued to swear to the existence of "goon squads" of Negroes, for instance, although police were unable to make a single arrest on that charge. Whites also heard that all Negro workers were plotting to suddenly quit their jobs "on a certain day." Negroes, in turn, heard that their white employers intended to fire them all, "on a certain day."[8]

Rumor-mongering also fell on the business community with a heavy impact. Word often circulated that a particular firm, usually a national concern, was a contributor to the NAACP and this might cause whites to informally boycott its goods and services. Negroes were liable to avoid a company which was said to donate to the White Citizens Council. This phenomenon was not peculiar to Montgomery at the time; several national firms were the target of such boycotts across the South in the nineteen-fifties. But in Montgomery the incidence of this was certainly high. Those companies known to be so affected included Philip Morris cigarettes, Ford Motor Company, Philco appliances, Falstaff Beer, Coca Cola, Colonial Bread, Holsum Bread, and International Harvester.[9] Some people suggested that competitors of these firms began the damaging rumors purposely, and it was reported that some distraught businessmen found themselves the objects of contradictory tales that caused both races to boycott them.[10]

Other stories, equally persistent, circulated among whites that struck at the character of the MIA's leaders. The belief hung on, for example, that Mrs. Parks planned her arrest. Many believed the whole protest to be the work of "outside agitators." There were also abundant accounts of how various leaders used MIA money for personal items. Rev. King was often the butt of these stories, which had it that he had purchased Cadillacs or Buicks for himself and his wife, Coretta. Cruder stories made the rounds that accused King or other leaders of moral lapses, sexual misconduct, gambling and the like. Rev. Abernathy was also prominently featured in such rumors. MIA leaders worried about the effect of these but decided that the only practical course was to ignore them.[11]

Although it is ahead of the narrative, it is interesting to note that for many white people the substance of these charges was proved later in the year. On June 11 the volatile U. J. Fields abruptly blasted unnamed MIA leaders for "misusing money sent from all over the nation." Deploring a situation "in which the many are exploited by the few," Fields resigned his post and proclaimed complete disassociation from the organization.[12] This was a serious accusation, but it convinced few in the Negro community. King cut short a vacation in California to confront Fields, who subsequently recanted before a specially-called mass meeting. He admitted that his charges were false and were motivated by personal enmity for some leaders. He apologized and was taken back in to the fold, but never again held office in the MIA.[13]

This darkened atmosphere of distrust and hostility was further complicated by the emergence of a new group in Montgomery, the White Citizens Council. The Citizens Council movement had grown up in Mississippi in reaction to the Supreme Court's decision on school segregation in 1954. It spread into Alabama and the Montgomery chapter, the Central Alabama Citizens Council, was founded only a few years before the boycott began. This branch was headed by State Senator Sam M. Englehardt, a fiery segregationist from Shorter in Macon County, and embraced the six counties surrounding Montgomery.

The Council officially advocated carrying the fight against segregation into the courts. Resistance to the civil rights movement was also to be conducted by any other legal means, including the use of dominant white economic power and the race's preponderance at the polls.

During the early stages of the boycott the Council was concerned with increasing membership and publicizing its doctrines. By late January it boasted of an enrollment approaching 9,000, by mid-February it claimed 12,000.[14] Its leaders, Englehardt and Luther Ingalls, former member of the special Mayor's Committee, continually lashed out at the boycott and called for white solidarity in the face of the Negro threat. Rewards were posted for information about "goon squads" and about the unsolved sniping at buses.[15] Rallies were held at which speakers attacked the MIA, the NAACP, and other such groups. In February a large meeting was held where 15,000 people heard Senator James O. Eastland of Mississippi attack the entire Negro civil rights movement from a pro-Council position.[16] Members of the Council also frequently attended meetings of the City Commission to urge continued resistance to MIA demands.[17]

The Council was not universally approved by Montgomery whites. As mentioned previously, the *Advertiser* was mildly opposed to its advocacy of economic sanctions against Negroes. Other moderate elements were afraid the Council might develop into a violent force similar to the Ku Klux Klan, despite its official renunciation of illegal means. Governor Folsom, for instance, disapproved of the organization for this reason. He also thought there was no need for such a group, since whites would continue to control society in the South, anyway. He saw the Council, too, as a dangerous innovation which made its appeal on an "emotional basis" for the purpose of controlling local politics.[18]

Despite these objections the Council received a boost in prestige in January by the addition of Clyde Sellers to its ranks. Sellers, of course, was much troubled by the boycott. He believed, and frequently stated in public, that the great majority of Negroes adhered to the protest only because of intimidation by "goon squads." He also thought that if the city yielded on the first come-first served plan violence and bloodshed would erupt because of increased racial friction. Montgomery would have to double its present police force to contain the situation.[19]

Sellers decided he must do something to impress the white public with his fears. He had been asked to join the Council before but had refused from a reluctance to "lend his name as a public official" to the group. His joining might also put him in an embarrassing position politically. Nevertheless, as his sense of urgency grew, and as he recognized the danger of the Council falling into the hands of intemperate and irresponsible elements, he changed his mind. At a Council meeting on January 6, before a crowd of 1,200, he spoke out in a vivid attack on the boycott and the civil rights movement in general. Declaring that he no longer wanted Negro votes, he announced his intention to join the Council because "if people don't wake up to what's going on, it will be too late to wake them up at all."[20]

This dramatic move did have a sobering effect, and seemed a bad omen for the MIA. As the *Alabama Journal* assessed it, "In effect, the Montgomery police force is now an arm of the White Citizens Council." The paper advised "cool Negro heads" to realize the full implication of this for the protest.[21] Sellers hoped that his colleagues on the Commission would follow his lead, but did not think it proper to ask them to join. In a few days, however, his wish was fulfilled, as a result of one of the most bizarre incidents of the boycott.

On Saturday, January 21, the City Commission held an unscheduled meeting and summoned three Negro ministers to its chambers. These were W. K. Kines, a Baptist, B. F. Mosley, a Presbyterian, and D. C. Rice, a bishop of a small A.M.E. church. The three were well known in the Negro community, but were no way connected with the boycott leadership. The pretext for their attendance at the meeting, allegedly something to do with a pending insurance policy, was never adequately explained. However, at the end of the meeting the Commission released a statement to reporters claiming that the boycott had been settled. The names of the ministers were withheld, and they were described simply as a "group representing the Negroes of Montgomery." The statement said that these representatives had agreed to three proposals formerly put forward by whites: first, that the ten front seats on each bus be reserved for whites, the last ten for Negroes, with each race filling toward the center; next, that courtesy would be extended to all passengers; finally, that the City Commission had no right to tell the bus company to hire drivers of a particular race. It was also announced that the bus service would be restored to all sections as soon as enough Negroes petitioned the company for resumption.[22]

This unexpected development came too late to meet Saturday's press deadline, but was picked up by the Associated Press and sent over its wires under the heading: "Capital Bus Boycott May Be Near End."[23] The story was read that evening by Carl Rowan, Negro editorial writer for the *Minneapolis Tribune*, who was puzzled by it. He telephoned King for confirmation, who replied that this was the first he knew of the story. Rowan hung up and called Mayor Gayle for the names of the men involved. Gayle would not divulge them but did say they were ministers and told their denominations. This was enough for King and the other leaders to guess their identities. The three were contacted and denied having "settled" the boycott. King, Nixon, and others worked though Saturday night and Sunday morning to make sure that every Negro in town that the story was false.[24]

On the following Monday, January 23, King called a news conference to dispute the Commission's claim. Rev. Mosley told the press that he had been "hood-winked" by the commissioners; all three ministers denied having agreed to the Commission's proposals. King then declared, "The bus protest is still on and it will last until our proposals were given sympathetic treatment."[25] This announcement incidentally wrecked the bus company's plans, because bus service had been restored to Negro areas that morning in expectation of an end to the boycott.[26] More important, King had practically branded the Commissioners as liars, who were willing to resort to chicanery to break the protest's momentum.

On that same day the Commission met routinely to approve an extension of the bus company's charter, which was due to expire soon. Gayle used the occasion to hit back at King and the MIA, and the other Commissioners followed suit. It was announced that Gayle and Parks were joining the Citizens Council, and Gayle next lashed out at the protest. He warned all whites that the boycott was part of a campaign "to destroy our social fabric." He vowed that there would be no more talks with the MIA until it was ready to end the boycott. He asked whites to stop providing rides for their domestic workers by chauffeuring them to and from work or by giving them "blackmail transportation money." The public must see that "the Negroes are laughing . . . behind their backs" at the sight of whites subsidizing the boycott. He thought that the Commission had "pussy-footed around on this boycott long enough, and it has come time to be frank and honest." Fair proposals had been offered to Negro leaders, who treacherously reported "one thing to a white person and another to a Negro . . ."[27]

Clyde Sellers spoke up next and concurred with the Mayor. He Announced that from now on he was ordering police to disperse "loitering" groups at Negroes at pickup points in white areas. This was necessary, he said, because such groups frequently trampled on lawns and created too much noise in quiet residential sections. He was also ordering his men to put and end to "mass hitch-hiking" by the boycotters.[28] As revealed later Sellers transmitted a general order that day to his police chief, which was posted for the entire force to read. This order told police to "take steps to make certain no incidents arise to cause any additional trouble," while being careful to maintain "the best of relationships with the Negroes."[29]

Franklin Parks was the last to speak and, naturally, condemned the MIA's stand. He alluded vaguely to assurances he had received from businessmen that they would "lay off Negro employees who are being used as NAACP instruments in this boycott." He gave no specific information on this threat.[30]

When news of the Commissions's outburst was received by the white community, reaction was generally quite favorable. Messages of congratulation poured into City Hall for the "strong stand" taken. One newspaper applauded Gayle's statement as one that "put into words the thoughts in the minds and hearts of our citizenship."[31] Whites generally expressed relief that the Commission cleared the air and approved the pledge to toughen its response to the protest.

As seen in retrospect though this hardening of attitude had mixed results. In a sense the "get tough" policy, as Negroes called it, was only window-dressing. Talks with Negroes had already played out and no more seemed likely unless one side capitulated to the other. The rhetorical fury of the Commission did not diminish the Negro public's loyalty to the MIA and the boycott, and may even have strengthened it. The subsequent crackdown by police on loiterers and hitch-hikers, with a tightening of traffic law enforcement against the car pool, was ineffectual. The Negro press charged that over a hundred pool drivers were arrested for minor violations in the first week after announcement of the "get tough" policy.[32] The MIA had sufficient funds to pay these fines, and only a few dropped out of the pool because of the pressure. As an example of this "crackdown" Rev. King was arrested on January 26 for driving 35 miles an hour in a 25 mile-per-hour zone. He was taken to jail, frisked for weapons, finger-printed, and released on bond.[33] King's case and the others were resented by Negroes as harassment of their protest and misuse of lawful authority by white officials.

On the night of January 30 a far more serious thing happened, which added to the sum of rising anger among Negroes. That evening, while her husband was away from home presiding over a mass meeting, Coretta King heard an object strike the porch of their house. As she rushed to a back bedroom where their little daughter lay sleeping, an explosion rocked the house. Fortunately, the bomb or device was a weak one and little damage was done, and no one was injured. King, of course, hurried home and was joined there by the City Commissioners and Police Chief Ruppenthal. A crowd of 300 Negroes gathered outside the house, and milled about in a defiant, angry mood. King came out to address them and urged them to disperse. He warned them not to "do anything panicky," and reminded them of their commitment to non-violence: "Don't get your weapons . . . We want to love our enemies . . . Be good to them, love them and let them know you love them." The crowd obeyed his plea for them to disperse, and the danger passed.[34]

Sellers expressed his regrets to King and promised to uncover the guilty party. He also offered police protection to King, "to defend you against acts such as this."[35] On the next morning Mayor Gayle got a resolution through the regular Commission session which deplored the bombing, and offered a $500.00 reward for arrest of the guilty.[36] The local White Citizens Council even spoke out on the incident, denouncing "such strange and foreign acts," and posting an equal reward.[37]

Two nights later, however, a second bomb went off, this one in the driveway of E. D. Nixon's home. Again little damage and no injury occurred. But Negroes now charged that these outrages were the direct result of the City Commission's "recalcitrant" attitude and "get tough" policy.[38] Roy Wilkins, national director of the NAACP, publicly called on Governor Folsom to use his authority to prevent more violence in Montgomery. Folsom, however, remained aloof from the controversy.[39] Some important newspapers around the state deplored the bombings, but the two in Montgomery were comparatively unconcerned. There was a suspicion among many local whites, one which Commissioner Sellers shared, that MIA leaders or some other Negroes had arranged the bombings for propaganda purposes.[40] Perhaps reflecting this suspicion the *Alabama Journal* published an article commenting on the incident at King's home, which read "Bombs are wholly ineffective as arguments, especially when they are so placed as not to hurt anybody."[41]

The next development in the boycott situation was an attempt by the MIA to get around the log-jam of snarled negotiations, and to settle the matter permanently in the courts. King later said that this move, a civil suit in Federal Court, was undertaken in reaction to the bombings, the "crudeness of the 'get tough' policy," and the intransigence of the City Commission."[42] However, the evidence is that this decision was actually made before the bombings, or even the Commission's outburst of January 21. If this is correct it does not, in any case, absolve the Commission of making a grave tactical error by the pronouncements and crackdown in late January. As will be seen, the MIA used these as partial grounds for the suit.

On about January 14, E. D. Nixon discussed the subject of such a suit with King and Abernathy. Nixon suggested that they not try to carry through with Mrs. Parks' case, as originally planned. He thought they might do better with a suit for practical reasons. He told them of an instance in the mid-nineteen forties, when a similar arrest had occurred. He believed that case, too, had been scheduled for appeal, but that ten years later it was still pending in the courts. He feared they might have as much trouble getting the Parks case on a docket in Alabama.[43]

Fred Gray was thinking about this, too. About the middle of January he decided that an "end run" was advisable. He knew there was a quicker "vehicle" to the Supreme Court than the Parks case, and it was obvious they had to go to the highest tribunal for complete satisfaction of their demands. The Parks case was a local criminal matter, which would first have to be taken through the intervening state courts before coming under federal jurisdiction. A suit filed in Federal Court would by-pass these time consuming obstacles. Also, through a civil suit the MIA could probably get an injunction against the segregation law along the way, which they could not get in a criminal case. It was possible too, that the best result they could get from the Parks case would be the setting aside of her conviction, without the desired anti-segregation ruling.[44]

The logic of this argument was convincing, and the MIA decided in favor of it. Gray accordingly filed suit in the United State District Court in Montgomery on February 1, 1956. This was done in behalf of five Negro women who had experienced some form of racial discrimination on local buses. They were Amelia Browder, Susie McDonald, Jeanetta Reese,

Claudette Colvin, and Mary Louise Smith. Defendants named in the suit were the City Commissioners individually and as a legal body, Police Chief Ruppenthal, the bus company, and two drivers. It was charged that these defendants had formed "a conspiracy to interfere with the civil and constitutional rights of the Negro citizens" of Montgomery. This conspiracy employed "force, threats, violence, intimidation, and harassment," and was designed to prevent Negroes from using private transportation, therefore depriving them of the rights, privileges, and immunities guaranteed by the Fourteenth Amendment to the United States Constitution. Defendants, and particularly the City Commission were accused of harming plaintiffs in five specific ways. First, they had urged whites to refuse transportation to Negro employees. Also, the Commissioners had joined the White Citizens Council. Defendants had also enforced traffic regulations too stringently against Negroes, while not doing the same to whites. The police had questioned and harassed Negro taxi drivers. Finally, defendants had promoted economic reprisals against Negroes in various ways, such as by giving information on boycotters to their employers.[45]

The suit asked that defendants be prevented from conducting such interference in future. The court should also define the legal rights of the parties involved, and brand the interference cited above as a violation of the Fourteenth Amendment. Also, it was asked that the sections of the Montgomery City Code and the Code of Alabama pertaining to segregation on intra-state buses be ruled "null and void." The court was asked to enjoin defendants from enforcing those sections any longer, on grounds that they were unconstitutional.[46]

As provided for by federal law the suit was scheduled to be heard by a panel of three federal judges. J. C. Hutcheson, Jr., chief judge of the United States Fifth Judicial Circuit seated in Houston, took the case under advisement. He was empowered to choose the panel, and took over a month to release his decision.[47] By that time three amendments had been made to the original suit.

First, Gray added to the list of defendants the members of the Alabama Public Service Commission. C.C. "Jack" Owen, Sibyl Pool, and Jimmy Hitchcock, as the A.P.S.C., had jurisdiction over utility companies operating in the state, which included bus companies. It was necessary for them to be enjoined from enforcing segregation statues, if those laws were to be nullified effectively. Next, Gray deleted the charge that the defendants had actually conspired together to abridge Negro rights. This was probably done to tighten up the case in light of a recent experience the NAACP had suffered in Birmingham. In an attempt to force Autherine Lucy's re-admission to the University of Alabama, NAACP lawyers unwisely accused officials of conspiracy to keep her out. When this could not be proved the case was lost.[48]

The third amendment to the suit arose over a confused incident that sparked much furor and caused Gray serious trouble. This was the deletion of Jeanetta Reese's name from the list of plaintiffs. Mrs. Reese withdrew from the action on February 2, one day after the suit had been filed. In doing so she told Mayor Gayle and reporters "You know I don't want nothing to do with that mess." She charged that Gray had tricked her into signing suit papers and stated she didn't even know what the papers were for. Gray answered that she had understood the nature of the papers and the suit, and said she had been frightened into withdrawing by the police.[49]

Because of Mrs. Reese's charge a grand jury indicted Gray on February 18 for malpractice and "unlawful appearance as an attorney." If convicted he would face a possible fine of $500.00 and permanent disbarrment. Fortunately for Gray it was discovered early in March that the state was without jurisdiction in the case. Since suit had been filed in a federal office building the offense fell under federal control and was out of Alabama's hands. On March 2, Montgomery Circuit Court dismissed the charge against Gray.[50] The United States District Attorney refused to press charges and the incident was closed.

This was not the end of Gray's worries, however, as another incident also threatened to remove him from participation in the boycott. On February 3, he granted an interview to a local reporter and mentioned that he had not been in military service. He had been deferred from the draft as a part-time minister of the Church of Christ. On February 8, Alabama's Selective Service Director, James W. Jones, announced that Gray had been reclassified as 1-A.[51] Gray had expected to lose his deferment a year before, when he informed his board that he was taking up the practice of law. However, he opposed reclassification at this late date because he believed it was simply an attempt to "silence dissent." He was not prepared to admit the precedent of using the draft to punish boycotters.[52]

On February 22, an appeals board upheld his new classification. On the next day, therefore, Gray asked Clarence Mitchell, head of the NAACP's Washington bureau, to intercede in his behalf. The NAACP obliged and took his case through another series of appeal and reviews. Finally, General

Lewis Hershey, director of National Selective Service, intervened. He overruled lower decisions and returned Gray to a deferred status. In protest of this fourteen Alabama draft officials resigned their offices and the Autauga and Bullock county boards refused to induct anyone until Gray was drafted. Senator Lister Hill demanded a Congressional inquiry into Gray's case as the controversy mounted. Nevertheless, Hershey made his decision stick, and Gray was not drafted.[53]

On February 13, a more dangerous effort to break up the boycott came to light, when the regular February session of the Montgomery County Grand Jury convened. Since mid-January Circuit Solicitor William F. Thetford had been preparing to bring boycott leaders to trial. He was confident it could be shown that these leaders were in clear violation of the state's 1921 anti-boycott law. He asked the City Commission in January to assist him, and Sellers delegated two city detectives to the Solicitor's office. These men worked with Thetford full-time investigating the MIA's activities. Movies were made of car pool operations, tape recordings were obtained of mass meetings, and other evidence was gathered.[54]

The grand jury, composed of seventeen whites and one Negro, were charged on opening day by Judge Eugene B. Carter to examine the boycott and to determine if indictments were warranted. He told the jurors that he was concerned about the recent deterioration of racial matters in "a city that both races have had pleasure living in." He spoke of the imminent danger of violence and warned that "the doctrine of hate has no place here." He also wanted the jury to decide if the boycott was a "wrongful interference with traditional property rights." and concluded, "if the boycott is illegal, it must be brought to an end."[55]

The jury heard evidence presented by Thetford and also took testimony from 200 witnesses. Among these witnesses were U. J. Fields of the MIA and several pool drivers. Presentment was made on February 21.[56]

The grand jury responded that, indeed, a critical antagonism was evident between the races in Montgomery, from which bloodshed might soon erupt. Jurors believed that "the NAACP attack on segregation is the primary cause of the unrest . . . " They proclaimed, "We find that there has been an illegal boycott existing in this county since the early part of December, 1955. Indictments have been returned where guilt was shown."[57]

The list of persons indicted was the longest ever presented in the county. It included King, Nixon, Abernathy and most of the other leaders, and many of the car pool drivers. The total number of names, in fact, originally was

115, but it later found that duplication of names had occurred in some cases. The final number of the indicted stood at 89. Of these, 75 were arrested on the first day that warrants were available, February 2, and the remainder were brought in next day. All of those arrested were ordered to post bond of $300.00 each, and were released.[58] Ten years later King admitted that by accepting bond the MIA had committed "a tactical error." He realized only after it was done that, if they had remained in jail, "it would have nationally dramatized and deepened our movement even earlier."[59]

Despite this "tactical error" the mass arrests proved to be a windfall for the MIA, anyway. Many local whites privately thought it was mistake to indict so many.[60] Nationally, the reaction was even more critical. For the first time news of the boycott rated front page treatment by the *New York Times*. The American Civil Liberties Union denounced the arrests as "clearly unconstitutional." Congressman Adam Clayton Powell of Harlem described the affair as "a new low in American barbarism," and demanded that President Eisenhower give protection to boycott leaders. Civil rights groups, liberal associations, and ministerial alliances across the North sent money and messages of encouragement to headquarters.[61]

Another important result of the indictments was the direct intervention of the NAACP in the boycott for the first time. Prior to this the MIA and the NAACP had remained officially separate. Officials of the larger organization often met with MIA representatives for briefings on the situation in Montgomery, and local NAACP branches often contributed money for the boycott, but little other contact was maintained. There was even speculation among liberals that the larger group was jealous of the Montgomery group's success, or disapproving of its direct action, non-legalistic approach.[62] Whatever the truth of this conjecture, the two organizations began to work together almost immediately after indictments were returned.

E. D. Nixon telephoned Thurgood Marshall, chief counsel for the NAACP, on February 21. Marshall was old acquaintance of Nixon's, and after hearing of the indictments, promised that he would lend a hand in defending the MIA.[63] At the same time Fred Gray called Robert Carter, Marshall's assistant, for the same purpose.[64] Shortly thereafter, Roy Wilkins made it official by cabling King that "all the resources" of the NAACP, including "its entire legal staff," were at his disposal during the crisis. Arthur Shores, a Birmingham Negro attorney who had handled the Autherine Lucy case, was delegated to assist Gray and Charles Langford in pre-trial preparations.[65]

Meanwhile Adam Clayton Powell was organizing a national protest against the indictments. He proposed a "National Deliverance Day of Prayer" to be held on March 28. He asked Negroes and white sympathizers to stop work for one hour on that day, as an indication of their support of the boycotters' cause. This idea gained acceptance throughout the North, as prayer meetings, speeches, and memorial services were scheduled. The Massachusetts Board of Representatives voted by a three to one margin to suspend business for an hour that day.[66] A newspaper in Communist China editorialized about the MIA's "heroic struggle."[67]

Increasing pressure was placed on President Eisenhower to authorize federal intervention in Montgomery. One Northern ministerial group urged him to go there "personally," to lend his prestige to the protest.[68] Eisenhower, indeed, was privately "outraged" at the recent events in Montgomery, but remained silent in public.[69] Alabama Negroes heard reports that he had directed Attorney General Herbert Brownell to check on ways federal power might be brought to bear, but if this was true nothing ever came of it.[70]

"Ike's" steady refusal to condemn the arrests drew sharp criticism from some liberal quarters. In early March Powell attacked him as a "Pilate" for his unconcern.[71] But the President's only public response to queries on his position was to urge approval by Congress of his plan for a bi-partisan civil rights commission. He finally laid to rest any notion that he would intervene in Montgomery at a news conference on March 20. When asked his opinion of the situation there Eisenhower said that Alabama law covered the matter, and he expressed the wish that both races would learn to understand each other, and to work together.[72]

Arraignment proceedings for the indicted were held February 24. All 89 defendants pleaded not guilty, and waived rights to jury trials. Judge Eugene Carter set the date for trial as March 19.

On that day the chambers and halls of Circuit Court were filled with curious whites, anxious Negroes, and newsmen from the United States, France, England, and India. William F. Thetford stood ready to prosecute, aided by two assistant solicitors. Defendants were represented by Gray, Langford, Ozell Billingsley, Arthur Shores, and Peter Hall. These last three were provided by the NAACP, as was Robert Carter, Marshall's assistant. Judge Carter refused to let the other Carter approach the bar, however, since he was not licensed in Alabama. He did allow him to sit at the defense's table and help in preparing their arguments.[73]

In preliminary proceedings Judge Carter ruled the indictments valid and dismissed Gray's several demurrers. He allowed the defense's request for separate trials for the 89. Since King's name had headed the list of the first indictment bill, it was ruled that he should stand trial first.[74]

For the next four days each side pressed its respective contentions. The prosecution examined 27 witnesses. Thetford gradually built up his accusation that King was the leader of a group whose aim was to foment and sustain the boycott. By the testimony of J. H. Bagley and W. A. Gayle he showed that King always acted as head of the MIA and spokesman for Negroes in all negotiating sessions. Erna Dungee, financial secretary for the group, brought along subpoenaed checks, deposit slips, and bank statements to show that King, as well as she and Nixon, was responsible for MIA financial transactions. U. J. Fields, recording secretary, produced minutes of meeting, including records of the initial meeting, where King was elected president.[75]

Thetford had little trouble piecing together proof of his self-evident thesis that King was leader of the MIA and influential in maintaining the boycott. Repeated objections by the defense and failing memories of some of his witnesses could not set back his case. At one point during the first day's testimony, Judge Carter declared, "There is enough evidence at the present to connect the material with a charge of conspiracy against the defendant."[76] Prosecution also elicited testimony that would show the coercive nature of the boycott. Several bus drivers told of shots fired at their vehicles during early days of the protest. Several Negroes told of attacks or threats of violence against them if they did not cooperate with the boycott. Carter disallowed much of this testimony, however, since such acts could not be connected with the MIA.[77]

The state rested its case on February 21. Gray then moved for dismissal, contending that insufficient proof had been presented to prove a conspiracy or to connect King with one. When this was disallowed Gray presented his case. He summoned 5 witnesses, most of whom were Negroes who had had humiliating or physically damaging experience on buses, due to the segregation system. Gray sought to show by this that Negroes had "just cause" for their boycott, which was an allowable defense under the 1921 law. He also countered Thetford's picture of a violent, coercive boycott by bringing forward several creditable witnesses, who attested to its nonviolent character. Joe Azbell, city editor of the *Montgomery Advertiser*, recounted his personal observations of King's call for nonviolence. Rev. Robert Graetz, only white member of the MIA's executive board, agreed, and told of several instances when King had expressly condemned threats and intimidation.[78]

Finally, King took the stand. He denied encouraging Negroes to boycott; rather he said, he had always told them to let their own consciences guide them. Thetford struck at this assertion by showing a copy of the MIA's resolution of December 5, which called for continuance of the first day's boycott. King denied authorship of the document, explaining that he had been on the committee which fathered it, but that he had been engaged in other business when it was produced.[79]

After the defense rested, Carter quickly announced his decision. He found King guilty as charged and fined him $500.00 or 386 days at hard labor. He explained that he gave King only half of the possible maximum fine because he had tried to oppose violence in the protest. Gray announced that the decision would be appealed and posted a bond of $1,000.00 for security. Carter therefore granted continuance in all the other cases until King's appeal should be completed.[80]

After the decision, on February 23, King went to an "emotion charged" mass meeting. He vowed to continue fighting for "justice and equality" until the cause should prevail.[81] News of his conviction was making headlines around the country, again. His trial produced the largest transcript (over 500 pages) and received the most extensive coverage of any in Montgomery's history.[82] His conviction again fired the sympathies of liberals and stimulated contributions to the MIA. A small newspaper in Asbury Park, New Jersey, for example, denounced the verdict as "a disgrace to the state of Alabama," and started a collection to pay King's fine.[83]

As Gray and his assistant started preparations for appeal attention shifted to an arena where prospects for the MIA were brighter. Shortly before King's trial had begun Judge Hutcheson in Houston had announced the composition of the three-man panel to hear the civil suit filed on February 1st. All three judges were native Alabamians. They were: Richard T. Rives, 61 year old judge on the Fifth Circuit Court of Appeals; Seybourn H. Lynne, 48 year old District Court judge for Northern Alabama; 38 year old Frank M. Johnson, of the District Court for Central Alabama. Rives and Lynne were Truman appointees while Johnson was the lone Republican among them, having been elevated by Eisenhower in 1955. Judge Hutcheson scheduled hearing of the suit for May 11.[84]

But before the suit could be heard the United States Supreme Court issued a decision in a similar case which created a great deal of confusion, and which caused the first break in the ranks of the anti-boycott forces.

In December, 1955, the NAACP sponsored a suit in Columbia, South Carolina, which aimed at eliminating segregation on buses in that city. Thurgood Marshall and Robert Carter took that case, *Flemming* vs. *South Carolina*, to a District Court in Richmond, Virginia. In late January, 1956, this court struck down Columbia's segregated seating requirements.[85] The bus company involved took that decision to the Supreme Court, which handed down a ruling on April 23. With no explanation, the Court only said "The appeal is dismissed. *Slaker* vs. *O'Conner*, 278 U.S. 188."[86]

This was interpreted by observers, including the *New York Times*, as an invalidation of segregation and was trumpeted as another land-mark decision.[87] In Chicago the National City Lines immediately issued orders to its Southern companies to cease enforcing segregation on their buses. This order was posted by the Montgomery branch on the day of the Court's decision.[88]

However, to the embarrassment of many earlier commentators, in a few days the *Washington Post* and other papers were saying that the Court's ruling had been widely misinterpreted. The appeal had been dismissed for purely procedural reasons, since there had been a legal error in the format of its presentations. In short, there had been no decision on bus segregation, per se.[89]

The National City Lines stuck to its original order, regardless. It was believed that segregation would be struck down soon enough, anyway, and the company should avoid expensive court battles by preparing for that ruling now. The Montgomery City Lines, of course, had to abide by the parent corporation's decision.[90] Jack Owen of the Alabama Public Service Commission had other ideas though. He believed from the first that the Supreme Court's decision applied only to South Carolina at most, whether it outlawed segregation or not. On April 24 he sent a wire to the bus company's Chicago headquarters in which he ordered that firm and "all public carriers in Alabama" to retain segregated seating "or suffer the consequences."[91] W. A. Gayle supported Owen by announcing that the city would enforce segregation laws "just as we have been doing."[92] The national firm refused to budge, however, and replied that it had "no choice but to comply with the decision of the Supreme Court."[93] Clyde Sellers applied more pressure to the company by ordering his police to keep enforcing segregation, and to look only to him for authority on the question. Any driver who disobeyed the city and state laws, he announced, would face arrest.[94]

To compound the confusion at this juncture, J. H. Bagley of the bus company was stricken with a severe heart attack and went to the hospital. His representatives met with the City Commission on April 27 but they could make no headway. The company was caught between the conflicting demands of the city and its own headquarters.[95]

The City Commission took stronger steps to enforce its will. On April 30 it passed a resolution citing segregated seating as necessary for "public health, morals, comfort, and peace of the community." Gayle was empowered to seek an injunction against the bus company to secure this end.[96] Suit was filed, therefore, in Circuit Court on May 1, and Judge Walter B. Jones began hearings two days later. The bus company argued that it faced ruinous court costs if it defied the Supreme Court's ruling; the city replied that social chaos would result if segregation was destroyed. After 45 minutes of arguments Jones promised to release a decision soon.

On May 9 Jones delivered his ruling. He accepted the city's thesis, and enjoined the bus company from disobeying state and local segregation laws, which "no straight out decision of the Supreme Court of the United States" had invalidated.[97]

At 9.00 A.M. two days later, May 11, hearings were opened in United States District Court on the case of *Browder* vs. *Gayle*, the MIA's suit against public officials and the bus company. This hearing, too, was a short one, lasting only three hours. Gray, Langford, and Robert Carter stood for the plaintiffs. Gray conducted most of the examination for them, and simply called the four women to the stand in turn. Each told of a particular incident she had been party to, where she was forced to yield her seat to whites, or otherwise discriminated against on account of her race.[98]

Attorneys for the A.P.S.C., the City Commission, and the bus company contended that "harmony between the Negro and white races in this city depends upon continued segregation." They also argued that suit in Federal Court was unnecessary, since plaintiffs had had a chance to "adjudicate all matters" in state courts. Further, no irreparable damage had been done to plaintiffs by defendants; alleged damages were the result of legitimate enforcement of existing laws.[99]

Walter Knabe, attorney for the City Commission, handled most cross-examination of the four plaintiffs. He told the court that "one of our contentions is that all this is one scheme and plan." He tried to elicit, through questioning, details which would show that King and other MIA leaders had influenced the women to support the boycott. He suspected that they could have sought redress for their grievances, some of which went back several years, long ago. He thought they had come forward only to suit the purposes of the MIA.[100] Clyde Sellers and W. A. Gayle were also brought to the stand and repeated their conviction that relaxation of segregation laws would lead to bloodshed. Finally, an official of the bus company was brought forward and at the request of judges explained to them in detail the practical points of the bus companies segregation procedures.[101]

At noon the panel of judges ordered adjournment. They promised an early decision and retired with a mass of subpoenaed documents relating to the Parks case, the Colvin case of early 1955, and orders and decisions of the City Commission.

Both sides anxiously awaited word of the court's decision, which finally came on June 5, six months to the day after the boycott began. The decision was reached by a split vote, with Judge Lynne dissenting from the ruling opinion of Johnson and Rives. The majority opinion, which was limited in application only to Montgomery, was what the MIA had hoped for. Johnson and Rives held that Montgomery's segregated buses did violate the "equal protection" and "due process" guarantees of the Fourteenth Amendment. They believed that the doctrine of separate but equal facilities as embodied in *Plessy* vs. *Ferguson* had been "impliedly overruled" in several previous decisions of the Supreme Court. Therefore, the City of Montgomery was "permanently enjoined and restrained" from enforcing any sections of the city or state code, or any other law, "which may require plaintiffs or any other Negroes similarly situated to submit to segregation in the use of bus transportation facilities in the City of Montgomery."[102]

However, the injunction was temporarily suspended for ten days to give defendants' lawyers time to mount an appeal to the Supreme Court. Suspension of the injunction would also ensure that the case would receive quick attention by the Supreme Court, since by this device the case automatically was given preferred status on that Court's docket.[103]

Needless to say the Negroes in Montgomery were jubilant at receipt of the news. The court's decision gave meaning to their sacrifices of the past six months. It was realized, however, that the final hurdle had not yet been cleared. The Supreme Court, which was then in summer recess, would have to approve the lower court's verdict at its next October session. There was

271

always the possibility the Supreme Court would overturn the ruling, although Negroes believed that odds against this were high. It was decided, then, that even though the injunction would take operation in a few days, they would not go back to the buses until that final, irreversible decision in Washington. The MIA had ample financial resources now to operate the car pool for the several months necessary, and the general mood among Negroes after this victory was that, having boycotted so long, they could boycott a little longer. The City Commission and the A.P.S.C. announced intention to appeal as soon as possible, and lawyers for both sides began preparation of their cases. Montgomery's citizens, white and Negro, sat out the summer anxiously, and looked to the fall for a final end to the boycott.[104]

FIVE

Conclusion of
the Boycott

There were few important events in the boycott during the summer months after the District Court's decision in June. By this time the MIA had enough money to finance its operations and the car pool required little effort to maintain as it functioned. Morale was high among boycotters because it was expected that the Supreme Court would grant them final victory in the fall.

These warm months were the time when leaders could more nearly relax than at any other. They used part of their free time to travel around the country speaking to interested groups. On these occasions various leaders explained the methods of mass protest worked out in Montgomery and extolled the virtues and advantages of nonviolence. Rev. King was a celebrated figure and was much in demand as a speaker. He addressed large audiences in Chicago, Los Angeles, San Francisco, and other cities.[1] Several times he also went with other MIA leaders to New York to participate in rallies for the NAACP at Madison Square Garden. Flanked by such distinguished supporters as Eleanor Roosevelt, King and others spread the doctrine of nonviolent protest.[2] In August of that year Rosa Parks, J. E. Pierce, and Rev. Robert Graetz represented the MIA at a civil rights seminar at the Highlander Folk School. Located in Grundy County, Tennessee, this was a controversial training school for civil rights workers and labor organizers. Parks, Pierce, and Graetz conducted a week-long workshop at which they shared practical knowledge gained in Montgomery with sympathizers from other cities.[3]

As time drew closer for the anticipated climax to the legal fight, however, the MIA was forced to meet several threats to continuance of the boycott. The attempt to draft Fred Gray into the Army, as previously mentioned, was underway. And on August 25 Robert Graetz's home was bombed, though not severely, while he was at the Highlander Folk School. Negroes of course were outraged by the incident, and saw it as another attempt to intimidate their leaders. Mayor Gayle, however, dismissed it as a "publicity stunt." He told reporters, "It's a strange coincidence that when interest appears lagging in the bus boycott, something like this happens." He pointed out that boycott leaders were not at home when bombings occurred and charged that such acts were staged to stimulate lagging contributions.[4]

In September a serious menace to the car pool developed. Local white agents began to cancel liability insurance policies on automobiles driven in the pool. Alabama law required each car to have $11,000.00 worth of such protection, and some way had to be found to provide it.[5] King finally got around this obstacle by engaging the help of a Negro insurance broker in Atlanta, who persuaded Lloyds of London to accept the risk.[6]

In October a campaign began to attack the car pool, which was perhaps the most vulnerable point in the MIA's operations. In the middle of the month the local press reported that white housewives were receiving threatening telephone calls in which they were warned not to drive their maids to and from work anymore. Letters were also circulating through the community which purported to list the names of housewives who continued to ferry domestic workers.[7] This particular effort to break up the pool was unsuccessful and soon died away. It was followed, though, by another campaign which enjoyed more backing and which was ultimately triumphant.

An influential member of the anti-boycott forces was Jack D. Brock, editor of *Alabama Labor News*. Brock was a former president of the Alabama State Federation of Labor, who consistently opposed the boycott because of its adverse effects on the local union of white bus drivers. He was also a staunch segregationist and a leading figure in the Central Alabama Citizens Council. He saw no contradiction between the interests of the Council and that of organized labor, and publicly attacked George Meany, head of the national AFL-CIO, for stating that the two groups were basically inimical.[8]

On October 2 Brock presented an editorial in his paper in which he lashed out at the defeatist attitude among local whites. He believed that the cause of white supremacy and segregation on buses was not lost, and announced that he was working with certain unnamed groups "to correlate the efforts" of each to defeat the boycott. This attack would be directed against the MIA's car pool which was, he said, clearly illegal and which had been allowed to operate much too long.[9]

Three days later, on October 26, Brock went before the City Commission to demand that the pool be stopped. He was supported by John Kohn, attorney for an interested group of citizens. Kohn told the Commissioners that they could do what had been done recently in Tallahassee, Florida. A few months before Negroes in that city had organized a boycott of buses much like the one in Montgomery. They had even operated a similar car pool. City fathers there had stifled the protest by getting an injunction against the pool. Brock, Kohn, and their supporters urged the Commission to follow suit in Montgomery.[10]

The Commission had compiled much information on the car pool months before when evidence was being gathered for the trial of Rev. King. They now consulted with Walter Knabe, city attorney, and decided that such an injunction as Brock and the others wanted might be obtained. On October 30, therefore, they passed a resolution ordering Knabe to file proceedings designed to "stop the operation of car pools or transportation systems growing out of the bus boycott."[11] This decision apparently satisfied the petitioners but was greeted elsewhere with criticism. The *Advertiser*, for example, feared that the Commission was about to commit "another blunder" comparable to the mass arrests in February. It agreed that the car pool was an illegal jitney service as the Commission had declared, but claimed that "the timing of this legal action is questionable." The *Advertiser* believed that this move should have been taken a year ago when the boycott first began. Now, everyone expected the Supreme Court to strike down bus segregation soon. Since "nobody is paying any attention to the boycott anymore," the commission should have left the matter alone.[12]

On November 2 the MIA tried to head off this threat by appealing again to the United States District Court. Gray, Langford, Billingsley, Hall, and Shores asked Judge Frank Johnson for an injunction to prohibit the city from seeking an injunction of its own. The court was also asked to issue a restraining order to keep the city from interfering with the pool in other ways. It was argued that the pool was a legal, voluntary operation and that hindrance of it violated the equal protection clause of the fourteenth Amendment.[13] Johnson did not agree with the MIA this time, however. On the next day he denied the request for an emergency restraining order because the Negroes had failed to show that any real harm was threatened by the Commission's move. As for the appeal for an injunction, he said, this could be granted only after a hearing had been held on the question. He scheduled that hearing for November 14.[14]

On November 13, though, hearings began under Eugene B. Carter in Montgomery Circuit Court on the city's petition for an injunction against the car pool. Knabe argued for the city that the pool constituted a "public nuisance and private enterprise." He cited the two previous instances in which the city had refused to grant the MIA a jitney license, and charged that the Negroes had gone ahead with their plans regardless. The pool used paid drivers and dispatchers, he said, and therefore was a business operating without a license. He pointed out, too, that the boycott and car pool had drawn considerable revenue away from the bus company, which paid a royalty of two percent of its income to the city. Therefore the city had lost about $15,000.00 because of the boycott. The MIA answered these charges by arguing that the pool was legal. Drivers and other workers in the pool donated their services voluntarily and received only compensation for their time and expenses.[15]

After seven hours of testimony Judge Carter rendered a verdict which accepted the city's arguments. He issued a temporary injunction to become effective at midnight of that same day, which ordered the pool to cease its operations. This was a "desolate moment" for King and the others and seemed to be the most serious obstacle they had yet encountered. There was a danger that the loss of the pool would necessitate a return to the buses.[16]

Carter's verdict would have seemed much worse to Negroes, had it not been for a joyous piece of news delivered that same day, as the hearing recessed for lunch. It was learned that the Supreme Court had finally released its decision on *Browder* vs. *Gayle*, the suit originated by the MIA in District Court. Speaking on the MIA's motion that the lower ruling be allowed to stand the court unanimously decided that "the motion to affirm be, and it is hereby, granted." Three previous cases were cited to support the decision, including the historic *Brown* vs. *Board of Education* (347 U.S. 483), as well as *Mayor and City Council of Baltimore* vs. *Dawson* (350 U.S. 877) and *Holmes* vs. *Atlanta* (350 U.S. 879).[17]

King received news of this decision during lunch recess in the court room in Montgomery. He was naturally jubilant and hailed the ruling as a "glorious day-break" in the "long night of enforced segregation."[18] Negroes involved in the boycott and others around the country shared his reaction. The NAACP declared this to be "the one outstanding substantive gain" in the fight for civil rights in 1956, "for the Supreme Court, by this decision, delivered the coup de grace to the 'separate but equal' doctrine laid down three score years ago in the *Plessy* vs. *Ferguson* case."[19]

Response to the decision among whites in Montgomery was predictably less approving. It was realized that although the Supreme Court's pronouncement dealt specifically only with local and state laws on bus

276

segregation it provided the precedent to integrate buses all over the South, and thereby was a severe blow to the segregation system as a whole. Jack Owens of the Alabama Public Service Commission saw the order as paving the way for violence and bloodshed. He urged bus companies in the state to find some way to keep harmony among passengers by arranging seats in such a manner that the races will be kept separate."[20] W. A. Gayle vowed that the City Commission would continue the fight against integration by every legal means. But Governor Folsom noted that there was really little that could be done about the Court's ruling, and that the only way to preserve segregation in other areas was to "keep such cases out of the courts."[21]

The joy that prevailed among Negroes in Montgomery helped to lessen the gloom surrounding Judge Carter's injunction. It would be several weeks before a desegregation order reached town, because the losing side in the suit would be given a chance to apply for rehearing. It was necessary to work out a substitute transportation method until that order arrived since the car pool was now enjoined. On November 14 Judge Frank Johnson emphasized this need by refusing to issue an injunction against the City Commission's interference with the pool. He stated that his court had the power to grant such a request but that "the circumstances of the case do not warrant it."[22]

On November 14 the MIA held two simultaneous mass meetings to vote on a substitute proposal. About 8,000 Negroes attended the sessions and voted first to end the boycott officially, but not to ride the buses until the desegregation order was put into effect. They next approved a plan by which residents of each street or block would set up their own voluntary car pools, to last until a return to buses. This was called the "share-a-ride" system, and was in operation for over a month. Rev. Solomon S. Seay was given the job of coordinating the different pools.[23]

In the meantime lawyers for the MIA tried to get the Supreme Court to step up delivery of the integration order. Gray, Langford, Thurgood Marshall, and Robert Carter asked that the order be made effective immediately. Justice Hugo Black, speaking for the Court, refused them on November 19. He reminded them that motions for rehearing must be heard first. This meant that it would be the middle of December before the case would finally be disposed of.[24]

While awaiting that step the MIA conducted an "Institute on Nonviolence and Social Change" early in December. This was a series of lectures and classes showing Montgomery's Negroes how to approach their new status on buses, and how to handle problems sure to arise when integration took hold.[25] A few days after that the United States Attorney General, Herbert Brownell, presided over a meeting of 33 Federal District Attorneys from 14 southern states. Brownell told them that the Supreme Court's ruling would apply to the whole section, and asked them to see that it was enforced in their districts.[26]

The final action by the Supreme Court came on December 17. The Court considered motions for rehearing filed by the City Commission and the Alabama Public Service Commission, but decided that there were insufficient grounds for any further business on the case. Accordingly, an order embodying the decision of November 13 was dispatched to the Federal Court in Montgomery.[27] This paper arrived on December 20. King immediately called J. H. Bagley at the bus company when he heard of its arrival, and asked the manager to restore service on all lines for the next day, December 21. A mass meeting was called on the night of the 20th in which a happy, singing crowd approved the resolution to return to the buses on the next day.

At 5:55 A.M. on December 21, 1956, King, accompanied by Abernathy, Nixon, and Glenn Smiley, a white minister who was a friend of King's, boarded the first bus. As reporters and cameramen watched the driver turned to the MIA leader and asked "I believe you are Reverend King, aren't you?" King replied that he was, and the driver said, "We are glad to have you this morning."[28] The Montgomery bus boycott was over.

Although December 21 marked the formal end of the boycott, events connected with it made news well into 1957. Several buses were fired on by snipers in the early days of integrated seating, forcing the City Commission on December 29 to suspend bus service after 5 P.M. for a few days.[29] The sniping picked up again in early January and Mayor Gayle replied with another temporary curfew. But the most unfortunate instance of violence came on the night of January 9 of the new year, when four Negro churches and the homes of Rev. Abernathy and Rev. Graetz were severely damaged by bombs.[30] Although no one was hurt by the blasts these acts kindled again the wrath of Negroes; and this time many whites were incensed, as well, who believed that Montgomery had seen too much violence in the past year. The February term of the grand jury, which twelve months before had indicted so many MIA leaders, in 1957 ordered trials for four of seven white men accused of the crimes. The grand jury reported its deep aversion to the bombings, and stated, "We prefer that the problems of maintaining segregation be met openly and honestly rather than with cowardly stealth and violence under cover of darkness."[31]

Although two of the men accused signed statements admitting their roles in the bombings of January 9, a white jury refused to convict them. The other two were consequently not tried. Nor was anyone ever brought to justice for the several bombings of Negro houses in 1956. However, in a spirit of general amnesty none of the other leaders was brought to trial for violation of the anti-boycott law. King launched an unsuccessful appeal of his conviction on that charge. His lawyers failed to file appeal papers until the August following conviction, which was well beyond the sixty-day period allowed by Alabama laws. Therefore King was made to pay the original $5,00.00 fine levied in March. Mrs. Rosa Parks' case was carried into the Court of Appeals, as well. Her conviction as eventually set aside after the Supreme Court established its ruling on bus segregation.[32]

As seen from a vantage point a decade later the Montgomery bus boycott still stands as a unique and dramatic event. Although this period of time may be too short to allow a full understanding of its historical significance, some observations concerning the boycott's importance are possible.

It is obvious that the Montgomery Improvement Association must be credited with a remarkable achievement for its part in organizing and sustaining the protest. But even more remarkable was the mood among Montgomery's Negroes that led to the spontaneous conviction that a boycott was necessary in the first place. The reasons for the courage and spirit of sacrifice that they showed for over a year are not wholly clear. It is true that they had a real sense of grievance toward, and a hatred of, bus segregation, but so did Negroes in almost every other southern city. The black public in Montgomery knew that considerable mass protests had been tried in Harlem and Baton Rouge, among other places, and they knew that the Supreme Court was their new ally in the case of equality. They enjoyed able and intelligent leadership, although it was to an extent fragmented or divided before the protest began. But all of these factors were present in other places; only in Montgomery did the Negro masses act with determination to eliminate bus segregation. As Rev. King has said about the motivation of the boycotters, "every rational explanation breaks down at some point. There is something about the protest that is suprarational . . . ."[33] In keeping with his training as a minister King concludes that a "divine dimension" was the catalyst responsible for setting off the boycott where and when it occurred.

Less difficult to understand are the various practical factors which kept the boycott going once it began, and which worked for its eventual success. Besides the sense of grievance and psychological momentum among Negroes, the most important of these was the guiding medium of the MIA. Through it leaders of the black community were able to focus their efforts more effectively. The car pool, the mass meetings, and the various operating committees that it conducted were indispensable aids to the boycott. The attitude of cooperation among leaders and masses was another key factor. Almost as important as these were evidences of moral and financial support given by Negroes and whites outside the South. The use of nonviolence, which was seen by King and some others as a moral imperative but which all Negroes understood to be a practical necessity, was in turn of great benefit in securing outside help. And some credit, too, must go to the city fathers of Montgomery, whose blunder in bringing Negro leaders to trial did much to stimulate that support.

Another problem for the observer is to decide on the true success of the boycott in relation to the goals it set. Although it was undoubtedly a successful campaign, since it lasted until buses were desegregated, some critics have tried to show that it was largely a meaningless event. The *Montgomery Advertiser* shortly after the Supreme Court's decision sought to analyze the hectic year of protest. That paper concluded that "the boycott has not seated a single colored citizen beside a white citizen . . . Nothing has been achieved except the inconvenience of colored citizens . . ." The Court's ruling had been the result of a civil suit and "could have been obtained without a single colored citizen walking a single block in protest."[34] The NAACP concurred partially in this view, asserting that "actual desegregation of Montgomery bus seating patterns came . . . in response to an NAACP suit."[35]

Strictly speaking this view is correct, and in that sense the boycott was meaningless, or at least unproductive. The bus company did promise to school its drivers in courtesy to all passengers; but it claimed that this had always been its policy. Negro bus drivers were not hired as a result of the protest, but because of later civil rights legislation in the nineteen sixties. And, as stated above, bus desegregation did not come about directly because of the boycott.

However, in another sense the boycott was much more successful than its detractors would admit. MIA leaders explain that they and the Negro public understood in February, when suit was filed in Federal Court, that the boycott was no longer necessary for tactical reasons. But they also understood that its continuance was necessary for more subtle, psychological reasons. Montgomery Negroes had sworn never to go back to segregated buses. It was a matter of pride to them that that vow be fulfilled. That was why King announced in February that although they were "depending on the courts to give the final answer," no end to the boycott was contemplated.[36] As E. D. Nixon put it, boycott leaders would not urge their people to return to buses after suit was filed, because to do so would be to lose the confidence of the masses. Also, continuing the boycott would ensure that every boycotting Negro would have a personal stake in the final victory. After a year of sacrifice and struggle Negroes would make sure that the Supreme Court's ruling would be no hollow, de jure decision. Whereas in some southern cities Negroes continued to sit in the rear of buses even after the case was settled, in Montgomery they asserted their right of integrated seating immediately.[37] After the boycott was over some 50,000 Negroes in Montgomery felt a sense of achievement and hope that made the year's struggle seem worthwhile. The NAACP concluded that in this way the boycott had been "an event of the greatest significance in the struggle of the Negro toward dignity and full citizenship.[38]

As Rev. King assessed it, the boycott was evidence too that the Negro in the South had "come of age" in the political and social life of his section. No longer could he be regarded by whites as part of a docile, inert mass outside of the councils of government. From now on he would be more insistent on the acquisition of his civil rights. King also believed that several more propositions were proven by the success of the boycott, all of which augured well for further campaigns. First, the boycott showed that Negroes in the South could organize and maintain the necessary unity for successful protests. Also, they could put more faith in their leaders, as Montgomery had shown that the masses were not always "sold out." Nonviolent resistance had been shown to be a "powerful weapon" which had propaganda value and which justified the faith of the protestors. It was also shown that the Negro church was becoming more "militant," or active in civil rights. The protest gave proof that Negroes had an increasing confidence in themselves. And, finally, it showed that economic power was another useful tool in the civil rights campaign; as *Time* magazine pointed out, the boycott proved to White Citizens Councils that "economic reprisal . . . is a double-edged blade."[39]

Since 1957 the South and the nation have witnessed scores of protests waged along lines developed in Montgomery. The use of nonviolent massive resistance has been prolific, and paralleling this development has been the emergence of Martin Luther King, Jr. as the foremost leader in the Negro's fight for equality. Virtually unknown when the boycott began, King's presidency of the MIA brought him to the country's attention. This was especially true after the bombing of his home in January, 1956, and his ordeal in court in February and March. The national press applauded his thesis of nonviolence, his learning and ability, and his commitment to civil rights.[40] Although some observers contend that almost anyone would have succeeded as head of the MIA because of the great cooperation among Montgomery Negroes, King undoubtedly contributed much to the boycott's success. And for millions of whites and Negroes King became a symbol of that campaign. These sympathizers quickly came to admire his "special vision" of Gandhian resistance.[41]

Within a few months after the conclusion of the boycott King, flushed with success, moved back to his home city of Atlanta. There he soon organized the "Southern Christian Leadership Conference." This organization drew together smaller church-related groups under his leadership, and has been the sponsor of many civil rights projects since 1957.[42] The profound influence he has had on the course of civil rights in this country began with the success in Montgomery. It is possible that the most important result of the boycott was the launching of King on that career.

Notes

CHAPTER ONE

1. *Montgomery Advertiser*, December 8, 1955, p.1
2. Lerone Bennett, *What Manner of Man* (Chicago: Johnson Publishing Co., 1964), p. 55.
3. Martin Luther King, Jr., *Stride Toward Freedom* (New York: Harper Brothers, 1958), p. 28. Hereafter referred to as King, *Stride*.
4. *Alabama Journal*, January 26, 1956, p. 2A.
5. Reynold Mills, assistant superintendent of the Montgomery City Lines, Inc., in *Aurelia S. Browder Et Al.* vs. *W.A. Gayle Et Al.*, Civil Action Number 1147-N, In the District Court of the United States for the Northern Division of the Middle District of Alabama, hearing May 11, 1956, transcript page 60. Hereafter referred to as *Browder* vs. *Gayle*.
6. *The Code of the City of Montgomery, Alabama*, 1952, (Charlottesville, Va.: Michie City Publishing Co., 1952), Chapter 6, Section 10, p. 42. Hereafter referred to as *Montgomery City Code*.
7. *Ibid.*, Section 11, p. 42.
8. *The Code of Alabama*, 1940, *Title 48* (Atlanta: West Publishing Co., 1941), Section 268, p. 477. Hereafter referred to as *Code of Alabama 1940*.
9. *General Laws (And Joint Resolutions) of the Legislature of Alabama Passed at the Organizational Session of 1947* (Birmingham: Birmingham Printing Co., 1941), No. 130, Sections 1 and 2, p. 40-41. Hereafter referred to as *General Laws of 1947*.
10. Personal interview with Jack Crenshaw, former legal counsel of the Montgomery City Lines, Inc., August 15, 1967. Hereafter referred to as Interview with Jack Crenshaw.
11. Reynold Mills in *Browder* vs. *Galye*, p. 65-67.
12. *Ibid.*, p. 65.
13. Interview with Jack Crenshaw.
14. Reynold MIlls in *Browder* vs. *Gayle*, p. 59.
15. *Alabama Tribune*, December 16, 1955, p.1.
16. Interview with Jack Crenshaw.
17. Reynolds Mills in *Browder* vs. *Gayle*, p. 68.
18. Personal Interview with Edgar Daniel Nixon, former Treasurer of the Montgomery Improvement Association, July 28, 1967. Hereafter referred to as Interview with E.D. Nixon.
19. *Ibid.*
20. Interview with Jack Crenshaw . . . As an example of the difficulties mentioned; one bus passed through a Negro section at the beginning of its run where it

invariably took on many Negroes. It then stopped at St. Margaret's Hospital where white nurses going off duty would board. The first six seats in the bus, three to a side, were placed at right angles to the front of the bus, that is, three were spaced on each side with their backs to the side of the bus. If a white nurse occupied either of the last two seats in this line, which were at right angles to seats seven through ten, then the possibility arose that the nurses would be rubbing knees with Negro men in seats seven through ten.

21. Interview with Jack Crenshaw.
22. Personal interview with Fred David Gray, former legal counsel of the Montgomery Improvement Association, August, 11, 1967. Hereafter referred to as Interview with Fred Gray.
23. Interview with Jack Crenshaw.
24. This view is concurred in by King, *Stride*, p. 34; interview with Fred Gray; interview with E.D. Nixon; personal interview with Rufus A. Lewis, former chairman of the transportation committee of the Montgomery Improvement Association, August 2, 1967, hereafter referred to as Interview with Rufus Lewis.
25. Rev. Major Jones in Tape 50-B, recorded August, 1956, in Tape recordings of the Highlander Folk School Audio Collection in Department of Archives, Auburn University. The original recordings of the Highlander collection were made on wax disks or wire recorder, and the entire collection is held by the Manuscript Division, Tennessee State Library and Archives, Nashville, Tennessee. Hereafter the tape recordings will be referred to as Highlander Folk School Tapes.
26. Interview with E.D. Nixon; interview with Fred Gray; *Birmingham Post-Herald*, February 2, 1956, p. 1.
27. *Alabama Tribune*, December 23, 1956, p. 8; interview with Fred Gray; interview with Rufus Lewis.
28. King, *Stride*, p. 30; interview with Rufus Lewis.
29. Interview with E.D. Nixon.
30. *Alabama Journal*, February 4, 1956, p. 1A and 8A.
31. Interview with E.D. Nixon; interview with Fred Gray; interview with Rufus Lewis.
32. See *Holmes* vs. *Atlanta* (350 U.S. 879); also *Mayor and City Council of Baltimore* vs. *Dawson* (350 U.S. 877)
33. *Anniston Star*, January 2, 1956, p. 1.
34. Anna Bontemps and Jack Conroy, *Anyplace But Here* (New York: Hill and Wang, 1966), p. 346.
35. J.E. Pierce in Highlander Folk School Tapes, 12-F.
36. See *Montgomery Advertiser* for 1900, especially July 3, p. 5; August 4, p . 7; August 7, p. 1; August 16, p. 7; see also *The Republican* (Huntsville, Alabama), September 22, 1900, p. 3.
37. *New York Times*, June 16, 1953, p. 15; June 21, 1953, p. 65.
38. *Ibid.*, December 26, 1953, p. 21.
39. Interview with E. D. Nixon; J. E. Pierce in Highlander Folk School Tapes, 12-F.

40. Police Department of the City of Montgomery, Alabama, Complaint against Claudette Colvin, March 2, 1955.

41. Interview with E.D. Nixon.

42. Rosa Parks in Highlander Folk School Tapes, 12-F; King, *Stride*, p. 41; Claudette Colvin was subsequently convicted on a consolidated charge as a delinquent in Juvenile Court and given an indefinite probation as Ward of the State. *Alabama Journal*, March 19, 1955, p. 5-B.

43. Rev. Thomas R. Thrasher, "Alabama's Bus Boycott," *The Reporter*, XIV (March 8, 1956), no. 5, p.13. Hereafter referred to as Thrasher, Alabama's Bus Boycott.

44. Rosa Parks in Highlander Folk School Tapes, 12-F; King, Nixon, Gray, and Lewis also deny that she was a "plant" by the NAACP.

45. Police Department of the City of Montgomery, Alabama, Complaint against Rosa Parks, December 1, 1955.

46. Interview with E.D. Nixon.

47. *Ibid.*

48. Rosa Parks in Highlander Folk School Tapes, 12-F.

49. Interview with E.D. Nixon.

50. *Ibid.*

51. J. E. Pierce in Highlander Folk School Tapes, 12-F; interview with E. D. Nixon.

52. Interview with Fred Gray.

53. King, *Stride*, p. 45.

54. *Ibid.*, p. 46; interview with Rufus Lewis; interview with E.D. Nixon.

55. *Montgomery Advertiser*, December 4, 1955 p. 1A.

56. J.E. Pierce in Highlander Folk School Tapes, 12-F; interview with E.D. Nixon.

57. King, *Stride*, p. 47-48; J.E. Pierce in Highlander Folk School Tapes, 12-F; interview with Rufus Lewis.

58. Interview with Rufus Lewis; King, *Stride*, p. 48.

59. *Birmingham News*, January 11, 1956, p. 1.

60. *Atlanta Journal*, December 3, 1955, p. 1A.

61. *Montgomery Advertiser*, December 4, 1955, p. 1A.

62. Personal interview with Clyde C. Sellers, former police commissioner of Montgomery County, July 31, 1967. Hereafter referred to as interview with Clyde Sellers.

63. *Ibid.*

64. *Montgomery Advertiser*, December 5, 1965, p. 1.

65. J.E. Pierce in Highlander Folk School Tapes, 12-F.

66. *Montgomery Advertiser*, December 5, 1955, p. 1.

67. *Ibid.*

68. King, *Stride*, p. 54; interview with E.D. Nixon.

69. *Alabama Journal*, December 5, 1955, p. 2A.

70. Aurelia S. Browder in *Browder vs. Gayle*, p. 3.

71. E.G. Jackson in *Alabama Tribune*, December 9, 1955, p. 1.

CHAPTER TWO

1. A new contract with drivers was signed on the next day. *Montgomery Advertiser*, December 7, 1955, p. 1.
2. *Alabama Journal*, December 5, 1955, p. 2A.
3. J.E. Pierce in Highlander Folk School Tapes, 12-F.
4. J. H. Bagley in *M. L. King, Jr. vs. State of Alabama*, In the Alabama Court of Appeals, 3rd. Div. 9, Appealed from Montgomery Circuit Court, Aubrey M. Cates, Jr., presiding, January 17, 1957, transcript in 4 volumes. Hereafter referred to as *King* vs. *State*.
5. as Chapter I, p. 198.
6. *Montgomery Advertiser*, December 6, 1955, p. 6.
7. *Ibid.*; *Alabama Journal*, December 5, 1955, p. 1.
8. Interview with Fred Gray.
9. Interview with E.D. Nixon.
10. Interview with Rufus Lewis.
11. *Montgomery Advertiser*, June 2, 1956, p.1.
12. Interview with Fred Gray; interview with E. D. Nixon.
13. Erna Dungee in *King* vs. *State*, I, p. 61.
14. Note: this group became the Montgomery Improvement Association, hereafter referred to as the MIA. Unfortunately, the official records of the MIA were unobtainable directly. Mrs. Johnnie Carr, current president of the group, and Mrs. Hazel Gregory, secretary, state that papers pertaining to the boycott have been lost or scattered, mainly through moving to new headquarters. Also, Rev. King's personal papers were removed by him and given to the Crozier Theological Seminary. Also, leaders such as Nixon and Lewis say that records kept at the time were not very detailed. However, when King was tried for conspiracy to commit illegal boycott the MIA's records were subpoenaed and appear as state's evidence in the transcript. These have been employed here and consist mainly of minutes of meetings, financial information, and the like.
15. Interview with Fred Gray; interview with E.D. Nixon; interview with Rufus Lewis.
16. Interview with E. D. Nixon.
17. Interview with Rufus Lewis.
18. King, *Stride*, p. 56.
19. *Ibid.*; Minutes of the MIA in *King* vs. *State*.
20. Minutes of the MIA in *King* vs. *State*; interview with E.D. Nixon; interview with Fred Gray, interview with Rufus Lewis, King, *Stride*, p. 58.
21. Minutes of the MIA in *King* vs. *State*.
22. King, *Stride*, p. 57.
23. *Ibid.*; interview with E.D. Nixon.
24. Interview with E.D. Nixon; interview with Fred Gray; J.E. Pierce in Highlander Folk School Tapes, 12-F.
25. Interview with E.D. Nixon; interview with Fred Gray; J.E. Pierce in Highlander Folk School Tapes, 12-F.

26. *Alabama Tribune*, December 16, 1955, p. 8.
27. Minutes of the MIA in *King* vs. *State*.
28. *Birmingham News*, February 19, 1956, p. A-6.
29. *The Code of Alabama, 1923*, Vol. II, Criminal (Atlanta: Foote and Davies Co. 1923), Chapter 91, 3447-3455, p. 98-100. Hereafter referred to as *Code of Alabama 1923*.
30. Interview with Fred Gray.
31. Gleaned from the Negro press, especially the *Alabama Tribune* in January, 1956.
32. Minutes of the MIA in *King* vs. *State*.
33. *Alabama Tribune*, December 16, 1955, p. 1; *Montgomery Advertiser*, December 7, 1955, p. 1.
34. Minutes of the MIA in *King vs. State*.
35. Emory Jackson in the *Alabama Tribune*, December 16, 1955, p. 8.
36. *Montgomery Advertiser*, December 6, 1955, p. 1.
37. King, *Stride*, p. 61.
38. *Alabama Tribune*, December 16, 1955, p. 1.
39. King, *Stride*, p. 64; interview with E.D. Nixon.
40. Interview with E.D. Nixon.
41. Joe Azbell in *Montgomery Advertiser*, December 7, 1955, p. 1.
42. Norman W. Walton, "The Walking City," in *The Negro History Bulletin*, Vol. XX (October, 1956), p. 18. Hereafter referred to as Walton, "The Walking City."
43. Interview with Fred Gray; interview with E.D. Nixon.
44. King, *Stride*, p. 72.
45. Interview with Fred Gray.
46. Interview with E.D. Nixon; interview with Rufus Lewis.
47. *Ibid.*
48. Aurelia S. Browder in *Browder vs. Gayle*, p. 5.
49. Minutes of the MIA in *King* vs. *State*.
50. *Ibid.*
51. *Alabama Tribune*, January 20, 1956, p. 1.
52. "Minutes, Board of Commissioners, City of Montgomery," October 3, 1955 to October 2, 1959, (bound by Paragon Press), meeting December 9, 1955, p. 69. Hereafter referred to as Minutes of the Commission.
53. Interview with Rufus Lewis.
54. *Montgomery Advertiser*, December 6, 1955, p. 6.
55. *Alabama Journal*, December 14, 1955, p. 5A.
56. Interview with Rufus Lewis.
57. *Ibid.*
58. *Ibid.*
59. Rufus Lewis in *King* vs. *State*, II, p. 340-342; King, *Stride*, p. 76.
60. Interview with Rufus Lewis.
61. *Ibid.*
62. *Ibid.*

63. *Ibid.*
64. William Demby, "They Surely Can't Stop Us Now," *The Reporter*, Vol. XIV (April 5, 1956), no. 7, p. 18. Hereafter referred to as Demby, "They Surely Can't Stop Us Now."
65. Interview with Rufus Lewis; King, *Stride*, p. 84.
66. Interview with Rufus Lewis.
67. *Ibid.*; interview with E.D.Nixon.
68. Interview with Rufus Lewis; Minutes of the Commission, January 31, 1956, p. 121.
69. *Montgomery Advertiser*, April 3, 1956, p. 1.
70. Interview with Rufus Lewis.
71. *Montgomery Advertiser*, November 14, 1956, p. 1.
72. Interview with Rufus Lewis.
73. Interview with E.D. Nixon; King, *Stride*, p. 80.
74. *Birmingham World*, December 23, 1955, p. 8.
75. Interview with E.D. Nixon.
76. *Birmingham News*, March 12, 1956, p. 8.
77. *Alabama Tribune*, March 2, 1956, p. 1.
78. Interview with Fred Gray.
79. *King* vs. *State*, II, 265-280.
80. Interview with E.D. Nixon.
81. *Montgomery Advertiser*, February 22, 1956, p.1.
82. Interview with E.D. Nixon.
83. *Ibid.*
84. *Ibid.*
85. Interview with Rufus Lewis.
86. *Ibid.*; interview with E.D. Nixon.

CHAPTER THREE

1. Interview with E. D. Nixon; Julie Seale Harris letter to the *Montgomery Advertiser*, January 4, 1956, p. 4A. Clyde Sellers states that on at least one occasion a body of Negroes approached the City Commission to complain of the boycott. They wanted the city to know that many of them disapproved of it.
2. *Montgomery Advertiser*, December 12, 1955, p. 4A.
3. Interview with Rufus Lewis; interview with E.D. Nixon.
4. *Anniston Star*, January 28, 1956, p. 4.
5. *Montgomery Advertiser*, December 8, 1955, p. 4A.
6. *Ibid.* Also December 7, 1955, p. 1.
7. *Ibid.*, December 13, 1955, p. 1.
8. *Alabama Journal*, January 8, 1956, p. 2B.
9. Interview with Clyde Sellers.
10. *Montgomery Advertiser*, December 8, 1956, p. 1.
11. Interview with Clyde Sellers.

12. *Alabama Journal*, December 10, 1955, p. 1A.
13. Interview with Clyde Sellers.
14. *Alabama Journal*, December 7, 1955, p. 13-A.
15. Interview with Clyde Sellers.
16. For the Claudette Colvin incident see Chapter I, p. 14; *Alabama Journal*, December 6, 1955, p. 1A.
17. *Montgomery Advertiser*, December 7, 1955, p. 1.
18. Thrasher, "Alabama's Bus Boycott," p. 14.
19. *Ibid*.
20. King, *Stride*, p. 108.
21. *Alabama Journal*, December 8, 1955, p. 1A.
22. Interview with Jack Crenshaw; interview with Clyde Sellers.
23. King, *Stride*, p. 109; *Alabama Journal*, December 9, 1955, p. 1A.
24. *Alabama Journal*, December 9, 1955, p. 2A; *Montgomery Advertiser*, December 9, 1955, p. 1.
25. Interview with Jack Crenshaw.
26. King, *Stride*, p. 111; interview with Jack Crenshaw.
27. *Browder* vs. *Gayle*, p. 55.
28. *Alabama Journal*, December 9, 1955, p. 2A; Thrasher, "Alabama's Bus Boycott," p. 14.
29. Interview with Clyde Sellers; interview with Jack Crenshaw.
30. *Alabama Journal*, December 9, 1955, p. 1A.
31. Interview with Clyde Sellers.
32. King, *Stride*, p. 112; interview with Jack Crenshaw.
33. King, *Stride*, p. 111.
34. Interview with Jack Crenshaw.
35. For the Act of July 1, 1947, see Chapter I, p. 4; interview with Fred Gray; *Birmingham World*, December 16, 1955, p. 8.
36. *Alabama Journal*, December 9, 1955, p. 2A.
37. *Montgomery Advertiser*, December 9, 1955, p. 2A.
38. *Ibid*.
39. King, *Stride*, p. 113.
40. Interview with Clyde Sellers.
41. Interview with Jack Crenshaw.
42. *Alabama Journal*. December 11, 1955, p. 1A.
43. *Montgomery Advertiser*, December 16, 1955, p. 8A.
44. Interview with Rufus Lewis.
45. King, *Stride*, p. 113.
46. *Montgomery Advertiser*, December 17, 1955, p. 1.
47. Interview with Clyde Sellers.
48. Thrasher, "Alabama's Bus Boycott," p. 14.
49. King, *Stride*, p. 114.
50. Emory Jackson, *Alabama Tribune*, January 13, 1956, p. 1.
51. King, *Stride*, p. 114; interview with E.D. Nixon.
52. *Birmingham World*, December 23, 1955, p. 1.
53. Interview with Jack Crenshaw.

54. *Birmingham World*, December 23, 1955, p. 1.
55. *Alabama Journal*, December 17, 1955, p. 1A.
56. *Ibid.*, December 18, 1955, p. 2A.
57. *Birmingham News*, December 18, 1955, p. 10; King, *Stride*, p. 116.
58. *Birmingham News*, December 18, 1955, p. 10.
59. *Montgomery Advertiser*, December 18, 1955, p. 1.
60. *Ibid.*
61. *Ibid.*, p. 1 and 2A.
62. *Birmingham World*, December 23, 1955, p. 1.
63. *Alabama Journal*, December 19, 1955, p. 1.
64. *Montgomery Advertiser*, December 20, 1955, p. 2A.
65. *Alabama Journal*, December 19, 1955, p. 1A.
66. *Ibid.*
67. King, *Stride*, p. 121.
68. *Alabama Journal*, January 18, 1956, p. 3B.
69. *Ibid.*
70. *Ibid.*, December 22, 1955, p. 1A.
71. *Alabama Tribune*, December 30, 1955, p. 8.
72. *Montgomery Advertiser*, January 5, 1956, p. 1.
73. Thrasher, "Alabama's Bus Boycott," p. 14.
74. *Birmingham World*, January 10, 1956 p. 1.
75. *Alabama Journal*, January 10, 1956, p. 8A.
76. *Ibid.*, February 8, 1956, p. 1A; *Montgomery Advertiser*, February 8, 1956, p. 1.
77. King, *Stride*, p. 122; interview with Fred Gray.
78. *Montgomery Advertiser*, February 21, 1956, p. 1.
79. *Ibid.*, 2A.
80. *Ibid.*
81. Dr. L. D. Reddick in the *Birmingham World*, February 7, 1956, p. 8.
82. Interview with James E. Folsom, former Governor of Alabama, November 6, 1967. Hereafter referred to as Interview with James E. Folsom.
83. *Ibid.*; *New York Times*, February 25, 1956, p. 10.
84. *Montgomery Advertiser*, January 25, 1956, p 2A.
85. Interview with James E. Folsom; *Alabama Journal*, February 24, 1956, p. 1A, and March 17, 1956, p. 1A.
86. *New York Times*, March 14, 1956, p. 34.
87. *Montgomery Advertiser*, March 16, 1956, p. 9A; Folsom's claim to have met secretly with boycott leaders and Gayle is the subject of much confusion and many conflicting stories. Folsom stated in a personal interview that he had called Gayle and asked him to find some common ground with the MIA so that the boycott might be ended peacefully and quickly. He asserts that Gayle answered that such approaches had been exhausted and that Clyde Sellers opposed any other attempts to negotiate. Folsom says he next met with a "delegation" from the MIA on at least one occasion, who wanted him to persuade the Commission to reconsider Negro demands. Folsom told them that

he could not intervene in the matter, and that his hands were tied. He does not remember the date of the meeting or details surrounding it. He does not remember, either, who composed the delegation, but believes King was a member. Sellers, however, states that he had had no personal communication with Folsom and does not know of any conversation between Gayle and Folsom. Fred Gray, Rufus Lewis and E.D. Nixon do not recall any communication with Folsom. Gray further states that he was present as legal counsel at every negotiating meeting the MIA took part in and that he would "ordinarily" have remembered talking the Governor. None of these Negroes remembers King mentioning any contact with Folsom, nor does King allude to any such meeting in his book, *Stride Toward Freedom*. Jack Crenshaw does remember Folsom issuing his statement that he had met with leaders, but does not remember Gayle mentioning it. Mabel Amos, Secretary of State of Alabama, was Folsom's personal Secretary at the time and believes such talks were held. She thinks Folsom arranged the meeting through his chauffeur, Winston Craig, who was a member of King's church. She recalls other details. Craig's widow, Ruth Briggs Craig, however, says that if her husband, who often performed business for Folsom and other governors he served under, did arrange such a meeting he never mentioned it to her. Annie Lola Price, Presiding Judge of the Alabama Court of Appeals, a Folsom appointee and close friend of the Governor, also thinks a meeting was arranged through Craig, but can remember nothing else.

88. *Birmingham News*, April 27, 1956, p. 1; interview with Fred Gray.

CHAPTER FOUR

1. Emory Jackson in the *Alabama Tribune*, January 13, 1956, p. 1.
2. *Montgomery Advertiser*, January 5, 1956, p. 4A.
3. *Ibid.*, January 19, 1956, p. 4A.
4. Minutes of the Commission, January 4, 1956, p. 91; March 9, 1956, p. 169.
5. *Mobile Press*, March 4, 1956, p. 6.
6. *Alabama Labor News*, February 14, 1956, p. 2.
7. Thrasher, "Alabama's Bus Boycott," p. 15.
8. *Ibid.*
9. *New York Times*, February 28, 1956, p. 22.
10. Thrasher, "Alabama's Bus Boycott," p. 15.
11. Interview with E.D. Nixon.
12. *Montgomery Advertiser*, June 12, 1956, p. 1.
13. *Ibid.*, June 19, 1956, p. 1; interview with E.D. Nixon.
14. *Alabama Journal*, January 2, 1956, p. 2A.
15. *Alabama Tribune*, January 20, 1956, p. 1.
16. *Montgomery Advertiser*, February 11, 1956, p. 1.
17. Interview with Clyde Sellers.
18. Interview with James E. Folsom.

19. Interview with Clyde Sellers.
20. *Ibid.*; *Montgomery Advertiser*, January 7, 1956, p. 1.
21. *Alabama Journal*, January 8, 1956, p. 2B.
22. *Montgomery Advertiser*, January 22, 1956, p. 1.
23. *Birmingham News*, January 22, 1956, p. 1.
24. King, *Stride*, pp. 125-126; interview with E.D. Nixon.
25. *Montgomery Advertizer*, January 24, 1956, p. 2A.
26. *Alabama Journal*, January 23, 1956, p. 1A.
27. *Ibid.*
28. *Ibid.*
29. *Browder* vs. *Gayle*, p. 50.
30. *Montgomery Advertiser*, January 25, 1956, p. 2A.
31. *Alabama Journal*, January 24, 1956, p. 4A.
32. *Birmingham World*, January 31, 1956, p. 1.
33. *Montgomery Advertiser*, January 27, 1956, p. 1.
34. *Ibid.*, January 31, 1956, p. 1.
35. *Ibid.*
36. Minutes of the Commission, January 31, 1956, p. 123.
37. *Montgomery Advertiser*, February 1, 1956, p. 1.
38. *Birmingham World*, February 3, 1956, p. 1.
39. *Ibid.*, February 7, 1956, p. 1.
40. Interview with Clyde Sellers.
41. *Alabama Journal*, January 31, 1956, p. 1.
42. King, *Stride*, p. 151.
43. Interview with E.D. Nixon.
44. Interview with Fred Gray.
45. *Browder* vs. *Gayle*, petition of suit.
46. *Ibid.*
47. *Browder* vs. *Gayle*, docket.
48. *Ibid.*; interview with Fred Gray.
49. *Alabama Journal*, February 2, 1956, p. 1.
50. *Montgomery Advertiser*, March 3, 1956, p. 1.
51. *Alabama Journal*, February 4, 1956, p. 1A; February 8, 1956, p. 1A.
52. Interview with Fred Gray.
53. *Ibid.*; *NAACP Annual Report for 1957*, p. 31; *Montgomery Advertiser*, October 3, 1956, p. 2A.
54. Interview with Clyde Sellers.
55. *Montgomery Advertiser*, February 14, 1956, p. 1.
56. *Ibid.*, February 22, 1956, p. 1.
57. *Alabama Journal*, February 21, 1956, p. 1.
58. *Montgomery Advertiser*, February 23, 1956, p. 1.
59. King, *Playboy Interviews*, p. 350.
60. Interview with Jack Crenshaw; interview with James E. Folsom.
61. *New York Times*, February 24, 1956, pp. 1 and 10.

62. Fred Routh, regional director of Southern Regional Council, in Highlander Folk School tapes, 12-D.
63. Interview with E.D. Nixon.
64. Interview with Fred Gray.
65. *Alabama Tribune*, March 2, 1956, p. 8.
66. *Montgomery Advertiser*, March 2, 1956, p. 11A.
67. *Ibid.*, March 26, 1956, p. 1.
68. *New York Times*, March 19, 1956, p. 23.
69. Dwight D. Eisenhower, *Waging Peace 1956-1961*, Volume II of *The White House Years* (Garden City, New York: Doubleday and Co., Inc., 1965), p. 152. Hereafter referred to as Eisenhower, *Waging Peace*.
70. *Birmingham World*, February 28, 1956, p. 1.
71. *New York Times*, March 3, 1956, p. 10.
72. *Alabama Journal*, March 21, 1956, p. 1.
73. *King* vs. *State*, I, p. 14.
74. *Ibid.*, I, p. 1.
75. *Ibid.*, gleaned from Volume II.
76. *Montgomery Advertiser*, March 20, 1956, p. 1.
77. *Ibid.*, March 21, 1956 p. 1; trial records.
78. *Alabama Journal*, March 22, 1956, p. 1A.
79. *Ibid.*
80. *King* vs. *State*, I, p. 11; III, p. 548.
81. *Alabama Journal*, March 23, 1956, p. 1A.
82. *Montgomery Advertiser*, March 24, 1956, p. 1.
83. *New York Times*, March 24, 1956, p. 15.
84. *Browder* vs. *Gayle*, docket; *Montgomery Advertiser*, May 31, 1956, p. 4A.
85. *Montgomery Advertiser*, February 2, 1956, p. 4A.
86. *Ibid.*, April 30, 1956, p. 4A.
87. *New York Times*, April 24, 1956, p. 1.
88. *Montgomery Advertiser*, April 24, 1956, p. 1.
89. *New York Times*, April 25, 1956, p. 1.
90. *Montgomery Advertiser*, April 26, 1956, p. 1.
91. *Race Relations Law Reporter*, Volume I, 1956, published by the Vanderbilt University School of Law (no other data printed), p. 673, Hereafter referred to as *Race Relations Law Reporter*.
92. *Montgomery Advertiser*, April 24, 1956, p. 1.
93. *Ibid.*, April 25, 1956, p. 8A.
94. *Browder* vs. *Gayle*, p. 55; *Montgomery Advertiser*, April 25, 1956, p. 8A.
95. *Montgomery Advertiser*, April 28, 1956, p. 1.
96. Minutes of the Commission, April 30, 1956, p. 221.
97. *City of Montgomery* vs. *Montgomery City Lines, Inc.*, In Equity No. 30358, In the Circuit Court of Montgomery County, Alabama, Walter B. Jones presiding, May 9, 1956, decision of Judge Jones.
98. *Browder* vs. *Gayle*, pp. 1-32.
99. *Ibid.*, demurrers filed by counsel for defendants.

100. *Ibid.*, p. 14.
101. *Ibid.*, pp. 32 and 67.
102. *Ibid.*, writ issued June 19, 1956.
103. *Ibid.*; *Montgomery Advertiser*, June 20, 1956, p. 2A.
104. Interview with E. D. Nixon; *Montgomery Advertiser*, June 21, 1956, p. 1.

CHAPTER FIVE

1. *New York Times*, June 25, 1956, p. 16.
2. *Montgomery Advertiser*, April 2, 1956, p. 1; *Alabama Labor News*, May 22, 1956, p. 1.
3. Highlander Folk School Tapes Register.
4. *Montgomery Advertiser*, August 26, 1956, p. 1 and 2A.
5. *Ibid.*, September 17, 1956, p. 1.
6. King, *Stride*, p. 158.
7. *Montgomery Advertiser*, October 17, 1956, p. 1.
8. *Alabama Labor News*, February 14, 1956, p. 2.
9. *Ibid.*, October 23, 1956, pp. 1 and 2.
10. *Montgomery Advertiser*, October 27, 1956, p. 1.
11. Minutes of the Commission, October 30, 1956, p. 448.
12. *Montgomery Advertiser*, November 1, 1956, p. 1.
13. *Ibid.*, November 2, 1956, p. 1.
14. *Ibid.*, November 3, 1956, p. 1.
15. *Alabama Journal*, November 13, 1956, p. 1A; *Montgomery Advertiser*, November 14, p. 1.
16. *Montgomery Advertiser*, November 14, 1956, p. 1; Martin Luther King, Jr., in "Interview with Martin Luther King," *Playboy Interviews* (Chicago: H.M.H. Publishing Co., 1967), pp. 349-50. Hereafter cited as King, *Playboy Interviews*.
17. *Browder* vs. *Gayle*, In the Supreme Court of the United States, October Term 1956, 77 Sup. Ct. 145, numbers 342 and 343.
18. *Montgomery Advertiser*, November 14, 1956, p. 1.
19. *NAACP Annual Report* for 1957, p. 29.
20. *Montgomery Advertiser*, November 14, 1956, p. 1.
21. *Ibid.*, November 16, 1956, p. 1.
22. *Ibid.*, November 15, 1956, p. 1.
23. *Ibid.*; King, *Stride*, pp. 160-163; interview with E. D. Nixon.
24. *Montgomery Advertiser*, November 20, 1956, p. 1.
25. *Ibid.*, December 4, 1956, p. 1.
26. *Ibid.*, December 11, 1956, p. 1.
27. *Browder* vs. *Gayle*, In the Supreme Court of the United States, October Term 1956, 77 Sup. Ct. 145, numbers 342 and 343.
28. King, *Stride*, pp. 170-73.
29. Minutes of the Commission, December 29, 1956, p. 491.
30. *Montgomery Advertiser*, January 10, 1957, p. 1.

31. *Alabama Journal*, February 16, 1957, 1A.
32. King, *Stride*, pp. 180-184; *King vs. State*, I, p. 1; personal interview with Aubrey M. Cates, Jr., Judge of Alabama Court of Appeals, presiding at King's hearing, December 22, 1967.
33. King, *Stride*, p. 69.
34. *Montgomery Advertiser*, December 9, 1956, p. 1.
35. *NAACP Annual Report for 1957*, p. 7.
36. *Montgomery Advertiser*, February 8, 1956, p. 1.
37. Interview with E. D. Nixon.
38. *NAACP Annual Report* for 1957, p. 7.
39. In Anna Bontemps, *One Hundred Years of Negro Freedom*, (New York: Dodd, Mead and Co., 1962), pp. 257-258; *Time* magazine, XLI (January 16, 1956), p. 20. Hereafter referred to as Bontemps, *One Hundred Years*.
40. *New York Times*, March 21, 1956, p. 28.
41. Bontemps, *One Hundred Years*, p. 257.
42. King, *Playboy Interview*, p. 347.

Bibliography

I. Primary Sources

1. *Personal Interviews*

Interview with Mabel P. Amos, Secretary of State of the State of
   Alabama and former personal secretary to Governor James E.
   Folsom, December 22, 1967.
Interview with Aubrey M. Cates, Jr., Judge of the Court of Appeals
   of the State of Alabama, December 22, 1967.
Interview with Jack Crenshaw, Former Legal Counsel for the
   Montgomery City Lines, Inc., August 15, 1967.
Interview with James E. Folsom, Former Governor of the State of
   Alabama, November 6, 1967.
Interview with Fred David Gray, Former Legal Counsel for the
   Montgomery Improvement Association, August 11, 1957.
Interview with Rufus A. Lewis, Former Chairman of the
   Transportation Committee of the Montgomery Improvement
   Association, August 2, 1967.
Interview with Edgar Daniel Nixon, Former Treasurer of the
   Montgomery Improvement Association, July 28, 1967.
Interview with Annie Lola Price, Presiding Judge of the Court of
   Appeals of the State of Alabama, December 22, 1967.
Interview with Clyde C. Sellers, Former Police Commissioner of
   Montgomery County, Alabama, and former Circuit Solicitor of
   Montgomery County, Alabama, January 3, 1968.

2. *Court Documents*

Aurelia S. Browder Et Al. vs. *W.A. Gayle Et Al.*, Civil Action
   Number 1147-N, in the District court of the United States
   for the Northern Division of the Middle District of Alabama.
   _____In the Supreme Court of the United States, October Term,

1956, 77 Sup. Ct. 145, Numbers 342 and 343.

City of Montgomery vs. *Montgomery City Lines, Inc.*, In Equity
Number 30358, In the Circuit Court of Montgomery County,
Alabama, Walter B. Jones, presiding, May 9, 1956.

M. L. King, Jr. vs. *State of Alabama*, In the Alabama Court of
Appeals, 3rd. Div. 9, Appealed from Montgomery Circuit
Court, Aubrey M. Cates, Jr., presiding, January 17, 1957,
IV volumes.

Rosa Parks vs. *City of Montgomery*, In the Alabama Court of Appeals,
Appealed from Montgomery Circuit Court.

3. *Public Documents*

City of Montgomery, Alabama. Police Department of the City of
Montgomery, Alabama, Complaint against Rosa Parks,
December 1, 1955; Complaint against Claudette Colvin, March
2, 1955; Complaint against Fred Daniel, December 5, 1955.

Montgomery County, Alabama. District Attorney of Montgomery
County's File Number 2279, "Bus Boycott," 3/19-22/56; Number
2270, "Sonny Kyle Livingston;" Number 1960, Raymond C. Britt.

_____."Minutes, Board of Commissioners, City of Montgomery,"
October 3, 1955 to October 2, 1959, bound by the Paragon
Press.

4. *Printed Codes and Statutes*

The City of Montgomery, Alabama. *The Code of the city of
Montgomery, Alabama, 1952.* Charlottesville, Va.: Michie City
Publications Co., 1952.

The State of Alabama. *The Code of Alabama, 1923.* Vol. II,
Criminal. Atlanta: Foote and Davies Co., 1923.

_____. *The Code of Alabama, 1940, Title 48.* Atlanta: West
Publishing Co., 1941.

_____.*General Laws (And Joint Resolutions) of the Legislature
of Alabama Passed at the Organizational Session of 1947.*
Birmingham Printing Co., 1948.

5. *Books*

Eisenhower, Dwight David. *Waging Peace, 1956-1961*. Vol II of *The White House Years*. Garden City, New York: Doubleday and Co., 1965.

King, Martin Luther, Jr. *Stride Toward Freedom*. New York: Harper and Bros., 1958.

_____. *Where Do we Go From Here: Chaos or Community?* New York: Harper and Row, 1967.

6. *Other Printed Sources*

Highlander Folk School Audio Collection. Nashville: Manuscript Division, Tennessee State Library and Archives, 1964.

Hughes, Rev. Robert E. *Alabama Council Newsletter*. Pub. by Alabama Council on Human Relations, Inc. 1956.

King, Martin Luther, Jr. *Playboy Interviews*. "Interview with Martin Luther King," edited by editors of *Playboy*. Chilcago: H.M.H. Publishing, Co., 1967.

_____.*Our Struggle—The Story of Montgomery*. New York: Pub. by the Congress of Racial Equality, 1956.

National Association for the Advancement of Colored People. *New Threat to Civil Liberties—1956*. 48th Annual Report of the National Association for the Advancement of Colored People. New York: 1956.

Race Relations law Reporter. Vol. I. Pub. by the Vanderbilt University School of Law, 1956 (no other data).

7. *Articles*

Demby, William. "The Surely Can't Stop Us Now," *The Reporter*, Vol XIV, No. 7 (April 5, 1956), 18-21.

Thrasher, Rev. Thomas R. "Alabama's But Boycott," *The Reporter*, Vol. XIV, No. 5 (March 8, 1956), 13-16.

Walton, Norman W. "The Walking City, A History of the Montgomery Boycott," *The Negro History Bulletin*, Part I in Vol. XX, (October, 1956), 17-20; Part II in Vol. XX (November, 1956), 27-33; Part III in Vol. XX,

February, 1957), 102-104; Part IV in Vol. XX (April, 1957, 147-152 and 166.

8. Newspapers

Alabama Journal. March 1, 1955-December 1, 1956.
Alabama Labor News. January 1, 1956-November 1, 1956.
Alabama Tribune. December 5, 1955-June 18, 1956.
Anniston Star. January 2, 1956-June 6, 1956.
Atlanta Journal. December 5, 1955-December 1, 1956.
Birmingham News. December 5, 1955-November 21, 1956.
Birmingham Post-Herald. December 5, 1955-December 1, 1956.
Birmingham World. December 5, 1955-December 1, 1956.
Mobile Press. February 1, 1956-March 31, 1956, *passim*.
Mobile Register. January 1, 1956-April 1, 1956, *passim*.
Montgomery Advertiser. July 1, 1900-November 1, 1900; December 1, 1955-December 1, 1956.
New York Times. June 16, 1953-June 21, 1953; December 5,-December 1, 1956.
New York Times Magazine. December 16, 1956 and December 29, 1957.
Republican (Huntsville, Alabama). September 22, 1900.

II. Secondary Sources

1. Books

Bennett, Lerone, Jr. *What Manner of Man?* Chicago: Johnson Publishing, Co., 1964.

Bontemps, Anna. *One Hundred Years of Negro Freedom*. New York: Dodd, Mead and Co., 1962.

Bontemps, Anna and Conroy, Jack. *Anyplace but Here*. New York: Hill and Wang, 1966.

Bowen, David. *The Struggle Within—Race Relations in the United States*. New York: W.W. Norton and Co., Inc., 1965.

Clayton, Edward T. *The Negro Politician—His Success and Failure*. Chicago: Johnson Publishing Co., 1964.

Gay, William T. *Montgomery, Alabama, a City in Crisis*. New York: Exposition Press, 1957.

Hughes, Langston. *Fight for Freedom—The Story of the NAACP*. New York: W.W. Norton and Co., Inc., 1962.

Parsons, Talcott and Clark, Kenneth B. (editors). *The Negro American*. Cambridge: Houghton-Mifflin Co., 1966.

Stang, Alan. *It's Very Simple—The True Story of Civil Rights*. Boston: Western Islands Publishers, 1965.

From Harlem to Montgomery

The Bus Boycotts and Leadership of

Adam Clayton Powell, Jr. and

Martin Luther King, Jr.

DOMINIC J. CAPECI, JR.

While much has been written about Martin Luther King, Jr., and the Montgomery Bus Boycott of 1956, historians have ignored Adam Clayton Powell, Jr., and the Harlem Bus Boycott of 1941. The two boycotts were marked by similar leadership and occurred in decades of despair but in periods of major socioeconomic change. Although it was much smaller in size and more local in impact, a study of the Harlem boycott yields important information on Powell's leadership before his political career and, more significantly, on earlier protest philosophies and tactics. A comparison of the boycott reveals both the continuity and unity in black protest and leadership and the diversity that marks different eras and locales.

Though Powell and King came of age in different generations and regions, they experienced similar formative influences that ultimately led them to nonviolent protest. Both were named after their fathers, each of whom had risen from sharecropping to become renowned Baptist ministers in Harlem and Atlanta, respectively. Reverend Adam Clayton Powell, Sr., and Reverend

Martin Luther King, Sr., were assertive, protective parents. Thus young Powell was spoiled "utterly and completely," while King, Jr., enjoyed life's comforts in "an extraordinarily peaceful and protected way."[1] Both were precocious, entering college in their mid-teens and earning advanced degrees in religion. More significant, both underwent serious racial and religious growing pains. As a youngster, Powell had been roughed up by blacks for being "white" and by whites for being "colored."[2] Later at Colgate University, he passed for white until his father came to lecture on race relations. The negative reaction of Powell's white roommate to his true identity was a "tremendous" shock. Perhaps the trauma was almost as great as the earlier, unexpected death of his sister Blanche, which triggered in Powell a religious reaction: "The church was a fraud, my father the leading perpetrator, my mother a stupid rubber stamp." King, too, was scarred during his early years. When the mother of his white playmates informed King (then six years old) that as they grew older they could no longer play together, he ran home crying.[3] Although never estranged from his father, as a teenager King considered the church irrelevant, and wondered whether religion "could serve as a vehicle for modern thinking."[4]

As young adults, Powell and King overcame these problems. At Colgate, Powell experienced a revelation, which led to his ordination in 1931. He served as assistant pastor of his father's Abyssinian Baptist Church and earned a master's degree in religious education at Columbia University. In 1937, he succeeded his father as pastor. Adopting the elder Powell's commitment to the social gospel, he forged his congregation into "a mighty weapon" and led numerous nonviolent direct action protests for black employment opportunities during the Great Depression.[5] As part of the larger "Jobs-for-Negroes" movement, Powell joined with Reverend William Lloyd Imes of the St. James Presbyterian Church and A. Philip Randolph of the Brotherhood of Sleeping Car Porters to organize the Greater New York Coordinating Committee for Employment.[6] By 1941 Powell overestimated that four years of picketing by the committee had brought Harlem "ten thousand jobs."[7] This commitment and leadership earned him enormous popularity and, among church women, the title "Mr. Jesus."[8]

King matured along similar lines, for Dr. Benjamin E. Mays and others at Morehouse College successfully molded his concept of religion. King was ordained and became the assistant pastor at his father's Ebenezer Baptist Church. He then attended Crozer Theological Seminary and received a doctorate in theology from Boston College. Although the elder King was only infrequently involved in organized protest, he and Alberta King had instilled dignity and pride in their son. King remembered his father admonishing a policeman for calling him "boy"; pointing to his son, the elder King ejaculated, "That's a boy there. I'm Reverend King."[9] Eventually, King drew on nonviolent direct action for the Montgomery boycott and became immensely popular. "L.L.J.," or "Little Lord Jesus" as church women called him, had moved to the center stage of black leadership.[10]

While Powell and King, then, experienced similar upbringings, a comparison of the bus boycotts in Harlem and Montgomery provides an opportunity to analyze their leadership, protest philosophies, and tactics.

The Harlem bus boycott of 1941 was prompted by black degradation, rising expectations, and a heritage of black protest. Throughout the 1930s, black New Yorkers subsisted on marginal economic levels.[11] As late as 1940, 40 percent of the city's black population received relief or federal monies for temporary jobs.[12] Moreover, most blacks were relegated to menial positions.[13] In Harlem, the largest black community of over two hundred thousand persons, hope was generated, nevertheless, as black leaders and white officials—like Mayor Fiorello H. La Guardia—pressed for change and as World War II held out promise for greater black employment opportunities.[14]

Blacks had a longstanding grievance against the Fifth Avenue Coach Company and the New York Omnibus Corporation. In 1935, the Mayor's Commission on Conditions in Harlem reported that the Coach Company was "fixed in its policy of the exclusion of Negroes from employment."[15] At the time of the bus boycott six years later, the Coach Company and the Omnibus Corporation together employed only sixteen blacks, mostly as janitors, none as drivers or mechanics, out of a labor force of thirty-five hundred persons.[16] Hence, on March 10, 1941, when the Transportation Workers Union (TWU), under the leadership of Michael J. Quill, went on strike against the bus companies, black leaders moved quickly to the union's support. The National Negro Congress, for example, "wholeheartedly" supported the strike, which lasted for twelve days and halted the service of thirteen hundred buses.[17]

Under Roger Straugh's leadership, the Harlem Labor Union (HLU) began picketing local bus stops before the TWU strike had ended, demanding the employment of black bus drivers and mechanics.[18] The Greater New York Coordinating Committee for Employment led by Powell and the Manhattan Council of the National Negro Congress directed by Hope R. Stevens joined with HLU to form the United Bus Strike Committee (UBSC). The formal boycott, however, did not begin until March 24, four days after TWU had agreed to arbitration and two days after bus service had resumed. Moreover, Powell emerged as the spokesman for the boycotters, providing, in Urban Leaguer Elmer A. Carter's estimation, "dynamic leadership."[19]

Before the boycott began, Powell received a quid pro quo from Quill. In return for black support of the TWU strike, the boycott would receive union backing.[20] Later, on March 24, Quill assured Powell that blacks employed by the bus companies would be considered for union membership so long as they had clean records and had never been scabs.[21] That evening, over fifteen hundred persons gathered at the Abyssinian Baptist Church and agreed to boycott the buses until blacks were hired as drivers and mechanics.[22]

Powell's tactics drew from the Jobs-for-Negroes movement, in which many members of the United Bus Strike Committee had participated. Picket lines surrounded Harlem's bus stops, soup kitchens fed volunteers, and black chauffeurs and mechanics were registered.[23] An "emergency jitney service" of privately owned automobiles transported some boycotters, but the key to the boycott's success was New York City's subway system and taxi companies which provided efficient, relatively inexpensive alternative transportation. Before the boycott terminated, volunteers painted placards, donated approximately $500, and gave use of their automobiles.[24] The month-long campaign kept sixty thousand persons off the buses each day at a loss of $3,000 in daily fares.[25] It also drew together five hundred persons from various backgrounds and both races, as bandleaders, ministers, postal clerks, housewives, beauticians, and nurses walked the picket line.[26] Celebrities, like musician Duke Ellington, actively supported the boycott.[27]

Well aware of the significance of the church in black society, Powell made the Abyssinian Baptist Church one of two boycott headquarters. It was the location of the first and second boycott rallies. It provided volunteers experienced in protest, communications, and physical resources and, of course, became the base of Powell's operations and the center of his power.

Powell stressed the philosophy of nonviolent direct action. Blacks were to use only peaceful, legal avenues of redress. By appealing to "the Grace of God" and "the power of the masses," Powell combined religious and political themes; this combination of righteousness and self-help would enable "a black boy . . . to roll a bus up Seventh Avenue." Picket lines, as well as Powell's rhetoric, however, implied militancy. Those flouting the boycott, he declared, should be converted, "one way or another."[28] Three years after the boycott, Powell summarized his nonviolent, though strident, philosophy in *Marching Blacks*: "No blows, no violence, but the steady unrelenting pressure of an increasing horde of people who knew they were right" would bring change.[29]

The boycott was threatened first by violence and then by a misleading newspaper story. Following a UBSC rally at the Abyssinian Baptist Church on March 31, individuals hurled objects at several buses along Lenox Avenue. Fifty patrolmen dispersed those responsible, some of whom had attended the rally. "FEAR ANOTHER HARLEM RIOT," screamed the *Age*'s headlines.[30] Of more concern to Powell and others was the *Amsterdam News* story of April 5.[31] It announced that the bus companies had agreed to employ over two hundred black drivers and mechanics, providing that TWU waive the seniority rights of more than three hundred former bus employees waiting to be rehired. Such an agreement had been discussed, but no final decision had been reached. UBSC leaders moved quickly to maintain their boycott. They labeled the story "a lie," reorganized pickets, distributed leaflets, asked ministers to inform their congregations of "the true facts," and planned a mass meeting.[32]

Despite crisis, the boycott and negotiations continued. Once Ritchie agreed to hire blacks, the major obstacle was TWU seniority policies. On April 17, Powell informed five thousand persons at the Golden Gate Ballroom that an agreement was imminent.[33] Signed twelve days later, the agreement waived the seniority rights of all except ninety-one TWU drivers furloughed by the bus companies; after these men were reinstated, one hundred black drivers were to be hired.[34] The next seventy mechanics employed would also be black, and thereafter, blacks and whites would be taken on alternately until 17 percent of the companies' labor force—exclusive of clerical staff—was black. This quota represented the percentage of black residents in Manhattan. Black workers would be enrolled as TWU members, although the bus companies exercised "sole discretion as to the type of Negro employees to be hired." The agreement would not take precedence over prior management-labor commitments provided they were nondiscriminatory. Of course, all boycott activities would cease. Powell declared that the agreement was made possible by new TWU contracts providing shorter hours and by additional municipal franchises enabling the bus companies to employ three hundred more persons.[35]

Several factors made the Harlem boycott successful. Powell's agreement with Quill prevented bus company officials from playing blacks against whites in the TWU strike and the bus boycott. Throughout the strike, Quill raised the possibility of the bus companies employing strikebreakers.[36] Blacks traditionally had been exploited as scabs, and some of the bus terminals were strategically located in Harlem.[37] Indeed, at least one Harlem correspondent informed Mayor La Guardia that two thousand black men could "start the bus lines in 5, 10, or 20 hours."[38] Powell's agreement significantly reduced the possibility of TWU's strike being broken by force, and reciprocally, it assured that the bus boycott would not fail because of traditional union opposition toward blacks.

Powell's agreement with Quill also held out the hope that blacks would support labor in the upcoming subway negotiations between La Guardia and TWU leaders. During the previous June, the municipal government had bought and unified the Brooklyn-Manhattan Transit Corporation and the Interborough Rapid Transit Company, which had been operated by TWU and the Brotherhood of Locomotive Engineers. When La Guardia contended that neither the right to strike nor a closed shop could be permitted among civil service employees, labor officials retorted that the mayor had reneged on his obligations and anticipated a precedent-breaking conflict with the municipal government when the original contract expired on June 20, 1941.[39] TWU leaders believed that mayoral reference to the bus strike as "bull-headed, obstinate and stupid" was designed to weaken their position in the coming subway negotiations.[40] Obviously, public opinion would be crucial in that dispute. Hence, some blacks, like the *Age* editor, saw TWU support for the bus boycott as a trade-off for black support in the forthcoming union battle with the mayor.[41]

Changing opinions and the impact of World War II helped make the Powell-Quill agreement possible. The racial attitudes of TWU leaders had been improving since 1938 when the union unsuccessfully sent blacks to be employed as drivers at the World's Fair.[42] By World War II, Powell understood how uncomfortable society was in opposing a totalitarian, racist Nazi regime while practicing racial discrimination. "America," he stated later, "could not defeat Hitler abroad without defeating Hitlerism at home."[43] Of equal importance, TWU leadership could pare seniority lists by three hundred unemployed members and make room for black employees because defense orders stimulated the economy and selective service calls reduced union ranks. According to the *Afro-American* editor, the difficulty in finding bus drivers and mechanics provided blacks with unforeseen opportunities.[44]

The boycott assured those opportunities. By early May, seven black mechanics had been hired by the bus companies and ten blacks were expected to begin chauffeur training within a week.[45] Six months later, forty-three blacks had been employed in various classifications, including mechanic's helpers.[46] Finally, on February 1, 1942, after all the ninety-odd furloughed white operators had been given opportunity for reemployment, the first ten black drivers employed by the Coach Company and the Omnibus Corporation began their routes.[47]

That victory was historical. It drew blacks, labor, and management together in a successful effort to break down discriminatory employment practices in privately owned bus companies, and indirectly, it accelerated a similar trend that had already begun in the municipally owned transportation systems under La Guardia'a leadership.[48] The boycott also held out promise for "Negro-labor solidarity."[49] Moreover, it effectively utilized the tactics and philosophies of the Jobs-for-Negroes movement, focused on the concept of equal opportunity, established the idea of a quota system, and provided safeguards for protecting blacks in their newly won jobs. All these elements were also attempted in the 1930s and 1960s, indicating the continuum of black protest that links militant means with traditional ends and nonviolent direct action tactics with greater participation in larger society. By exploiting both TWU ambitions and war manpower exigencies, Powell, Straugh, and Stevens created numerous jobs for black workers. But it was Powell who played the leading role, as he had done for the past decade, speaking out and organizing protests that brought approximately seventeen hundred jobs to Harlem.[50] Exactly because of that record, blacks enthusiastically supported his successful candidacy for City Council in November 1941. His delivery of tangible gains merits mention, for as councilman and, later, congressman he had the reputation for imparting only catharsis to his constituents.[51] Finally, Powell's boycott sparked other protests; numerous blacks agreed with the editor of the *Pittsburgh Courier*, who said, "If this can be done in New York, it can be done in other cities."[52] Indeed, in May the National Association for the Advancement of Colored People launched a nationwide picket campaign against defense industries that held government contracts but refused to hire blacks; Powell journeyed to Chicago to help the Negro Labor Relations League launch a jobs campaign; and the Colored Clerks Circle of St. Louis prepared to boycott a local cleaning company.[53] Official entry of the United States into World War II prevented the emergence of what might have been widespread black protest akin to that of the 1950s and 1960s.

Nearly fifteen years later, when Rosa Parks refused to give up her seat to a white passenger on the Montgomery Bus Line, another phase of black protest began. It was led by Martin Luther King, Jr., who was unknown and inexperienced when leadership of the Montgomery Improvement Association was thrust on him in December of 1955. When he arrived in Montgomery during the previous year to accept the pastorate of the Dexter Avenue Baptist Church, it was "the cradle of the Confederacy." Of one hundred and thirty thousand residents, blacks comprised 40 percent. Segregated and scattered throughout the city, they were exploited economically and lacked even the semblance of geographic, political, or social unity.[54] Jim Crow practices prevailed, particularly on the bus lines where operators possessed police powers for enforcing segregation. A long history of passenger abuse by bus drivers was well known to blacks who had been beaten, ridiculed, and stranded. Coretta Scott King accurately contended that black passengers were treated worse than cattle, "for nobody insults a cow."[55] Earlier efforts to protest this treatment had failed because of black disunity and white power.

Juxtaposed to years of degradation, however, were rising expectations. If the United States Supreme Court's decision against segregated public school systems in *Brown v. Topeka* (1954) did not affect Montgomery immediately, it signaled a major change in race relations. More immediate, however, was the emergence of what King termed "a brand new Negro" whose struggle for dignity was obstructed by self-deceiving whites who continued to live in the past.[56] Hence some blacks and many whites were surprised when the arrest of Rosa Parks triggered protest. During the eighteen years that he had lived in the South, columnist Carl Rowan "had never seen such spirit among a group of Negroes."[57]

That spirit was mobilized by the Montgomery Improvement Association (MIA) which grew out of the efforts of E. D. Nixon, a pullman porter who presided over the local NAACP, and Jo Ann Robinson, an English professor at Alabama State College and president of the Women's Political Council.[58] They arranged a meeting of black ministers, who adopted Reverend Ralph Abernathy's idea of the MIA, elected King as its president, and organized a mass meeting of black residents. On Monday, December 5, over four thousand people crammed into the Holt Street Baptist Church to endorse a boycott until the bus lines guaranteed (1) courteous treatment, (2) a first-come-first-served seating arrangement (blacks in the rear, whites in the front), and (3) employment of black operators on predominantly black routes. Moderate, mostly symbolic, alterations in the Jim Crow system were sought.

The MIA tactics resembled those of earlier black protest movements, including Powell's.[59] As Lawrence D. Reddick has pointed out, Montgomery was "ideally fitted" for a bus boycott; its sizable black population comprised 70 percent of all bus passengers, while its layout of 27.9 square miles enabled residents to reach most places by foot.[60] An effective boycott, however, needed alternative means of transportation. In its initial stages, black cab companies agreed to carry black passengers for the price of the ten cents bus fare. A car pool supplemented the taxi service, becoming the major mode of transportation after municipal officials outlawed the lower taxi fares. Over three hundred automobiles moved in and out of forty-eight dispatch and forty-two collection stations.[61] Financial support originated among the protestors, but as their efforts drew national and international attention, donations came from various sources. In one year, the MIA had spent $225,000.[62] From December 5, 1955, to December 21, 1956, the boycott cost the Montgomery Bus Lines over a quarter of a million dollars in fares, the City of Montgomery several thousand dollars in taxes, and the downtown white merchants several million dollars in business.[63] It also boosted black businesses and reduced the social distance between classes within the black society.

It was no coincidence that the protest spirit emanated from the church, southern black society's most independent institution and primary means of communication. It became routine for blacks to share a ride or walk daily and attend mass meetings at a different church each Monday and Thursday.[64] The boycott became inseparable from the secular and religious life of black society, maximizing the participation of everyone from domestic to clergymen. Not surprisingly, church-owned vehicles in the car pool were dubbed 'rolling churches.'

Emphasizing the concepts of love and justice, King forged a philosophy of nonviolent direct action, stressing self-help, condemning violence, focusing on evil—rather than evil-doers—and espousing "love for America and the democratic way of life."[65] He realized the limits of black power, the history of white repression, and the need for legitimacy in the eyes of white America. Perhaps for these reasons, MIA leaders originally sought a first-come, first-served seating arrangement "under segregation" and watched those blacks who might have resorted to violence.[66] Both the demands for desegregation in seating arrangements and the Gandhian dimension of King's philosophy evolved after the boycott had begun. Nonviolence, already implicit in the Christian teaching that underlay the boycott, was formally articulated by

311

King as a result of the influences of Bayard Rustin and the Reverend Glenn E. Smiley of the Fellowship of Reconciliation.[67]

Despite solid organization and philosophical appeal, the boycott confronted several problems. King later admitted having been "scared to death by threats against myself and my family."[68] Indeed, on January 30, 1956, as Coretta King and baby Yolanda inhabited the premises, the King home was bombed. In addition, King had to deal with a legal system that sanctioned Jim Crow. As a result of Title 14, Section 54, of the Alabama Code prohibiting boycotts, King and eighty-eight others were convicted of unlawful activities.[69] Later the car pool was halted by court injunction. What saved the boycott was the slow wit of the municipal officials and the federal injunction banning segregated buses which was upheld by the United States Supreme Court.[70] Nor did the boycott receive meaningful support from the white community. A handful of whites, like Reverend Robert Graetz, pastor of the black Lutheran Trinity Church, "paid dearly" for participating in the boycott.[71] Other whites assisted the protest unwittingly by chauffeuring their domestics to and from work. For the most part, however, whites either opposed the boycott or, if sympathetic to it, were afraid to say so publicly.

Internal pressures also proved troublesome. Early in the boycott, as abusive phone calls, long hours of work, and relentless efforts to maintain unity began to mount, King despaired and confided in God, "I've come to the point where I can't face it alone." At this time King experienced a revelation, which enabled him "to face anything."[72] Jealousy on the part of some black ministers threatened the boycott periodically. The gravest incident occurred on January 21 when King was informed that Mayor W. A. Gayle and three black ministers had agreed on a settlement to end the boycott. That evening and the following Sunday morning, MIA leaders successfully alerted the black community to this hoax.

These pressures notwithstanding, the boycott was successful, with support coming from numerous quarters. Congressman Adam Clayton Powell, Jr., for example, pressed President Dwight D. Eisenhower to protect the eighty-odd blacks indicted for boycott activities.[73] When Eisenhower refused to comply, Powell publicly chided him for "trying to wash his hands like Pilate of the blood of innocent men and women in the Southland."[74] He then organized a "National Deliverance Day of Prayer" for March 28, which was commemorated in several cities, including Atlanta, Chicago, and New York. Powell collected and sent $2,500 to MIA.[75] Early the next month, he asked all members of the House of Representatives for contributions to help rebuild seven black churches in Montgomery that had been bombed by terrorists, and later recorded that only two Congressmen honored his request.[76] Before the year ended, he and several other nationally known blacks spoke in Montgomery. In sum, the Montgomery bus boycott brought to the surface black awareness that had been stirring since World War II.

As significant was the recent shift in the United States Supreme Court under Chief Justice Earl Warren. Just as Mayor Gayle had deduced that the boycott could be crushed by enjoining the car pool for being unlicensed, the higher court upheld a United States District Court decision that laws in Alabama requiring segregation on buses were unconstitutional. This decision of November 13, 1956, meant victory for MIA, but King continued the boycott until a federal order arrived in Montgomery six weeks later; on December 21, MIA leaders rode the bus in victory.

That victory sparked the Civil Rights Movement. The Montgomery bus boycott provided a leader in King, a philosophy in nonviolence, a tactic in direct action, and, as important, a tangible triumph. Blacks were poised for change, needing, in Lerone Bennett's words, "an act to give them power over their fears."[77] The boycott, of course, did much more, for under King's leadership it achieved legitimacy and prepared both races for a prolonged assault on inequality. That King succeeded in the South, and succeeded with the United States Supreme Court's assistance, underscored a major theme for the coming decade. That the Montgomery City Bus Line so adamantly and successfully refused any agreement regarding the hiring of black bus drivers indicated both the obstacles and limits for changes that lay ahead. Nevertheless, the boycott spawned the Southern Christian Leadership Conference, "a sustaining mechanism," and elevated the struggle for racial equality to the national level.[78]

The Harlem boycott of 1941 came nowhere near achieving this, for it was much smaller and failed to sustain a national protest movement. Nor was it supported throughout the black community. Yet similarities between it and the Montgomery experience abound, particularly those dealing with leadership. Powell and King came from deeply Christian, middle-class families that provided physical security while imposing high parental expectations. As precocious youngsters, both Powell and King experienced anxiety and guilt.[79] Each questioned his father's vocation, perhaps feeling incapable of living up to the parental reputation or, as most likely in Powell's case, repressing hostility toward a domineering father. Each tried to escape: Powell by passing for white and King by engaging in masochistic tendencies. (King

313

jumped out of an upstairs window once, blaming himself for an accident involving his grandmother; at another time, he blamed himself for being at a parade when she died of illness.[80]) As young adults, however, both men sublimated this inner turmoil and embraced the church and their fathers, becoming independent from the latter, yet reflecting them. Perhaps, as psychoanalyst Erich Fromm has theorized about other historical figures, their long-sought-after personal independence emerged in their struggle for collective black liberation.[81]

Powell and King believed that collective liberation could only come through the black church with its "enormous reservoirs of psychic and social strength."[82] Such liberation would free both races, for blacks possessed the divinely inspired mission of achieving equality through the redemption of white society.[83] As the largest black Protestant church in the United States, the Abyssinian Baptist Church boasted a membership of thousands, which provided Powell with impressive human and financial resources. King's Dexter Avenue Baptist Church, however, was more representative of black congregations, comprising one thousand persons and limited finances.[84] In order to be effective, Powell and King successfully established coalitions with other religious and secular groups.

If the church became the vehicle for change, it was black folk religion that provided the sinew for protest. Powell and, more directly King, converted traditional black religiosity into "a passion for justice."[85] Speaking to northern, urban congregations, Powell avoided "Valley-and-Dry-Bones sermons," stressing instead "nicely chosen Negro idioms about everyday issues."[86] Powell could be moved by his own words and weep publicly. King spoke a more "religious language" that struck at the heart of southern black culture.[87] Reverend Andrew Young, a member of the Southern Christian Leadership Conference, observed that no one could have mobilized black southerners by arguing about segregation and integration, but when King preached about "leaving the slavery of Egypt" or "dry bones rising again" everybody understood his language. Both Powell and King possessed what historian Joseph R. Washington, Jr., has called "that Baptist hum which makes what is said only as important as how it is said."[88] The inflections of their voices, the cadence of their deliveries, the nuances of their messages, the animation of their gestures were eagerly anticipated and instinctively understood by multitudes who shared a special cultural and historical relationship with their preachers. Powell and King, then, mobilized black people and became their surrogates, "interpreting their innermost feelings, their passions, their yearnings" as well as channeling their emotions into viable protest.[89]

Protestant theology and Gandhian tactics provided the means by which Powell and King could channel the passion for justice. Both men advocated the social gospel, contending that any religion ignoring the socioeconomic conditions that shackle humanity was, in King's rhetoric, "a dry-as-dust religion."[90] Nonviolent direct action was not a new tactic in black protest, but it was one that permitted Powell, King, and their supporters to become social gospel activists. Following King's successful boycott, blacks increasingly favored an active role by the church in social and political issues during the years 1957 to 1968.[91]

If the boycotts shared a similar religious heritage, they also reflect the respective personality characterizations of Powell and King. Political scientist Hanes Walton, Jr., notes that Powell used nonviolence for practical reasons as "a potent, energetic tool," while King embraced it as "an end in itself, endowed with superior moral qualities."[92] Powell did not advocate violence, but on occasion his rhetoric was intimidating and implied the use of intimidation. King, of course, would tolerate no such deviation from passive resistance.[93] King's commitment notwithstanding, Powell more accurately reflected the reasons for which blacks utilized nonviolent direct action. In the aftermath of the Montgomery boycott, for example, over 70 percent of the black respondents surveyed in that city recognized the usefulness of nonviolence since black people lacked the "power to use violence successfully."[94] According to sociologist E. Franklin Frazier, "Gandhism as a philosophy and a way of life is completely alien to the Negro"; black religious heritage accounts for the presence of nonviolent direct action in the civil rights movement.[95]

That King much more than Powell envisaged—as did Mahatma Gandhi—"a life of service to humanity on a level which called for a self-discipline of rare order" was partly due to socioecological factors.[96] Even in 1941, Harlem, the "Negro Mecca" of the world, was a more secure environment for black people than was Montgomery fifteen years later. Powell had been raised in that security and had successfully used the avenues of redress that were available in the North. King had been brought up in southern segregation, where survival depended upon staying in one's place and where protest efforts had little result. Powell never experienced the pressures and fears that haunted King daily; Powell had enemies, but none who threatened his family or bombed his home. Exactly because of his own background and fears, King understood the need to allay southern white fears if blacks were to avoid pogroms and race relations were to progress: "If you truly love and respect an opponent, you respect his fears too."[97]

King's upbringing emphasized inner control, the kind that enabled him to bear parental whippings with "stoic impassivity."[98] Reverend King, Sr., stressed discipline, and the precarious social environs demanded self-regulation. Hence King originally questioned the emotionalism in the black church and later, in the boycott, took great pains to direct it into safe arenas. Finally, the religious and secular elements in the southern black church appear to have been much more interdependent than elsewhere, which partly accounts for King's commitment to nonviolence as a way of life. This commitment may have been—as in Gandhi's experience—marked by ambivalence, for King stressed love partly for the purpose of controlling hate (perhaps his own).[99] In Powell's case, the opposite was true. As a child, he was spoiled, and lived in an environment that did not demand inner control for survival. He never led a humble life, but, rather, publicly flouted the racial mores of white society. Nor was his religion as all-encompassing as King's; it was more secular and compartmentalized, reflecting the tremendous impact that migration and urbanization had had upon the northern black church. Powell released anger more directly by stressing direct action, while King tended to displace it by putting emphasis on nonviolence, or, more precisely, on what Gandhi called Satyagraha—love-force. It is, then, no coincidence that Powell later singled out Marcus Garvey as the greatest mass leader, demonstrated his independence by clearly identifying an enemy, and spoke militantly of change.[100] King, however, referred only to Booker T. Washington in his first major address in the boycott—"Let no man pull you so low as to make you hate him," stressed racial reconciliation by describing forces of evil, and prayed for opponents.[101] Hence it is not surprising that the name of Powell's organization, the United Bus Strike Committee, projected an assertive, challenging image and that the Harlem boycott focused on the tangible bread-and-butter issue of jobs. By contrast, King's efforts emphasized uplift, as implied in the title, Montgomery Improvement Association, and sought more symbolic, civil rights objectives.

Powell had undertaken the Harlem boycott as his last major protest as a social gospel activist at the end of the Jobs-for-Negroes campaign. He would soon begin a political career as councilman in New York City, and World War II would soon reduce protest to rhetoric as black leaders feared that their efforts would be labeled traitorous. King was thrust into the

Montgomery boycott, his first meaningful protest, which began the civil rights movement. Larger and more significant historically than anything that Powell had done, King embraced that movement and its principles until they died together on April 4, 1968. While the contributions of King are obvious, those of Powell have been forgotten by many. Nevertheless, King knew of Powell's efforts. "Before some of us were born, before some of us could walk or talk," King recalled in the 1960s, "Adam Powell wrote *Marching Blacks*, the charter of the black revolution that is taking place today."[102] One can imagine Powell, in his accustomed modesty, ejaculating an "Amen."

NOTES

1. Adam Clayton Powell, Jr., *Adam by Adam: The Autobiography of Adam Clayton Powell, Jr.* (New York, 1971), 14; James Baldwin, "The Dangerous Road before Martin Luther King," *Harper's Magazine*, February 1961, 38.
2. Powell, *Adam by Adam*, 24, 30, 32.
3. William Robert Miller, *Martin Luther King, Jr.: His Life, Martyrdom, and Meaning for the World* (New York, 1968), 8.
4. "Attack on the Conscience," *Time*, 18 February 1957, 18.
5. Adam Clayton Powell, Jr., *Marching Blacks: An Interpretive History of the Rise of the Common Black Man*, rev. ed. (New York, 1973), 92.
6. For the Coordinating Committee's most important contract with the Uptown Chamber of Commerce in 1938, see Ira De A. Reid, "The Negro in the American Economic System," Reel 11, Book 1, 150-55, The Carnegie-Myrdal Study of the Negro in America—1940, microfilm series, Southwest Missouri State University Library; for the "Jobs-for-Negroes" movement, see William Muraskin, "The Harlem Boycott of 1934: Black Nationalism and the Rise of Labor-Union Consciousness," *Labor History* 13 (Summer 1972): 361-73.
7. Powell, *Marching Blacks*, 100.
8. Roi Ottley, *'New World A-Coming': Inside Black America* (New York, 1943), 220.
9. Quoted in Miller, *Martin Luther King, Jr.*, 9.
10. David L. Lewis, *King: A Critical Biography* (New York, 1970), 83.
11. New York State Temporary Commission on the Condition of the Urban Colored Population, *Second Report of the New York State Temporary Commission on the Condition of the Urban Colored Population to the Legislature* (New York, 1939), 35, 38.
12. New York Urban League, *Annual Report of the New York Urban League for 1940* (New York, 1941), 1.
13. "Placement of Negroes in the State," *Employment Review* 5 (May 1942): 235, for example.
14. Dominic J. Capeci, Jr., *The Harlem Riot of 1943* (Philadelphia, 1977), chapters 1-3.
15. Mayor's Commission on Conditions in Harlem, "The Negro in Harlem: A Report on Social and Economic Conditions Responsible for the Outbreak of March 19, 1935" (typescript, 1935), 23, Fiorello H. La Guardia Papers, Municipal Archives and Records Center, New York City (hereafter cited as FHLP).
16. *Afro-American* (Baltimore), 22 March 1941, 8.
17. William Gaulden to Michael Quill, 13 March 1941, Box 830, FHLP; *New York Times*, 8 March 1941, 21. The thirteen hundred buses accounted for 95 percent of the franchised bus service in Manhattan Borough.
18. *Amsterdam News* (New York), 22 March 1941, 17.
19. Elmer A. Carter, "Smashing the Color Line," *Opportunity*, May 1941, 130.

20. Powell, *Adam by Adam*, 66. Although Powell's autobiography is marred in places by error, he appears to have been the important link to Quill.
21. *Amsterdam News*, 29 March 1941, 17.
22. *Ibid.*
23. *Ibid.*
24. Ollie Stewart, "Harlem Bus Strike Still Unsettled, despite Rumor," *Afro-American*, 19 April 1941, 2; *Pittsburgh Courier*, 10 May 1941, 24; Morgen S. Jensen, "Harlem Wages Unrelenting War on Buses," *Pittsburgh Courier*, 12 April 1941, 24.
25. *Daily Worker* (New York), 11 April 1941, in "Scrap Book," 184: 150, FHLP.
26. *Afro-American*, 19 April 1941, 2.
27. Neil Hickey and Ed Edwin, *Adam Clayton Powell and the Politics of Race* (New York, 1965), 61.
28. Quoted in *Amsterdam News*, 29 March 1941, 17.
29. Powell, *Marching Blacks*, 98.
30. *Age* (New York), 5 April 1941, 1.
31. *Amsterdam News*, 5 April 1941, 9.
32. Stewart, "Harlem Bus Strike Still Unsettled," 1-2.
33. *Afro-American*, 19 April 1941, 6.
34. For the contents of the agreement, see Edgar T. Rouzeau, "Harlem Wins Out," *Pittsburgh Courier*, 26 April 1941, 1, 4.
35. *Amsterdam News*, 19 April 1941, 17.
36. *New York Times*, 11 March 1941, 20, and 17 March 1941, 1.
37. *Age*, 22 March 1941, 6.
38. Sherman S. Furr to La Guardia, 18 March 1941, Box 830, FHLP.
39. La Guardia to Franklin D. Roosevelt, 28 March 1940, Box 2572, FHLP; *New York Times*, 9 March 1941, 37.
40. Quoted in *New York Times*, 12 March 1941, 13; *New York Times*, 11 March 1941, 20.
41. *Age*, 12 April 1941, 6. Ultimately the bus companies did not hire strikebreakers and the threatened strike among municipal subway employees did not occur as TWU agreed to remain under contract pending a judicial decision on its right to bargain collectively or to strike while engaged in municipal service.
42. William Gaulden, Malcolm Martin, and Hope Stevens to John A. Ritchie, 13 March 1941, Box 830, FHLP.
43. *People's Voice*, 2 May 1942, 5.
44. *Afro-American*, 19 April 1941, 4.
45. *Pittsburgh Courier*, 10 May 1941, 5.
46. Edmund Collins to Ethel S. Epstein, 7 November 1941, Box 774, FHLP.
47. *New York Times*, 1 February 1942, 39; John E. McCarthy to Ethel S. Epstein, 16 February 1942, Box 774, FHLP.
48. For example, see *Crisis*, May 1940, 150; the correspondence of Malcolm G. Martin and Lester B. Stone, Box 808, FHLP; and *Age*, 5 July 1941, 1.
49. *Daily Worker*, 27 April 1941, in "Scrap Book," 186; 44, FHLP.
50. *Amsterdam News*, 1 November 1941, 9.

51. James Q. Wilson, "Two Negro Politicians: An Interpretation," *Midwest Journal of Political Science* 4 (November 1960): 346-69.
52. *Pittsburgh Courier*, 3 May 1941, 6.
53. *Afro-American*, 3 May 1941, 6, and 10 May 1941, 6; *Pittsburgh Courier*, 12 April 1941, 18.
54. "Attack on the Conscience," 18.
55. Coretta Scott King, *My Life with Martin Luther King, Jr.* (New York, 1969), 111.
56. Martin Luther King, Jr., and Grover C. Hall, Jr., "Arguing the Bus Boycott: Two Views of Alabama's Race Troubles," *U.S. News and World Report*, 3 August 1956, 87.
57. Carl Rowan, *Go South to Sorrow* (New York, 1957), 125.
58. For information in this paragraph, see Lewis, *King*, 49-58.
59. For streetcar boycotts that predated both Harlem and Montgomery, see August Meier and Elliott Rudwick, "A Strange Chapter in the Career of 'Jim Crow'," in their *Making of Black America: Essays in Negro Life and History* (New York, 1969), 2: 14-19.
60. Lerone Bennett, Jr., *What Manner of Man: A Biography of Martin Luther King, Jr.* (Chicago, 1964), 56; Lawrence D. Reddick, "The Bus Boycott in Montgomery," *Dissent* 3 (Spring 1956): 108.
61. Bennett, *What Manner of Man*, 66; Lewis, *King*, 63.
62. "Attack on Conscience," 19.
63. Norman W. Walton, "The Walking City, A History of the Montgomery Boycott–Part III," *Negro History Bulletin* 20 (February 1957): 103; Miller, *Martin Luther King, Jr.*, 50.
64. For information in this paragraph, see Walton, "The Walking City–Part II," *Negro History Bulletin* 20 (November 1956): 29, 32.
65. For King's philosophy, see Martin Luther King, Jr., *Stride Toward Freedom: The Montgomery Story* (New York, 1958), 90-117; for the quotation, see King, "Arguing the Bus Boycott," 89.
66. Preston Valien, "The Montgomery Bus Protest as a Social Movement," in *Race Relations: Problems and Theory*, ed. Valien and Jitsuichi Masuoka (Chapel Hill, 1961), 116; Rowan, *Go South to Sorrow*, 124.
67. Lewis, *King*, 72.
68. Quoted in Walton, "The Walking City–Part IV," *Negro History Bulletin* 20 (April 1957): 152.
69. Walton, "The Walking City–Part I," *Negro History Bulletin* 20 (October 1956): 19.
70. Lewis, *King*, 78.
71. Coretta Scott King, *My Life*, 128.
72. King, *Stride Toward Freedom*, 134-35.
73. *New York Times*, 24 February 1956, 10.
74. *Ibid.*, 3 March 1956, 10.
75. *Ibid.*, 17 April 1956, 29.
76. Powell, *Adam by Adam*, 39.

77. Bennett, *What Manner of Man*, 60.
78. Bayard Rustin, *Strategies for Freedom: The Changing Patterns of Black Protest* (New York, 1976), 38.
79. Powell, *Adam by Adam*, 22-35, details the anguish and implies the guilt experienced over his racial identity, adolescent development, and familial relations, particularly love for his sister and rebellion against his father; Lewis, *King*, 3-26, describes a more stable childhood, but one marked by periodic bouts of insecurity and guilt and underlined by paternal dominance.
80. Miller, *Martin Luther King, Jr.*, 7.
81. Erich Fromm, *Escape from Freedom* (New York, 1945, 1965), which pertains to Calvin, Luther, et al.
82. Bennett, *What Manner of Man*, 67.
83. Powell, *Marching Blacks*, passim; Hanes Walton, Jr., *The Political Philosophy of Martin Luther King, Jr.* (Westport, Conn., 1971), 31.
84. Abel Plenn, "Report on Montgomery a Year After," *New York Times Magazine*, 29 December 1957, 36.
85. Gayraud S. Wilmore, *Black Religion and Black Radicalism* (Garden City, 1972), 242, which refers to King but is also applicable to Powell.
86. Ottley, *'New World A-Coming'*, 231.
87. Andrew Young, in *The Black Preacher in America*, Charles V. Hamilton (New York, 1972), 132-33, for this and the following quotation.
88. Joseph R. Washington, Jr., *Black Religion: The Negro Christianity in the United States* (Boston, 1964), 3.
89. Donald H. Smith, "Martin Luther King, Jr.: In the Beginning at Montgomery," *Southern Speech Journal* 34 (Fall 1968), 16, refers to King but is also applicable to Powell.
90. King, *Stride Toward Freedom*, 36.
91. Hart M. Nelsen and Anne Kusener Nelsen, *Black Church in the Sixties* (Lexington, 1975), 98.
92. Walton, *Political Philosophy of Martin Luther King, Jr.*, 26, 33.
93. For the absence of coercion by the boycotters in Montgomery, see Rowan, *Go South to Sorrow*, 128.
94. Jacquelyne Clark, *These Rights They Seek: A Comparison of the Goals and Techniques of Local Civil Rights Organizations* (Washington, 1962), 69.
95. E. Franklin Frazier, *The Negro Church in America* (New York, 1963), 75.
96. Erik H. Erikson, *Gandhi's Truth: On the Origins of Militant Nonviolence* (New York, 1969), 237.
97. Quoted in "Attack on the Conscience," 20.
98. Miller, *Martin Luther King, Jr.*, 9.
99. For Gandhi's ambivalence, see Erikson, *Gandhi's Truth*, 251-53; for King's use of love as a "negative factor" to control hate, see Washington, *Black Religion*, 9. During the boycott, King consciously suppressed anger which he admitted verged on hatred. King, *Stride Toward Freedom*, 139.
100. Powell, *Marching Blacks*, 49.
101. King, *Stride Toward Freedom*, 62.

102.Quoted in Powell, *Marching Blacks*, v.

Challenge and Response in the Montgomery Bus Boycott of 1955-1956

J. MILLS THORNTON III

Shortly after five o'clock on the evening of December 1, 1955 Mrs. Raymond A. Parks boarded the Cleveland Avenue bus of the Montgomery City Lines at Court Square in Montgomery, Alabama. She sat next to the window on the side opposite the driver, in the first row of seats in the black section of the bus. The bus driver, James F. Blake, wrenched the yellow bus into gear and headed it up Montgomery Street towards its stop in front of the Empire Theater—towards that moment when Mrs. Raymond A. Parks and James F. Blake would change the course of American history.[1] In order to understand how their disagreement could have had such an effect, one must understand the context of past experiences and relationships that shaped the reactions of Montgomerians to it.

At the end of 1955 municipal politics in Montgomery was in the midst of a fundamental transformation. For essentially the preceding half century Montgomery had been led by the Gunter Machine, headed for most of that time by William A. Gunter, Jr., the city's mayor from 1910 to 1915 and from 1919 to his death in 1940. Mayor Gunter had come to power after more than a dozen years of bitter factional warfare between two groups of the city's wealthy older families. Thereafter, he turned back all challenges to his rule. He could always rely upon the unwavering support of the city's morning newspaper, the Montgomery *Advertiser*, whose editor, Grover C. Hall, Sr., was one of his closest advisers, and upon the allegiance of the majority of Montgomery's older families. In the final two decades of his life he also had the unanimous support of city employees, whom—as a result of an act which he pushed through the state legislature—he could in effect hire and fire at will.[2]

If there were no successful challenges to the Machine after 1919, however, the unsuccessful challenges were many. During the 1920s Gunter's uncompromising opposition to the Ku Klux Klan made him a special object of Klan hatred. His repeated expressions of disapproval for the prohibition experiment placed the Anti-Saloon League in the ranks of his enemies, and fundamentalists condemned him for his generally lax enforcement of public morality. During the 1930s he turned the city government into a relief operation, putting hundreds on the public payroll and earning the bitter hostility of fiscal conservatives for unbalancing the city budgets. At the time of his death in 1940 he was admired by much of Montgomery's upper class and by large numbers of the city's unemployed. But he was also detested by many owners of small businesses and conservative citizens, strict Baptists and Methodists, and others to whom his values—rooted in the easygoing tolerance and aristocratic paternalism of his planter and Episcopalian background—were anathema.

After Gunter's death the Machine spent the next decade searching for a leader. The mayor was immediately succeeded by Cyrus B. Brown, who had long been one of Gunter's most powerful lieutenants and was at the time president of the Montgomery County governing body, the Board of Revenue. But Brown, an elderly man, died in 1944. David Dunn, who had earlier been a political protege of former Governor Bibb Graves, obtained Machine endorsement to succeed Brown but resigned in 1946 to go into private business.

The mayoralty then passed to City Attorney John L. Goodwyn, a cousin of Gunter's wife, whom Gunter had appointed city attorney in 1930. Goodwyn resigned in 1951 to accept a position in the state government; this position led eventually to his being appointed to the state Supreme Court. Goodwyn was succeeded by William A. "Tacky" Gayle, a Machine stalwart who had been a member of the City Commission since 1935.[3]

During this decade of rapid changes in leadership the Machine grew steadily weaker. The rapidity of these changes itself contributed to the process. Another factor in the Machine's decline was Gunter's penchant for surrounding himself with colorless, if often quite competent, administrators. Early in the century the Gunter forces had secured the abolition of the mayor-council form of government for the more easily controlled three-man commission.

In addition to the mayor there was a commissioner of public affairs, who administered the police and fire departments, and a commissioner of public works, who had charge of parks, libraries, street maintenance, and garbage collection. During the 1930s Gunter turned to two retired military men to fill these posts. Gayle, a veteran of World War I, had subsequently served as Alabama's adjutant general and had returned to active duty in World War II. In 1943 while serving in Britain as an air force colonel, Gayle was elected to his third term on the City Commission in absentia. The other commissioner, General William P. Screws, had been the commander of the Alabama contingent in the famed Rainbow Division during World War I. This tradition continued when George L. Cleere, another former state adjutant general, was selected to succeed Gayle as commissioner of public works when Gayle became mayor in 1951. These men, for all their efficiency, were by no means Gunter's equals as politicians, and without him they had trouble in holding the voters' affection.

By far the most important reason for the Machine's decline, however, was the changing character of the city's population and residence patterns. During the first half of the twentieth century Montgomery grew rapidly, at an average of 30 percent a decade. This steady growth concealed after 1940 an important change in the city's racial composition. In 1910, as Gunter was first taking office as mayor, Montgomery's white population for the first time achieved parity in numbers with blacks. During the remainder of the Gunter years the relative proportion of the two races remained stable at 55 percent white and 45 percent black. But after Mayor Gunter's death the proportions began to change, under the impact both of increased black emigration to the North and of increased rural white movement into the city. In 1950 Montgomery was 60 percent white and 40 percent black; the white population grew by 47 percent during the 1940s and the black by only 23 percent. This trend continued during the 1950s. By 1955 Montgomery contained about 120,000 people, of whom some 63 percent were white and 37 percent were black.

The increasing white population meant that the number of residents in the city who could vote was growing even faster than was the population at large. The Machine had no hold upon either the gratitude or the affection of many of these new voters. Moreover, changing residence patterns reinforced this development. Resentments of Gunter's policies on the part of the lower middle class had existed in the 1920s and 1930s, but the resentment had found little institutional support. The town was small and could sustain few institutions alternative to the ones controlled by the well-to-do. During the 1940s and early 1950s the development of housing subdivisions on the edges of the city with small homes intended for the white lower middle class, effectively separated that group from the institutional control of the upper class and the upper middle class. In the eastern section of Montgomery—Capitol Heights, Dalraida, and Chisholm—there developed churches whose congregations did not contain a mix of classes and within which leadership could therefore fall to the lower middle class. In 1931, for instance, there were only seven white Baptist churches in the city, and in 1940 there were still only eleven, but by 1952 there were twenty. The number of white churches belonging to the Pentecostal sects, always a refuge for poorer elements of the population, also advanced rapidly. In 1931 white Pentecostal congregations constituted less than a fourth of the city's white churches, but by 1940 they were a third of the total, and by 1952 almost 40 percent of it.[4]

Similarly, East Montgomery developed alternative men's clubs; the Lions Club and the Exchange Club, for instance, both established separate East Montgomery units, leaving the downtown clubs in the hands of the businessmen who had dominated them. The growth to the east also demanded new schools, and with them came PTAs to be run by men and women unlikely to be leaders in a PTA in which the various classes were commingled—as had been the case with the PTAs of the few schools in the earlier, smaller city. Power in these earlier organizations had gravitated toward social leaders. East Montgomery also developed separate shopping and entertainment areas. In these and countless other ways the simple growth of the city gave the white lower middle class a separate community life and allowed it some measure of self-consciousness as a unit.

Meanwhile, this institutional "de-intermixture" of white classes was proceeding from the other side as well when subdivisions for wealthier residents were developed in South Montgomery, particularly in the Cloverdale section. Between 1951 and 1954 no less than sixty new subdivisions were completed in East and in South Montgomery, and in 1955 another thirty-three were reported to be in the planning stages.[5]

The first hint of what these developments portended for the Machine came in the city elections of 1947, when General William P. Screws, a member of the City Commission since 1931, was challenged by a young East Montgomery schoolteacher and football coach, Earl D. James. James's connection with physical education at Capitol Heights Junior High School placed him in an excellent position to capitalize upon the emerging sense of community in that section of the city. Screws beat James in Cloverdale, while James swamped all of his opponents in Capitol Heights and also ran well in an older, lower middle class ward, Oak Park. James thus erected a majority upon a basis not previously seen in Montgomery politics. The division between South Montgomery and East Montgomery that was demonstrated in these returns was to become characteristic of municipal elections for the next thirty years.[6]

Nevertheless, the Machine did not yet foresee its doom. It still controlled two of the Commission's three seats. James proved an able and relatively tractable official. He was elected to a second term in 1951 but resigned in 1953 to enter business. In the special election to choose James's successor the newly emerging shape of city politics first became completely clear. State Representative Joe M. Dawkins gathered endorsements for his candidacy from Montgomery's most prominent citizens. In the first primary Dawkins carried every precinct in the city and missed winning without a run-off by only 523 votes. In the second primary Dawkins faced Dave Birmingham, a man whose candidacy was regarded by the city's upper class as a bad joke. Birmingham had been an early and zealous supporter of former Governor James E. Folsom, and he shared much of Folsom's aggressive hostility to the wealthy. Birmingham was a classic demagogue. During his campaign he suggested that the chlorination of the city's drinking water had caused the preceding summer's devastating polio epidemic. He charged—contrary to well-documented fact—that the red color that sometimes appeared in the water was not iron but mud. The burden of Birmingham's appeal was an attack on the Machine. Dawkins was, Birmingham said, "hogtied to the old ring masters. . . . It is never good for a city to let one 'click' [sic] completely dominate it. Progress would stagnate." He opposed appointive municipal boards: "The ring masters through the board masters are strangling you to death with taxes without any responsibility to you as to how they will spend this tax money." He unremittingly attacked "that cesspool of gangsters at City Hall" and particularly decried the taxes that had been levied in order to finance the extension of services to new areas of the rapidly growing city.

Birmingham beat Dawkins in the run-off by a margin of 53 percent to 47 percent. Dawkins carried the wealthier precincts; his best ward was Cloverdale. Birmingham swept the lower middle class and lower class white precincts; he ran best in Capitol Heights and did well in precincts in which a substantial minority of the voters was black. The meaning of this election for the fortunes of the disintegrating Machine was unmistakable. *Advertiser* editor Grover C. Hall, Jr., commented that, with Birmingham a member of the Commission, "The City Hall is going to be notably different for the foreseeable future." Doubtless, Hall had no real conception of just how right he was.[7]

The principal reason for the Machine's demise was the growing independence of the white lower middle class. Politicians called this phenomenon "the silent vote." In a 1955 article the *Advertiser's* city editor, Joe Azbell, explained the meaning of the term. In the 1920s and 1930s, in a city dominated by personal acquaintance, family alliances and personal favors rather than issues really decided the outcome of elections. But the growth of the city had added many voters to the rolls who were not members of the family alliances. The abolition of the city spoils system in favor of appointment by civil service examination had deprived the Machine of much of its power to bind voters to it by favors. By 1955, Azbell noted, voters lacked personal knowledge of the candidates and had thus begun to make voting decisions on the basis of issues, as filtered through the mass media. Politicians therefore lacked any real sense of where the voters were moving until the election returns were counted. In 1953, 1954, and 1955 knowledgeable observers had repeatedly guessed wrong about the election outcome because the voters no longer were members of cousinries or other blocs whose behavior could be predicted. Of the 1955 municipal elections Azbell commented, "No one seemed to care how the Hills were moving. No one seemed concerned about the political blocs. But twenty years ago a political observer would not dare comment on an election without first determining how the blocs were going. For the first time in city political history, ring politics played no important part in the local election, because the old ring politics has been overshadowed by a growing city where there is no control or method of determining how the voters will cast their ballot." As a result, city administrators feared their new constituents.[8]

If the growing independence of the white lower middle class was the principal factor that had altered the structure of municipal politics, another factor of almost equal significance was the newly important black vote. The white lower middle class might be unfamiliar to the politicians, but the black community was virtual terra incognita. The state Democratic primary of 1946 represented the first primary in which blacks could legally vote; earlier such elections had been conducted under the white primary rule, which the Supreme Court had forbidden in 1944. Because they could now participate in the only elections that mattered in Alabama, blacks sought to register in increasing numbers during the late 1940s and early 1950s, particularly in the cities. The number of blacks registered in Montgomery grew slowly but steadily, and by 1955, 7.55 percent of the city's 22,210 registered voters were black. This percentage was well above the 5 percent ratio statewide. Moreover, in some wards black voters represented a substantial proportion of the total: 31 percent in Beat 7W, almost 25 percent in Beat 2, and 20 percent in Beat 6. Seven and a half percent is quite a small figure, but given the near equiponderance in the rivalry between South Montgomery and East Montgomery during these years, blacks could easily represent a balance of power.[9]

The returns in the special election of November 1953 appeared to black leaders to demonstrate that Birmingham owed his margin of victory over Dawkins to blacks, and they prepared to press the new commissioner for interest on this debt. Moreover, Birmingham stood ready to respond, both because he needed to hold the political allegiance of the blacks and because his racial views appear to have been genuinely, remarkably liberal.[10] The inauguration of Dave Birmingham as a city commissioner therefore, marked the beginning of a heady period for the black leadership in which it found itself with genuine access to the city government for the first time.

The most important black spokesman in making demands upon the newly constituted City Commission was Edgar D. Nixon, a sleeping-car porter who was also president of the Montgomery local of the International Brotherhood of Sleeping Car Porters. Moving beyond his union power base, Nixon in the late 1940s and early 1950s had become more and more publicly active in demanding amelioration of conditions for members of his race. Throughout these years he was the dominant figure in the Montgomery chapter of the NAACP and was state president of that organization in 1948-49. He was also president of the Montgomery chapter of the Alabama Progressive Democratic Association, which had been organized during the 1940s as a black alternative to the regular party apparatus. In 1954 he created a great stir in Montgomery as a candidate for the County Democratic Executive Committee, the first black in living memory to seek public office. Though

329

he lost to a white candidate, Joseph W. Carroll, he won more than 42 percent of the vote in the precinct, only a fourth of whose voters were black. In 1955 Nixon sought unsuccessfully to purchase a ticket to a Jefferson-Jackson Day dinner in Birmingham; the evening's principal speaker, Governor G. Mennen Williams of Michigan, abruptly cancelled his appearance in protest against Nixon's exclusion. Such highly visible efforts made Nixon the best known "activist" in Montgomery and gave him a considerable following in the black community.[11]

Equally as prominent in the dealings with the City Commission were two other blacks, Rufus A. Lewis and Mrs. Jo Ann Robinson. A former football coach at Alabama State College, Lewis was at the time a successful businessman and the chairman of the Citizens' Steering Committee, a group that had been formed in the fall of 1952 to press for better treatment for blacks. Mrs. Robinson, an English teacher at Alabama State College, was the moving spirit behind the black Women's Political Council, a group organized in 1949 to urge black women to register to vote; thereafter, the Council became the most militant and uncompromising organ of the black community. Led by Mrs. Robinson, Mrs. Mary Fair Burks, and Mrs. Thelma Glass, all of the Alabama State College faculty, and Mrs. A. Wayman West, Jr., the wife of a dentist, and sometimes aided by the more moderate Federation of Negro Women's Clubs, the Council repeatedly protested to the City Commission against discrimination and injustice in Montgomery. Indeed, with exceptions such as Nixon and Lewis, the blacks who addressed complaints to the City Commission in this period usually were women.[12]

The election of Dave Birmingham encouraged these groups for the first time to seek redress from the city government for long-standing grievances: the lack of black policemen, the inadequacy of parks and playgrounds in black sections of the city, and the conditions on the city buses. Immediately after Birmingham's election the Montgomery County Grand Jury and the Montgomery *Advertiser* had both urged the city to join Dothan, Anniston, and Talladega in hiring black policemen. Possibly supporters of the Machine saw this action as a way to cope with Birmingham's popularity in the black community. But the two Machine commissioners apparently remained dubious. After Birmingham's inauguration a delegation of black leaders met with the Commission; at this meeting Birmingham extracted from his colleagues a promise to hire black officers if funds could be found to pay their salaries. Birmingham continued to press the proposal and finally, in early May 1954, succeeded in obtaining the addition of four blacks to the force. Their hiring caused consternation among the city's extreme segregationists, whose resentment expressed itself two years later, during the boycott, when the home of one of the four, Patrolman Arthur G. Worthy, became a target for bombers. In the summer of 1955 Police Chief Goodwyn J. Ruppenthal sought to placate still hostile citizens by reassuring them that the new policemen were "just niggers doing a nigger's job."[13] But the doubts of many Montgomerians were not so easily assuaged, and the controversy rendered Birmingham's two colleagues increasingly unwilling to join him in taking other similar actions. The Machine could not afford to alienate either black or white segregationist voters. This difficulty virtually immobilized the two Machine commissioners on every racial issue from late 1953 through early 1955, as the city prepared for the crucial municipal elections of late March 1955. In addition, their position was rendered even more awkward by the considerable heightening of white fears and black hopes that followed the Supreme Court's school integration decision in mid-May 1954.

Meanwhile, no such hesitation bound Birmingham or the black leadership. The question of parks in black areas escalated to a new level of public controversy in January 1955, when a delegation from the Women's Political Council appeared at a City Commission meeting to urge the appointment of a black to the city Parks and Recreation Board and to suggest Council member Mrs. A. Wayman West, Jr., for the position. Commissioner Birmingham immediately moved that the next vacancy go to a black, but Mayor Gayle persuaded him to withdraw the motion until a vacancy actually occurred. The mayor, who had actively supported a city program under which three new playgrounds for blacks had been recently built, assured the delegation that its request would be given every consideration when there was a vacancy. He continued his effort to define a medial position later in the same week when he appeared before a large group of blacks gathered to celebrate the inauguration of Governor James E. Folsom and there praised the work of the city's black policemen. But the question of black representation on the Parks and Recreation Board could not be dismissed so easily. It was to become a principal issue in the city elections in March. In August, Commissioner Birmingham, now a lame duck, offered a motion to expand the Parks and Recreation Board from five to seven members and to designate the two new places for blacks, but Gayle and Cleere voted the resolution down. However, the mayor in July and the Parks and Recreation Board in September assured angry black delegations that if the city's voters would approve the proposed issuance of a million dollars in parks bonds, significant improvements in Negro parks would immediately be forthcoming.[14]

While the public was concerned with the issues of black policemen and black membership on the Parks and Recreation Board, tension over racial relations on the city's buses had quietly been mounting. At the end of 1953, encouraged by Birmingham's recent election, the Women's Political Council met with the City Commission to lodge three complaints: that blacks sometimes had to stand beside empty seats, in cases where the black section was filled but the white section was not; that black passengers were compelled to get on at the front door to pay their fare and then to get off and to reboard at the back door to take a seat, rather than being permitted simply to walk down the aisle of the bus ; and that buses stopped at every corner in white neighborhoods but only at every other corner in black neighborhoods. Allegations of discourtesy by drivers and of buses' passing by waiting black passengers were also made. The meeting was inconclusive, but representatives of the bus lines, who were present, evidently offered to investigate specific charges of discourtesy. Several months later, in the spring of 1954, the Women's Political Council again met with the Commission and representatives of the bus company to reiterate its three complaints and to offer a list of specific instances of abuse by bus drivers. At this meeting the delegation from the Political Council was accompanied by Rufus Lewis representing the Citizens' Steering Committee, by a delegation from the Federation of Negro Women's Clubs, and by a large group representing black trade union locals. At this meeting as at the earlier one the principal spokesman for the blacks was Jo Ann Robinson of the Political Council.

As a result of this meeting the problem of buses' stopping only at every other corner in black areas was remedied. Addressing the issue of seating, the Commission, on the advice of City Attorney Walter Knabe and bus company attorney Jack Crenshaw, informed the blacks that it was legally powerless to do anything about the problem of black passengers' being compelled to stand beside empty seats. The city ordinance and the state statute on the subject were both read aloud to the petitioners. The meeting was evidently a stormy one. Subsequently, Mayor Gayle testified that several days later Mrs. Robinson called him angrily "and said they would just show me, they were going in the front door and sitting wherever they pleased." In April 1954 the Reverend Uriah J. Fields, a militant young black minister who was later to break spectacularly with Martin King, brought the seating complaints before the public with a letter to the Montgomery *Advertiser* demanding that the policy be altered. There the matter rested until the following spring.[15]

Meantime, the elections that could kill the already moribund Machine were approaching. Gayle and Cleere both sought re-election. Gayle's only opponent was Harold McGlynn, a candy wholesaler who was a political associate of Commissioner Birmingham. Cleere's principal opposition came from Frank Parks, an East Montgomery interior decorator who was a former Grand Master of Alabama's Masons. Parks set out to create an electoral coalition like that which had enabled Birmingham to upset Dawkins a year and a half earlier. Though Gayle and Cleere supported each other, and Birmingham supported McGlynn and Parks, it is unclear whether or not Gayle and Cleere supported one of the candidates opposing Birmingham; at any rate, they did not do so publicly. Birmingham drew two principal opponents. Sam B. Stearns, the owner of a downtown parking garage and a nephew of a former Montgomery County sheriff, ran a vigorous and well-financed campaign, but the returns showed him much less popular than observers had thought. The real threat to the incumbent was former State Representative Clyde C. Sellers, a resident of South Montgomery and the owner of an exterminating business. Sellers effectively emphasized his extensive experience in law enforcement; he had joined the state Highway Patrol shortly after its formation, had worked his way up through its ranks, and in 1945 had been appointed director of the department by Governor Chauncey Sparks. His four years in the state legislature also strengthened his credentials. That he had been a star football player for Auburn University in the 1920s gave him additional popularity. But the issue that was to carry him to victory was provided by the events of the canvass.

Birmingham launched a typically demagogic campaign. His two colleagues on the Commission had voted to increase the city sewerage fee in order to finance the extension of sewer mains into the Allendale-Wildwood section, a South Montgomery area. Birmingham denounced this decision as class legislation and demanded that the wealthy homeowners in the section pay for the sewers themselves. Frank Parks loudly echoed this argument. Birmingham revived his accusation that chlorination of the water supply was dangerous; he alleged as proof that city water would kill camellia bushes. He also charged that Gayle and Cleere might have favored the construction of a city sewage treatment plant only in order to make a private profit by selling the plant's effluent for fertilizer. With such allegations Birmingham hoped to hold, and Parks to build, constituencies of whites of the lower class and the lower middle class. McGlynn refused to stoop to this level, and perhaps for that reason his campaign against Gayle never really gained momentum. McGlynn did join Birmingham and Parks in a strong effort to gain the allegiance of the black vote.[16]

As the campaign of 1955 began, black leaders hoped to use the black balance of power between South Montgomery and East Montgomery to extract real concessions from the candidates. They had just passed through a year in which the city government had shown unprecedented willingness to listen to their proposals. Birmingham, Parks, and McGlynn were eager for black support. One of Birmingham's opponents, Stearns, was equally as willing to seek black votes. Nor, indeed, were Gayle and Cleere hostile. Though more reticent than were their opponents about openly campaigning for black ballots, still both men were racial moderates. The remnants of the Machine that they represented could command a certain residue of good will in the black community. Mayor Gunter's actions in the 1920s and 1930s had endeared him to many blacks, and after World War II the Machine-dominated city government had constructed a number of low-rent public housing projects for poor blacks. By 1955 the Montgomery Housing Authority, which was headed by the late Mayor Gunter's son-in-law Charles P. Rogers, administered four such developments and had a fifth in the planning stages. Its public housing record was not an unmixed asset for the Machine, however, because many blacks resented the demolition of their homes and their removal into crowded apartments, however modern.[17]

All of these circumstances so emboldened the black leaders that they decided in February to hold a public meeting in order to question the various Commission candidates about their stands on racial issues. The candidates subsequently also appeared before organized labor and the Junior Chamber of Commerce.[18] But the spectacle of office seekers appearing before blacks to submit to interrogation was a sight for which the electorate was unprepared.

The meeting, held under the auspices of Nixon's Progressive Democratic Association, convened in the Ben Moore Hotel, the city's only black hotel, on the evening of February 23. All of the candidates were present. The session commenced with Nixon's distributing to them a questionnaire asking their position on a number of specific black grievances. The first area of complaint on the list was "the present bus situation. Negroes have to stand over empty seats of city buses, because the first ten seats are reserved for whites who sometime never ride. We wish to fill the bus from the back toward the front until all seats are taken. This is done in Atlanta, Georgia, Mobile, Alabama and in most of our larger southern cities." Next came requests that a black be appointed to the Parks and Recreation Board and that blacks be considered for all municipal boards. The third subject mentioned was the lack of middle-class housing subdivisions for relatively well-to-do blacks. The authors of the questionnaire had been upset by the city's decision a week earlier to forbid the development of such an area because of the protests of neighboring whites. The fourth plea was that qualified black applicants be considered for civil service jobs with the city. "Everybody cannot teach," the questionnaire noted, in reference to the limited professional opportunities available to Montgomery's middle-class blacks. The document concluded with three complaints about the inadequacy of city services in black neighborhoods. It asked for the installation of more fireplugs in these sections, the extension of sewer mains to eliminate outdoor privies, and the widening and paving of streets and the addition of curbing.

In their responses Birmingham, McGlynn, and Parks all agreed to appoint a black member of the Parks and Recreation Board. Stearns, who had adopted the strategy of attempting to defeat Birmingham by outbidding him for the allegiance of the city's various groups, also agreed, and added a proposal for a sixteen-member all-black advisory board as an adjunct of the Parks Board. The press reported that black leaders were as a result closely divided as to whether they should endorse Birmingham or Stearns. Gayle and Cleere remained noncommittal on the Parks Board issue. Sellers gave a general talk that did not speak to any of the points in the questionnaire; he said later that he did not see the document until the end of the meeting. Accounts of the session do not indicate any reply by any of the candidates to the questionnaire's proposal on bus seating.[19]

After the candidates had completed their presentations, the meeting adjourned, but its repercussions were still being felt years later. Clyde Sellers quickly saw that the black proposals and their deferential handling by his two opponents presented him with the issue that would allow him to win a majority. It appeared that Stearns and Birmingham were going to divide the black vote. Sellers, as a South Montgomerian, could count on a large vote from that section in response to Birmingham's vociferous attacks on its residents. Previously, though, there had seemed to be no way to cut into Birmingham's solid following in East Montgomery. Now, demagogic exploitation of racial tensions promised to counter Birmingham's exploitation of class tensions and thus to capture support in the eastern wards. During

March, before the election on the 21st, Sellers made the most blatantly and insistently racist addresses heard in Montgomery since the days of J. Johnston Moore, the Ku Klux Klan's candidate against Mayor Gunter in the 1920s. Sellers converted the Ben Moore Hotel meeting into the principal issue of the canvass. He answered the questionnaire point by point in his speeches and advertisements. He asserted flatly that the blacks' bus seating proposal would violate state law—not bothering to explain how, in that case, the system could be used in Mobile. He pledged himself to oppose the appointment of blacks to city boards. To the request that qualified blacks be allowed to apply for civil service jobs, he said, "If the commission were to comply with this request, it would be only a short time before negroes would be working along side of whites and whites along side of negroes ...I have always felt that if a man wanted a job bad enough, he could go where the job, for which he is qualified, is available. There are places in this nation where civil service jobs for negroes in cities are available but not in Montgomery. I will expend every effort to keep it that way."[20] Sellers's campaign was aided by the first of the bus incidents, the arrest on March 2 and the trial on March 18 of Claudette Colvin for violation of the segregation ordinance.

Sellers had been correct about the effect of his racial appeal upon the electorate. In the returns he took 43 percent of the poll, to 37 percent for Birmingham, 16 percent for Stearns, and 4 percent for a minor candidate, John T. Weaver. Birmingham carried the wards with substantial black registration and also took the poorest white wards. But the white lower middle class areas of East Montgomery that he had swept in 1953 now went to Sellers. Capitol Heights, which had given Birmingham 62 percent of its vote in 1953, making it his banner precinct, now gave him only 31 percent, to 44 percent for Sellers. At the same time South Montgomery voted heavily against Birmingham; Sellers took 60 percent of the poll in Cloverdale. Despite Sellers's solid lead over Birmingham, a run-off between the two men would have been necessary. However, two days after the election Birmingham collapsed while preparing to give a television speech; his doctor diagnosed his condition as "overexertion and exhaustion" and advised him to withdraw from the race. Birmingham did so, and Sellers was declared elected. We can never know whether Birmingham could have defeated Sellers. Birmingham had come back from an even more substantial deficit to defeat Dawkins in 1953, but Birmingham's chances of repeating this accomplishment in 1955 were poor. Sam B. Stearns, the third important candidate in the race, had made shrill personal attacks on Birmingham. It is unlikely that a white voter who had cast his ballot for Stearns in the first round would thereafter have moved to the support of Birmingham.

In the mayoral election McGlynn had seldom indulged in the demagogic appeals of Birmingham and Parks. He may have been hurt by the fact that he was a Roman Catholic, but on that point evidence is lacking. Although McGlynn received 40 percent of the vote and carried the wards with substantial black registration and also the city's poorest white ward, West End, nevertheless Mayor Gayle won easily.

In the election for commissioner of public works the incumbent, George Cleere, had refused to follow Sellers in exploiting the racial issue. Instead, he had attempted to answer with reason the strident class-oriented accusations of Parks, particularly with reference to the sewerage fee. The result was that Parks was elected on returns whose geographical distribution was virtually identical to the distribution of the support for Birmingham in his race against Dawkins in 1953. Cleere swept the South Montgomery wards, taking more than 75 percent of the vote in Cloverdale, but Parks carried the substantially black precincts and those of the white lower class and lower middle class.[21]

The election's outcome puzzled Grover C. Hall, Jr.; why should the voters have elected Parks, Birmingham's ally, over Cleere, Gayle's ally, but then have repudiated Birmingham himself and returned Gayle?[22] The meaning of the election was probably much clearer to Gayle, now the sole Machine survivor in municipal politics, seated between an uncompromising segregationist on his right and an adversary of Montgomery's wealthy on his left. The Machine's traditional policies of moderate, paternalistic racial attitudes, and a firm alliance with the city's upper class had failed to sustain it, and they held little likelihood of endearing Gayle to the constituencies that had elevated either of his two colleagues. Clearly, Gayle needed a new strategy immediately. The lesson of Parks's victory appeared to be that, given the new social realities produced by the city's rapid postwar growth, an East Montgomerian would always defeat a South Montgomerian when the issues remained class oriented. The lesson of Sellers's victory appeared to be that the vigorous exploitation of racial antipathies could give a South Montgomerian at least a fighting chance of defeating an East Montgomerian. Gayle was, of course, a South Montgomerian. But Gayle's dilemma was much more complicated than this analysis would imply. First, he was unlikely to abandon a set of beliefs that he had held sincerely for many decades merely because political strategy seemed to dictate this course. Second, developments within the business community rendered it less than certain that a sound strategy actually dictated this course. To understand this factor, we must briefly explore the attitude of Montgomery's businessmen towards their city government.

The business community believed that the source of all genuine social ills was the lack of industrialization. Montgomery's economy rested primarily on the presence of the state government and of two air force bases, Maxwell and Gunter. One in every seven families in the city was an air force family in 1955. Aside from income generated by federal and state government expenditures, Montgomery relied almost exclusively on its role as a marketing center for the surrounding agricultural area.[23] By 1955 businessmen were armed with legislation passed during the preceding decade providing Alabama municipalities with powerful tools for attracting industry to the state, particularly in the form of tax advantages and of public financing of plant construction. Business leaders therefore had high hopes of broadening Montgomery's economic base.

This zealous commitment to industrialization was the source of the tension between businessmen and the city government. Business leaders believed that the city's politicians had been inept in attracting industry. Near the end of October 1953 the *Advertiser* had broken the story that DuPont had purchased 850 acres near Montgomery, "as a prospective site for an industrial plant." The article had concluded excitedly, "Announcement is expected soon on the type of plant to be constructed." Months passed, and no such announcement was forthcoming. Reportedly, four other "very large companies" that had considered building factories in Montgomery had been lost to other cities during 1954 and 1955. Worried businessmen sought to discover what they were doing wrong. The Chamber of Commerce desperately debated ways to attract favorable national publicity for the city. Chamber of Commerce President James G. Pruett ominously warned the Rotary Club that "industry will come to Montgomery and Alabama only when there is a healthy climate for it and when government on all levels is not hostile to it." In this atmosphere of frustration at the repeated recent failures in the drive for industrialization, forty of the city's most important businessmen met in mid-October 1955 to organize the Men of Montgomery. Adopting the frank motto "We Mean Business," they chose as their first project a campaign to compel the City Commission to act on a proposal that had languished in the City Hall bureaucracy for years: to construct a new terminal for the municipal airport to give visitors to the city a more favorable first impression.[24]

Mayor Gayle had always counted on business support. The Gunter Machine had been closely allied with business interests. Gayle himself was a brother-in-law of one of the most influential businessmen in Alabama, Birmingham industrialist Donald Comer of Avondale Mills.[25] Now the mayor faced a business community organized with a new efficiency and motivated by a new hostility. By the fall of 1955 his dilemma was acute. His colleagues on the Commission each represented constituencies only recently defined, and Gayle had no real access to either. The black leadership was making militant demands upon the city for the first time and was asking for public responses. The business community was suddenly dubious of his competence and disposed to press him for positive action. If he moved towards one of the newly emerging constituencies, he risked permanently alienating the elements in the city upon which he had relied ever since he had first entered politics. Against this background the city moved towards the events of early December.

At the Ben Moore Hotel meeting on February 23 bus seating had headed the list of grievances. On the afternoon of March 2 came the arrest of Claudette Colvin, a fifteen-year-old black girl who refused to vacate her seat when ordered to do so by a bus driver, Robert W. Cleere. Miss Colvin, who was returning from school, was seated far back in the bus, just forward of the rear door, on a seat with an older black woman, a Mrs. Hamilton. The bus was entirely filled, and Cleere ordered the two blacks to stand in order to give their seats to boarding whites. Mrs. Hamilton refused, and Cleere summoned police. When the police arrived, a black man got up, gave his seat to Mrs. Hamilton, and left the bus. Miss Colvin, who apparently was led into her resistance by the actions of Mrs. Hamilton, now found herself deserted to face the music alone. She became hysterical, kicked and scratched the arresting officers, and had to be carried bodily from the bus.[26]

Because of her age Miss Colvin was brought to trial before Juvenile Court Judge Wiley C. Hill, Jr., a first cousin of U.S. Senator J. Lister Hill. She was not the first person to be arrested for violation of the bus seating ordinance, but according to Commissioner Birmingham she was the first person ever to enter a plea of not guilty to such a charge. Her twenty-four-year-old attorney, Fred D. Gray, one of two black lawyers in Montgomery, interposed two defenses. The first, that segregated seating violated the U.S. Constitution, was overruled in short order by Judge Hill. The second defense was more troublesome. When the city ordinance requiring segregation on public conveyances had first been adopted in 1900, it had provoked a black boycott of the city trolley lines. This boycott had lasted throughout the summer of 1900 and had ended only when the City Council agreed to amend the new ordinance to forbid compelling anyone to vacate his seat unless there was another seat to which he could move. This proviso remained a part of the city code. Because both sides in the Colvin case agreed that the bus had been entirely filled, the bus driver, rather than Miss Colvin, had violated the segregation ordinance.

State laws supersede city ordinances, however. In 1945 the state legislature had enacted a statute requiring the Alabama Public Service Commission to see that all bus companies under its jurisdiction enforced racially segregated seating. This statute, unlike the city ordinance, gave bus drivers absolute power to seat passengers. It was unclear whether or not the Public Service Commission had jurisdiction over municipal bus lines. A year later the state was to contend in federal court that the state law was inapplicable in such situations in order to avoid having it at issue in the suit seeking to declare the segregation of Montgomery buses unconstitutional. Now Circuit Solicitor William F. Thetford moved to meet Gray's defense by amending the complaint so as to allege a violation of the state law rather than of the city ordinance. Judge Hill overruled Gray's objection that the state law did not apply, found Miss Colvin guilty both of violating the state bus segregation statute and of assault and battery on the arresting officer, declared her a juvenile delinquent, and ordered her placed on probation. Gray filed an appeal to Circuit Court, but on the appeal the state pressed only the charge of assault and battery, and on that ground Miss Colvin's sentence of probation was affirmed. As a result Gray was deprived of any way to use this case as a means to contest the various questions that had been raised with regard to the segregation laws.[27]

Meanwhile, Miss Colvin's arrest had moved the city's black leaders to make one more effort to deal with the bus problem through the political mechanism. In mid-March, as the municipal election campaign climaxed, blacks arranged two meetings with white officials. At the first one Commissioner Birmingham and the bus company's manager James H. Bagley met in Bagley's office with a delegation that included the Reverend Martin L. King, Jr., a twenty-six-year-old Baptist minister who had moved to Montgomery the preceding September to take up his first pastorate, and who in the intervening six months had become quite active in the city's

NAACP chapter. It appears that, at this meeting as at earlier ones, the principal spokesman for the blacks was a conspicuous member of King's new congregation, Jo Ann Robinson.

This encounter was relatively amicable. Birmingham was eager to conciliate the blacks, and Bagley did not wish to offend his customers gratuitously. The black delegation pointed out that forcing a passenger to stand in order to seat another passenger violated both company policy and the provisions of the city code. Bagley acknowledged that the policy did forbid such action; he promised to investigate and to reprimand the bus driver in the Colvin case if it was warranted. The blacks evidently brought up the seating plan proposed in the questionnaire presented at the Ben Moore Hotel meeting; Birmingham promised to secure a formal opinion from City Attorney Walter Knabe on what seating arrangements were legally permissible. Unfortunately, nothing came of either of these promises.[28]

Birmingham's failure to act is understandable; within two weeks he was a lame duck, his influence greatly diminished and his health precarious. Bagley's inattention to the matter was simply shortsighted. A principal source of friction on the buses was the company's loosely defined seating policy. In practice the policy varied enormously from route to route and from driver to driver. Even under the company's official policy, the middle sixteen seats of the bus had no fixed racial designation; it was the responsibility of the driver to shift the racial line forward or back in order to provide a number of seats roughly proportionate to the racial composition of the group of riders at any given moment. Under these circumstances the drivers had to reseat passengers rather frequently. The embarrassment and humiliation to blacks of being thus publicly forced to acknowledge and accept legal discrimination was exacerbated by the fact that the harried drivers usually adjusted the seating simply by shouting peremptory commands over their shoulders. If Bagley had attempted to specify the seating policy more fully and had sought more vigorously to enforce company rules requiring courtesy from drivers, he could have eliminated much of the ill will between the bus line and the black community. If he had emphasized to the drivers the company policy against unseating passengers when other seats were unavailable, he would have forestalled both the Claudette Colvin and the Rosa Parks incidents.[29]

The second meeting in response to Miss Colvin's arrest appears to have been much stormier than that with Bagley and Birmingham. Bagley arranged this meeting for the blacks. The black delegation included, as usual, members of the black Women's Political Council and the Federation of Negro Women's Clubs. It also included Rufus A. Lewis of the Citizens' Steering Committee and attorney Fred Gray. Mayor Gayle and City Attorney Knabe represented the city. The bus company was represented by its attorney, Jack Crenshaw. The blacks apparently pressed the seating proposal contained in the questionnaire distributed at the Ben Moore Hotel meeting. Gray believed that the proposal violated no existing law. Crenshaw adamantly maintained that the proposal flouted both the city ordinance and the state statute, an opinion in which Knabe concurred.

The importance of Crenshaw's intransigence both in producing and in sustaining the bus boycott can hardly be overstated. He was an excellent lawyer, educated at Harvard. He was a political ally of the racially moderate Governor Folsom. Despite this background, however, he proved incapable of understanding the strategic advantage of accepting a modest compromise in order to forestall a full-scale assault on segregation. He dismissed Gray's arguments out of hand and informed his client Bagley that the law left the bus company absolutely no room for compromise. The meeting adjourned with the complaints of the blacks still unanswered.[30]

Through the summer and fall of 1955 a series of events kept the bus question before the public. Early in the year a black woman, Sarah Mae Flemming, had sued the city bus line of Columbia, South Carolina, for damages for its having enforced the segregation laws against her. In mid-July the U.S. Court of Appeals for the Fourth Circuit ruled in this case that segregated seating on buses was unconstitutional—a decision that received headline treatment in the Montgomery *Advertiser*. Later in July a young black, James M. Ritter, had defied the order of a bus driver in Richmond, Virginia, to move to the rear and had been fined ten dollars for his action. In Montgomery itself another black teenager, Mary Louise Smith, was arrested on October 21 for refusing to yield her seat to a white woman. This case did not create the furor which the Colvin incident had, however, because Miss Smith chose to plead guilty; she was fined five dollars.[31]

Equally important in focusing attention on the bus company was the fact that its franchise was about to expire. National City Lines, Inc., of Chicago, owned the Montgomery bus company. That firm had been granted a twenty-year city franchise in 1936; the franchise would come up for renewal in March of 1956. In late October an official of the company came to Montgomery to open negotiations. He and the city commissioners surveyed the city from the air in order to plan revisions in the bus routes, and delegations from a number of the new subdivisions on the city's outskirts appeared before the Commission to seek the extension of bus service to their areas. At the same time the bus company was bargaining with the bus drivers' union for a new two-year contract. Montgomerians who recalled that all bus service had been suspended during a brief strike in December 1953 watched the progress of the negotiations apprehensively.[32]

In the fall of 1955 the press was filled with accounts of events in Selma. There a group of twenty-nine blacks in September petitioned the city board of education urging the integration of the schools. In mid-September the head of the recently organized Dallas County White Citizens Council, attorney M. Alston Keith, reported that the efforts of the Council had resulted in the firing of sixteen of the twenty-nine petitioners from their jobs. Blacks retaliated by refusing to buy the milk of a dairy that had agreed to discharge a petitioner. Next came incidents of arson and kidnapping, both directed against a black grocer who had been a participant in the boycott of the dairy. Finally, in late October six young white men, two of them members of the Selma police force, were arrested and indicted for the actions directed at the grocer, and one of the accused policemen thereupon committed suicide.[33]

In early November black Congressman Adam Clayton Powell visited Montgomery to speak to the Progressive Democratic Association. Congressman Powell spent the night at the home of Edgar D. Nixon. In his speech Powell warned the Citizens Councils that their economic pressure "can be counter met with our own [black] economic pressure." The example of the events in Selma and the force of Powell's remark doubtless made an impact upon Nixon, who because of his background in the labor movement and because of his long association with and intense admiration for his union's president, A. Philip Randolph, was predisposed in any case to believe in the efficacy of economic action.[34]

The arrest of Rosa Parks struck a spark to this tinder. When Mrs. Parks boarded the bus, it was divided into twenty-six seats for blacks and ten for whites. Two blocks farther on, when the bus stopped in front of the Empire Theater, it was completely filled, and both whites and blacks were standing; all white standing room was taken. Driver James F. Blake undertook to readjust the seating to a more equitable ratio by clearing one row of seats, altering the racial division to fourteen white and twenty-two black. Since the four unseated blacks would have to stand, Blake's action violated both company policy and the city code. At the same time, inasmuch as company policy forbade allowing whites to stand in the black section, if Blake had not taken his action, none of the whites waiting to board could have been accommodated, although standing room was available in the rear of the bus.

Rosa Parks had been for most of the preceding decade the secretary of the Montgomery chapter of the NAACP. She had grown up on a farm in southern Montgomery County. Against great odds she obtained a high school diploma in 1933. Montgomery then provided no public high school for blacks. But Mrs. Parks's family, ambitious for her advancement, had arranged to send her to the laboratory school of Alabama State College. Although she thus became one of a very small number of black high school graduates in the city, she found herself unable to obtain employment commensurate with her educational level. She worked at a number of relatively menial jobs; in 1955 she was a seamstress altering ready-to-wear clothes in the city's principal department store, the Montgomery Fair. This situation very probably produced a certain bitterness in her and contributed to her decision during World War II to become an active member of the NAACP. She was elected the chapter secretary in 1943 and later also became the adviser to the chapter's youth auxiliary. She had therefore been particularly concerned with the arrest of Claudette Colvin. In the summer of 1955 she had attended an integrated seminar on race relations at the Highlander Folk School, an invitation she had received at the suggestion of Mrs. Clifford J. Durr, the wife of a liberal white attorney. Mrs. Parks worked for Mrs. Durr on a part-time basis as a seamstress. All of these circumstances had made Mrs. Parks peculiarly sensitive to the importance of the series of meetings, petitions, and remonstrances in relation to the bus situation during the years before 1955. We may well suppose that, had she not been so intimately connected with the controversy, she might have been inclined to join the other three blacks on the row of seats in obeying Blake's instruction. But she, alone of the four, did not move. Blake summoned the police, who took her to the city jail. From the jail she contacted her colleague in the NAACP chapter, Edgar D. Nixon. Nixon made bond for her.[35]

If Mrs. Parks had not been a close friend of Nixon's and a prominent figure in the black community, Nixon might not have been moved to such decisive action, and the people whom he contacted might not have responded so readily. But Mrs. Parks and her husband, a barber at Maxwell Air Force Base who had resided in the city for more than a quarter of a century, were distinctly civic leaders and, at least socially, members of the middle class. Nixon returned from the jail and began calling the city's most prominent blacks to suggest that blacks stage a strike of the buses. Those called phoned others. One of these calls took the matter out of Nixon's hands. Attorney Fred Gray called Jo Ann Robinson.

Mrs. Robinson and her associates in the Women's Political Council saw Rosa Parks as one of their own, a woman of similar social status and community standing. The Council did not await the outcome of Nixon's consultations; it acted. Early the next morning, December 2, Mrs. Robinson mimeographed at her office at Alabama State College a call for a boycott of city buses on December 5, the day of Mrs. Parks's trial: "Another Negro woman has been arrested and thrown into jail because she refused to get up out of her seat on the bus and give it to a white person. It is the second time since the Claudette Colbert [sic] case that a Negro has been arrested for the same thing. This must be stopped . . . until we do something to stop these arrests, they will continue. The next time it may be you or you or you." Council members busied themselves throughout the afternoon and evening of December 2 distributing these handbills in the black sections of the city.[36]

Meanwhile, Nixon's calls to black civic leaders during the night of December 1 and the morning of December 2 had produced sufficient support for a boycott to set up a meeting for the night of December 2 at the Dexter Avenue Baptist Church. But when the forty or so leaders convened, they found themselves faced with a *fait accompli* because of the action of the Women's Political Council during the afternoon. The meeting was reduced to attempting to assure that the boycott that had been called by the handbills would be successful. Committees were appointed to attend to various organizational details, and a mass meeting was scheduled for the night of December 5 to consider future action in the light of how successful the boycott that day might prove.[37]

When sixteen black leaders met on the afternoon of December 5 to plan the evening's mass meeting, they considered two new pieces of information. The boycott had been brilliantly successful, far more so than leaders had permitted themselves to hope. And Rosa Parks had been convicted and fined ten dollars. At the trial City Prosecutor D. Eugene Loe had faced the problem of the city code's prohibition of unseating a passenger unless another seat was available and had met it as had Solicitor Thetford in the Colvin case, by moving to amend the complaint so as to allege a violation of the state law rather than of the city ordinance. Mrs. Parks's attorney, Fred Gray, had again contended that the state law did not apply to municipal bus lines, but his argument had been overruled by Recorder's Court Judge John B. Scott, a nephew and appointee of the late Mayor Gunter.[38]

The success of the boycott's first day and the conviction of Mrs. Parks made it clear that the boycott would continue, at least until the blacks received conciliatory overtures from the city. The sixteen persons present at the afternoon meeting decided to create a formal organization to run the boycott. At the suggestion of the Reverend Ralph D. Abernathy, twenty-nine-year-old pastor of the First Baptist Church (black), they adopted the name Montgomery Improvement Association. They constituted themselves the Association's Executive Board and proceeded to choose officers. Presiding at this meeting, as at the meeting on December 2, was the Reverend L. Roy Bennett, a Methodist who was the president of the black Interdenominational Ministerial Alliance. Bennett's gavel had been wielded in an extremely high-handed fashion at the December 2 session, thus provoking much resentment. When Bennett opened the floor for nominations for president of the new organization, Rufus A. Lewis of the Citizens' Steering Committee saw an opportunity to depose Bennett gracefully. He suggested Martin L. King. Lewis, as a member of King's church, had some knowledge of King's talents; King had recently submitted a dissertation to Boston University for the S.T.D. degree, which marked him as considerably better educated than most of Montgomery's black ministers. The selection of King did not proceed, however, from any clear recognition of his potential for leadership but rather from general hostility to Bennett. Lewis chose King largely because King was Lewis's pastor. King was quickly and unanimously elected, and Bennett was then made vice-president. King's election determined the element within the MIA that would become dominant in shaping its policy. Bennett was an older man and a Methodist. King's advisers were almost uniformly Baptists and were usually young, often not out of their twenties. It is also interesting to note that, in February, Bennett was to become the sole member of the black leadership to urge the acceptance of the business community's proffered compromise.[39]

The Board next named a committee to draft a resolution for the consideration of the mass meeting that evening. The resolution explicitly attributed the boycott to the failure of the bus company to clarify its seating policy following the two March meetings and to the resultant misunderstandings that had produced the Smith and Parks arrests. It called on "every citizen in Montgomery, regardless of race, color or creed" to participate in the boycott, and urged employers voluntarily to afford transportation to their employees.[40]

The Montgomery chapter of the Alabama Council on Human Relations, the Alabama branch of the Southern Regional Council, arranged a meeting with the MIA, the City Commission, and the bus company on December 8—a success due primarily to the ironic circumstance that the ACHR's most prominent white member in the city, the Reverend Thomas Thrasher, an Episcopalian, was the rector of Mayor Gayle's church. The task before the meeting was large. Both the bus company's manager James H. Bagley and its attorney Jack Crenshaw had emphasized in their public statements their belief that the company could not legally alter bus seating arrangements. Crenshaw had maintained that blacks "have no quarrel with our company. If they don't like the law we have to operate under, then they should try to get the law changed, not engage in an attack on our company." To this position King had replied, "We are not asking an end to segregation. That's a matter for the Legislature and the courts. We feel that we have a plan within the law." Thus a principal question before the December 8 meeting, as before all the earlier ones, was whether the law allowed its enforcers any discretion.[41]

The meeting began with Martin King's reading a list of three demands, satisfaction of which was a prerequisite to the end of the boycott: more courtesy from bus drivers; the hiring of black drivers on the four predominantly black routes; and the seating of blacks from the back towards the front and of whites from the front towards the back without insisting that a section always be kept clear for each race. The demands appear to reflect the thinking of Edgar D. Nixon; the seating proposal was lifted from the questionnaire of the Ben Moore Hotel meeting, and the request for black drivers was consistent with Nixon's long-standing commitment as a labor leader to opening additional occupations to blacks.

Crenshaw replied by denying that drivers were discourteous, except in the rarest instances; by flatly rejecting the idea of black drivers, at least for the coming decade; and by declaring the seating proposal illegal. On this last point he joined battle with Gray. Gray offered a full-scale legal brief attempting to demonstrate that the 1945 state statute did not apply to Montgomery City Lines and urged the City Commission to seek a formal opinion from the state attorney general on the question. In any case, he noted, both city code and state statute simply required separate but equal accommodations; they made no attempt to specify the precise arrangements by which this goal was to be accomplished. As King put it in a statement issued two days later, presumably written in consultation with Gray, "The Legislature, it seems clear, wisely left it up to the transportation companies to work out the seating problem in a reasonable and practical way . . . We feel that there is no issue between the Negro citizens and the Montgomery City Lines that cannot be solved by negotiations between people of good will. And we submit that there is no legal barrier to such negotiations." At the meeting King emphasized that the suggested seating plan was in use in Mobile and other Southern cities. Crenshaw did offer to have every other bus on the heavily black Washington Park route designated exclusively for blacks, but beyond this concession he simply reiterated that the company could not "change the law."

After some hours of these exchanges, Mayor Gayle suggested that it might be useful if a smaller group conferred in private. He then withdrew, taking the press, television cameramen, spectators, and peripheral participants with him. King, Gray, and perhaps other blacks remained to talk with Bagley and Crenshaw and the two new commissioners, Sellers and Parks. According to King's account of this session, as soon as the reporters had gone, Parks—who had defeated Cleere with black votes—ventured, "I don't see why we can't arrange to accept this seating proposal. We can work it within our segregation laws." At once Crenshaw replied, "But Frank, I don't see how we can do it within the law. If it were legal I would be the first to go along with it, but it just isn't legal. The only way that it can be done is to change your segregation laws." Then he added, "If we granted the Negroes these demands, they would go about boasting of a victory that they had won over the white people, and this we will not stand for." Facing this determined opposition from Crenshaw and knowing that Sellers could not be brought to compromise, Parks crumbled, and the next day resignedly informed the press that he regretted that the conference had produced no settlement but that "We cannot break the law."[42]

This sequence of events had been most peculiar. Although all the blacks were integrationists, the thrust of their efforts was so to reform the actual practice of segregation as to make it acceptable and thus to remove the impetus for its elimination. Crenshaw, a firm segregationist, was by implication urging the blacks to seek the complete abolition of segregation in the courts.

Since March the blacks had repeatedly pointed out that their plan was in effect in many Southern cities, including Mobile. King had reiterated this point at the meeting on December 8. Yet, Bagley subsequently testified that he had been unaware of this fact on December 8 and found it out only later. When the *Advertiser* printed on December 31 an article confirming the accuracy of the blacks' statements, the article was thought worthy of prominent treatment and seems to have caused surprise among whites. Nevertheless, the illogic of maintaining that the state law permitted in Mobile what it forbade in Montgomery escaped the white citizenry; when Bagley was asked about the inconsistency, he replied merely, "I cannot testify what they would do in Mobile, or what they can do, but I know what we can do in Montgomery." True, the Mobile City Code specifically required the seating plan in use in that city. But it is also true that the Montgomery City Code prescribed no specific seating plan.[43]

Similarly, Gray had argued at length at both the Colvin and the Parks hearings that the state statute did not apply to municipal bus lines and had submitted a brief to the Commission and the bus company expounding this position. No one in authority, except possibly Frank Parks, appears to have paid any attention. Gray had suggested that the Commission seek a ruling from the attorney general; the Commission toyed with the idea of doing so but in the end took no action. The following spring, however, when Gray joined the Public Service Commission as a defendant in his federal court suit to void bus segregation, in order to have the state law as well as the city ordinance declared unconstitutional, the state suddenly took up Gray's earlier argument in its entirety. At the trial the president of the Public Service Commission, C. C. "Jack" Owen, flatly denied that his agency had any jurisdiction over municipal bus systems. The Court read the state statute of 1945 to Owen and asked him if his construction of the act was that it "does not include common carriers such as buses in the City of Montgomery?" Owen, evidently nonplussed by the question, stammered in reply, "I had never thought of it in that particular line of thinking. This is the first time that point has ever been brought up. It seems to me like that means segregation as far as segregation is concerned."[44]

Whites simply did not reflect carefully on the legal points which the blacks raised. Indeed, President Owen—a Montgomerian whose position ought to have made him more than ordinarily concerned with this aspect of the controversy—did not even know that the question of the applicability of the 1945 act had been at issue throughout the preceding year. These attitudes appear particularly puzzling because what Gray and his associates were actually trying to do was to rationalize the segregation system. Why did segregationists find it so difficult to accept the modest reforms which the blacks suggested—reforms whose acceptance would clearly have strengthened segregation itself, by diminishing opposition to it? Consideration of three efforts to reach a compromise will help provide an answer to this question.

Mayor Gayle's copy of the resolution adopted by the black mass meeting on December 5, which Fred Gray had handed to the mayor at the December 8 meeting, was offered in evidence at King's trial for violation of the anti-boycott law. On its back someone, presumably the mayor, had jotted in pencil, "How about again appointing [a] com[mittee] of Retailer[s] etc. to meet with [K. E.] Totten [vice-president of National City Lines of Chicago] to bring some recommendations to [the] City Com[mission]?" The reference was to the course which the commissioners had successfully followed in the bus drivers' strike of December 1953. At that time the Commission had named a committee of six—the presidents of the Chamber of Commerce, the Retail Merchants Association, the white Ministers Association, and the PTA, an attorney, and a prominent black—to mediate the conflict. When the December 8 meeting produced no settlement, the Commission evidently decided to make use of this precedent.

Totten returned to Montgomery on December 15 to continue negotiations for the renewal of the company's expiring franchise. After conferring with him the Commission called a meeting of all parties to the controversy on the morning of December 17, and there the mayor suggested the appointment of a ten-member committee—eight whites and two blacks—to act as mediators between the MIA and the bus company. Jo Ann Robinson at once insisted that the number of whites and blacks on the committee be equal. Apparently, the commissioners conceived of the dispute as being between the bus company and the MIA, and of the committee as a neutral mediator, while the MIA thought of the dispute as being between Montgomery's whites and blacks, and of the committee as a sort of collective bargaining arrangement. After some discussion the mayor agreed to add six MIA members to his original ten. These sixteen people met on the afternoon of December 17 and again on December 19 but reached no agreement.[45]

The blacks included King, Abernathy, Robinson, attorneys Fred Gray and Charles D. Langford, the Reverend Hillman H. Hubbard, pastor of one of the city's largest black congregations and one of the few older black preachers prominent in the MIA's leadership, and the two well-to-do black businessmen who were Gayle's choices, Pluie M. Blair, who owned a dry-cleaners and who was called the "Negro Mayor of Montgomery," and

Dungee Caffey, a realtor with diverse interests. The white delegation, balancing the black one, included also three ministers: Dr. Henry Allen Parker of the First Baptist Church (white), the Reverend G. Stanley Frazer of St. James Methodist Church, and the Reverend Henry Edward Russell of Trinity Presbyterian Church, brother of U.S. Senator Richard Russell of Georgia. There were two businessmen: James J. Bailey, the manager of a furniture store and president of the Furniture Dealers Association, and William H. Fields, the manager of a local J. C. Penney store and president of the Retail Merchants Association. Mrs. Earnest R. Moore was the wife of a dental technician and the president of the city-county PTA. Mrs. Logan A. Hipp, Jr., the wife of an insurance adjuster, worked as a secretary in the office of the city Chamber of Commerce. The final white member was William G. Welch, a bus driver for the Montgomery City Lines and president of the bus drivers' local union.[46]

King charged that the mayor had "not appointed a representative committee of whites." At first glance the allegation would appear unfounded. But an investigation of the committee's deliberations casts the notion into a different light. The blacks advanced their seating proposal, and Gray argued that it could be effected within existing law. At the initial session the white delegation, unlike the black, contained no lawyers. The whites relied for legal advice upon City Attorney Walter Knabe, who attended the meetings. Knabe had been involved in the negotiations stretching back to the preceding spring and was committed to the position that the seating proposal was illegal. He informed the whites that Gray was simply wrong, and the whites adopted this position in their final report, issued on January 18. King states that K. E. Totten acknowledged to him privately that the black proposal was used by National City Lines' Mobile affiliate; Totten, King reports, said that he could not see why what worked in Mobile could not work in Montgomery. If Totten made this admission privately, he refused to do so publicly. Instead, he declined to become involved in the local negotiations, saying only that National City Lines would abide by any arrangement accepted by Montgomerians. Understandably, a national firm that dealt with cities across the country would wish to avoid becoming entangled in heated municipal controversies. This motive must have been particularly strong in the Montgomery situation because Totten was at this very time attempting to secure a new franchise from the city government. However, Totten's refusal to intervene, coupled with the whites' reliance upon Knabe's advice, left the committee within the limits of the controversy that had previously been defined, unable to approach the problem from a new perspective.

Of course, the whites on the committee were segregationists; had they not been, they would not have reflected accurately the sentiment of the community which they represented. Yet segregationist attitudes in themselves were no real barrier to a settlement, because the black delegation emphasized that it had no desire to disestablish segregation. Ill will between the two sides on the committee was exacerbated by the inability of Frazer and Russell to resist the urge to lecture the blacks on the morality of segregation and the immorality of ministerial involvement in politics. The black clergymen responded with lectures of their own. Still, the white committee members were not opposed to compromise. Frazer presented what he took to be a compromise: that fixed lines of racial division be marked on every bus, determined by the proportion of the races on each route, but that riders be permitted to sit forward or back of the line until the seats were needed by the other race. The proposal, as Charles Langford noted, ignored the principal black complaint, the unseating of passengers already seated. At least Frazer's proposal demonstrated a willingness to try to find a solution. Bailey even stated to the committee, "I came here prepared to vote for liberalization of interpretation of the city's laws with certain conditions."[47]

The failure of the committee to discover a compromise was not entirely attributable to the racial attitudes of the committee members, though such attitudes doubtless contributed to the impasse. None of the whites on the committee was a member of Montgomery's upper class; Bailey, the member of the white delegation who seems to have been most favorable to compromise, was the one member who was at all prominent in the city's business community. This fact is significant. When King called the whites unrepresentative, what he evidently meant was that they were all too representative. The situation demanded men and women who were sufficiently confident of their social position to allow them to be original in their approach to the problem. The committee contained no such members, and it is primarily for that reason that its deliberations proved sterile.

The mayor had not appointed any of the city's social and economic leaders to the committee because of his weak political position. The March elections had emphasized that Gayle could no longer permit himself to seem a front man for Montgomery's upper class. Rather, he needed to seek the support of other social elements among the whites. He certainly could not permit himself the luxury of an action that flew in the face of white community sentiment. A compromise suggested by the committee he did appoint would give some promise of generating community consensus. Precisely because the committee was representative, its deliberations were doomed without the intervention of some outside figure like Totten. Gayle may initially have hoped that Totten would help, but when Totten refused, the Committee became an exercise in futility.[48]

The encounter between the city and its black citizens entered a new stage in late January, when attitudes in both camps had hardened considerably. After the December 19 meeting the biracial committee held no further sessions. On January 6 Clyde Sellers appeared at a meeting of the White Citizens Council and dramatically announced that he was joining the organization. On January 9 the City Commission met with an MIA delegation for two hours at King's request, but neither side would modify its position. On January 18 the white members of the biracial committee issued a final report publicly acknowledging the failure of their efforts and urging all parties to accept Frazer's compromise proposal. At least by the same time in mid-January some MIA leaders were concluding that further negotiations would be fruitless and were beginning to discuss the possibility of a federal court suit to have bus segregation declared unconstitutional.[49]

During this period discontent had been growing among those black ministers who were not a part of the MIA's leadership. The boycott had so captured the imagination and the loyalties of the city's blacks that the failure of a black minister to be included occasionally as a speaker at the frequent mass meetings which were the movement's backbone demeaned him in the eyes of his congregation. Probably, jealousies thus generated lay behind the decision of three black ministers to contact white officials with the offer to negotiate a settlement. The Reverend Benjamin F. Mosely, pastor of the First Presbyterian Church (black), Bishop Doc C. Rice, pastor of the Oak Street Holiness Church, and the Reverend William K. Kind, pastor of the Jackson Street Baptist Church, one of the few prominent black preachers in the city who had not been chosen a member of the MIA's executive board, perhaps expected that, if they were able to engineer the creation of a compromise acceptable to the black community, they might gain for themselves a portion of the public attention being focused upon King, Abernathy, Gray, and their associates.

On January 21 the City Commission met with the three ministers, together with Paul B. Fuller, the executive secretary of the Chamber of Commerce, and the Reverend Thomas Thrasher of the Alabama Council on Human

Relations. The meeting produced a compromise under which ten seats in the front would always be reserved for whites, ten seats in the rear for blacks, and the remaining sixteen seats would be filled as the MIA proposed, blacks sitting from the rear and whites from the front; in addition, all-black buses would be provided during rush hours on three predominantly black routes. The proposal did not specify whether passengers seated in the middle sixteen seats could be unseated. It stated that the City Commission had no authority to alter the bus company's hiring policies; the company had repeatedly refused to hire blacks, so this statement implied the rejection of the request for black drivers.

The MIA promptly denounced this agreement and stated that the three ministers did not speak for the city's blacks. It soon became apparent, moreover, that virtually the entire black community supported the MIA's position in this regard. The three ministers thereupon repudiated the compromise; they told King that they had not understood the proposal and had attended the meeting under the impression that it was to discuss the city's insurance. The commissioners were livid with rage at this turn of events. Mayor Gayle subsequently swore that both Fuller and Thrasher had read the agreement carefully to the ministers who had fully understood and approved of it. On this basis the commissioners had publicly committed themselves to the compromise. All three commissioners were increasingly in awe of Montgomery's rapidly growing White Citizens Council, whose membership local newspapers reported to be 6,000 at the beginning of February and 12,000 by the end of that month. By that time it had become the largest single organization in Montgomery County. Sellers, in a speech to the council on January 6, had pledged to continue fighting the blacks' demands and had repeated the promise in even stronger terms on January 17. Gayle and Parks had been somewhat less vocal but naturally wished to avoid offending council members unnecessarily. Now all three commissioners found themselves revealed to the voters as willing to compromise but deprived at the same time of any compromise to show for their pains. They felt betrayed.[50]

On January 23 Mayor Gayle announced, "The Negro leaders have proved they will say one thing to a white man and another thing to a Negro." He said, "The City Commission has attempted with sincerity and honesty to end the bus boycott in a businesslike fashion. We have held meetings with the Negroes at which proposals were made that would have been accepted by any fair-minded group of people. But there seems to be a belief on the part of the Negroes that they have the white people hemmed up in a corner and they are not going to give an inch until they can force the white people of our community to submit to their demands—in fact, swallow all of them . . . We attempted to resolve their reasonable complaints but they proved by their refusal to resolve the reasonable ones that they were not interested in whether the bus service was good or not. What they are after is the destruction of our social fabric." He called the black leadership "a group of Negro radicals" whose only real goal was to "stir up racial strife." He stated, "The white people are firm in their convictions that they do not care whether the Negroes ever ride a city bus again . . ." He concluded, "When and if the Negro people desire to end the boycott, my door is open to them. But until they are ready to end it, there will be no more discussions."

This statement appears to have been the product of a moment of anger, but the astonishing approbation with which whites greeted it transformed it into fixed policy. Appreciative calls swamped the City Hall switchboard; hundreds of congratulatory telegrams flooded in, and voters eager for the opportunity to shake Gayle's hand crowded the mayor's office. Commissioner Parks reported himself "amazed with the avalanche" of approval. He concluded, "There is no need for us to straddle the fence any longer. I am taking a stand and so are the other commissioners." Both Gayle and Sellers moved at once to identify themselves even more firmly with the "get tough" stand. Gayle called for whites to refuse to drive their domestics to and from work or to pay their taxi fare; "the Negroes are laughing at white people behind their backs" because of the whites' willingness to do so, he warned. Sellers instructed the police to arrest blacks waiting to catch a ride and to charge them with loitering. "A person has a perfect right to wait for a ride," he noted, "but the practice of six or eight Negroes huddling together for an hour or more, trampling lawns and making loud noises in white residential districts must cease." On January 24 Mayor Gayle and Commissioner Parks announced that they, too, had joined the White Citizens Council. Within weeks all members of the County Board of Revenue also had joined. The council's attorney proclaimed that the group was now so large that blacks would never again be able to influence candidates for local office by "dangling their bloc votes" before aspirants.[51]

Stronger and stronger statements followed, as politicians rushed to associate themselves with the City Commission's popular stand. The pronouncements soon bore fruit. On the night of January 30 a stick of dynamite was thrown onto the porch of Martin L. King's home; his wife and a visitor narrowly escaped injury. The MIA leadership had been discussing the advisability of a federal court suit for at least two weeks, as a political settlement seemed increasingly illusory. However, the bombing of King's home convinced the MIA that simply to continue pressure on the city through the boycott to force agreement to the blacks' demands was no longer a reasonable strategy. If negotiations ever could produce an agreement, it would be in the far future. Meantime, the boycott would be fraught with excessive risk. On February 1 Fred Gray filed suit challenging the constitutionality of bus segregation.[52] Mayor Gayle denounced the suit as "proof beyond any doubt that Negroes never wanted better bus service as they were claiming, but complete integration." The blacks, he said, stood convicted of double-dealing.[53]

These events strikingly illuminate the commission's ignorance of sentiment among both blacks and extremist whites. First, the events emphasize how tenaciously the commissioners and their advisers believed that the MIA did not actually speak for the city's blacks. The commissioners had repeatedly urged the masses of blacks to repudiate King and other spurious leaders who owed their apparent positions as spokesmen for the black community only to the apathy of many blacks and to the intimidation of the remainder by MIA goon squads. Commissioner Sellers estimated that 85 to 90 percent of the city's blacks would immediately resume riding the buses if there were no danger of physical reprisal. "The innocent Negroes should wake up," Commissioner Parks warned. "They don't know what they are doing, but I'm afraid they're going to find out. The white people have been their friends, and still want to be, but we can't sit here and watch them destroy our transportation system." Mayor Gayle accepted both Parks's emphasis on ignorance and Sellers's emphasis on fear, although there is relatively little evidence of intimidation and none linking the intimidation to the MIA. Unfortunately, one of the few instances in which intimidation was alleged involved Mayor Gayle's father-in-law's cook. The mayor's closeness to this particular incident perhaps increased his sense of the violence surrounding the boycott. Whether because of Sellers's dark, conspiratorial explanation or because of Parks's more benign one, the city's political leaders were convinced that the MIA's claims to represent Montgomery's blacks were false.

This attitude accounts for the commissioners' otherwise inexplicable notion that the three non-MIA black ministers constituted, as the statement of January 21 claimed, a "group representing the Negroes of Montgomery." At the time of the appointment of the biracial committee on December 17

Gayle had insisted on appointing two prominent blacks, Blair and Caffey, who had not been nominated by the MIA, perhaps partly in the hope that he would tap the reservoir of anti-MIA feeling which he thought to exist. This expectation failed; Blair and Caffey proved to be completely committed to the MIA's demands. When the three ministers approached white leaders in late January, the commissioners evidently felt that they had at last forced from hiding a leadership alternative to King. Of course, the commissioners knew that no organized group had appointed the three ministers. On the other hand, the commissioners regarded the views of the three ministers as more fully consonant with those of the black masses. If the commissioners had been correct in their analysis, it would have been reasonable to have supposed that the conclusion of a settlement with the ministers would give most blacks sufficient encouragement to return to the buses. The compromise produced no such result simply because the Commission was wrong; Montgomery's blacks were dedicated to the achievement of the MIA's program. Unfortunately, the repudiation of the settlement by the three ministers obscured this fact for city political leaders.[54]

The Commission betrayed similar ignorance in failing to gauge the effect upon the city's racist extremists of the intemperate statements issued in late January. The extremist element evidently took the "get tough" policy and the resulting public ovation as a license for violence. In addition to the bombing of King's home on January 30 the home of Edgar D. Nixon was bombed on February 1, though the latter explosion caused no damage. In later months, incidentally, the belief became general in Citizens Council circles that blacks themselves had staged both of these bombings to gain sympathy and contributions from Northerners.[55] The absence of any sense of the state of sentiment among blacks and among white racial extremists is a complementary phenomenon with a single culprit: these segments of the population were essentially excluded from political life, and the Commission had such limited contact with them that it lacked any mechanism for understanding their motives and assumptions.

Contemporary with the events of January, the third and last effort to formulate a compromise acceptable to the MIA emerged from the business community. The Men of Montgomery, already dubious of city politicians, were persuaded by January that the Commission's mismanagement of the crisis had prevented a settlement and that businessmen might well succeed where politicians had failed. Moreover, the organization had three good reasons to try. The boycott had intensified racial hatred in the city, damaged trade, and directed such unfavorable publicity to the city as to complicate any effort to attract industry to the area. Mayor Gayle's announcement on January 23 that the Commission would not negotiate further made the politicians' inability to secure an agreement explicit. The bombing of Dr. King's home clearly announced that the entire affair had gotten out of hand and that unless a compromise could be found quickly, seriously unfavorable reports in the national press would be inevitable.[56] These two events moved the Men of Montgomery to intervene in the boycott. Thus, rather ironically, the same set of circumstances convincing the black leadership that additional negotiation would be fruitless, finally moved the city's economic powers to undertake the mediation of the controversy.

During the first three weeks of February a committee of the Men of Montgomery held two full-scale negotiating sessions with MIA leaders and at least one with the City Commission. It was also in almost constant informal contact with the two groups in an effort to locate tenable middle ground. The Men of Montgomery members advanced no proposals of their own; they apparently saw themselves as brokers rather than as parties to the conflict. King later wrote of them that they had proved themselves "open-minded enough to listen to another point of view and discuss the problem of race intelligently," and in reference to their arbitration he concluded, "I have no doubt that we would have come to a solution had it not been for the recalcitrance of the city commission." However, the obstacles to any such happy outcome appear genuinely insuperable. The commissioners' statements during the last week of January had made it virtually impossible for them to agree to any substantial concessions; and their receptiveness to compromise was not increased by the fact that on February 10, at a White Citizens Council rally which filled the state coliseum, a crowd of some 12,000 gave both Mayor Gayle and Commissioner Sellers sustained, emotional standing ovations.[57]

For its part the MIA was no longer in a position to negotiate. At no time would it have been easy for the MIA to have made concessions; as King had noted in mid-January, "We began with a compromise when we didn't ask for complete integration. Now we're asked to compromise on the compromise."

The filing of the federal court suit on February 1, however, had eliminated even the small basis for an accord that had been present. The MIA's initial requests had sought only a reform of specific practice within the general framework of segregation; the MIA had repeatedly and strenuously affirmed its view that its proposals were in keeping with city and state law. But the suit sought the elimination of segregation. It so changed the MIA's position that King had evidently given serious consideration to recommending that the boycott be called off. The boycott had been intended to move the City Commission and the bus company to action. If the MIA were going to rely on a court order to produce the action, there was no longer a reason for a boycott. Indeed, the only difficulty with this logic was that the MIA could not be certain that the federal courts would declare bus segregation unconstitutional. Despite the decision of the MIA to continue with the boycott, the organization could hardly be expected to agree to a compromise perpetuating segregation while it was at the same time asking the courts to compel full integration. The Men of Montgomery's efforts would appear therefore to have been doomed from the outset.[58]

Nevertheless, the Men of Montgomery pressed mediation because the city's good reputation could be restored only if Montgomerians solved the boycott themselves. Their task was made especially urgent when some prominent Montgomery lawyers began to advocate a course that would almost certainly destroy whatever respect for the city remained among national opinion leaders: the mass indictment of virtually all the city's most prominent blacks for violation of the Alabama anti-boycott law.

The anti-boycott law had been passed in 1921 as a part of a series of statutes provoked by a bloody strike of Birmingham coal miners in that year. From the beginning of the bus boycott the applicability of this act to the situation had been discussed, but the question was not taken very seriously because, as the *Advertiser* noted editorially on December 8, "As a practical matter, we doubt that either the bus company or the solicitor will attempt to jail 5,000 Negroes." As the hatreds generated by the dispute deepened, some Montgomerians considered prosecution as a realistic weapon. On January 9 Frederick S. Ball, an important figure in both legal and social circles in the city, dispatched a letter to the *Advertiser* demanding the boycotters' indictment. "An individual has the right to ride a bus or not as he or she sees fit and that right should not be interfered with and should be protected by the police," he wrote, "but when certain so-called leaders call a group together and organize a boycott, they are taking the law into their own hands and should be prosecuted. Whether the bus company or its drivers have or have not always themselves obeyed the law and given colored passengers their rights is not the question at all, because two wrongs do not make a right and there is always legal redress against the bus company for anything it does wrong. The question is whether the officials whose duty it is to enforce the law are going to sit idly by and permit the illegal destruction of a transportation system which is most certainly needed by both races." He added pointedly, "A copy of this letter goes to the county solicitor with the suggestion that he give consideration to presenting this matter to the grand jury . . ."

Grover C. Hall, Jr., clearly shared the view of the business leaders that this course would be sheer folly. Hall attempted to dispose of Ball's argument with gentle ridicule. "Atty. Ball . . . is against lawlessness. So he has asked Solicitor Thetford to prosecute. What leaves us confused is the question whether Atty. Ball is also opposed to the lawlessness of defying the U.S. Supreme Court, the supreme law. . . . We ask then, is Atty. Ball for law-abiding at the local level and lawlessness at the Supreme Court level? And, as we asked Dec. 8, what if Atty. Ball got some bus boycotters convicted in a Montgomery court? Would not the Supreme Court automatically reverse the convictions? Another perplexity left by Atty. Ball's brief letter is whether he is against all persons who have entered an 'arrangement' to boycott? For example, Police Commissioner Clyde Sellers is a card-carrying member of the White Citizens Council, an organization dedicated to boycott and economic sanctions against Negroes. Does Atty. Ball want White Councilman Sellers indicted also?"

But Ball was not so easily dissuaded. On January 12 he replied, "The question is not, as put in your [editorial], how far to 'cast the net' of law enforcement, or whether we should abide by our own state laws or the most recent ruling of the federal Supreme Court on segregation in public schools. The question is not what the White Citizens Council stands for. . . . The law against boycotting is not a segregation law. It applies to all instances where people organize to prevent the operation of a lawful business. The single question here is whether certain religious and other misguided leaders who are openly and publicly violating the law against boycotting should be permitted to do so at the expense of the risk of our city losing a much-needed bus system, or whether the law against boycotting should be enforced. I think it should be enforced, and soon, before it is too late."

Hall continued to believe that sensible officials would not pursue Ball's suggestion. On January 15 Hall referred to "the contradictions and impracticality of Lawyer Ball's vexed demand that the solicitor jug the bus boycott leaders for violation of the anti-boycott law," and noted, "The polite silence of the solicitor substantiates our reservations about the Ball formula."

On January 17 an *Advertiser* reader, George C. Poulos, wrote the paper, "If an organized boycott is against the law, as Mr. Fred Ball states . . . , then why should anyone have to present his letter to the Circuit Solicitor? Doesn't the Solicitor know his job? Why does he have to be reminded of his duty? Maybe he is worried about the Negro vote. He had better start worrying about the white vote."[59]

Hall's confidence and Poulos's fear were both misplaced. On January 10, the day after Ball's initial letter appeared, Circuit Solicitor Thetford contacted Commissioner Sellers and asked that two detectives be assigned to the solicitor's office to investigate the boycott. Sellers agreed at once, and the investigation was launched on January 11. That it was being conducted did not become public knowledge during January, but by February 13 it had become clear that officials had determined to seek indictments; on that day Circuit Judge Eugene W. Carter charged the new county grand jury to determine whether the bus boycott violated the anti-boycott law.[60]

The negotiating efforts of the Men of Montgomery now became a race against time to find a settlement before the forces seeking prosecution could obtain the adoption of their strategy. On February 8 the Men of Montgomery published in the newspapers the name and telephone number of their executive secretary, William R. Lynn, and urged anyone having a suggestion for a compromise formula to contact him. In the end the City Commission was not in a position politically to offer much more than it had previously conceded to the three non-MIA black ministers: the reservation of ten seats at front and rear, with blacks seating from the rear and whites from the front in an unreserved middle section of sixteen seats. The Men of Montgomery sought to make this proposal more palatable to blacks by adding other reforms, such as mechanisms for more effectively institutionalizing the right of blacks to enter complaints against drivers. After a two-hour meeting on the morning of February 20 the Men of Montgomery succeeded in extracting from the Commissioners a public promise "that there will be no retaliation whatsoever resulting from the bus boycott"—almost certainly a reference to the grand jury investigation then entering its final stages. The concessions, which might well have satisfied the black leadership a year earlier, came far too late. At an MIA mass meeting on the evening of February 20 the audience shouted the proposals down; only the Reverend L. Roy Bennett and his assistant pastor openly supported the compromise. On February 21 the grand jury returned indictments of eighty-nine blacks, twenty-four of whom were ministers, for the misdemeanor of conspiring to boycott.[61]

The collision between the business community and the bar over the correct tactics to pursue in the crisis is worth some comment. The Men of Montgomery contained but a single lawyer among its forty founding members; it was composed of merchants, realtors, land developers, contractors, insurance men, bankers, brokers, and other men of similar occupations.[62] From the outset the most inflexible of the whites were lawyers. The differences in attitude which the differing vocations produced is one of the most puzzling aspects of the episode. We may in part explain the attitudes of Judge Carter and Circuit Solicitor Thetford by pointing to the pressures of an elective position; though Judge Carter was quite strong politically, Solicitor Thetford was a young man just beginning his second term in office. That explanation does not account for the stance of such men as Crenshaw, Knabe, and Ball. One might think that they would have seized upon the black proposals as a way to preserve segregation. In fact, however, they repeatedly displayed an absolutist predisposition that precluded compromise.

Nor is their temperament to be explained by a narrow devotion to the letter of the law. Gray's reading of the text of the act was at least as reasonable as Crenshaw's and Knabe's—a fact proved when the contending parties actually later switched sides, as a result of the federal court suit, on the question of the applicability of the state statute. Ball's construction of the anti-boycott law involved considerable legal difficulties as well. The constitutionality of the law had been specifically considered and affirmed by the Alabama Supreme Court in 1943. However, in that opinion Justice William H. Thomas, writing for the court, had saved the act by interpreting it very strictly. The statute prohibited conspiring to boycott "without a just cause or legal excuse." Such a law could be upheld, Justice Thomas said, when regarded as an effort by the legislature to prohibit the use of force, violence, or other unlawful activities to prevent someone from engaging in his business. If the statute were so construed as to permit the state to interfere with protest carried out by lawful means, it would be unconstitutional. But when limited in its scope and application simply to conspiracies to hinder a lawful occupation by actions otherwise illegal, the statute was within the state's police power. The U.S. Supreme Court had indicated its satisfaction with this decision by denying certiorari in the case. When Martin King was brought to trial in March—the first and only one of the boycotters to be tried—the prosecution was clearly aware of Justice Thomas's opinion and sought to prove that the boycott had indeed been accompanied and maintained by violence: shots had been fired at buses and a number of blacks had been forcibly restrained from riding, the testimony alleged. There was, however, no evidence connecting the MIA to these actions. In fact, at the conclusion of the trial Judge Carter, though convicting King, refused to sentence him to prison on the grounds, explicitly stated, that King had worked to prevent violence. At the very least the applicability of the anti-boycott law to the Montgomery situation was debatable.[63]

One might, of course, attribute the lawyers' maladroit handling of the boycott situation to ignorance or to poor legal training. But Crenshaw and Knabe had both received their legal education at Harvard. Knabe had been an undergraduate at Yale. Ball had been graduated from Princeton and had attended law school at Columbia and Emory. If these men desired to preserve segregation, as they certainly did, it was surely not a lack of mental acuity that prevented their seeing that acceding to the modest demands would strengthen, rather than weaken, the system.

Racism is no adequate explanation for the phenomenon; Montgomery's attorneys were no more nor less racist than were her business leaders, who were eager to compromise. Neither a literalist reading of the law nor a defective legal education provides an explanation; indeed, the facts contradict both contentions. Perhaps the answer lies in the role demanded of a lawyer as a representative of his client. Lawyers are poorly prepared to participate in the give-and-take of negotiations because they are trained to think of themselves as defending their clients' interests from the assaults of hostile adversaries. Such an attitude does not lend itself easily to the search for common ground. Rather, it almost inevitably conceives of the parties to a negotiation as enemies and tends to emphasize the elements in each position that are irreconcilable. In the boycott this tendency was exacerbated by racial prejudice and by the threat which the black effort seemed to pose to the white attorneys' own social position. But prejudice and social position could as readily have become motives to seek some settlement that would have preserved segregation in an ameliorated form, as the example of the business community shows. The key to the puzzle must be the legal turn of mind upon which the prejudice and the fear of social disintegration were acting, not merely the racial and class positions themselves.

However that may be, by the end of February 1956 both black and white leaders had abandoned the search for compromise and with it the political process and had determined to trust their respective causes to the rigid and unconditional judgment of the courts. The pressures leading to this decision among the whites have already been explained. Equally perplexing is why the blacks had not reached this decision much earlier. As logic would indicate that the whites should have been willing to compromise to preserve segregation, so logic would appear to dictate that blacks should have turned to the courts at once to attack the system which they despised. Indeed, as the *Advertiser* noted editorially at the conclusion of the boycott, the boycott itself accomplished absolutely nothing; only a decision of the courts ended the encounter, and that decision could have been obtained at any time, without the necessity for a boycott, simply by entering suit.

This riddle is solved in part by the observation that Montgomery's blacks had not yet developed the faith in the federal court which future years would generate. The city's federal judge, Frank M. Johnson, Jr., was still an unknown quantity, not a legend. He had held his position for just three months and had received Senate confirmation only the day before Gray filed the suit seeking to enjoin bus segregation. Southern federal judges certainly had not proved particular enemies of segregation in previous years. In fact, in the Montgomery bus suit itself, one of the three federal judges who heard it, Seybourn H. Lynne of Birmingham, dissented strongly from his colleagues' holding that the school integration decision of 1954 was applicable to bus seating.[64]

Yet lack of faith in the courts is not the most important explanation for the initial willingness of the black leadership to settle for a compromise within the framework of segregation. The real reason is that the bus boycott in its origins was much less a social than a political movement. During the year and a half that Dave Birmingham served on the City Commission black leaders developed a strengthened sense of the malleability of the system. The size of the black vote grew every year, and the city government paid new attention to black complaints. The decision to hold a public session to interview candidates for commissioner in 1955 and to release a list of endorsements reflected this growing confidence that politics could be made to subserve the needs of blacks. However, the outcome of the election dealt a considerable blow to this optimism. Black leaders had been permitted a brief experience of a happier relationship with their rulers, only to have it snatched away.

Bus seating had been one of the areas in which blacks had genuinely expected that they would be able to make progress. In the conferences that had followed the arrest of Claudette Colvin they had been promised public clarifications, which would have represented a clear acknowledgment of their ability to compel the city to respond to their concerns. No clarifications were forthcoming; the Commission formally rejected Birmingham's motion to add black members to the Parks and Recreation Board; the segregationist Sellers was inaugurated; and Mrs. Parks was arrested under the same circumstances as Miss Colvin. The MIA's statements at the beginning of the boycott emphasize unmistakably the connection between the city's failure to define the precise requirements of the segregation ordinance following the Colvin incident and the decision to boycott. The city elections, which had seemed in the spring so likely to produce an amelioration of the blacks' lot, had produced instead a situation that if anything was the worse for having earlier seemed so hopeful.

If government was ever really to benefit blacks, it now seemed, black leaders would have to discover some mechanism other than the electoral process by which to influence politicians. The boycott was intended to be such a mechanism. In the minds of its organizers, at least, it appears to have been analogous to a strike—a way for persons individually weak to bring collective pressure to bear upon the powerful once negotiations have failed. The boycott was not a revolution; it was merely an extension of the negotiations. The black leaders persisted in offering in December their seating proposal advanced in March precisely because they initially conceived their movement not so much as a direct action against bus segregation itself as rather a search for a means to manipulate the political process. They genuinely believed that, faced with this proof of how seriously blacks took the grievance, the City Commission would be compelled to seek a remedy.[65] For this device to work successfully, the blacks could only ask for something which the commissioners could legally grant—an amelioration of segregation.

Both the Ben Moore Hotel meeting and the boycott were politically naive. Under other circumstances the black leaders surely would have known that public endorsement of a candidate by blacks was likely to be counterproductive. They would similarly have known that for the commissioners to respond to pressure applied openly through a boycott—to knuckle under to blackmail, as it would have seemed to segregationists—would have infuriated a large part of the electorate. One cannot condemn the black leadership for its naivete in these matters;

inasmuch as blacks had been almost entirely excluded from political life in Alabama for two generations, it could hardly have been otherwise. Yet, the political process was clearly not analogous to an industrial dispute precisely because the interests involved were so many and varied and the conflicting pressures upon the Commission were so manifold. Surely, there was never any real likelihood of achieving a negotiated settlement of the boycott. At the outset of the boycott the *Advertiser* had stated editorially, "The boycott makes an innocent sufferer of the bus company. Had the company defied city and state laws, its franchise would have been canceled. The quarrel of the Negroes is with the law. It is wrong to hold the company a hostage."[66] The blacks replied over and over again—though the whites never seemed to listen—that their quarrel was not at all with the law, that they had no intention of asking the company to abandon segregation, that they merely wished to have the company apply the law in Montgomery as it did in Mobile. In a peculiar sense, however, the *Advertiser* was right, and the blacks were wrong. What the boycott taught the city's black leaders as it dragged on was that their quarrel was—had to be—with the law. Compromise with segregation was impossible because segregation so forged and underlay social relationships that even the most modest reform of its requirements threatened—just as the white politicians claimed—the entire social fabric. In such a situation reform was impossible; only "revolution" would do. The white response to the boycott revealed this truth forcefully to the blacks; that revelation is the boycott's supreme achievement, and it is something which no court suit could ever have accomplished.

Perhaps the most interesting single aspect of the boycott is that the inflexibility of segregation was something which black leaders had to learn. It was so much the fundamental presumption of the civil rights movement in later years that we find it difficult to believe that there could have been a time when a black—when anyone—was unaware of this characteristic of the system. Indeed, it is this difficulty that makes the MIA's position in the initial stages of the boycott seem so peculiar. But segregation revealed the true extent of its inflexibility only under the pressure of the civil rights movement itself. For those who had lived inside the segregation system, black and white, the pervasiveness of its impact was not so readily apparent. It is not the author's intention to maintain that blacks were not acutely aware of the constant humiliation that segregation entailed. Yet, the enormous variety of interracial associations even under segregation made the institution seem less fundamental to the shaping of attitudes than in fact it was. Particularly in a city like Montgomery, in which the Gunter Machine had defeated the Ku Klux Klan and ruled with relative benevolence, it was easy not to know how exceedingly far, into how many unrelated organs, the infection had spread. Black leaders had been too ready to believe that the brief thaw that Dave Birmingham's tenure had represented for them marked the beginning of spring. The writer believes that they made this mistake because they, in common with most white Southerners, had conceived of their world, though suffused with segregation, as fictile. Only after segregation came under assault and its supporters roused themselves to fight back were blacks, and later whites, able to discover the omnipresence and the rigidity of the system.

In a sense Martin King, having learned these lessons during the bus boycott, spent the rest of his career arranging demonstrations of them for others. Blacks, especially older blacks, in other Southern cities had to be shown that they were more fully imprisoned than they had believed. Moderate whites had to be shown that, whatever the extent of their good will, segregation had the power to render their best efforts vain. In these demonstrations the medium was the message; the immediate goals in a given city were less important than the process of placing segregation under stress in order to reveal the nature of its hold upon society. Iconoclasts sometimes note that King did not create the boycott, as a way of questioning his greatness. But King's greatness actually lies in the fact that during the boycott, by observing what was happening, he grew. He, far more than any of his contemporaries, white or black, learned the truths which the events of the boycott contained about the nature of the Southern dilemma.

In the end, the bus boycott teaches that segregation could have been disestablished only in the way in which it was disestablished: by internal pressure sufficient to compel intervention from outside the South. For all its diversity and complexity—in large part because of its diversity and complexity, since any fundamental reform would affect an infinite variety of interests—the South did not possess within itself the capacity to save itself. The strength of segregation was bound up with the pluralism of Southern society. As no man could untie the Gordian knot, so segregation would not—could not—yield to negotiation. Thus the boycott, because it failed to achieve its initial goals, succeeded for that reason in changing the course of American history.

Notes

1. Montgomery *Advertiser*, December 2, 1955; Montgomery *Alabama Journal*, December 5, 1955; Trial Transcript, *Rosa Parks v. City of Montgomery* (Records of the Alabama Court of Criminal Appeals, Office of the Clerk, Supreme Court Building, Montgomery), 9. This article has greatly benefited from interviews conducted with the following people on the dates noted: Ralph D. Abernathy, February 28, 1979; Joe F. Bear, March 9, 1979; Eugene W. Carter, October 16, 1978; Jack Crenshaw, July 15, 1977; Virginia F. Durr, May 2, 1979; C. T. Fitzpatrick, January 11, 1979; Fred D. Gray, October 17, 1978; Mark W. Johnston, July 19, 1977; Walter J. Knabe, August 5, 1977; Rufus A. Lewis, July 27, 1977; William V. Lyerly, September 2, 1976; William R. Lynn, December 29, 1976; Edgar D. Nixon, August 2, 1977; Rosa L. Parks, May 22, 1978; James G. Pruett, Sr., January 2, 1977; Jo Ann Robinson, January 27, 1978; William F. Thetford, September 4, 1976. At the request of Mr. Pruett, I have regarded his interview as confidential.

2. Thomas M. Owen, *History of Alabama and Dictionary of Alabama Biography* (4 vols., Chicago, 1921), III, 716; Montgomery *Advertiser*, April 1, 2, 1911, May 18, 20, 1919; *Acts of Alabama*, 1911, pp. 289-315, 1915, pp. 52-76, 1919, pp. 97-102; *House Journal* 1915, pp. 1461-66; *Senate Journal*, 1915, pp. 1144-49, 1170-71, 1173-75.

3. Montgomery *Advertiser*, March 15, 16, 1943, August 9, 12, September 5, 6, 1944, March 8, May 5, 9, 1946, March 18, 1947, March 19, 20, 1951; Montgomery *Alabama Journal*, May 9, 1946, March 18, 1947. Dunn had resigned in order permit returning soldiers to participate in the choice of their mayor—one of his campaign pledges in 1944—but had declined himself to become a candidate in the special election "as I am entering private business here in Montgomery."

4. The figures as to churches were developed from Montgomery city directories. After 1952 city directories ceased to designate their entries by race. Dalraida and Chisholm were not within the city limits at this period.

5. Montgomery *Advertiser*, February 20, March 15, 1955.

6. Montgomery *Alabama Journal*, March 18, 1947; Montgomery *Advertiser*, August 28, 1953, October 28, 1955.

7. Montgomery *Advertiser*, September 15, October 3, 4, 18, 24, 27, November 1, 3, 4, 1953.

8. *Ibid.*, March 27, 1955; cf. May 12, 1954.

9. *Ibid.*, May 8, 1946, November 9, 1953, March 25, 1955; *Smith v. Allwright*, 321 U.S. 649.

10. E.g., Dave Birmingham to James E. Folsom October 28, 1955 James E. Folsom Papers, Manuscripts Division, Alabama State Department of Archives and History, Montgomery.

11. Montgomery *Advertiser*, February 6, March 21, April 20, May 6, 1954, September 23, 30, 1955; Montgomery *Alabama Tribune*, September 30, October 14, 1955; Montgomery *Alabama Journal*, February 2, 1956; Clifford J. Durr to Hubert T. Delany, September 4, 1955, Durr to Herbert H. Lehman, March 25, 1957, both in Clifford J. Durr Papers, Alabama State Department of Archives and History, Montgomery; Thomas J. Gilliam, "The Montgomery Bus Boycott of 1955-1956" (M.A. thesis, Auburn University, 1968), 12-13. Nixon today believes that he may have been counted out in the executive committee race (interview, August 2, 1977).

12. Trial Transcript, *M. L. King, Jr. v. State of Alabama* (Records of the Alabama Court of Criminal Appeals, Office of the Clerk, Supreme Court Building, Montgomery), 256-57, 349-59; Martin Luther King, Jr., *Stride Toward Freedom: The Montgomery Story* (New York, 1958), 34, 73; Montgomery *Alabama Tribune*, December 23, 1955. Mrs. Burks and Mrs. Robinson organized the Council when they were refused membership in the League of Women Voters. Mrs. Robinson suggests that black women were able to be more aggressive in dealing with whites than were black men because in the environment created by segregation, women were under somewhat fewer strictures (interview, January 27, 1978). Lewis had been employed by the Montgomery Board of Education at the end of World War II to organize classes under the GI Bill for returning black veterans, and the veterans whom he taught became the backbone of his organization (interview, July 27, 1977).

13. Montgomery *Advertiser*, November 7, December 17, 1953, April 15, 17, 23, June 20, 1954; Juliette Morgan to William A. Gayle, July 13, 1955, Juliette Morgan Scrapbook, Alabama State Department of Archives and History, Montgomery.

14. Montgomery *Advertiser*, December 20, 1953, January 19, July 20, August 10, September 14, 1955; Montgomery *Alabama Tribune*, January 28, August 19, 1955. The *Advertiser* alleged editorially that Birmingham's August resolution was merely the opening gun in his rumored race for a seat on the County Board of Revenue. At the July meeting with the blacks Cleere and Birmingham almost came to blows and had to be separated by the mayor. The land that was promised as the site of a large new Negro park at the September meeting ultimately became a parking lot for a white football stadium.

15. Trial Transcript, *King v. State*, 141, 256-57, 349-59; Montgomery *Advertiser*, April 6, 1954.

16. Montgomery *Advertiser*, February 1, 6, 9, 13, 16, 20, 27, 28, March 10, 13, 16, 20, 23, 24, 27, 1955.

17. 1956 Montgomery City Directory; Montgomery *Advertiser*, May 9, 1954, February 1, 9, 1955. An additional highly visible alteration in race relations, though one unconnected with politics, was the hiring in the winter of 1953-54 of black players for the city's professional baseball team.

18. Montgomery *Advertiser*, February 9, 16, March 16, 1955, January 13, 1956.

19. *Ibid.*, February 18, 24, 25, March 1, 16, 20, 1955. Abernathy gives the membership of the committee that drafted the questionnaire as including himself, Nixon, Lewis, Robinson, Mrs. A. Wayman West, and James F. Pierce,

a professor of political science at Alabama State (interview, February 28, 1979). Nixon, who presided at the meeting, says that all of the candidates chose to duck the bus-seating question (interview, August 2, 1977).

20. *Ibid.*, March 16, 20, 1955.

21. *Ibid.*, February 9, 13, March 16, 20, 22, 24, 25, 29, 1955. Because of the presence on the ballot of a minor candidate, George J. Rivers, the race between Parks and Cleere was forced into a run-off, but the geographical distribution of the vote was identical in both elections.

22. *Ibid.*, March 30, 1955.

23. Montgomery *Alabama Journal*, January 13, 1956.

24. Montgomery *Advertiser*, October 28, 1953, January 15, 1954, February 20, 24, March 7, 10, October 19, December 11, 1955, March 4, 1956; Montgomery *Alabama Journal*, November 3, December 9, 1955, January 10, 1956.

25. Montgomery *Advertiser*, December 11, 1955.

26. *Ibid.*, March 6, 1955; Trial Transcript, *Aurelia S. Browder v. William A. Gayle*, Civil Action 1147-N, U.S. District Court, Middle District of Alabama (Federal Records Center, Atlanta, Georgia, FRC Box Number 426114), 17-20, and Colvin arrest warrant and complaint contained in case file.

27. Montgomery *Alabama Journal*, March 18, 19, 1955; Montgomery City Code of 1952, Chapter 6, Sections 10-11; Code of Alabama, 1940, Recompiled, Title 48, Section 301 (31a); Gilliam, "Bus Boycott," 17. Gray had only returned to Montgomery six months earlier, after attending law school in Cleveland, Ohio. The Colvin case was his first joust with the segregation laws (interview, October 17, 1978). But he quickly became a leader of the black community; that summer found him serving as a spokesman for the black delegation in the meetings with the city concerning the parks.

28. King, *Stride* 41-42; Trial Transcript, *King v. State*, 240, 344-46; Gilliam, "Bus Boycott," 18-19; Montgomery *Alabama Tribune*, March 16, 1956.

29. Trial Transcript, *King v. State*, 360-486, 510-47; Trial Transcript, *Browder v. Gayle*, 58-69.

30. Trial Transcript, *King v. State*, 256-57, 344-46, 357-59, 539-40. On Crenshaw's and Knabe's opinions of the legality of the Negro proposal, see below, notes 43, 47. Crenshaw and his brother had handled Governor Folsom's suit to compel the Dixiecrat presidential electors to vote for Harry Truman: *Folsom v. Albritton*, 335 U.S. 882; *State v. Albritton*, 251 Ala. 422.

31. *Flemming v. South Carolina Electric and Gas Co.*, 128 F. Supp. 469, 224 F. 2d 752; Montgomery *Advertiser*, July 15, 1955; Montgomery *Alabama Tribune*, July 22, 29, 1955; Trial Transcript, *Browder v. Gayle*, 10-12.

32. Montgomery *Advertiser*, December 12-16, 1953, October 25, 27, December 7, 20, 1955, January 25, February 16, 1956.

33. *Ibid.*, September 8, October 22, 23, 26, 1955; Montgomery *Alabama Tribune*, September 16, October 28, 1955. A petition seeking the integration of Montgomery's schools was also presented to the local board of education in August, and similar petitions were submitted throughout Alabama, evidently at the instance of the national NAACP. These petitions appear to have been

the trigger for the establishment of a great many of the Alabama chapters of the White Citizens Council.

34. Montgomery *Advertiser*, November 6, 1955; Interview with Nixon, August 27, 1977. In the 1930s both Powell and Randolph had organized black boycotts of Northern merchants who refused to hire blacks.

35. Interview with Rosa L. Parks, May 22, 1978; interview with Virginia F. Durr, May 2, 1979; Trial Transcript, *Parks v. City of Montgomery*, 7-9; Montgomery *Advertiser*, December 2, 6, 1955; Montgomery *Alabama Journal*, December 5, 1955. From the jail Mrs. Parks telephoned her mother, who located Nixon. Nixon called his close friend Durr, a former member of the Federal Communications Commission during World War II, and together they arranged the bond.

36. Gilliam, "Bus Boycott," 22-23; B. S. Thompson, Sr., ed., *A Century of Negro Progress in Montgomery City and County, 1863-1963* (Montgomery, 1963), 2; interview with Jo Ann Robinson, January 27, 1978. Furious, Alabama State's president H. Councill Trenholm threatened to dismiss Mrs. Robinson for having placed the college in danger of white retaliation by her actions. She retained her job only by swearing to keep her role secret. In this she was eminently successful; Solicitor Thetford stated that despite his most diligent efforts, he was never able to discover the origin of the handbill (interview, September 4, 1976). Rufus Lewis believes today that the real source of the boycott was the prominence and popularity of Mrs. Parks, which moved the city's black women to take action (interview, July 27, 1977).

37. King, *Stride*, 43-49; Trial Transcript, *King v. State*, 446-48; Montgomery *Alabama Tribune*, December 9, 16, 1955. Additional copies of Mrs. Robinson's handbill were run off by King and Abernathy in the church office after the meeting that night and were distributed on December 3 and 4. The text of the handbill also was reprinted on the front page of the Montgomery *Advertiser* on December 4 and was read from the pulpits of many black churches that day, a Sunday. The persons whom Nixon called after the arrest were largely people who had been active in the NAACP and thus had known Mrs. Parks. But Nixon evidently recognized that this group of activists—many of whom were Alabama State faculty members—was unlikely to be successful in involving the black masses without the support of the clergy. Nixon had very little contact with the black clergy, but he did know Abernathy well. Abernathy was one of the few ministers who was also a leader of the NAACP. He was therefore the ideal bridge between the two groups. Nixon requested Abernathy to arrange for the attendance of the leading black ministers, and Abernathy did so. Abernathy states that King offered his church as the site of the meeting in the hope that he would not be asked to do anything further for the cause. But because the church was King's, he necessarily was appointed along with Abernathy to prepare the additional copies of the handbills that night, thus involving him reluctantly in organizing the boycott (interview, February 28, 1979).

38. Montgomery *Alabama Journal*, December 5, 1955; Montgomery *Advertiser*, December 6, 1955. On Judge Scott, see Montgomery *Advertiser*, September

25, 1955. Gray states today that whether the prosecution was carried out under the state law or the city ordinance seemed a matter of no real importance to him (interview, October 17, 1978). Abernathy states that none of the boycott's leaders had ever dreamed that the boycott could last longer than four days (interview, February 28, 1979).

39. King, *Stride*, 30, 46-58, 72-74; Montgomery *Advertiser*, January 19, 1956; Trial Transcript, *King v. State*, 106-28, 334. Abernathy reports that at the outset of the December 2 meeting there were perhaps 125 people present, but that Bennett's conduct of the meeting had reduced the attendance to 40 by the time that the vote was taken on the resolution endorsing the boycott. Lewis states that in suggesting King, he was merely searching for another name as an alternative to Bennett; he calls the nomination the luckiest accident of his life. Nixon claims that he had early recognized King's talents and was planning to nominate King if Lewis had not done so. But Abernathy says that Nixon barely knew King at the outbreak of the boycott; he says that when Nixon telephoned him on December 2, he himself suggested King's name to Nixon as a minister who might be cooperative. I am inclined to believe that Nixon's memory of his early appreciation of King's talents is influenced by the bitter struggle for King's mantle of leadership in which Nixon and Lewis engaged between 1961 and 1968—a struggle that culminated in Lewis's victory and that has left Nixon rather embittered. Indeed, Abernathy believes that Lewis suggested King's name as a way of preventing Nixon's own election as president, but I think that Abernathy is reading the later fierce rivalry back into an earlier time (interviews with Abernathy, February 28, 1979, Lewis, July 27, 1977, Nixon, August 2, 1977).

Nixon says that when he called the president of the Montgomery NAACP chapter, Robert L. Mathews, to report Mrs. Parks's arrest, Mathews refused to allow the chapter to become involved in a boycott without the approval of the NAACP national headquarters. Nixon states that it was this attitude of Mathews which forced the creation of a separate organization to run the boycott. But Abernathy reports that he and King had been discussing for months the need for an umbrella organization to bind Montgomery's blacks together, and that he seized the opportunity afforded by the boycott to suggest the creation of one.

40. Trial Transcript, *King v. State*, 59-61 , 344-46; Montgomery *Alabama Tribune*, December 16, 1955.

41. Montgomery *Advertiser*, February 1, December 7, 1955; Montgomery *Alabama Journal*, December 7, 1955.

42. King, *Stride*, 108-13; Trial Transcript, *King v. State*, 239, 248-50, 336, 346-47; Montgomery *Advertiser*, December 9-11, 1955; Montgomery *Alabama Journal*, December 8, 9, 1955; *Browder v. Gayle* case file, Exhibit A: "Legal Requirements Concerning the Segregation of Races on City Buses." Abernathy states that the three demands were composed at a meeting at noon on December 5 consisting of Abernathy himself, Nixon, and Edgar N. French, director of the pensions office of the A.M.E. Zion churches in Montgomery, and were subsequently accepted by the MIA Executive Board (interview,

February 28, 1979). He may, however, be confusing the demands with the resolution of the December 5 mass meeting. King's statement that the demands were adopted by the mass meeting (*Stride*, 63-64, 108-09) is erroneous. Gray cannot today recall whether he helped King prepare the statement issued on December 10 (interview, October 17, 1978), but its argument clearly is derived from Gray's brief. Crenshaw does not recall the interchange with Parks which King reports, but he does confirm that Parks was more amenable to accepting the MIA's demands than were the other two commissioners—particularly Sellers. As Gayle and the reporters left the meeting, Gayle told those remaining that he wanted them to find a settlement as quickly as possible. Crenshaw even today rather resents that remark, feeling that it was an effort on the mayor's part to pass the buck to the bus company, which Crenshaw still regards as an innocent third party in the dispute (interview, July 15, 1977).

43. Trial Transcript, *King v. State*, 539-41; Montgomery *Advertiser*, March 20, December 31, 1955; King, *Stride*, 110; Mobile City Code of 1947, Chapter 20, Article 1. Crenshaw continues to believe today that the Montgomery Code required in detail the bus company's specific seating arrangement; when I told him that the Code merely required that the seating be separate and equal, he replied that he was positive that I was wrong. He is also under the impression that Mobile had adopted its seating plan only a few months before the outbreak of the boycott. He states that the Montgomery company had always been willing to accept the Mobile plan if the City Commission would amend the ordinance to permit the arrangement, but that the Commission adamantly refused to do so (interview, July 15, 1977).

44. Trial Transcript, *Browder v. Gayle*, 46-48; Motion of Public Service Commission for Dismissal of Complaint, in *Browder v. Gayle* case file. This reversal of positions was so complete that it has left Crenshaw confused about what his position had been on the issue earlier in the boycott. He believes that he had argued to the City Commission that the state statute was not applicable and that Gray had maintained that it was (interview, July 15, 1977).

45. Trial Transcript, *King v. State*, 346; Montgomery *Advertiser*, December 13, 1953; Montgomery *Alabama Journal*, December 16, 1955; King, *Stride*, 117-18. Just as the commission apparently thought of the MIA and the bus company as the principal disputants, so the bus company thought of the MIA and the Commission as the principal disputants. This odd situation tended to inhibit both the company and the city in the negotiations with the blacks.

46. At the second meeting Luther Ingalls, an attorney prominent in the Montgomery White Citizens Council, was added to the white delegation, and Mrs. Hipp became a non-voting secretary of the committee—an alteration that provoked an outraged protest by King.

47. King, *Stride*, 114-21; Montgomery *Advertiser*, December 18, 20, 1955; Montgomery *Alabama Journal*, December 17, 19, 20, 1955, January 18, 1956; Trial Transcript, *King v. State*, 233-36, 248-50, 336, 539-41. Knabe states today that he never doubted the legality of the MIA's seating proposal. He says that he opposed granting the concession only because he was convinced that doing so would not really produce an end to the boycott (interview, August

5, 1977). But if he held such an opinion at the time, he certainly never gave any public hint of it. Crenshaw believes that Knabe supported his position (interview, July 15, 1977).

48. Crenshaw states that National City Lines hoped that by refusing to get involved, it could avoid making anyone mad (interview, July 15, 1977). The national company's determinedly noncommittal position is well illustrated by B. W. Franklin [executive vice-president] to Wilhelmina D. Long, March 20, 1956, enclosed in Wilhelmina D. Long to James E. Folsom, May 9, 1956, in Governors' Correspondence: Folsom II, Civil Archives Division, Alabama State Department of Archives and History, Montgomery.

49. Montgomery *Advertiser*, January 7, 10, 1956; Montgomery *Alabama Journal*, January 18, 1956; Montgomery *Alabama Tribune*, January 20, 1956; Gilliam, "Bus Boycott," 114-16, The origins of the idea for a federal suit are disputed. Gray states that he had favored filing a federal suit from the outset but had been unable to convince the MIA Executive Board to authorize the action, both because the strategy was new and untried for Montgomery blacks and because many MIA leaders had high hopes for negotiations in the early weeks (interview, October 17, 1978). Abernathy states that the idea of a federal court suit was first suggested to him near the end of December, he believes by Gray (interview, February 28, 1979). Nixon states that the idea of a federal court suit was suggested to him by his friend Clifford J. Durr. Nixon says that he passed the suggestion along to King and Abernathy; he dates this exchange to mid-February, however, which is impossible (interview, August 2, 1977). Mrs. Durr says that her husband originally suggested the idea to Gray after Ball's letter of January 9. She also states that Durr helped Gray with all the briefs and submissions in the boycott suit and that she personally typed them (interview, May 2, 1979). Lewis states that no one proposed a suit until shortly before it was actually filed, after the negotiations had proved unsuccessful (interview, July 27, 1977). Despite these differing accounts, it would appear certain that MIA leaders were discussing filing suit at least by mid-January, and it seems highly unlikely that the idea was much considered before late December.

50. Trial Transcript, *King v. State*, 252-53; Montgomery *Alabama Tribune*, January 27, 1956; Montgomery *Advertiser*, January 7, 18, 19, 22, 24, February 5, 28, 1956; Montgomery *Alabama Journal*, January 23, 24, 1956. My account of this episode differs considerably from that in King, *Stride*, 124-26. King accepted the three ministers' explanation at face value. I am led to reject it and to credit Gayle's testimony at King's trial on the point for two reasons. Most important, King's version does not adequately account for the nature and content of Gayle's statement of January 23. Secondly, an attempt by the city to perpetrate a hoax is inconsistent with the presence of Thrasher at the meeting. The Montgomery chapter of the White Citizens Council had been organized at a meeting on October 3, 1955 with about 300 persons in attendance. It was the tenth chapter to be organized in Alabama (Montgomery *Advertiser*, October 3, 4, 1955).

51. Montgomery *Advertiser*, January 24-26, February 14, 1956; Montgomery *Alabama Journal*, January 24, 1956.

52. Montgomery *Advertiser*, January 31, February 2, 1956; Montgomery *Alabama Journal*, January 31, 1956. Between January 26 and January 29, with the situation obviously deteriorating rapidly, Governor James E. Folsom attempted a secret mediation. Abernathy states that Folsom intervened after a delegation of blacks requested him to do so. But the governor's efforts proved fruitless (interview with Abernathy, February 28, 1979; interview with William V. Lyerly, September 2, 1976; Trial Transcript, *King v. State*, 254-55, 496-97). Gray confirms that the bombing was the trigger for the filing of the federal suit. He states that many in the MIA leadership remained hopeful even through January that the boycott would produce concessions and so, though he had begun preparing the suit, the MIA Executive Board had continued to hesitate about filing it. But the bombing, he says, clearly made it necessary for the MIA to appear to be taking firm retaliatory action, and therefore the Executive Board, at a meeting the morning after the bombing, instructed him to file, which he did later the same day (interview, October 17, 1978).

53. Montgomery *Advertiser*, February 3, 1956.

54. *Ibid.*, December 5, 1955, January 18, 26, 1956; Montgomery *Alabama Journal*, January 24, 27, 1956; Trial Transcript, *King v. State*, 213-27; Trial Transcript, *Browder v. Gayle*, 32-36; King, *Stride*, 115, 118, 120. White Montgomery leaders repeatedly told me that they knew there had been intimidation of many blacks to keep them off the buses because they had been told so by their servants or other employees. I am inclined to believe that these stories were usually told employers in an effort to offer acceptable explanations for cooperation with the boycott. But the tales, while protecting the individual black from reprisal, had the harmful effect of preventing whites from recognizing the extent of black support for the MIA. Abernathy reports that the commissioners made repeated efforts to divide King from the remainder of the MIA leadership as well (interview, February 28, 1979).

55. Montgomery *Advertiser*, February 2, August 26, 1956; Gilliam, "Bus Boycott," 114, 137. Clifford J. Durr to Corliss Lamont, February 7, 1957, Durr Papers. Jack Crenshaw believes even today that rivalries among various factions within the MIA leadership produced the bombings (interview, July 15, 1977). At the other extreme, Fred Gray still suspects the City Commission of having ordered the bombings (interview, October 17, 1978). Many of the whites whom I interviewed believe that the boycott was prolonged unnecessarily as a sort of confidence game through which sympathetic Northerners were being rooked for contributions.

56. It is worth noting in this regard that stories about the boycott had not yet reached the front page of the New York *Times* and did not do so until the indictment of MIA leaders for violation of the anti-boycott law, except for one article on the White Citizens Council rally at the state coliseum on February 10.

57. King, *Stride*, 121-22; Montgomery *Advertiser*, February 11, 1956. A considerable number of businessmen participated in the negotiations at one

stage or another, but the principal business negotiators appear to have been Joe F. Bear, owner of a lumber and construction firm, C. T. Fitzpatrick, owner of a laundry and dry-cleaning business, James G. Pruett, president of the local division of the Trailways bus system, and Mark W. Johnston, vice-president of a bank. Bear was the Men of Montgomery chairman for February; the organization's chairmanship rotated monthly, on an alphabetical basis. Fitzpatrick, Pruett, and Johnston were the presidents of the Chamber of Commerce for, respectively, 1954, 1955, and 1956.

58. Montgomery *Advertiser*, January 19, February 8, 9, 1956. Despite King's statement most of the surviving black leaders agree with my assessment (interviews with Abernathy, February 28, 1979, Gray, October 17, 1978, Robinson, January 27, 1978). Rufus Lewis adds the interesting point that because white leaders, after years of ignoring blacks, were at last taking them seriously, the MIA was rendered quite reluctant to end the boycott that had finally given them access to power (interview, July 27, 1977). The business negotiators are unanimous in stating that, though they approached the negotiations with high hopes, convinced that a settlement could be found, they quickly came to see that the blacks were unwilling to make any concessions. I should also note Gray's statement that after February 1, all elements of the white community expressed to him privately a willingness to accept the MIA's original proposals if he would withdraw the federal suit and even offered him bribes to secure his agreement (interview, October 17, 1978). The sequence of events during February and early March makes this assertion seem implausible to me.

59. Montgomery *Advertiser*, December 8, 1955, January 11, 12, 15, 17, 19, February 15, 1956. Code of Alabama, 1940, Recompiled, Title 14, Section 54.

60. Trial Transcript, *King v. State*, 161-62, 186-87, 190; Montgomery *Alabama Journal*, February 13, 1956; Montgomery *Advertiser*, February 14, 1956. Thetford states that he was deeply dubious of indictments under the anti-boycott law as a tactic; he felt that, after a series of lengthy and emotional trials, the prosecution would result only in small fines for the boycotters or at most brief jail terms, without doing any real damage to the boycott itself. His own preference was for the bus company to seek a broad injunction against the MIA on the ground that its carpool operation was violating the company's exclusive franchise. If the MIA then disobeyed the injunction, its leaders could be jailed indefinitely for contempt. This strategy, he believes, would have broken the boycott. But he was unable to convince Crenshaw to adopt it. Crenshaw states that he was equally dubious of prosecuting under the anti-boycott law, but that he was unwilling to sue for an injunction because doing so would have involved abandoning the company's position as an innocent, neutral third party and was not, he thought, likely to end the boycott in any case. Thetford says that his hand was finally forced on the anti-boycott law when, as a result of the Ball letter, Judge Carter became convinced of the necessity to enforce the statute and came to him with the information that he intended to charge the next grand jury on the subject. Judge Carter does not recall the Ball letter, but he confirms that he decided to charge the grand jury

about the act and thereupon informed Thetford of his intention (interviews with Thetford, September 4, 1976, Crenshaw, July 15, 1977, Carter, October 16, 1978).

61. Montgomery *Advertiser*, February 6, 21, 22, 28, 1956; Montgomery *Alabama Journal*, February 8, 20, 21, 1956. The MIA Executive Board's only white member, the Reverend Robert Graetz, also favored the compromise but did not support it publicly (Trial Transcript, *King v. State*, 486-92). There may have been unpublished elements in the compromise; in his letter to the Men of Montgomery reporting the compromise's rejection, Abernathy refers to the "proposals submitted by your organization approved by the City Commission and City Bus Line and with the fare conveyed to me by telephone . . ." Abernathy no longer recalls what he meant by the latter phrase (Abernathy to Men of Montgomery, February 20, 1956, in file 2279, Records of the Solicitor's Office, Fifteenth Circuit, Montgomery County Courthouse, Montgomery; interview, February 28, 1979). Lynn reports that the Men of Montgomery did not receive a single suggestion as a result of its appeal (interview, December 29, 1976) Thetford says that he was convinced that the Men of Montgomery mediation would fail, but that if the blacks had accepted the compromise, he would have entered a *nolle prosequi* as to the indictments (interview, September 4, 1976).

62. Montgomery *Advertiser*, October 19, 1955; Montgomery City Directories for 1955 and 1956.

63. Montgomery *Advertiser*, March 23, 1956. Trial Transcript, *King v. State*, 193-227; *Lash v. State*, 244 Ala. 48; *Lash v. Alabama*, 320 U.S. 784, 814.

64. *Browder v. Gayle*, 142 F. Supp. 707; Montgomery *Advertiser*, October 23, 25, November 6, 1955, February 4, December 9, 1956, June 6, 1959; Montgomery *Alabama Journal*, October 24, 1955, January 31, 1956.

65. Montgomery *Alabama Tribune*, December 30, 1955. The purpose of the boycott is a matter of some dispute among surviving MIA leaders. Mrs. Robinson states that, because of the progress which the Women's Political Council had already been able to secure, she was initially quite optimistic about the prospects for negotiations. Gray says that he never had any hopes for the negotiations and "favored a federal suit" from the beginning, but he also says that most of the members of the MIA Executive Board believed that the negotiations would produce a settlement. Abernathy says that because the city and bus company officials had seemed willing to listen at earlier meetings and because the black proposals seemed to him so modest, he expected the whites to accept the MIA's position. Lewis states that at the outset no one really thought about whether or not the boycott was likely to produce concessions; he says that the boycott was born in the anger over Mrs. Parks's arrest and that its initial purpose was not to gain alterations in the bus seating policy but to demonstrate forcefully the extent of black resentment. Nixon says that the exchanges at the time of the Colvin arrest had convinced him of the futility of negotiating, and that he supported the boycott not because he thought it "likely to produce" concessions but because he thought that by making Mrs. Parks's case a *cause celebre*, blacks would be able to prevent the white courts

from shunting her case aside. He feared, he says, that white judges would never consider a test of the segregation laws seriously unless the test was so surrounded with publicity that they were compelled to do so (interviews, January 27, October 17, 1978, February 28, 1979, July 27, August 2, 1977). Each of these positions is entirely plausible, and very probably each reflects some aspect of the historical reality. At the same time the memory of each participant has necessarily been shaped to some extent by his knowledge of and reaction to the subsequent events. In the final analysis the historian must ground his judgment in the sense which he has derived from the contemporary documents.

66. Montgomery *Advertiser*, December 8, 1955.

The Montgomery
Bus Boycott
A Case Study in the Emergence
and Career of a Social Movement

STEVEN M. MILLNER

This paper was originally written as a Ph.D. dissertation in Sociology at the University of California at Berkeley in 1981. It has been edited and substantially revised for publication here.

Steven M. Millner is Associate Professor and Chairman of the Afro-American Studies Program at San Jose State University. He has taught at the University of Mississippi and at the University of California at Berkeley. His articles have appeared in such journals as *The Western Journal of Black Studies* and *New Perspectives*.

Contents

ONE

Introduction

> Among the laws that rule human societies there is one which seems to be more precise and clear than all others. If men are to remain civilized or become so, the art of associating together must grow and improve in the same ratio in which the equality of conditions is increased. [1]

Struggles to achieve equality or to improve the conditions of how Americans associate with each other have come to characterize this society. In an earlier age, Alexis de Tocqueville was surprised by the tendency of Americans to form voluntary associations in their efforts to achieve social equality. Such struggles continue to intrigue contemporary students of social change. In the language of the social sciences, these attempts are usually categorized as social movements.

The case analysis that forms the basis of this study describes and assesses one such movement. It was an effort that emerged only after decades of social and interracial transformation in America's Deep South. By the early 1950s several circumstances had been gradually established that facilitated the growth of hope and determination that new measures of equality should be extended to all Americans regardless of color. How these hopes and determination were harnessed and productively channelled was a fascinating process to study but is difficult to explain. Nonetheless, social scientists must attempt explanations; in the chapters that follow I present a modest account of a crucial movement. Such analysis, relatively new when pursued by de Tocqueville, has assumed standards that have been discussed in social scientific journals for years. Reviewing this material was essential to the successful completion of this study. That process prepares one to properly see how social movements unfold from the point of view of the insider. This was a guiding principal used as I studied the boycott.

I have become convinced that one of the most effective ways to conduct such research is to try and comprehend the main features of and changes in what C. Wright Mills called historic social structures.[2] Mills referred to a need for studies that would probe how shifts in such structures would promote both new forms of human consciousness and resultant social action. The suggestion was an excellent one and the spirit of Mills' advice prodded me as I decided to undertake this project. Social change itself also contributed to that decision.

In the 1950's and 1960's, while academic mavericks such as Mills and Alvin Gouldner were calling for probes to study major social changes, thousands of social activists around the world were struggling to achieve the types of goals that visionaries had only been discussing decades earlier. In Vietnam, a war between the French and forces led by an obscure leader named Ho Chi Minh was first coming to the attention of this country's political leaders; in Africa, decolonization sentiment was blossoming in British, Belgian, and Portuguese colonies; and here in the United States the South's system of racial segregation sentiment was coming under renewed attack from various quarters. In all these instances the resulting conflicts produced the kinds of social movements that scholars need to devote time and energy to as we seek to comprehend the social world. This study reflects that obligation and provides a model for how such analysis can be done.

For purposes of this analysis, I decided to utilize Herbert Blumer's seminal ideas about social movements. Blumer's theories about collective behavior and social movements have long been recognized as valuable contributions to sociological theory.[3] However, when I undertook this study not enough attention had been directed at measuring whether his notions reflect circumstances as they actually develop in societies. Blumer's ideas, important as they may be, are not the only ones assessed in the chapters that follow. Critical questions his theories omit are also presented and discussed in detail. Looking at this social movement allows one to explore issues of a general theoretical nature while also answering questions about American history. Students of both sociology and history should find it to be useful and informative. It provided me with surprises that now fit a certain logic.

The chapters that follow discuss the role of women in the genesis of the Montgomery bus boycott and the less publicized leadership qualities of Martin Luther King, Jr. When I started this analysis I had no preconceived plans to highlight such factors; their emergence and significance rests solely on the merits of their importance to this movement. This is, of course, how it must be. Such discoveries suggest however, why readers might be well advised to study movements such as the one I report on. Analysis of this sort contributes to a more general understanding of how all people, not just racially oppressed blacks, behave when acting collectively. The behavior of such "little people" really registers on the scale of history.

In the Montgomery movement, unknown women and others such as black taxicab drivers made critical contributions to the boycott's effectiveness. Obviously they would have impeded such efforts if they had been apathetic. So too, charismatic leaders such as King also carried out important functions when they were "off-stage". Before this study little attention had been paid to King's masterful bureaucratic maneuvers. Since this study pinpoints such factors, it should gently assist readers to understand their own potential for contributing to actions that may turn out to have historical significance.

To understand either social behavior or the actions of those involved in collective movements requires that concepts be properly understood. In this analysis the most critical concept employed is that of the "social movement".

Specifying a Basic Concept

Paul Wilkenson's working concept of what a social movement is provides three important insights about that dynamic.[4] Wilkenson notes that a social movement (1) is a deliberate collective effort to promote change in any direction and by any means; (2) exhibits an organizational structure which may be either loose or highly formalized; and (3) has adherents who act on the basis of their conscious volitions. Wilkenson's broad definition contains elements that have achieved something approaching a consensus in the field. Joseph Gusfield, writing in the late 1960's, had also touched on all three of the variables that Wilkenson carefully elaborates.

> The concept of a social movement is thus suggestive of people who, on the one hand, are in the process of rejecting existing social values and arrangements while on the other, they are both striving to make converts to their way of seeing things and dealing with the resistance that their activities inevitably call forth. But while the movement is often carried by associations, it is not wholly an associational phenomenon. It is in the system of generalized beliefs and in partisan commitment to such beliefs that we find the characteristics of a social movement.[5]

The ideas of Wilkenson and Gusfield accurately describe what took place in Montgomery, Alabama in 1955 and 1956. While the terms of Wilkenson's criteria seem to be rather easily met, the Montgomery protest also satisfies Gusfield's more stringent definitional standards. A more systematic definition of the "social movement" term had been developed, and its use proved to be most helpful in sorting out the multitude of activities that fall under the general heading of the Montgomery bus boycott. This is the description of what a social movement involves suggested by Herbert Blumer in the early 1960's.[6]

Going further than many social theorists, Blumer implies that social movements must be properly viewed as actions mounted in the face of intensely hostile audiences. While indicating that movements generally face opposition, Blumer also noted that any authentic movement typically leaves an important legacy for both its active members and the society in which it occurs. Blumer's belief is that fully developed social movements are able to do this only because they contain certain essential components. Thus, before any episode of collective behavior can be properly labelled a "social movement," it must exhibit certain stages and conditions.

Blumer notes that a mature social movement is purposeful behavior where the participants have well-defined objectives or goals that they consciously pursue. Additionally, such movements are thought to pass through stages of development that can be grouped under these headings: (1) agitation, (2) development of *esprit de corps*, (3) development of morale, (4) formation of an ideology, and (5) development of operating tactics. Finally, he posits that movements can be considered complete when they (6) leave behind a body of functionaries, new objects and views, and a new set of self-conceptions.[7]

In the chapters that follow I describe how such criteria make sense when analyzing the protest activities mounted by Montgomery's blacks. For purposes of stylistic continuity, the terms boycott, protest, and movement should all be understood as referring to the social movement that emerged in Montgomery, Alabama in December of 1955. These terms are used interchangeably in the text that follows. Social scientists should always clearly describe the methods they employ when collecting and analyzing data.

Methodology

Leonard Schatzman and Anselm L. Strauss accurately commented on field research in the social sciences. They said that

Once the decision has been made to inquire into some social process in its own natural context, the researcher creates much of both his method and the substance of his field of inquiry. To say that the researcher creates his method as he works may seem unbecoming, yet we are discussing this very point. Method is seen by the field researcher as emerging from operations—from strategic decisions, instrumental actions, and analytic processes—which go on throughout the entire research enterprise.[8]

I decided to undertake this study in 1976 while teaching a class at the University of Santa Clara that was titled "Contemporary Black Thought". The course content focused on discussions of the strategies, ideologies and personalities that emerged during the Civil Rights Movement. Towards the end of the class, I was particularly dissatisfied with my inability to explain the origins of the direct action phase of the Civil Rights struggle. I sensed that much more had happened than I had been able to report. After reading as much as I could about conditions in the South I realized that the first major campaign of the Civil Rights Movement, the Montgomery bus boycott, had not been adequately and accurately explained. The best available work on the boycott, Martin Luther King, Jr.'s *Stride Toward Freedom*, struck me as a valuable, if somewhat self-serving, publication.[9] As a student interested in social movements I sensed that accepting an account by one who had been as deeply involved in leadership as King had would not be wise. Since the protest occurred in the 1950s I also realized that other participants, perhaps critical ones, might still be available to present the facts as they had experienced them. I decided I would attempt to perform the most comprehensive analysis of that boycott that my training and resources allowed.

By the summer of 1977 I finished my survey of the literature and proceeded to the field. Entering Montgomery for the first time I had no contacts other than a few lists of people gleaned from King's book. Equipped with a rather broad checklist of important discussion items, I proceeded to survey the local phone directory and made some initial phone contacts. The warmth of my respondents and their willingness to discuss their movement days was gratifying. I spent dozens of hours talking with residents of Montgomery about their boycott experiences. All interviews were long, probing ones that were taped in the homes of respondents. The transcripts of a number of these interviews are included in this volume, pages 519-584.

In addition to these discussions I did library research while in Alabama. I repeatedly visited the Alabama State Archives in Montgomery, the campus library at Alabama State University (also in Montgomery), and ultimately surveyed the materials available at Atlanta University. All those efforts substantiated the wisdom of Schatzman and Strauss as mentioned above. While I was usually thorough in my field preparation techniques, I discovered that I should always be ready to rearrange my schedule to accommodate an additional respondent who just happened to be around when I came calling. Some of those interviews turned out to be among the most informative ones.

At the conclusion of my first field visit I had more than fifteen taped interviews I felt to be usable. After more than a year of analyzing this data I returned to Montgomery for more interviewing and library work. In the winter of 1979 I conducted several more weeks of field work. During the two periods of field work I spent more than three months in Montgomery, and conducted twenty-two taped interviews. My interviews included the recollections of the most critical living leaders from the Montgomery boycott except for the Reverend David Abernathy. Reverend Abernathy refused my efforts to interview him when I was unwilling to pay a fee of several hundred dollars. This did not surprise blacks who knew King's closest friend and confidant.

In addition to the field work in Montgomery, I travelled to Detroit, Michigan in January 1980 to interview Mrs. Rosa Parks. While in Detroit I also examined the Rosa Parks papers at Wayne State University. Mrs Parks proved to be an exceedingly honest and gracious respondent. Her life story deserves more attention that it receives in this or other accounts of the boycott. My interview with Rosa Parks [published here, pages 553-567] strongly suggests that the seeds of her 1955 actions were planted by both unusual family members and peer associates as early as the 1920s.

During the course of my data collection I interviewed two former boycott figures who now live in Los Angeles, California. These interviews, especially one with Mrs. Jo Ann Robinson, proved to be extremely useful in the analysis that follows.

Although there was no attempt made to achieve a "random" sample, a broad cross-section of former boycott participants was interviewed. The interviews were loosely structured with questions designed to ask respondents about several major areas, including: (1) social background, (2) motives for involvement in the protest, (3) boycott activities, (4) attitudes toward other members of the protest, (5) attitudes about white opposition, (6) feelings about Martin Luther King, Jr., (7) reflections about the impact the boycott had on personal life, and (8) feelings about present race relations in Montgomery. Additional questions relevant to individuals were included during each interview.

As I conducted my on site data collection insights about earlier struggles in Alabama developed. I became convinced that because I spent so much time in Alabama and shared a 1970s version of feeling racially oppressed with respondents, my field research improved. It is important to add that many whites in Alabama offered me unceasing assistance. Increasing numbers of Alabama's whites have come to recognize that they too shared an episode of collective behavior that signalled the start of a more progressive era. The pride that many took in this was a heartening development. While I make no claim of adequately exploring the actions and motives of the protest's opponents, I recognize that such analysis is necessary. As was true of the hidden boycott story, that opposition also requires a serious and sympathetic assessment. While this is so, the purpose of this analysis is to explain why a particular social movement emerged when it did and why it took the form that it displayed publicly. As in all social movements this was a public form that belied a very private reality.

The Problem

Equipped now with a better understanding of the concept of a social movement and informed about the methods employed in the data collection, it is now possible to briefly discuss the general problem.

The movement selected for analysis has come to be called the Montgomery bus protest. Taking place in the heart of Alabama's Black Belt in 1955-56, the incident was referred to as such because, at the time, an Alabama state law strictly prohibited such secondary boycotts. Montgomery, Alabama is the symbolic cradle of the old Confederacy, and the movement that emerged there had to overcome several major obstacles. The mere emergence of the boycott startled most citizens, black and white, and caught most scholars off guard as well. Why a social movement emerges has always been a significant question, and examining the bus boycott's origins clarifies how that process occurs. Superficial accounts of the Montgomery boycott's emergence tend to emphasize a spontaneous outburst of indignation by black citizens over the callous arrest of Mrs. Rosa Parks, a black seamstress who had refused to give up her seat to a white man. While there is some truth to that notion, a more detailed analysis reveals that Mrs. Parks's own consciousness plus her social status in Montgomery's black community may have been more crucial in sparking the protest. At that time her occupation was considered among blacks a high prestige one; she had also been the secretary of the local NAACP chapter and was well acquainted with members of the most prominent black women's clubs. These facts, in combination with others, proved critical in precipitating her actions and the protest that followed.

There was much indignation when Mrs. Parks was arrested, but it came principally from blacks who were already organized to seek change; they quickly mobilized the masses in support of their efforts. Once started, the protest's leaders, unknown to the public and as yet unexamined by scholars, had serious internal disputes that threatened the very success of the boycott. Such disagreements were a reflection of the different class interests and ideological currents among Montgomery's leading blacks. For years, Montgomery's black leaders had been unable to settle their differences or work cooperatively. Several unique circumstances, discussed in detail below, contributed to a temporary truce in what was often bitter infighting among the competing leaders and facilitated a successful boycott.

It was from the ranks of those leaders that Martin Luther King, Jr. first came to national attention. His philosophical orientation, which emphasized nonviolence, and his strategy for achieving social progress, a reliance on direct mass action, matured in the crucible of the Montgomery bus boycott. King successfully countered, as he did throughout much of his career, opposition to his approach from other Montgomery leaders. Some opposition leaders wanted to accept less than the boycotters eventually won and privately criticized King for allegedly prolonging the protest. Others questioned the honesty of some of the boycott's leaders and gave potentially damaging support to the opposing white power structure. King's ability to neutralize such opposition while coping with the normal pressures associated with managing a quickly formulated bureaucracy, demonstrated talents rarely acknowledged in later years. While some accounts of King's ultimate stature and ability to command allegiance focus on his personal charisma, his role in heading the Montgomery Improvement Association demonstrates that he and others involved in that movement possessed key characteristics necessary to be effective black leaders. Those leadership characteristics are described in more detail in later chapters.

To fully understand the boycott's career and its relevance to social theory, some important facts must first be known about the evolving nature of social and economic conditions in Alabama's Black Belt. These were culminating in the years just prior to the boycott. This culmination, plus events on the national and international scenes, played a crucial role in the boycott's emergence and success. The second chapter of this study is devoted to an examination of this background.

TWO

Alabama Before the Boycott

Alabama, because of both geography and history, provides unique possibilities for startling contrasts. The state extends north-eastward from a narrow access to the Gulf of Mexico at Mobile Bay and includes in its center a rich agricultural region that has come to be called the Black Belt.[1] Proceeding north from the former plantation-dominated Black Belt of Alabama, one encounters the red hills district. This area holds some of the South's richest deposits of coal and iron ore. This area, where industrialization occurred relatively late, was once characterized by widespread rural poverty.[2] In Alabama's far North the hill country slopes gently toward the Tennessee Valley. This northernmost area of the state is also a region noted historically for agricultural productivity.[3] Alabama is blessed with a mild climate, and its natural transportation network features numerous river systems plus access to the Gulf of Mexico. These features facilitated Alabama's growth as a producer of cotton and other agricultural staples. This pattern started in the early 1800's.

The Alabama Territory, officially opened to white settlement in 1814, had a population estimated to be 15,000 by 1815.[4] Between 1814 and 1819, white migration to the territory took on aspects of a boom with settlers coming into the area from all sides. By 1820, a year after its admission as a state, Alabama's residents numbered 129,227, of which 42,450 were slaves.[5]

Alabama's virgin lands were especially attractive to Virginians and Carolinians, and many prominent natives from those states moved to the Territory. The Black Belt region proved most attractive to these new settlers. Cotton became its major cash crop with its cultivation eventually dominated by planters who owned vast tracks of bottom land. Theodore Henley Jack noted that this region represented only a small portion of the state's area but was responsible for more than half of Alabama's cotton crop by 1840.[6]

The more affluent new residents of the Black Belt brought bondsmen with them, purchased them from travelling merchants, or obtained slaves from markets in cities such as Mobile or New Orleans. As a result, Alabama's slave population and for later decades its black population was concentrated in this "Black Belt." This is an area of thirteen counties where Davis and Donaldson found whites outnumbered by nearly three to one, there being 171,176 blacks compared to 64,474 whites.[7] Montgomery is located in the Black Belt's center.

The Black Belt is best understood if one is sensitive to the interplay of geography, history, and politics. In antebellum Alabama, planters who owned the largest and richest tracts of bottom land dominated the region's economic and political structures. Horace Mann Bond asserts that before the Civil War, slave ownership was the crucial index of elevated social class in Alabama.[8] The census data indicated that only a few planters owned substantial numbers of slaves, while three-fourths of the state's whites held none.[9] More critically, owners of large numbers of bondsmen frequently manipulated a locality's affairs to their advantage. This occurred throughout Alabama's Black Belt as the "slavocrats" assumed control of this region. It should be noted that such planters, though often dominant locally, were a very small proportion of the South's overall white population. On the eve of America's Civil War, less than 3,000 whites in this country owned more than 100 slaves.[10] As could be expected, the areas of their concentration took on unique characteristics. This was true of Alabama's Black Belt in the 1800's and persisted afterwards.

In politics, Alabama's planter-dominated Black Belt split early from other areas of the state with its voters consistently supporting the anti-democratic Whigs.[11] This set a pattern, with the political representatives of the Black Belt remaining consistently conservative until recent decades.

While the planter class dominated Alabama's Black Belt, most whites who lived in that region were not aristocratic, nor were they "poor white trash." A significant number of these Black Belt whites were either small merchants or yeoman farmers.[12] It is important to grasp this aspect of Alabama's antebellum community to avoid stereotypes that would obscure reality about subsequent class and racial dynamics.

While the antebellum South's economy was based on agriculture and dominated by planters, the very nature of its crops (rice, cotton, tobacco, sugar, etc.) required a variety of commercial roles which produced a well-differentiated white community. It was the temporary post-Civil War economic devastation of the planters that allowed the masses of whites and blacks to first contend for political dominance in the region.[13] While meaningful political competition in the postwar era became possible, conditions faced by the new competitors—non-planter whites and the recently emancipated blacks—were quite different. In the long run, such differences proved to be crucial, as the generally racist non-planter whites and impoverished ex-slaves were unable to mount any lasting coalition against the planters and members of an emerging commercial class. Several factors contributed to suspicions between poorer whites and Alabama's blacks. Most important was their historic separation. When coupled with fierce competition for scarce educational dollars, this factor proved especially important in sowing distrust and hatred between the two groups. Though economic hardships of the 1880's led many from both groups to support radical doctrines espoused by Alabama's Populists, that party lost the major political contests of the 1890's. When the Populist cause stalled Alabama's blacks struggled merely to retain their vote.

The Political Submergence of the Freedmen

Throughout the late 1800's, Alabama's blacks voted in significant numbers for Republican candidates; held a variety of local, state, and congressional offices; and otherwise participated in party affairs. This participation occurred despite the widespread poverty characterizing the Black Belt. While impoverished conditions were not new to the ex-slaves, such was not the case for the planters.

The Civil War cost Alabama's planters both their captive laborers and the paper value of their land. The dollar value of Alabama's cultivated farm acreage had been $175,824,622, or $9.20 per acre, in 1860; by 1880 the total value of a slightly reduced cultivated land had declined to $78,954,648, or to $4.19 per acre.[14] The per capita loss in the Black Belt was probably higher than in other sections of the state and social dislocation was intensified because more battles had been fought in the area. These problems persisted for decades. Faced with such difficulties the large planters attempted to devise means to regain their economic leverage and thus retain their political advantages. The resources they had on hand to realize their ends remained essentially unchanged—land and blacks who would have to be made to work it. But how could planters get blacks, who now had the vote and other civil rights, to work at rates that would allow for the extraction of significant profit? The creation of the tenant system was the mechanism that proved most successful in maintaining the planters' hold over the black masses. This system, which ultimately involved the overwhelming number of Alabama's blacks, minimized their ability to vote freely by limiting their economic autonomy. An example of how this worked was the widespread practice of planters physically transporting their tenants to the polls and closely supervising their ballot casting.[15] Other abuses were built into the share-crop system.

It seems ironic, but there is evidence that many of the ex-slaves preferred the tenant system and played a part in its establishment. The motivating factor for these Freedmen may have been their desire to avoid the gang labor system. This work arrangement had predominated during the slave era.[16] In the tenant system, individuals were seldom subjected to daily supervision and thus they could better regulate their own work pace. To a people just out of bondage, this was a critical measure of freedom. This should be no surprise, as control of the work pace remains important to modern man.[17] A tenant system was also believed to facilitate a more distinct division of labor based on sex, and it appears that many ex-slaves wanted their wives to be freed from the back-breaking routines associated with daily field work.[18] While the tenant system had provisions that appealed to and were insisted on by some ex-slaves, its evolution was one that led Booker T. Washington to characterize it as resembling the anaconda snake, which kills its prey slowly by squeezing it until all life is gone.[19]

The system demanded that landlords and tenants struggle against one another to realize any return on their investment. Such conflicts exacerbated the economic difficulties of the region. Since the South suffered from a serious capital shortage throughout the last decades of the nineteenth century, non-cash crops were neglected and farming techniques remained primitive.[20] The tenant system exacerbated other problems as cotton was the sole staple, but ultimately destructive cash crop of the Black Belt. Cotton is a labor-intensive crop and its cultivation in the gently rolling hills of the Black Belt caused especially serious problems of erosion and declining soil fertility. While the tenant system was uniquely suited to such a crop approach, that system also retarded the development of human creativity. The tasks associated with cotton cultivation were simple to learn but the repetitiveness of the work routine produced boredom and dissatisfaction.[21] Cotton's cultivation depleted both soil and the human spirit. While lands could be and were frequently abandoned, human victims were bound to this agricultural complex by strong tethers. Nonetheless many were glad to move to cities such as Montgomery. In those emerging cities they often found blacks who were their "leaders". Alabama's Black Belt was the region that produced the famous Booker T. Washington.

The Growth of Accommodationist Black Leadership

Booker Taliferro Washington was one of the most complex black leaders in this nation's history. After he established Tuskegee Institute in Macon County, Alabama it became the most publicized training school for blacks in the nation. Washington, as the principal of Tuskegee Institute, dominated Alabama's blacks in ways similar to how he controlled many of this country's blacks between 1895 and 1915.[22] By using his connections with influential whites, selectively distributing substantial amounts of philanthropic funds and punishing his "enemies" by various forms of coercion, Washington influenced black leadership styles for decades in many parts of the South. This was especially true of Alabama, where his impact lingered for years after his 1915 death.[23]

Washington's style was one calculated to win the favor of the South's then emerging industrial elites, while retaining the approval of the old planter classes. Always projecting himself as a humble, pragmatic representative of his people, Washington espoused the then popular doctrine of self-help while also emphasizing training devoted to mechanical trades and improved agricultural skills. He publicly eschewed the importance of blacks' voting rights while encouraging his constituency to avoid affiliations with either Populists or labor unions. Washington indicated that "agitation of questions of social equality is the extremist folly." Such an approach to leadership made it convenient for those Southern whites who wanted to ignore the limited conditions of life and opportunity available to that region's blacks.

Washington was so committed to the task of building Tuskegee that he even humored rich whites by telling them "darky" jokes as he appealed to their sense of charity.[24] To a remarkable degree, Washington's approach struck a responsive chord with the nation's prominent capitalists. Andrew Carnegie declared him to be a combined Moses and Joshua of his people.[25] Others like Julius Rosenwald, favored Washington's submissive demeanor and ideology as perfectly fitting the circumstances of this country's blacks.[26] Americans of literary and intellectual stature, such as William Dean Howells, expressed the belief that Washington's approach was, at the time, "the only way for his race."[27] His reception by Alabama's whites, especially those in the

Black Belt, is especially important to this analysis. An editorial that appeared in the *Montgomery Advertiser* during the late 1890's captured the essence of local white sentiment regarding Booker T. Washington. Describing him as a "safe Negro," the paper's editor observed

> From the day of his arrival at Tuskegee . . . Booker T. Washington has had the absolute Confidence of the White people of that community. There is never a word of harsh criticism of him or his methods. He has been singularly imbued with a desire to cultivate good relations between the two races, and to be of lasting benefit to his people. He is succeeding in both undertakings. There is nothing of the agitator about him. His ways are always those of pleasantness and peace, and as far as his voice and example prevail, there will always be the best of feeling between the White and Black people of the country.
>
> It is a blessing for the control of the colored schools to fall into the hands of such a man as Booker T. Washington. It can be said to his credit that colored teachers are found all over Alabama who were educated at his institution, and in every instance, the White people commend them for instilling correct notions into their pupils and for impressing upon them the fact that they cannot prosper unless their White neighbors prosper and unless a proper understanding exists between them. It is infinitely better to have teachers who have such notions than to have those who would seek to create prejudice which would lead inevitably to trouble.[28]

Inculcating Alabama's young blacks with "correct notions" and assisting them to develop the "proper understanding" of how racial subjugation was to be maintained were indeed important to whites at the opening of the new century. There were ritual forms of behavior that whites demanded blacks exhibit if they were to act as representatives of their race. While the public rituals of deference were retained several decades into the twentieth century, the attitudes of succeeding generations of black leaders were slowly undergoing change. While C. Vann Woodward implies that Black Belt white men were frequently casual in attitude and interaction with blacks, social distance between the races increased as the years passed.[29] While there is convincing evidence that social custom preceded the formal enactment of Jim Crow laws, states across the South began to formally require that railroads provide blacks and whites with separate accommodations by 1887.[30] Alabama passed this provision in 1891 and joined other southern states in ultimately erecting a legal system of segregation that sought to minimize racial contacts in virtually all social areas. While the erection of legal barriers to interracial contacts was not limited to a particular era or region these dynamics merely hint at the prevailing white dogmas that Alabama's blacks had to contend with. This was especially true of politics.

Members of an Alabama Constitutional Convention of 1901 rejected black petitioners' plea and effectively stripped the state's blacks of their voting rights. Ironically this development was justified as reflecting the mid 1890's conciliatory rhetoric of Booker T. Washington.[31] Even more interesting was how Washington's influence continued to grow as the circumstances of southern blacks declined. Washington's publicly espoused educational philosophy for blacks, with its emphasis on limited exposure to the liberal arts, was shared at the national level by President Theodore Roosevelt. Roosevelt, whose 1901 White House dinner with Washington caused a public furor, spoke frankly about the type of education he thought best suited for the country's blacks. Washington's influence can be detected in Roosevelt's words

> Of course the best type of education for the colored man, taken as a whole, is such education conferred in schools like Hampton and Tuskegee; where boys and girls, the young men and young women, are trained industrially as well as in the public-school branches. The graduates of these schools turn out well in the great majority of cases, and hardly any of them become criminals, while what little criminality there is never takes the form of that brutal violence which invites lynch-law. Every graduate of those schools—and for that matter every other colored man or woman—who leads a life so useful and honorable as to win the goodwill and respect of those Whites whose neighbor he or she is, thereby helps the whole colored race as it can be helped in no other way; for next to the Negro himself, the man who can be most help to the Negro is his White neighbor.[32]

While Roosevelt and others supported the educational policies pursued by the leaders of institutions like Virginia's Hampton and Alabama's Tuskegee, the masses of blacks were assisted neither by their "neighbors" nor by natural developments. By 1917, faced with the boll weevil, general agricultural decline, dismal educational opportunities, and no longer equipped with the ballot, thousands of blacks began leaving first the farms and later Alabama altogether. Their movement reflected a realization that migration was one of the few available means of effectively redressing their grievances. Seen this way, migration of a people may actually represent a profound political statement about their perception of their collective social circumstances.

While expressions of black protest can be gleaned from such behavior and from sources such as the *Chicago Defender*, others who opposed the harsh racial status quo were emerging.[33]

Much has been made of the criticism northern intellectuals, especially blacks from Boston, leveled at Booker T. Washington. A few natives of the South also voiced strong objections to his response to the tightening vise of Southern racial oppression. Such opposition was voiced as early as 1896 when John Hope, president of Atlanta University, analyzed Booker T. Washington's tactics

> I regard it as cowardly and dishonest for any of our colored men to tell white people that we are not struggling for equality . . . now catch your breath, for . . . I am going to say we demand social equality. In this republic, we shall be less than freemen if we have less than a white, less than that which thrift, education, and honor afford other freemen. If equality, political, economic and social is the boon of the other men in this great country of ours, then equality, political, economic, and social is what we demand . . . come, let us possess this land . . . let our discontent break mountains high against the wall of prejudice, and swamp it to the very foundation. Then shall we not have to plead for justice nor on bended knee crave mercy; for we shall be men.[34]

While Hope was not alone in militantly opposing Washington's style of leadership, conditions were such that developing any mass following for direct opposition was extremely difficult. Opposition usually took other forms, with those who found Alabama's circumstances most alienating before the Great Depression still tending to migrate north in search of better circumstances. Migration remained extremely attractive to many southern blacks, who still tended to reside in isolated cabins in rural areas and were thus more easily intimidated by threats of terror and other forms of reprisal. After Washington's 1915 death the re-emergence of the Ku Klux Klan in the 1920's further tempered outspoken resistance to a solidifying Jim Crow system, yet in the early 1930's stiff opposition did emerge and did so with some force. This particular episode of black resistance to the racial status quo signaled the beginning of changes that would culminate two decades later in Montgomery.

The Alabama Sharecroppers Union, which grew out of the internationally publicized Scottsboro Boys case, was an attempt to organize impoverished blacks in the State's Tallapoosa County during the early summer of 1931. By then the migration of blacks to the urban North had reversed itself with so many sojourners encountering unemployment. In the bleak year of 1931 growing numbers of Alabama's rural blacks recognized that they would have to directly confront their circumstances. The effects of the continuing Depression, local black outrage over death sentences handed down to nine teenagers falsely accused of raping white prostitutes, and the skills of racially integrated pairs of organizers from the Communist Party contributed to the emergence of this Sharecroppers Union.[35] Protesting the shameful circumstances of the Scottsboro defendants' trial was a principal motive for their initial decision to organize but union members quickly sought to redress their own grievances. Tallapoosa County's black sharecroppers, living about fifty miles northeast of Montgomery, sought better credit arrangements and improved food allocations, a nine-month school term with free bus transportation, and wages of a dollar a day for agricultural laborers.[36] Over a two-year period, the Sharecroppers Union attracted close to five thousand members in Tallapoosa and adjoining counties. This was, in the words of Dan T. Carter, a "revolutionary" development. Carter indicates that the emergence of such mass-based black opposition to Tallapoosa County's existing racial structure generated intense fear among whites partially as a consequence of the Scottsboro trials hysteria and also because of the genuine efforts made by "reds" from the "outside" to enlist the support of the state's blacks. The official response from the local and State's agents was swift and violent.

In the aftermath of a shootout between the county sheriff and a black union member, Tallapoosa County officials organized a posse of five hundred whites who roamed Alabama's rural areas questioning "suspicious" blacks and "searching for communist agitators." The church where the union's meetings had been held was burned, as were the homes of some suspected "reds," but casualties were described as minimal. Withstanding such harsh measures, a few of the county's blacks maintained their organization only to encounter renewed repression after events that took place a year later.

After an attempt by local whites in late 1932 to exert economic pressure on Cliff James, one of the area's few black landowners and by then the union's leader, Tallapoosa County deputies killed James and two other union members in a gun battle. A white posse, led this time by the sheriffs of Tallapoosa, Elmore, Macon, and Montgomery Counties, then went on another "nigger hunt." Casualties were described as being much higher than in the previous year's operation. Although the state's newspapers and officials tended to attribute such conflicts to "ignorant" blacks being stirred up by outside agitators, specifically "reds," significant new patterns emerged during what were described as the "Camp Hill incidents." One important new trend was the willingness of a few of Alabama's "moderate" whites to publicly support what they considered to be valid concerns of the impoverished blacks. While the emergence of a few native white "moderates" was rare, the development of militant black leaders such as Cliff James was even more critical. The masses of blacks in Alabama, as indicated by the emergence and widespread acceptance of the Sharecroppers Union, found themselves thrust into situations that forced them to seek ways to bring about change. The leaders of these desperate sharecroppers alternated between the old style of accommodationism as pioneered by Booker T. Washington and newer more militant techniques as they sought to achieve their generally moderate goals. Goals were becoming different though in urban centers.

By the late 1940's, the principal goal of most of Alabama's black leaders was voter registration. This realistic goal and strategies to achieve it did not require a direct assault on the economic system, nor did it directly confront the still elaborate structure of segregation. Voter registration was also a goal generally accepted by "moderate" whites in Alabama. In the Black Belt's cities, some of the more educated and courageous blacks achieved the "privilege" of voting by the early 1950's. Such an unusual achievement often came about as a result of political organizations that were established in the mid and late 1940's. When hundreds of blacks returned from the Second World War, a war that had been publicized as necessary to preserve "democracy," many returned with a strong desire that they be able to take full advantage of all the forms of democracy Alabama offered its citizens. Thus one of their primary goals was the right to vote. Private clubs of black veterans mushroomed throughout Alabama in the late 1940's, with many focused entirely on attaining voting rights.[37] In Montgomery leaders of such groups were going to prove crucial. The significance of what such clubs wanted should not be discounted, for their goals and strategies for achieving them did represent an ultimate threat to the long-term maintenance of the racial status quo in Alabama's Black Belt.

While the earlier form of public militancy had been systematically crushed among Black Belt sharecroppers in the 1930's, the attempts during the 1940's to increase the number of black voters in the state met with some success. Most of those blacks who benefited from those gains, however, were relatively privileged compared to the masses. Their special privilege did not mean that they separated themselves from the problems of the masses. With rigid segregation still in place this was impossible.

The movement of the South's rural blacks to urban centers like Montgomery allowed those professionals who provided services to these newcomers to strengthen their economic positions. Since this process had been going on for several decades, the racial caste system had slowly spawned a class of economically privileged blacks who, along with their children, ended up leading the assaults on the system of segregation. This class' economic solidification, when coupled with the surprisingly positive self-images Alabama's blacks maintained, set the stage for the development of militant and responsive leadership. Such a newly empowered urban-based black elite had, by the early 1950's, the flexibility of a substantial population base to work with, some covert white support, and the growing belief that segregation was beginning to crumble. This class emerged throughout the urban South and their actions in the 1950's and 1960's clearly demonstrate a determination to work fundamental changes in the segregated social structure. As subsequent discussion will reveal, these circumstances were especially true in Montgomery's black community. While such significant class developments were occurring throughout the region, a realignment in Alabama's white leadership, itself long in the making, also marked the decade immediately preceding the boycott.

Within the Black Belt's white community, the descendants of the planter class had experienced a substantial loss of economic and political power. This was partly because the largest plantations were slowly broken up by the inheritance process or by having land sold off to meet obligations incurred as a consequence of the general decline in agriculture. After the 1930's economic hegemony in Alabama shifted in favor of urban-based white merchants. Many such merchants and the remnants of the old planter class preferred living close to urban centers like Montgomery for social reasons. While many traditionally conservative whites found economic opportunity and comfort in Montgomery, by the early 1950's statewide political influence had shifted decidedly north toward booming Birmingham and newer urban centers in places such as Huntsville, Tuscaloosa, Anniston, and Gadsen.

This shift signaled the final triumph of industrial-based elites over plantation-style agriculturalists. While the shift was irreversible after World War II, those conservative-oriented whites who maintained economic and political dominance in the Black Belt were generally oblivious to developments taking place in Montgomery's black community. As urban communities like Montgomery evolved new patterns, the chance for meaningful communication between whites and blacks tended to lessen. Such earlier contacts and relationships, often involving considerable white paternalism, had provided a forum, albeit a distorted one, for communication between the leaders of the respective races. The gradual decline of such contacts on a local level in Montgomery was critical and is one reason why local whites badly misjudged the emerging moods of blacks. The long-range consequences of these modernization patterns and the ultimate response of the nation were all going to surprise and confuse Montgomery's leading conservative whites. That a few local whites would support such efforts also proved surprising and disturbing to the majority of Montgomery whites. Such processes represented a disruption in all phases of traditional societal arrangements and was most evident in the ways blacks and whites perceived how members of the races should relate to one another.

By the mid-1950's Alabama's blacks, like those throughout the South, were restive and convinced of the need for significant changes in race relations. The vast majority of Alabama's whites looked forward to an era of enjoying the region's blessings, convinced that after successive wars the country, and the South, should maintain "normalcy" during the bland administration of Eisenhower. The clash of individuals motivated by such diverse collective perceptions occupied the nation's attention for much of the 1950's and 1960's. Montgomery, after its boycott began, became the first major battleground.

As mentioned in the introduction, changes in relations between the South's whites and blacks have spawned numerous theories to explain these changes. Some of the more important of these explanations focus on the issue of the personality characteristics exhibited by the South's blacks.

The view that the South's blacks had collectively "accommodated" themselves to the racial status quo, had come close to achieving a consensus among social scientists in the years before the boycott. Such a misperception demands some comment and can be best explored if accompanied by illustrations from the lives of some of those who became participants in the Montgomery boycott. The following chapter focuses on how some of those who became restive might have been moved toward that form of consciousness.

THREE

Ripening for Revolt

Assessing the context from which reform movements emerge is best done when the social scientist assumes a type of dual analytic focus. At times one's evaluative frame might best be trained on a society's evolving superstructure. This is because changes in basic institutions such as the economy ultimately reorder the actions and meanings humans attach to aspects of their day-to-day behavior. At other times, correct social analysis depends upon paying close attention to critical shifts in a group's collective consciousness. Ignoring opinion shifts among key sectors of a citizenry precludes any possibility of predicting mass behavior. The outcome of such a failure can be measured by the series of "surprise movements" that have grabbed center stage in recent decades. The explosive circumstances of South Africa in the mid 1970's, Iran in the early 1980's, or America's South in the 1960's were occasions of change that produced shocking developments not predicted by professional observers. These were all societies that combined aspects of modernization processes with deeply masked public opinion shifts that ultimately ignited opposition movements against entrenched authorities. In each case these movements were fueled by a social logic that finally become undeniable. This reality is demonstrated by the Montgomery, Alabama bus boycott of 1955 and 1956. Like its counterparts this reform effort had an internal logic tied to evolving social dynamics that characterize many localities in the modern world. This fact, perhaps more than any others, makes understanding the bus boycott an important matter. For part of what sparked the Montgomery protests were the suppressed longings of those who spent lifetimes enduring the twin disruptions caused by dire poverty and a rural-to-urban migration. The rural-to-urban process is especially important because it exposes those fleeing a peasant-like status, whether they finally settle in Teheran, Iran or cities like Los Angeles or Montgomery, to a wider variety of opportunities for expressing their pent-up grievances. Understanding such movements, though, requires assessing the meanings participants attribute to their new conditions. This seems especially true of various movements that emerged in the South that were designed to change the system of white-black relations.

407

Such an issue is best illustrated by describing how this took place in Montgomery.

In the remaining sections of this chapter important preconditions that contributed directly to the emergence of the bus boycott are reviewed and assessed.

The Momentum of Black Belt Dissatisfaction

An issue for this study was deciphering how evolving social trends in Alabama's Black Belt influenced the bus protest's emergence and its subsequent form. Such effects should be accounted for because of their connections to this reform movement's development. In addition to providing opportunities for the reorganization of daily life, economic and residential shifts exposed thousands to powerful ideological undercurrents in the years before the protest. Other patterns beginning to characterize the lives of Alabama's blacks in the 1930's might best be described as lifestyle shifts. City life especially provided new patterns of exposure that contrasted with the isolation that so often characterized the lives of those who had been sharecroppers. Being introduced to Alabama's blacks in the late 1930's and 1940's were radios, more visits from relatives who were reading papers like the *Chicago Defender*, the liberating effect of private automobiles, and countless other aspects of modernization. While the impact of these new patterns varied, their existence combined with an American post-World War II euphoria to lead many of Alabama's blacks to question their circumscribed status.

Listening to Montgomery's citizens talk about the personal ferment that characterized those transitional years after World War II, it became evident to me why protests became symptomatic of the 1950's and 1960's. That the grievances were pent-up over decades is beyond doubt. The particular conditions that prevailed among Afro-Americans who tilled Alabama's Black Belt soil were important because these human transplants joined the movements of the 1950's and 1960's and pushed them to success.

Almost all who would become boycott participants had some previous connections to the soil. Most, as was true throughout the Deep South, had ample reason to turn their back on the hardships of rural life. Few could claim not to have been periodically effected by the hopelessness and dismal heartaches that plagued the region's poorest agricultural workers. Even so it was certainly not unusual for black farmers to remain doggedly determined to succeed against nature's odds. More than a trace of this strength would be detected later in the protest actions of the middle 1950's. Such a tradition of rural persistence would prove critical to the boycott's ultimate outcome. The strength of such determination can be judged both by the number of blacks who had become significant land owners, and by the number of others who stayed on the land despite faint hopes for success.

Blacks throughout the entire South owned and operated about 183,000 farms in 1930. Far more though were tenants or sharecroppers. In 1930, 306,000 blacks and 709,000 whites fit the census department's criteria for being called tenant farmers, a mode of relations whose terms were only slightly more beneficial than bottom rung sharecropping. In that same year 393,000 Southern blacks and 383,000 whites remained tied to the even more discouraging sharecropping system.[1] While such figures apply to the Region as a whole, in Alabama's ten-county Black Belt 91.9% of tenants and sharecroppers were black.[2]

While land ownership among Alabama's blacks increased somewhat between 1910 and 1920, in the decade of the 1920's the number of black farm owners declined by 7.4% and the value of their holdings dropped by 14%.[3] As is easy to gauge, agricultural circumstances for Alabama's blacks, especially those in the Black Belt, became more wretched in this pre-boycott era. The average per capita income for blacks in 1920, reported in Table 3-1 (see following page), reflects the prevailing economic circumstances of blacks that spurred them to move to centers like Montgomery.

Even these dismal figures do not fully reflect the demoralizing conditions of work associated with premechanized Black Belt cotton farming. The principal tasks associated with cotton production—plowing, hoeing and picking—could be learned by most, but the repetitiveness of that work routine produced widespread boredom and bitter dissatisfaction. This was especially true, as one would expect, among Alabama's farm youth during the 1930's. Members of this group are key because they would form a backbone of support for the bus protest in their adult years. Clues about their attitudes during this early era appear in the literature describing Deep South race relations in the 1930's.

Expected to toil long hours while subsisting on substandard diets, rural black families of that era were often riddled by dissension. As was true nationally, black youth on farms were rejecting their "future" in massive

Table 3-1

Black Per Capita Income, By Region, 1920

Location	Annual Income
New England States	$436
Mid-Western States	331
Pacific States	231
North Carolina	160
Louisiana	136
South Carolina	91
Alabama	81
Texas	64
Mississippi	56

Source: Abram L. Harris, "Negro Migration to the North," *Current History Magazine*,20 (Sept. 1924), 923.

numbers. In large part this rejection of farm life was directly related to the scant chances for financial gain reported in Table 3-1, but other traditional features of life in the South figured prominently in this growing black distaste for rural life. Charles S. Johnson in both of his classic 1930's studies, *Shadow of the Plantation* and *Growing Up in the Black Belt*, provided graphic evidence of how Alabama's black youth were coming to view their future prospects.[4] Johnson's quote from an eighteen year old he called Jimmie Hill illustrates this point:

You jes' can't make anything at it. A man has a better chance if he rents. Then he can manage his own business and it's up to him to get out what he can. They don't even let you see the accounts, and you know they're cheating you but you can't do a thing about it.

I was with my uncle one time when he was settling, and the White Man had cheated him out of pract'ly everything. We told him to go back and tell the man that he thought he had made a mistake in figgering up the settlement. That ole peckerwood scratched his head and said, 'Wal, now les' see. There was the time you got this, and then you got this on such and such a day.' Well, time he got back through figgering again my uncle had to give him back

$6.00 of the settlement. I was mad as a hen 'cause the crop wasn't nothing and he sure needed all he could get; but I had to laugh. My uncle jes' said, 'Yassuh, thank you, suh'; and went home. They don't let you keep books on 'em, and if you dispute 'em, that's how they do you. But there ain't gonna be no farm for me. [5]

Perhaps there was no farm future for "Jimmie Hill." Like thousands of others he may have "voted with his feet" and migrated first to "town" and later to the North. But all of Alabama's Jimmie Hills did not leave the state. Large numbers of them migrated to urban settings like Montgomery during the pre-World War II era. Importantly, others who had left the South during the 1920's returned when the Great Depression wrecked economic havoc during the 1930's. When they did return, whether to relocate or just to visit, they often painted startling if exaggerated images of the North to entertain their "home folks." In this way too, old conceptions of racial role and segregationist ritual began to be reexamined and discarded by blacks in states like Alabama. Slowly, these new urban residents became convinced that there were alternative life styles to the ones they were often times forced to endure. Slowly, their initial relief at being free from the tedium of rural life gave way to a refocusing of dissatisfaction on the most oppressive aspects of life in segregated cities. This was especially true of those who wandered extensively before returning to the support networks provided by their extended families. Many had to rely on such family ties because they had been ill-prepared to cope with the requirements of urban complexity. Improved educational opportunities and decent employment emerged as twin hopes among these young blacks in the early 1940's. These goals were not at all unusual given the struggles to make a living that members of that group faced.

Many of those who struggled through these battles were poorly trained for survival in the city. Frequently semiliterate, they were among the initial victims of the national economic collapse in the 1930's. The paltry sums allocated to educate Afro-Americans (Table 3-2) residing in Alabama's Black Belt by the 1920's contributed to the reasons many could not successfully compete during the Great Depression. This was a pattern that showed little evidence of change in the 1930's. In the opening year of that decade only 5.8% of the region's black high school age youth were registered in school. This compared with 29.8% of similarly aged whites.[6] Montgomery itself offered no public high school for blacks, though in 1930 it had a population that included 29,970 Afro-Americans.[7] Birmingham, with its special, segregated "Industrial Tech," enrolled half of the entire state's black high school students in 1930. That facility was unusual in a state that had done little for its black pupils in the opening decades of the twentieth century.

Table 3-2

Alabama Black Belt Per Capita Allocation for Teacher Salary, Per Child

	White	Black
1910	$14.55	$ .80
1930	32.99	2.73

Source: Horace Mann Bond, *Negro Education in Alabama*, (Atheneum, 1939), p. 259.

Allocations for blacks, as illustrated by Table 3-2, frequently meant school facilities that were both dilapidated and without basic equipment. With such paltry sums available, school was often held in abandoned tenant shacks, where nature's elements were as much a part of the normal class routine as recitation. In such shacks pupils frequently had to write on crude slates that were held on their knees. Alabama's officials often considered slate boards to be a luxury blacks did not need. During winter, the State's Black Belt teachers frequently had to stop instruction so they could lead forays to the local woods to secure fuel for the classroom stove. Yet most of Alabama's blacks, despite these and numerous other disabilities, remained convinced that education was the key to escaping their prevailing conditions.

While some managed to elevate themselves by diligent attention to their lessons, most found the educational process to be a dismal charade that merely reinforced the effects of the prevailing oppressive racial status quo. These patterns caused widespread resentment among Alabama's black youth. Such feelings emerged throughout the region in the 1930's and 1940's.

These were patterns emerging throughout the South among its citizens of color. Educational discrimination was an especially troubling aspect of the regional racial status quo. Strong parallels can be drawn between the educational circumstances Arthur Raper found in his Depression era study of Georgia's heavily black districts and Alabama's Black Belt region. Raper was shocked when he discovered that officials of Green County, Georgia annually spent more money transporting 510 white pupils to school, than they did to educate the county's 5,368 black students![8] Similar patterns of neglect characterized Alabama's Black Belt counties. Nowhere was this more evident than in length of school term.

For Afro-Americans the average school year in Alabama's rural Black Belt in 1920 had been a paltry eighty-seven days.[9] By 1930 this had increased but to only one hundred and thirteen days. In contrast, Montgomery's public schools for blacks convened an average of one hundred and seventy-five days in the 1930's. This widely known pattern pulled blacks to the States's capitol and helped keep them from fleeing North. This was also a pattern that caused racial friction in Alabama as in many localities rural white schools also ran a bit "short." Such contrasting educational circumstances also prodded urban migration among that group.

Importantly, the fact that Montgomery's black schools functioned in a more comprehensive manner assured that urban students received more thorough exposure to abstract ideas about citizenship rights and idealized versions of American democracy. When social analysis of evolving Southern black consciousness is done, comparative dimensions such as this need to be noted. This helps in understanding how such factors contributed to the more general processes that sensitized and made specific Southern blacks more alert to the necessity for significant change in the region's overall racial order.

As this consciousness developed it began to be more openly manifested among the young of the era. Johnson described a typical rural Black Belt fourteen year old in the mid-1930's who got angry each time she saw whites riding past on a school bus. Johnson's "Beulah King" confided

> Now if they ain't got money enough to buy a bus for both White and colored children to ride in I don't see why they couldn't let some of the colored children have some of the seats in "the White bus", and ride. It just doesn't seem fair to me for them to let the White children ride and make us walk. 'Cose it ain't so bad when the weather is good, but I just get so mad I want to cry when it's rainy and cold. The little ones at home can't go at all when the weather is bad.[10]

This growing distaste for the prevailing rural racial order felt by the Jimmie Hills and the Beulah Kings was widely shared by their peers in the early 1930's. That their resentment frequently centered on the tangible forms of discriminatory treatment was certainly to be expected. Discrepancies in school bus facilities such as expressed by "Beulah King" formed a strong basis for widespread dissatisfaction among those Black Belt youth who were to become potential bus boycotters.

In the remaining portion of this chapter personality formation among a few of those who became important boycott participants is explored. While the connections that tie shifts in superstructure and individual mental context continue to resist final analysis, the profiles that follow reestablish that such links were durable and influential in the case of Montgomery bus boycott participants. By reviewing the development of a small number of those who became participants, a full appreciation of these links can be achieved. In this way too the reader will recognize that shifts in a local group's racial consciousness, though sometimes decades in the making, can be as critical as the transformation of a set of labor relations.

Profile One: A Denial of a Formal Title

By the late 1970's Mrs. Johnnie Carr became the president of the Montgomery Improvement Association. Though still not accepted by some because of lingering sexism, Mrs. Carr's roots in Alabama's Black Belt were firm. She was native to Montgomery County, being born in a rural south county settlement. As was true for many other Black Belt families, early death claimed her father and two siblings. Mrs. Carr's mother then moved to "town" in the 1920's seeking access to job opportunities and hopeful about other changes.

Arriving in Montgomery proper, Mrs. Carr was nurtured in a kin network that placed a premium on children achieving educationally. Ambition to improve through educational attainment, a strong value among the emerging black lower-middle class, characterized Mrs. Carr's childhood. The youthful Johnnie Carr bonded strongly with a mother who made "every sacrifice" to insure that her children could stay in school.[11]

The refuge of school took on added importance as the young black female gradually experienced more of the barriers that reinforced Montgomery's rigid racial caste barriers. The mundane aspects of that segregation system were especially grating for a youth who had formed moderate expectations of a better life. Mrs. Carr recalls

We were always very depressed. 'Cause our people didn't have any opportunities to participate in things that we felt as citizens we should've been given . . .

414

> For instance I would go downtown and if I wanted to buy a hamburger, and sometimes I did, I'd have to find a black hamburger shop, unless I wanted to go down into a little hole in a basement.[12]

Grievances such as these were to be reported in profusion in the 1930's. They were important. To young teens such customs were especially embittering. Ironically, it encouraged some of them to search for all other discriminatory practices. Unknown to their parents some black teens explored the limits of Montgomery's segregation system as if they were adventurers. These mid-1930's social "explorers" found the limitations that their more cautious parents often only alluded to. When they found them in profusion the resentment of each new discovery had renewed impact. In this manner handfuls of Montgomery's black teens of the 1930's began developing a perspective that predisposed them to support anti-segregation movements.

Though she did this in her early womanhood, the passing of the decades has not dimmed Mrs. Carr's ability to recall minute details. Discussing them causes the old distresses to be graphically described

> They really used to treat black women wrong. If you'd go into a store and wanted to try on a hat they'd tell you that you better put a stocking cap on your head. Then if you'd go into a store to try on shoes and you didn't have stockings they'd go and find you an old filthy footlet to put on and that kind of stuff. There was so much of that stuff. All those types of things made us bitter, bitter.[13]

When citizens of color began frequenting Montgomery's commercial establishments in growing numbers such contacts and negative reactions to them increased. In Mrs. Carr's case, she had significant early interactions that prevented her from developing a generalized anti-white frame of reference. Mrs. Carr's years at the Montgomery Industrial School provided confirmation that positive interracial contacts were possible. The critical importance of this private training school for black females deserves special emphasis.

This school, established by a white New England woman at the turn of the century, was praised very early as one of the best industrial schools for black girls in the South.[14] Run by a woman known simply as Miss White, the school placed primary emphasis on domestic service skills, with most attention devoted to developing techniques for proper cooking, nursing, and sewing. Local whites also feared that "racial equality" was taught. It was. Since the school also taught the traditional virtues of "civic responsibility," Miss White and the New England "outsiders" were ostracized by other

415

whites but revered by Montgomery's blacks. Miss White kept her school functioning until, blind and infirm, she retired in 1928.

Though Mrs. Carr left the school in her early teens to marry, the standards she was exposed to helped to shape her subsequent attitudes and continue to guide her behavior. Chief among these was the impetus both Miss White and Mrs. Carr's mother had given to leading a life involving "Christian Charity". Both women also taught that all citizens, females included, should strive to promote social reforms. The intensity of these ideas, coming at a time that coincided with progressive exposure to the rigid caste customs, helped set Mrs. Carr on a course toward activism. In the late 1930's she became the first black woman to join the Montgomery branch of the National Association for the Advancement of Colored People. She explains that action as being prompted specifically by yet another of the more mundane aspects of the caste system. Mrs. Carr recalled

> I remember me and a friend went into a store that was having a sale. And we applied for some credit. I wrote my name as Mrs. J.R. Carr and the clerk, she wrote J.R. Carr, and I just looked at her. Then finally I said, "I put Mrs. J.R. Carr" and she said, "Oh." And I never got that credit. And until this day I haven't shopped at that store, even though they have excellent material.

She chuckles before adding sarcastically

> My friend didn't put Mrs. on her application and she got her credit.[15]

Widespread practices such as that contributed to the especially militant tone of Montgomery's local NAACP chapter. When Mrs. Carr joined that group she met Edgar Daniel Nixon.

Profile Two: "Not Even the Fishing"

E. D. Nixon, born in 1899, walks in the 1980's with a pronounced stoop. In the 1950's he was a muscular six-feet four inches tall. As a pullman porter he had acquired the habit of standing ramrod straight. Being grievance handler for his union forced the development of what became a knack for negotiating with irate Southern whites. Travel and duty hours spent reading discarded newspapers broadened his social consciousness. Submersion in the political maneuvers of the 1941 March on Washington Movement provided

Nixon national connections with labor leaders and New Deal Democrats.[16] Seemingly primed for race leadership by the 1950's, he would quietly join a push for a compromise candidate, M.L. (Mike) King, Jr., to become group spokesman. It was a practical decision at the time but years of contemplation have caused Nixon to ponder what he might have achieved personally. At a crucial moment though, he had not hesitated because he sensed what had become a modern requirement. Nixon speaks with traditional Black Belt diction patterns. This was an insurmountable leadership handicap for many older blacks during the mid-1950's dawn of the television age. Quite wisely, Nixon conceded to the new technology.

Speaking of his early life Nixon describes a difficult childhood with a father who was both a Baptist preacher and sharecropper. Despite these occupations he "never had anything." Unlike many from the early era Nixon omits reference to his mother but describes his early years in graphic terms

> I was born in Montgomery. And at that time my father was employed for a company, I understand, by the name of Sable's Steel and Iron Company. Couple of years after my birth, he left. Went on back to the country. His sister named me and when he left he left me with her.
> She was a single woman, a widow. So I fought it out here up and down for six or eight years and, of course, during the summer my father would come down, pick me up, carry me down and I'd spend part of the summer with him.[17]

When asked whether life in rural Autauga County had enjoyable aspects he replied, "not even the fishing."

When Nixon was twelve, and he emphasizes the exact date of October 5, 1911, he left home to be on his own. By his own account he had less than twenty months of school. In search of work he traveled first to Mobile and later to Birmingham.

In Birmingham, Nixon took a job in a grocery store that paid him a dollar a day. Becoming dissatisfied he opened his own store, but a lack of the skills needed to manage accounts and other complicated matters contributed to its failure. With no further dreams of contributing to the development of a "thriving Negro business community" as B.T. Washington had once proposed, Nixon returned to Montgomery. He eventually worked as a railroad baggage handler before achieving the rank of pullman porter. With this job Nixon had attained a position close to the top of the then prevailing racial job ceiling. He was to remain at that post from 1923 until 1964.[18]

During his early years on the job Nixon expressed in hints, thinly veiled innuendos and other unmistakable allusions, the feelings of protest hundreds of pullman porters harbored toward those white riders who engaged in boorish behavior. He too hated the more general system of segregation. His was an ethos and subtle mode of behavior that was growing stronger with successive generations of pullman porters. In the 1930's, Nixon became a rising star among these younger black pullman turks. His political consciousness was also spurred by an art form that characterized the culture of the South's Afro-Americans. Like countless other young porters, Nixon especially enjoyed the satirical blues styles that were increasingly popular nationally in the 1920 's and 1930's. Such songs were not new to the Black Belt native.

Reviewing how Alabama's Afro-American culture unfolded is important because it gives strong evidence about values that were ascending in these formative decades. Nixon had heard the "bitter blues" all over Alabama in his youth. They impressed him as much as the material he later read as he surveyed an increasingly militant national black press in the 1920's and 1930's. An argument might be made in Nixon's case that such blues were even more important in galvanizing his anti-Jim Crow beliefs. While this point might be debatable where E. D. Nixon is concerned, for thousands of others from his generation it is a general truth. The pervasive influence of "bitter blues" messages was most pronounced on the increasing numbers of urban blacks in the South during the 1930's. Such a pattern represented the continuation of a long established trend. In Alabama, black political commentary expressed through music was a well established tradition long before Nixon's youth. Lawrence W. Levine, whose analysis of the elements of protest in Deep South Afro-American culture is especially revealing, recounts a typical lyric from a 1915 Auburn, Alabama song

If a White man kills a Negro, they hardly carry it to court,
If a Negro kills a White man, they hung him like a goat.[19]

Nixon, sharing in the collective bitterness about the circumstances of black educational life, described himself as being receptive to the sentiments of another typical Black Belt song of that early age. One morning in 1979, sitting in one of Montgomery's apartment units known as "the projects," he sang this tune to me

White man goes to college,

Nigger to the field,
White man learns to read and write,
Poor Nigger learns to steal, honey babe,
Poor Nigger learns to steal.[20]

Pullman porters like Nixon, confronting face to face white arrogance far more frequently than most other blacks, remembered finding such satirical songs especially appealing and meaningful. Theirs was also a world, like many other closed black occupational groups, that contained countless jokes about white customers. Patterns of such black humor facilitated the healthy release of the porters' suppressed hostility and pent-up aggression. E. D. Nixon became a vocal and critical contributing member to this important status group which produced many of the America's most militant black activists in the 1930's and 1940's.

As he was to be later, Nixon's membership in the group of young turks had been influenced in part by the charismatic speaking abilities of a black orator and then ardent Socialist, A. Philip Randolph. Recalling a mid-1925 speech Randolph delivered in St. Louis, Nixon remembered

He was the most ablest speaker I ever heard. That's including Reverend King. Of course people don't want to hear me say that. But that's true.[21]

Randolph's charisma was combined with a frank appeal to the porters' economic self-interest. According to Nixon, Randolph promised those assembled at St. Louis' Black YMCA that

Those of you who'll stick with me. The day'll soon come that I'll have you making a hundred and fifty dollars a month.[22]

Nixon said he "couldn't believe it." Pullman porters were then making seventy-five dollars a month plus tips. This was a wage that put them within range materially of the educated black elite. Seven months later he joined and became very active in the intrigues of the Brotherhood of Sleeping Car Porters. Ironically, one reason Nixon joined was because he felt he could risk being fired. At the time he had no major family responsibilities. Within two years he became president of the Montgomery local. Nixon started taking unusually courageous stands then because

I figured I could get me something else. I didn't have a wife or nothing. They had me on the carpet a whole lot of times then.[23]

With each encounter Nixon developed more confidence in his ability to handle pressure. As president of that local Nixon learned the ins and outs of his labor contract, "like a book. Had to."

By the late 1930's Nixon was increasingly active in Montgomery's black community organizations. His role as president of his union local was supplemented by the presidency of the local chapter of the NAACP in the mid 1940's. That was still a time when only a few blacks were interested in such a dangerous post. Yet this was also a time of enormous national growth for the NAACP, and Nixon's Black Belt local increased from four hundred to two thousand members. His abilities recognized, Nixon became the statewide president of the NAACP in the late 1940's. During his tenure twenty-two chapters were added in Alabama, many in the Black Belt. Managing such growth provided E. D. Nixon with valuable skills and enough personal assurance to try to stir change in the racial caste system. He would always remain what he was in his twenties. He remained essentially a cohort and leader of working men who knew him as a fearless and tireless labor activist.

Coming from a background that had denied him opportunities for close relationships, Nixon gradually achieved a stronger sense of self-dignity and coherent protest ideas largely as a consequence of his involvement in the community of the Pullman Porters Brotherhood. Importantly, his militant union brothers would be available for sensitive duty during the long days of the protest. The existence of this type of national network, and blacks' ability to command it without concern with issues such as ideological purity, was an important reason that the bus boycott would have a chance for success while a 1930's tenant's union, as discussed in the last chapter, could be easily crushed.

E.D. Nixon was a central figure in this and many of Montgomery's black organizations. By the eve of the boycott's emergence he had become a well-known community figure commanding attention and respect among those who wanted rapid racial change. Nixon remained especially aware though of his personal limitations. Both his speech patterns and previous political rivalries figured in why it was unlikely that he could have played the role of being Montgomery's boycott spokesman. Those dynamics are discussed in detail in later chapters.

Profile Three: We Were As Good As Anybody

While E.D. Nixon and Mrs. Carr endured stifling poverty as children, Mrs. Erna Dungee Allen fared better. She shared the pattern of a rural Black Belt birth, but it was to a family with a father who was a "country school teacher." Importantly, he was a teacher at a Rosenwald school.[24] Employment at such schools provided rural teachers exceptional economic security. The Dungees confirmed their special status in 1917 with an automobile purchase. Their relative advantage promoted positive self-worth and the formation of intrafamily warmth. Mrs. Allen benefited from such circumstances and later married one of Montgomery's most prosperous black physicians.

Mrs. Allen had other advantages unavailable to most of Alabama's blacks. Like Mrs. Carr, she attended Montgomery's rural black schools before her admission to Miss White's Montgomery Industrial School. She described the impact Mrs. White's school had while she suppressed a gentle chuckle

> All those women. They didn't talk to us much about color. The biggest thing they emphasized was cleanliness was next to Godliness. And they taught us we were as good as anybody. That you had a responsibility. That nobody was better than us. That's how we came up. Our folks taught us the same thing.[25]

Consistency reinforced the importance of accepting such an alternative standard. Over time such patterns of positive thought came to characterize the Montgomery Industrial School pupils. By the early 1920's the esteem they received in Montgomery's black community had become as noticeable as their highly visible polka dot uniforms. Black parents with an eye to the future throughout the Black Belt moved to Montgomery and strove to provide their daughters the chance to attend this school. Private matters such as acting out one's family ambition were critical to speeding the eventual doom of the Black Belt's racial order. Motivated by reasons such as these, as well as the more documented farm mechanization squeeze, people deserted Alabama's Black Belt for the special setting Montgomery was becoming.

Mrs. Allen's parents moved to Montgomery proper in the 1920's and she later attended Alabama State University. Upon graduation and marriage, she taught six years in rural black schools before devoting her full attention to the activities of Montgomery's black "society." Despite becoming engulfed in a type of social world that would later be described as "frivolous" by E. Franklin Frazier, Mrs. Allen remained more than vaguely aware of her responsibilities to racial uplift. She became especially interested in voting during the 1930's and 1940's. Mrs. Allen describes an incident her father endured in the mid 1930's as a catalyst for these thoughts. She recounts his difficulties

I remember Papa went down to see about registering and was told that while he was qualified they couldn't let him do it because his friends would want to. He attempted several times and finally paid his poll taxes back twenty-one years. Mr. Nixon was one who did too.[26]

A seemingly moderate political climate in Montgomery during the World War II years contributed to growing numbers of the more educated blacks registering. Despite the prestige, Mrs. Allen waited until 1949 to become an active voter. She had sworn she would never pay a poll tax so she waited until after the U.S. Supreme Court repealed it. Despite these small signs of progress, the racial atmosphere in Montgomery left her with a vague uneasiness. She recalled

Black people were kind of coasting along, everything was segregated. We had just accepted that. We didn't like it because sometimes it was most inconvenient. You would avoid using some things like transportation because of this. You would drive as long as you could on a trip because there was no accommodation along the way. You'd drive until you go to some place where you knew someone.[27]

Such nuisances were most grating, of course, on those blacks able to travel. Importantly, members of this slowly growing black privileged class were able to chance joining Southern protest groups that began mushrooming in the late 1930's. The appearances of such groups in Alabama, some inspired by the Camp Hill militancy, marked a critical turning point in blacks' efforts at reform.

Mrs. Allen became a casual member of Montgomery's NAACP in the middle 1940's. Largely inactive, she paid dues, though now claims she believed that the tactical approach of legalism was overly slow. Nonetheless, occasional involvement such as hers provided another means of sustaining many blacks' basic assumptions about the need for racial change. Many others in Montgomery shared her perspective while other professionals used such membership merely as a means to mingle socially.

Whether they were sincere in their desire for affiliation is beside the point. Merely by being members in such groups they, like Mrs. Allen, became available for rapid mobilization. She was forty-two at the time of the boycott and childless. Like most of her social cohorts, Mrs. Allen had crafted a cautious life that allowed her to remain insulated from certain of Montgomery's segregation ordinances. Such careful black lives were often devoid of psychic, meaning however, and Mrs. Allen was one of dozens who quickly responded to the activities generated by the boycott's emergence. With normal rules of status suspended during this crisis she mingled freely with lower class blacks in a fashion unknown to her since a happy Black Belt youth. In later musings she focused on the excitement generated by the collective effort to carry the boycott forward. She remembered

> Oh, you just worked. You worked . . . Sometimes I'd get there in the morning and I'd be there until midnight. And I'd leave and Mr. Nixon and some of the others they'd still be there. I don't know when they'd sleep.[28]

Despite the grueling schedule her involvement was as satisfying as the "play-work" she had performed in her beloved father's garden plot. While Mrs. Allen found new opportunities for expressing long established sentiments in the protest of the 1950's, Joe Reed was a young, raw ex-soldier returning to Alabama.

Profile Four: Be A Man

While young, Joe Reed was provided with well-defined ideas about his chances in the Black Belt's racial order. Born in the late 1930's in Evergreen, Alabama, Reed learned that life had a clear purpose. In sum, it was the simple American struggle to get ahead. Growing up surrounded by black males who constantly mocked each other for staying tied literally to mule teams, Reed soon learned that "getting ahead" meant getting away from Southern soil. As so many others would, he joined the military as a means of escape. When finished with his first military hitch he attended Alabama State University and resettled permanently in Montgomery. His consciousness, though, remained infused with rural values.

Evergreen is a tiny village that serves as a county seat, mid-way between Montgomery and Mobile. While Conecuh County straddles Alabama's piney woods region and the southern fringe of the Black Belt, residents such as Reed were embedded in a web of institutional connections to the latter.

Reed takes special pride in his home region based on his assertion that "people believed in education there."[29] While Southern blacks have often

423

viewed education as a panacea for progress, in Reed's case it has worked. A pragmatic politician who had been a delegate to several national Democratic conventions, he took special pride in having addressed his fellow delegates from the floor in 1976. At the time of the interview he served as the highest ranking black in the Alabama Educational Association. This biracial teachers' Association wields considerable political clout in contemporary Alabama politics. Reed receives and enjoys deferential treatment from all staffers.

His style of interaction with employees reflects a sense of self-confidence that some unrepentant white supremacists find abrasive. Reed is indifferent to such reactions. This stems in part from his desire to maintain his home community's orientation. He insists that "his Evergreen" was known throughout the local area as a place with

> . . . no Uncle Toms, here. Nope . . . none . . . couldn't have made it with us. [30]

In the late 1930's Reed's Evergreen was a Saturday gathering spot for black shoppers. One could almost always hear Saturday afternoon complaints about the treatment "them Scottsboro Boys" received. Such was the quality of chatter that swirled around a young Reed's head as he scampered between adult's legs. A keen observer would also have noted black men in Evergreen who slipped behind stores in those years for "clear refreshments." After sufficient alcoholic fortification, this "rabble" returned to swear even louder that such a circumstance "wouldn't go here." Such was the verbal pattern throughout the Black Belt region.

While such "fortified" boasting was often no more than collective catharsis, the vehemence, volume, and wildly demonstrated enjoyment associated with such weekly sessions were especially influential on those who quietly ate candy while listening and waiting for their fathers. There were other important messages being delivered to Reed by significant others at this time. These were a bit more formal.

Typical of many black American parents in the late 1930's and early 1940's, Reed's parents preached to him about being "prepared." He heard that children would have to be ready to do things that their parents never imagined would be available. Children like Reed did have new chances because America's economy finally stirred and began reviving in the late 1930's. Reed's childhood also coincided with a number of widely publicized "firsts" for blacks and he was encouraged by them. Such dynamics spurred future hopes within Reed and members of his generation. Adding to these patterns were other important ideas that were becoming more readily accessible. By the late 1930's, Alabama's blacks were acquiring more radios and used cars and access to such devices lessened the impact of rural isolation. Reed's family struggled but eventually had them all.

Such developments heralded the general effects that all forms of modernization were having throughout the rural South. It is now clear that as tractors began revolutionizing the south's agricultural order in the 1930's and 1940's, so too did the sly racial innuendoes being radio broadcasted by Fats Waller and others like him from points beyond the cotton curtain.[31] In this and countless other ways, the racial consciousness of Alabama's Black Belt residents like Reed was being shaped and reshaped in the decades before the protest's emergence.

In rural areas these modernizing trends slowly became reflected in how customer transactions were conducted in small villages and at crossroad stores. As Black Belt residents, such as Reed's parents, became more involved in a world of cash rather than a sharecropper provision supply system, many quietly expected that they would be waited on in the order they entered Evergreen's stores. Stores where this pattern was rejected lost significant patronage from blacks. This developing dynamic spurred a predictable reaction from many whites. It involved the day of the week when most blacks in Evergreen shopped: Saturday.

Many Southern whites stopped shopping on Saturdays altogether rather than tolerate such weekend "impudence." Others slowly adjusted to the practical realities of the new day. More importantly, as a few commercial outposts changed, doubts emerged among other white merchants heavily dependent on black customers. Over time, merchants in Evergreen and other locales grudgingly accepted the new practices. In this way and others, racial customs began to be quietly reassessed in Reed's home area. Small changes like this, seldom discussed in the Civil Rights literature, contributed to the generally growing momentum for change that would later characterize the 1950's and 1960's.

At some point, however, minor adjustments in a system of racial etiquette such as the ones a school-age Reed witnessed lose their potential to pacify. The collective accumulation of grievances over decades, the constant rehashing of those grievances in front porch conversations, sermons, songs, and during school recesses, finally becomes sufficient so that one develops a strong predisposition to support all plausible efforts to promote racial change. This happened with Reed as it did with others.

This quality of mind among Alabama blacks was enhanced by minor local variations in the segregation system. It has been amply demonstrated that blacks in southern border states in the 1930's and 1940's faced fewer confining restrictions than did those from the Deep South.[32] Within Deep South states like Alabama slight variations occurred and these often took on exaggerated importance. Among youth with developing or still fragile egos, establishing one's status often included debating the ways of white folks in one's home place.

Children and teens going to regional church mixers, athletic contests, etc., were often especially vicious in their verbal attacks about the alleged backward racial character of Black Belt localities. Reed and others responded in kind, but such outside assertions rang true far too often. In partial defense, Reed developed a strong distaste for any contact with whites that contained the possibility for the ritual imposition of segregation requirements.

While his psyche-protection strategy of avoidance worked to a point, a festering determination for change came to characterize Reed's views. The intensity of these desires contributed to his eventual evolution as a political activist. His parents, whom Reed describes simply as "plain folks," constantly reinforced a telling message. He recalls

> They told us to be a man. If you tell somebody something, do it. Nobody ever beat us. Nobody told us to be afraid of anyone. They stressed common sense.[33]

It was by recalling such "common sense" that Reed, and hundreds like him, joined in the collective efforts to achieve racial change in the mid 1950's. When the call to action came he was perfectly prepared to respond.

Individual Discontent:
Its Significance in the Black Belt

The four "personalities" presented above symbolize some of the diverse elements that came together in support of the bus protest in Montgomery. Each had some private torments that were the bane of the Southern black world. More importantly, they had all come to share in the desire for significant change in race relations. Their beliefs lacked consistency and coordination, but that would come. The essence of each was a multiple identity. Able to assume the roles of employee, church steward, soldier,

426

organizational head, student, parent, etc., all later would be able to assume varying roles in the boycott itself. They would do this because of a long-simmering common consciousness. All were profoundly resentful about the ritually enforced roles of denigration required of them by a segregated social order. None dissented on this issue. Close inspection reveals there was nothing about them that resembled a simple, "accommodated" Southern black personality described in an earlier era by Robert E. Park.[34] Briefly reviewed, three shared in the wide-spread material poverty that characterized the Black Belt. One, the least educated, became a labor and political activist with crucial national political connections. The other male, after acquiring important non-accommodative attitudes as a child in the Black Belt, had his views reinforced by events in Montgomery. The other two profiled are black women. Later chapters will demonstrate that such women were expected and able to assume important roles in the boycott. They would do this successfully because of the long developing common consciousness about the Jim Crow system. There could have been no successful boycott without the key organizational skills and determination of such black women. While both women were to play critical roles in the protest, one was from a poor, "broken" household, while the other had advantages known to few of the region's blacks.

These four, and thousands of Montgomery's other blacks, by the middle 1950's had come to share an ever keener sense of discontent. Such an underlying mood was communicated only sporadically in the decade before the bus protest. Such collective discontent is one of several ingredients necessary if a major social movement is to take coherent form. Community organization and precipitating events are also essential. In the chapter that follows, those issues are explored.

FOUR

A Boycott Consciousness Takes Form

Widespread dissatisfaction with life may characterize the worldview of a people for generations and not be translated into action designed to promote social change. Such quiescence may be accounted for in a variety of ways. Some social orders have populations who adhere rigidly to belief systems, such as India's Hindus with their focus on reincarnation, that effectively channel sentiments of discontent in an otherworldly direction.[1] Other societies may be structured in a fashion that lessens the prospect that resistance efforts can be mounted. Repressive police states such as Duvalier's Haiti or the Spain of the Franco era come to mind. Regimes such as these are capable of maintaining a degree of stability for reasons other than mere terror. In both, relatively large segments of their populations remain dispersed in rural settings and provincial in other ways. Given such structural conditions, organizing and sustaining opposition from below becomes comparatively difficult.[2] While these illustrations give clues about factors that usually promote the appearance of stability, the circumstances that were coming to characterize the black community of Montgomery, Alabama in the post-World War II era were radically different. Because of this the potential that a sustainable black opposition movement could be mounted was more pronounced than many realized. As the conditions that preceded the actual mobilization are reviewed, the initial support the movement received from Montgomery's black masses begins to be more comprehensible.

A crucial factor in this potential to mobilize resistance was that the persistent dissatisfaction described in the preceding chapter could now be more readily organized and channelled within an urban context.[3] This chapter provides a review of the attributes of Montgomery's black community so that the reader can appreciate how several important social dynamics contributed to the momentum that preceded the boycott's announcement. Such a review makes it easier to understand why Montgomery, as opposed to a site such as Birmingham, became the cradle for the emergence of the direct action phase of the modern Civil Rights Movement.[4]

Reorganization of black Life in Urban Enclaves

Between 1920 and 1950 Montgomery experienced the type of growth that characterized many American state capitals. As Table 4-1 illustrates, the decade of the 1920's was especially critical in the transformation of Montgomery from a moderate size town to an urban center. This trend of population growth continued through the early 1950's, but it was during the sustained growth of the 1920's that Montgomery's black community infrastructure developed qualities that would be crucial during the subsequent boycott. Traditional black organizations such as lodges, small businesses, churches, social clubs, and other voluntary associations, took root and grew during this dynamic era of population growth. Their development slowed but continued despite the deadening economic depression that ravaged the 1930's. A primary reason these organizations were able to persist is because of the continued migration of the rural black poor to Montgomery. The persistence of this migration provided an economic base important to support the growth of an aspiring lower-middle class of blacks. These middle-class strivers would in turn provide a fertile recruiting base for social uplift groups. An even larger rate of white growth also occurred in Montgomery during this era but the essential levers of white politics and influence remained largely intact.[5] The outlines of Montgomery's population growth are illustrated in Table 4-1. (See following page.)

Since the major portion of the black population increase took place in the 1920-1940 era, the disruptions that tend to plague a community's institutions during rapid population expansion had been experienced and consolidated before the boycott's emergence. Members of Montgomery's black community had a chance to develop a shared consciousness based on mutual experience and opportunity. This was especially true of those who were forming elements of what might best be described as "Negro Society." Members from such groups would later play

430

Table 4-1

Population Growth of Montgomery, By Race

	Total	Growth	white	Growth	black	Growth
1920	43,464		23,631		19,827	
1930	66,079	52.0%	35,474	50.1%	29,970	51.1%
1940	78,084	18.2%	43,547	22.7%	34,535	15.2%
1950	106,525	36.4%	63,114	44.0%	42,538	23.1%

Source: U.S. Census

critical roles in the movement's early stages. What was happening in black Montgomery is important because it reflects a process that evolved throughout the Deep South. Pivan and Cloward described the significance of this development in the following terms

Concentration and separation [also] generated a black economic base, despite the poverty of most of the black urban wage workers who contributed to that base. One significant result was the gradual emergence of a black occupational sector which was relatively invulnerable to white power, a sector consisting of clergymen, small entrepreneurs, professionals, and labor leaders. In an earlier period, and particularly in southern rural society, very few—if any—blacks were located in these occupations, and those few were usually dependent on whites. The emergence of an independent leadership sector was accomplished by institutional expansion and diversification, and by greater institutional independence of the white community.[6]

While Pivan and Cloward may overstate the independence of this emerging black class, by the early 1950's the first signs of their appearance were everywhere, especially in black Montgomery. This process had long-term implications for local race relations patterns. In many localities members of this "new" black class were especially hostile to the normal functioning of the segregationist social order. Though harboring such sentiments, members of this growing group in Montgomery remained cautious in their public demeanor. Feeling themselves forced to be circumspect in such a fashion was especially aggravating to these "new blacks." As the decade of the 1950s dawned, Montgomery contained dozens of individuals who suppressed their desires to attack the symbols and the structure of the system of segregation.

Though militant sentiments reflected this class's emerging value system, there is never a guarantee that social action precisely follows a group's values.[7] More important to comprehending this boycott's emergence is that local members of these black elites were coming to share the belief that small steps could be taken to alleviate the particulars of their city's prevailing racial system. Until the middle 1950's they lacked any coherent means to act on their emerging collective view. Moreover, members of this new class of Deep South blacks, in Alabama and elsewhere, remained aware of the special wrath they generated from most of the South's whites. Such a perception was realistic given the response of whites when racial customs began to be publicly challenged by Southern blacks in the early and late 1940's. During this time white suspicion of blacks who even affected the appearance of professional status increased.[8] Though overt white hostility toward middle class blacks toned down a bit in the early 1950's, this was principally a function of such blacks' genius at avoiding potentially threatening circumstances.

In Montgomery, the decade of the 1940's had included a few middle class blacks increasing their contacts with reform-minded forces outside the South and establishing a token, though growing, number of semi-public contacts with liberal-minded old family whites of the "better class." These contacts usually took highly innocuous forms such as planning sessions for civic events and generally avoided ritually proscribed interactions such as the sharing of meals. That such meetings occurred at all, however, gave credence to the notion that Montgomery's blacks were becoming recognized as members of the "civic community." Thus these were highly significant, if still largely symbolic, interactions. Though such signs of recognition began to increase by the late 1940s, racial taboos remained too strong to permit "reputable" white organizations to have biracial memberships. Thus these civic strivers within Montgomery's black community still remained virtual outsiders. Given this continued status, feelings of hostility slowly mounted within this group. Before the mid-1950s these sentiments were seldom openly displayed. Though denied important forms of interaction they felt entitled to, this new class of "tie and collar" blacks was faring much better than other Montgomery blacks.

Urban life for the masses of Montgomery's blacks was far more harsh than it was for the relatively privileged. In the early 1950's the age-old struggle for economic survival remained paramount for most who had arrived in the city after being displaced by the transformation of the Black Belt's agricultural order. Most solved their ever pressing economic problems by acquiring service jobs, unskilled or day labor, or other forms of low status employment. This type of work, along with menial jobs at local military installations, formed the bulk of employment that was available to the masses of blacks. Like many other Southern cities Montgomery remained largely devoid of heavy industry or private firms that would have had to compete for workers. This proved to be a major factor in the especially poor economic circumstances that plagued Montgomery's black masses. When the income circumstances of Montgomery's blacks are compared with their counterparts from other urban centers of the state, these important differences are revealed. Table 4-2 illustrates this point.

Table 4-2
Median Family Income of Alabama Blacks, Selected Cities, 1949

Birmingham	$1,609
Gadsen	1,480
Mobile	1,173
Montgomery	908
Selma	865

Source: U. S. Census

This was a major reason for the special importance that economic-tinged issues would assume during the early course of the boycott. The figures from Table 4-2 also begin to suggest why the especially job-stifled masses of blacks in Montgomery turned out to be more likely candidates for social mobilization than did ex-Black Belt residents who moved to more prosperous Alabama settings. It should also be noted that unlike many industrial sector jobs offered at the steel mills in Birmingham or the unskilled labor jobs on the docks in Mobile, Montgomery's service-oriented jobs for blacks usually required far more frequent doses of demeaning face-to-face encounters with whites. This is not a minor point. The nature of demeaning interracial job etiquette, a more frequent experience for the average black Montgomerian, seems to have provided additional momentum to the rapidly developing resistance consciousness. While an issue such as this can be debated indefinitely, there were other special factors that contributed to a developing mobilization impulse directed at the restrictive customs imposed on black patrons of the Montgomery City Lines. Feelings against the bus system were fairly uniform and proved to be especially telling in the Montgomery case. They deserve a brief examination.

Bus Codes: Harsh Even By Deep South Standards

The grievances Montgomery's black masses harbored toward the segregation system that was imposed on the bus system were of long standing.[9] Montgomery's laws regulating seating were thought to be particularly harsh and humiliating by local blacks. Owen Butler, a railroad worker who migrated to Montgomery from rural Georgia, described these stringent laws and how discomforting they were to him. Butler's sentiments reflect the black views that had become widespread

> Boycotting the buses had been on my mind a long time even before it started. I had seen so many things, you know? Such as getting on a bus downtown, and you know . . . it's be crowded, three white people would be sitting in the front and Negroes couldn't even get on the bus right!
> He had to get up there, hand the man the money, then get back down, go to the rear and get in. Try to get in. Sometimes they pulled off and left you.[10]

Rituals such as the ones Butler described were important indicators of the especially cumbersome system that was used to maintain passenger segregation on Montgomery's buses. For purposes of comparison, bus segregationist ordinances in Richmond, Virginia, Atlanta, and Nashville, were all less restrictive than Montgomery's in that regulations in those locales provided for seating on a first-come, first-served basis with blacks filling buses from the rear toward the front and white passengers required to follow an inverse pattern.[11] Additionally, in none of these cities were blacks expected to follow the rigidly demeaning practice of boarding through a rear door. Nor were blacks in those cities asked to relinquish their seats to later-arriving white passengers.[12] All these behaviors could be demanded of Montgomery's bus-riding blacks. Montgomery's bus ordinances then were especially demoralizing when compared to either national or regional standards. More critical was the fact that the local black ridership was becoming increasingly aware of and restive about these special patterns. If that city's blacks had made up an insignificant percentage of the bus system's passengers their growing dissatisfaction might have remained unimportant. What had been true of the 1930s no longer applied. By 1955 these harsh rules were being imposed on a bus ridership that was three-quarters black. Thus they were having an especially negative impact. By the year in question these "local bus customs" were felt by seventeen to eighteen thousand daily black riders. These twice-daily bus rides became frequent reminders to masses of Montgomery's blacks that they were an especially oppressed group. In this way questions about interracial bus patterns assumed far more importance and immediacy than other potential points of contention such as drugstore lunch counter customs.

It should be understood that while other issues were present, and strong resentment about some would ultimately become evident, the bus question was a natural to become a collective obsession with Montgomery's blacks. Such a natural that it became the first grievance collectively addressed by Montgomery's blacks in the 1950's. When Alabama blacks had been overwhelmingly rural residents and a single weekly Saturday visit to town had been the social rule, a bus system such as Montgomery's would not have had the same impact. With the mass relocation of poor and autoless blacks, though, came repeated exposure to harsh urban realities. Thousands of experiences such as Owen Butler's and countless daily conversations about them gradually convinced blacks that Montgomery's bus seating had to change to make it more reasonable. Despite these realizations Montgomery's especially impoverished blacks could not, as local whites had largely done by the mid 1950's, easily abandon the bus system.[13]

While the bus system's degrading practices irritated thousands of men like Butler, the rough and callous treatment white bus drivers routinely meted out to black women was an even more troubling source of mass frustration. In a social order where strong patriarchal values prevailed, and men of color shared such orientations, black women were characteristically denied the ritual courtesies that were deemed proper in the South. White bus drivers, many of whom were overworked and rushing to meet unrealistic expectations, remained largely oblivious to the effects their harsh and often vulgar commands had on black female passengers. Examining the sexual composition of Montgomery's black community allows one to understand why these patterns were especially critical to Montgomery's black female organizations. Table 4-3 describes the sexual composition of Montgomery's black community in the decades before the boycott's emergence.

Table 4-3
Sexual Composition of Montgomery's black Community

	Total	Male	Female	Males/100 Females
1920	19,827	8,553	11,274	75.9
1930	29,970	13,054	16,916	77.2
1940	34,535	14,942	19,593	76.3
1950	42,538	18,698	23,840	78.4

Source: U. S. Census

There is reason to suspect that of the daily riders, black females provided a proportion even higher than the sex ratio reflects. Thus any movement to protest bus treatment would have to have strong appeal with black women. It should be emphasized that the importance black women would assume during the protest was related as much to their calculated efforts to foment change as it was to their ratio in Montgomery's black population.

A small core of black women long dissatisfied with the particulars of local racial conditions began organizing themselves as the Woman's Political Council after several had been refused membership in the Montgomery chapter of the League of Women Voters. Such a rebuff was not unexpected, and minor forms of cooperation persisted between the black females and a few of the League's most liberal members. The refusal of the white organization to admit them, however, pushed the black woman to pursue a far more militant course in the years before the boycott's emergence. This is an important point in terms of the tone of political consciousness that emerged among Montgomery's local blacks. It is now obvious that since this group operated without the caution that was the hallmark of biracial groups of this era, Montgomery had a more highly aggressive and rhetorically militant group available to its black community. Their existence subtly forced other black leaders in Montgomery to develop corresponding appeals. Though militant, the Women's Political Council focused on minor reforms as they rapidly increased their membership and shaped their goals in the late 1940's and early 1950's. In this they were similar to other black organizations that mushroomed in Montgomery and throughout the South in the post-World War II era.[14]

Two other black grassroots organizations that had important following in Montgomery during the pre-boycott 1950s were the local chapter of the statewide Alabama Progressive Democratic Association and a group of black small businessmen organized as the Citizens Steering Committee. The fact that groups such as these were in place was a crucial social ingredient in Montgomery's black community. Such male groups were fairly diverse in their class makeup and affiliation patterns, thus contacts with a wide range of Montgomery's black citizens could be handled rapidly, which enhanced the protest action that was soon to emerge. More importantly, such groups provided valuable training for black secular leaders in an age and region where a conservative clergy had often been the dominant leadership force for both whites and blacks.

The personal qualities and experiences of the leaders of these groups, E. D. Nixon of the Progressive Democrats and a Fisk University-trained black mortician named Rufus Lewis of the Citizens Steering Committee, were such that connections throughout the state and region had been developed in the years before the boycott's emergence. All would be quickly but quietly utilized during the initial hectic stage of boycott organizing.

These decade-long developments took on added significance once a heightened pattern of bus driver-black female antagonisms began to tap bitter but previously latent resentments among Montgomery's blacks in the spring of 1955. This local pattern, appearing against a general backdrop of shifts in America's over-all approach to race relations that were generally heartening to blacks, provided final ingredients in the setting so that collective resistance became a distinct possibility for Montgomery's blacks.[15] As in other rapidly developing movements a series of dramatic incidents contributed to a final escalation of racial tension before the emergence of the active phase of the movement. Such a process is similar to stages long noted by social analysts.

The Series of Precipitating Incidents

As Neil Smelser notes, aggrieved groups may undergo a variety of experiences that create a sense of urgency and hasten mobilization for action in the formative stage of a social movement.[16] Smelser also indicates that precipitating incidents, whether they be points upon which rumors are built or catalytic events by themselves, are often among the final important collective experiences presaging a movement's formal appearance.[17] In the case of the bus protest a series of widely discussed arrests of black women for alleged misconduct galvanized sentiment among blacks in the months before December, 1955. It should be noted that incidents such as these had occurred rather routinely in the past, but by 1955 not all of Montgomery's blacks were willing to respond passively. A principal reason for this change was that by 1955 local leaders had created among their following a more heightened sense of willingness to act. This had been done by focusing internal organizational debate on the bus company and its policies. The impact of each arrest was correspondingly heightened since all were discussed by local leaders in their semi-public forums. These practices promoted a growing momentum of support for bus seating reform from diverse sectors of Montgomery's black community. The Woman's Political Council, because they met more frequently than other black organizations, were especially important in this building crescendo of debate and focus.

This leadership pattern influenced the black masses to recognize each arrest as fitting an overall and unfair bus seating pattern. Over time virtually none of Montgomery's blacks would believe official white positions that arrested passengers had engaged in misconduct. Perceptual change such as this is always a crucial final stage before a social movement can be successfully launched. When it had been achieved among black Montgomerians the stage was nearly set for activism to emerge. Given the underlying strain and diffused discontent long widespread among Montgomery's black citizens, an emerging leadership diagnosis that a boycott was needed would finally lack only an effective call for action. In time that too would be made. The particulars of the three arrest incidents suggest why this process was developmental and gradual and not immediate. The first arrest in 1955 was not especially unusual.

Claudette Colvin, a fifteen-year-old black student, was arrested on March 2, 1955, for refusing to give up her seat so a later arriving white passenger could be seated.[18] Ms. Colvin's arrest followed closely in the wake of an extraordinary February 23rd meeting between black and white candidates for municipal office. During that meeting local blacks, following the agenda of Progressive Democrat leader E. D. Nixon, had listed improved bus passenger treatment as their leading grievance. The assembled white candidates ignored that issue entirely while they offered competing promises about improved recreation facilities for local blacks. Since arranging and holding this first overtly political meeting was viewed as a major symbolic achievement by most of Montgomery's middle-class blacks, many were not put off by the white candidates' unwillingness to address their substantive grievances.[19] The leaders of the Woman's Political Council, however, were not easily pacified by what they considered to be mere token gestures.[20]

That group's president and vice-president, Jo Ann Robinson and Mary Fair Burks, were both members of the English Department at Alabama State University, and among the most militant of Montgomery's black intelligentsia. Bonds of friendship between the pair enhanced their organization's ability to pursue grievances with a vengeance and the Colvin arrest, because of her youth, was especially irksome. Thus Robinson and Burke advocated a temporary boycott of the buses in early March, 1955, to demonstrate the seriousness of concern blacks felt about this issue. E. D. Nixon, fearful that such actions might impair the re-election chances of a white liberal democrat his association was aligned with, quickly arranged for Colvin to plead not guilty to her arrest charge. Nixon then arranged for Ms. Colvin to be represented by one of Montgomery's only two black attorneys, twenty-four year old Fred Gray.[21] Nixon's actions and persuasion convinced Robinson and Burks that this March "crisis" could be handled more effectively through the local courts. While the pair of leaders and members of their group had doubts about the "legalistic" strategy Nixon had come to embrace as an NAACP official, they reluctantly recognized that no effective action could be launched without that legendary leader's support.[22] Thus the Colvin case, though frequently commented on within black community networks, became enmeshed in the Alabama court system.

By mid-summer 1955, drawn out legal maneuvers left the young female convicted of assault and battery on a police officer and placed on probation as a juvenile delinquent. This unsatisfactory resolution of the Colvin case nettled blacks, especially women like Burke and Robinson, throughout late summer and early fall. Most troubling to the leadership was the fact that despite two spring meetings with white bus officials no concessions had been won. Yet overt black opposition to bus patterns considered unsatisfactory was maturing, fueled by each such rebuff. Importantly, such failed negotiations, coupled with what most considered to be the totally unsatisfactory resolution of the Colvin case, enhanced the militant posture being staked out by the female leaders Robinson and Burke. The arrest of eighteen year old Louise Smith on October 21, 1955, reignited festering resentments among members of the Women's Political Council.[23] Smith, like Colvin, had refused to vacate her bus seat to allow a white more comfort. It was her curt refusal to comply with a bus driver's barked command that assured she would be arrested. In previous instances such as this, blacks would have been unceremoniously ejected, but by the fall of 1955 some white drivers appear to have begun enforcing their own informal version of a get-tough policy in the increasingly polarized atmosphere on the buses. They too had become more aroused in the wake of the Claudette Colvin case controversy.

The Louise Smith arrest increased pressures on E. D. Nixon and other black male leaders to address the grievance of bus passenger abuse in a more drastic fashion. When Nixon interviewed Smith to determine her suitability as a symbol to organize protest around, he found her residence to be a tar paper shack on the fringe of town, complete with a porchsitting father who remained in a continual drunken stupor.[24] By general but reluctant consensus, no effort was made to thrust Louise Smith forward as a symbol of an aggrieved black community. Quietly, mutual arrangements were made for Smith to admit her "guilt" and pay a token fine of five dollars.[25] Reaction to her case and the number of courtroom spectators it generated, alerted some of Montgomery's whites that things were seriously astir in local black ranks.

The intensity of feeling emerging from blacks angry about the bus system was to become fully expressed only after Mrs. Rosa MacCauley Parks was arrested the afternoon of December 1, 1955. Her arrest, the third in the series, proved to be the final spark needed to begin the process of movement activation.

A Third Dignity Seeker That Refused

In subsequent years Rosa Parks would be referred to as "ideal for the role assigned to her by history," "courageous," the "Mother of the Civil Rights Movement," or, surprisingly, as a woman with a "certain bitterness in her."[26] These characterizations are in sharp contrast to a few of the initial depictions of the bus boycott that omitted reference to her altogether.[27] It is this analyst's contention that both the post-boycott hyperbole and the earlier press omission of Rosa Parks' role in the protest distort the essence of her act. More importantly such a labeling phenomenon fails to contribute to a more general understanding of the significance of the Parks arrest and why it was especially able to generate decisive action from Montgomery's black leaders. To fully appreciate why that December 1, 1955 arrest proved so electrifying entails assessing Rosa Parks' social character and local reputation, while framing it within the context of the on-going bus seating controversy.

The Rosa MacCauley Parks of the mid-1950's should be viewed as one who shared several of the characteristics that typified the life-style of those previously referred to as Montgomery's emerging black middle-class. What Rosa MacCauley Parks lacked in objective economic measures necessary to confer such status, she made up for in value orientation. In this she was representative of thousands of black aspirants.

Rosa Parks placed a premium on sustaining family ties. She had learned and practiced the survival techniques all Southern blacks had to employ to avoid contacts with potentially abusive whites. Mrs. Parks was a quiet and reliable employee but one who was also an incessant reader of the increasingly pro-integrationist national black media. She, like others of her inner circle, had viewed with alarm the futile effort of the Ku Klux Klan to make an Alabama comeback in the late 1940's. In all these realms her life was fairly typical. Such biographical bits alone might have dictated her refusal to comply with a custom she had long abhorred, but other factors figured prominently in the December 1, 1955 Rosa Parks refusal. Chief among these other features was an evolving mother-daughter relationship that had set into motion the development of a worldview that had its final culmination that December day. Mrs. Parks describes her birthplace and the central figure in her early socialization in the following way

> My mother was a teacher in the rural schools of Montgomery County. For about two or three years she was my own teacher. She attended school at Selma, Alabama and in Montgomery at Payne University. The school there was organized by the A.M.E. Church and she attended the State Normal School (in Montgomery) which is now Alabama State University.
> She taught for awhile before she married. She met and married my father and moved to Tuskegee, Alabama. That's where I was born.[28]

Mrs. Parks speaks with the soft drawl of a Black Belt resident as she describes the painful days of her parents' marriage dissolution. Revealed is the leave-taking of a father whose spirit was broken by the Deep South's limited opportunity structure. The mother left behind seems to have refocused the family's hopes on young Rosa, an only and often lonely child. Mother-daughter conversations became serious at an early age, and were designed to gently instill in the young Rosa lofty goals and specific values. The most critical goal the young Rosa internalized was the necessity for educational achievement. A specific value orientation she quietly learned to treasure was that one had a moral obligation to resist dehumanizing treatment.[29] It should be noted that this orientation was not taught to the young Parks in direct fashion as the "Be A Man" philosophy was to Joe Reed. Rosa Parks' mother instilled ideas about personal dignity in ways that were more ambiguous, selective, but ultimately just as influential. Because of this there was a consistency in the development of Parks' consciousness that provides clues about how thousands like her formed values during the decades before the boycott. Only for reasons such as this should sociologists be intrigued by detailed personality analysis. Mrs. Parks recalls specifics of her mother's parenting strategy

> I think the only person she spoke very much about would be Dr. George Washington Carver and what he could accomplish as a scientist. She could've mentioned Dr. DuBois, but the very first thoughts I remember regarding public resistance to being humiliated as a slave was from Richard Allen, the founder of the A.M.E., when they set up the A.M.E. Church in Philadelphia.[30]

Her reference is to a religious leader who, along with a fellow black named Absalom Jones, founded the African Methodist Episcopal Church.[31] Rosa Parks had begun hearing such tales in Sunday School as a young member of Montgomery's A.M.E. Church. Mrs Parks, a life-long member of that denomination, was involved in a religious tradition that is considered one of the most conservative in public expressiveness among black Christians. Typically, members of A.M.E. Churches severely limit emotional display in their services and as a general rule promote public stoicism. The A.M.E.'s traditional theological approach also places heavy emphasis on the need of members to create an earthly domain where achieving human dignity becomes a real possibility.[32] Such an orientation remained very attractive to those, like Rosa Parks, who as adults longed for social respectability while finding themselves engulfed in a sea of racially degrading segregation practices.

In the years before her arrest, Rosa Parks, like thousands of others in her generation and congregation, stubbornly sought means to jettison anxieties about her self-worth. Religious orientations, which many clung to almost slavishly, usually provided some solace. Yet the persistence of segregationist customs was a constant irritant to her as she struggled to sustain a positive self-image. Given such shared tendencies, isolated acts of noncooperation by other A.M.E. members were not unheard of before her arrest. Importantly, when one became publicly labelled as a deviant for abridging the South's racial customs, the A.M.E. membership, both locally and nationally, tended to consecrate one as a true adherent.[33] Mrs. Parks was well aware of this traditional process, having long been announcements secretary in her Montgomery church.

While this religious emphasis was present in Mrs. Parks' personality, other personal qualities made her arrest especially galling to local blacks. Jo Ann Robinson, attempting to explain why this third in the series of arrests, the Parks case, aroused such bitter revulsion among the community's blacks declared simply:

Mrs. Parks she was a lady. You know what I mean? She was too sweet to even say damn in anger.[34]

While many viewed Mrs. Parks as epitomizing a tranquil, respectable female member of the emerging black "tie and collar" group in Montgomery, Parks was far more complex than that. She was also a "lady" with a long demonstrated progressive consciousness, and one with important ties to a community of activists built over time. These portions of her make-up did not become critical until after a childhood spent learning some essential values. Rosa Parks was an authentic product of the Black Belt.

She had been exposed to a variety of rituals and ideas that helped her to grasp the notion that black resistance to racial oppression had been a constant American theme. Like others in the rural Black Belt, she spent many youthful hours immersed in Afro-American music. This was an experience that seemed to reinforce the strong mother-daughter relationship. Rosa Parks recalled important specifics from the character of the music that permeated her youth:

Well we didn't have much to listen to. At the time the thing that was becoming popular was the victrola. But we never owned one. The most popular music was the church singing, the hymns, spirituals, and the blues. The blues were very popular. My mother used to sing a great deal. It came back to me so vividly at the King birthday celebration (in 1979). One thing she sang was O, Freedom Let It Ring, and Before I'd be a Slave I'd Be Buried in My Grave. She also sang We Shall Overcome.. But it was a different arrangement, didn't sound like today's.[35]

The young Rosa was not encouraged to sip from any "bitter blues" stream. Her mother followed what was locally a conventional if still rare pattern, as she sought to insure upward social mobility for her daughter. Mrs. MacCauley moved with the ten-year-old Rosa to Montgomery in the 1920's where Rosa was enrolled in Miss White's Montgomery Industrial School. This opportunity was a treasured one for black females in Alabama's Black Belt. In acting in this fashion Mrs. MacCauley had to make personal sacrifices that were highly unusual for one who had been a country school teacher. Rosa's mother had to both work as a domestic and take in sewing. The traditional skill of sewing had become what a young Rosa learned both at home and during the quiet years at Miss White's school. As she learned the skills that would later enable her to work respectably as a downtown seamstress, Rosa Parks resisted strong encouragement to be a public school teacher. Mrs. Parks' discussion of her reasons for resisting that career indicates that this reluctance was based principally on the quality of life she knew to be available to rural blacks in Alabama. As we sat in cold and drab Detroit in the late 1970s she remembers

> My mother wanted me to go into teaching and maybe I could have if I put my mind to it. But I thought the schools were just too segregated and oppressive. You didn't get much money for that.
>
> In my younger days I had wanted to be a nurse. I felt inclined to look after sick people. It could've been because I had been around so much illness with my grandfather and grandmother.[36]

The sensitive youth was unable to realize her career objective for a variety of reasons. Miss White's industrial training center closed before Rosa could graduate. While she later transferred to the black high school laboratory being run by Alabama State University, she left to care for an invalid grandmother before she could finish.

Within a few years of the termination of her education, she entered the restricted world of employment open to Montgomery's blacks. She also married. Despite minor changes in life she quietly retained an interest in migrating to the North. Rosa Parks' husband, who had a secure job as a barber at the local military installation and her mother, who continued to live with her, preferred that the family stay in the South. Both husband and mother, playing the role of "significant others" to Rosa Parks, also wanted to change the local racial status quo. Their actions seem to have provided basic ideals that Mrs. Parks continually reconfronted as she moved through the grey, dreary days of Montgomery's segregation as a maturing adult in the years before her December 1, 1955 arrest. This point is illustrated by the

444

process that led to Mrs. Park's joining the NAACP. She discusses that decision with some reluctance:

> My husband had been one of the charter members of Montgomery's NAACP. But by the time I joined he was no longer active. I never did hear him say why he lost interest, it could've been personal reasons. I . . . I can't say.[37]

As with most black political organizations, Montgomery's local NAACP was rife with factional disputes. While such wrangling often disillusioned individuals, in Mrs. Parks' case her husband never successfully interfered with her decision to try actions that might contribute to black progress in the post-World War II era. While her husband remained estranged from the organization, an old connection from her Montgomery Industrial School days strongly influenced her to consider joining the NAACP. Mrs. Parks remarked:

> I joined the NAACP after I saw Mrs. Johnnie Carr's picture in one of the newspapers. I saw Mrs. Carr's picture in the black paper, not the white paper. It was the *Alabama Tribune*. I remembered that she and I had been classmates at school so I thought to myself that . . . Johnnie Carr is a member.
>
> Actually that was my initial reason for going to the meeting, and eventually becoming a working part of the organization. I had plenty to do at the time, but I think what I was concerned about was what could be done to relieve the oppressive racial situation. I had also read in *Look* magazine about Walter White.[38]

Joining was not as automatic as Mrs. Parks' statement suggest. When she joined the NAACP in 1945 she was only the third black woman locally to do so. Besides Mrs. Johnnie Carr, Rosa Parks' mother joined the NAACP during the same week of her daughter's affiliation. Their involvement with the local NAACP introduced them to political activists like E. D. Nixon and other community leaders. In the late 1940's Mrs. Parks' continued involvement in the NAACP slowly expanded to include the all around duties associated with being a local chapter's secretary. In this role she annually compiled and forwarded to national headquarters dozens of field reports on mysterious deaths, unpublished rapes of black women by white males, instances of voter intimidation, and numerous other such incidents. Over time she became quietly embittered by such repeated exposure to the sordid underside of Montgomery's race relations. Mrs. Parks' feelings were seldom shared with others, but with her mother she was able to discuss them in detail as those two gradually sorted through ideas about how Montgomery's blacks should respond to such circumstances.

By the early 1950's Rosa Parks became the organizer of youth activities for the local NAACP and was becoming widely known for her gentle and generous devotion to the community's black youth. Mrs. Parks' rejection of all forms of segregation became progressively more fixed in those years after her first visit to the North and as a consequence of a Deep South experience that would later become famous as a result of its connection to Martin L. King, Jr.

In the summer of 1955, Martin L. King, Jr. was a guest at an interracial retreat sponsored by a white liberal group from Tennessee known regionally as the "Highlanders."[39] Years later when reactionary whites discovered a photograph of King taken during his visit to the Highlander Folk School, they pronounced it proof positive that he was a "tool of the Soviet-inspired conspiracy to bring about racial integration."[40] In the 1960's billboards with a blown-up photo of King fraternizing with the Highland Center's "known communists" became commonplace in the Deep South. Though it went largely undetected, Mrs. Parks was sitting next to King in that pre-boycott photograph. In another interview she described how that Tennessee experience influenced her

> That was the first time in my life I had lived in an atmosphere of complete equality with the members of other races, and I did enjoy going up there, and I felt it could be done without the signs that said "white" and "Colored"—well, without any artificial barriers of racial segregation.[41]

By late 1955 Rosa MacCauley Parks was moving rapidly toward her "historic moment" with an accumulating will to resist the arbitrary customs associated with Montgomery's system of segregation. Since she was deeply involved with Montgomery's black teenagers through her activities as the NAACP's youth director, Mrs. Parks had been especially rankled by the first two bus arrests in the series that would only end with a final one on December 1st. She had shared in the talk that lingered locally about the unfair circumstances blacks encountered on those vehicles. For Mrs. Parks, discussions of such issues evoked memories of sentiments inculcated both in youth and throughout a life that had become increasingly organized psychically against Montgomery's racial status quo.

On the afternoon of December 1, 1955, after a strenuous pre-Christmas rush day of kneeling at the feet of whites as a seamstress at Montgomery's largest department store, Rosa MacCauley Parks settled into one of the few remaining seats, anticipating another crowded, stomach-churning bus ride home. Two blocks later she was abruptly ordered to "get up, move back and stand", so that later arriving whites could sit. This as the bus moved through hilly, downtown Montgomery. Wearily, she quietly but firmly refused. This third 1955 refusal, the most quiet one, would be made into a mighty historic shout within a few days. This day, though, she was quickly arrested and rather gingerly booked by a few of the more well-behaved police of Montgomery.

When confronted that day, Rosa Parks had reached a psychic state that provided no option other than quiet refusal. While it seems obvious that a number of circumstances cascaded to a climax in the months before her refusal, assessing an incident that Rosa Parks' mother, an ever-present influence, discussed decades before that December 1, 1955 arrest may further clarify why this especially shy woman of color chose resistance. When asked if her mother had ever complained of being mistreated on account of her color, Mrs. Parks quietly recalled:

> She didn't accept it either. I remember her talking about something that happened in Montgomery. She was standing at the streetcar stop. Some white man came up and stood next to her. She wasn't noticing him at all. So he just started using a lot of profanity. He was cursing at her and, of course, she was really helpless. I heard her mention how upset she was but the only thing she could do was move further from where he was standing.
>
> She never mentioned everything that happened because those things would be pretty hard to discuss. Sometimes she'd be talking to someone else and I'd hear. I don't know if those things happened frequently but whenever they did I guess they left quite an impression.[42]

Such "things" from the 1920's and 1930's certainly did leave quite an impression. Not merely on a youthful Rosa Parks, but on thousands of other blacks throughout Alabama and Montgomery—as would that third and climatic arrest of December 1, 1955. Perhaps in the fleeting instant after the driver's command to move was given and her realization that she could not obey, Mrs. Parks recalled such memory fragments. To consider the previous plight of a mother who had also joined the "dangerous" NAACP and shared so many hurts, would seem somehow logical—as logical as refusing to move at the command of a rushing, "just doing his job" bus driver. But while such a third refusal, historically critical as it was, can be assessed narrowly in individual terms, Parks' case was most significant because it provided the essential spark that ignited a movement.

In the preceding chapter I described the crumbling social structure of Alabama's Black Belt. This chapter has given more of an indication of how key individuals began to form tentative conceptions of how they could shape the emerging order to achieve long desired gains. Montgomery's blacks were gradually coming to recognize that collective action was necessary if significant, as opposed to token, improvements were to be realized. Over a period of several months activist-prone leaders such as Jo Ann Robinson, Mary Fair Burks, and others came to believe that drastic measures must be taken against the important social lynchpin of the bus system. With these concerns in mind those who were action-oriented hoped to spur a massive response as Rosa Parks' arrest became known. While this turned out to be the case, there was nothing automatic about the process. With either social change or social movements there never is. A single act, or series of precipitating acts, do not a movement make. The pieces of this social movement still had to be brought together and a variety of means found to hold those elements in place until they solidified. That process is described in the following chapter.

FIVE

The Leap to
Activation

Analyzing the first stages of a social movement's emergence and ultimate routinization is a standard requirement for students of that phenomenon.[1] As I reviewed the events that transpired in the aftermath of the Rosa Parks arrest, it became obvious that classic patterns common to resistance efforts of this type were involved. The most significant of these developments had to do with the transformation in consciousness among the masses of Montgomery's blacks.[2] This shift in consciousness was indicated behaviorally in a multitude of ways. Among them were the appearance of thousands of participants at an initial mass rally; the near total withdrawal of black patronage from the bus system, and the substantial level of support given to the private carpool that had been quickly established by blacks. These actions all occurred within days of the December 1, 1955 Parks arrest. None of these circumstances would have been possible without a growing momentum for bus seating reform. Such momentum had grown throughout the series of three arrests discussed in Chapter Four. This verifies the maxim that to be authentic a social movement must emerge from the concrete grievances of a people. A group's emerging disposition requires focus and direction before effective protest actions can be made. For this to be accomplished leaders must perform vital functions and services when mass discontent allows the window sealed to social change to be nudged slightly ajar. Black Montgomery offered an abundance of individuals with these necessary skills and potential.

While Montgomery had a reservoir of black leaders who shared the community belief about the need for race relations change, there had never been a consensus about tactics. As word spread of the Rosa Parks arrest so too did the belief that a real victory might now be won. This early optimism and the masses' anger forced agreements upon local leaders long split by petty differences. This too is a commonly observed process during initial phases of social movements. While expectations among both masses and leaders varied tremendously during those initial days (as also seems typical of social movements) there was to be only a short period of euphoria before the reality of struggle was fully grasped. Students of social movements recognize that collective quests for change are very fragile and seldom successful. This effort, though, seemed destined for success just as it seems inevitable that a Rosa Parks "type" would not forever endure segregation.

Analysis of reform movements also yields the truth that these episodes of behavior invariably develop unique modes of expression and styles of participation in their earliest stages. This chapter's primary focus will be on the Montgomery bus boycott's initial active phase.

The Poised Women Seize the Perfect Arrest

As was noted earlier, members of Montgomery's Women's Political Council had been active in efforts to change local bus regulations throughout the summer and fall of 1955. Their activities after the Parks arrest escalated enough so that they deserved to receive the classic label of "social agitators." These activists came to regard such labels as terms of honor. Such a description fits because this small core of black women demonstrated great political moxey while operating within bureaucratic structures designed to inhibit any race relations reform. These women also forced decisive action from many black male leaders who had grown apathetic and timid. It is worth noting, however, that "agitators" such as these are only rarely able to directly implant the seeds of unrest. Blumer surmised that more often a movement's "agitators" are the type who, "intensify, release and direct the tensions which people already have."[3] Such "agitation," following Blumer's logic, facilitates collective morale and in other ways enhances *esprit de corps*. In the Montgomery boycott case, this was a task assumed immediately by the Women's Political Council through individuals such as Jo Ann Robinson and Mary Fair Burks.

Robinson had been among the first to be phoned by E. D. Nixon as he notified the small core of black activists in Montgomery following the Rosa Parks arrest. While Nixon sputtered with rage about this latest arrest, Robinson shrewdly agreed to attend the emergency meeting he was attempting to convene. She then began acting on her own to force at least a one-day boycott of the buses. This had been a joint Robinson-Burke hope during the previous summer of disappointment. Discussing the actions she took after Rosa Parks' arrest, Jo Ann Robinson remembers

> I called all of the officers of the group, all three of them, then I called the principals of schools because these women were members of the organization (Women's Political Council) . . . They were thrilled to help. At Alabama State University we had to be careful because we were under the direct control of the (State) Board of Education. So anyway, I called everybody who could get in touch with the young women. I also called every man who had made a contribution in helping us. I said to them, 'We the women have talked about this. Now what I would like to do is get these stencils made into about 20,000 fliers and get them out.'
>
> I took the responsibility for that, and I couldn't afford to let anybody help. I'm a good typist and after I typed them I ran them off. That was really difficult work doing that much. I got those things done and they were taken to the schools, every little black storefront, and corner by Friday. It just couldn't fail.[4]

Robinson's behavior was more complicated than that. With two trusted students, she had slipped into the basement of the Alabama State University administration building with only hours to spare before the leaflets were to be distributed. There they used the university's machines to duplicate the leaflets. Taking such a risk was necessary or the full impact of Robinson's plan would have been threatened. When the three departed they split up to deliver parcels of leaflets to the dozens of women who belonged to the association Robinson and Burke headed.[5] This was bold action within the context of the 1950s. All participants knew that possession of such material could cause immediate dismissal for those who were public school teachers. While dismissals of public school teachers would later became almost commonplace in the South no such reprisals were made in Montgomery. Sensitive acts such as these could be carried out successfully only because of the strong cohesion that had developed after years of organizational solidarity. Predictably, a few of the black women became nervous simply because they were holding "hot" material, and this too facilitated the quick action Robinson believed was necessary. Those who were most nervous got rid of their packets especially fast.

By early Friday evening, December 2, hundreds of Robinson's leaflets announcing a mass meeting and calling for a December 5, 1955, one-day boycott of the buses had been distributed. Ironically, most went to Montgomery's black settlements via the hands of children who were never to benefit from the 1954 *Brown v. Board of Education* Supreme Court

451

decision. Thus the persistence of racial segregation actually facilitated acts that chipped its foundation away. More important from Jo Ann Robinson's perspective was that this tactic assured that the word would begin spreading during the crucial hours of the weekend's start. Such an acute sense of timing would assist those who were just learning how to become effective protestors on numerous occasions during the course of the boycott.

Some of the credit for informing Montgomery's blacks about plans for the protest has been given to a politically moderate journalist named Joe Azbell, a white who wrote for the *Montgomery Advertiser*. Azbell reprinted the contents of the Robinson leaflet in a December 4, 1955 *Advertiser* column.[6] While phrasing his description of the pending boycott in a way that remained acceptable to the generally white readership, Azbell's message also reached some local blacks who were unaware of the pending "crisis." This was in line with the wishes of E. D. Nixon, the source of Azbell's tip. This "Azbell-Nixon" news connection, established during the early 1950s when Nixon became active in Montgomery's local politics, proved to be an especially important link in the early stages of the protest. The existence of such a relationship in Montgomery takes on added importance when it is realized that so few close "local black-local white journalist" connections were available in later civil rights campaigns. The implications of such rare alliances needs to be seriously explored. During the initial days of the boycott's emergence such a news plant was, because of Nixon's numerous other actions, merely one of several tactics used to inform and arouse Montgomery's blacks about both the Parks arrest and the evolving plans for a protest. Nixon, and his political allies, Robinson and Burke, continued to move rapidly because they sensed they had to outflank the generally conservative local black clergy.

After the Parks arrest it seems clear that Nixon, who immediately mobilized old allies from the Progressive Democrat club and local Pullman Porters, and Robinson and Burke, through their leadership of the Women's Political Council, were issuing a twin challenge. Being put on notice were those whites who controlled the bus system, as well as the most timid of Montgomery's black "leaders" who had previously been reluctant to question any white authority figure. As the leafletting and Azbell's column circulated word of an impending action these old-line black conservatives were snared. They found themselves being forced to publically support the "reasonable" one-day protest or they could run the risk of appearing to be either indecisive or a racial traitor. Few chose the latter. This pattern also allowed more militant black leaders to retain effective control of the movement as it was becoming active.

With the Montgomery activists in firm initial control, their top priority became elaborating a strategy that would elicit mass support. Issues such as rearranging the local leadership hierarchy had to be ignored as the enormous task of coordinating the escalating activities began to be assumed. In those first few hours chaos seemed to reign. If a "movement" was to be seized from jumbled circumstances the militants believed they had to have the support of the entrenched black leaders. This reality was faced squarely by activists who initially sublimated powerful ego drives in hopes of achieving the goal of generating a popular movement. While most focused on the necessity to avoid allowing the emerging momentum to be lost, two activist-oriented blacks quietly moved to create an important role for one who would go on to have a major impact on both the boycott and the direction of modern American history.

A (M.L.) King (Jr.) is Anointed

Martin Luther King, Jr.'s evolution as a Montgomery boycott participant marked a critical turning point in his career. This bus boycott was his baptism in social activism, and its general characteristics shaped his consciousness in ways that remained consistent until his death.[7] While the Montgomery events had a serious influence on King's career, his effect on the boycott's development is more difficult to gauge. A central cause of this problem has been that much of King's earliest leadership behavior remains unexamined. King, like leaders of all modern movements, soon found himself with bureaucratic responsibilities to handle, dissident elements to placate, and a variety of other periodic crises to contend with. Though King's claim that he was aware of such burdensome responsibilities before his Montgomery experience now seems dubious, he had ample reason to be familiar with such requirements by the conclusion of that struggle.[8] While judging King on how he handled such role expectations is important, so too is exploring the maneuvers that thrust him toward the front line of race leadership.

The process that resulted in King's nomination as spokesman for blacks in Montgomery owes something to his being "discovered" in the months prior to the arrest of Mrs. Rosa Parks. There are several contenders vying for the prestige associated with having made the discovery of King's leadership

453

potential. With this being the case self-serving accounts have to be scrutinized carefully. Evidence suggests that two individuals were most critical in this process.

In recent years E. D. Nixon has become recognized as one who might have been an alternative to Martin L. King, Jr. to lead the Montgomery protest. While reasons discounting this possibility have been discussed in Chapter Four, Nixon's version of King's rise to the top implies that it was he who hoped to lure the young minister into accepting the role of protest spokesman. Nixon claims that his strategy of leadership "entrapment" began the night of the Parks arrest as he started circulating word of that matter. Martin L. King, Jr., the twenty-seven year old minister of the church that Nixon, Robinson and Burke all attended, was the third person Nixon phoned. After informing King of the catalytic Parks arrest, Nixon inquired if King were willing to get involved. In his book, *Stride Toward Freedom*, King claimed to have "agreed at once" and to have offered his Dexter Avenue Baptist Church as a meeting place.[9] Nixon remembered their conversation differently. He chuckled while insisting that King's response was "Brother Nic, let me think about it for awhile."[10]

Nixon claims he phoned sixteen others before talking again with King to discover if he had decided to cooperate with the actions being planned. After King's affirmative response Nixon claims he joked with the recent arrival that

I'm glad of that 'cause I've called eighteen other people and they all said yes, and I told them we were all gonna meet at your church this evening.[11]

While King's hesitation made Nixon initially wary of his reliability under pressure, the choice of Dexter Avenue Baptist Church as a meeting place was calculated. Dexter Avenue Baptist was and remains black Montgomery's most prestigious religious institution. It fit a category that was beginning to characterize the South of the 1950's: a community with urban blacks supporting at least one politically progressive church. In Montgomery, Dexter Avenue Baptist had filled this role since the mid 1940's. By slyly arranging to have the initial meeting of leaders at Dexter, Nixon knew that he had a good chance to consolidate the support of its all-crucial "tie and collar" crowd. Nixon also recognized that his selection of this site would probably give strong impetus to King's selection as spokesman for the emerging protest. This too figured in his decision to meet at Dexter Avenue Baptist. While he would not be the one to formally propose the nomination,

Nixon was among a handful who had heard King speak specifically about race relations in Alabama in the early months of 1955. Such exposure had left Nixon convinced that King's appointment as spokesman would be more than just satisfactory. Another local black who shared Nixon's view of King's political potential, but who had become an organizational rival of Nixon's Pullman Porters, was responsible for the actual strategy that propelled King into the role of the protest spokesman.

A soft-spoken mortician named Rufus Lewis, at the time one of Montgomery's most affluent blacks, was also very aware of King's personal qualities. He too conspired to push the newcomer forward. Lewis, as was true of many of his associates, had strong reservations about the splintered ranks of religious figures who had traditionally been thought of as local black "leaders." That group's tradition of jealousies and petty wrangling had occasionally undercut previous protest efforts. Being a mortician had allowed him ample first hand evidence of these patterns and Lewis was especially worried that these old "know-nothings" be outflanked. To get around this generation of older, conservative black ministers Lewis conspired with a friend to replace the temporary chairman of the still-organizing group, Reverend Roy Bennett, with King. Lewis describes how the tone of the first leadership meeting at Dexter Baptist Church prompted his action

> I knew many of the other ministers and some of the other persons who headed the organizations, 'cause I had been active here all my life. and the meeting . . . was such a dissatisfying thing to me that P.E. Conley and I went to talking about it. And I said this Reverend Bennett, he, he can't direct this thing. And, well I suggested that we try and get Reverend King.
>
> Now I had made no contact with Reverend King or nobody else. But I was reacting to the confused situation we faced in that first week. And that was the sole reason for my nominating Reverend King. I hadn't talked to E. D. Nixon or anybody else. No one except P.E. Conley. He and I decided that . . . let's get somebody else. I mentioned King's name and told him to try and get some support and that I would try and get some support.[12]

Before the second meeting Lewis insured support for a Martin L. King, Jr. chairmanship by making certain that key members of the Citizens Club (a voter registration lobby group Lewis headed) were there to vote for his "candidate." In this action the then fiftyish Lewis and his followers recognized that in King they were proposing a candidate similar to dozens of other aspiring black leaders in the South during the mid-1950's. They had watched carefully as the young churchman had been tested in the emerging

Montgomery political trends throughout 1955. They saw both talent and poise and hoped he had courage. Lewis was as impressed as E.D. Nixon had been and he decided to act. Though unaware of it King had been pushed into a political corner, one that left him little room to avoid being "anointed." Given the history of the church he pastored, he undoubtedly anticipated playing a role as an activist, but this move must have seemed too sudden for him.

As a natural consequence of heading the local "political " church, Martin L. King, Jr. found himself deeply immersed in such circles. The events at Dexter Avenue the week prior to the Parks arrest suggest what was coming to typify the black political vanguard that King had to minister to. *The Birmingham World*, the only statewide black newspaper of the 1950's reporting on Montgomery's community currents with depth and clarity, noted that on November 27, 1955, an evening program at Dexter Avenue Baptist would feature Dr. T. R. M. Howard. As president of the Mississippi Regional Council of Negro Worship, Howard had become a regionally known orator with skills honed from hundreds of speeches delivered throughout the South of the 1950s. Howard chose as his topic that week "Mississippi Shame Story: Desegregation A Way Station, Integration Our Goal." Howard's Dexter Avenue Baptist Church statements typified sentiments that were coming to characterize the views of the South's new blacks. He advocated strong resistance to archaic racial customs and insisted that 1955 might be a time when Southern blacks begin to plan a "March on Washington."[13] The young, hosting minister King listened quietly as he was exposed to yet another speaker with a militant frame of reference that would influence his worldview. T. R. M. Howard, however, was not around when the boycott's public leader had to be selected.

King's youthful demeanor and speaking abilities, however, were sufficient to convince his "sponsors" that he might be an adequate spokesman for what was still, in the first days of December, 1955, a very uncertain social movement. As King quietly accepted what Nixon and Lewis had accomplished he did so with a simple "If that's what y'all want I'll do my best . . ."[14]

King's performance after finding himself "drafted" chairman and spokesman of the newly christened Montgomery Improvement Association verified the wisdom of his elders.

Getting the Spirit to Walk

With an organizational structure being erected and a leader with potential in place, the Montgomery activists continued to mobilize support for what was being announced initially as a one-day boycott of Montgomery's public buses. During the weekend of December 3-4, 1955, local blacks were still hearing details of the "perfect" arrest of Rosa Parks as Nixon and his close associates made plans for what they secretly hoped would be a protracted struggle. Mary Fair Burks and Jo Ann Robinson continued exchanging ideas with local ministers so that instructions could be delivered from pulpits on the morning of Sunday, December 4, while Nixon's Pullman Porter associates made contacts with black taxi drivers to begin convincing them to help. All wondered whether local blacks would resist the temptation to ride the buses on the 5th of December. Though the activists worried, the vast majority of those masses needed little help to recognize that the indignities of rural segregation had been replaced by a cruel form of urban injustice. They needed even less assistance deciding that one day of walking might be "good medicine for Montgomery's white folks." Their decisions made, many of those who supported the protest begin to feel an excitement that resembled the state of mind sociologists refer to as contagion.[15] The events of Monday, December 5, spurred this development.

The December 6, 1955 afternoon edition of the *Montgomery Advertiser* carried a report with the headline, "5,000 At Meeting Outline Boycott; Bullet Clips Bus." The article goes on to describe masses of "hymn-singing Negroes" in a "packed" Baptist church, voting to continue the bus boycott against the Montgomery City Lines. The article touches on several aspects of the initial day's activity that need analysis. This clarification is essential because several patterns that would enable the protest to be a long term success were in evidence. First, mass participation in previously established cultural practices—in this case hymn singing and other forms of traditional ritual expression—helped sustain comfort and solidarity as Montgomery's blacks began to experience direct involvement in protest activities. In a sense the use of such familiar religious settings and rites provided further legitimacy to the notion that a secular protest movement was now acceptable. Setting was important because generations of Southern blacks had been instructed to bring all their grievances to the Lord's altar. As the boycott was breaking black churches were now centers encouraging political activism in what was, in the mid 1950's, a marked departure from their past. Actually the rapidly unfolding developments in Montgomery had positioned that community's black churches so that they had little choice in supporting the "new day's dawn." Thus by organizing through these social vehicles Montgomery's militants put themselves in league both with the "almighty" and, more practically, forced the hand of local black clergy.

Secondly, the "packed and overflowing" turnout, demonstrated conclusively that support for continued protest actions was readily available and that bold leadership had become acceptable. With such a massive outpouring of support, fears conservative black leaders had about their involvement were effectively dissipated. Such a turnout, so carefully engineered by the militant leaders, also verified that, at least in Montgomery, the time had come for action. Additionally, these militant leaders were astute enough to engage in procedures, in this case a ritual "vote" among a group still largely ignored politically, that sought to instill in those masses the notion that both their support and active participation mattered. With a people still not used to being "counted" such procedures themselves, even if only perfunctory, were bound to strike a responsive chord.

Finally, the second part of the headline, "Bullet Clips Bus," illustrates a point that is often overlooked when the Civil Rights movement is analyzed. Real or implied threats of retaliatory black violence aimed at either random whites or race "traitors" influenced the course of events. Though this dynamic resists measurement, its existence must be acknowledged. While personal responsibility for firing the shot was never established, its occurrence demonstrated that Montgomery contained at least a few blacks with such strongly-held beliefs that behavior of this type threatened to ignite a blood bath. Though Montgomery contained blacks such as this the protest's leaders refused to acknowledge them publicly. Yet the shot sobered the protest's leaders since it forced them to recognize that their rapidly recruited ranks included some anonymous zealots who might use any means to express their support for this newest of causes. Mindful of this possibility the protest's organizers began the arduous task of reinforcing among neophyte followers that only "Christian" protest tactics were to be used. Support from Montgomery's black "tie and collar" groups and the traditionally religious masses depended on such "plain commonsense" tactics. Malcolm X and his tactical advice would not be attractive or, indeed, heard of in Montgomery for several more years.

Though arcane quibbling about the issue of nonviolent tactics would eventually preoccupy the boycott's pragmatic leaders, no such debate was necessary on that first, fragile day. Within hours of that shot dozens of church deacons, pullman porters, and ex-soldiers attending Alabama State University had been sent through Montgomery's black settlements on their own "hot head" control mission. While they found only a few who needed such counseling this wave of personnel seized another opportunity to reinforce the general strategy and remind the people about the Monday night mass meeting. This would be the meeting that would provide the final ingredients necessary for turning an incipient movement into a sustained crusade.

While that December headline captured essential elements of that meeting's significance other events occurred that helped sustain the group's initial morale. During the course of that Monday night meeting the assembled throng, already electrified by their one day triumph, was presented a Rosa Parks who had become a fully processed "judicial martyr." Following the then traditional swift and sure approach in responding to black infringements of its racial caste barrier, Montgomery's local judiciary had convicted Mrs. Parks of violating the City's bus segregation ordinance that very morning. Thus when the prim Mrs. Parks was presented to the collected throng they now saw her as an important local example in a long line of Southern black "innocents" who had been falsely arrested and rapidly convicted for breaking unjust laws. Blacks who can be effectively presented as "judicial martyrs", whether they be the Scottsboro Boys of the 1930's or members of the black Panther Party in the 1960's, have often provided a powerful stimulus for sustained public resistance. Thus by processing Rosa Parks with such rapidity, Montgomery's white power structure unwittingly handed the mobilizing group a "completed" heroine.

A final factor that provided Montgomery's blacks with the *esprit de corps* necessary to sustain active resistance was the effect of Martin L. King, Jr.'s initial boycott address. While it is probable that the dynamics already discussed were sufficient to promote support for a continued protest, King's speech provided a coherent set of ideas to justify that decision. A systematic set of ideals and justifications for them are often among the crucial features of a sustainable movement. Montgomery's protest as it moved now toward becoming a sustained boycott was no exception.[16]

The Ideas of Noncooperation Brilliantly Espoused

While Martin L. King, Jr. had been recognized as having enough leadership potential to be selected as public spokesman for the MIA, he was still generally unknown before what was to be his first major address. Assessing the impact that mini-sermon had on its audience is important because this was the speech that clearly established King and his "vision of protest" as legitimate. This speech would also give strong hints of the charismatic style that would be part of his appeal for the rest of his life.

The young Martin L. King, Jr., like Southern Baptist preachers black and white, worked hard at the craft of rhetorical flamboyance.[17] After years of speech contests and small talks to intimate audiences he understood perfectly when to use a strategic pause, sensed the possibilities that might be elicited if his head tilted with the correct line, and had mastered nuances of intonation that gave his impressive vocabulary even more flexibility.

Though it is difficult to assess whether King's personal style had more of an impact on assembled masses than did the content of his ideas, it is clear that over time their combined effect could be telling. As is often the case with a social movement, the direct consumers of King's messages were unconcerned with such issues. King's deft blend of style and ideals generated immediate and intense popular support from Montgomery's blacks. After that first mass meeting all participants, King included, would recognize this to be the case. While the youthful King had considered it undignified and manipulative to utilize emotional preaching ploys to stir support from an audience, on many occasions, including this first speech, his intellectual instincts gave way when it became practical to use rhetorical splendor. By the end of this Montgomery campaign King would understand better that the effective race leader in the South was one who could help transform collective excitement into mobilized resistance. At times this had to be done even if it meant adopting a "preacher's approach," where traditional emotionalism was resorted to.

In an important discussion of this issue, Hortense Spillers indicates that King's sermon style typically placed heavy emphasis on "picturesqueness" and "grandness" of speech.[18] This combination plus King's persistent use of metaphors was thought to be an especially effective way of drawing stark symbolic contrasts between the forces of good and evil. Those tendencies were evident in his address to those who assembled at the Holt Street Baptist

Church for that first mass meeting. King's address that evening included the following extended passage

> There comes a time. (long pause) There comes a time when people get tired—tired of being segregated and humiliated, tired of being kicked about by the brutal feet of oppression. (long pause as response builds)
>
> We had no alternative but to protest! For many years we have shown amazing patience. We have sometimes given our white brothers the feeling that we liked the way we are being treated. But we come here tonight to be saved from that patience that makes us patient with anything less than freedom and justice. (long pause as response to speaker reverberates throughout church)
>
> One of the great glories of democracy is the right to protest for right. The white Citizen's Council and the Ku Klux Klan are protesting for the perpetuation of injustice in the community. We are protesting for the birth of justice in the community.
>
> Their methods lead to violence and lawlessness. But in our protest there will be no cross burnings. No white person will be taken from his home by a hooded Negro and brutally murdered. There will be no threats and intimidation. Our method will be that of persuasion, not coercion. We will only say to the people: 'Let your conscience be your guide!' Our actions must be guided by the deepest principles of our Christian faith. Love must be our regulating ideal. Once again we must hear the words of Jesus echoing across the centuries: 'Love your enemies; bless them that curse you, and pray for them that despitefully use you.' (audience on its feet shouting in response)
>
> If we fail to do this our protest will end up as a meaningless drama on the stage of history, and its memory will be shrouded with the ugly garments of shame. In spite of the mistreatment that we have confronted, we must not become bitter and end up hating our white brothers. As Booker T. Washington said: 'Let no man pull you down so low as to make you hate him.' (overwhelming response including shout)
>
> If you will protest courageously and yet with dignity and Christian love, when the history books are written in future generations, the historians will have to pause and say: 'There lived a great people—a black people—who injected new meaning and dignity into the veins of civilization.' This is our challenge and our overwhelming responsibility.[19]

This message was delivered to a crowd who had been spurred to defiance by long-standing grievances with segregation's circumstances in general and by a year-long spiral of events that occurred on the strategically sensitive Montgomery bus lines in particular. While they had become aroused by intolerable conditions King's coherent explanation and call to action provided the movement an important ideological tone. If movements are to negotiate the social territory from outraged response to coherent and sustained resistance such a complex of ideas is necessary.[20]

King's mini-sermon, while delivered spontaneously, provided the necessary, but highly effective condemnation of an existing social pattern—"the brutal fact of oppression"—while also giving clear insights about what Montgomery's blacks had to do if they were to deserve the prized status of "moral citizen"—"protesting for the birth of justice in the community." Other rhetorical techniques also made King's talk especially effective. King's use of rhythmic repetition, as when he made clear the contrasts between injustice and justice and the whites' historic use of extralegal coercion versus his new call for persuasion, were well within the traditional range of rhetorical devices used by Southern Baptist preachers. Finally, what made this first address highly unusual was that King, while using traditional black religious rituals, did so to justify a secular movement. As he explained so effectively, Montgomery's blacks were faced with ". . . no alternative but to protest" after years of "amazing patience." He reminded his listeners that to do less would be to clothe themselves in the "ugly garments of shame."

While King defended the legitimacy of the protest's actions his speech scarcely mentioned the long-range policies or tactics that would have to be employed. This omission was not an oversight. The emerging movement's leader, aware of local past failures, did not wish to be overly precise about such matters. As King's stirring message propelled the masses with renewed fervor, those who operated behind the scenes moved feverishly to fill the boycott's tactical void. As E. D. Nixon, Jo Ann Robinson, Rufus Lewis, and other activist-oriented blacks worked through the night of December 5, 1955, to erect a more permanent protest structure, they did so buoyed by the knowledge that in King they had found a highly effective communicator for the group's evolving ideals and goals.

As the one-day "protest" became recognized as a bus boycott in the first days of December, 1955, it received national publicity in the weeks that followed. As America's attention began to be focused on the novelty of Southern blacks protesting effectively in the traditional citadel of the old Confederacy, Martin L. King, Jr.'s stature would grow along with support for the movement. This was not accidental—on the contrary it can best be understood as a consequence of tactics adhered to during the middle stages of the boycott. If the boycott had collapsed at this point so too might have any national career for King. That the movement did not falter had to do both with its ability to generate material support from other regions, and with tactics pursued by whites who were responsible for leading the local opposition. Chapter Six describes important aspects of this phase of the movement.

SIX

The Failure
of Moderation:
The Crackdowns
that Followed

Days after entering its active phase the protest's participants began to exhibit behavior that would justify the application of social labels such as (1) recognized leaders (2) activist followers (3) passive supporters and (4) skeptical sympathizers.[1] Rapid routinization of this sort is rather unusual but given the circumstances discussed in Chapter Four, the boycott's pattern is not surprising. As that chapter made obvious, strong momentum for change had been latent among Montgomery's blacks. Though the intensity of those sentiments had finally been acted on, several problems had the potential to disrupt the still fledgling movement.

One issue the newly recognized leaders had to immediately address was the logistical problem of providing assistance to the thousands whose urban work rhythms required modern transit. If this issue had not been quickly confronted serious consequences would have followed. This is so because the normal euphoria associated with a popular movement's emergence wears thin quickly when critical personal routines are disrupted as severely as they were being in Montgomery. As previously noted the protest's leaders clearly understood that something had to be done to cope with this potential problem. Though arrangements had been made with local black cab drivers to provide cheap rides for commuting workers, none of the protest's leaders imagined that resolving this issue would ultimately require several weeks. Such an interim step had been taken because the protest's leaders were convinced initially that their struggle would last only a few weeks. They were soon to discover that even a "reasonable" protest such as theirs also produced a series of harsh measures designed to weaken and ultimately destroy their movement's foundation. This chapter explores such issues and related dilemmas that surfaced during the early rounds of negotiations between Montgomery's black and white leaders.

The results of those negotiations, compounded by several short-sighted tactics engaged in by the protest's opponents, provided a powerful stimulus to the movement's growing internal cohesion. In that sense the verbal sparring that characterized the early face-to-face encounters strongly reinforced the resolve of the protest's adherents while giving its leaders more time to effectively structure their opposition. Those negotiations are important to review before the boycott's evolving inner dynamics can be fully understood.

The Apologetic Approach is Rejected

Mid-1950s Montgomery, like few Southern localities of its size, had a developed pattern of black-white negotiations before the protest's emergence.[2] While these interchanges had not produced substantive race reforms, the fact that they had occurred was important to the boycott's evolution. Because of this history only a few of Montgomery's white leaders doubted that such talks should actually occur. Numbers played an important role in motivating this initial appearance of white reasonableness. As has been noted, with blacks forming such a substantial proportion of the bus system's patrons their periodic request for "grievance discussions" had begun to be seriously, though perhaps grudgingly, considered in the early 1950's. As a result some black residents considered the bus company to be a relatively enlightened corporation for permitting this type of interchange. Enlightenment had little to do with this then rare policy. After the protest's start the empty buses demonstrated in raw terms just how much dependence on black patronage could matter. As all began to recognize that the protest was a real racial crisis, city officials hoped that Montgomery's white citizenry would be sophisticated and tolerant enough so that few questions would be raised about whether talks should occur. Though the bus company's management had little choice in this matter, their willingness to negotiate may also have been predicated on their more general belief that since no major concessions had been granted blacks in previous interchanges, little might now have to be offered to resolve this latest bus crisis. These newest circumstances, however, were those of a forming movement, and not merely another temporary crisis. This reflected the local variation of a larger trend that most of the South's white leaders neglected to detect or accept in the 1950's and early 1960's. Before this protest Southern whites generally refused to acknowledge that a new corps of Southern black leaders had matured and that these new types could pursue grievances with skill and determination. In Montgomery local blacks of this kind were in the boycott's forefront from its start.

Even before the boycott's active phase many of Montgomery's more militant blacks had gradually become convinced that talks with bus officials or other white leaders would probably be futile unless blacks were in a bargaining position with some strength. The protest's emergence now provided one of the first opportunities for these emerging blacks to seek racial change. With unprecedented black unity being daily demonstrated these local leaders now believed that they had achieved sufficient leverage to win important reforms in the bus system. What they would seek to change still remained to be determined. Holding meetings between their chaotic efforts to bring order to the developing private carpool arrangement, E. D. Nixon, Ralph Abernathy, Rufus Lewis, King, Jo Ann Robinson and about a dozen of their counterparts hammered out a minimum set of principals they believed local whites could gracefully accept. The group's goals were generally modest because many of the more traditional black leaders retained lingering doubts about the long-term possibility of sustaining an effective boycott. Trying to preserve unity, key local militants agreed to a package of requests that they had strong reservations about.[3] Some would later say they acquiesced because a set of grievances had to be quickly presented, given the natural demands of the social drama underway. The protestors' "requests" do seem minimal considering the long standing psychic abuses the bus system's customs had inflicted. These matters were to be addressed on December 8, 1955.

In the first negotiating session following the boycott's formal inception, Montgomery's blacks indicated their willingness to call off the four-day-old protest action if three largely symbolic reforms were adopted by the bus company.[4] Speaking for the protestors, King's first request was that bus seating be provided all patrons on a first-come, first-served basis with blacks filling buses from rear to front and whites reversing that pattern. No sections would have been specifically reserved for either race according to this remedy.

467

More importantly, the forced reassignment of seats, the policy at the crux of the three precipitating arrests discussed in the previous chapter, would have been discarded if this suggestion had been agreed to. While protecting the dignity of black riders in this regard was obviously thought to be important, so too was the second request King made for the group he represented.

Montgomery's blacks, as King explained, wanted renewed and specific assurances that in the future normal courtesy from all drivers would be extended to patrons regardless of their race. This too was an important dignity issue reflecting an abusive pattern that had rankled local blacks over the years. Such dignity issues seemed at the heart of this current dispute. As mentioned earlier, the news of the specifics of the final arrest and quickly emerging protest had rekindled local blacks' bitter memories of bus drivers using vulgar language, their refusal to open doors and make scheduled pick-ups and stops for black patrons, and a range of other complaints that had simmered for years. King's position as spokesman now obligated him to convey both the content and renewed intensity of these specific grievances though he, like hundreds of other middle-class blacks, had never set foot on a local bus. Though this was the case, King and his colleagues effectively presented the harsh specifics that fueled this grievance.

Finally, a third request was made, aimed at satisfying those who were chiefly concerned with the issue of black economic advancement. In this matter, King communicated the desire that "negro drivers" be hired to serve Montgomery's predominately black routes. This request was of extreme importance to E. D. Nixon, whose grass-roots organizing had put him in contact with hundreds of black men who had hopes that they could hold dignified and clean jobs. Many of these, who were called the "forgotten fellows" by Nixon, had been servicemen in Korea in the early 1950's and possessed documented skills in driving large vehicles. Largely ignored by their government and many local "tie and collar" blacks, these individuals were appealed to by this request, and in other ways by leaders like E. D. Nixon.

Interestingly, such initial requests, even if they had been agreed to, would have left the core of the bus system's segregation customs largely intact. In that respect they represented a distinct departure from the promises King had made to the thousands who had gathered for the mass meeting held earlier in the week. Their mild tone also reflected the strong internal pressure being directed at King to restrain his personal inclination to advocate complete desegregation of the bus system. That the youthful King abided by this collective dictum amply demonstrates that at this point he was still a "spokesman" and not the group's unquestioned leader. Even King's personal bearing during this first negotiating session was in marked contrast to his behavior of a few days earlier in the week.

For the first time King faced the sobering task of face-to-face negotiations with Southern whites. Whether deliberate or not, King completely jettisoned his integrationist bombast. Carefully avoiding topics he had outlined during the first mass meeting, King now stiffly insisted that the group he was speaking for was not actually seeking the demise of segregation. Instead, rapid and progressive solutions to local grievances were more critical according to the now circumspect King. Remarkably, so mild had this "negotiator" King become that he failed even to mention that blacks also wanted always to be allowed to board Montgomery's buses through the front door! But all could not be remembered during those initial days of countless meetings that had stretched for hours. King was exhausted as were others during the December 8 meeting.

Others who were involved in the backroom deliberations that had produced the three initial black "requests" later expressed mild amusement when reminded of the relative modesty of their earliest bargaining position. Rufus Lewis smiled broadly at the memory of those earliest sessions. Then he implied that several in the black group hoped to allow whites to respond in a positive way so that bad feelings would not forever poison local race relations. Lewis tried to explain why certain blacks preferred a low key approach in the following manner

The only reason I can give is that we were reacting to something that to our way of thinking was very bad. We were trying to do the reasonable thing to stop it. And the thing we asked for was to be seated from the back of the bus to the front. I think we were trying to be reasonable. Remove what the past had been. We were trying to take a gradual approach then.[5]

When asked to speculate about what might have occurred if King's initial call for full integration had been forcefully pursued Lewis noted

It's hard to say. But the thing is that it was a growth. We were greeted with a situation where we were treated very badly and we wanted to correct this step by step. But as we moved forward *the whole horizon seemed to open wider for us. And the wider it is the further you're going to go*. That was the type of development.[6]

While Lewis' assertion that local blacks were trying to move "step by step" is basically accurate, no horizons opened vista-like in the boycott's initial days. This was especially true of relations between the negotiators. One factor contributing to what soon became an impasse was the hardening posture being taken by Montgomery's white city commissioners. This was in contrast to trends that had seemed favorable in previous months.

During early 1955 deliberations, many months before this protest's emergence, a white "moderate" named David Birmingham had sought to sooth interracial antagonisms about bus arrangements in the hope that a few seating "adjustments" might be granted. Birmingham, acting in his capacity as a Montgomery city commissioner, had played a conciliatory role in a futile attempt to reconcile blacks and whites after the Colvin arrest of February 1955.[7] As negotiations were initiated in this atmosphere of acute crisis though, David Birmingham was unavailable. Strong political pressure and related health problems combined to force Birmingham out of a race for reelection in 1955, leaving the protestors with no white elected "friend" willing to try and moderate the City Commission's drift toward a less tolerant approach to race relations.[8] Indeed, as the increasingly dramatic boycott continued, resentment among local whites escalated sharply. Responding to this pattern and reflecting their own views, bus officials and a segregationist hardliner elected to replace David Birmingham, Clyde Sellers, began experimenting with counter-pressures as they tried to break the protestors' resolve. For appearances' sake these white "hard-liners" had allowed the formal process of interchange to go forward. In fact this surface agreeableness was little more than a diversionary gesture. Men like Sellers had no intention of "losing". What is interesting is that they would talk at all with leaders like King, Nixon and Robinson.

Such a response was probably inevitable since the local whites had become fully alert and were giving increased attention on these startling matters. Media coverage also accentuated the pressure leaders of both sides felt. While the national media's attention to Montgomery's emerging social drama was a harbinger of patterns that would occur again and again in later years, its focus on Montgomery's "problem" became important in convincing local whites that what many had hoped was merely a minor "nigger flap" might not be a casual problem. As the nation was becoming informed about the bus protest, Montgomery's local media outlets also began to pay increased attention. At this early stage such local attention may have been more important. This too forced the December 8, 1955 session to be drama and not exchange.

Since the first negotiations were conducted amid local television coverage, it was a virtual certainty that any proposals King advanced for the MIA would be summarily rejected by the white officials. While all the social actors understood this, the behavior of one broke the protocol of local civility and needlessly inflamed tensions. Acting as though mere rejection was not sufficient, the bus company's attorney, Jack Crenshaw, also mugged and leered before the cameras. Crenshaw deliberately rebuked King when he informed him that his corporate client had no intention of hiring black drivers within the coming decade.[9] Media hijinks such as Crenshaw's would be repeated throughout the course of the protest. As the four-hour meeting of December 8, 1955 wound to a close, all of the protest's leaders recognized that despite their having made the local television news, the effort to settle this dispute "reasonably" had resulted in failure and insult. As the chastened black leaders left with their hats literally in hand, a few resolved that it would be a long while before they again tried a step by step "reasonable" approach to negotiations. The bus boycott's leaders also faced the harsh reality that blacks in Montgomery would be forced to intensify the group's boycott consciousness as opposed to pursuing a flexible negotiating stance. It was also clear that bus company officials were on the verge of pursuing a counter-offensive. Their counter-measures would be designed to quickly and efficiently destroy the still days-old protest. While rejection of the protestors' modest requests had not been completely unexpected, the first blatant efforts by local whites to destroy the movement would startle many of the protest's partisans. They would find it merely the first in a series of such tactics. For vehement resistance to racial change, always a factor in the South's social order, was re-emerging as a regional as well as local phenomenon.

The Reflexive Crackdown: The Inevitable Boomerang Effect

The holiday season of late 1955 proved to be a dead time in newsrooms across the country. Reports on issues highlighting the South's race relations have frequently been used as "filler" during such times. With little happening nationally, a continuing story about "new Negro types" in Alabama had a chance to retain an important audience. This was so because issues of race

471

always generate some public attention. During the days that the boycott's leaders had spent struggling to hammer out an effective negotiating stance, several other Deep South race-angle stories, with varying degrees of newsworthiness, were being reported on nationally.

Throughout the week of the protest's first mass meeting and initial stalled talks, the *New York Times* reported that in Atlanta two thousand Georgia Technology students had rioted in response to an effort by then Governor Marvin Griffin to bar their football team from accepting an invitation to play in the Sugar Bowl.[10] The sports-crazed students had declared themselves outraged by Griffin's "meddling" in University affairs. The Georgia politician rationalized his behavior by insisting that the University of Pittsburgh had a black reserve player and that the Pennsylvania school was determined to sell its bowl ticket allotment on a nonsegregated basis. Within days, the politically posturing Griffin relented and permitted Tech's team to accept the bowl game bid. Small concessions by politicians such as Griffin were becoming more rare as the South's racial climate took a decided turn for the worse in December of 1955. Reading the *Times* during the week of the emerging bus boycott provides other clues about the seriousness of what had become a regional white backlash. The race-angle story the *Times* carried adjacent to the student riot report was even more indicative of the general white counter-trend that seemed to emerge throughout the South in this transitional period.

That story reported on the Virginia response to the 1954 Supreme Court decision mandating school desegregation. Earlier that State's rural-dominated State Legislature had passed a bill promising tax assistance to private schools (that is, newly formed segregated academies) and this measure was now being prepared for a general voter referendum. In subsequent months Virginia's voters, after becoming inflamed by fears of racial change, narrowly approved the measure. Such twin *Times* reports illustrate variations of dominant sentiments that were being reasserted during the mid 1950's as the South's whites began registering their response to the first cracks in the walls of segregation.[11]

Montgomery, with defiant blacks walking along its streets, now began to offer its version of this more general trend as local white leaders began to forcefully assert and abuse their traditional authority. Such a counter-trend met little opposition from America's national leaders in the mid-1950's as they too responded to the growing pattern of regional reaction. Given this bitter dynamic a final report from the *Times* on the day in question begins to be more comprehensible.

Buried on page eighty-seven in the same *Times* edition is a third race-angle story describing the reluctance of both major political parties to make the civil rights of Southern blacks an issue in the 1956 national elections. Under the headlines, "No Push Expected for Civil Rights," this final article described the general reluctance of either then Republican President Eisenhower and soon-to-be Democratic Presidential nominee Adlai Stevenson to push for full citizenship rights for the South's blacks. Throughout the 1940's and 1950's, national political leaders vacillated when race-based insurgency began to be expressed. Neither party reacted strongly to this boycott. With neither Montgomery's whites or blacks getting early national support the contending forces continued to bob and weave in the local arena. Thus the art of generating and sustaining local support remained all-important during this early protest period. Both sides would eventually experience surprises.

The overwhelming support the boycott received from local blacks continued to shock the city's whites and the latter's leaders quickly took a reflexive hardline in tactics consistent with their stonewall negotiation stance. However, in their haste to crack down Montgomery's white leaders committed surprising blunders. In a silly move leaving the few hundred black bus passengers who had not become boycott supporters no option, city and bus company officials announced that beginning December 10, 1955, no further bus pickups would be made in black neighborhoods.[12] While this plan may have been calculated as a face-saving gesture by whites, this confusing response had the unintended effect of assisting the boycott's partisans. First, this new "get tough" stance represented a complete turnaround from a white negotiation approach that had been announced only the day before. This gambit also drew renewed attention to local blacks' newfound ability to act consistently in a unified manner. The protest's adherents became gleeful as they realized that as at no time in the recent past they were now able to influence the course of local events. Indeed, this panicky white response seemed to convince blacks that they were, in the words of the former participants, "really starting to get to 'em now."[13] This early shutdown of bus service to Montgomery's black settlements also allowed the protest's leaders to concentrate renewed attention to issues other than preventing new, and sometimes still confused converts from reverting to old bus riding habits. With this important symbolic battle "won," or handed over, the protest's leaders were able to devote their full attention to the onerous task of providing thousands of local blacks with an alternative means of transportation. A segregation practice once forced upon them now offered Montgomery blacks a short-term solution to this immediate problem.

The dual taxicab system the local racial customs demanded had spawned a significant number of independent black cab drivers by the mid 1950's. Members of this closed occupational group now quickly responded to appeals made by the protest's leaders and quietly began providing pooled rides for bus boycotters while charging very nominal fees. In retrospect, the positive results of this procedure were more significant than was initially recognized. Formerly abused bus riders now found themselves receiving door-to-door courteous service for the same ten cent fee they had routinely deposited in faceless corporate fare boxes. Coming when they did, such pooled services reinforced the still fragile realizations among local blacks that they could protest against Jim Crow laws without seeing their entire social world destroyed. In the Alabama of the mid 1950's, such ideas still had only a tenuous hold among historically oppressed blacks. This was an important outcome of the taxicab drivers' behavior but there was much more to be gained than this.

Perhaps as critical to the movement's long-term success was the strong sense of cohesion generated by the countless conversations that took place between boycotters in the back seats of those cabs. Though these types of interactions promoted the development of group morale in ways far less dramatic than King's or others' speeches, their impact was just as critical. Such pooled cab rides, coming early in the protest's development, provided necessary cohesion and a strong sense of "righteousness" for hundreds who were never able to attend the rituals associated with the protest's public events.

Naturally, the cumulative effects of such patterns were recognized by Montgomery's increasingly vigilant white community within a short time. Days after the bus company's withdrawal of services local black cab drivers began receiving formal notification that their business licenses would be revoked if they failed to charge passengers standard rates. Faced with this overt threat most of the local black cabbies reluctantly complied with the law. Only the really daring drivers continued to provide services for the duration of the protest.[14]

When the news circulated that the black cab drivers had been threatened, even more of the masses of Montgomery's blacks began to realize that if the protest was to achieve any of its stated goals, sacrifices would have to be made on a long-term basis. The willingness to engage in protracted sacrifices, the stage arrived at by thousands of Montgomery's blacks about the time of the taxicab warnings, signaled that the protest was passing an important early juncture. The temporary boycott had become a collective action maturing and developing internal stability with exceptionally strong membership allegiance. Such characteristics were to prove absolutely essential. Without them, the bus boycott might not have survived the escalating resistance it would receive from local whites during the weeks of January 1956. The latter recognized that with the moderate "crackdown" having failed to disrupt the protest, more extreme counter-measures might have to be applied. The boycott's opponents were not above using guile though, as the next several days demonstrated.

A Phony Settlement Followed by Unofficial Terror

While the cold dampness of an Alabama January settled over Montgomery in early 1956, the stalled negotiations and cutoff of bus services to local blacks led to increased tensions between and within both groups. There seemed no way out of the dilemma as blacks stood steadfast for seating changes and white representatives remained committed to a generally counterproductive crackdown. Positions were hardening.

Recognizing the dangers of stalemate, a group of civic-minded white moderates, fearful that negative publicity was affecting Montgomery's ability to attract new industry, arranged for renewed meetings between the contending forces.[15] Still neither group's leaders felt that any compromise was possible and unsatisfactory results were predictable. Thus on January 9, 1956, the Montgomery City Commission again refused to change their position on bus seating arrangements after a two-hour parley with Martin L. King, Jr., and other MIA officials. This result was predictable given the increasing national attention the five-week-old protest was beginning to command. Such attention made genuine compromise politically unthinkable for local whites and this latest rebuff led Montgomery's blacks to suspect anew that reasonable efforts to settle the dispute were a waste of time. Nonetheless, neither side was satisfied with the state of stalemate and, given Montgomery's racial history, an incident such as the one that occurred was probably inevitable.

The events that contributed to the surprising announcement of the boycott's "settlement" during late January seem sure to forever remain murky. However, a few of the circumstances are undisputed and their impact can be fairly established. The most important of these was the effect that the surprising announcement of a "solution" had on the relationship between the protest's leaders and their followers.

As alluded to by respondents in Chapter Five, the ranks of black ministers in Montgomery included some individuals who were flagrant opportunists. These classic "Uncle Toms" existed in most Southern communities but their ranks in Montgomery were supplemented by others who were financially tied to local white patrons. Those who were dependent like this had become so after years of support from a handful of local white "angels" who had supplied them with small favors and token donations. In many instances, black church groups seemed unaware that their "leaders" were on the take in this fashion. By the mid-1950s, these types of arrangements reflected a lingering though increasingly denounced pattern that most of the South's blacks had rejected. Even so such "neo-Uncle Tom" ministers would remain a special community liability throughout the active phase of the civil rights movement and the Montgomery protest gave early evidence of how potentially destructive such "leaders" could become. White leaders in Montgomery used all "resources" they had at their disposal. For what good are puppets if they cannot be made to dance when a show starts?

On January 21, 1956, a mere eleven days after their categorical public rejection of King and his cohorts' renewed efforts to settle the dispute, the Montgomery City Commission announced that they had held a conference with a group of "prominent Negro ministers" that produced a solution to the bus problem and a "plan to end the boycott."[16] Beyond the announcement of the "settlement" itself the incident's dynamics were telling. The unusual timing of this announcement, late on a Saturday afternoon, seemed designed to maximize confusion among local blacks who were unable to discover from news reports who the "prominent ministers" were who had agreed to the "definite policies" that were promised "to be fair to all citizens, white and colored."[17]

Terms of the "solution" were announced as including courtesy to all passengers, the continuation of reserved front seats for whites and reserved rear seats for Negroes, separate buses for Negroes during rush hours, and the immediate resumption of service to black sections of Montgomery. Such terms actually came close to representing the slight departures from the old customs that the MIA's leaders had initially requested. They were being announced now to a black public that had endured weeks of both sacrifice and movement building, circumstances that had left both the masses and their leaders in no mood to accept such a symbolic pittance. Weeks of national media attention had also helped harden local blacks' attitudes so that accepting terms other than a complete change of seating arrangements was now perceived to be a sellout. To a people who had quickly developed pride as the country began to take note of their unique courage, this surprise "solution" seemed unthinkable. Immediately, Montgomery's black masses began to clamor for a clarification of these surprising terms. White officials pretended to be shocked to discover that they were not trusted, but this "deal" was also discreditable because of the obvious manner in which they had tried to circumvent the legitimate leaders of the boycott. The commissioners understood this and it accounts for their refusal to reveal the identity of those "leaders" who had agreed to the peculiar "solution." A variety of other circumstances also contributed to this subterfuge quickly failing.

To their credit, local news reporters, who remained generally neutral throughout the boycott, immediately checked the accuracy of the alleged breakthrough with E. D. Nixon, Martin L. King, Jr., and others.[18] But the paper then published the story despite knowing it to be false. The protest's leaders, after being informed of the false settlement story, toured local black communities that Saturday evening spreading word of the story while also arranging to have denials issued from church pulpits the next morning.

The three black "leaders" who had cooperated in this abortive "settlement" were eventually identified and coaxed into publicly denouncing the "agreement." Their defense? A claim that they had been "tricked" into accepting.[19] The three "turncoats," the Reverend William K. Kind, of the Jackson Street Baptist Church, an obscure "Bishop" Doc C. Rice of the Oak Street Holiness Church, and the Reverend Benjamin F. Mosely of the First Presbyterian Church, remained objects of local scorn from the City's blacks years after their independent venture. Incidents such as this, though, frequently work to the advantage of social movements. In retrospect the protestors benefitted in several ways from the phony settlement encounter.

The outpouring of resentment toward the three "turncoats" provided many of the movement's most involved members with a convenient release for tensions that had begun building as local white pressures had been applied. The released frustrations referred to were more complex than those typically associated with reform movements of this type. Many of the protest's veterans had been silently tortured by worry as they had waited patiently for some of the local "Toms" to be used against them. Now that they had survived the long-expected trick they felt they could press forward. This was always a movement that reflected patterns of the American South.

The incident did limit the range of options available to the MIA's leadership. For the black masses' angry response to this incident served as a pointed warning to the MIA's leaders that they too had no room for shabby backroom deals that might be perceived as the proverbial sellout. The protest's leaders were thus put on notice that a firm refusal to back down was their sole leadership alternative. This strengthened the faction of militants that King was increasingly aligning with in the backroom debates. Fallout from this incident also influenced the MIA's opponents. Within days of the "settlement's" collapse the city commissioners began considering aligning with the local chapter of the White Citizens Council that was then being organized. While Thornton's account of this false settlement encounter suggests that the city commissioners felt betrayed and only then joined the local Council, major responsibility for this fiasco and the circumstances that followed must ultimately be assigned to those who set up discussions with such purported leaders.[20] Those leaders were thus implicated in the escalating terror that followed because they unleashed a rhetorical rampage after their settlement strategy failed. The terror that followed was both officially sponsored and of a variety that was all too familiar to the participants.

While police harassment of the boycott's participants had increased after the first crackdown on black cab drivers it was again accelerated after the commissioners' pseudoagreement was publicly rejected by the MIA. This intensified crackdown was accompanied by violence on January 30, 1956. On that night, while he was addressing the MIA's weekly mass rally, a dynamite bomb was exploded at King's home. The blast's occurrence marked yet another turning point in the protest's evolution.

When informed of the attack, King rushed from the meeting to see if members of his family had been hurt. After being assured of his family's safety, he emerged from his heavily damaged home to address a large crowd that had gathered at the scene. This gathering was not merely a group of curiosity seekers. The makeup of the assembled group made the crowd more potentially volatile than normal. The parsonage King inhabited sits on South Jackson Avenue in the heart of Montgomery's downtown black area. It is within a half mile of Alabama State University. This being the case, angry young black students made up a large proportion of those who gathered, and many of them shared the values expressed by Joe Reed in Chapter Four. As dozens of those youthful boycott zealots stood picking through the shambles of King's porch they thought that being a man meant "taking nothing."[21] King recognized their mood immediately and quickly began delivering an impromptu speech, admonishing the crowd to avoid violence and to return home peacefully. His talk was crucial for a variety of reasons other than the obvious purpose of dispelling immediate retaliatory violence. It also marked one of the first occasions that King spoke in a nonchurch setting to a large gathering of the movement's supporters. Importantly, his message that night contained elements of a proto-nonviolent ideology that eventually came to characterize his still-maturing personal social philosophy. All scholars of King should study that address.

King's mini-sermon emphasized that Montgomery's black protestors must accept such earthly transgressions because they had to ". . . love their white brothers no matter what they did to them."[22] He also implored those who had gathered to remember that if he was killed, "this movement will not stop, because God is with the movement." After much more soothing talk, he instructed the crowd's members to "go home with this glowing faith and this radiant assurance." King would only rarely find himself at a loss for such flowery eloquence throughout his career but the response to this particular message, given by an angry crowd that had only gradually become an audience, first cheers, then a rather rapid dispersal, illustrates other important points about the followers of what was now an active and maturing movement.

King's abbreviated talk was convincing to the potential mob primarily because most were coming to recognize that they were mutual participants in an important on-going protest. Recognitions such as this mean a lot to any movement's members. Allegiance to collective efforts such as the bus protest also frequently facilitates the development of a coherent ideology. In the bus boycott's case, several of these emerging ideas reinforced the wisdom of local blacks remaining self-controlled, since whites' actions were promoting respect for local leaders. While those who quickly gathered in anger that night might not be able to reconstruct explanations for their acts in the language of the social sciences a pattern was becoming clear. Montgomery's blacks were now responding to King, as if he were a figure who had very special charismatic qualities.

Social scientists have long understood that at critical stages in a social movement's progression, its recognized leaders, especially when they have such obvious qualities as King did, begin to enjoy unquestioned authority and even command awe from the collective's committed members. The willingness of these Alabama State "hotheads" to obey King's "return home" instructions on the night of the porch-bomb incident signaled that such a stage had been reached by the boycott's members. Given what followed two nights later and then again and again, obedience of this type had to become a critical feature of the consciousness of the bus boycott's adherents. As the masses in Montgomery were soon to learn, terror tactics had just begun to be used against their reform movement.

On February 2, 1956, E. D. Nixon's home was dynamited.[23] While far less publicity was attached to this second attack and though Nixon later became resentful because of that fact, blacks in Montgomery still refused to be provoked. Instead, a curious type of spontaneous ritual began to develop. Dozens of the boycott's "walkers" began to make unusual efforts to stroll past the sites of both bombings. Other groups rode by in cramped cars on their way to or from work. Small unplanned prayer meetings were held before King's home and, as now seems obvious, these two bombing assaults proved to be counter-productive. In fact, the bombers' targets, and King's home was immediately repaired, began to take on shrine-like qualities in their symbolic ability to reinforce local blacks' collective commitment.

While several other black churches and private homes were ultimately destroyed or heavily damaged by such terror in Montgomery, this pattern no longer deterred local blacks who had become fully determined to confront their harsh circumstances. Such determination would prove essential as local whites of all classes became more ruthless in their desperate efforts to preserve Montgomery's crumbling racial status quo. This had been reflected locally in the rapid establishment of an affiliate of the previously mentioned mushrooming White Citizens Council. That new group attracted thousands of local whites including all the city commissioners who joined by late January. When the commissioners did so they became aligned with professional hate-mongers of an extreme sort. The highly visible boycott provided these white race-baiters both a convenient target and organizing spur.

On February 10, 1956, Montgomery was the setting for a mass meeting of some twelve thousand whites. This gathering had been called by members of the local White Citizens Council whose circulars contained graphic and pointed references to views local whites were encouraged to ritually reconfirm. The following quote illustrates the White Citizens Council leaders' assessment of the protestors

> In every stage of the bus boycott we have been oppressed and degraded because of black, slimy, juicy, unbearably stinking niggers. Their conduct should not be dwelt upon because behind them they have an ancestral background of Pygmies, Headhunters and snot suckers . . .
> If we don't stop helping those African flesh eaters, we will soon wake up and find Reverend King in the White House.[24]

With support growing rapidly from Montgomery's whites for demagogues who would use such imagery the local grand jury was empowered, on February 13, 1956, to investigate all aspects of the boycott. The consequences of this particular strategy would be the most serious in the series of crackdowns being directed at the boycotters. Yet, when the law is used as a deliberate tool to stifle opposition as it was during this boycott, those who become targets realize that legal proceedings do not warrant unthinking support. Blacks in the Deep South had a developed history of skepticism about local judicial proceedings and in the Montgomery case their lack of awe assisted the group's cohesion. Such solidarity would be necessary as Montgomery's grand jury moved rapidly to the attack. While ostensibly empaneled to investigate whether State or local laws were being broken, the Grand Jury's proceedings and subsequent action helped create a new corps of what might best be understood as "boycott celebrities." The creation of these recognizable targets helped keep the protest on track.

Best Clothes for a Corps of Martyrs

As the previous analysis of Rosa Parks' arrest indicated, social movements appealing to Southern blacks have often been sustained by the visibility of what I will call "judicial martyrs." In the boycott's case, a second cast of such victims began to emerge in late February of 1956. On the twenty-first of that month the local circuit court grand jury handed down eleven indictments naming 115 defendants. Those named in these blanket indictments found themselves charged with breaking a 1921 law making it a misdemeanor to conspire, without just cause or legal excuse, to hinder a company in the conduct of its business. The restrictive nature of laws

481

limiting civil liberties, such as the local one wielded in Montgomery, reflected a strong regional tradition.

Such laws had been erected throughout the South in earlier decades with the intent of preventing both labor organizing and race-based movements of opposition.[25] While the use of these codes had been a rarity the response of Montgomery's now fully mobilized blacks indicates that such legal measures are futile in the face of determined mass opposition. Opposition, however, must be properly coordinated if it is to accomplish more than merely registering simmering discontent. This is especially true in a social order such as the Deep South's where legal assaults had become a major part of the repertoire of repression. Thus, the boycott's leaders had to use keen insight as they maneuvered to contend with the application of this latest variation on the crackdown theme. If they had made a tactical blunder, chaos and collapse of their movement might have followed. Avoiding such pitfalls is one measure which can be used when assessing the effectiveness of a movement's leaders. For it is the constant pressure of responding creatively and correctly to the fine details of an opponent's plans that can separate a social movement's leadership from their followers. Responding to this latest development was another major test of the quality of the boycott's leaders. Montgomery's blacks were the beneficiaries of several leaders, besides King, who contributed to the strategic decisions on how the group should respond to the February indictments. An old technique was trotted out because these indictments had neither stunned nor surprised the protest's organizers. In fact this crisis was seized and used to reignite sagging morale. The events were played out inside Montgomery's black churches.

Borrowed straight from the black church revival tradition, holding a mass meeting seemed especially capable of providing the movement's leaders with a momentary respite so that plans could be derived for confronting this formidable problem. It should be noted that the indictments loomed as one of the most serious threats the protestors had to grapple with. At this point in the boycott's evolution it was especially important to present unified, public opposition to the indictments since the fear of going to the South's jails had long been an especially effective technique of social control. In Montgomery though, this pattern was on the verge of being reversed. In each subsequent campaign that Martin King would lead he and his followers confronted the threat of jail. He learned how to handle that in Montgomery as well as from Gandhi. Though this would be the case, ideas for confronting the indictments were still being sorted through by the movement's leaders as they groped for an effective response. Thus, to maintain appearances it was thought that another, and very special, mass meeting would have to be staged.

In the mass meeting held the night after the indictments were announced, a crowd conservatively estimated to be twenty-five hundred heard the Reverend Ralph David Abernathy deliver a fiery sermon about the necessity for continued racial unity. In his most important boycott moment, the baritone-voiced preacher, who was to remain King's first lieutenant, roamed across the pulpit calling effectively for the boycott's followers to display even stronger resistance. Abernathy bellowed reassurance to the crowd that measures as drastic as mass indictments really meant that local whites were getting desperate in their efforts to end what was by then an eleven week-old protest. After skillfully wringing the packed house to the point of frenzy, Abernathy called on the local residents to observe a "Double P" day. This ceremonial observation would have entailed local blacks refusing to use any motorized transportation as they engaged in a "prayer and pilgrimage" day. Abernathy's appeal generated peak crowd reaction when after a lengthy harangue he semi-shouted the following plea

Every race-loving Negro is being asked to walk everywhere he goes so those who always walk may know we are walking with them.

Not a single race-loving Negro will turn a switch or touch a starter . . .

Not a single race-loving Negro will take a cab . . .[26]

Finally Abernathy brought the crowd to its feet by mining the last vein of his audience's emotions. He did so with a rousing closing line delivered after a long "Kinglike" pause. Following his cab reference, Abernathy quietly added, "And you know . . . nobody will ride the buses."

While Abernathy's performance provided momentary exhilaration, the "Double P" day was less successful than the boycott's leaders hoped. No conclusive plans had been made and though rhetorically effective Abernathy's plea for a commemorative day, delivered on the very eve of the planned occasion, was not enough to insure its success. Strategies involving movements having thousands of participants, even those based in a single urban center, require proper lead time if followers are to respond correctly to calls for sacrifices. Though the boycott was almost three months old at this point, parts of its infrastructure were still wobbly and this too contributed to the failure of the "Double P" day. That potential embarrassment was masked by an interesting subplot created by Montgomery's blacks as they responded to the indictment process itself. In several important respects examining their response provides an accurate gauge of the boycott's continuing vitality despite the wave of terror and the other crackdowns to which the movement had been subjected.

It should come as no surprise that the 115 who were indicted found themselves instantly transformed into movement martyrs. This is a normal dynamic observable in countless other reform movements. But this pattern was just emerging in the South when it was applied in Montgomery to the protesters. Their reaction demonstrated a keen sense of organizational wisdom. Here too these boycotters established a pattern. Indeed it became such a normal response that by the early 1960s, some opposition groups deliberately sought ways to provoke such official measures in hopes of solidifying their positions. Those episodes owe something to lessons learned from the Montgomery experience. After weeks of protesting the bus boycotters were fully prepared to seize this latest opportunity to promote their cause. Their plan focused on getting family members, church associates, and fellow workers to converge on the downtown courthouse so that the indicted leaders could surrender amidst wildly-cheering throngs. This plan emerged from deliberations among the boycott's veteran leaders. Rufus Lewis described details of those talks in the following fashion

> When all those people were indicted we made a special effort to get everyone of them to go down at one time—and we did. Reverend Hubbard suggested that we put on our best clothes and go down.
> And it was such an effective thing that the court couldn't deal with it at all. We didn't meet on this. Reverend Hubbard just made the suggestion that we dress for the occasion and go down en masse—so it would appear that we were together. And that was an impressive thing as far as we were concerned.[27]

The Reverend H. H. Hubbard was one of several who provided such key strategic suggestions. Preferring to remain out of the spotlight, Hubbard eventually became a consistent supporter of Martin L. King. Hubbard's reverence for King grew despite a strong reservation about the latter's views regarding the philosophy of non-violence. H. H. Hubbard, like several of his ministerial colleagues, forever remained a gun-packing preacher who considered such equipment necessary if blacks were to assure their personal survival in the deep South. Though it was well known locally that he was always prepared for any ultimate showdown, Hubbard's contributions to the boycott's strategic deliberation were always carefully considered. When implemented, as with his suggestion to arrive as a group to be indicted, his advice usually proved helpful. This "preacher to the common man" also worked in a community where his views regarding self-protection, at least in the mid 1950's, were widely shared. This was especially evident on the morning that Montgomery's blacks gathered to witness their leaders turn themselves in to be indicted.

The Reverend B. J. Simms, who witnessed the unfolding indictment drama from early in the morning until its evening conclusion, described an especially revealing interchange between the crowd and several of Montgomery's police officers. Simms recalled the social texture of that morning in the following manner

> Blacks had come from every section of town. Black women with bandannas on, wearing men's hats with their dresses rolled up. From the alleys they came. That is what frightened white people. Not the tie and collar crowd. I walked into there (to be indicted) and the cops were trembling.
>
> Said, 'you got mah name? I'm B. J. Simms.'
>
> Cop said 'yeah, yeah . . . here, your name is here.'
>
> Said, 'alright what do I do?' Said, 'you get in that line there.'
>
> I got in line behind the late Mrs. A. W. West.[28]

Simms went on in his recollections to describe an interchange between the edgy local police and the crowd of boycott supporters. As had so frequently been the case during the course of this protest, the interchange involved white male police officers and black women. Simms' description of what occurred when a policeman tried to move the surging masses back from the courthouse steps is as follows

> One of the police hollered 'all right you women get back.'
>   Three great big old women with their dresses rolled up over work pants told him and I will never forget their language,
> 'We ain't going nowhere. You done arrested us preachers and we ain't moving.'
> He put his hands on his gun and his club. They said, 'I don't care what you got. If you hit one of us you'll not leave here alive.' That was the thing we had to work against, keeping those blacks from killing these whites.[29]

Those, like Simms, who were working as leaders to maintain a tenuous racial peace while also pushing the cause of continuing bus boycott had roots overwhelmingly in Alabama's rural Black Belt region. Data from the files of those indicted clearly demonstrate the extent to which this was a local grass roots movement. Almost all indicted had been born on area farms or in nearby small villages; and most were between thirty-five and fifty years old.[30] Importantly, as discussed in Chapter Five, most also fit the general characteristics of that group of emerging blacks who began assuming leadership roles throughout the South in the mid 1950s. That is, the indicted protestors were relatively well-educated, had experienced some life or travel outside the deep South, and most held occupations that left them generally immune to the coercive economic power of local whites.

All those indicted pleaded not guilty to the conspiracy charges, and the initial trial was set for the week of March 19, 1956. Not surprisingly, black ministers formed the largest occupational group charged; with twenty-four arraigned. Public school teachers, physicians, college professors, middle-aged housewives, morticians, and white-collar types constituted the bulk of the other blacks who were indicted. Examining the results of that process also reveals how little local whites knew about the grassroots leaders of those who had finally confronted them. While the blanket indictments had listed 115 defendants, the total number of those booked ended up being eighty-nine. Among those charged were Rosa Parks, Jo Ann Robinson, E. D. Nixon, Rufus Lewis, B. J. Simms, Ralph Abernathy, and dozens of others, including a most important one who had remained out of town on the "day of days." The absent leader had been Martin L. King, Jr.

When King returned to Montgomery the next day, he returned in the company of his very protective father. By late March it had becoming obvious to all involved that Martin L. King, Jr. was being treated as the leading black target. All subsequent strategy by local whites made this clear. Despite being the last to be indicted, King was immediately scheduled to be the first tried. By being singled out as the test case, Martin L. King, Jr., found himself being thrust ever upward as the visible leader of this protest. His March trial would also become the focus of more national attention than the boycott had generated to that point. Quietly, however, the inner mechanics of the movement had become so chaotic during this period that the more important "trial" might have been whether the protest itself could be indefinitely sustained. While reviewing trial transcripts of a case as crucial as *Martin Luther King, Jr., vs. State of Alabama*[31] might be important to understanding the boycott's ultimate legal impact, comprehending this other "trial" is more fundamental for those whose interest is analyzing social movements. Details of this "trial" are discussed in Chapter Seven.

SEVEN

Sustaining Black Support
and
Generating White Dollars

There were so many things. We paid rent. We paid water bills.
We bought food. We paid people's doctor bills. We even buried
somebody. Not as a result of any activity. Those were free rides
as far as I was concerned. But they seemed to think this is what
we had to do. We even bought washing machines. (Erna Dungee
Allen, Montgomery, Alabama, July 1977)

In some respects, sustaining local black support for the boycott was as
difficult as winning the attention and sympathy of the North's whites proved
to be. Scholars have long recognized that sustaining popular support for a
movement is critical.[1] Many movements can attract a mass following during
their initial, euphoric days only to lose supporters as the novelty of
involvement declines.[2] This proved to be the case in Montgomery. Despite
the concern protest leaders felt they engaged in the type of behavior Mrs.
Allen describes above. Considering that mutual support systems have
traditionally been associated with the southern black church—and the MIA's
leaders came primarily from the pulpit—such forms of sharing should not be
surprising.[3] Undoubtedly there was a lot of unnecessary largess, but given
the inadequate system of government welfare that prevailed in states like
Alabama during the mid-1950s, that abuse was probably inevitable. While
the more obnoxious of these abuses offended those members of the "tie and
collar" crowd who witnessed them, it is likely that a segment of the masses
would have resumed riding the buses if there had not been some minimal
sharing of the movement's resources. This occurred because everyone
involved came to know that a lot of money was pouring into the MIA's mail
room. Others sought such aid because there was and there remains gut-

wrenching poverty in Montgomery. But such tactical support was not nearly as critical as other strategies that evolved.

Patterns of Local Support

Strategies had to be developed that would produce results effective enough to sustain a movement that was experiencing major problems as early as February 1956. As discussed in Chapter Six, by then the boycott's leaders were under indictment, the loosely organized car pool was faced with financial uncertainty as it sputtered and threatened to collapse, and numerous other nagging problems confronted Martin L. King, Jr. and his fellow leaders. If they had been any less determined, the boycott's leaders might have been tempted to try and quietly compromise with their opponents. However, by selecting the energetic and eloquent King, the veteran leaders positioned themselves to utilize a tactic that had last been successful during the Scottsboro Boys trials of the early 1930s.[4] This involved the strategy of dispatching the boycott leaders on forays to the North. Such journeys "up the road" were designed to generate much-needed money and accompanying public support. Given King's rapidly developing qualities, he, along with some few others, was a natural for this role.

Initially, some of the boycott's leaders thought that since they had been given firm local support, a relatively self-contained boycott might be possible. The less experienced leaders assumed that all that was needed was the temporary maintenance of race unity. King's early statements illustrate this point. In them he seemed concerned primarily with his local constituency. Frequently King sought to sustain the boycotters' enthusiasm and unity by dramatically invoking memories of the Ku Klux Klan's night-riding days.[5] For a time, King's ritualistic invocations regarding "terroristic whites" were effective in sustaining the appearance of near total unity among Montgomery's blacks. In an ironic twist, those January 1956 bombings of King's and Nixon's homes served as principal reminders that such fears were realistic. But as time went by and the masses of Montgomery's blacks did not directly experience such senseless violence, King's appeals began to wear thin. Nonetheless, local support for the protest remained strong. This was especially true of an organization called the No-Name Club.

The No-Name Club emerged during the first few weeks of the protest and consistently contributed a hundred dollars a week to help finance the car pool. The club's president, Mrs. Georgia Gilmore, had little formal education but was intensely committed to opposing racial segregation. Mrs. Gilmore, though president of the club, supported her family in a very traditional way: she was a very talented cook and a daily vendor of lunches that were a staple item for dozens of black Montgomery's "tie and collar" crowd. One of Mrs. Gilmore's steadiest customers, and one whose compliments for her excellent cooking were undoubtedly sincere, was Martin Luther King, Jr. Cooking aside, King had a particular reason to pay frequent visits to Mrs. Gilmore's table.[6] Georgia Gilmore was not only president of the No-Name Club, but was also its sole member.[7]

The entire Gilmore family had heard King speak at the first mass meeting, and though electrified by his style, were more attracted by a slogan he used in the first few weeks of the protest. King, wise ideologist that he was, recoined a number of morale-sustaining slogans he had heard during his youth. In a continuing effort to keep class relations harmonious in black Montgomery, King was fond of using the slogan, "You can't go up without taking me with you."[8]

Hearing such slogans and witnessing the "tie and collar" crowd practicing what was being preached strongly encouraged the masses of blacks in Montgomery. Countless contributions, most much smaller than the No-Name Club's, came from impoverished followers. While the Georgia Gilmore types of Montgomery have still not seen their finances improve relative to others, the protest did provide them with an effective means of expressing their opposition to the racial status quo. Though there were numerous other "no-name" contributors who provided sustained support to the boycott, it soon became obvious that financial resources from followers in the North would be essential. King's talents were enlisted within weeks in the pursuit of this new goal. The decision to utilize a fundraising approach that frequently took MIA's leaders out of town demonstrates an important point. Important decisions were routinely made in the absence of top MIA officials. Since there was no initial pattern of over-reliance on a small number of top officials, many competent participants were able to participate in the movement's management. Sharing leadership in this manner promoted group cohesion while dissipating competition for power. While internal solidarity was promoted, the need for outside support was also increasingly evident. The private carpool being provided cost thousands every week.

Generating Support from Northern Whites

By February 14, 1956, Martin Luther King, Jr. was involved in his first northern mission seeking funds and public sympathy. The importance of such actions should not be discounted. On the issue of tactics, the fifth major mechanism essential to a social movement's development and maintenance, Herbert Blumer says

> Obviously, the tactics are evolved along three lines: gaining adherents, holding adherents, and reaching objectives. Little more can be said than this . . .[9]

Nonetheless, in the practical world of managing and building northern support for the movement, the boycott's social significance had to be publicly clarified and perhaps elevated. In his effort to elevate the actions unfolding in Alabama's Black Belt to international importance, King's February speech in Chicago emphasized that the type of resistance that emerged in Montgomery was "happening all over the world"[10] and that

> The oppressed peoples of the world are rising up. They are revolting against colonialism, imperialism, and other systems of oppression.[11]

While glibly making such heady comments, King was speaking in the comfortable, conservative surroundings of a black Baptist church. Initially it was the North's prosperous blacks who proved ready, indeed eager, to embrace these new ideas about their counterparts in the South. Somewhat later, a significant portion of the North's liberal whites also accepted the reality that a Southern reform movement had emerged.

In the mid-1950s the North's whites were not threatened by such actions. There seemed no possibility that any such black revolt might emerge above the Mason-Dixon Line. However, if northern whites or conservative blacks became alarmed, King always made efforts to soothe them. In that early Chicago sermon he also assured his audience that, while the boycott might have "world-wide implications," it was not meant to be a blood-stained affair. He insisted that

> This is a movement of passive resistance. We have kept violence out of the picture from our standpoint.[12]

As for the primary objective of King's first northern foray, he stated the need succinctly and with little subtlety. After sadly declaring that some tentative steps were being taken to call off the bus boycott, King mentioned that the car pools had cost Montgomery's blacks "a lot of money."[13]

In responding to such appeals to help those "down home," northern blacks proved exceedingly generous in their support to the movement. In reality, King's threat that the boycott might have to be called off was an empty one. When a vote at a mass meeting regarding the question of ending the boycott was taken a week after King's Chicago speech, only two people among the four thousand attending supported calling off the protest.[14] Threatening to capitulate was formally considered only as a final means to avoid having the movement's leadership indicted. That even two protesters would vote to give in seems surprising.

One of the two who publicly supported giving in was Reverend L. R. Bennett, pastor of Mt. Zion A.M.E. Church. This was the same Bennett who had chaired the first leadership organizing meeting that had generated such dissatisfaction that he had been replaced by the youthful King. Bennett's act strongly suggests why it was so crucial that this boycott have a leader who would not crack when the pressures from whites began to escalate. Perhaps Bennett was sincerely motivated by a desire to lessen the racial tension that all Montgomerians were feeling; but others in Montgomery insinuate that this was not a factor in his behavior. Those still alive said that King's first rival for local leadership simply wanted to stop the movement because of personal jealousy. An issue such as this might not be answerable at this point but how support from northern citizens was generated can be explored further.

Overwhelming support for the movement from northern blacks was generated by several means. These included extensive coverage in the black press, church speaking tours by a broad cross-section of the movement's leaders, and making use of the strong identification felt by northern blacks who maintained close ties with their southern relatives. Other strategies had to be employed to gather support from northern whites.

To fully understand how the boycott's leaders generated support from northern whites requires an analysis of the segments of that population that ultimately made significant financial contributions to the movement's success. Not surprisingly, they tended to be those organizations and individuals historically associated with progressive causes. These included labor groups from the old CIO, churches from the more liberal Protestant denominations, Jewish groups based in New York City, and those Democrats who identified with the racial egalitarian spirit of the New Deal. These were groups (and it was becoming a generalized trend with television's development) that responded appreciatively to articulate black spokesmen. Martin L. King, Jr. proved he was a natural. But there was another technique that legitimized the movement in northern white minds. This strategy had nothing to do with King's charisma.

The boycott's veteran leaders quietly encouraged sympathetic northern whites to come and observe firsthand the circumstances in Montgomery. E. D. Nixon was confident that these inspections would work only to the movement's advantage. Typical of these inspection groups were three clergymen from affluent suburbs in and around Chicago. After being exposed to King's initial Chicago address, these three were invited to spend a few days visiting Montgomery during early March 1956.[15]

The three were affiliated with the Unitarian and Universalist churches, liberal Protestant sects with very few black members. All were extremely prominent members of those denominations. They were the Reverend Albert A. Harkins of Elgin, Illinois, who was a former president of the Universalist Ministers Association of America; Dr. David H. Cole, who was then president of that association, and Dr. Homer A. Jack, who was a Unitarian minister and contributing writer to the important magazine *The Humanist*.

The ministers spent three days observing the mechanics of the boycott and they were thoroughly impressed by the massive black support those actions enjoyed. The three left Montgomery after promising to speak in support of the boycott in other northern locations, to write articles justifying the boycott, and to generally assist in what they considered a just action. This tour, followed by similar ones, helped galvanize public opinion among northern white liberals to support the boycott. As could be expected, most of Montgomery's whites, including some in the local press, described such visitors as meddlesome "outsiders" whose presence only encouraged the continuation of impudent acts by misguided local blacks.[16] Despite receiving rhetorical hostility, white visitors figured prominently in generating tangible support for the boycott.

The sentiments taken back to Illinois by these clergymen typified the strong support the Montgomery movement ultimately enjoyed with liberal Protestant and some other northern religious groups. Other strategies also assisted in promoting this growing interest. During late March 1956, a "National Deliverance Day of Prayer" was organized to commemorate the circumstances being protested in Montgomery.[17] Initially timed to coincide with the conspiracy trials of the movement's leaders, the commemorative day generated prayer-protest rallies from Los Angeles, where ten thousand blacks and whites gathered, to Boston, where the white Episcopal bishop, Norman B. Nash, addressed eight hundred worshipers. Though Nash's address perceptively highlighted racial problems in Boston, dozens of speakers around the country focused attention that day on what Rabbi Joseph S. Shabow called ". . . the shame of segregation in the South . . ."[18]

This artfully orchestrated commemorative day generated widespread public support and indicated the growing interest the boycott was receiving among whites and blacks in the North and West. It should be noted, however, that the most important strategy in stimulating sustained support in the North remained the public speaking appearances of the movement's leaders.

While reminiscent of the strategies used by fundraisers during the Scottsboro Boys case of the 1930's, the pattern the movement leaders developed was actually as old as the approach used by the "moral suasion" branch of the anti- slavery abolition movement.[19] This approach had leading blacks from the boycott's ranks—especially King—speaking to groups of left-leaning whites who could be counted on to support a "correct" cause.

While paralleling earlier patterns, the ideas for this fundraising approach among the North's whites was generated by leaders who had had significant involvement with the labor movement. This included E. D. Nixon, Owen Butler, and others who had held strategic positions in the Brotherhood of Sleeping Car Porters Union. This proved to be one of the principal strategies that sustained the Montgomery protest—unlike a 1953 bus boycott in Baton Rouge, Louisiana, which had failed.[20] Though critical to the boycott's success, such a fundraising approach also eventually generated, perhaps inevitably, strife among the movement's leaders.[21]

Dissension within a social movement's leadership ranks is normal; different issues generate it. To the extent that such disagreements and splits can be concealed from a movement's followers, morale and momentum can more easily be sustained. In Montgomery, disagreements among leaders escalated after the role of "visiting protest celebrity" was firmly established.

By the end of April 1956, numerous missionaries from the protest's leadership ranks had travelled outside Montgomery to speak before black churches and other gatherings. Initially such forays created little jealousy due to their newness and to the limited money and attention involved. However, as more northern white groups began to request speakers, a "star system" developed. Many of those groups offered large cash contributions and generous reimbursement for a speaker's travel expenses. Many of those organizations now also insisted on being addressed only by Martin Luther King, Jr.

As King's personal fame heightened and the best engagements were increasingly directed his way, others began to miss the prestige of being the "visiting protest celebrity." This envy, which was quite normal given Alabama blacks' previous lack of access to either financial resources or public acclaim, also generated suspicions of financial chicanery.

E. D. Nixon, who admits that his perspective might be somewhat harsh, recalled

> A lot of times a minister would make a speech and would think that he's entitled to some of it. Everybody didn't do like I done. Why I've known of even Reverend King . . .
> Reverend King, he spoke up in Canada and he told me, "Brother Nic, when the check come from Canada, that's my personal check." And when it come I gave it to him. No, weren't no question about it . . .[22]

Such behavior bothered Nixon and other insiders since not all participants engaged in it. He explained

> Mrs. Parks, whatever she collected she turned in. She come in three or four o'clock in the evening and turn in anything she'd collected and I'd give her a receipt for it. Everybody didn't do that.[23]

Finally willing to be completely candid, Nixon admitted that he once accepted six hundred dollars from a speaking engagement and retained it for his personal use. Such behavior, while generally isolated, would have seriously jeopardized the success of the protest if it had become widely publicized. While such top-level moral aberrations were generally concealed from public scrutiny, a different relationship—one that was also crucial symbolically in generating public support from northern whites—was deliberately publicized by the boycott's leaders.

The Boycott's Token White Leader and His Impact

During the 1950's and early 1960's, liberal whites remained convinced that if solutions were to be found to what was then generally considered to be the South's "race problem," such answers would have to be generated by a coalition of blacks and whites. This philosophical approach, completely consistent with the political ideals that sustained the New Deal, was shared by the movement's leaders. Thus, the symbolic importance of a young, white Lutheran pastor named Robert S. Graetz cannot be discounted.[24]

Graetz, twenty-seven at the time, was pastor of an all-black congregation, Trinity Lutheran Church on Cleveland Avenue. This church was in the center of one of Montgomery's most important black neighborhoods. Like King, the young Lutheran had been in Montgomery only about a year before the protest erupted. His biography paralleled King's in other interesting ways.

Graetz, like the other outsider, though not from Montgomery, was familiar with the South—having been born in West Virginia. It was while being educated in a liberal northern seminary that Graetz, again like King, had his first involvement with members of another race. While attending seminary in Ohio, Graetz also flirted with—and later rejected—socialism. This too was a pattern that would become very familiar to liberal Democrats and some members of the South's emerging black middle class. King, who also first toyed with thoughts about economic democracy during his northern years, shared another important characteristic with Graetz. Both had fathers who were substantial achievers and major influences on their sons. Graetz's father, an engineer for a large corporation, once told his son in discussing economic matters

. . . someone once said that a young man who doesn't become a socialist at some time before he is twenty-five has no heart and one who clings to that view after twenty-five has no brain.[25]

Graetz gave considerable importance to such values, but by his post-seminary years he referred to himself as being an "Eisenhower-democrat."[26] While he became politically conventional, Graetz did not entirely give up on idealism and this disposition, as was also the case with King, was largely inspired by his father. While Graetz relinquished ideas of economic redistribution he easily redirected his sense of idealism toward the general quest to bring about changes in the South's system of race relations.

When the boycott emerged, Graetz became deeply and publicly involved. He suffered mightily as a consequence. Weeks before King was to face it, Graetz was taken to jail, threatened, and only reluctantly released after Montgomery's police detected him transporting boycotting blacks.[27] His home too was later bombed and Graetz's family had to endure the nightly telephone threats that were directed at all those who became publicly identified as movement leaders. The psychological warfare directed at Graetz was particularly bitter. In a twist that seems only logical, given the South's historic anti-black thought, Graetz's involvement as a movement leader was publicized locally even before King's was. Many of Montgomery's more racist whites were and remain convinced that some sinister white mastermind had to be behind the boycott's emergence. This type of bigot could not accept the notion that blacks could do intelligent things on their own. Initially, many of them thought of Graetz as the prime "culprit."

While the mere mention of Graetz's name eventually came to cause many white Montgomerians to curse, around the country he was projected as a symbol of hope. While generally sincere, this tactic was especially effective on the North's Lutherans and those of other liberal denominations. The boycott's leaders, including King, recognized this early, and visiting journalists were steered to activities that highlighted Graetz's involvement. In an ironic twist, the medium that had initiated this focus on Graetz was the black press. Widely circulated photographs and discussions of Graetz's involvement, giving him novelty treatment, appeared in the black press as early as December 22, 1955.[28] Graetz, however, brought important skills and sincere dedication to the movement and was later added to the Executive Board of the MIA. His rise did not stop, as within a year of the boycott's conclusion, Graetz had become that organization's secretary.

In other areas Graetz was important to the movement for reasons that went beyond mere symbolism. His quiet success as a raiser of needed funds is an example. Graetz's correspondence with northern Lutherans helped to generate more than seven thousand dollars in the first month of the boycott.[29] While some of the veteran black ministers remained jealous of Graetz's prominence and thought him to be generally naive, both his race and his ability to raise funds assured him an important role in the movement's leadership constellation.

As could be expected, Graetz made frequent appearances in the North to help solidify that region's support for the boycott. By being publicly identified as having engaged in such activities, the young Lutheran was involving himself in a very delicate process. While there may now be a tendency to regard whites such as Graetz with cynicism, at that time his well-publicized example also helped legitimize the idea among a few of Montgomery's non-racist whites that support for the boycott—if only covert—might be the Christian thing to do. While there were only a few such people, their emergence also helped sustain this boycott.

The few whites who were considered guilty of breaking racial ranks came principally from Montgomery's upper class. The author has heard reports that less-advantaged whites also provided support, but this support was typically described as being verbal encouragement. An important, albeit small, group of upper-class white Montgomerians did gave tangible support to the protest. Their social status characteristics were, as was the case with the Womans Political Conference, most unusual.

Most were female and employers of domestic servants. Many defiantly provided rides to those who worked for them. While some were undoubtedly motivated by an intense personal disdain for performing what was considered "Negro work", others were genuinely, if secretly, sympathetic to the protesters' cause. This points out an important fact: personal attachments between the South's upper-class whites and their domestic employees, though often dismissed as having been demeaning and exploitative, were sometimes more than that. On occasion, serious discussions about issues of race were engaged in by those who, perhaps because of length of the relationship, felt comfortable talking about such matters. As might be imagined, many of these discussions took place only between upper-class white women and their black female servants. Such woman-to-woman relationships are frequently critical in any movement's success; this was certainly true in the Montgomery case.

Proof that the employers were not merely being selfish was demonstrated by the frequent practice of giving rides to both employees and the employee's friends. Such practices were so common that they generated caustic public rebukes from Montgomery's Mayor W. H. Gayle. The problem was so serious that as early as late January 1956, Gayle was publicly imploring whites to cease "the practice of paying 'blackmail' transportation money in any form or fashion."[30] Though publicly rebuked by Gayle and other white officials, this support pattern became so well-established that it re-emerged as a public issue in the waning months of 1956. It was then tinged with a viciousness that hinted at the deep cleavages that had developed among Montgomery's whites.

In late October 1956, the *Birmingham News* reported that numerous upper-class white women who had persisted in providing rides to their domestic employees were being harassed by threatening phone calls. Such calls and other efforts at intimidation often frightened and disillusioned this handful of whites. There is even evidence that such activity contributed to the suicide of one of the city's librarians.[31] While white support tactics could produce ugly reactions, they also provided some comic relief to the boycott's primary supporters.

As could be expected, after a short while many of Montgomery's blacks had developed tremendous pride because they had not given in to the intense pressure from local whites. They also found some humor in the more awkward and ineffective coercive tactics whites used. By the summer of 1956, protesters were sharing countless jokes about "big- shot" whites. Such jokes increased after Mayor Gayle's heart attack in April of 1956. Montgomery's blacks openly wondered if the mayor had "heart enough" to prolong his opposition to what they considered to be their inevitable victory.

While such humor might now seem mildly vicious, it served the important social function of preserving in-group solidarity. Other jokes circulated about the hoped-for cracking of the all-powerful white establishment. Some work-weary blacks found small comfort by chuckling about how they managed their good white folks in order to get door-to-door rides. Indeed, as in all parts of the country, a certain amount of prestige had long been given to those blacks who were most adept in such maneuvers. While some of the movement's leaders also occasionally giggled about how they manipulated support from northern whites, such actions in Montgomery again give clues to how a locality's most mundane routines can be profoundly affected by the inner workings of a social movement.

Despite the midsummer emergence of sustaining humor, the boycott was still problematic. Efforts to maintain it and to win an ultimate victory were no longer limited to Montgomery's blacks. The world was now watching. Even so, some of the most critical events and individuals remained hidden.

While the dynamics of how support for the protest was generated have largely been ignored before this study, this chapter's discussion verifies ideas that scholars have long regarded as applying to social movements. Social scientists who have closely analyzed opposition movements have often been amazed at how struggles have been sustained despite the fragmentation of leadership energies occurring when envy and distracting opportunities arise. In the boycott's case, most participants wisely ignored minor abuses and focused on the long-range goal of victory. The leaders also tended to maintain a daily concern with how to sustain the often fragile unity between Montgomery's black haves and have-nots. Critically, this protest's leaders also demonstrated a keen understanding of how to most effectively utilize their symbolic weapons (e.g., Robert Graetz). Such wisdom generated working ties with sympathizers around the country, thus providing the movement critical financial support. More importantly, the national consciousness was being influenced in ways that would continue to generate support for the reform efforts southern blacks were to undertake in the years ahead. This begins to speak to the overall significance of the boycott. In the summary chapter that follows, the task is more systematically completed.

EIGHT

"Just a Start"

> The one thing that we had decided, and this is what King said, that we were not going to take anything except total integration. I had gotten tired and some others had too and wanted to take this and that but Martin L. King said we would not take anything except total integration.
>
> *How did the whites react to this goal?*
>
> They feared that anything they gave would be viewed by us as just a start. And, you know, they were probably right. (Jo Ann Robinson, July 1977)

Social movements as discussed in this and other studies exhibit various phases of development throughout what J. Victor Baldridge calls their life careers.[1] Scholars generally agree that mass-based movements typically reach a stage where participation slowly declines as aspects of the protest activity lose their novelty. While certainly not a law of history, it is rare for reform movements to retain their initial form as they pursue their principal goals. Instead, most movements become transformed as they become bureaucratized. Many dynamics explain this; several operated in Montgomery. For instance, important "personalities" were created and became openly worshiped. Organizational structures, many painfully constructed, became held dear after they demonstrated effectiveness. The Montgomery Improvement Association, created in the first days of this protest, was still functioning in the late 1970s. When victories are achieved, some of a movement's adherents immediately set and strive for new goals. That also happened in this case. Here the victors included Martin L. King, Jr. As stated, all these dynamics surfaced in the post-boycott era. Collectively, these and other such dynamics constitute what might be called the boycott's residue.[2]

Typically a movement's legacy is more appreciated and experienced by those who play central roles during the various crisis stages. Those participants are frequently the ones who are most involved in the formal establishment of a movement's traditions and the symbolic enshrinement of its popular heroes. Again, what has been true in other movements was true in the Montgomery protest. It was clear to this outsider that people who had been "insiders" were forever changed and forever reliving their movement memories. To many, E. D. Nixon or King were still guiding beacons despite their having never talked or walked with either. This chapter focuses on important aspects of these patterns. It briefly describes how the boycott was resolved, and reviews what happened when the protesters returned to the buses. Finally, it is important to identify some of the more critical factors that contributed to the movement's success, before assessing the impact this boycott had on the Civil Rights Movement.

The Non-Issue of "Legalism" in the Movement's Success

Resolving the conflicts that had emerged in Montgomery was not simple. As is so often the case in American society, the contending parties resorted to the courts. This was an arena where the protest's leaders were confident of ultimate victory. If victory had not been achieved there, the long range consequences for the Civil Rights Movement might have been severe. But that movement too was bound to occur. Martin King may not have ever led it, but there are many who say he did not lead in Montgomery either.

During the final months of the Montgomery protest the boycott's continued existence often seemed uncertain. The tactics of police harassment, the delay of deliberations by city officials, and other forms of opposition gradually took their toll on the movement's participants.[3] It is now clear that if the boycott's leaders had failed to utilize a variety of protest tactics, including legal ones, the movement's outcome might well have been reversed. The results of legal tactics were especially critical in the boycott's final weeks. This reliance on legal maneuverings, a strategy traditionally employed by the NAACP, has come to be referred to as "legalism" by movement insiders. While radicals and even King would use that term jokingly during 1960s, in this protest's case, it proved to be a salvation. Perhaps E. D. Nixon's old ties with the NAACP saved King's skin and his reputation, as B. J. Simms would say in 1977.

A final victory would not be achieved until December of 1956 after shrewd legal maneuverings by a team of lawyers working for the protesters prevailed in this country's highest court. It is also worth noting that the movement's legal approach was ultimately possible only because of the monetary resources and public attention generated by the "big" and "little" people who were boycotters. Given these advantages, critical legal steps could be taken that pushed the protest toward a gratifying and important symbolic victory. While "legalism" produced such results in Montgomery, it was not to enjoy unquestioned popularity later among southern activists. The long delays, prohibitive costs, and uncertainty of results dissuaded many activists. Other circumstances would also prevent later reliance on this tactic.

By the early 1960s the astute use of legal maneuvering would be matched tactic by tactic by foes of racial change. The simultaneous campaigns in dozens of Deep South localities would also frequently stretch a thin line of Movement lawyers beyond their breaking point.[4] As a result many activists would be left on their own to try and devise legal defenses when confronted with the inevitable local arrests. This did not happen in Montgomery and that would really help this protest to be successful. These Montgomery protesters remained convinced that "legalism" worked for the rest of their political days. In contrast, some early 1960s campaigns would feature zealous activists who eschewed legal tactics altogether. Many would choose to fill the jails as a means of demonstrating to the nation the judicial barbarity of the Deep South.[5] Many others would become convinced that courtrooms were no longer as significant battle places as were struggles at lunch counters, movie theaters, or less visibly, voter registration offices. To these later activists going to jail would provoke no sense of shame; indeed, confinement for the cause would became a significant badge of honor. Martin L. King, Jr. was destined, as were some others from this protest, to share this perspective. Such a consciousness, manifested during the boycott by the indicted leaders, was not severely tested. The limitations of "legalism" were not immediately apparent after the bus boycott. For in Montgomery, "legalism" was confirmed as protest strategy.

In this early protest, legal tactics of the type traditionally employed by the NAACP received near unanimous approval. This approach was altogether logical to veteran boycott leaders who had utilized such tactics throughout their activist careers. Given the spirit of the Warren Court's then-emerging pattern regarding racial integration, it also made clear tactical sense to pursue this direction.

E. D. Nixon, attorneys Fred Gray and Clifford Durr, and others had quickly recognized that because of how Mrs. Parks was booked upon her arrest, they could make a strong legal assault on Montgomery's law requiring bus segregation.[6] Within the first weeks of the protest several lawyers began the task of positioning the MIA so that a legal victory would be virtually assured. A member of this legal team, a black attorney then in his early thirties, was Charles Langford. In the late 1970s Langford was to recall

> We had the assistance of the best legal minds locally and throughout the country. That helped us . . . We cooperated one hundred percent with the NAACP.[7]

Langford attended law school at the Catholic University in Washington, D.C., and he, like several other members of the legal team, always intended to return to the South to practice. The Montgomery native was a member of a group that sometimes included a dozen lawyers. That eight of them were black and practiced in the state indicates a crucial difference between the bus boycott and previous legal struggles between blacks and whites in Alabama. In earlier eras, most notably the 1930s Scottsboro Boys and Camp Hill incidents, overworked white attorneys from outside Alabama had to present complex defenses, while often also trying to generate the popular support their cases needed. Despite tireless efforts those attorneys frequently lost both in the Alabama courts and in their subsequent appeals. They also left Alabama as quickly as they could because they were marked men. This would not be the case with the boycott's attorneys although they too would become targets.

Unlike those earlier white attorneys, Langford and the other members of the boycott's legal team remained in Alabama and prospered. Langford became a partner in Gray, Seay, and Langford. The firm has a branch located on Dexter Avenue just a block from the church formerly pastored by Martin Luther King, Jr. Theirs is a black firm that has "arrived." Based on the adulation they received during the boycott's trials and afterwards, such a development was predictable. Grey and Langford also had talent, training and courage. But they only became "celebrities" after the Warren Court found for them in 1956.

While the crime of which Rosa Parks was initially found guilty was not nearly as serious as the criminal charges in the Scottsboro Boys or Camp Hill cases, ultimate victory in her case had more important long term ramifications. All involved in the litigation recognized the possible repercussions of their courtroom struggles. What was on trial in the case stemming from Mrs. Parks' arrest was whether the legal momentum gathering against *dejure* segregation as announced in *Brown vs. Board of*

Education could be maintained. Given the significance of that potential outcome, her black lawyers, who hailed from all over Alabama, plus Robert Carter of the NAACP's New York headquarters, had to quickly organize a coherent legal strategy.

Clifford Durr, a liberal white of the New Deal Era who assisted in these deliberations, was a former member of the Federal Communications Commission and gave valuable legal advice to the movement's leaders throughout the campaign. A long and close friend of E. D. Nixon, Durr provided advice on briefs that was readily incorporated by the MIA legal team. While contributing substantially in strategy sessions, Durr remained in the background.[8] Strategically, he knew that the actual legal arguments would be better if made by others. Thus, the dramas that unfolded in Montgomery's courts always publicly pitted a team of black legal experts against a team of white lawyers. Such imagery further consolidated support and contributed to pride among the boycott's supporters. Most importantly the MIA's lawyers had circumstances that let them concentrate fully on the legal issues at hand. There was no problem with resources, and local blacks were willing enough to be witnesses. Able to pay close attention to detail, legal missteps were avoided.

The legal issues in Montgomery were complex. All litigation stemming from Mrs. Park's arrest had to be handled separately from the legal charges leveled at King and his fellow conspirators. Appeals of Mrs. Parks's case, which the boycott's lawyers amended and supplemented with additional litigants, were quickly moved to the federal courts and dealt narrowly with the issues of desegregating the city's buses. King and, indirectly, the indicted "celebrities" were forced on two separate occasions to defend their legal right to conduct what became a highly effective economic boycott. While the boycott's legal team filed petitions in federal courts during May of 1956 attacking local bus segregation, the boycott's leaders were forced to defend their actions when charged under an old Alabama law prohibiting secondary economic boycotts. Interestingly, the existence of this law explains why the movement's leaders consistently avoided any public reference to their protest as being a "bus boycott."[9]

In a major tactical blunder, it was not until the middle of November 1956 that the city's lawyers successfully sought to enjoin the MIA from operating its boycott-sustaining car pool. That would be the city's third legal attack designed to destroy the bus protest. As the earlier attempts had failed, so would this effort. It was an attack that, by that late date, would not harm the protest's ultimate outcome. By then other forces were about to intercede.

In an ironic twist the U.S. Supreme Court announced its decision affirming an earlier federal court order outlawing Montgomery's system of bus segregation on the very day, November 13, 1956, that the city was successful in getting the MIA's car pool outlawed. Despite their defeat in the Supreme Court, Montgomery's elected officials refused to allow desegregated buses until official legal notification was formally received. During this interim period, those blacks in Montgomery who had depended on the buses and a now-enjoined private car pool resumed walking. They did this rather than return to still segregated buses. The protestors felt that their victory should not now be tainted by a final lack of resolve. In those waning days of the boycott the movement's leaders shifted their emphasis to preparing the masses for returning to a bus system that would be, at least formally, desegregated.

Much effort was put into organizing "good conduct" workshops and preparing instructional leaflets on proper bus etiquette. There was also much quiet revelry in the wake of the Supreme Court's decision. While celebrations occurred, other patterns, normal for this stage of a social movement's career, also began to emerge. The satisfaction of those first days of victory would, at least for some, begin to be tempered by a growing sense of loss. Not surprisingly this lassitude contributed to efforts by some to hang on to the movement's protest forms indefinitely.

The mass meetings and the stimulus of seeing empty buses were only reluctantly being relinquished. Rufus Lewis, though normally a very reserved man, gestured profusely as he described how such circumstances affected him.

> The most stimulating thing of the whole process was that there were so few black people who would get on those buses. To see the reactions of blacks. To know that the message had gotten over, to the world and to the other folk. You can't imagine how that felt. It was like we said, well we can do anything now.
>
> You couldn't keep that high all the time. But the mass meetings were stimulating too. You'd say that you were going to have the meeting at seven and people would have the church filled at five o'clock.[10]

Given the intensity of such experiences, the boycott's most active participants tried to hold on to the spirit and rituals, the feelings, of the protest activities. New emotions developed in the "victory days" period as well. Those feelings were not brought on by how they were treated once they returned to the buses.

A Final Violent Salvo, Then White Retreat

By late fall 1956, the boycotters had severely reduced the number of mass meetings being held. Car pool ridership also showed a drop as the cool, crisp days of Alabama's fall replaced summer's swelter. The presidential election of 1956, rematching the candidates of 1952, took the nation's and much of Montgomery's attention away from the lingering bus boycott. The Supreme Court had not then acted, but many who had joined in the protest had become emotionally fatigued. King and other boycott figures continued to give out-of-town talks before interested audiences, but the newness of the movement was wearing off. There were only sporadic incidents that totally reinvigorated the morale of the movement's masses in those waning months. The appearance in Montgomery of the Ku Klux Klan in late November 1956 was such an occasion.

The Klan had made a comeback of sorts in central Alabama beginning in the late 1940s.[11] Fractured by internal corruption, the new Klan of the 1950s was barely tolerated by the majority of whites in the Black Belt. Alabama's whites had quickly come to perceive that group's tactics as needlessly crude and generally ineffective. Nonetheless, that group managed to attract about a thousand spectators to a Saturday night rally at a motor speedway just outside Montgomery on November 24, 1956. Robed speakers admonished those in attendance to be wary of integrationist-oriented "burr-headed niggers," but their blustery rhetoric and other efforts to intimidate Montgomery's blacks proved futile.[12] This Alabama Klan of the 1950s was so comically disorganized that when its members made an attempt to motorcade through Montgomery's black communities, they lost their way and eventually became separated from each other. Witnessing that spectacle, blacks heckled and waved at the ragtag Klansmen as they meandered through the streets of the Alabama capital. Though the Klan seemed comical in its outmoded intimidation efforts, serious violence did erupt in Montgomery after blacks returned to the now-integrated buses. It was to be violence of a type similar to acts that would later bring death to many during the Selma protest year of 1965.

Several desegregated buses became targets of rifle fire in late December 1956. The City Commission reacted to these ambushes by ordering a halt to all night bus service. It is interesting to note that once again black women seemed selectively targeted during these waves of reactionary terror. Several incidents involved black female passengers being beaten or passengers being beaten by small groups of white males. King described the assault victims as including a teenage girl beaten by "white thugs" and a pregnant woman who was shot in the leg.[13] This wave of terror was not limited to passengers getting off buses. During the last days of 1956 a series of bombings rocked Montgomery. The targets included the homes of Robert Graetz and Ralph Abernathy, and four churches that had been used for mass meetings. Unlike King's and Nixon's homes these victims suffered extensive property damage.

The members of Montgomery's governing City Commission quickly moved to reassert their authority. Prompted by a recovered Mayor Gayle, the city posted a reward for the apprehension of those responsible for these latest bombings. Within a matter of days seven whites were arrested and charged with the bombings. Despite signed confessions from two of those indicted and a strong prosecution effort, an all-white jury acquitted all the accused.[14] Montgomery's blacks, though further embittered, were not surprised by that demonstration of local justice, nor were most of the city's blacks surprised at the white response to bus desegregation.

After King had led Montgomery's blacks back to the buses on December 21, 1956, local whites began staying off those vehicles altogether. While not organized in their actions, Montgomery's whites got strong encouragement from important opinion makers.

Alabama State Senator Sam Englehardt, a key figure in Montgomery's White Citizens' Council, publicly advocated that all whites now turn their backs on the bus system.[15] Propelled by such sentiments and increasingly able to rely on private automobiles, Montgomery's whites tended to avoid the buses altogether as the 1950s became the 1960s. While such a move was not unanticipated by Montgomery's blacks, it did cause continued economic hardship for the Chicago-based bus company. As for black Montgomerians, many were already focusing on other long-held goals. Before commenting on their directions some summary comments about factors that contributed to the generally successful protest operation should be stated.

Some Critical Differences That Made the Difference

While the residents of Montgomery's black community had characteristics common in Alabama's Black Belt, there were differences about that city setting that proved critical to the emergence of opposition to the racial status quo. Montgomery had long been a site of militant, albeit quiet, black opposition to the most degrading aspects of racial segregation, giving that community an established constituency ready for this episode of resistance. A striking early parallel pertinent to this study's findings has been ably described by August Meier and Elliott Rudwick.[16]

In their interesting article they describe how one form of black political opposition was expressed at the turn of the century. Meier and Rudwick note that Montgomery was one of a very few southern cities where a trolley car "boycott" was temporarily successful. That effort, made to protest the initial imposition of segregation on municipal carriers, was sustained over the years 1902 and 1903. Their article establishes that this early transit protest was led principally by black ministers. They also indicated that despite the "surprising persistency" shown by the trolley car boycotters, segregation was later "quietly imposed."[17]

While segregation was ultimately rigidly enforced in the decades after the trolley car boycott, Montgomery's black community remained a social arena where a militant leadership could be successfully nurtured. While much of this leadership emerged from the normal Black Belt processes that produced E. D. Nixon, Joe Reed, Rosa Parks and others, six additional factors about Montgomery contributed to its uniqueness.

While similar conditions might have prevailed in other locations, these particular patterns made the bus protest's success more likely. Among the most important of these was (1) Montgomery's symbolic legacy as the first capital of the old Confederacy. This contributed to Montgomery's reputation as a "hardcore" city with both northern blacks and whites. This reputation was wisely played upon by the protest's leaders as they used every means to generate necessary support. Though described as an especially repressive southern city, Montgomery by the mid-1950's was actually controlled by relatively moderate whites. Though "moderate" only if compared to racial hardliners such as Bull Connor of Birmingham, these white leaders were willing to occasionally deliberate with their black counterparts. This practice lent credibility to the protest leadership and allowed key members of that group, especially King, to mature under fire. These white officials also made repeated strategic errors as they sought alternately to crack down on, then conciliate Montgomery's bus boycotters. It is now clear that the white leaders' most persistent mistake was a faulty estimation of the resolve of the black masses. The white officials also failed to appreciate the ingenuity of their leadership counterparts. Individuals such as Jo Ann Robinson and others might not have been "counted" by the opposition but their actions proved critical. Also crucial to the success of the protest was (2) the existence in Montgomery of a substantial, and organizable, black population of roughly 50,000.

Montgomery's blacks were concentrated in several spatially dispersed, though compact, neighborhoods. Communication among leaders of these black areas was easily maintained during the boycott, but this population dispersion made implementing social control tactics more difficult for those opposing the movement. This was an especially critical point since these neighborhoods had been gradually supplemented by migrants from other areas of the Black Belt. By the mid-1950s many of these newcomers had successfully adjusted to the relative security they found in black neighborhoods of Montgomery. Additionally, such a population shift added to a growing confidence among both leaders and followers that collectively opposition to the more brutal forms of white racial oppression might now be possible. The existence of these increasingly restive masses facilitated the growth and helped shape the character of (3) a moderately militant black middle class.

The emergence of this relatively independent black professional class marked the culmination of a process occurring throughout the South in the 1940s and 1950s. It was especially critical in Montgomery. What made middle-class blacks in Montgomery different from their counterparts elsewhere, however, was their political perspective. Many had been educated in the North or were affiliated with Alabama State University, an institution where "proper" race consciousness was much more militant than at comparable facilities such as Booker T. Washington's Tuskegee Institute. In the months before the boycott, Alabama State University had hosted Adam Clayton Powell, Jr. and several other speakers who were viewed at the time as very militant "race men."[18] Enhancing the development of such relative race militancy was the disrespectful and abrasive treatment local whites still accorded members of this "tie and collar" crowd. As a result racial, not class, consciousness remained their prevailing point of reference. While middle-class blacks retained this strong sense of racial identity, they had developed the organizational skills typically associated with professionals. The highly visible behavior of the "tie and collar" crowd in Montgomery gave strong impetus to similar activity by their class counterparts in later civil rights struggles.

As the largest black college in the state, Alabama State University also provided an especially well-educated and relatively politicized faculty available for potential mobilization. Members of this class of professional blacks contributed to an additional key factor: (4) the numerous black voluntary associations, self-help groups, and politically-oriented clubs in Montgomery. Membership in these groups often crossed class lines in black Montgomery and provided important training opportunities for those who played roles in the boycott's leadership structure. Rufus Lewis, E. D. Nixon, and others headed political action groups that were relatively unique in the Black Belt. Such groups were in place when the boycott began and their importance became obvious when the MIA needed additional office space to house its rapidly growing clerical staff. That problem was quickly solved when the Black Bricklayers Union allowed the new organization the use of their private meeting hall. Such groups played critical roles throughout the career of the protest.

Just as crucial was (5) a small group of activist religious leaders. They provided essential leadership qualities and the spiritual legitimacy (a critical factor in a region like the Black Belt) necessary to maintain the struggle during the movement's more difficult phases. More important for the future, the behavior of these religious leaders in Montgomery gave strong impetus to similar actions throughout the South. After the boycott ended, black ministers throughout the South found that their followers expected them to be and do "right" on movement issues. This new expectation is attributable in part to the example set in Montgomery during 1955 and 1956.

Both Martin Luther King, Jr. and Robert Graetz personified these elements, but they were widely shared by other well-known ministers in Montgomery's black community. Importantly, the community's adulation was so intense and the spotlight was so broad that few petty jealousies intruded on the MIA's cohesion. On those rare occasions when jealousy emerged it was deftly handled by a rapidly maturing King and other experienced leaders. Finally, there was (6) the relatively nonthreatening form that the protest itself took.

This final factor has to be understood as being as critical as any previously discussed. The boycott, directed as it was at withdrawing from, rather than assaulting, a system of segregation, had little direct daily impact on the city.

513

For while important symbolically, reforming a bus seating system did not significantly threaten the racial interest of local whites. Additionally, it was a form of activism that was, as were all the methods used by these protesters, completely respectable in the eyes of most living in this country and to the citizens of the world. The appearance of using wholly legitimate methods helped the protesters' cause immeasurably. While a mounted posse could attack rural blacks in the 1930s, the bus boycotters' tactics denied whites many retaliatory options. The white response to the black victory, a significant withdrawal of bus patronage, presaged what would happen throughout the Black Belt when that region's public schools were finally integrated in the late 1960s.

That the boycott required only that blacks refrain from an activity that had previously became fraught with anxiety also operated to strengthen the boycott leaders' position. This low level of demand on participants facilitated mass inclusion rather than exclusion. These were all important factors in sustaining the boycott. Given the benefit of Montgomery's example, activists in subsequent struggles would frequently emphasize tactics that also provided opportunities, though sometimes only symbolic, for mass involvement.

By listing these factors I do not mean to imply that their existence was sufficient cause for either the movement's emergence or success. Throughout this analysis care has been taken to focus on previously unexamined factors that contributed to the boycott's evolution. The interaction of these and factors discussed in previous chapters contributed to the general patterns the boycott exhibited. But it is not always possible to describe precisely how all such factors interacted. Just as aspects of human behavior continue to defy explanation, so it is with social movements, but clarification of a social movement is possible when one applies useful theoretical tools. In this work's introductory chapter Herbert Blumer's ideas about social movements were briefly discussed. In many ways this study's findings confirm the accuracy of those views. Blumer's ideas about social movements, however, have serious limitations in some areas. His framework barely acknowledges the inner turmoil frequently felt by people before their involvement in social movements. Blumer's ideas also provide rather sketchy notions about how activists and societies are affected once a movement enters its declining stage. Though Blumer was not preoccupied with such matters, they are important. In the final section that follows, these topics are touched upon as they relate to this movement.

The Post-Boycott Years

Jerry D. Rose has observed

> A major focus of sociological interest in social movements that make specific demands has been the question of the fate of such movements in relation to the fate of the goals they are pursuing. It might seem obvious that if the aims of a movement were accomplished, the movement would cease to exist. Actually, this seems frequently not to be the case. People who have fought together for a cause may develop affective attachments to one another and may be reluctant to break up their association when the original cause of the movement ceases to be an active motivation.[19]

While Rose correctly notes that movements that achieve their aims rarely disband immediately, he fails to address how those residual organizations and affective ties function as activity declines. In the case of the bus boycott three post-protest patterns are seen: (1) the boycott's contributions and symbolic significance to the developing Civil Rights Movement; (2) the impact, or lack of one, the movement had on local affairs through the continued operation of MIA; and (3) the effect the protest had on reshaping the personal beliefs, values and activities of its participants. Each of these deserves some brief comment.

The Montgomery movement prompted emulative efforts throughout the Deep South. While more than twenty localities quietly desegregated their bus lines as a direct consequence of the Montgomery protest, most large cities held firm.[20] Where blacks tried to organize boycotts similar to the one in Montgomery, they generally received negative responses. The most noted of these imitative boycotts occurred in Tallahassee, Florida in early 1957. That protest failed to achieve either the national attention or the local support needed to push it to a victory. When Florida's governor suspended bus service in that capital city, the Tallahassee movement floundered before ultimately collapsing.[21] The leader of that failed Florida protest effort, Reverend C. K. Steele, did ultimately make a valuable contribution to the ongoing Civil Rights Movement. It was Steele who called for a meeting of activist black ministers to be held in Atlanta during early January, 1957. Buoyed by the still recent success of the Montgomery movement, Steele's conference call produced the Southern Christian Leadership Conference, with Martin Luther King, Jr. as its president.

King transferred the tactics and organizational structure of the Montgomery movement virtually intact into this new organization. With

King as its principal spokesman, this new organization provided numerous aspirants hope and advice as they approached what would be the turbulent 1960s. The SCLC was to grow and remain King's organizational base for the remaining years of his life. While the SCLC was to fall on hard times after King's death, for a while it was a major force in the South. It owed a lot to the Montgomery protest's pattern.

The Montgomery movement produced much more than just a regional, voluntary association. It provided the South's blacks with clear evidence that direct opposition to the racial status quo would produce positive results. Indications of this contribution were widely expressed in the early 1960s. William H. Peace III, himself a black activist in Raleigh, North Carolina in the early 1960s, suggests that the Montgomery protest did more than just stimulate an already emerging consciousness. Peace, in discussing the student sit-in-movement in the early 1960s, asserts

> Throughout the South, associations were formed in each city along the lines of the Montgomery Improvement Association which had played such a key part during the bus boycott in Montgomery, Alabama. These associations, working in close conjunction with the Negro churches, became the backbone of the student movement which would not have been able to start or to maintain itself without the aid of these local groups.[22]

Scholars as well as black participants have since noted how critical the Montgomery movement was in effecting such future directions. James W. Vander Zanden, Robert H. Brisbane, Everett C. Ladd, Jr., and numerous others have described the boycott's impact.[23] While the boycott helped foster a legacy of the tactical wisdom of direct action, it had a less definite impact on Montgomery itself.

By the boycott's final days, the "tie and collar" crowd and local ministers had become the dominant forces in the MIA. Grass roots leaders such as E. D. Nixon and Reverend Cherry became increasingly bitter about being pushed aside and left the MIA's leadership circle. Though King and his successors tried, no major effort paralleling the bus protest emerged in Montgomery. Lacking local issues to organize around and faced with a growing usurpation of organizational positions by status seekers, the MIA became further removed from the local black masses. This process escalated after King's permanent departure for Atlanta in early 1960.

With King's departure the MIA, already in decline, slid further toward organizational irrelevancy. No longer able to easily generate a significant demonstration of support from the local citizens, the MIA had trouble following up the boycott victory. As late as 1962 the organization's president was still pleading with the City Commission to hire black bus drivers. While this had been one of the initial requests in December 1955, by then only two had been hired.[24] By the mid-1960s, the MIA was being led by its fourth president, Reverend Jesse L. Douglass, and was directing much of its organizational energy to an ineffective campaign for voter registration. While holding annual commemorative services coinciding with the arrest date of Mrs. Parks, the MIA had become generally ignored by the masses of Montgomery's blacks. Though this was so, there was still a lingering amount of prestige involved with being officially connected with the organization. By the mid-1960s its annual public program was largely organized by committees dominated by black society women and a handful of ministers from the more prosperous of the local black churches.[25] The inclusion of King as the keynote speaker in 1966, one of his rare post-boycott ventures to Montgomery, was the only event that attracted much of a crowd.

The decline of the MIA accelerated in the 1970s. That group now lacks even a meeting place. Led by Mrs. Johnnie Carr beginning in the mid-1970s, the organization has been abandoned by both the "tie and collar" element as well as the general masses.

While the MIA was approaching organizational extinction by the late 1970s, memories of the boycott and its effect on local citizens could still be detected in Montgomery. As they recalled the glory days of the boycott, many of the former activists expressed bitterness with Montgomery's present. Not surprisingly, it is similar to the bitterness that was widespread before the boycott. Disgust with a lack of economic opportunity, hurt from a continuing refusal by many whites to extend them respect, and a fear that expecting any real change was futile, were prevalent attitudes among the boycott's former activists.

Mrs. Hazel Gregory, who played a critical role in MIA's bureaucratic functioning, later had trouble gaining employment because of her activities. Mrs. Gregory now often wonders about those who, like herself, were such staunch boycott supporters. Years later she still experienced negative effects from her boycott involvement but expressed bitterness primarily toward other blacks, not whites in Montgomery. She said

I'm still known as Hazel Gregory, the MIA's secretary. The blacks who actually take part in things here, want to keep me out. I ask the question, what is it?

They are almost as determined as whites that I will continue to suffer because of my participation. But this will not deter me from going forward.

I do have mixed emotions many times about the movement, but the rewards were worth it. And I would do it again.[26]

Mrs. Gregory expresses such thoughts because she remains haunted by a circumstance that largely explained her initial boycott involvement. Hers was a predicament shared with many other boycott participants, including Rosa Parks, Jo Ann Robinson, Martin Luther King, Jr., Joe Reed, and others; the inner conflicts and troubles associated with what Tamotsu Shibutani calls "marginal status."[27] Those who became activists, and countless others in Montgomery, reached a stage where, given the conditions of the Black Belt, they felt compelled to make moral decisions about their personal conduct regarding segregation. When an organized protest opportunity presented itself, such decisions followed easily, given the social logic that had been incubating for decades.

Feelings of marginality most often become acute under conditions where one has to choose between contrasting behaviors expected by various reference groups. In Montgomery, the ideas, behaviors and new expectations associated with expanded education, travel and outside support, made it easy to reject the daily, degrading rituals of racial segregation. Though a precipitating incident was necessary to make the decision official, Montgomery's blacks, both elites and masses, had finally reached the stage where no other behavior except protest seemed reasonable or acceptable. Most may not have been aware of this when the rumblings began. Some few, however, had plans from the beginning. E. D. Nixon suggests that, from the start, "Our goal was to break down segregation, that's what we really started for."[28] Now little seems to be stirring in an area where much still needs to accomplished.

That job was not completed by the boycott nor were all as affected by that movement as were Rosa Parks, Martin Luther King, Jr., Rufus Lewis, and others. That social episode did however profoundly influence the nation's consciousness and the strategies for change that would be used in the years ahead. In that regard, as the author quoted Jo Ann Robinson when opening this chapter, the bus boycott of Montgomery, circa 1955-56, was

" . . . just a start . . . "

Interviews

Erna Dungee Allen

AUGUST 6, 1977

[Allen was secretary of the Women's Political Council and did mimeographic work for voter registration.]

Millner: What was Montgomery like before the boycott?

Allen: As I recall, black people were kind of coasting along, everything was segregated. We had just accepted that. We didn't like it because sometimes it was most inconvenient. You would avoid using some things, like transportation, because it was so inconvenient. You would drive as long as you could because there was no motel accommodation along the way. You'd drive until you got to some place where you knew someone.

Millner: What was the basic goal of the Women's Political Council?

Allen: Primarily voter registration. We had been in touch with the League of Women Voters in Washington, D.C. about getting a second chapter here in Montgomery for ourselves, but they said they could not have two in one city. So we set up the Women's Political Council. It was mostly professional people like teachers, social workers, secretaries. Jo Ann Robinson, Mary Fair Burks, and others were real smart and active.

Millner: How did Montgomery's whites compare to whites in Birmingham, Mobile, etc.?

Allen: Some cooperation, we didn't eat together, didn't socialize together, though I feel whites in those cities were basically the same.

Millner: When did you hear of the idea of the boycott?

Allen: I'm a member of the A.M.E. Zion. We were having a one-day meeting on the corner of High Street and Hall Street. Reverend Abernathy came in and interrupted the meeting with these pamphlets that said "Stay off the buses Monday." So we took those leaflets over to our church, Reverend Bennett and I, and duplicated them and passed out hundreds of them on this side of town.

Millner: Which of the ministers had the most influence?

Allen: Reverend Bennett was president of Ministerial Alliance, then there was Reverend A. W. Wilson and Reverend Hubbard and Reverend King. Reverend King hadn't been in the community long, but he was really making an impact on the community. Mr. Nixon, though, was the first person I heard who said boycott.

Millner: Were you surprised by the idea of the boycott?

Allen: I hadn't thought about it. But no, I wasn't. It seemed like the logical thing to do.

Millner: What did you think of the initial goals?

Allen: The initial goals were for first come, first served. And at that time that seemed a fair solution. But it was not accepted. So then they went for the whole thing. If they had accepted the other goals we might've been doing that yet.

Millner: How important were black women in those first few meetings?

Allen: Women listened to men. They passed the ideas to men to a great extent. Mary Fair Burks and Jo Ann Robinson were very vocal and articulate, especially in committee meetings. But when it came to the big meetings, they let the men have the ideas and carry the ball. They were kind of like the power behind the throne.

We really were the ones who carried out the actions. Driving the cars, though men eventually took over that. But we organized the parking lot pick-ups and many things like that. Finally, Mr. Rufus Lewis and Reverend B. J. Simms took over that transportation committee.

522

It just seemed as if a lot of women, good people like Mrs. Georgia Gilmore and others, were just waiting for something like this.

Millner: How did the protestors operate behind the scenes?

Allen: You talk about women in the boycott. When all the dust settled the women were there when it cleared. They were there in the positions to hold the thing [MIA] together. We took the position that if anything comes up, all you have to do is whistle and the men will be there. They'd come. But the little day-to-day things, taking care of the finances, things like that, the women still take care of that.

Millner: How long did it take for the MIA to become a smooth-running operation?

Allen: Not too long. There was always somebody to work out any snags. The biggest problem was police harassment. It just seemed we had never done anything like this, but it turned out to be just like it was run by professionals.

Millner: What kind of administrator was Reverend King?

Allen: He listened a lot and he thought a lot. He got by himself a lot. But he had a lot of help from the other men. And they exchanged ideas and he accepted ideas. And they usually came up with a good decision out of all of the exchanging of ideas.

Millner: What about the other leaders? What were your impressions?

Allen: Reverend Fields was kind of temperamental, jealous, rivalry. I think that's what set him off.

Mr. Nixon, he didn't have the education that most of the men had and that's what, I think, frustrated him. His was more of a frustration than any meanness or resentful. But he did question things because he had been the one who had gotten Mrs. Parks out of jail. But he was the one who suggested Dr. King be president.

Millner: What was it like working in the MIA?

Allen: Oh, you just worked. You worked . . . Sometimes, I'd go there in the morning and I'd be there until midnight. And I'd leave and Mr. Nixon and some of the others, they'd still be there. I don't know when they'd sleep. I'd never seen that before or since.

Millner: How did people get hired as protest workers?

Allen: The drivers, for instance, were ministers by and large. The other people had jobs but the ministers could drive all day.

Millner: What was the protest's long-term impact on you?

Allen: Yeah, I would say it showed me that if you want to do something and want it enough, that you can do it. I teach my child the same thing.

Millner: Had you heard about the philosophy of nonviolence before Reverend King got here?

Allen: Only through India, Gandhi. But in our case we had no choice. We had no guns, they had everything. [laughs] It was the only thing we could've done.

Millner: Did everyone go along with nonviolence?

Allen: On the surface.

Millner: What were some of the things that haven't been reported about the boycott?

Allen: There were so many things. We paid rent. We paid gas bills. We paid water bills. We bought food. We paid people's doctor bills. We even buried somebody. Not as a result of any activity. Those were free rides as far as I was concerned. But they seemed to think this is what we had to do. We even bought washing machines. We did everything trying to get along with the people.

And usually the folks who weren't participating, who didn't belong to a church or anything, were the ones who came for help. They were usually the poorest ones.

Reverend King, he was real sympathetic. But he was against some of that. But the majority of that, he felt he had to go along with most of it.

Johnnie Carr

Millner: What was Montgomery like before the boycott?

Carr: We were always very depressed. 'Cause our people didn't have any opportunities to participate in things that we felt that as citizens we should've been given. The lack of opportunity to go to school bothered us. Myself, I went to a school where the teachers always taught us that the color of your skin had nothing to do with the content of your heart. Your character is what you go by. So we had something in us that made us feel, you know, that we ought to be allowed to participate in various things in the community.

For instance, I would go downtown and if I wanted to buy a hamburger, and sometimes I did, I'd have to find a black hamburger shop unless I wanted to go down into a little hole in a basement.

Of course we also had the problem of police brutality and even of young girls who were raped by policemen here. The NAACP and others would carry it to court. But it was always that the granddaddy was a judge or the uncle was a sheriff, it was an all-white family affair.

But if it was a black man accused of raping a white woman, you just knew that was the electric chair! All these types of things just made us bitter, bitter!

And we would have our conventions and things and we wouldn't think of trying to go downtown to a place like the Jefferson Davis Hotel. We just had our meetings in our churches.

A lot of black people just resigned themselves to this. But the NAACP and others would just try and get us to fight. And I can remember one of the first fights we had was when the ministers tried to get us to fight to get the curtains removed that separated us on the trains' dining cars. At the time we kinda had the cart before the horse because we thought that if you had achieved in life, you shouldn't have to face this. Well, we finally realized that

527

it's not whether you have achieved in life, but whether you are a human being, that you should have an opportunity.

We also went into stores and you would put down your name as Mrs. Johnnie Carr and the clerk she'd write it Johnnie Carr. I remember me and a friend went to a store that was having a sale. And we applied for some credit. I wrote my name as Mrs. J. R. Carr and the clerk she wrote J. R. Carr and I just looked at her. Then, finally, I said, "I put Mrs. J. R. Carr," and she said, "Oh." And I never did get that credit. And until this day I haven't shopped in that store, even though they have excellent material. My friend didn't put Mrs. on her application and she got her credit.

They really used to treat black women wrong. If you'd go into a store and wanted to try on a hat, they'd tell you that you better put a stocking cap on your head. Then if you'd go into a store to try on shoes and didn't have stockings, they'd go and find you an old footlet to put on and all that kind of stuff. There was so much of that stuff. All those types of things made us bitter, bitter. So, when the protest started, it wasn't anything new for me 'cause I had protested and boycotted all along. I was just happy that something had finally come along.

Millner: Tell me something about the Women's Political Council.

Carr: They had the Women's League of Voters and blacks could not join. So black women formed their own league. People like Jo Ann Robinson, Mary Fair Burks, and Mrs. A. W. West worked very hard as leaders to get us organized. We had been working for years together.

Millner: What about what happened in early December 1955?

Carr: Mr. Nixon said that when they arrested Mrs. Rosa Parks that they had arrested the wrong woman.

When Mrs. Parks was arrested, this seemed to have been the thing that sweetened the cheese. It got people started.

I remember my first contact after Mr. Nixon called and told me about Mrs. Parks. It was from Mrs. A. W. West who called and asked if I would take an area to distribute the leaflets. I told her I was going out of town to Birmingham for a meeting but that I would see to it that there would be people in the community that got those leaflets out. So I got about five people in my neighborhood to do that.

Millner: What was your initial exposure to Martin Luther King, Jr.?

Carr: It was at an NAACP meeting in August 1955. He just got up and made a few remarks after he had been introduced by Mr. Robert Nesbit. Rosa and I were there and I just turned around and said, "Listen to that, he's something, isn't he?" The flow of his words and the way that he expressed them while just talking about ordinary things. We discovered something in him that just made him seem a little bit different from others. Now Mr. Nixon was a hardworking man, a fine leader and everything, but he doesn't have that thing that could weld people together in a movement like ours.

Millner: When did you hear King speak again?

Carr: That first night at the mass meeting when people came together. There was a flowing out from one to another and Dr. King, when he spoke, well, his leadership was just something else.

Millner: What did you think about the initial goals of the MIA?

Carr: That was when the whites put their foot in their mouth. Because when the committee went down, with Dr. King as their leader, they were trying to stop people from being harassed and being made to give up their seats. When the whites refused that, they had done what we called put their foot in their mouth. The movement would've never gotten so strong as it got. And we would have not moved as fast as we did and the MIA would not have ever existed today. They rejected us meanly.

But they just made us so much more determined. So determined that we wouldn't give up. Some of them said that we'd be back on the buses the first day that it rained hard. I can just remember that so. And the first day it rained, I got in my car and drove down and saw a group of people down on Decatur Street and I stopped and said, "As many of you as can, get in this car." And they said, "No, no, Mrs. Carr, just let us walk in the rain." Rain just dripping down off of 'em and I just sat in the car and cried like a baby. Because people were willing to do these things, to sacrifice. And I just knew that God was going to do something for us.

Millner: How did people react when the Mayor and the three ministers announced the first settlement?

Carr: Well, those ministers were really what you would call Uncle Tommish. And the people just rejected it. You could tell as soon as their names came out who they were. None of them was real leaders in our communities. It was like an old-time joke to us. Did they think we were fools?

Millner: What about U. J. Fields? How did you react to his statements and charges about leaders abusing their positions and so on?

Carr: Well, let me give you a little background on Reverend Fields. This church on the corner, Hall Street Baptist Church, our minister had gone and we needed a minister to carry on. So they used Reverend Fields from Alabama State. He was kind of a young minister and the people kind of latched on to him. That's all that Hall Street had ever done, was make young ministers. He started us off by having us bring up the money to him to be blessed. We had never done that kind of thing before and that and three or four other things led people to want to seek out someone else. He was not the pastor, and after he left he really low-rated Hall Street. So I knew him from there.

After they got started, well, naturally, they [the MIA] called him in and even made him secretary. Now there may have been some money spent unwisely, but I don't think no money was spent any other way. But he had got his head so big that he said those things anyway. Now anybody with any sense at all knows that you will make mistakes and blunders and things. And I think very little of anybody who was part of the inside who would go out and try and destroy. And that's all he was doing. And if it could've been proven that people were doing wrong, it might've destroyed people's minds and hearts.

Millner: Were there any others who were jealous?

Carr: I have heard Mr. Nixon say that "When I walk into an MIA meeting, don't nobody clap or say anything, but when Dr. King walks in, everybody stands up and claps." Now he had been here working down through the years and all, but it was just one of those things. And I got all over him about that.

Ralph Abernathy had a tinge of that in him. And we found it out and we would try and cure him. 'Cause he was Dr. King's right-hand man.

Millner: What's become of today's MIA?

Carr: Well, now we have the Board of Directors that has twenty-seven. We have doctors, lawyers, postmen, housewives, ministers, just a cross section of people. We just don't have the masses or the money to do everything we want. We'd like to send a busload to Atlanta for the SCLC's birthday celebration, but we just can't do it. Maybe six or seven of us will go.

Millner: Do you think any of the MIA's difficulty might be that some don't want to have a woman president?

Carr: Well, it has occurred to me. Because I've heard so much about this women's lib. And I have even offered that if they want to remove me, they can, 'cause it doesn't make that much difference to me. But then people say no, because they wouldn't find anyone who would be as interested as me. I've been the president now for ten years.

Millner: What kinds of things is the group involved with now?

Carr: Well, we're kind of involved with this housing discrimination thing. We'll go into suits and things where the MIA will go in and join. At one time we were deeply involved in desegregation of the schools. Schools were integrated all around, Mobile, Tuskegee, just all round. And we finally found some litigants and got things moving here. One of them was a Methodist minister, Reverend B. S. Thompson, and as soon as his bishop found out, he was moved to Mississippi. That left the Carrs to carry that burden. My son Oliver Carr, Jr. was a litigant against the schools.

Millner: Had you been a bus rider before the protest?

Carr: Yes, I had been a bus rider. And I had argued with those drivers about the seats. I was real ornery about that. I wasn't in any hurry about going back. I just wanted it so that people could go and be properly served.

Millner: What about when the boycott ended?

Carr: I was so proud when they put black bus drivers on that I just said I want to get on and just go with him.

But I'm still a little disillusioned because I think we are losing a little bit of ground in 1977.

Millner: Are you still active in organizations other than the MIA?

Carr: I'm still a member of the NAACP. There are now two branches of it. It doesn't seem like the East Side branch is too active, but the West Side branch is doing quite a bit.

The MIA meets once a month. But not in the summer. We tried that before but it just doesn't seem to work then. We need new blood. Young blood. Maybe something will happen again.

U. J. Fields

NOVEMBER 25, 1977

Millner: Tell me some things about your background.

Fields: I was born in Alabama. A small town called Sunflower. It's forty miles north of Mobile. Later I lived in Chicago. Served in the military and had my service extended during the Korean conflict. I returned to Chicago, considered going to Roosevelt College, but as it cost too much, I returned to Alabama and went to Montgomery's Alabama State University.

I found no relief from segregation in either Chicago or the military.

I did a lot of thinking in the military about racism. And as a freshman at Alabama State College I became a leader. I became the president of my class. After a couple of years I became a minister. I was "called" while in the military. I had been a chaplain's assistant. I was ordained just before I "took over" the Bell Street Baptist Church.

[Fields went on to claim he was highly respected at Alabama State by his professors because he could do things about his disenchantment, while they couldn't. Fields then claimed that at Bell Street Baptist Church he had a "power base" while being "economically secure" because he had both a student body position and the G.I. Bill.

He was called to Bell Street in 1953, and ran for president of the student council at Alabama State University. He had been inspired by E. D. Nixon's election campaign for a Ward Leader's seat in 1954. Fields claimed Nixon was the first black on the ballot in Montgomery County since Reconstruction. He then emulated Nixon's campaign at Alabama State and became a member of the Progressive Democrat Club. U. J. Fields won that 1954 election despite not being a black "Greek." He claims that before the boycott he had to try three times before he could become a registered voter.

533

During that student campaign Fields claimed that Jo Ann Robinson and Mary Fair Burks got an Alabama State voting machine on which to conduct the student vote. This was to raise the consciousness of students.

Curiously, U. J. Fields was a member of another church while he pastored the Bell Street Baptist Church. During that time Claudette Colvin was a member of his congregation.]

Fields: She was a high school student at Booker T. Washington High School, and the way I understand she had been encouraged by her parents to "be a real person," although her parents probably did not encourage her to defy the Alabama State segregation ordinance. But what happened was that she did take a seat. She was put on probation after being found guilty.

I was among a number of persons who got involved in going to court over the Claudette Colvin case, but it just wasn't the time.

Millner: Reverend Fields, would you tell me why King was selected?

Fields: I've heard different versions. Being MIA secretary doesn't mean that my recollection is foolproof. But I believe that I have a recollection that is as well or better than many around me for various reasons. But some things I won't go into. Yet, as I recall, the first choice, Reverend Bennett, didn't want to get involved. As you can recall it was something that could involve death. He declined because he feared. Really feared.

Then it was given to King because some older ministers didn't want it.

I feel that there was a strong feeling as to whether King or I should've had that position. Because of what I had been involved in. But it went to King. And notice that immediately after they selected King president, they elected me secretary. It's like saying, "All right, he didn't get president, I'll give him secretary." Now, I was very pleased that Reverend King was elected president.

[Fields claimed that he knew King prior to the boycott and that the two had occasionally chatted while he was a student. But such talks were only occasional, since King was "in and out of town too much." He had much more to say about King.]

Fields: When money came into the situation, and as egos began to expand, people getting a sense of importance, there came what I call a kind of a seeking to use the masses in a way . . . for the advantage of those who wanted power. This was some of the leadership of the organization. This is what caused me to sever my relationship with the MIA

Millner: Would you summarize your assessment of Reverend King?

Fields: Well, Dr. King was a good man, but Dr. King was a man, as I see it, who played to the grandstand. And he had a sense of pride, and I believe in pride, but I think he had the sense that he . . . well, King had an ego. I think Dr. King did some good work, but he was a person who wanted it to be really known, and yet sometimes in a very subtle way, that he was the person who had the power and that he was responsible for what good was being achieved. And I did not believe that. And I do not believe it many years after.

[U. J. Fields then claimed that there was a significant misuse of funds as well.]

Fields: The truth has never come out on that one. I had some personal knowledge of money that was drawn out, reportedly, to do certain things, make certain purchases, including purchasing a station wagon, that ended up not purchasing a station wagon. But certain other items that was used by people in the leadership. I had strong reactions that this was not the thing to do. At one time the principle of that really bothered me.

After they saw that I wouldn't go along with this, they started to call meetings without involving me. It was like having meetings on the side. King knew of this but did nothing. There were also phony trips that never took place.

Millner: What was your assessment of participants such as Ralph Abernathy?

Fields: Well, there are a number of ways to look at Abernathy. I recall looking at Abernathy when I first met him. He wanted to impress me that he was the most educated black minister in Montgomery, simply because he had a college degree from Alabama State. And he seemed to have taken a great deal of satisfaction from that.

There were people who strongly felt that Abernathy was a person you really had to keep your eyes on. I certainly thought so. And I think that the ways monies were used, Abernathy was one of the persons very much involved making those determinations.

Nobody dared to say a word against Ralph or Dr. King. Now I think we have to give Dr. King some credit. But I would say a word against my Momma if I thought there was something I should say a word against.

Millner: You resigned your post and later criticized the MIA.

Fields: I did not really recant what I had said. There was a lot of emotion that if you spoke against Dr. King on anything like that, was like speaking against the creator. I was aware of that. I was not an insane man, nor a maniac. I started once not to go to that meeting period. The reason I decided to go is because I did not want to do anything that would interrupt the continuation of the Montgomery protest. I was part of that protest. I had put a lot into Montgomery. And I didn't want to do anything that would destroy it.

They say King came to my rescue but I think there's two sides to that. I think King, also recognizing something in my ability and courage, felt that if I did not really, in any way, come back to the organization, that this could actually be just the straw that could break the camel's back. That really it would cause the movement to wane.

I later found there's no pressure like pressure from the inside group. The masses, the poorer people, they deserve a great deal of credit. In a way they were not given it. They were not given it.

Rufus Lewis

JULY 18, 1977

Millner: What types of things were you doing in Montgomery before the boycott years?

Lewis: I was part of the Citizens Club, a group of veterans who organized into a political group and formed a club. This club served for a short while as headquarters of the bus protest.

Millner: What other kinds of clubs or organizations were active in Montgomery before the bus boycott?

Lewis: There were the Progressive Democrats. That was a group of blacks who were trying to get into the Democratic Party. I was the chairman of that group.

Millner: How large were the groups?

Lewis: I couldn't say for sure. They were not large groups. At this time it was a difficult task to get blacks into politics. We spent much of our time trying to get people registered and trying to get them organized and trying to make contact with the larger Democratic Party. We even sent some messages to the Convention. The Progressive Democrats were really alive.

Millner: Were they still active right before the boycott?

Lewis: Yes. They were quite active. They were not too large. They were mainly interested in working in the community politically. Encouraging people to take an active part and to get involved politically. Many were right out of Korea.

537

Millner: Were there any ministers in the Progressive Democrats?

Lewis: No, no. The Citizens Club was the sort of club that was sort of a nightclub. It had dancers, that sort of thing. And the ministers were not involved in that. We worked with churches to have discussions and meetings, but besides giving us that kind of support, they weren't active in the organization. Though they did encourage the people to get registered. Many of these guys were young vets who wanted their rights at home.

Millner: Were you surprised that the ministers got involved in the bus boycott?

Lewis: In a way I was, in a way I was not. It was the personality and force and intellectual level of Reverend King that mostly drew them. He was such a high man above them that they strove to get closer to him. So I wasn't surprised because I knew from the attitudes of some of the ministers. You see, he was doing such an excellent thing that they couldn't pull back. He almost drew them with his personality. And then all the ministers had to join in or they'd be labelled as Toms.

Millner: How did you hear about the boycott?

Lewis: I am a member of Dexter Avenue Baptist Church. I had been prior to Reverend King's coming. And JoAnn Robinson and Mary Frances Burke were members of the church. I think I got it from JoAnn Robinson. I think I got called about Mrs. Parks's arrest. Then everybody wanted to know just what do we do to do something about this thing. I don't know exactly who suggested a meeting and that we talk about it at Dexter.

Millner: Were you surprised that people would consider a boycott of even one day's duration?

Lewis: No. You got to have some understanding of the background before Reverend King. There was a minister, Vernon Johns, before Reverend King who had set the stage, I suppose, for a lot of reaction to white misbehavior, so to speak. And it wasn't such a surprise to react to that sort of thing. We had been reacting to that sort of thing before in a disorganized way. So it wasn't such a big surprise that a group would come and suggest that sort of thing. You knew something had to be done. You try to do something to solve the problems you're involved with.

Millner: During that first meeting at Dexter, what did people talk about doing?

Lewis: During that first meeting we were so disgusted with the results of the meeting because of the chairman, named Reverend Bennett, that not too much was done. It was too confused.

Millner: Why was Reverend Bennett the person who chaired that first meeting?

Lewis: I couldn't answer that. I think the ministers were trying to get in and I think a lot of ministers were called. It was tending toward a ministers' approach. And I think that was why.

Millner: What do you mean by a ministers' approach?

Lewis: Well, you wouldn't of had laymen taking such an active part. All the key positions would've been ministers' positions. And that would've cut some people out who were willing and able to get something done.

You can't have just ministers. You've got to get people. It doesn't matter who you are. I daresay I wouldn't of been chairman of transportation if it would've been solely on the ministers. Although Reverend Simms was assistant to me and he eventually became the chairman. But that wasn't the way to get the best job done and I think Reverend King knew that. A lot of times he didn't want them old ministers any more than us.

Millner: Were there any difficulties between Methodist and Baptist ministers?

Lewis: There may have been a very little. I think it didn't have time to develop. And when the time came for it to develop, King was in such a position so high above everybody that it couldn't congeal.

Millner: Why the initial mild goals?

Lewis: The only reason I can give is that we were reacting to something that to our way of thinking was very bad. We were trying to do the reasonable thing to stop it. And the thing we asked for was to be seated from the back of the bus to the front. I think we were trying to be reasonable. Remove what the past had been. We were trying to take a gradual approach then.

Millner: During the early meetings what would have happened if people had pushed for full integration on the buses?

Lewis: It's hard to say. But the thing is that it was a growth. We were greeted with a situation where we were treated very badly and we wanted to correct this step by step. But as we moved forward the whole horizon seemed to open wider for us. And the wider it is the further you're going to go. That was the type of development.

Millner: Were there any leaders who wanted to push for integration initially?

Lewis: I doubt it, but I can't answer.

Millner: What did you do in the boycott?

Lewis: Getting a group of people together to provide transportation for people. Helping those who did not ride the buses. We worked day and night contacting people who had cars that would volunteer to take people places. And we'd see about getting gathering places for pick-up stations. There weren't any churches that refused us this because at that time most of the people were involved because it was such a stimulating thing. We also had to get places in the alien white community for them to congregate at in order to come home. There were some real problems.

Millner: How often did your Transportation Committee meet?

Lewis: Almost daily. As often as necessary. It wasn't a matter of time. I was a part of the funeral home and had a lot of time I could take. Mrs. Adair, she was completely free. And several others. They could give a lot of time to it.

Millner: Were most of your committee members active?

Lewis: Yes, yes. Very helpful, very active. And the other committees were too. The board was the main thing and it was active too.

Later on I became chairman of the voters registration committee that sent people from door to door, to churches and other places. We finally had enough materials to do it and we had the transportation to take people down to try and register. Once the boycott started, people were much more willing to do this. The whole community just came alive. You were happy to be a part of just anything. This was ten years before Selma.

Millner: What did people say about the boycott's leaders?

Lewis: Well, we know the whites were against it. Some blacks were afraid that things were being pushed too far and too fast. A few were afraid for their job or their relations with some certain whites. Some had these adverse attitudes because of fear.

Millner: When would they express these fears?

Lewis: Well, never at the mass meetings. The mass meetings were so stimulating that it just engulfed everybody. You couldn't resist the influence of the mass meetings. Mainly because of the dynamic personality of Reverend King. No person could inspire the people like him. We had some good people, Reverend Hubbard, Reverend Fields, Reverend Anderson, who's in Mobile now, was an excellent minister, Reverend Hooks, but there was no other man who could compare with Reverend King.

Millner: How did you come to nominate Reverend King as chair?

Lewis: The only answer I can give, I was a member of the church before he came. I had been a churchgoer for a long time, although I'm not sure at this point. I knew many of the other ministers and some of the other persons who headed the organizations, 'cause I had been active here all my life, and the first meeting was such a dissatisfying thing. That's when P. E. Conley and I were talking about it. So I said that this Reverend Bennett, he can't direct this thing. So I suggested that we try and get Reverend King. Now I had made no contact with Dr. King or nobody else. But I was reacting to the confused situation we faced in that first week. And that was the sole reason for my nominating Dr. King. I hadn't talked to E. D. Nixon or anyone else. I mentioned King's name and told him to try and get some support and that I would try and get some support. Nixon and others liked this idea too. So we all went to the meeting and as soon as the part was open for nominating the chairman, I was rushing because I didn't want some of the other folks I knew who were anxious to do it—because I knew what sort of persons they were. I didn't want anybody to get ahead of that so for that reason I nominated Reverend King and Connelly seconded that.

Millner: What other people wanted that position:

Lewis: Well, I couldn't say for sure. But I'm almost sure, I won't call names, but yeah, other people wanted that position.

Millner: What do you think the others' motives were for wanting the position?

Lewis: It's an honor to be a chairman of this, the chairman of the other. Irrespective of whether you're doing the job or not. And sometimes chairmen get an attitude that stifles action instead of generating it.

Millner: Had that happened in Montgomery before?

Lewis: Yes, yes. Persons would get in positions mainly for selfish reasons and just stifle the whole movement. And they weren't doing anything. Some were ministers, some were not. This was the reason I wanted to get a jump on them. I did not talk to Martin King. He did not know what I had in mind. And when he found out I understand he said, "if that's what y'all want, I'll do my best."

Millner: Why did you put such emphasis on voting?

Lewis: That's a good question. I just knew, see. I had a feeling that voting was extremely important. When I was teaching veterans my job was government and civics, and my civics was mainly voter registration. The white VA supervisor was a man who never came into my classroom 'cause he didn't want me to teach it, but he couldn't stop me. He was not a bad white man.

Millner: Would you change anything about the boycott?

Lewis: The only thing would be to have had enough leadership left after Reverend King went away to the SCLC to have a cohesive group here in Montgomery. I think we lost a great deal after Reverend King and Reverend Abernathy went away from here.

Millner: What other kinds of things did you do during the boycott?

Lewis: I went all over, held a lot of meetings and things, but the only effective thing was voter registration.

Once I was in Lowndes County during the boycott. I was told I'd be shot if I came back and tried to get any more blacks to register.

Millner: How did the common people experience this protest?

Lewis: There were many women who lost their jobs because their bosses would tell them if they couldn't rides the buses they weren't needed.

But some were sympathetic to the boycott.

Millner: Do you have any special memories of the boycott?

Lewis: The most stimulating thing of the whole process was that there were so few black people who would get on those buses. To see the reactions of blacks. To know that the message had gotten over. To the world and to the other folk. You can't imagine how that felt. It was like we said, "well, we can do anything now."

You couldn't keep that high all the time. But the mass meetings were so stimulating too. You'd say that you were going, having the meeting at seven, and people would have the church filled at five o'clock.

E. D. Nixon

[E. D. Nixon was a lifelong citizen of Montgomery and a leader of the black community for more than forty years. Insiders said that Nixon's work as a pullman porter played a critical part in his political development. Nixon himself believed that many cities were a lot worse than Montgomery. He began "fighting during Roosevelt's time" and insisted that he believed that more black lawyers were needed before the struggle could be successful.]

Millner: Was the arrest of Rosa Parks planned in advance?

Nixon: Rosa Parks didn't plan it, and she didn't just free the Negro, she freed the white man too. But I hates the fact that the people of Montgomery didn't have a dime's worth of foresight and they let Rosa Parks leave Montgomery. They made me so mad that I cussed in church that night. They took up only eight hundred some dollars on Rosa Parks Night.

Millner: Mr. Nixon, why were you so upset when Rosa Parks left? Wasn't she under intense pressure?

Nixon: They didn't realize the fact that if I had paid Rosa Parks's fine like I'd done hundreds of other people's, you'd never known of Martin King. And if I hadn't been tied in to organized labor like I was, you'd never get the money to operate. Nobody gave a preacher that kind of money. We should've honored a thousand other people like Mrs. Parks. Just one of others honored could've been me. Now, Reverend King done a good job, I'm not arguing that point. But he weren't the only man. When you look around there ain't a man in Montgomery who can say that Martin King got

545

'im out of jail. There's thousands of people who can say E. D. Nixon got 'em out of jail.

Millner: What was one of your most important contributions to the protest's development?

Nixon: I'm gonna be frank with you. I wrote the early demands 'cause I wanted to be sure we got something started. I knew if we went into a meeting and didn't have something wrote down, we'd stay there all night fighting over this or that. And number two, I wanted to have something our people would accept so we could build an organization around. The young folks like King didn't know to do this. Now, I know Montgomery, brother, and black people would do a whole lotta talking but when it came time to do something, people wouldn't be there. Young ones like King had to be tested. I even told Abernathy, these mild recommendations wouldn't be accepted by black ministers. King wasn't in on it at that time. Reverend French went along. I also thought that local preachers could be gotten to by the whites. And that's the reason Martin King got drawn into it. The other preachers, their masters would get them a pair of shoes, a coat, and they'd a-ruined something that needed starting.

Millner: Why weren't the earlier arrests from 1955 used to spark the protest?

Nixon: OK, the case of Louise Smith. I found her daddy in front of his shack, barefoot, drunk. Always drunk. Couldn't use her. In that year's second case, the girl, very brilliant but she'd had an illegitimate baby. Couldn't use her. The last case before Rosa was the daughter of a preacher who headed a reform school for years. My interview of her convinced me that she wouldn't stand up to pressure. She were even afraid of me. When Rosa Parks was arrested, I thought "this is it!" 'Cause she's morally clean, she's reliable, nobody had nothing on her, she had the courage of her convictions.

Millner: Did you, Rufus Lewis, and others push King to leadership?

Nixon: In the first evening meeting, at a critical time I threatens to tell the people the ministers were cowards if they didn't go along with us. King jumped up and said he wasn't no coward. And that's when he was nominated. Rufus Lewis did the actual nominating but that was all understood, Reverend Abernathy, Reverend French, and I had already agreed to that. Before then it was Abernathy who had said, "Brother Nick, you gonna serve as president?" I said, "not unless you all don't accept my man. If you all don't accept my man, I'll stay in the chair." I had seen King in August. Took his measure.

Millner: Please describe the first mass meeting.

Nixon: On December 5, 1955, the black man was born again in Montgomery. On that morning when they tried Mrs. Rosa Parks, the whole courtroom and all out in the street was crowded with black men. They was saying, "Brother Nick, Brother Nick, what's happening?" I tells them she's found guilty. They was mad then. They said, "Brother Nick, if you don't come out, you know what we gonna do? We gonna come in there and get you." There must've been over five hundred men there. But you know, King, he wasn't there. Man, the police were out there with sawed-off shotguns, people all upstairs looking out they windows with guns, and a guy walked up to me and said, "Brother Nick, I believe I can jump that son of a bitch right there." I said, "man, look upstairs, don't you touch 'im, look upstairs, don't even spit on the street." I couldn't believe it. But now I think about it, King wasn't around that day.

Millner: How did the black people of Montgomery find out about the pending boycott? Many didn't even have radios, etc.

Nixon: Well, on Sunday, December 4, 1955, Montgomery's police commissioner broke in on the radio and TV, every hour, and said "it's been brought to my attention that the niggers"— and that's what he said—said the niggers had a bunch of goon squads to keep other niggers off the buses. But my people didn't all hear that. If they had had radios and TVs and all that, a whole lot of 'em would've took sides with the polices. If they'd heard it on the radio, some would. And also every black minister preached it that Sunday morning.

Millner: How did other people hear about it so rapidly?

Nixon: We said a slogan, "Don't ride the bus till you hear from us." We said this all over the day before, so even winehead men would go along. Had to have 'em too. I remember once it was pouring down rain. Winehead man said, "Brother Nick," everybody called me that, he said, "I know you ain't gonna like it, it's pouring down rain, we had enough money to make it home, but we took the bus. I was gonna buy wine with it, but what you gonna do to us? So I said, "Nigger, you know what the slogan is—'Don't ride the bus till you hear from us.'" I slipped up that day. Cussed them.

Millner: Would you give me your opinion about U. J. Fields?

Nixon: U. J. Fields? You ain't going to agree with me about Fields. He just didn't agree with the way Reverend King done things. He had a right to disagree with him if he wanted to. I don't think all the folks oughta agree with everything Reverend King did. Or all the things I did. Now I have maintained contact with Fields. I have spoken for Fields at various times. I have even helped him get money for many of his projects and things. It's sad, but some of King's supporters run that man off.

Millner: How was the protester's unity cemented?

Nixon: We didn't have any difficulty. You know, the only thing that would've, if I'd been dumb enough to use it, that would've destroyed the organization, in the first board meeting they left me off in the election of officers. I wasn't there, so I didn't know anything about it. Ted Poston of New York called me about one o'clock in the morning and asked me about it. I said I didn't know anything about it. He asked did I want to make a statement about it? So I said, "no comment." Then this other guy who wrote some book about Jackie Robinson, he called and I said again, "no comment."

Next morning I walked into the church office, everybody expected me to be mad. I heard Martin King say to Abernathy, "we can't do it, you can't do that," he said. King said, "Somebody notified United Press [International] and this other guy and both of them called Brother Nick last night and they told me point blank that Brother Nick said 'no comment.' If Brother Nick had issued a statement, he could've destroyed this organization." King said this, I heard him.

Millner: Did you ever think the boycott was going to fail?

Nixon: No, I never thought it was gonna fail. When I saw Mrs. Parks that morning, when they tried Mrs. Parks, I knew we had it made, and then that Monday night we went to church and saw all these people. We couldn't fail and two days later the press was in here from all 'cross the country. That's one of the things I could foresee that led me to want Reverend King to serve. I knew he was intelligent. That he would be able to meet with any class of people, and I knew that. I foresaw that. You might think, he's saying that now. But if they taped my speech the night of December 5, 1955, at Holt Street Church. I said, "I'm glad to [see] you all out here, including you, Commissioner of Police." Then I said, "I want to tell you something. If you're scared, you better get your hat and coat and go home because this is going to be a long drawn-out affair and before it's over, somebody going to die, and if it's me, don't let it be in vain."

Millner: Were there other difficult times?

Nixon: Yeah, when the taxi services were enjoined. Then I goes up to Detroit to buy a station wagon. Plus a guy in New York gave his old station wagon to us. Later they tried to stop us from using them station wagons.

Millner: Mr. Nixon, what do you think explains the protest's success?

Nixon: I don't know how much you believe in religion, but the Lord used me to reach King. Why would I think about him the second Sunday in August 1955 and tell J. E. Pierce about it if it wasn't? Why would I think about King more so than anybody else when it come time to select the leaders? You see what I'm talking about? I'm not deeply religious, but I believe it.

Millner: Did you get support from others beside the local residents?

Nixon: Some whites supported us when push came to shove. I remember there once that I had three thousand dollars of white folks' money. Plus I had two to three thousand dollars of my money, and four to five thousand dollars of MIA money. These white folks loaned us they money. But they never asked for it back. We had so many bills they couldn't get it back.

Millner: If you could change anything about the boycott, what would it be?

Nixon: We had a whole lot of money at that time and some of it we handled unwisely. There wasn't nobody stealing much of anything, but we just handled it unwisely.

Millner: What about U. J. Fields's allegations about black ministers pocketing money?

Nixon: I wouldn't argue with that. A lot of times a minister would go and make a speech and he'd think that he's entitled to some of it. Everybody didn't do like I done. Why I've known Reverend King to, you know? Reverend King, he spoke up in Canada and he told me, said, "Brother Nick, when the check come from Canada, that's my personal check." Sure 'nough, when it came I gave it to 'im. No, weren't no question about it. A lot of that happened. But Mrs. Parks never accepted anything. Whatever she collected she turned right in. She'd come in three or four o'clock in the evening [afternoon] and turn in anything she'd collected and I'd give her a receipt for it. Everybody didn't do that.

Millner: Why did you resign as treasurer of the MIA?

Nixon: I disagreed with how the records were kept. And I thought that King's were somehow remiss. I wanted to protect my "open book" reputation.

Millner: Anything else about the money business?

Nixon: Yes, once Reverend King said something like this to me. Said you let the people know how much money you got, they won't give you no more, or they'll sue for it. But I don't care what they said, there ought to have been records kept. Even if they would've kept two record books. And we'd grown pretty good, pretty fast. At the time when I resigned, I think we had $184,000 in cash, $56,000 in a mortgage on a store.

Millner: How did King maintain his position of prominence?

Nixon: I used to often hear the joke about Reverend King and how he gripped them positions. People would look on TV and he'd be someplace else. Down on his knees praying. The point is, King, he'd identify these things because if he hadn't, he'd faded out. He had to latch on to everything that came along.

Millner: Are you suggesting that King should be viewed as a man, not as a demigod?

Nixon: Dr. King was not the same man when he left here as when he took over the boycott. When he first came here, he was humble, he didn't know his way around, hadn't been nowhere but to school and came out. We really pushed him a whole lot. Right now people don't like to hear me say this, . . . but it isn't what Reverend King did for the people of Montgomery, it's what the people of Montgomery did for Reverend King. I'll say that anywhere and without reservations.

Millner: Do you sometimes feel as if you became a forgotten man?

Nixon: My house was bombed on February 2. They didn't have no picture of me in the paper. Nobody asked me nothing about whether my wife was scared to stay there by herself. Nobody asked me if I had enough money to put my windows back in. Even Dr. King never even talked to me about it.

Millner: Was it possible he was too busy after that?

Nixon: To be truthful, Dr. King never even said a word about me helping to put him in that position. I saw him many times after that. When Reverend King left here, I never seen nor heard a word of thanks.

I don't know whether he wanted to push me down or not. And I had really helped him. It were me who made arrangements for him to go to the Democratic Convention in '56. Got him hotel reservations next to Stevenson. Now he's gone. Soon I will be too.

Rosa Parks

JANUARY 20, 1980

Millner: This taping is being done in Detroit on January 20, 1980. Mrs. Parks, would you start by describing your youth?

Parks: My mother was a teacher in the rural schools of Montgomery county. For about two or three years, she was my own teacher. She was very interested in higher education. She attended school at Selma, Alabama, and in Montgomery at Payne University. The school was organized by the A.M.E. Church, and she attended the State Normal School, which is now Alabama State University.

She taught for a while before she was married. She met and married my father and moved to Tuskegee, Alabama. That's where I was born.

Millner: Did your parents ever discuss Booker T. Washington?

Parks: My mother was very much impressed by Booker T. Washington. She admired his ability. Since my mother and father did not stay together after I was born, I don't have a memory of him. I never did hear what his opinion was about Booker T. Washington. I do think I recall hearing my mother say that at one time, since my father was a very skilled carpenter, Washington did offer him work on the campus and a place to live and an assurance that the children would get a chance at training at Tuskegee. But he did not accept this offer. He left the South, went North, apparently to find more lucrative work, and my mother never did join him.

There's very little I could tell you about him.

Millner: Did your mother ever mention W. E. B. Du Bois?

Parks: I think the only other person she spoke very much about would be Dr. G. W. Carver. And what he could accomplish as a scientist. She could've mentioned Dr. Du Bois but the very first thoughts I remember regarding a public resistance to being humiliated as a slave was from Richard Allen, the founder of the A.M.E., when they set up the A.M.E. Church in Philadelphia.

We had what we called the Christian and Allen League in the evening after church. It was before I was in my teens. I remember joining. . . .

Millner: What would your mother have you read?

Parks: The first thing I read beyond school books was called *Is the Negro a Beast?* It belonged to either my mother or her sister. I was fascinated by it.

We also had a copy of Booker Washington's book. I've been a reader for a long time. First of all you had to learn that there was something different back then and that there was such a thing as slavery and a difference in us and the people who were white.

One interesting memory I have was of people talking about the movement back to Africa under the leadership of Marcus Garvey. Yes, they were talking about that. I recall my grandfather, when I was about six years old, this was before the Armistice Day of World War I. And later at some point, about 1923, some representatives of Garvey's came through and held a meeting. My grandfather, who had been a slave when he was a little boy, he looked exactly like the white people did. He did attend the meeting but he was rejected because of his white appearance. That ended our talking about our going to Africa. We used to use the expression "going back to Africa." But they wouldn't accept him and I can remember that very well. That was my mother's father.

From then on I remember the Klan activity in the neighborhood with the men coming back from World War I.

Millner: Can you tell me more about your family?

Parks: My grandfather was the son of the slave master. The master had died when he was very young and also his mother died. He was raised in a harsh way, almost starved.

Millner: Did you ever visit the North when you were young?

Parks: No, I didn't come into the North until I was full grown. The first time I visited Detroit was in the 1940s. My mother was here, that was just after the end of the second War. My brother had been discharged and my mother was here. While she was here I came up to visit.

Millner: *What did you think of the North when you came up in the 1940s?*

Parks: Well, I saw that there was some difference. A somewhat different atmosphere than the South. There you had to adhere to racial segregation, everywhere publicly. On the buses, everywhere you went. And there was some difference here, you could find a seat anywhere on a bus. You could get better accommodations in Detroit.

Millner: *When people left Alabama in the 1940s, what did they say led them to leave?*

Parks: Why they were leaving? I think a great many were leaving because they heard they could earn more money. Better opportunities.

Millner: *Was your family involved in farming? Or sharecropping?*

Parks: There was a small piece of land owned by the white people my grandmother had worked for when she was a youngster, the same people that had owned my grandfather and great-grandmother. She had taken care of one of their children and had lived with them. When she was in her declining years, she was given use of what had been their home house and there was a small piece of land her father had actually purchased after he was set free. You see, after being set free he remained with these people, and he purchased a small piece of land, I think about twelve acres, that adjoined the house. Enough acreage for a garden and a small farm.

We were just children doing work in other people's fields.

Millner: *Did you ever do any of that work?*

Parks: Yes, I did. We would chop cotton, we called it hoeing the cotton, to get the grass out in the spring and in the fall we'd pick it.

We raised peanuts but not to a great extent. I don't think we ever raised enough to sell. We had our regular garden and quite a few fruit trees, peach and apple. And plums grew wild along the road. We'd pick blackberries in the woods, do canning, whatever.

Millner: What kind of music did you listen to as a child?

Parks: Well, we didn't have much to listen to. At that time the thing that was becoming popular was the victrola. But we never owned one. The most popular music was the church singing, the hymns, spirituals, and the blues. The blues were very popular. My mother used to sing a great deal. It came back to me so vividly at the King birthday program, one song she sang they sang, "Oh, Freedom Let It Ring!" and "Before I'd Be a Slave I'd Be Buried in My Grave." She also sang "We Shall Overcome," but it was a different arrangement, didn't sound like today's.

Millner: What was your life like as a youth?

Parks: When I moved to Montgomery I was living with my aunt along with my mother and grandmother. My grandfather had passed when I was ten.

My aunt did domestic work. At one time she was working at a Jewish home. Her young children and I would go and help her. And there was sewing to be done. My mother did quite a bit of that when she was done teaching. She also took a course in beauty culture. There was always something we were trying to do to earn something.

And of course we lived sort of neighborly. If any of the neighbors had provisions or something we needed we would be welcome and the same way with us. This was out in the country.

In Montgomery we sold food from a basket; this was called a grab basket. We'd take them to fairs and places to sell.

Millner: How did your mother feel about being mistreated about her color?

Parks: She didn't accept it either. I remember her telling me about something that happened in Montgomery. She was standing at the streetcar stop. Some white man came up and stood up to her. She wasn't noticing him at all. So he just started using a lot of profanity. He was cursing at her and of course she was really helpless. I heard her mention how upset she was but the only thing she could do was move over further from where he was standing.

She never mentioned anything that happened because those things would be pretty hard to discuss. Sometimes she'd be talking to someone else and I'd hear. I don't know if those things happened frequently but whenever they did I guess they left quite an impression.

Millner: Can you tell me something about your husband?

Parks: When I first met my husband I heard about the Scottsboro Boys from him. It was in 1931. My husband was born in Randolph County, Alabama, up toward the Georgia line.

Millner: What kind of ideas did your husband have about the racial situation in Alabama?

Parks: He had some problems too. He was very fair. People didn't think he was black. One of the things that seemed to bother him was that he didn't have a chance to finish school. Because he could not attend the white school and they did not have one in his community that he could attend. He went to school for the first time when he was twenty-one years old. He had many problems. When he was very young his mother and grandmother both passed away and he had a young sister and he had to let one of his cousins bring her up.

He told me about one incident where some man in the Klan had run his car into a ditch. The man called my husband to help him with the car and he went over to the man and called him by his name. He knew who he was. My husband was just a youngster.

I don't know what would've happened to him if he hadn't of helped the man. I guess he was about fifteen.

Though I never did see any, I remember the Klan was quite active in our neighborhood. Even until today I have never seen a picture of a member of the Klan other than on T.V. But I was aware of them by the time I was about six years old. It was a very serious matter.

If people said the Klan was going to come, you'd stay inside. And my grandfather would keep his gun ready. I think they'd just want to keep people afraid.

557

My mother once said that there was a church building not far from where she was teaching and the Klan had taken a Negro man to the church and made him burn it down. So her school children would think that they better take their little belongings with them so that they wouldn't get burned down.

Millner: What kinds of things did you do at Miss White's school?

Parks: Oh, there was home economics, and there was arts and crafts, we'd make things, and there was sewing. They had sewing machines, which we did not have at the rural school. And they had a kitchen.

It was my mother's idea to send me to school there so I could get [a] better education. I was quite young then.

Miss White was an old maid, and she established the school for the purpose of educating young black girls. By her having an all-white faculty, all women, and her teaching the Negro girls, it set her apart from the white community. She was not accepted or welcomed in the white community. She was from Massachusetts. Melrose was her home. She wrote me a letter, long before the boycott, from there after she had closed her school.

I wasn't able to finish there because she closed when I was in the seventh grade. This was about 1927 or 1928 that she gave up. I then went to Booker Washington School and finished the ninth grade, and later to Alabama State's high school until my grandmother was so ill I had to stop and take care of her. Then my mother was ill and I had to care for her. So I wasn't able to finish high school.

My mother wanted me to go into teaching and maybe I could have if I put my mind to it. But I thought the schools were just too segregated and oppressive. You didn't get much money for that.

In my younger days I had wanted to be a nurse. I felt inclined to look after sick people. It could've been because I had been around so much illness with my grandfather and grandmother.

Millner: When you were younger, did you ever think about going to the North? You're shaking your head.

Parks: Yes, I did—well, hearing people come back and they'd be dressed well, some would be living much better than if they'd have stayed in the South. Enjoying more freedom.

After I married, it seemed my husband had no inclination for leaving. Because I guess we didn't have enough money together to even think about leaving. My mother actually was more interested in leaving.

We just didn't make the move. One thing I dreaded was the winters. All that snow and ice.

Millner: How did you become involved in the NAACP?

Parks: My husband had been one of the charter members of Montgomery's NAACP. But by the time I joined, he was no longer active. I never did hear him say why he lost interest, it could've been because of personal reasons. I just can't say.

[She later shared a picture of herself at an NAACP meeting with her mother, Johnnie Carr, and one or two other women present. Prominent among the thirty males in the photograph was E. D. Nixon.]

Millner: Were there any restrictions against your joining the NAACP because you were a woman?

Parks: No. I joined the NAACP after I saw Mrs. Johnnie Carr's picture in one of the papers. She was secretary, and I went to a meeting, it was election day, and I was selected secretary.

Millner: When did you become a registered voter?

Parks: In 1945 I became a registered voter and before that time, in 1943 or 1944, we had started a registration drive, but when I filled out my application and answered all the questions and turned it in, I was still not sent a registration certificate. But I didn't give up.

Millner: Was it hard to get people to go down and try to register in the 1940s?

Parks: Yes, it was. It was difficult. Even under the leadership of Mr. Nixon, who worked along with Attorney Madison of New York. He was a black attorney who came down and gave us some instructions and helped us to get started. For this, someone was pressured into saying he was representing him without permission, and of course he was thrown into jail and disbarred in Alabama.

I joined the NAACP after I saw Mrs. Johnnie Carr's picture in one of the newspapers. I saw Mrs. Carr's picture in the black paper, not the white paper. It was the *Alabama Tribune*. I remembered that she and I had been classmates at school so I thought to myself that Johnnie Carr is a member.

Actually that was my initial reason for going to the meeting, and eventually becoming a working part of the organization. I had plenty to do at the time, but I think what I was concerned about was what could be done to relieve the oppressive racial situation. I had also read in *Look* magazine about Walter White.

Millner: Was the segregation situation something you thought about on a daily basis?

Parks [long pause]: I guess so. After I had grown up. It did become a major part of my thinking. Especially during 1955. One of the first cases I worked on with Mr. Nixon involved a young serviceman whose father came to Mr. Nixon because his son had been arrested for raping a white woman in Georgia.

Millner: How was Mr. Nixon thought of in the community at that time?

Parks: He was thought of as a person who had enough courage and dedication and concern to approach the white people in power on issues that concerned us. We thought he had plenty of courage and nerve.

Millner: Did people look up to him?

Parks: It all depended upon who it was. Even those people who did not look up to him because of his lack of formal education—but when it came down to it, I think even those people admired him for what he could do and for how dedicated he was.

Millner: Did you ever work on or hear about the Viola White case?

Parks: I remember Viola White was the woman whose small daughter was assaulted by a white man. I can't remember how much I actually did on it. I remember hearing talk about that case.

Millner: Did you know Reverend King before the boycott?

Parks: Yes, I had met him when he was the speaker at the NAACP meeting in August of 1955. That was the very first time I heard him speak. I was very impressed with his eloquence and I was also surprised he was the new pastor at Dexter Street Baptist Church because he was so young. He looked like he might have been a student in college instead of a minister at this very prestigious church.

It had the reputation for being a very cultured church. I was very much impressed, very favorably impressed, by his manner and his appearance.

I did hear mention he declined to be president of the NAACP. Because he was rather new to Montgomery and had a lot of work to do in his church. He had set up a social action committee within the church where the members would become involved with the community.

At that point I guess it was realistic. By being unknown within the community, his first contact would be with his church members. That was a decision he would have to make himself.

When I first heard him speak, I thought that he had . . . I didn't know what he would be doing, but I thought he was well prepared educationally to take a role of leadership in the community. But I didn't have any thoughts about how high he would go.

Millner: What did your husband and mother say about your arrest?

Parks: My husband was very upset. My mother was too. After they found that I was OK and I hadn't been physically manhandled they felt better.

Mr. Nixon was quite interested in this being a test case. A case to test the segregation laws.

Millner: Did he have to convince you? Did he have to convince your mother?

Parks: I don't remember if I had any great reluctance. First of all, I had to get used to the fact that I had been in jail. And I had my work to do. Also

I had my mind on the youth council workshop that I had planned for the workshop. I was more concerned with that.

Millner: Did you go through with that workshop?

Parks: Yes, I did. Even though it was very poorly attended. Then I talked more with Mr. Nixon and so after Mr. Nixon talked about it and explained it, he didn't have to do any great amount of talking, I just agreed it would be the thing to do. I was ready to do it. Neither one of them [her husband and mother] objected.

The very next morning I got up and went back to work. There was this little article in the paper. The young man, the tailor, he had heard about me being arrested and was surprised I was there. He thought that I would be too nervous or too upset to ever show up at work. I think I told him, "You don't think that going to jail is going to keep me home, do you?" Something like that. Sort of light.

So many people had called me that I asked him why hadn't he called. He said, "Oh, I just thought that you'd be too nervous and upset and I certainly didn't expect you to work today." So a very short while later the man who was in charge of that department came up. He didn't say anything at all. He seemed like he was very bothered or disturbed. He just saw me there. So I just stayed on to work until noon. At noon I left and went to Fred Gray's office. That's where I saw so much activity. The *Jet* magazine was there. Fred was moving about. Talking with me. The *Jet* people started taking my picture and asking questions.

The *Montgomery Advertiser* called Mrs. Rosa Smith, a woman who ran the elevator in the store. They thought she was the one. They wanted me to answer some questions. So she said that they wanted me to call the paper. But I never called to make any statement. So the local paper didn't locate me for the first few days.

Millner: What do you remember about the first mass meeting?

Parks: It was very difficult for me to get in. I could hardly get through the crowd. I had stayed at Fred Gray's office that Monday after my trial was over and answered the telephones for him.

The people were calling to talk to me but I never told them who I was. I knew what they were calling about but I just didn't give out any information. They didn't know my voice so I just took the messages. While I was there a man came in who said he had just come from over at Alabama State College where he heard the students speaking about not riding the buses. That was the first mention that I had heard of a possible protest by not riding the buses. Also while I was there Mr. Nixon called and he was asking about me, and asked me if I was going to the meeting that night at Dexter Avenue Church. I asked him what was the meeting about. He said it was about this "thing." Mentioning my arrest. That was Friday.

All the speeches that night were very well received. I can't recall if I said anything that night. I do recall asking someone if I should say anything and someone saying, "Why? You've said enough." I did make a statement at the first meeting at Dexter Avenue Baptist Church.

Millner: Had you done any public speaking before then?

Parks: Yes, I had. I had made some remarks in church, especially in Sunday School Conventions. But I never was what you'd call a person who was out to speak. At school you would have to at verbal recitations.

Later I was invited to come to Detroit. It was my first plane ride. It was Local 600, the local Mrs. Tappes' husband was in. I had been at the Highlander School in July of 1955.

Millner: The U. J. Fields charges—what did you hear about them?

Parks: I just felt that he was maybe jealous of Reverend King's popularity. He himself was not getting any recognition. He thought he should have it. I don't recall anyone else taking the same attitude that he did.

Mrs. Georgia Gilmore was very upset with him. It took Reverend King to persuade her not to do him any bodily harm.

He [Fields] admitted in the meeting that he was wrong. He wrote a book about the negative things but I haven't read it.

Millner: Do you think any money was misused?

Parks: I don't know. I never did know and couldn't say.

Millner: Why did you move to Detroit in 1957?

Parks: I moved because my brother was here. He never did go back to Alabama after his discharge from the service. He was quite concerned about our well being. My mother and I and my husband thought that we'd leave.

During the time of the bombing of the church, we did have quite a few unpleasant telephone calls. My mother and husband took most of them because they would be at home. When she was home it was pretty frustrating and unpleasant. By the time I decided to move, things like that had lightened up a great deal. I didn't leave just because of that.

I always felt that I wanted to go somewhere else to live. But I probably couldn't have convinced my husband.

Millner: How did the boycott and all the events affect your husband?

Parks: Well, pretty badly. It caused him to worry a great deal. He wasn't well and you know when you have poor health.

Millner: Did anyone try and persuade you not to leave?

Parks: Yes, the person who came to my house when he found out I was planning to leave was Reverend Abernathy. Mrs. Virginia Durr was the first person I told outside my family. She became very much concerned. Actually I didn't have any family there besides my husband and mother. She had some first cousins.

Millner: Did Reverend King and you ever have any conversations about your leaving?

Parks: No. He and I never had any conversations about that. Because I think he was getting ready to leave for Atlanta.

We were not what you would call extremely close personally. I would see him at the meetings, we'd talk, ask about each other's families.

Millner: What would happen in MIA board meetings? Did you attend often?

Parks: Occasionally. I didn't attend too many. I was too busy at home. My job was discontinued at the store in the first week of January 1956, so I would be busy with distributing food and clothes in the community, then I'd do a little bit of work as a dispatcher in the car pools.

Millner: When you got to Detroit, what were your feelings?

Parks: Everything had quieted down in Alabama. Naturally I missed the people I had been seeing. Going to the various meetings. Something to think about. But very shortly after I got here I was approached about a job at Hampton Institute by their president. I accepted that. I was there about a year but came back in the Fall of '58. My mother and husband stayed here. I was the hostess of the off-campus guests. To see that their rooms were comfortable. I had charge of the dining room too.

Millner: How was the North different than the South?

Parks: Well, I know there were problems here, probably not in the same way. But especially in the school system. The schools would be overcrowded. The job situation wouldn't be none too good.

[Her husband did janitorial work and, though lacking a license, taught barbering in Detroit at a local barber college.]

I knew some people here. I had visited here a few times. We settled down over on the Near East Side [in] the upper flat of a two-apartment house.

Millner: Did you attend the mass meeting of '63 in Detroit?

Parks: I was a part of that. And the one in Washington in 1963. There was a great crowd that marched here in Detroit. Their conduct was very good. Great speeches.

Millner: What about the March on Washington in 1963?

Parks: I marched in both of them. In Detroit someone gave me a seat on the platform. And in Washington too. I was given a seat on the platform.

I heard about John Lewis, from Pike County. He was head of SNCC at that time. I also knew John Forman and we once had lunch in the Atlanta airport.

And I especially recall that I heard Malcolm X a week before he was assassinated. That was the first time I heard him speak and was introduced to him. That was here in Detroit. He spoke one Sunday evening and the next Sunday he was shot.

I admired him for the stand that he took. And also because he had had a pretty rough background and he [had] been able to bring about a change within himself. And he was a very eloquent and forthright speaker. And just like Dr. King he seemed to be a good family man, a good father and husband who was very fond of his family.

Millner: Do you also recall when you last saw Dr. King?

Parks: That was also just a few days before he was assassinated. Mrs. Tapps and I went to hear him in Grosse Pointe. There was a horrible mess when he tried to speak out there. They disrupted the meeting. There were whites. It was an all-white city. That was after mid-March 1968. I didn't even get an opportunity to speak with him then.

Usually whenever he was here I would go to hear him speak. He would ask me to call. He used the expression that he was as close to me as the telephone.

When I was in Atlanta I would visit his home. That happened two or three times.

Millner: Were you in Detroit in 1967? When it had its hot summer?

Parks: It really upset both of us almost beyond description. We couldn't work, sleep, eat. We could watch from our house one of the grocery stores being looted. It was owned by good, good whites.

My husband worked in the barbershop right across from them. It hurt my husband so, they were just regular whites, they had been customers of my husband.

All around that looting was just something. This same store was set fire about three or four times but the people living upstairs would put it out.

All that time the police would be driving right by while they were looting, and they wouldn't stop. So finally, late that night about 1:00 the police rounded up everybody. The neighbors said that a lady who earlier that day had tried to persuade others to loot was arrested.

It was a sad sight. But it was hard to keep my husband in. I had to drive him to get a shot, a sedative to quiet him down. One of the troopers threatened to hit him on the head with a rifle. This was right at our house. He was trying to watch the barbershop. He had a knife that a judge whose hair he took care of in Alabama had given him. And the trooper took it. He said that he always regretted that. It wasn't something dangerous.

That was pretty sad.

Millner: Please tell me about the Rosa Parks Foundation.

Parks: There's a committee that's raising funds for a house that will be my permanent home. Then when I pass on it will be a shrine. To keep my mementoes.

I'm hopeful it will be not just a shrine but something that will help people be closer knit in their families. Something that will help people avoid being institutionalized when they're older.

Then there's the idea of some training center for careers. And things could be on display. And works. But life is really the most important art work.

Jo Ann Robinson

[This interview took place in Jo Ann Robinson's sunny apartment in Los Angeles.]

Millner: What did you do to help start the protest?

Robinson: I called all of the officers of the group, all three of them, then I called the principals of schools, because these women were members of the organization. Yes, the principals were women! They were thrilled to help. At Alabama State we had to be careful because we were under the direct control of the Alabama Board of Education. So anyway, I called everybody who could get in touch with the young women. I also called every man who had made a contribution in helping us. I told them that the women had talked about this. That we would like to get these stencils made into about 50,000 flyers [Interviewer's note: My guess is that a figure of 10,000 is more likely.] and get them out. I took the responsibility for that, and I couldn't afford to let anybody help. I'm a good typist, and after I typed them I ran them off. That was really difficult work doing that much. I got these things done on Thursday evening and they were taken to the schools, every little storefront and corner, by Friday.

It just couldn't fail.

Millner: What almost toppled the protest before it started?

Robinson: I made a mistake and left one copy in my car. I was reported and by the time I got ready to teach my afternoon class, it was ten minutes to two, I got this telegram. It said not to hold my classes, but to come to the president's office. Well, I was tired, I was hungry, so the only thing I could think of was just to get on my knees and say, "Lord, push some nerves into my body and let me go meet him."

President Trenholm was so angry his cheeks just quivered. So he told me that I had exposed the college. That I wouldn't be able to stay, and so on. I calmly said I had not exposed the college, and that nothing in the notice involved the college. So we argued for a while and finally you could just see his face relaxing. So I told him what had happened to Rosa Parks, and I said somebody had to do it. I told him about the Woman's Council, that there were 200 and some women who supported this.

Finally he said, "Well, from now on try not to let yourself be exposed." Eventually he was a strong supporter, though behind the scenes.

Millner: Describe what your pre-protest life was like.

Robinson: I had been a teacher in the public schools before the boycott. I had separated from my husband, continued my education. Then I had been teaching at Alabama State since 1949.

Millner: Had you seen what the bus system was like before the boycott?

Robinson: People accepted the discrimination. They stood on the bus, over empty seats. They paid their money and got off and got on the back.

Millner: Did the local leaders accept these circumstances?

Robinson: The leaders here were not political leaders. They were businessmen. Sometimes they were given little tokens that kept them satisfied.

Mr. Nixon was one of them but Mr. Nixon was very limited educational wise. And that affected him as a potential leader. And he was sort of an agitator. But then when the whites recognized it he sort of cooled it down.

People respected Mr. Nixon for his bravery. But he wasn't always able to follow up. See, he could expose trouble but then he couldn't take it from there. He just couldn't go any further. He was willing, I've never seen anyone more willing, but I think his leadership stopped where he couldn't go anywhere further.

Millner: Can you recall what happened the night of the Rosa Parks arrest?

Robinson: I called Mr. Nixon about two o'clock that night. He was the only man who had done, whatever was done, for making things known. He was known for supporting us. When I called Mr. Nixon he was cleaning up for the next morning. I respected Mr. Nixon, he was really the only older man who had done whatever was to be done. So when I told him the women had agreed to get the letters out, he told me he would not be there the next morning. But he would call Reverend Hubbard and get Hubbard to do anything he could to help this.

When Mr. Nixon got back, the meeting had already been held that Friday night. The men took it over, with Reverend Bennett presiding. They offered the chairmanship to several. I think Reverend Fields even said they offered it to him, before Dr. King took it.

***

Mrs. Parks, she was a lady, you know what I mean. She was too sweet to even say damn in anger.

***

Millner: How would the MIA leadership prepare for its meetings with the bus company and city officials?

Robinson: We would meet before. The one thing that we had decided, and this is what King said, that we were not going to take anything except total integration! I had gotten tired and some others had too, and some wanted to take this and that but Martin Luther King said we would not take anything except total integration!

Millner: How did the whites react to your insistence on change?

Robinson: They feared that anything they gave would be viewed by us as just a start. And you know, they were probably right.

We thought that by coming off the buses that Monday would have made them yield to our demands. We had not planned to come off the buses but one day. But when we met Monday night people said, "We'll do it all week."

Millner: What was Reverend King like in those early years?

Robinson: Some of it I can't tell. I will not tell. But as a man he was one of the most kind and humble men I had met. The way he could stand up in the presence of threats. You know? And he would never lose his equilibrium. I guess it was charisma. The way he could be cursed out and never raise his voice. You know? And never show his anger. Now if I get

571

mad, I will raise my voice. You would have never known it when he was angry.

***

Millner: What was really happening behind the facade with the protestors?

Robinson: The money that came into office, now they had a recording secretary that took care of that. Now nobody can say what happened to money that was carried in by envelope. But I really believe that a little bit of money was taken.

I have the feeling that jealousy may have caused some ministers to maybe do some things. But I couldn't really say that I saw it myself.

Millner: What happened at the weekly mass meetings?

Robinson: Everybody would just clap and hold hands in the meeting. Oh, you just loved everybody. A Ph.D. and anybody could just sit together. Nobody got mad with anybody. You know, that kind of thing.

That feeling lasted until I left there. And that was '60. It really united them. Made them feel part, you know, of one another's problems and successes.

Millner: How did the boycott affect your career at Alabama State?

Robinson: I wasn't fired. But I think, this was '59, the boycott had been over three years. There was another group feeling that they had to demonstrate. There had been a public announcement by Police Commissioner Sellers that there would be no demonstrating around the Capitol. Well, naturally, everybody wanted to test that law. The demonstration then was one where naturally people at Dexter Baptist wanted to be in on it. We said we'd march from Dexter up to the Capitol. Then people from other parts of the city would be able to come and congregate on the steps of it [the Capitol] and have a prayer service. Sellers said no! And the blacks decided to defy his order. Now I didn't see any need to do it. But I went to church and by the time the service was over, all of the area around Dexter was blocked. Ku Klux Klan and every other kind of organization. The streets were blocked.

Someone decided to march anyway. Decided to go from Dexter up there. Whites were armed with shotguns all the way up to the Capitol. Waiting for someone to come out there. There was no way in the world to get out. My car was all blocked up. Finally I left and walked right through them. They opened up and let me by. But it just wouldn't of made sense to go there and march. But Abernathy and a few others went out there and got knocked about. It was stupid of them. People had baseball bats. The crowd was ready for them. That would've been it. But this boy had gotten hit, was bleeding, and others still wanted to go up there We eventually got out. A few days later President Trenholm called us in.

In the meeting he said that it had been reported to him that, and he called a few people's names, we were starting more trouble. When I was asked if I was there, I said yes. Then we all got angry and asked him why he wasn't there!

Later, I explained my position, told him that I couldn't get to my car. I understand that while some people close to Trenholm were very sympathetic, well, a couple of us got letters saying we would not be rehired. Everybody who had been involved in either protest paid for it.

Rev. B. J. Simms

JULY 16, 1977

[Reverend Simms was the chairman of the Transportation Committee, which ran the car pool.]

Millner: What was it like here before December 1955?

Simms: The pre-boycott atmosphere in Montgomery was typical of many southern cities. A "repressive air" was here. You had a feeling of impending danger as you walked the streets. There was no "feeling of freedom." When the buses were crowded, you'd have to get back off and reboard in the rear.

Millner: What were the peculiar circumstances of the buses?

Simms: The buses would be especially full afternoons, and many times there wouldn't be room for either whites or blacks.

Millner: Had you ever personally been a bus rider?

Simms: I refused to ride the buses because I wouldn't pay my money and then stand.

There had been much trouble on the buses before. Remember, 90% of Montgomery's blacks depended on those buses.

Millner: Tell me a few things about your pre-movement days.

Simms: I came to Montgomery as a student at Alabama State in 1931, and made it my home. I worked on government surveys of black unemployment in Montgomery. Later I was the first principal at a free black high school here in Montgomery.

Millner: Tell me how that high school operated.

Simms: Alabama State had a high school, but students from all over the state would come there by application. They had the cream of the crop. But they had to pay. The better class of blacks would send their children there. But the masses, their education ended at the sixth grade.

Millner: Tell me how that school started in the 1930s.

Simms: Finally, some well-intentioned whites and blacks got permission to use Alabama State's facilities for Montgomery's black public. They held classes from late afternoon to nine o'clock at night.

I quit as principal after I got a scholarship to Oberlin. I was being sponsored by the Dexter Avenue Baptist Church. I'm very proud of that.

I worked at an upper-class all-white church in Newark, New Jersey, before I came back. My assistants were all white. I then did USO work during the war. I worked out of New York, before going to Mobile. They were having racial troubles there because northern blacks wouldn't accept discrimination. I established a USO for blacks in Mobile.

Millner: How did you first hear of the boycott?

Simms: There was a knock on my door. This was about 11:30 Sunday night and I went to the door and there was a pamphlet sticking in the screen door handle. I got it and brought it in.

That Monday morning when I went to school, the boycott was in progress. But a lot of blacks would've never known about it if the *Advertiser* hadn't of said something about it in their Sunday edition. It went like wildfire all over town.

Millner: Who was at the first meeting?

Simms: It was just plain Joe Jones who worked in a filling station, a cook, a yardman, the nurses, and all that, those were the people who caught fire. It's astounding, just masses of people.

Millner: Explain your idea about King's involvement.

Simms: King had one helluva fight, he was pushed into this. Because he was new. So that if it failed, the established ministers would not have been to blame. They would've retained their positions of leadership. It was that old rascal E. D. Nixon and others who wanted King.

Millner: What did King know about his impending role?

Simms: King did not know what he was getting into. It was only after he had his vision that he was going to meet his death, in his kitchen on Jackson Street, that he knew where he was going.

Millner: Describe King's impact as you saw it.

Simms: King could touch the most bigoted, ignorant, illiterate black. And get over what he was saying. And it frightened a lot of ministers because after King began his inspiring talks that would just set people afire, some churches began clamoring for more educated ministers.

Millner: When you took over the transportation system, what did you find?

Simms: A lot of people were taking advantage of the MIA in the first two months. They'd charge people and then get free gas from the MIA. They also had trouble getting enough drivers to run our car pool. It was hell.

Nobody would volunteer. And I just walked in from my classes at Alabama State. But Dr. S. S. Seay had known me since I was a boy. He had gone to school with a sister of mine. He stood up and said, "I got a young man, and if anybody can handle this mess he can." Everybody wondered who it was. I was sitting in back of him and he said, "this man right here." I was stunned.

Martin King said, "Yeah, I believe that is the man." He said, "Brother B. J., will you handle it?" I said, "I don't know whether I can handle that."

King got Abernathy to take over. And we went out in the hall and we talked and talked and talked. He said, "Now, you know the situation. People respect you, people know that you're a pastor and that when you say something, that's that. And you can handle this thing. We need you, Brother B. J., don't fail us."

We spent twenty minutes out there. And I said, "Mike, I'll tell you, I don't know." He said, "Do it for me and for your people."

I said, "Mike, I'll do it if you'll let me run it. If I have to have any interference from the front office up there, from a couple of fellas who harassed Lewis, I can't handle it. If you let me run it, you can draw up certain guidelines, and I'll consult with the board, but I've got to have the last words within the limits."

He said, "Yes, I'll back you to the hilt." He went in and told the board. They said, "Well, all right."

Millner: What were your first actions after taking over?

Simms: I eliminated all of the spongers. Oh, there was a hue and a cry. Nope, only ones I would approve could get gas. I sent a list to the service stations. Said "These are the persons who gets X amount of gas. This is your copy and they are to be allotted so many gallons a day. If extra gas is given, we will have a card which will be punched and duly signed. Then they can get more gas. An extra five gallons if necessary. If you give 'em any more than that, you pay for it." They didn't believe it at first.

We only used black gas stations because we thought we better keep our business to ourself.

Millner: Tell me how the spongers from within would operate.

Simms: A guy would come in and get two tires. Two days later he'd come back and get two more, he'd sell them. Rufus Lewis didn't have time to keep up with 'em. Nobody kept up. We set up a book.

We set up an office, three dispatchers who would get in at 5:30 a.m., and I gave them some authority.

I had come up working in an automobile shop. I knew repairs, tires, etc., and so I stopped the draining of thousands of dollars the MIA lost to overcharging on phony repairs. Another sad thing we've never talked about is filling stations had been sending in phony invoices. It was pretty rotten for a while.

Millner: What did your secret reforms do for the protest?

Simms: These actions brought on support because people knew they could count on the system. Pretty quick I turned it around.

Millner: Can you identify some of the inner circle who were important to the protest?

Simms: Reverend A. W. Wilson. At first he may have been a little leery. His church was brand new, they were still paying on it. But we used it several times. There was never any open opposition to King by A. W. Wilson.

Then there was this man named U. J. Fields. [He] was a nut to start with. He was jealous. He wanted to be number one. He was a crackpot to start with. He had wanted to be a leader but he never had the charisma, the knowhow, and nobody knew him except that he was a peculiar kind of fellow who went to Alabama State University.

Fields was one of the reasons we had to lay down a rule that no one except King would issue statements. And then only after the board had passed on it. That was a cardinal rule. Fields decided if he couldn't run it, he'd ruin it.

Millner: What was the attitude here in the early months of the boycott?

Simms: These blacks were so militant that if articulate people hadn't of taken charge, it would've ended in a blood bath.

Millner: Did that militance show up during the movement? Tell me about the mass arrests.

Simms: Blacks had come from every section of town. Black women with bandannas on, wearing men's hats with their dresses rolled up. From the alleys they came. That is what frightened white people. Not the collar and tie group.

I walked into there and the cops were trembling. Said, "You got my name? I'm B. J. Simms." Said, "Yeah, yeah. Here your name is here." Said, "All right, what do I do?" Said, "You get in that line there." I got in behind the late Mrs. A. W. West.

When a policeman tried to move the crowd back, this is what happened.

One of the police hollered, "All right, you women get back." These great big old women with their dresses rolled up told him, and I never will forget their language, "Us ain't going nowhere. You done arrested us preachers and we ain't moving."

He put his hands on his gun and his club. They said, "I don't care what you got. If you hit one of us, you'll not leave here alive."

That was the thing we had to work hard against, keeping these blacks from killing these whites.

Millner: Why were the initial goals so modest?

Simms: There was a feeling that that was all we could get. There was a point in the boycott when we just asked them to obey the law! They said, "Aw, no, we're going to reserve some seats for whites." So, much to their surprise we became hard-hearted. We said, "If you won't obey the law, we want them [the buses] completely desegregated."

King and all of us were initially willing to follow the law. This was early on in the boycott's existence. Before huge sums of money started coming in.

Millner: Were there individuals who objected to King's nonviolent approach?

Simms: I, for one. But I didn't object loudly. He never converted me. He'd say, "Brother B. J., can't you go along with me?" I said, "Yes, to a point." But in a meeting where he'd ask those who believed in nonviolence to hold up their hands, I and a few others couldn't.

I agreed with it as a tactic but not as a philosophy. If they'd of laid their hands on me, and I'd of been in a position to retaliate, I would have. I was ready to die.

Millner: Were there others like you back then?

Simms: People had guns, knives, clubs, and they were ready if the KKK had come.

Millner: How did whites try to oppose the protest?

Simms: A lot of whites thought they would hurt Negroes by cutting the buses off. But you couldn't attract businesses and manufacturers to a city with no buses. But dumbbells never think. Businessmen knew. The businessmen were mad with the politicians because downtown was just dying.

Rev. B. J. Simms

JANUARY 9, 1979

Millner: What happened to the MIA's records?

Simms: We had to hide all that stuff, and some of it was destroyed. But I didn't mean for the books, the books that I'm talking about was a record book of all the drivers, all of the repairs on automobiles, and the purchasing of tires and batteries, the amount of gasoline allotted to each driver for his routes, even for extra gas.

Millner: How did people make connections?

Simms: We hired about eight or ten persons from over at Alabama State. We paid them twelve dollars a week to act as dispatchers. For instance, at each place there was a person there, and there was a car assigned. Their job was, as each car came in they were to load them, handle the passengers, and list their destination, the time they left, and everything. [They worked at the large gathering points; they were mainly his students] I thought that was the only way to get our money's worth. And also to keep chiselers from getting gas and then going off with the gas. And that's what was happening when I took over. We were losing hundreds of dollars a week, thousands of dollars a month. And I purged a whole list. Purged 'em. They were dismayed.

I also assigned drivers to churches with stringent requirements. Transportation became so smooth that after a short while, the data on the number of the previous day's passengers, destinations, etc. was available by 11:00 a.m. [He had never done anything like this. He got few suggestions.]

The drivers were volunteers. But each church selected its own driver for its station wagon. They were all members of the church. Holt Street's driver was employed by the church as a part-time janitor. Of course they got someone else when he became a full-time driver. Now, people who drove their own private automobiles, or persons who volunteered to become our drivers, of course we paid them too.

Millner: When did you take over?

Simms: After people began griping that they couldn't get proper transportation. And they were just throwing away money. There was no system at all. People were getting charged, threatening to go back to the buses. A special meeting was held. They were about to cave in. King was a worried young man.

[Absent from the meeting during which he was appointed was Rufus Lewis. The soft-spoken Lewis was out on a voter registration effort. King ushered B. J. Simms into that meeting. When they finished Simms was King's new transportation man.]

Simms: Some of King's opposition looked askance at anything he did. Especially his mingling with college-trained Negroes. Some of 'em were hoping against hope that the thing would go down the drain. As they had suspected and predicted. [That was] the reason they agreed for King to be the president.

See, he just got here, a little squirt, so to speak. As they said, "He'll never do nothing. We can't do nothing 'cause folks not going to follow us." King and any other who had a fair deal of education created jealousy, and there was secret fighting directed against them. Jealousy was behind this and a desire for notoriety.

[Simms insisted on having total power over his committee. He made observations about others in positions of leadership.]

Simms: Hubbard was a supporter of King. He was a mulatto who didn't like white folks. He was just down to earth. He didn't like white folks at all. Yet he could pass. The Ku Klux [Klan] stopped Hubbard one night. And they had 'im. And they weren't sure what he was. Old Hubbard used to laugh, when he'd tell it. They'd said, "What are you? You white or black?" He said that he told 'em "White folks, I don't know what I am. What are you?" So they turned him loose.

Old Hubbard liked the bottle too. He was just down to earth.

Millner: Another important participant was the Rev. J. H. Cherry.

Simms: Cherry was the dispatcher at the downtown feeder point. The other one was at Normandale's, where they got permission from the merchants so the police wouldn't harass them. They were on private property and outside the city limits there. Cherry was a good old-fashioned Methodist minister. He was just so dedicated. Nobody ever bothered him.

Millner: Adam Powell visited here before the boycott. What happened?

Simms: Black people thought Powell had cut a hog, so to speak. That means he had made a colossal mistake.

Powell was scheduled [to] and did address the student body at Alabama State. And he laughingly told 'em about the scotch and soda he had just had with the governor. Well, naturally, the *Montgomery Advertiser* jumped all over it. Blacks were down on Powell because they thought that Powell had put the governor on the spot. And the governor had honored him and treated him with correct protocol. And that hurt the governor too.

Blacks thought that Powell had done a disservice to all the blacks in the state. Very few blacks in the South ever thought much of Powell at all, except that he was a lot of mouth.

Millner: Reverend B. J., are you sure?

Simms: Well, I admit there were some who applauded him for his bravery. And I'll tell you something else. Here in Montgomery the local NAACP never figured in the boycott as an organization—it disdained that type of tactic—but a few of its members were supporters. King thought that their slow approach would never really do, given the way Southern judges functioned. We used to laugh at the justice system throughout the South.

Millner: Reverend Simms, how was Alabama State run?

Simms: Trenholm had to make all the decisions. He made out all the students' schedules. Students had to get him to sign and often weren't able to be in class until three weeks after school started.

Millner: Was President Trenholm a boycott supporter?

Simms: Trenholm just understood. He did not give any orders. Did not mention it. Did not try to curtail anybody. He was all for it. But officially he would never acknowledge it. He just didn't know, so to speak. He could be hypocritical just like white folks were.

He knew I would leave campus as soon as my classes ended. He just overlooked it. He was no Uncle Tom.

Millner: How many rides were provided on a daily basis?

Simms: There were 15,000-20,000 rides per day, is my estimate.

Millner: What about the economics of the car pool?

Simms: We did business with the whites but it had to be done through a black. They did this so the black could get something out of it. They dealt only with black gas stations. Word got out that Simms "wasn't playing," so all the bloodsuckers dropped away.

Millner: What happened during the last months?

Simms: Some people were actually hurt when this thing ended. No more mass meetings. Some people would be there as early as 11:00 o'clock in the morning to get a seat.

Millner: Describe for me how your committee functioned.

Simms: The Transportation Committee was essentially me. It very seldom met. Never did anything. First they thought it might be necessary. But after transportation policy was made, there was very little reason to meet. Some of my people were just ghost members. A lot of people just wanted their name on the board. They never came. They just wanted to be on there after the boycott became widely known.

Millner: Thank you, Reverend Simms.

Notes

CHAPTER ONE

1. Alexis de Tocqueville, *Democracy in America* (New York: Vintage Books, 1945), ed. by Philip Bradley, Volume II, p. 118.
2. C. Wright Mills, *The Sociological Imagination* (New York: Oxford University Press, 1959).
3. Herbert Blumer, "Social Movements" in Alfred McClung Lee's *Principles of Sociology* (New York: Barnes and Noble, Inc., 1955), pp.199-220.
4. Paul Wilkenson, *Social Movements* (New York: Praeger Publishers, 1971), p. 27.
5. Joseph R. Gusfield, "Studying Social Movements," *International Encyclopedia of the Social Sciences*. (New York: Macmillan Company and the Free Press, 1968), Volume 14, p. 445.
6. Blumer, *op. cit.*, pp. 199-202.
7. *Ibid.*, p. 203.
8. Leonard Schatzman and Anselm L. Strauss, *Field Research: Strategies for a Natural Sociology* (Englewood Cliffs, New Jersey, 1973), p. 7.
9. Martin L. King, Jr., *Stride Toward Freedom: The Montgomery Story* (New York: Ballantine Books, 1958).

CHAPTER TWO

1. J. D. Pope, "Types of Farming Areas," *Agriculture of Alabama*, Alabama Department of Agriculture and Industries. (Montgomery, Alabama, 1930), pp. 53-65.
2. *Ibid.*
3. *Ibid.*
4. Quoted in Theodore Henley Jack, *Sectionalism and Party Politics in Alabama, 1819-1842* (Menasha, Wisconsin: George Banta Publishing Office, 1919), p. 7.
5. U. S. Bureau of Census, Third Census, 1820 (Washington, D.C.: Government Printing Office, 1820).
6. Jack, *op. cit.*, p. 19.
7. George A. Davis and O. Fred Donaldson, *Blacks in the United States: A Geographic Perspective* (Boston: Houghton Mifflin Company, 1975), p. 35.
8. Horace Mann Bond, *Negro Education in Alabama* (New York: Atheneum, 1939).

9. Leslie Howard Owens, *The Species of Property, Slave Life and Culture in the Old South* (Oxford, England: Oxford University Press, 1976), p. 9.

10. *Ibid.*

11. Jack, *op. cit.*, pp. 21-36.

12. *Ibid.*, p. 34.

13. *Ibid.*, pp. 47-51.

14. *Ibid.*

15. Walter L. Fleming, *Civil War and Reconstruction in Alabama*, (New York: Columbia University Press, 1905), pp. 710-734. While Fleming's account of the evolution of that system is permeated with its author's attitude that blacks are inherently inferior, it does provide a mechanism to follow the broad details of that system's development in Alabama. For a better description of how the tenant system developed in other parts of the South, see Arthur F. Raper's *Preface to Peasantry* (New York: University of North Carolina Press, 1936). Raper provides an excellent account of how the sharecrop system functioned in Georgia's Black Belt. He describes how some ex-slaves, wishing to avoid the gang labor system and hoping to allow their wives to escape from fieldwork, actively sought a system of tenancy. That this would occur is a telling commentary about the post-slave era in the Deep South.

16. Raper, *op. cit.*, pp. 96-97.

17. Robert Blauner, *Alienation and Freedom* (Chicago: University of Chicago Press, 1964). Blauner's study provides a thorough discussion of how important control of the work pace is in general to wage earners. While not discussing black workers or sharecroppers specifically, there is no reason to suspect that they would differ in their concern for work pace control from the wage earners Blauner describes.

18. Fleming, *op. cit.*, pp. 710-734. Again, Fleming wrote in a derogatory fashion of this desire by black men to protect their women. For a more sympathetic explanation of this phenomenon, see Theodore Rosengarten's *All God's Dangers: The Life of Nate Shaw* (New York: Avon Books, 1974). Rosengarten's biography of Nate Cobb, an ex-sharecropper who lived in northern Alabama during the late 1800s and through the early years of this century, contains a vivid account of the motives of Alabama's black sharecroppers. See also William S. McFoley's "Unfinished Business: The Freedman's Bureau and Federal Action in Race Relations," in Nathan I. Huggins, Martin Kilson, and Daniel M. Fox, eds., *Key Issues in the Afro-American Experience* (New York: Harcourt Brace Jovanovich, Inc., 1971), pp. 14-15.

19. Booker T. Washington, "The Anaconda," from Milton Meltzer, ed., *In Their Own Words: A History of the American Negro*, Vol. 2 (New York: Thomas Y. Crowell Company, 1965), pp. 102-106.

20. *Ibid.*, pp. 105-106.

21. Rosengarten, *op. cit.*, pp. 103-361. Davis and Donaldson, *op. cit.*, pp. 66-84, also discuss the demoralizing aspects of the sharecropping routine.

22. Louis R. Harlan, "The Secret Life of Booker T. Washington," *Journal of Southern History*, Vol. 37 (August, 1971), pp. 343-416. In this article Harlan and other scholars provide ample evidence of the strategies Washington used

to maintain his power. See also Francis L. Broderick, "The Fight Against Booker T. Washington," in Hugh Hawkins, ed., *Booker T. Washington and his Critics: Black Leadership in Crisis* (Lexington, Massachusetts: D. C. Heath and Company, 1974), pp. 67-80.

23. Bond, *op. cit.*, pp. 205-219, 224-225.
24. Holman Hamilton and Gayle Thornbrough, "Washington's Humor," in Emma L. Thornbrough, ed., *Booker T. Washington: Great Lives Observed* (Englewood Cliffs, N.J.: Prentice-Hall, Inc., 1969), pp. 84-85.
25. Andrew Carnegie, "The Negro in America." An address delivered before the Philosophical Institute of Edinburgh (Inverness, 1907), pp. 30-31, 39-40.
26. Thornbrough, *op. cit.*, p. 8.
27. William Dean Howells, "An Exemplary Citizen," *North American Review*, CLXXIII (August, 1901), pp. 281-288.
28. *Montgomery Advisor*, quoted in Max Bennett Thrasher, *Tuskegee: Its Story and Its Work* (Boston, 1900), p. 193.
29. C. Vann Woodward, "The Genesis of Segregation," in Joel Williamson, ed., *The Origins of Segregation* (Lexington, Massachusetts: D. C. Heath and Company, 1968), pp. 1-6.
30. Vernon Lane Wharton, *The Negro in Mississippi, 1865-1890* (Chapel Hill, North Carolina: University of North Carolina Press, 1947), pp. 227-233.
31. Harlan, *op. cit.*, pp. 393-416.
32. Theodore Roosevelt, "Sixth Annual Message," Washington, D.C., December 3, 1906.
33. Emmett Jay Scott, *Negro Migration During the War* (New York: Oxford University Press, 1920).
34. Quoted from Daniel Walden, "The Contemporary Opposition to the Political Ideals of Booker T. Washington," *Journal of Negro History*, Vol. XLV, No. 2, April, 1960, p. 109.
35. Daniel T. Carter, *Scottsboro: A Tragedy of the American South* (Baton Rouge, Louisiana: Louisiana State University Press, 1969), pp. 123-132.
36. *Ibid.*, pp. 123-127.
37. Charles V. Hamilton, *Minority Politics in Black Belt Alabama*, (New York: McGraw-Hill Company, 1960), pp. 2-8.

CHAPTER THREE

1. Calvin L. Beale, "The Black American In Agriculture," in Mabel M. Smythe, ed. *The Black American Reference Book* (Englewood Cliffs, New Jersey: Prentice-Hall, Inc., 1976), p. 294.
2. Horace Mann Bond, *Negro Education in Alabama: A Study in Cotton and Steel* (New York: Atheneum, 1939), p. 228.
3. Bond, *Ibid.*, p. 229.
4. Charles S. Johnson, *Growing Up In the Black Belt* (New York: Schocken Books, 1967) and *Shadow of the Plantation* (Chicago: University of Chicago Press, 1934).

5. Johnson, *Growing Up In the Black Belt*. p. 219.

6. Bond, *op. cit.*, p. 257.

7. *Ibid.*

8. Arthur F. Raper, *Preface to Peasantry* (New York: Atheneum, 1936).

9. Bond, *op. cit.*, p. 256.

10. Johnson, *Growing Up in the Black Belt*, p. 113.

11. Conversation with Johnnie Carr, Montgomery, Alabama, July 17, 1977.

12. Interview with Johnnie Carr, Montgomery, Alabama, July 17, 1977, p. 527 in this volume.

13. *Ibid.* p. 528.

14. J.C.M. Curry papers, Manuscript Collection, File 7, Alabama State Department of Archives and History, Montgomery, Alabama. The Curry collection describes a 1902 visit to Miss White's school.

15. Carr interview, p. 528.

16. Interview with Edgar Daniel Nixon, January 17, 1979 in Montgomery, Alabama.

17. Interview with Edgar Daniel Nixon, January 17, 1979 in Montgomery, Alabama.

18. *Ibid.*

19. Lawrence W. Levine, *Black Culture and Black Consciousness* (Oxford: Oxford University Press, 1977), p. 251.

20. *Ibid.*, p. 250.

21. Nixon interview of January 17, 1979.

22. *Ibid.*

23. *Ibid.*

24. Interview with Erna Dungee Allen, January 18, 1979 in Montgomery, Alabama.

25. *Ibid.*

26. *Ibid.*

27. *Ibid.*

28. Erna Dungee Allen interview, August 6, 1977. Page 524 in this volume.

29. Interview with Joe Reed, January 20, 1979 in Montgomery, Alabama.

30. *Ibid.*

31. Levine, *op. cit.*, pp. 195, 232.

32. C. Vann Woodward, *The Strange Career of Jim Crow* (New York: Oxford University Press, 1974), pp. 161-163. Woodward's account is one of many that describe this pattern.

33. Reed, *op. cit.*

34. Robert E. Park, *Race and Culture* (Glencoe, Illinois: The Free Press, 1950), pp. 280-281.

CHAPTER FOUR

1. T. Scarlett Epstein, *Economic Development and Social Change in South India*, (Manchester, England: The University Press, 1962), especially pp. 154-189.

2. For discussions of these examples see Francois Latortue's article "Reflections on the Haitian Labor Force," in *The Haitian Potential: Research and Resources in Haiti*, edited by Vera Rubin and Richard P. Schaedel (New York: Teachers College Press, 1975), pp. 221-239, and Eduardo Sevilla-Guzman's "The Peasantry and the Franco Regime" in *Spain in Crisis: The Evolution and Decline of the Franco Regime*, edited by Paul Preston (Sussex, England: The Harvester Press Limited, 1976), pp. 101-124.

3. Michael Lewis' article "The Negro Protest in Urban America," in *Protest, Reform, and Revolt: A Reader in Social Movements*, edited by Joseph R. Gusfield (New York: John Wiley and Sons, Inc., 1970), especially pp. 176-182, reemphasizes how critical this point would be in the 1960s.

4. While much more needs to be done to explain why black communities varied in this fashion, Montgomery, as a state capital, had established a tradition for being the center of political intrigues for Alabama blacks.

5. J. Mills Thornton, III makes this point about Montgomery's white community in his article, "Challenge and Response in the Montgomery Bus Boycott of 1955-1956," in *Alabama Review* 33(July, 1980), pp. 163-235. Reprinted in this volume.

6. Frances Fox Piven and Richard A. Cloward, *Poor Peoples' Movements: Why They Succeed, How They Fail* (New York: Vintage Books, 1979), p. 204.

7. As discussed in the previous chapter, generations of southern blacks had expressed their anger about social oppression in various folk art forms before political activism became feasible. This point is given detailed attention in Lawrence W. Levine's *Black Culture and Black Consciousness* (Oxford, England: Oxford University Press, 1977), especially see his chapter on "Black Laughter," pp. 298-366.

8. Charles S. Johnson, *Patterns of Negro Segregation* (New York: Harper and Brothers Publishers, 1943), pp. 289-293.

9. August Meier and Elliott Rudwick describe a turn of the century trolley car protest by Montgomery's blacks in their article, "The Boycott Movement Against Jim Crow Streetcars in the South, 1900-1906" in *The Black Experience in America* (Austin, Texas: University of Texas Press, 1970), edited by James C. Curtis and Lewis L. Gould.

10. Owen Butler, interviewed in Montgomery, Alabama, January, 1979.

11. Johnson, *op. cit.* pp. 44-50.

12. This especially harsh custom had also been the prime factor instigating discontent among blacks who organized a short-lived bus boycott in Baton Rouge, Louisiana, in 1953. See Martin L. King, Jr.'s brief discussion of this protest in his *Stride Toward Freedom* (New York: Ballantine Books, 1958).

13. As previously described, Montgomery's blacks were generally impoverished and thus forced by circumstance to rely on the bus system as urban work locations demanded long distance commutes.

14. Piven and Cloward, *op. cit.*, p. 204.

15. How overall national changes contributed to political tendencies among the South's blacks is discussed by Numan V. Bartley, *The Rise of Massive Resistance: Race and Politics in the South in the 1950s* (Baton Rouge, Louisiana:

589

University of Louisiana Press, 1969) and Robert H. Brisbane, *Black Activism: Racial Revolution in the United States, 1954-1970* (Valley Forge, Pennsylvania: Judson Press, 1973).

16. Neil Smelser, *Theory of Collective Behavior* (New York: The Free Press of Glencoe, 1963), p. 271.
17. *Ibid.*, pp. 292-296.
18. Thornton, *op. cit.*, pp. 187-191.
19. Interview with E. D. Nixon, Montgomery, Alabama, January 18, 1979.
20. Conservation with Jo Ann Robinson, Los Angeles, California, August, 1977.
21. Nixon interview, January 18, 1979.
22. Robinson conversation, *op. cit.*
23. *Ibid.*
24. Nixon interview, July 27, 1977. Page 546 in this volume.
25. Nixon interview, January 18, 1979.
26. See King's account, *op. cit.*, p. 35. See also L.D. Reddick, "The Bus Boycott in Montgomery," reprint from *Dissent* (Spring, 1956), p. 2, and *San Jose News*, January 16, 1980. The Reddick piece is included in the present volume.
27. For an example of an initial news report that completely omitted reference to Mrs. Parks, see the front page of the nationally circulated black newspaper, the *Chicago Defender* of December 17, 1955. The *New York Times*' December 6, 1955, initial report mentioned Mrs. Parks, but only to specify that she was a forty-two year old seamstress.
28. Interview with Rosa MacCauley Parks, Detroit, Michigan, January 20, 1980. Page 553 in this volume.
29. Conversation with Rosa Parks, Detroit, Michigan, January 20, 1980.
30. Parks interview, page 554 in this volume.
31. Mary Frances Berry and John W. Blassingame, *Long Memory: The Black Experience in America* (New York: Oxford University Press, 1981, Advance review copy), p. 92.
32. *Ibid.*, pp. 96-101.
33. *Ibid.*
34. Robinson interview, *op. cit*, page 571 in this volume.
35. Parks interview, *op. cit.*, page 556.
36. *Ibid.*, page 558.
37. *Ibid.*, page 559.
38. *Ibid.*, page 560.
39. Howell Raines, *My Soul is Rested: Movement Days in the Deep South* (New York: G.P. Putnam's Sons, 1977), pp. 395-400.
40. *Ibid.*
41. *Ibid.*, pp. 30-40.
42. Parks interview, *op. cit.*, pages 556-557.

CHAPTER FIVE

1. Herbert Blumer, "Social Movements," in Alfred McClung Lee, ed.), *Principles of Sociology* (New York: Barnes and Noble, 1955), pp. 199-202.
2. *Ibid.*
3. *Ibid.*
4. Interview with Jo Ann Robinson, Los Angeles, California, August, 1977. Page 569 in this volume.
5. *Ibid.*
6. *Montgomery Advertiser*, December 4, 1955. Azbell had been an associate of E. D. Nixon over the years and was remarkably professional in his coverage of the protest.
7. After this protest King's approach to social change always included the participation of masses of citizens.
8. Martin Luther King, Jr., *Stride Toward Freedom* (New York: Ballantine Books, 1958), pp. 20-33.
9. *Ibid.*, p. 36.
10. Interview with Edgar Daniel Nixon, Montgomery, Alabama, January 18, 1979.
11. *Ibid.*
12. Interview with Rufus Lewis, Montgomery Alabama, July 18, 1977. Page 541 in this volume.
13. *Birmingham World*, November 27, 1955.
14. Interview with Rufus Lewis, page 542.
15. Neil Smelser, *Theory of Collective Behavior* (New York: The Free Press, 1963), p. 7.
16. Herbert Blumer, "Social Movements," in Alfred McClung Lee (ed.), *Principles of Sociology* (New York: Barnes and Noble, 1955), p. 210.
17. Hortense Spillers, "Martin Luther King and the Style of the Black Sermon," in C. Eric Lincoln (ed.) *The Black Experience in Religion* (Garden City, New York: Anchor Books, 1974), pp. 80-85.
18. *Ibid.*, p. 80.
19. This excerpt is quoted from Jim Bishop, *The Days of Martin Luther King, Jr.* (New York: G.P. Putnam's Sons, 1971), p. 140.
20. Blumer, *op. cit.*, p. 210.

CHAPTER SIX

1. Herbert Blumer, "Social Movements," in Alfred McClung Lee (ed.), *Principles of Sociology* (New York: Barnes and Noble, 1955), p. 203.
2 The pattern of contacts between local white officials and blacks escalated in the 1950s as blacks became more active politically. E. D. Nixon's run for a ward beat seat in the early 1950s helped spur this development. As previously mentioned, Nixon, Jo Ann Robinson and others had also negotiated with officials about the pattern of driver abuse on the Montgomery City Lines.

3. Conversations with E. D. Nixon, January 18, 1979, in Montgomery, and Jo Ann Robinson, August 28, 1977 in Los Angeles verified how the more militant protest leaders felt about these initial goals.

4. Martin Luther King, Jr., *Stride Toward Freedom* (New York: Ballantine Books, 1958), p. 52.

5. Interview with Rufus Lewis, Montgomery, Alabama, July 18, 1977. Page 540 in this volume.

6. *Ibid.*

7. J. Mills Thornton, "Challenge and Response in the Montgomery Bus Boycott of 1955-1956," *Alabama Review* 33 (7/80): pp. 163-235, is the best description of these negotiations. This essay is reproduced in this volume, pages 323-379.

8. *Ibid.*

9. Although Thornton's account identifies Crenshaw as the major stumbling block to the MIA, he fails to describe how Crenshaw's personal style affronted local blacks.

10. *The New York Times*, December 4, 1955.

11. Numan V. Bartley, *The Rise of Massive Resistance: Race and Politics in the South During the 1950s* (Baton Rouge, Louisiana: Louisiana State University Press, 1969), pp. 67-81.

12. See *Montgomery Advertiser*, December 9, 1955, and December 16, 1955 for comprehensive summaries of the MIA's and white official's positions.

13. Interview with Reverend J. H. Cherry, Montgomery, Alabama, January, 1979.

14. Montgomery's black cabdrivers began receiving mailed notices of a "cease and desist" nature on December 16, 1955. As an easily identifiable group, the white officials targeted the black cabdrivers for special abuse.

15. There were some public voices of white moderation in Montgomery. The "Men of Montgomery" offered to try and mediate the dispute. They sought an end to "force, intimidation and reprisal" by both whites and blacks. See *Alabama Journal*, February 8, 1956.

16. See *Alabama Journal*, January 23, 1956.

17. *Ibid.*

18. King, *op. cit.*, pp. 100-101.

19. *Ibid.*, pp. 101-102.

20. Thornton, *op. cit.*

21. Interview with Joe Reed, Montgomery, Alabama, January, 1979. Interview with Mark Gilmore, Montgomery, Alabama, August, 1977.

22. King, *op. cit.*, p. 109. See also the *Alabama Journal* of January 31, 1956.

23. *Ibid.*, pp. 113-114.

24. Quoted from Robert H. Brisbane, *Black Activism: Racial Revolution in the United States, 1954-1970*. (Valley Forge, Pennsylvania: Judson Press, 1973), pp. 41-42.

25. See *Montgomery Advertiser*, February 24, 1956.

26. *Ibid.*

27. Interview with Mr. Rufus Lewis, Montgomery, Alabama, January 18, 1980.

28. Interview with Reverend B. J. Simms, Montgomery, Alabama, July 16, 1977. Page 579 in this volume.

29. *Ibid.*, pp. 579-580.
30. See *Montgomery Advertiser*, February, 23, 1956.
31. *Martin Luther King, Jr. v. State of Alabama*, 1956.

CHAPTER SEVEN

1. Lewis Coser in his work *The Functions of Social Conflict* (New York: The Free Press, 1956), pp. 39-48, describes how the expression of hostility often binds together a social movement's members. Hanes Walton's discussion of the NAACP's opposition to Judge John J. Parker's 1930 nomination to the Supreme Court discloses how southern white opposition assisted that organization in maintaining cohesion during the trying times of the Depression. As Coser theorized and Walton confirmed, such principles prevail in movements involving blacks.
2. Neil Smelser in his *Theory of Collective Behavior* (New York: The Free Press of Glencoe, 1963), especially pp. 253-261, discusses the critical factor of organizational direction during a social movement's emergent stage.
3. E. Franklin Frazier's account of the economic cooperation function of the black church remains the standard treatment of this subject. See *The Negro Church in America* (New York: Schocken Books, 1964), pp. 34-38. Frazier's account depends heavily on W. E. B. DuBois's *Economic Cooperation Among American Negroes* (Atlanta: Atlanta University Papers, 1907).
4. Daniel T. Carter's *Scottsboro: An American Tragedy* (Baton Rouge, Louisiana: Louisiana State University Press, 1970), provides an excellent account of the fundraising procedures used and abused in that earlier Alabama campaign.
5. King's references to the Ku Klux Klan appeared in his first address to a mass meeting on December 5, 1955, and continued throughout the campaign.
6. David L. Lewis, *King: A Biography* (Urbana, Illinois: University of Illinois Press, 1978), p. 38.
7. Interview with Mark Gilmore, Montgomery, Alabama, August 10, 1977.
8. *Ibid.* Mark Gilmore reports that this was a prime element of King's presentation style that attracted support from those blacks less privileged than others. Gilmore was particularly adamant in noting the class cleavages that existed among Montgomery's blacks before King's emergence.
9. Herbert Blumer, "Social Movements," in *Principles of Sociology*, Alfred McClung Lee, ed. (New York: Barnes and Noble, 1955), p. 211.
10. *Montgomery Advertiser*, February 15, 1956. Special File—Library, Department of Archives and History, Montgomery, Alabama. The article is headlined: "King Says Boycott Part of Revolt by Oppressed."
11. *Ibid.*
12. *Ibid.*
13. *Ibid.*
14. *Montgomery Advertiser*, February 23, 1956.
15. *Montgomery Advertiser*, March 9, 1956.
16. *Ibid.*

17. *Montgomery Advertiser*, March 29, 1956.
18. *Ibid.*
19. *Ibid.*
20. Jim Bishop, *The Days of Martin Luther King, Jr.* (New York: G. P. Putnam's Sons, 1971), pp. 153-158, discusses the Baton Rouge boycott and its leader, Reverend Theodore Jemison. See also Martin Luther King, Jr.'s *Stride Toward Freedom* (New York: Ballantine Books, 1958), p. 59.
21. Interview with Hazel Gregory, former secretary of MIA, Montgomery, Alabama, July, 1977.
22. E. D. Nixon, Montgomery, Alabama, July 27, 1977. Page 550 in this volume.
23. *Ibid.*
24. *Montgomery Advertiser*, January 10, 1956. An article by Tom Johnson discloses some very interesting facts about Graetz. That article also provides one of the earliest accounts of a story that has become a boycott classic. Johnson's article refers to an older black woman who, after walking a long distance in support of the protest, was asked if she were tired. According to Graetz, the woman replied:

    Well, my body may be a bit tired, but for many years now my soul has been tired. Now my soul is resting. So I don't mind if my body is tired, because my soul is free.

    In later years this morale-sustaining story has been simplified many times as it has been retold. This story has also been credited to Martin Luther King, Jr. Howell Raines's version of the story is an example.

    Martin asked this old lady, he said, "Now listen . . . you have been with us all along, so now you go on and start back to riding the bus, 'cause you are too old to keep walking . . ."

    She said, "Oh, no." Said, "I'm gonna walk just as long as everybody else walks. I'm gonna walk till it's over."

    So he said, "But aren't your feet tired?" She said, "Yes, my feets is tired, but my soul is rested."

    Raines's version, incorrectly attributed to King, has King posing the quaint question during the concluding days of the protest, while Johnson's article appeared within a few weeks of the boycott's inception.

    This legendary story was striking enough, though, for Raines to title his book, *My Soul is Rested*.
25. *Ibid.*
26. *Ibid.*
27. *Ibid.*
28. *Jet Magazine*, December 22, 1955.
29. *Op. cit.*, *Montgomery Advertiser*, January 10, 1956.
30. *Alabama Journal*, January 25, 1956.
31. Bishop, *op. cit.*, p. 72

CHAPTER EIGHT

1. J. Victor Baldridge, *Sociology: A Critical Approach to Power, Conflict, and Change* (New York: John Wiley and Sons, 1975), p. 307.
2. Herbert Blumer, "Social Movements", in *Principles of Sociology*, Alfred McClung Lee, ed. (New York: Barnes and Noble, Inc., 1955), p. 214.
3. The pressures on those most involved with the boycott's leadership were such that complaints of fatigue were expressed in the early months of the boycott. Mrs. Coretta Scott King expressed such fatigue in an article in the black press. See *Richmond Afro-American*, March 31, 1956.
4. For excellent reports on contrasting views of the NAACP legalism approach, see Pat Watters' and Reese Cleghorn's *Climbing Jacob's Ladder* (New York: Harcourt, Brace and World, Inc., 1967), especially the chapter on "Field Report—Telling It Like It Was," pp. 171-209.
5. Martin Luther King, Jr., utilized such a tactic during the Birmingham, Alabama, campaign conducted during the summer of 1963. Robert Brisbane discusses that and similar examples in his book *Black Activism: Racial Revolution in the United States, 1954-1970* (Valley Forge, Pennsylvania: Judson Press, 1974), see especially pp. 43-72.
6. Jim Bishop, *The Days of Martin Luther King, Jr.* (New York: G. P. Putnam and Sons, 1971), p. 133-134.
7. Charles D. Langford, interviewed in Montgomery, Alabama, August 14, 1977.
8. *Ibid.*
9. Martin Luther King, Jr., advised of the legal nuances, when writing for the April 1956 issue of the *Liberation* magazine, referred consistently to the boycott as "our protest." King's statement is in a pamphlet reprinted by the Congress of Racial Equality in March, 1975.
10. Rufus Lewis, interviewed in Montgomery, Alabama, July 18, 1977. Page 543 in this volume.
11. For an example of this comeback, see the *Montgomery Advertiser* of August 24, 1950. That edition contains an article describing the selection of Montgomery as the site of a coalition of Klan groups that were based in six states.
12. *Montgomery Advertiser*, November 25, 1956.
13. Martin Luther King, Jr., *Stride Toward Freedom* (New York: Ballantine Books, 1958), p. 140.
14. David L. Lewis, *King: A Biography* (Urbana, Illinois: University of Illinois Press, 1978), p. 83.
15. *Montgomery Advertiser*, December 20, 1956.
16. August Meier and Elliott Rudwick, "The Boycott Movement Against Jim Crow Streetcars in the South, 1900-1906," in *The Black Experience in America*, James C. Curtis and Lewis L. Gould, eds. (Austin, Texas: University of Texas, 1970), pp. 87-115.
17. *Ibid.*, p. 113.
18. Adam Clayton Powell, Jr., also made militant statements in support of the boycott. Powell, characteristically, predicted that the Montgomery movement

would spawn imitative efforts. For an example of Powell's continuous comments on the boycott, see the *Birmingham News* of March 2, 1956.

19. Jerry D. Rose, *Introduction to Sociology* (Chicago: Rand McNally College Publishers, 1980), p. 416.

20. Bishop, *op. cit.*, p. 190.

21. *Ibid.*, p. 19.

22. William H. Peace III, "The South Reacts," in *The Angry Black South*, Glenford E. Mitchell and William H. Peace III, eds. (New York: Corinth Books, 1962), pp. 118-119.

23. James W. Vander Zanden, *Race Relations in Transition* (New York: Random House, 1965), p. 56. Robert H. Brisbane, *Black Activism: Racial Revolution in the United States, 1954-1970* (Valley Forge, Pennsylvania: Judson Press, 1973), p. 41. Everett C. Ladd, Jr., *Negro Political Leadership in the South* (New York: Athenfeum Press, 1969), p. 47.

24. Montgomery Improvement Association's Tenth Anniversary Program, printed December, 1966, p. 5.

25. *Ibid.*, pp. 29-30.

26. Hazel Gregory, interviewed in Montgomery, Alabama, January, 1979.

27. Tamotsu Shibutani, *Society and Personality: An Interactionist Approach to Social Psychology* (Englewood Cliffs, New Jersey: Prentice-Hall, Inc., 1961), p. 574.

28. E. D. Nixon, interviewed in Montgomery, Alabama, January 18, 1979.

Bibliography

Baldridge, J. Victor
    1975   *Sociology: A Critical Approach to Power, Conflict and Change*
         New York: Wiley and Sons

Bartley, Numan V.
    1969   *The Rise of Massive Resistance: Race and Politics in the South During the 1950's*
         Baton Rouge, La.: University of Louisiana Press

Bishop, Jim
    1971   *The Days of Martin Luther King, Jr.*
         New York: G. P. Putnam's Sons

Blauner, Robert
    1964   *Alienation and Freedom*
         Chicago: University of Chicago Press

Bond, Horace Mann
    1939   *Negro Education in Alabama*
         New York: Atheneum

Brisbane, Robert
    1973   *Black Activism: Racial Revolution in the United States, 1954-1970*
         Valley Forge, Pa.: Judson Press

Carter, Daniel T.
    1969   *Scottsboro: A Tragedy of the American South*
         Baton Rouge, La.: University of Louisiana Press

Clark, John B.
    1927   *Populism in Alabama*
         Auburn, Ala.: Auburn Printing Company

Coser, Lewis
    1956   *The Functions of Social Conflict*
         New York: The Free Press

Davis, Allison; Gardner, Burleigh B. and Mary R.
    1941   *Deep South: A Social Anthropological Study of Caste and Class*
         Chicago: University of Chicago Press

Davis, George A. and Donaldson, O. Fred
  1975   *Blacks in the United States: A Geographic Perspective*
          Boston: Houghton Mifflin Company
Dollard, John
  1937   *Caste and Class in a Southern Town*
          Garden City, N.Y.: Doubleday Anchor Books
DuBois, William E. B.
  1973   *Black Reconstruction in America*
          New York: Atheneum
Ellison, Ralph
  1964   *Shadow and Act*
          New York: Random House
Fleming, Walter
  1905   *Civil War and Reconstruction in Alabama*
          New York: Columbia University Press
Frazier, E. Franklin
  1957   *The Negro in the United States*
          New York: MacMillan
  1964   *The Negro Church in America*
          New York: Schocken Books
Frazier, Thomas R. (ed.)
  1971   *The Underside of American History: Other Readings*
          New York: Harcourt, Brace and Jovanovich
Geschwender, James
  1978   *Racial Stratification in America*
          Dubuque, Ia.: William C. Brown Company
Glazer, Nathan and Moynihan, Daniel P.
  1963   *Beyond the Melting Pot: The Negroes, Puerto Ricans, Jews, Italians and Irish of New York City*
          Cambridge, Mass.: MIT Press
Grant, Joanne
  1968   *Black Protest: History, Documents and Analyses*
          Greenwich, Conn.: Fawcett Premier
Hamilton, Charles V.
  1960   *Minority Politics in Black Belt Alabama*
          New York: McGraw-Hill Company

Holloway, Harry
    1969   *The Politics of the Southern Negro: From Exclusion to Big City Organization*
        New York: Random House
Hook, Sidney
    1943   *The Hero in History*
        New York: The John Day Company
Jack, Theodore Henley
    1919   *Sectionalism and Party Politics in Alabama, 1819-1842*
        Menasha, Wis.: George Banta Publishing Office
Johnson, Chalmers A.
    1962   *Peasant Nationalism and Communist Power*
        Palo Alto, Ca.: Stanford University Press
Jordan,Winthrop
    1969   *White Over Black: American Attitudes Towards the Negro, 1550-1812*
        Baltimore, Md.: Penguin Books
King, Martin Luther, Jr.
    1958   *Stride Toward Freedom: The Montgomery Story*
        New York: Ballantine Books
Ladd, Everett C.
    1966   *Negro Political Leadership in the South*
        Ithaca, N.Y.: Cornell University Press
Levine, Lawrence W.
    1977   *Black Culture and Black Consciousness*
        Oxford, England: Oxford University Press
Lewis, David L.
    1978   *King: A Critical Biography*
        Urbana, Ill.: University of Illinois Press
Litwack, Leon F.
    1965   *North of Slavery: The Negro in the Free States, 1790-1860*
        Chicago: University of Chicago Press
Logan, Rayford W.
    1954   *The Betrayal of the Negro*
        New York: Collier Books
Lyman, Stanford
    1972   *The Black American in Sociological Thought*
        New York: G. P. Putnam's Sons

Meier, August and Rudwick, Elliott
  1966   *From Plantation to Ghetto*
           New York: Hill and Wang
Mills, C. Wright
  1959   *The Sociological Imagination*
           New York: Oxford University Press
Owens, Leslie Howard
  1976   *The Species of Property: Slave Life and Culture in the Old South*
           Oxford, England: Oxford University Press
Osofosky, Gilbert
  1968   *Harlem: The Making of a Ghetto*
           New York: Torch Books
Piven, Frances Fox and Cloward, Richard C.
  1979   *Poor Peoples' Movements: Why They Succeed, How They Fail*
           New York: Vintage Books
Powdermaker, Hortense
  1939   *After Freedom: A Cultural Study in the Deep South*
           New York: Atheneum
Price, H. D.
  1957   *The Negro in Southern Politics*
           New York: New York University Press
Raines, Howell
  1977   *My Soul Is Rested: Movement Days in the Deep South*
           New York: Bantam Books
Raper, Arthur F.
  1936   *Preface to Peasantry*
           New York: University of North Carolina Press
Reid, Whitelaw
  1866   *After the War, a Tour of the Southern States, 1865-1866*
           New York: Harper and Row
Rose, Jerry D.
  1980   *Introduction to Sociology*
           Chicago: Rand McNally College Publishers
Rosengarten, Theodore
  1974   *All God's Dangers: The Life of Nate Shaw*
           New York: Avon Books
Ryan, William
  1971   *Blaming the Victim*

New York: Random House

Schatzman, Leonard and Strauss, Anselm L.
1973   *Field Research: Strategies for a Natural Sociology*
        Englewood Cliffs, N.J.: Prentice-Hall

Scott, Emmett Jay
1920   *Negro Migration During the War*
        New York: Oxford University Press

Smelser, Neil
1963   *Theory of Collective Behavior*
        New York: The Free Press of Glencoe

Tocqueville, Alexis de
1945   *Democracy in America*, ed. by Philip Bradley
        New York: Vintage Books

Thornbrough, Emma L.
1969   *Booker T. Washington: Great Lives Observed*
        Englewood Cliffs, N.J.: Prentice-Hall

Walls, Dwayne E.
1971   *The Chickenbone Special*
        New York: Harcourt, Brace and Jovanovich

Walton, Hanes, Jr.
1971   *The Political Philosophy of Martin Luther King, Jr.*
        Westport, Conn.: Greenwood Publishing

Watters, Pat and Cleghorn, Reese
1967   *Climbing Jacob's Ladder*
        New York: Harcourt, Brace and World

Wharton, Vernon Lane
1947   *The Negro in Mississippi*
        Chapel Hill, N.C.: University of North Carolina Press

Wiggins, Sarah Woolfolk
1974   *The Scalawag in Alabama Politics, 1865-1881*
        Tuscaloosa, Ala.: The University of Alabama Press

Wilkenson, Paul
1971   *Social Movements*
        New York: Praeger Publishers

Williams, John A.
1970   *The King That God Couldn't Save*
        New York: Coward-McCann

Williamson, Joel

1965   *After Slavery: The Negro in South Carolina During Reconstruction, 1861-1877*
          Chapel Hill, N.C.: The University of North Carolina Press
Wynes, Charles E.
1961   *Race Relations in Virginia, 1870-1902*
          Charlottesville, Va.: The University of Virginia Press

ARTICLES

Beale, Calvin
1976   "The Black American in Agriculture," in Mabel M. Smythe, ed., *The Black American Reference Book*
          Englewood Cliffs, N.J.: Prentice-Hall
Blumer, Herbert
1955   "Social Movements," in Alfred McClung Lee, ed., *Principles of Sociology*
          New York: Barnes and Noble
1969   "Attitudes and the Social Act," in Herbert Blumer, *Symbolic Interactionism: Perspective and Method*
          Englewood Cliffs, N.J.: Prentice-Hall
Broderick, Frances
1974   "The Fight Against Booker T. Washington," in Hugh Hawkins, ed., *Booker T. Washington and His Critics: Black Leadership in Crisis*
          Lexington, Mass.: D. C. Heath and Company
Den Hollander, A. N. J.
1934   "The Tradition of 'Poor Whites,'" in W. T. Couch, ed., *Culture in the South*
          Raleigh, N.C.: University of North Carolina Press
Gusfield, Joseph R.
1968   "Studying Social Movements," in *International Encyclopedia of the Social Sciences*
          New York: MacMillan Company and the Free Press
Hamilton, Holman and Thornbrough, Gayle
1969   "Washington's Humor," in Emma L. Thornbrough, ed., *Booker T. Washington: Great Lives Observed*
          Englewood Cliffs, N.J.: Prentice-Hall
Harlan, Louis R.

1971   "The Secret Life of Booker T. Washington," in *Journal of Southern History*, (August)

Heberle, Rudolf
1946   "A Sociological Interpretation of Social Change in the South," *Social Forces*, 25 (October)

Howells, William Dean
1901   "An Exemplary Citizen," in *North American Review*, CLXXIII (August)

Janowitz, Morris
1965   "Review of Shadow and Act," in *American Journal of Sociology*, LXX (May)

Kristol, Irving
1972   "The Negro Today Is Like the Immigrant of Yesterday," in Peter Rose, ed., *Nation of Nations: The Ethnic Experience and the Racial Crisis*
        New York: Random House

MacDonald, Dwight
1965   "A Theory of Mass Culture," in Bernard Rosenberg and David Manning White, eds., *Mass Culture: The Popular Arts in America*
        New York: The Free Press

McFoley, William S.
1971   "Unfinished Business: The Freedman's Bureau and Federal Action in Race Relations," in Nathan I. Huggins, Martin Kilson, and Daniel Fox, eds., *Key Issues in the Afro-American Experience*
        New York: Harcourt, Brace and Jovanovich

Meier, August and Rudwick, Elliott
1970   "The Boycott Movement Against Jim Crow Streetcars in the South, 1900-1906," in James C. Curtis and Lewis L. Gould, eds., *The Black Experience in America*
        Austin, Texas: University of Texas Press

Park, Robert E.
1950   "An Autobiographic Note," in *Race and Culture: Collected Papers of Robert E. Park*, Everett C. Hughes, Charles S. Johnson, Jitsuichi Masuoka, Robert Redford and Louis Wirth, eds.
        Glencoe: The Free Press
1950   "Education in Its Relation to Cultures," in *Race and Culture*

1950   "Our Racial Frontier on the Pacific," in *Race and Culture*

1950   "Racial Assimilation in Secondary Groups," in *Race and Culture*

1950   "The Race Relations Cycle in Hawaii," in *Race and Culture*

Pope, J. D.

1930   "Types of Farming Areas," in *Agriculture of Alabama*, Alabama
Department of Agriculture and Industries.
Montgomery, Ala.: State of Alabama

Reuter, Edward B.

1939   "Why the Presence of the Negro Constitutes a Problem in the
American Social Order," in *The Journal of Negro Education*, VII
(July)

Rowan, Carl

1967   "Martin Luther King's Tragic Decision," in *Readers Digest* (June)

Schaefer, Richard T.

1958   "The Ku Klux Klan: Continuity and Change," *Phylon* (Summer)

Spillers, Hortense

1974   "Martin Luther King and the Style of the Black Sermon," in C.
Eric Lincoln, ed., *The Black Experience in Religion*
Garden City, N.Y.: Anchor Books

Tower, J. Allen

1948   "Alabama's Shifting Cotton Belt," in *Alabama Review* (January)

Walden, Daniel

1960   "The Contemporary Opposition to the Political Ideals of Booker
T. Washington," in *Journal of Negro History* (April)

Washington, Booker T.

1965   "The Anaconda," in Milton Meltzer, ed., *In Their Own Words:
A History of the American Negro*

1966   "Democracy and Education," in Howard Brotz, ed., *Negro Social
and Political Thought: 1850-1920*
New York: Basic Books

Woodward, C. Vann

1968   "The Genesis of Segregation," in Joel Williamson, ed., *the
Origins of Segregation*
Lexington, Mass.: D. C. Heath and Company

Zanden, James W. Vander

1958-9 "Resistance and Social Movements," *Social Forces* (October-
May)

RECORDS AND SPEECHES

Carnegie, Andrew
  1907 "The Negro in America," delivered before the Philosophical Institute of Edinburgh.
Courlander, Harold
  1951 "I'm Going Up North," from *Negro Songs from Alabama*, Folkways Records, Band 6, Side 2.
Roosevelt, Theodore
  1906 "Sixth Annual Message," December 6, Washington, D.C.
X, Malcolm
  1963 "Message to the Grassroots," September, Detroit, Michigan.

GOVERNMENT DOCUMENTS

U.S. Bureau of Census, Third Census, 1820.
U.S. Bureau of Census, Fourteenth Census, Alabama Compendium.

MAGAZINES AND NEWSPAPERS

Alabama Journal
Birmingham News
Chicago Defender
Jet Magazine
Montgomery Advertiser
New York Times
Richmond Afro-American
San Jose News

The Origins of
the Montgomery
Bus Boycott

DAVID J. GARROW

Jo Ann Gibson Robinson moved to Montgomery, Alabama, in the late summer of 1949 to join the English Department at all-black Alabama State College. A thirty-three year old native of Culloden, Georgia, twenty-five miles from Macon, she was the twelfth and youngest child of Owen Boston Gibson and Dollie Webb Gibson, land-owning black farmers who prospered until Owen Gibson died when Jo Ann was six years old. As the children moved away, operating the farm grew more difficult for Mrs. Gibson, who eventually sold the property and moved into Macon with her younger offspring. Jo Ann graduated from high school there as the class valedictorian, and went on to earn her undergraduate degree at Fort Valley State College, the first member of her family to complete college. She took a public school teaching job in Macon and married Wilbur Robinson, but the marriage, heavily burdened by the death in infancy of their first and only child, lasted only a short time. Twelve months later, after five years of teaching in Macon, Jo Ann Robinson moved to Atlanta to take an M.A. in English at Atlanta University and then accepted a teaching position at Mary Allen College in Crockett, Texas. After one year there, Mrs. Robinson received a better offer from Alabama State and moved to Montgomery.

Mrs. Robinson was an enthusiastic teacher and responded energetically to her new position at Alabama State. She also became an active member of Dexter Avenue Baptist Church, which many Alabama State professors attended, and she joined the Women's Political Council, a black professional women's civic group that one of her English Department colleagues, Mrs. Mary Fair Burks, had founded three years earlier when the local League of Women Voters had refused to integrate.

It was a blissful fall, Mrs. Robinson later remembered. "I loved every minute of it." Just prior to Christmas she made preparations to visit some relatives in Cleveland for the holidays. Storing her car in a garage, she boarded a Montgomery City Lines public bus for the ride to Dannelly Field, the municipal airport. Only two other passengers were aboard, and Mrs. Robinson, immersed in holiday thoughts, took a seat towards the front of the bus. Suddenly, however, she was roused from her thoughts about her family by angry words from the driver, who was ordering her to get up.

"He was standing over me, saying 'Get up from there! Get up from there,' with his hand drawn back," she later recalled.

Shaken and frightened, Mrs. Robinson fled from the bus. "I felt like a dog. And I got mad, after this was over, and I realized that I was a human being, and just as intelligent and far more trained than that bus driver was. But I think he wanted to hurt me, and he did . . . I cried all the way to Cleveland."

That experience convinced Mrs. Robinson that the Women's Political Council ought to target Montgomery's segregated bus seating for immediate attention. "It was then that I made up . . . my mind that whatever I could add to that organization that would help to bring that practice down, I would do it," Mrs. Robinson recalled. "When I came back, the first thing I did was to call a meeting . . . and tell them what had happened."

Only then did Mrs. Robinson learn that her experience was far from unique, that dozens of other black citizens, primarily women, had suffered similar abuse from Montgomery bus drivers. Over the previous few years several black women, Mrs. Geneva Johnson, Mrs. Viola White, and Miss Katie Wingfield, had been arrested and convicted for refusing to give up their seats. Earlier in 1949, two young children, visiting from the north and unfamiliar with Montgomery's practice of reserving the first ten seats on each bus for white riders only, even if black passengers were forced to stand over vacant seats, also were hauled in for refusing a driver's command to surrender their seats. Some oldtimers in Montgomery remembered how the black community had mounted a boycott in the summer of 1900, when the city had first imposed segregated seating on Montgomery's street cars, a boycott that had won a refinement of the city ordinance so as to specify that no rider had to surrender a seat unless another was available. Nonetheless, drivers often made black riders who were seated just behind the whites-only section get up and stand so that all white passengers could sit.

Mrs. Burks thought black toleration of those seating practices and other driver abuse, such as forcing black passengers to pay their dime at the front, and then get off and board the bus through the rear, side door, was scandalous. "Everyone would look the other way. Nobody would acknowledge what was going on," Mrs. Burks remembered. "It outraged me that this kind of conduct was going on," and that so far no black community organizations had done anything about it.

Black activism did exist in Montgomery, even though it had not yet focused upon bus conditions, despite the widespread complaints. Several years earlier Arthur Madison, a New York lawyer who came from one of black Montgomery's most prominent families, had returned home and tried to stimulate black voter registration, but white legal harassment had forced him to return to New York. The outspoken pastor of Dexter Avenue Baptist Church, Rev. Vernon Johns, who had come to Montgomery in 1948, regularly denounced the bus situation, but many blacks viewed Johns as too unpredictable and idiosyncratic to assume a leadership role in the community. The brutal rape of a black teenager, Gertrude Perkins, by two white policemen earlier in 1949 had led Rev. Solomon S. Seay to repeated efforts to obtain justice in the case, but white officials had brushed off his complaints.

Another visible black activist was Pullman porter Edgar Daniel Nixon, a member of A. Philip Randolph's Brotherhood of Sleeping Car Porters and a local leader of the National Association for the Advancement of Colored People (NAACP). Nixon served as Alabama state president of the NAACP in 1948-1949, and also devoted much time to his Alabama Progressive Democratic Association, a black alternative to a state Democratic Party that continued to discourage black participation despite the 1940s' demise of the "white primary." Nixon regularly mounted one initiative after another; in 1954 he succeeded in winning 42 percent of the vote in a losing race for a seat on the party's Montgomery County Democratic Executive Committee, a tribute not only to the more than 1,500 black voters that Nixon and other activists like businessman Rufus A. Lewis had helped register, but also to the grudging respect that many whites felt for Nixon's tireless efforts.

Lewis, a well-known former football coach at Alabama State College, had been especially active not only in encouraging black registration but also in trying to unify black Montgomery's civic activism. Although some colleagues viewed Lewis and Nixon as low-key rivals for top leadership, Lewis' Citizens Club served as a regular hang-out for politically-minded blacks; his Citizens Steering Committee, formed in the fall of 1952, looked to find ways to exert some black political influence over Montgomery's city policies.

Equally if not more important to the political life of black Montgomery than Nixon's Progressive Democrats, the NAACP branch, or Lewis' Citizens Committee, however, was Mrs. Burks and Mrs. Robinson's Women's Political Council. By the early 1950s Robinson had succeeded Burks as president, and the core membership of regularly active participants numbered at least thirty women such as Thelma Glass, Mary Cross, Irene West, Euretta Adair, Elizabeth Arrington, and Zoeline Pierce, who were either faculty members at Alabama State, teachers in the local, segregated public schools, or wives of relatively well-to-do black professional men. More than either Nixon's circle or Lewis', these middle-class women were the most numerous, most reform-minded group of black civic activists in Montgomery.

The first notable opportunity for black political influence to make itself felt came in November, 1953, in a special election to fill one vacant seat on the three-member Montgomery City Commission. The black-supported victor, Dave Birmingham, a genuine racial liberal, won fifty-three percent of the vote in a contest that involved little discussion of race and allowed Birmingham to construct an electoral coalition of blacks and lower-class whites.

Impressed by their success in representing the balance of power, black civic activists, led by the WPC, met in late 1953 with Birmingham and his two racially moderate colleagues, Mayor W.A. "Tacky" Gayle and George Cleere, to voice three complaints about the racial practices of the municipally regulated and chartered bus company, Montgomery City Lines. Blacks having to stand over empty, white only seats on crowded buses was a constant insult and problem. So was most drivers' practice of forcing blacks to board through the rear door. Additionally, while buses stopped at every block in white sections of town, it was only every other block in black neighborhoods.

The three commissioners, Birmingham in particular, listened politely, but nothing came of the session.

Undaunted, Mrs. Robinson, who served as the WPC and black community's principal spokesperson, obtained another audience with the commission in March, 1954, and reiterated the three complaints. The WPC, which historian of Montgomery J. Mills Thornton III has accurately termed "the most militant and uncompromising organ of the black community" in pre-1956 Montgomery, also presented the commission with specific details of driver abuse of black passengers. This time the city officials agreed to alter the bus company's practice of stopping only at alternate blocks in black areas, but they and the city's lawyers insisted there was no way, under Alabama's state segregation statutes, that any changes or improvements could be made in bus seating practices. Robinson and other black representatives contended that elimination of the reserved, whites only seats, and a halt to the practice of making blacks surrender seats to whites on overcrowded buses would eliminate the most serious problems, but the white officials rejected the WPC's proposal that the front-to-back seating of whites, and back-to-front seating of blacks, with no one having to stand over an empty seat or give up one after being seated, would in no way offend the state segregation law.

Mrs. Robinson and her colleagues were unhappy over the city's refusal to show any flexibility. In early May, the Commission did approve the hiring of Montgomery's first four black police officers, but many black Montgomerians attached greater importance to the ongoing prosecution of a black teenager, Jeremiah Reeves, who faced the death penalty for the supposed rape of a white woman in 1951.

Mrs. Robinson was already thinking of how to put more pressure on the Commission to improve bus conditions when, on May 17, came a news announcement that strengthened her determination. The United States Supreme Court, in *Brown v. Board of Education of Topeka* and five companion cases challenging racially segregated public schools, ruled that governmentally-mandated school segregation was unconstitutional and that the sixty-year-old doctrine of "separate but equal" was no longer valid.

Four days after the landmark *Brown* decision, Mrs. Robinson typed a letter to Montgomery's Mayor Gayle, with a copy to Montgomery City Lines manager J.H. Bagley. She thanked Gayle for the March meeting and for the change in the buses' alternate block stopping practice, but reiterated the WPC's great unhappiness at the ongoing seating policies. Then she politely voiced the threat she had quietly been recommending to her black leadership colleagues.

Mayor Gayle, three-fourths of the riders of these public conveyances are Negroes. If Negroes did not patronize them, they could not possibly operate.

More and more of our people are already arranging with neighbors and friends to ride to keep from being insulted and humiliated by bus drivers. There has been talk from twenty-five or more local organizations of planning

611

a city-wide boycott of buses. We, sir, do not feel that forceful measures are necessary in bargaining for a convenience which is right for all bus passengers. We, the Council, believe that when this matter has been put before you and the Commissioners, that agreeable terms can be met in a quiet and unostensible manner to the satisfaction of all concerned.

Mrs. Robinson pointedly noted that many Southern cities, including Mobile, already were using the front-to-back, back-to-front segregation seating plan that Montgomery refused to implement. "Please consider this plea, and if possible, act favorably upon it," she concluded, "for even now plans are being made to ride less, or not at all, on our buses. We do not want this."

Despite the extremely gentle and tactful language she employed in her letter to Gayle, Mrs. Robinson was hoping that black community sentiment would support a bus boycott to force the Commission's hand. Another meeting with the white officials on June 1 registered no progress, but Mrs. Robinson found only modest interest in her boycott idea throughout much of the black community, and placed the idea on a back burner for the time being.

Next to bus conditions, the second civic concern troubling the WPC and other black activists was the decidedly inferior quality of the segregated parks and recreation facilities available to black Montgomerians. One step the WPC had identified as a partial remedy was the appointment of a black member, such as WPC member Mrs. Irene West, to the city's Parks and Recreation Board. Mrs. Robinson voiced this request at a January, 1955, meeting of the City Commission, but despite supportive comments from Birmingham and Mayor Gayle, nothing happened. Instead, attention turned to the upcoming mid-March city elections, and a public candidates' forum that E. D. Nixon's Progressive Democratic Association held on February 23 at the black Ben Moore Hotel.

All three incumbents, plus their major challengers, Harold McGlynn for Gayle, Frank Parks for Cleere, and Sam Sterns and Clyde Sellers for Birmingham, attended the first-of-its-kind event and faced questions about bus conditions as well as the Parks and Recreation appointment. A majority of the contenders endorsed a black appointment to the Parks Board, while others avoided any specifics on either topic. Although the open soliciting of black votes by so many white candidates seemed impressive, one of Birmingham's challengers, former Auburn University football star and state highway patrol officer Clyde Sellers, saw the convocation, and Birmingham's sympathy for black concerns, as just the opening that was needed to cut into Birmingham's previously solid white working class electoral support.

Sellers' strategic desire to make race an election issue got a coincidental boost on March 2 when a fifteen-year-old black girl, Claudette Colvin, refused to give up her bus seat, well toward the rear of the vehicle, so as to accommodate an overflow of newly-boarding white passengers.

Police officers were able to drag Colvin from the bus only with considerable force. The incident immediately sent the black leadership into action. Mrs. Rosa Parks, a seamstress and longtime NAACP member who was adult advisor to the NAACP Youth Council, to which Claudette Colvin belonged, immediately began soliciting financial assistance for her legal defense, as did Mrs. Parks' good friend Virginia Foster Durr, one of Montgomery's few racially liberal whites.

Rufus Lewis' newly formed Citizen's Coordinating Committee, yet another leadership unity organization which included E.D. Nixon and the WPC's Thelma Glass among its top officers, quickly sent out a mimeographed letter, "To Friends of Justice and Human Rights," seeking Colvin's acquittal, a reprimand of the bus driver involved, and clarification of the oft-ignored city provision that no rider had to give up a seat unless another was available.

Nixon and Mrs. Robinson, thinking that Colvin's case might supply an opportunity for a court challenge to the constitutionality of Montgomery's bus seating practices, interviewed the young woman, but concluded that her personal situation and the particulars of the arrest precluded using the incident as a test case. Robinson and others met, unsuccessfully, with city and bus company officials to seek dismissal of the charges.

Claudette Colvin was quickly convicted for both assault and battery and violating the segregation statute at a March 18 trial, only three days before the city election. When Colvin's attorney, young Montgomery native Fred Gray—who had been one of Mrs. Robinson's Alabama State students before attending law school in Ohio—filed notice of appeal, the prosecutor indicated that he would pursue only the assault and battery charge, not the segregation issue.

On the 21st, Sellers narrowly bested Dave Birmingham, who declined a possible runoff because of bad health, while Frank Parks, who had received black support, defeated Cleere. Disappointed both by the Colvin outcome and Birmingham's loss, the black leadership hoped for other opportunities.

In June, Mrs. Robinson, Gray, and other black representatives met once again with city and bus company officials. Despite Gray's observations about

Mobile's practices, the white officials, particularly bus company lawyer Jack Crenshaw, adhered firmly to their contention that no changes could be made legally in bus seating practices. Popular complaints about the seating situation and driver abuse remained at high levels, but no further organized initiatives were undertaken.

One relative newcomer to the city, Rev. Martin Luther King, Jr., who had succeeded Vernon Johns as pastor of Dexter Avenue Baptist Church in mid-1954 and accompanied Robinson's delegation to the early March meeting with the city, attributed a good part of the inaction to what he later termed "an appalling lack of unity among the leaders" and a "crippling factionalism." More of a problem than competition among active leaders, King thought, was the pervasive indifference of many middle-class black Montgomerians to any political or civic concern. Economic vulnerability and fear of white retribution understandably inhibited some, but "too much of the inaction was due to sheer apathy," King later wrote.

Although Mrs. Robinson still husbanded her hope that the WPC could at some point launch a boycott of the buses, the late summer and fall of 1955 passed with relative quiet; the October 21 arrest of one black woman, Mrs. Mary Louise Smith, for refusing to surrender her seat became known to most of the black leadership only several months later.

On Thursday evening December 1, Mrs. Rosa Parks, the NAACP activist who had assisted Claudette Colvin's defense, felt tired and weary from her seamstress work at the Montgomery Fair department store when she boarded one of the Cleveland Avenue route buses at Montgomery's Court Square for her regular ride home. One stop later, after taking a seat in the first row behind the ten whites-only seats, Mrs. Parks and the three other black passengers in that row were ordered by the driver, J. F. Blake, to get up so that one newly-boarding white man—who could not be accommodated in the front section—could sit. Although the other three people complied, Mrs. Parks silently refused, and two police officers were summoned to place her under arrest and transport her to the city jail.

Word of the incident spread quickly. E. D. Nixon called the jail to learn about the charges, only to be refused an answer by the officer on duty. Knowing that attorney Gray was out of town for the day, Nixon called white lawyer Clifford Durr, who like his wife Virginia, already knew Mrs. Parks. The Durrs and Nixon drove to the jail to sign the bond for Mrs. Parks' release. A Monday trial date was set for the charge of violating the city's segregated seating ordinance.

While attorney Durr explained to Nixon and Mrs. Parks that they could win her acquittal since there had been no other seat available for her to take when driver Blake demanded hers, Nixon argued that the arrest of Mrs. Parks, a widely-known and well-respected person in black Montgomery, was precisely the opportunity the black leadership had long-awaited for challenging the entire bus seating situation. With some hesitance Mrs. Parks agreed, and Nixon went home to plan his next steps.

Later that evening Fred Gray returned to town, learned of Mrs. Parks' arrest and immediately called Mrs. Robinson, who he knew to be the "real moving force" among the black leadership. Mrs. Robinson in turn called Nixon. They quickly agreed that the moment for launching the long-pondered boycott of the buses was at hand.

Nixon would make the calls to set up a black leadership meeting Friday evening; Mrs. Robinson and her WPC colleagues would immediately start producing and distributing handbills calling upon black Montgomerians to stay off the buses on Monday, December 5. "We had planned the protest long before Mrs. Parks was arrested," Mrs. Robinson later emphasized. "There had been so many things that happened that the black women had been embarrassed over, and they were ready to explode." They knew immediately that "Mrs. Parks had the caliber of character we needed to get the city to rally behind us."

Wasting not a moment, Mrs. Robinson sat down at her typewriter with a mimeograph stencil and typed the same message on the sheet several times:

This is for Monday, December 5, 1955

Another Negro woman has been arrested and thrown into jail because she refused to get up out of her seat on the bus for a white person to sit down.

It is the second time since the Claudette Colbert (sic) case that a Negro woman has been arrested for the same thing. This has to be stopped.

Negroes have rights, too, for if Negroes did not ride the buses, they could not operate. Three-fourths of the riders are Negroes, yet we are arrested, or have to stand over empty seats. If we do not do something to stop these arrests, they will continue. The next time it may be you, or your daughter, or mother.

This woman's case will come up on Monday. We are, therefore, asking every Negro to stay off the buses Monday in protest of the arrest and trial. Don't ride the buses to work, to town, to school, or anywhere on Monday.

You can afford to stay out of school for one day if you have no other way to go except by bus.

You can also afford to stay out of town for one day. If you work, take a cab, or walk. But please, children and grown-ups, don't ride the bus at all on Monday. Please stay off of all buses Monday.

The stencil complete, Mrs. Robinson called one of her Alabama State colleagues, business department chairman John Cannon, who had access to the school's mimeograph room and readily agreed to join her for a long night of work. By daybreak they had run off thousands of sheets, cut them into single copies, and organized the brief flyers into batches for distribution to dozens of WPC members and their friends. After teaching her first morning class, Mrs. Robinson and two students set out in her car, dropping off the bundles to helpers all across Montgomery. Thousands upon thousands of the leaflets went from hand-to-hand throughout black Montgomery.

While the WPC's network put the boycott into effect, E. D. Nixon made dozens of phone calls to assemble the black leadership. Like Robinson and her WPC colleagues, Nixon knew that for their protest to win mass support, the city's ministers, not always in the forefront to black civic initiatives, would have to be convinced to give the effort their full and active support. The WPC's post-haste distribution of the announcements, Robinson and Nixon knew, ought to short-circuit any arguments that now was not a good time for a boycott, even before they could be voiced. As Fred Gray later emphasized, "the ministers didn't know anything about those leaflets until they appeared."

Although the Friday evening leadership caucus had some difficulties in overcoming the autocratic style of one black pastor, agreement was reached on further publicizing the Monday boycott and on holding a Monday evening mass rally to assess the first day's success. The leadership would meet again Monday afternoon to plan the rally, and amidst scores of weekend phone conversations between the various black activists, a consensus gradually emerged that perhaps a new, all-encompassing community organization ought to be created to oversee this unique effort.

Mrs. Robinson and the WPC membership knew that with the protest going public, their state-payroll positions at Alabama State, and the budgetary vulnerability of the college to white political retaliation, required that they remain in the background. As Mrs. Burks later noted in explaining why the origin of the boycott leaflets was treated as a closely guarded secret well into the 1960s, "the full extent of our activities was never revealed because of the fact that we worked at State."

Monday morning the amazing success of the protest was readily apparent as onlooker after onlooker observed no more than a handful of black bus riders on Montgomery's largely empty vehicles.

Also on Monday, Mrs. Parks, in a very brief trial, was convicted of failing to obey the driver's commands and to surrender her seat. Hundreds of black Montgomerians, in a remarkable scene, gathered at the courthouse to show their support. That afternoon, when the black leadership assembled, Rufus Lewis—to be certain that leadership did not fall into unskilled hands—quickly nominated his pastor, Rev. Martin Luther King, Jr., to be president of their new community group, the Montgomery Improvement Association. A surprised King hesitantly accepted, and the leadership agreed to make continuation of the boycott beyond their one day success, contingent upon mass sentiment at the evening rally.

A huge and enthusiastic turnout for the evening event quickly and convincingly answered that question. Now the community leaders turned their efforts to organizing substitute means of transportation for the thousands of black Montgomerians eager to forsake a transportation system that most had assumed was an unpleasant but unavoidable fact of daily life.

Thursday morning, with the boycott four days old, more than half a dozen MIA representatives, including King, Robinson, and Gray, met with city and bus company officials under the auspices of the biracial Alabama Council on Human Relations. Even though King emphasized to the whites that "we are not out to change the segregation laws," but only to win the driver courtesy and first-come, first-seated front-to-back and back-to-front seating policy that the WPC had been requesting for well over a year, the white officials would not budge from their insistent refusal that no changes in seating practices could be implemented.

The whites' complete intransigence, in the face of a black community effort of such impressive proportions, surprised the black leadership, who had entered into those first negotiations believing that their modest demands ought to make for a quick settlement. Since "our demands were moderate," King later recalled, "I had assumed that they would be granted with little question." Only in the wake of that unproductive meeting did the MIA leaders begin to realize that it was the very fact of their challenge, and not the particulars of their demands, that had meaning for white Montgomery.

To the city and bus company officials such as Commissioner Clyde Sellers and attorney Jack Crenshaw, the real issue was not which precise seating plan was legally permissible, but the defense of segregation's policies as an exemplar of the underlying doctrine of white racial supremacy. On that question no compromise could be possible; there either was superiority or there wasn't. "They feared that anything they gave would be viewed by us as just a start," Mrs. Robinson later reflected. "And you know, they were probably right."

An often shy and resolutely self-effacing person, Jo Ann Gibson Robinson is now almost seventy and lives quietly by herself in retirement in Los Angeles. Only with some gentle encouragement will she acknowledge herself as "the instigator of the movement to start that boycott." Even then, however, she seeks to avoid any special credit for herself or any other single individual. Very simply, she says, "the black women did it." And she's right.

Sources and Suggested Further Reading

First and foremost, my understanding of Montgomery is based upon my personal interviews with many of the principals—Mrs. Robinson, Mrs. Burks, Mr. Nixon, Mr. Lewis, attorney Gray, Rev. Seay, Mrs. Durr and the late Jack Crenshaw, as well as Rev. Ralph D. Abernathy, Juanita J. Abernathy, Robert D. Nesbitt, Robert Williams, Rev. Robert S. Graetz, Maude Ballou, Lillie Armstrong Thomas (now Brown), Elliot Finley, Rev. Robert E. Hughes, and Jack Shows. I have also benefitted greatly from the interviews with some of the principals that are on deposit in the oral history collections of the Moorland-Spingarn Research Center, Howard University, Washington, D.C.; the Martin Luther King, Jr., Center for Nonviolent Social Change, Atlanta; and the Highlander Center, New Market, Tennessee, as well as from the interviews that have been shared with me by David Levering Lewis, Milton Viorst, and Worth Long and Randall Williams. I also strongly recommend the Statewide Oral History Program collection of interviews, compiled in 1973 by the Alabama Center for Higher Education, copies of which are on deposit at all of Alabama's traditionally black colleges.

There are a number of invaluable, unpublished manuscripts which shed crucial light on the boycott, particularly Mrs. Robinson's "The Montgomery Story," which the University of Tennessee Press will publish later this year, and Ralph D. Abernathy's "The Natural History of a Social Movement: The Montgomery Improvement Association," a 1958 M.A. thesis in Sociology at Atlanta University. Also extremely valuable are Sheldon Hackney and Ray Arsenault's "The Montgomery Bus Boycott: A Case Book"; Peter C. Mohr, "Journal Out of Egypt: The Development of Negro Leadership in Alabama from Booker T. Washington to Martin Luther King," B.A. thesis, Princeton University, 1958; Thomas J. Gilliam, "The Montgomery Bus Boycott of 1955-1956," M.A. thesis, Auburn University, 1968; Gordon L. Hartstein, "The Montgomery Bus Protest 1955-1956: What Precipitated, Sustained, and Prolonged the Boycott," B.A. thesis, Princeton University, 1973; Lamont H. Yeakey, "The Montgomery, Alabama Bus Boycott,

1955-1956," Ph.D dissertation, Columbia University, 1979; Steven M. Millner, "The Montgomery Bus Boycott: A Case Study in the Emergence and Career of a Social Movement," Ph.D dissertation, University of California, Berkeley, 1981; and Donald H. Smith, "Martin Luther King, Jr.: Rhetorician of Revolt," Ph.D dissertation, University of Wisconsin, 1964.

Among published works, the serious student will benefit from not only chapter two of Dr. King's *Stride Toward Freedom* (New York: Harper & Bros., 1958), but also Preston Valien, "The Montgomery Bus Protest as a Social Movement," in Jitsuichi Masuoka & Valien, eds., *Race Relations* (Chapel Hill: University of North Carolina Press, 1961), pp. 112-27; Aleine Austin, "Behind the Montgomery Bus Boycott," *Monthly Review* 8 (September 1956): 163-67; and Ralph H. Hines and James E. Pierce, "Negro Leadership After the Social Crisis: An Analysis of Leadership Changes in Montgomery, Alabama," *Phylon* 26 (Summer 1965): 162-72. Far and away the most valuable and insightful published analysis of the protest, and the place where anyone with further interest should begin, is J. Mills Thornton, III's "Challenge and Response in the Montgomery Bus Boycott of 1955-56," *Alabama Review* 33 (July 1980): 163-235.

Bibliographical Information and Acknowledgements

1. The Walking City: A History of The Montgomery Bus Boycott, by *Norman W. Walton* was originally published in five issues of the *Negro History Bulletin*, as follows: 20(10/56): 17-21, (11/56): 27-33, (2/57):102-104, (4/57): 147ff., 21(1/58):75ff. It is published here by permission of the author.

2. Alabama's Bus Boycott, by *Rev. Thomas R. Thrasher* was originally published in the *Reporter* 14(3/8/56):13-16. It is published here by permission of the estate of the author.

3. The Bus Boycott in Montgomery, by *L. D. Reddick* was originally published in *Dissent* 3(Spring 1956):107-117. Reprinted by permission of *Dissent*.

4. The Montgomery Bus Protest as a Social Movement, by *Preston Valien* originally appeared in *Race Relations*, edited by Jitsuichi Masuoka and Preston Valien (Chapel Hill: University of North Carolina Press, 1961), pp. 112-127. Reprinted by permission of the Press.

5. The Natural History of A Social Movement: The Montgomery Improvement Association, by *Ralph D. Abernathy*, was originally written as an M.A. thesis in the Department of Sociology at Atlanta University, August, 1958. Published here by arrangement with the author.

6. The Beginnings of a New Age, by *Edgar N. French*, originally appeared in Mitchell & Peace, eds., *The Angry Black South* (New York: Corinth Books, 1962), pp. 30-51. Reprinted here by permission of the author's estate.

7. The Montgomery Bus Boycott of 1955-56, by *Thomas J. Gilliam*, was originally written as an M.A. thesis in the Department of History at Auburn University in 1968. Published here by arrangement with the author.

8. From Harlem to Montgomery: The Bus Boycotts and Leadership of Adam Clayton Powell, Jr. and Martin Luther King, Jr., by *Dominic J. Capeci, Jr.*, originally appeared in the *Historian* 41(8/79):721-737. Reprinted by permission of Phi Alpha Theta International Honor Society in History.

9. Challenge and Response in the Montgomery Bus Boycott of 1955-1956, by *J. Mills Thornton, III* originally appeared in *The Alabama Review* 33(7/80):163-235. Copyright by The University of Alabama Press. It is reprinted here by permission of the Press.

10. The Montgomery Bus Boycott: A Case Study in the Emergence and Career of a Social Movement, by *Steven M. Millner* was originally written as a Ph.D. dissertation in Sociology at the University of California at Berkeley in 1981. It is substantially revised in this publication and is included by arrangment with the author.

11. The Origins of the Montgomery Bus Boycott, by *David J. Garrow* was originally published in *Southern Changes* 7(10-12/85):21-27. It is published here by permission of the author.

A Note on the Index

The following index could easily have been a series of sub-entries under the main heading *Montgomery bus boycott*. Or, this entry could have been left out altogether. Instead, we have elected to include under this heading all of the events that were specific to the boycott, such as meetings, negotiations, the car pool injunction, etc. Note that meetings and negotiation sessions are entered by the month and year they took place and alphabetized by month. Events involving specific individuals will be found under the individual's names, for example, Rosa Parks's arrest is under *Parks, Rosa*.

We have, in general, tried to include every mention of an individual, no matter how insignificant, on the grounds that it will be useful to some readers to know how many times and in what context someone is referred to. These entries immediately follow the individual's name and, where there are a number of them, are indicated by the word *mentioned*.

This volume tells the story of the Montgomery bus boycott from many different viewpoints (or, maybe it really is different stories). We felt it was especially important to provide a comprehensive index which combines all the various discussions of a given topic or event under a single entry and have attempted to do so. We trust the reader will find it a useful access point.

Ralph Carlson
Carlson Publishing

623

Index

TITLES IN THE SERIES

Martin Luther King, Jr.

and the

Civil Rights Movement

DAVID J. GARROW, EDITOR